Avizandum Statutes on

# Scots Commercial and Consumer Law
## 2015–2016

**Thirteenth edition**

Avizandum Statutes on

# Scots Commercial and Consumer Law
## 2015–2016

### Thirteenth edition

Editor

**John MacLeod**

Lecturer in Commercial Law, University of Glasgow

Avizandum Publishing Ltd
Edinburgh
2015

Avizandum Publishing Ltd
58 Candlemaker Row
Edinburgh EH1 2QE


First published   2003
2nd edition       2004
3rd edition       2005
4th edition       2006
5th edition       2007
6th edition       2008
7th edition       2009
8th edition       2010
9th edition       2011
10th edition      2012
11th edition      2013
12th edition      2014
13th edition      2015


ISBN 978-1-904968-72-6

British Library Cataloguing in Publication Data
A catalogue record for this book is available from the British Library

Typeset by AFS Image Setters Ltd, Glasgow
Printed and bound by Bell & Bain Ltd, Glasgow

# EDITOR'S PREFACE

This is the second edition of the *Avizandum Statutes on Scots Commercial and Consumer Law* which I have edited and I remain very grateful to the previous editors Professor Jenny Hamilton and Dr Ross Anderson.

This year has seen the passage of two major pieces of domestic legislation: the Insurance Act 2015 and the Consumer Rights Act 2015. The former will come into force in August 2016; with regard to the latter the latest communications from government state that it will be brought into force in October this year. The Insurance Act is a largely standalone statute and effect has not been given to its amendments so that the present law can be easily discerned. The Consumer Rights Act, on the other hand, operates both by way of direct provision and by very significant amendment to existing statutes. As was the case with the Bankruptcy and Debt Advice (Scotland) Act 2014, my view is that it is very difficult to appreciate the impact of this Act without giving effect to its amendments. Also, failing to give effect to them would have resulted in significant duplication of material with implications for the cost of this volume. For these reasons, effect has been given to its amendments, albeit in italics.

The past year also saw a new European Union Regulation on Insolvency Proceedings. It will enter into force in June 2017 and it has been included in preference to its predecessor on the basis that the majority of students using this book will not be in practice until then.

There have also been numerous minor amendments to much of the legislation included in this volume, the most noteworthy of which is probably the introduction of rules for electronic presentment of negotiable instruments into the Bills of Exchange Act 1882.

As in previous editions, amendments have been indicated by square brackets. Repeals of material included in the original statute are indicated by [. . .]. Legislation not yet in force appears in italics.

As is always the case with collections of this nature, considerations of length and cost mean that limits must be placed on coverage, particularly since the collection is primarily aimed at undergraduate students. As in previous editions, European Directives have not been included where they have been implemented by domestic legislation and provisions imposing criminal liability have largely been omitted.

This edition has been updated to July 2015.

I am very grateful to Avizandum Publishing for all their help and care in preparing this volume.

John MacLeod
University of Glasgow
*July 2015*

# CONTENTS

# PART I
# STATUTES

### COMPENSATION ACT 1592
### (RPS 1592/4/83; APS III, 573)

Oure Souerane Lord and estaitis of parliament statutis and Ordanis that ony debt de liquido ad liquidum instantlie verifiet be wreit or aith of the partie befoir the geving of decreit be admittit be all Jugis within this realme be way of exceptioun bot not eftir the geving thairof in the suspensioun or in reductioun of the same decreit.

### DILIGENCE ACT 1661*
### (RPS 1661/1/433; APS VII, 317, c 344)

[A]ll compriseings deduced . . . befor the first effectuall compriseing or after but within yeer and day of the same Shall come in pari passu together [. . .].

* As applied to adjudications by Adjudications Act 1672 (RPS 1672/6/55; APS VIII, 93, c 45).

### LIFE ASSURANCE ACT 1774
### (14 Geo 3, c 48)

**1  No Insurance to be made on the lives of persons having no interest, &c**
From and after the passing of this Act no insurance shall be made by any person or persons, bodies politick or corporate, on the life or lives of any person, or persons, or on any other event or events whatsoever, wherein the person or persons for whose use, benefit, or on whose account such policy or policies shall be made, shall have no interest, or by way of gaming or wagering; and every assurance made contrary to the true intent and meaning hereof shall be null and void to all intents and purposes whatsoever.

**2  No policies on lives without inserting the persons names, &c**
And it shall not be lawful to make any policy or policies on the life or lives of any person or persons, or other event or events, without inserting in such policy or policies the person or persons name or names interested therein, or for whose use, benefit, or on whose account such policy is so made or underwrote.

**3  How much may be recovered where the insured hath interest in lives**
And in all cases where the insured hath interest in such life or lives, event or events, no greater sum shall be recovered or received from the insurer or insurers than the amount of value of the interest of the insured in such life or lives, or other event or events.

**4  Not to extend to insurances on ships, goods, &c**
Provided always, that nothing herein contained shall extend or be construed to extend to insurances bona fide made by any person or persons on ships, goods, or merchandises, but every such insurance shall be as valid and effectual in the law as if this Act had not been made.

## MERCANTILE LAW AMENDMENT (SCOTLAND) ACT 1856
### (19 & 20 Vict, c 60)

### 8 Cautioners not to be entitled to benefit of discussion

Where any person shall become bound as cautioner for any principal debtor, it shall not be necessary for the creditor to whom such cautionary obligation shall be granted, before calling on the cautioner for payment of the debt to which such cautionary obligation refers, to discuss or do diligence against the principal debtor, as now required by law; but it shall be competent to such creditor to proceed against the principal debtor and the said cautioner, or against either of them, and to use all action or diligence against both or either of them which is competent according to the law of Scotland: Provided always, that nothing herein contained shall prevent any cautioner from stipulating in the instrument of caution that the creditor shall be bound before proceeding against him to discuss and do diligence against the principal debtor.

### 9 Discharge of one cautioner, to operate as a discharge to all

Where two or more parties shall become bound as cautioners for any debtor, any discharge granted by the creditor in such debt or obligation to any one of such cautioners without the consent of the other cautioners shall be deemed and taken to be a discharge granted to all the cautioners; but nothing herein contained shall be deemed to extend to the case of a cautioner consenting to the discharge of a co-cautioner who may have become bankrupt.

## TRANSMISSION OF MOVEABLE PROPERTY (SCOTLAND) ACT 1862
### (25 & 26 Vict, c 85)

### 1 Personal bond or conveyance of moveable estate may be assigned in the form set forth in schedule A

It shall be competent to any party, in right of a personal bond or of a conveyance of moveable estate, to assign such bond or conveyance by assignation in or as nearly as may be in the form set forth in schedule A. hereto annexed; and it shall be competent to write the assignation or assignations on the bond or conveyance itself in or as nearly as may be in the form set forth in schedule B. hereto annexed; which assignation shall be registrable in the books of any court, in terms of any clause of registration contained in the bond or conveyance so assigned; and such assignation, upon being duly stamped and duly intimated, shall have the same force and effect as a duly stamped and duly intimated assignation according to the forms at present in use.

### 2 Certified copy to be delivered to person or persons to whom intimation may in any case be requisite

An assignation shall be validly intimated (1) by a notary public delivering a copy thereof, certified as correct, to the person or persons to whom intimation may in any case be requisite, or (2) by the holder of such assignation, or any person authorized by him, transmitting a copy thereof certified as correct by post to such person; and (in the first case) a certificate by such notary public in or as nearly as may be in the form set forth in schedule C. hereto annexed, and (in the second case) a written acknowledgment by the person to whom such copy may have been transmitted by post as aforesaid of the receipt of the copy, shall be sufficient evidence of such intimation having been duly made: Provided always, that if the deed or instrument containing such assignation shall likewise contain other conveyances or declarations of trust purposes, it shall not be necessary to deliver or transmit a full copy thereof, but only a copy of such part thereof as respects the subject matter of such assignation.

### 3 As to transmission of personal bond, &c

Nothing in this Act contained shall prevent the transmission of any personal bond or conveyance of moveable estate, or the intimation of any assignation according to the forms at present in use.

## 4   Interpretation of terms

The following words in this Act, and in the schedules annexed to this Act, shall have the several meanings hereby assigned to them, unless there by something in the subject or context repugnant to such construction; that is to say, the word 'bond' and the word 'conveyance' shall extend to and include personal bonds for payment or performance, bonds of caution, bonds of guarantee, bonds of relief, bonds and assignations in security of every kind, decreets of any court, policies of assurance of any assurance company or association in Scotland, whether held by parties resident in Scotland or elsewhere, protests of bills or of promissory notes, dispositions, assignations, or other conveyances of moveable or personal property or effects, assignations, translations, and retrocessions, and also probative extracts of all such deeds from the books of any competent court; the word 'assignation' shall also include translations and retrocessions, and probative extracts thereof; the words 'moveable estate' shall extend to and include all personal debts and obligations, and moveable or personal property or effects of every kind.

## 5   Short title

This Act may be cited for all purposes as the 'Transmission of Moveable Property (Scotland) Act, 1862.'


## SCHEDULES REFERRED TO IN THE FOREGOING ACT

### SCHEDULE A

I, A.B., in consideration of, &c [or otherwise, as the case may be], do hereby assign to C.D. and his heirs or assignees [or otherwise, as the case may be,] the bond [or other deed, describing it], granted by E.F., dated, &c, by which [here specify the nature of the deed, and specify also any connecting title, and any circumstances requiring to be stated in regard to the nature and extent of the right required], [Testing clause†

†Note—[In the case of a traditional document, subscription of it by the granter] will be sufficient for the document to be formally valid, but witnessing of it may be necessary or desirable for other purposes (see the Requirements of Writing (Scotland) Act 1995 [, which also makes provision as regards the authentication of an electronic document.]).]

### SCHEDULE B

I, A.B., in consideration of, &c [or otherwise, as the case may be], do hereby assign to C.D. and his heirs or assignees [or otherwise, as the case may be,] the foregoing [or within-written] bond [or other writ or deed, describing it,] granted in my favour [or otherwise, as the case may be, specifying any connecting title, and any circumstances requiring to be stated in regard to the nature and extent of the right assigned] [Testing clause†

†Note—[In the case of a traditional document, subscription of it by the granter] will be sufficient for the document to be formally valid, but witnessing of it may be necessary or desirable for other purposes (see the Requirements of Writing (Scotland) Act 1995 [, which also makes provision as regards the authentication of an electronic document.]).]

### SCHEDULE C

I (A.), of the city of notary public, do hereby attest and declare, that upon the day of , and between the hours of and , I duly intimated to B. [here describe the party] the within-written assignation [or otherwise, as the case may be], or an assignation granted by [here describe it] ,and that by delivering to the said A. personally [or otherwise] by leaving for the said A. within his dwelling house at E., in the hands of [here describe the party], a full copy thereof, [or if a partial copy here quote the portion of the deed which has been delivered], to be given to him; all of which was done in presence of C. [Testing clause]

## TITLES TO LAND CONSOLIDATION (SCOTLAND) ACT 1868
### (31 & 32 Vict, c 101)

**59  Unnecessary to libel and conclude for decree of special adjudication**
Whereas it is inconvenient in practice to libel and conclude for general adjudication of lands as the alternative only of special adjudication, in terms of an Act of the Parliament of Scotland passed in the year one thousand six hundred and seventy-two: It shall not be necessary to libel or conclude for special adjudication, and it shall be lawful to libel and conclude and decern for general adjudication without such alternative, anything in the said last-recited Act of the Parliament of Scotland, or in any other Act or Acts of the Parliament of Scotland or of Great Britain or of the United Kingdom of Great Britain and Ireland, to the contrary notwithstanding.

**[62  Effect of a decree of adjudication or sale**
In all cases a decree of adjudication whether for debt or in implement, or a decree of constitution and adjudication whether for debt or in implement, if duly obtained in the form prescribed by this Act, or obtained, if prior to the commencement of this Act, in the form then in use, or a decree of declarator and adjudication, or a decree of sale, shall, except in the case where the subjects contained in the decree of adjudication, or of constitution and adjudication, or of declarator and adjudication, are heritable securities, be held equivalent to and shall have the legal operation and effect of a conveyance in ordinary form of the lands therein contained granted in favour of the adjudger or purchaser by the ancestor of such apparent heir, or by the owner or proprietor in trust or otherwise, and whether in life or deceased, of the lands adjudged, or by the seller of the lands sold, although [under legal disability by reason of nonage] or [mental or other incapacity] and it shall be lawful and competent to such adjudger or purchaser to complete [title by recording the decree as a conveyance or by using the decree as a midcouple or link of title.]

**[155  Date on which inhibition takes effect**
(1)  An inhibition has effect from the beginning of the day on which it is registered unless the circumstances referred to in subsection (2) below apply.
(2)  Those circumstances are—
(a)  a notice of inhibition is registered in the Register of Inhibitions;
(b)  the schedule of inhibition is served on the debtor after that notice is registered; and
(c)  the inhibition is registered before the expiry of the period of 21 days beginning with the day on which the notice is registered.
(3)  In those circumstances the inhibition has effect from the beginning of the day on which the schedule of inhibition is served.
(4)  A notice of inhibition must be in (or as nearly as may be in) the form prescribed.]

**157  No inhibition to have effect against acquirenda, unless in case of heir under entail or other indefeasible title**
No inhibition to be recorded from and after the thirty-first day of December one thousand eight hundred and sixty-eight shall have any force or effect as against any lands to be acquired by the person or persons against whom such inhibition is

used after the date of recording such inhibition, or of recording the previous notice thereof prescribed by this Act, as the case may be: Provided always, that where such inhibition is used against a person or persons who shall thereafter succeed to any lands which, at the date of recording the inhibition or previous notice thereof, as the case may be, were destined to such person or persons by a deed of entail, or by a similar indefeasible title, then and in that case such inhibition shall affect the said person or persons in so far as regards the lands so destined, and to which he or they shall succeed as aforesaid, but no further.

**159 Litigiosity not to begin before date of registration of notice of summons**

[(1)] It shall be competent to register in the general register of inhibitions a notice of any signeted summons of reduction of any conveyance or deed of or relating to lands, and in the register of adjudications a notice of any signeted summons of adjudication or of constitution and adjudication combined [. . .] in implement, which notice shall [be in (or as nearly as may be in) the form prescribed]; and no summons of reduction, constitution, adjudication, or constitution and adjudication combined, shall have any effect in rendering litigious the lands to which such summons relates, except from and after the date of the registration of such notice.

[(2) A notice registered under subsection (1) on or after the date on which section 67 of the Land Registration etc (Scotland) Act 2012 (asp 5) (warrant to place a caveat) comes into force shall not have any effect in rendering litigious any land a title sheet for which is comprised in the Land Register of Scotland or in placing in bad faith any person acquiring such land.]

**[159A Registration of notice of summons of action of reduction**

(1) This section applies where a pursuer raises an action of reduction of a conveyance or deed of or relating to lands granted in breach of an inhibition.

(2) The pursuer shall, as soon as is reasonably practicable after the summons in the action is signeted—

(a) register a notice of that signeted summons in accordance with section 159 of this Act; and

(b) [. . .] record in the Register of Sasines a copy of that notice.

(3) Where a decree of reduction is not obtained in the action to which the notice relates, the pursuer shall, as soon as is reasonably practicable—

(a) register in the Register of Inhibitions; and

(b) [. . .] record in the Register of Sasines,

a discharge of that notice in (or as nearly as may be in) the form prescribed.]

[(4) This section does not apply in relation to lands for which there is a title sheet in the Land Register of Scotland.]

## WRITS EXECUTION (SCOTLAND) ACT 1877
### (40 & 41 Vict, c 40)

**1   Extracts of writs registered in Books of Council and Session to have, in certain cases, warrant for execution. Form of warrant of execution inserted in extracts of all protests, &c**

In all extracts of writs, deeds, or other documents which contain a clause of registration for preservation and execution, and which are registered in the register of deeds and probative writs and protests in the Books of Council and Session in Scotland, the keeper or assistant keeper of the said register shall insert a warrant for execution in the form, or as nearly as may be in the form, of the Schedule to this Act annexed.

The warrants for execution inserted in the extracts of all protests of bills, promissory notes or bankers notes, or certificates of judgment registered for execution under the Judgments Extension Act, 1868, shall be as nearly as may be in the form of the said Schedule to this Act annexed.

**2   Extracts of writs registered in Sheriff Court Books to have warrant of execution in certain cases**

In all extracts of writs, deeds, or other documents which contain a clause of registration for preservation and execution, and which are registered in the Sheriff Court Books of any county in Scotland, and in all extracts of protests of bills, promissory notes, or bankers notes registered in the Sheriff Court Books, the sheriff clerk shall insert a warrant of execution in the form, or as nearly as may be in the form, of the Schedule to this Act annexed.

**[3   Power to execute diligence by virtue of warrant**

The warrant inserted in an extract of a document registered in the Books of Council and Session or in sheriff court books which contains an obligation to pay a sum of money shall have the effect of authorising—

(a)   in relation to an ordinary debt within the meaning of the Debtors (Scotland) Act 1987, the charging of the debtor to pay to the creditor within the period specified in the charge the sum specified in the extract and any interest accrued on the sum and, in the event of failure to make such payment within that period, the execution of an earnings arrestment, a money attachment] and the [attachment] of articles belonging to the debtor and, if necessary for the purpose of executing the [money attachment or] [attachment], the opening of shut and lockfast places;

(b)   in relation to an ordinary debt within the meaning of the Debtors (Scotland) Act 1987, an arrestment other than an arrestment of the debtor's earnings in the hands of his employer; and

[(ba)   in relation to an ordinary debt within the meaning of the Debtors (Scotland) Act 1987, inhibition against the debtor;]

(c)   if the document is a maintenance order within the meaning of the Debtors (Scotland) Act 1987, a current maintenance arrestment in accordance with Part III of that Act.]

. . .

**5   Extracts of deeds registered in the Books of Council and Session, and Register of Sasines, to be authenticated**

Extracts of all writs, deeds, or other documents of what nature soever, which may be registered in the Books of Council and Session, shall be equivalent to the registered writs, deeds, or other documents themselves, except where any writ, deed, or other document so registered shall be offered to be improven, and such extracts shall be signed on the last page thereof, by the keeper or assistant keeper of the register of deeds and probative writs and protests in the Books of Council and Session; and extracts of all writs registered in and issued from the office of the

General Register of Sasines shall be signed, on the last page thereof, by the keeper of the said register, or by a deputy duly commissioned by him to that effect, and no further signature on any other page of such extracts shall be necessary. But each sheet of all such extracts shall be impressed with an office seal or stamp to be kept in the respective offices of the said keepers; provided that it shall be necessary and sufficient in the case of marginal additions occurring in any extract that the same shall be authenticated by the signature of the officer certifying such extract.

## 6 Writs registered in the Register of Sasines for preservation only may afterwards be registered for preservation and execution

Where any writ containing in gremio thereof a procuratory or clause of registration for preservation and execution shall have been registered in the General Register of Sasines [. . .] for preservation but not for execution, it shall be competent to present for registration in the said register an extract of such registered writ [with, written on the extract writ a statement to the effect] that such extract is to be registered for preservation and execution; and it shall be lawful to register such extract accordingly, and to issue one or more extracts thereof, with warrant of execution in terms (mutatis mutandis) of Schedule B. annexed to the Land Registers (Scotland) Act 1868, and every such warrant of execution shall have all the like force and effect as any warrant of execution issued in terms of the twelfth section of the said last-mentioned Act; and in making such subsequent registration it shall not be necessary to engross ad longum in the said register the extract so presented, but the registration thereof may be effected by the insertion of a memorandum of such extract in the appropriate division or divisions of said register, setting forth the volume of the register, and the folio or folios of such volume in which said original writ is engrossed, and the insertion of such memorandum shall be deemed equivalent to the full engrossment in the division or divisions of the register in which such memorandum shall be entered as aforesaid of the extract so presented for registration.

## 7 After transmission of volumes of records of Books of Council and Session to the Lords Clerk Register, the deputy keeper of records may issue extracts of any deeds recorded in said volumes and authenticate the same as well as other extracts

Whereas, in terms of the twelfth section of the Public Records (Scotland) Act 1809, the volumes of records of the Books of Council and Session are, along with the warrants thereof, periodically transmitted by the keeper of the register of deeds and probative writs and protests in the Books of Council and Session, to the Lord Clerk Register or his deputies; be it enacted, that the deputy keeper of the records or any officer holding a commission to that effect from the Lord Clerk Register may, at any time, issue extracts one or more of any writ, deed, or other document registered in said volumes of records transmitted as aforesaid, in the same or in a similar form to the extracts of such writs, deeds, or other documents which might have been issued previous to such transmission. And all such extracts and the warrants of execution therein contained shall have all the like force and effect as any extract from the Books of Council and Session, made and issued previous to such transmission, or as any warrant of execution contained in or appended to such extract; and in all extracts issued as aforesaid, and also in all extracts issued of writs contained in any record in the custody of the Lord Clerk Register, it shall be sufficient that the last page thereof shall be signed by the said deputy keeper of the records or by any officer duly commissioned by the Lord Clerk Register to that effect, and no further signature on any other page of such extracts shall be necessary, but each sheet of all such extracts shall be impressed with an office seal or stamp to be kept in the office of the Lord Clerk Register; provided that it shall be necessary and sufficient in the case of marginal additions occurring in any such extract that the same shall be authenticated by the signature of the officer certifying such extract.

## 8 Commencement and extent of Act

This Act shall take effect from and after the first day of October one thousand eight hundred and seventy-seven, and shall apply to Scotland only.

## BILLS OF EXCHANGE ACT 1882
### (45 & 46 Vict, c 61)

### PART I
### PRELIMINARY

## 1 Short title

This Act may be cited as the Bills of Exchange Act, 1882.

## 2 Interpretation of terms

In this Act, unless the context otherwise requires,—

'Acceptance' means an acceptance completed by delivery or notification.

'Action' includes counter claim and set off.

'Banker' includes a body of persons whether incorporated or not who carry on the business of banking.

'Bankrupt' includes any person whose estate is vested in a trustee or assignee under the law for the time being in force relating to bankruptcy.

'Bearer' means the person in possession of a bill or note which is payable to bearer.

'Bill' means bill of exchange, and 'note' means promissory note.

'Delivery' means transfer of possession, actual or constructive, from one person to another.

'Holder' means the payee or indorsee of a bill or note who is in possession of it, or the bearer thereof.

'Indorsement' means an indorsement completed by delivery.

'Issue' means the first delivery of a bill or note, complete in form to a person who takes it as a holder.

'Person' includes a body of persons whether incorporated or not.

['Postal operator' has the meaning given by [section 27 of the Postal Services Act 2011].]

'Value' means valuable consideration.

'Written' includes printed, and 'writing' includes print.

### PART II
### BILLS OF EXCHANGE

*Form and interpretation*

## 3 Bill of exchange defined

(1)  A bill of exchange is an unconditional order in writing, addressed by one person to another, signed by the person giving it, requiring the person to whom it is addressed to pay on demand or at a fixed or determinable future time a sum certain in money to or to the order of a specified person, or to bearer.

(2)  An instrument which does not comply with these conditions, or which orders any act to be done in addition to the payment of money, is not a bill of exchange.

(3)  An order to pay out of a particular fund is not unconditional within the meaning of this section; but an unqualified order to pay, coupled with (a) an indication of a particular fund out of which the drawee is to reimburse himself or a

particular account to be debited with the amount, or (b) a statement of the transaction which gives rise to the bill, is unconditional.

(4)  A bill is not invalid by reason—

(a)  That it is not dated;

(b)  That it does not specify the value given, or that any value has been given therefor;

(c)  That it does not specify the place where it is drawn or the place where it is payable.

### 4  Inland and foreign bills

(1)  An inland bill is a bill which is or on the face of it purports to be (a) both drawn and payable within the British Islands, or (b) drawn within the British Islands upon some person resident therein. Any other bill is a foreign bill.

For the purposes of this Act 'British Islands' means any part of the United Kingdom of Great Britain and Ireland, the islands of Man, Guernsey, Jersey, Alderney, and Sark, and the islands adjacent to any of them being part of the dominions of Her Majesty.

(2)  Unless the contrary appear on the face of the bill the holder may treat it as an inland bill.

### 5  Effect where different parties to bill are the same person

(1)  A bill may be drawn payable to, or to the order of, the drawer; or it may be drawn payable to, or to the order of, the drawee.

(2)  Where in a bill drawer and drawee are the same person, or where the drawee is a fictitious person or a person not having capacity to contract, the holder may treat the instrument, at his option, either as a bill of exchange or as a promissory note.

### 6  Address to drawee

(1)  The drawee must be named or otherwise indicated in a bill with reasonable certainty.

(2)  A bill may be addressed to two or more drawees whether they are partners or not, but an order addressed to two drawees in the alternative or to two or more drawees in succession is not a bill of exchange.

### 7  Certainty required as to payee

(1)  Where a bill is not payable to bearer, the payee must be named or otherwise indicated therein with reasonable certainty.

(2)  A bill may be made payable to two or more payees jointly, or it may be made payable in the alternative to one of two, or one or some of several payees. A bill may also be made payable to the holder of an office for the time being.

(3)  Where the payee is a fictitious or non-existing person the bill may be treated as payable to bearer.

### 8  What bills are negotiable

(1)  When a bill contains words prohibiting transfer, or indicating an intention that it should not be transferable, it is valid as between the parties thereto, but is not negotiable.

(2)  A negotiable bill may be payable either to order or to bearer.

(3)  A bill is payable to bearer which is expressed to be so payable, or on which the only or last indorsement is an indorsement in blank.

(4)  A bill is payable to order which is expressed to be so payable, or which is expressed to be payable to a particular person, and does not contain words prohibiting transfer or indicating an intention that it should not be transferable.

(5)  Where a bill, either originally or by indorsement, is expressed to be payable to the order of a specified person, and not to him or his order, it is nevertheless payable to him or his order at his option.

**9   Sum payable**

(1)   The sum payable by a bill is a sum certain within the meaning of this Act, although it is required to be paid—

(a)   With interest.

(b)   By stated instalments.

(c)   By stated instalments, with a provision that upon default in payment of any instalment the whole shall become due.

(d)   According to an indicated rate of exchange or according to a rate of exchange to be ascertained as directed by the bill.

(2)   Where the sum payable is expressed in words and also in figures, and there is a discrepancy between the two, the sum denoted by the words is the amount payable.

(3)   Where a bill is expressed to be payable with interest, unless the instrument otherwise provides, interest runs from the date of the bill, and if the bill is undated from the issue thereof.

**10   Bill payable on demand**

(1)   A bill is payable on demand—

(a)   Which is expressed to be payable on demand, or at sight, or on presentation; or

(b)   In which no time for payment is expressed.

(2)   Where a bill is accepted or indorsed when it is overdue, it shall, as regards the acceptor who so accepts, or any indorser who so indorses it, be deemed a bill payable on demand.

**11   Bill payable at a future time**

A bill is payable at a determinable future time within the meaning of this Act which is expressed to be payable—

(1)   At a fixed period after date or sight.

(2)   On or at a fixed period after the occurrence of a specified event which is certain to happen, though the time of happening may be uncertain.

An instrument expressed to be payable on a contingency is not a bill, and the happening of the event does not cure the defect.

**12   Omission of date in bill payable after date**

Where a bill expressed to be payable at a fixed period after date is issued undated, or where the acceptance of a bill payable at a fixed period after sight is undated, any holder may insert therein the true date of issue or acceptance, and the bill shall be payable accordingly.

Provided that (1) where the holder in good faith and by mistake inserts a wrong date, and (2) in every case where a wrong date is inserted, if the bill subsequently comes into the hands of a holder in due course the bill shall not be avoided thereby, but shall operate and be payable as if the date so inserted had been the true date.

**13   Ante-dating and post-dating**

(1)   Where a bill or an acceptance or any indorsement on a bill is dated, the date shall, unless the contrary be proved, be deemed to be the true date of the drawing, acceptance, or indorsement, as the case may be.

(2)   A bill is not invalid by reason only that it is ante-dated or post-dated, or that it bears date on a Sunday.

**14   Computation of time of payment**

Where a bill is not payable on demand the day on which it falls due is determined as follows:

[(1)   The bill is due and payable in all cases on the last day of the time of payment as fixed by the bill or, if that is a non-business day, on the succeeding business day.]

(2)   Where a bill is payable at a fixed period after date, after sight, or after the happening of a specified event, the time of payment is determined by excluding the day from which the time is to begin to run and by including the day of payment.

(3)   Where a bill is payable at a fixed period after sight, the time begins to run from the date of the acceptance if the bill be accepted, and from the date of noting or protest if the bill be noted or protested for non-acceptance, or for non-delivery.

(4)   The term 'month' in a bill means a calendar month.

### 15   Case of need
The drawer of a bill and any indorser may insert therein the name of a person to whom the holder may resort in case of need, that is to say, in case the bill is dishonoured by non-acceptance or non-payment. Such person is called the referee in case of need. It is in the option of the holder to resort to the referee in case of need or not as he may think fit.

### 16   Optional stipulations by drawer or indorser
The drawer of a bill, and any indorser, may insert therein an express stipulation—
(1)   Negativing or limiting his own liability to the holder;
(2)   Waiving as regards himself some or all of the holder's duties.

### 17   Definition and requisites of acceptance
(1)   The acceptance of a bill is the signification by the drawee of his assent to the order of the drawer.

(2)   An acceptance is invalid unless it complies with the following conditions, namely:
(a)   It must be written on the bill and be signed by the drawee. The mere signature of the drawee without additional words is sufficient.
(b)   It must not express that the drawee will perform his promise by any other means than the payment of money.

### 18   Time for acceptance
A bill may be accepted—
(1)   Before it has been signed by the drawer, or while otherwise incomplete;
(2)   When it is overdue, or after it has been dishonoured by a previous refusal to accept, or by non-payment;
(3)   When a bill payable after sight is dishonoured by non-acceptance, and the drawee subsequently accepts it, the holder, in the absence of any different agreement, is entitled to have the bill accepted as of the date of first presentment to the drawee for acceptance.

### 19   General and qualified acceptance
(1)   An acceptance is either (a) general, or (b) qualified.

(2)   A general acceptance assents without qualification to the order of the drawer. A qualified acceptance in expressed terms varies the effect of the bill as drawn.

In particular an acceptance is qualified which is—
(a)   conditional, that is to say, which makes payment by the acceptor dependent on the fulfilment of a condition therein stated;
(b)   partial, that is to say, an acceptance to pay part only of the amount for which the bill is drawn;
(c)   local, that is to say, an acceptance to pay only at a particular specified place;
An acceptance to pay at a particular place is a general acceptance, unless it expressly states that the bill is to be paid there only and not elsewhere:
(d)   qualified as to time;
(e)   the acceptance of some one or more of the drawees, but not of all.

## 20   Inchoate instruments

(1)   Where a simple signature on a blank paper is delivered by the signer in order that it may be converted into a bill, it operates as a prima facie authority to fill it up as a complete bill for any amount [. . .] using the signature for that of the drawer, or the acceptor, or an indorser; and, in like manner, when a bill is wanting in any material particular, the person in possession of it has a prima facie authority to fill up the omission in any way he thinks fit.

(2)   In order that any such instrument when completed may be enforceable against any person who became a party thereto prior to its completion, it must be filled up within a reasonable time, and strictly in accordance with the authority given. Reasonable time for this purpose is a question of fact.

Provided that if any such instrument after completion is negotiated to a holder in due course it shall be valid and effectual for all purposes in his hands and he may enforce it as if it had been filled up within a reasonable time and strictly in accordance with the authority given.

## 21   Delivery

(1)   Every contract on a bill, whether it be the drawer's, the acceptor's, or an indorser's is incomplete and revocable, until delivery of the instrument in order to give effect thereto.

Provided that where an acceptance is written on a bill, and the drawee gives notice to or according to the directions of the person entitled to the bill that he has accepted it, the acceptance then becomes complete and irrevocable.

(2)   As between immediate parties, and as regards a remote party other than a holder in due course, the delivery—

(a)   in order to be effectual must be made either by or under the authority of the party drawing, accepting, or indorsing, as the case may be:

(b)   may be shown to have been conditional or for a special purpose only, and not for the purpose of transferring the property in the bill.

But if the bill be in the hands of a holder in due course a valid delivery of the bill by all parties prior to him so as to make them liable to him is conclusively presumed.

(3)   Where a bill is no longer in the possession of a party who has signed it as drawer, acceptor, or indorser, a valid and unconditional delivery by him is presumed until the contrary is proved.

*Capacity and authority of parties*

## 22   Capacity of parties

(1)   Capacity to incur liability as a party to a bill is co-extensive with capacity to contract.

Provided that nothing in this section shall enable a corporation to make itself liable as drawer, acceptor, or indorser of a bill unless it is competent to do so under the law for the time being in force relating to corporations.

(2)   Where a bill is drawn or indorsed by an infant, minor, or corporation having no capacity or power to incur liability on a bill, the drawing or indorsement entitles the holder to receive payment of the bill, and to enforce it against any other party thereto.

## 23   Signature essential to liability

No person is liable as drawer, indorser, or acceptor of a bill who has not signed it as such: Provided that

(1)   Where a person signs a bill in a trade or assumed name, he is liable thereon as if he had signed it in his own name:

(2)   The signature of the name of a firm is equivalent to the signature by the person so signing of the names of all persons liable as partners in that firm.

### 24   Forged or unauthorised signature

Subject to the provisions of this Act, where a signature on a bill is forged or placed thereon without the authority of the person whose signature it purports to be, the forged or unauthorised signature is wholly inoperative, and no right to retain the bill or to give a discharge therefor or to enforce payment thereof against any party thereto can be acquired through or under that signature, unless the party against whom it is sought to retain or enforce payment of the bill is precluded from setting up the forgery or want of authority.

Provided that nothing in this section shall affect the ratification of an unauthorised signature not amounting to a forgery.

### 25   Procuration signatures

A signature by procuration operates as notice that the agent has but a limited authority to sign, and the principal is only bound by such signature if the agent in so signing was acting within the actual limits of his authority.

### 26   Person signing as agent or in representative capacity

(1)   Where a person signs a bill as drawer, indorser, or acceptor, and adds words to his signature, indicating that he signs for or on behalf of a principal, or in a representative character, he is not personally liable thereon; but the mere addition to his signature of words describing him as an agent, or as filling a representative character, does not exempt him from personal liability.

(2)   In determining whether a signature on a bill is that of the principal or that of the agent by whose hand it is written, the construction most favourable to the validity of the instrument shall be adopted.

*The consideration for a bill*

### 27   Value and holder for value

(1)   Valuable consideration for a bill may be constituted by,—

(a)   Any consideration sufficient to support a simple contract;

(b)   An antecedent debt or liability. Such a debt or liability is deemed valuable consideration whether the bill is payable on demand or at a future time.

(2)   Where value has at any time been given for a bill the holder is deemed to be a holder for value as regards the acceptor and all parties to the bill who became parties prior to such time.

(3)   Where the holder of a bill has a lien on it, arising either from contract or by implication of law, he is deemed to be a holder for value to the extent of the sum for which he has a lien.

### 28   Accommodation bill or party

(1)   An accommodation party to a bill is a person who has signed a bill as drawer, acceptor, or indorser, without receiving value therefor, and for the purpose of lending his name to some other person.

(2)   An accommodation party is liable on the bill to a holder for value; and it is immaterial whether, when such holder took the bill, he knew such party to be an accommodation party or not.

### 29   Holder in due course

(1)   A holder in due course is a holder who has taken a bill, complete and regular on the face of it, under the following conditions, namely,

(a)   That he became the holder of it before it was overdue, and without notice that it had been previously dishonoured, if such was the fact;

(b)   That he took the bill in good faith and for value, and that at the time the bill was negotiated to him he had no notice of any defect in the title of the person who negotiated it.

(2)   In particular the title of a person who negotiates a bill is defective within

the meaning of this Act when he obtained the bill, or the acceptance thereof, by fraud, duress or force and fear, or other unlawful means, or for an illegal consideration, or when he negotiates it in breach of faith, or under such circumstances as amount to a fraud.

(3)  A holder (whether for value or not), who derives his title to a bill through a holder in due course, and who is not himself a party to any fraud or illegality affecting it, has all the rights of that holder in due course as regards the acceptor and all parties to the bill prior to that holder.

### 30  Presumption of value and good faith

(1)  Every party whose signature appears on a bill is prima facie deemed to have become a party thereto for value.

(2)  Every holder of a bill is prima facie deemed to be a holder in due course; but if in an action on a bill it is admitted or proved that the acceptance, issue, or subsequent negotiation of the bill is affected with fraud, duress, or force and fear, or illegality, the burden of proof is shifted, unless and until the holder proves that, subsequent to the alleged fraud or illegality, value has in good faith been given for the bill.

*Negotiation of bills*

### 31  Negotiation of bill

(1)  A bill is negotiated when it is transferred from one person to another in such a manner as to constitute the transferee the holder of the bill.

(2)  A bill payable to bearer is negotiated by delivery.

(3)  A bill payable to order is negotiated by the indorsement of the holder completed by delivery.

(4)  Where the holder of a bill payable to his order transfers it for value without indorsing it, the transfer gives the transferee such title as the transferor had in the bill, and the transferee in addition acquires the right to have the indorsement of the transferor.

(5)  Where any person is under obligation to indorse a bill in a representative capacity, he may indorse the bill in such terms as to negative personal liability.

### 32  Requisites of a valid indorsement

An indorsement in order to operate as a negotiation must comply with the following conditions, namely:—

(1)  It must be written on the bill itself and signed by the indorser. The simple signature of the indorser on the bill, without additional words, is sufficient.

An indorsement written on an allonge, or a 'copy' of a bill issued or negotiated in a country where 'copies' are recognised, is deemed to have been written on the bill itself.

(2)  It must be an indorsement of the entire bill. A partial indorsement, that is to say, an indorsement which purports to transfer to the indorsee a part only of the amount payable, or which purports to transfer the bill to two or more indorsees severally, does not operate as a negotiation of the bill.

(3)  Where a bill is payable to the order of two or more payees or indorsees who are not partners all must indorse, unless the one indorsing has authority to indorse for the others.

(4)  Where, in a bill payable to order, the payee or indorsee is wrongly designated, or his name is mis-spelt, he may indorse the bill as therein described, adding, if he think fit, his proper signature.

(5)  Where there are two or more indorsements on a bill, each indorsement is deemed to have been made in the order in which it appears on the bill, until the contrary is proved.

(6)  An indorsement may be made in blank or special. It may also contain terms making it restrictive.

### 33  Conditional indorsement
Where a bill purports to be indorsed conditionally the condition may be disregarded by the payer, and payment to the indorsee is valid whether the condition has been fulfilled or not.

### 34  Indorsement in blank and special indorsement
(1)  An indorsement in blank specifies no indorsee, and a bill so indorsed becomes payable to bearer.

(2)  A special indorsement specifies the person to whom, or to whose order, the bill is to be payable.

(3)  The provisions of this Act relating to a payee apply with the necessary modifications to an indorsee under a special indorsement.

(4)  When a bill has been indorsed in blank, any holder may convert the blank indorsement into a special indorsement by writing above the indorser's signature a direction to pay the bill to or to the order of himself or some other person.

### 35  Restrictive indorsement
(1)  An indorsement is restrictive which prohibits the further negotiation of the bill or which expresses that it is a mere authority to deal with the bill as thereby directed and not a transfer of ownership thereof, as, for example, if a bill be indorsed 'Pay D. only', or 'Pay D. for the account of X.,' or 'Pay D. or order for collection.'

(2)  A restrictive indorsement gives the indorsee the right to receive payment of the bill and to sue any party thereto that his indorser could have sued, but gives him no power to transfer his rights as indorsee unless it expressly authorises him to do so.

(3)  Where a restrictive indorsement authorises further transfer, all subsequent indorsees take the bill with the same rights and subject to the same liabilities as the first indorsee under the restrictive indorsement.

### 36  Negotiation of overdue or dishonoured bills
(1)  Where a bill is negotiable in its origin it continues to be negotiable until it has been (a) restrictively indorsed or (b) discharged by payment or otherwise.

(2)  Where an overdue bill is negotiated, it can only be negotiated subject to any defect of title affecting it at its maturity, and thenceforward no person who takes it can acquire or give a better title than that which the person from whom he took it had.

(3)  A bill payable on demand is deemed to be overdue within the meaning and for the purposes of this section, when it appears on the face of it to have been in circulation for an unreasonable length of time. What is an unreasonable length of time for this purpose is a question of fact.

(4)  Except where an indorsement bears date after the maturity of the bill, every negotiation is prima facie deemed to have been effected before the bill was overdue.

(5)  Where a bill which is not overdue has been dishonoured any person who takes it with notice of the dishonour takes it subject to any defect of title attaching thereto at the time of dishonour, but nothing in this sub-section shall affect the rights of a holder in due course.

### 37  Negotiation of bill to party already liable thereon
Where a bill is negotiated back to the drawer, or to a prior indorser or to the acceptor, such party may, subject to the provisions of this Act, reissue and further negotiate the bill, but he is not entitled to enforce payment of the bill against any intervening party to whom he was previously liable.

### 38  Rights of the holder
The rights and powers of the holder of a bill are as follows:

(1)  He may sue on the bill in his own name:

(2)   Where he is a holder in due course, he holds the bill free from any defect of title of prior parties, as well as from mere personal defences available to prior parties among themselves, and may enforce payment against all parties liable on the bill:

(3)   Where his title is defective (a) if he negotiates the bill to a holder in due course, that holder obtains a good and complete title to the bill, and (b) if he obtains payment of the bill the person who pays him in due course gets a valid discharge for the bill.

*General duties of the holder*

### 39   When presentment for acceptance is necessary

(1)   Where a bill is payable after sight, presentment for acceptance is necessary in order to fix the maturity of the instrument.

(2)   Where a bill expressly stipulates that it shall be presented for acceptance, or where a bill is drawn payable elsewhere than at the residence or place of business of the drawee, it must be presented for acceptance before it can be presented for payment.

(3)   In no other case is presentment for acceptance necessary in order to render liable any party to the bill.

(4)   Where the holder of a bill, drawn payable elsewhere than at the place of business or residence of the drawee, has not time, with the exercise of reasonable diligence, to present the bill for acceptance before presenting it for payment on the day that it falls due, the delay caused by presenting the bill for acceptance before presenting it for payment is excused, and does not discharge the drawer and the indorsers.

### 40   Time for presenting bill payable after sight

(1)   Subject to the provisions of this Act, when a bill payable after sight is nego-tiated, the holder must either present it for acceptance or negotiate it within a reasonable time.

(2)   If he do not do so, the drawer and all indorsers prior to that holder are discharged.

(3)   In determining what is a reasonable time within the meaning of this section, regard shall be had to the nature of the bill, the usage of trade with respect to similar bills, and the facts of the particular case.

### 41   Rules as to presentment for acceptance and excuses for non-presentment

(1)   A bill is duly presented for acceptance which is presented in accordance with the following rules:

(a)   The presentment must be made by or on behalf of the holder to the drawee or to some person authorised to accept or refuse acceptance on his behalf at a reasonable hour on a business day and before the bill is overdue:

(b)   Where a bill is addressed to two or more drawees, who are not partners, presentment must be made to them all, unless one has authority to accept for all, then presentment may be made to him only:

(c)   Where the drawee is dead, presentment may be made to his personal representative:

(d)   Where the drawee is bankrupt, presentment may be made to him or to his trustee:

(e)   Where authorised by agreement or usage, a presentment through [a postal operator] is sufficient.

(2)   Presentment in accordance with these rules is excused, and a bill may be treated as dishonoured by non-acceptance—

(a)   Where the drawee is dead or bankrupt, or is a fictitious person or a person not having capacity to contract by bill:

(b)   Where, after the exercise of reasonable diligence, such presentment cannot be effected:

(c)   Where although the presentment has been irregular, acceptance has been refused on some other ground.

(3)   The fact that the holder has reason to believe that the bill, on presentment, will be dishonoured does not excuse presentment.

## 42   Non-acceptance

(1)   When a bill is duly presented for acceptance and is not accepted within the customary time, the person presenting it must treat it as dishonoured by non-acceptance. If he do not, the holder shall lose his right of recourse against the drawer and indorsers.

## 43   Dishonour by non-acceptance and its consequences

(1)   A bill is dishonoured by non-acceptance—

(a)   when it is duly presented for acceptance, and such an acceptance as is prescribed by this Act is refused or cannot be obtained; or

(b)   when presentment for acceptance is excused and the bill is not accepted.

(2)   Subject to the provisions of this Act when a bill is dishonoured by non-acceptance an immediate right of recourse against the drawer and indorsers accrues to the holder, and no presentment for payment is necessary.

## 44   Duties as to qualified acceptances

(1)   The holder of a bill may refuse to take a qualified acceptance, and if he does not obtain an unqualified acceptance may treat the bill as dishonoured by non-acceptance.

(2)   Where a qualified acceptance is taken, and the drawer or an indorser has not expressly or impliedly authorised the holder to take a qualified acceptance, or does not subsequently assent thereto, such drawer or indorser is discharged from his liability on the bill.

The provisions of this sub-section do not apply to a partial acceptance, whereof due notice has been given. Where a foreign bill has been accepted as to part, it must be protested as to the balance.

(3)   When the drawer or indorser of a bill receives notice of a qualified acceptance, and does not within a reasonable time express his dissent to the holder he shall be deemed to have assented thereto.

## 45   Rules as to presentment for payment

Subject to the provisions of this Act a bill must be duly presented for payment. If it be not so presented the drawer and indorsers shall be discharged.

A bill is duly presented for payment which is presented in accordance with the following rules:—

(1)   Where the bill is not payable on demand, presentment must be made on the day it falls due.

(2)   Where the bill is payable on demand then, subject to the provisions of this Act, presentment must be made within a reasonable time after its issue in order to render the drawer liable, and within a reasonable time after the indorsement, in order to render the indorser liable.

In determining what is a reasonable time, regard shall be had to the nature of the bill, the usage of trade with regard to similar bills, and the facts of the particular case.

(3)   Presentment must be made by the holder or by some person authorised to receive payment on his behalf at a reasonable hour on a business day, at the proper place as hereinafter defined, either to the person designated by the bill as payer, or to some person authorised to pay or refuse payment on his behalf if with the exercise of reasonable diligence such person can there be found.

(4)   A bill is presented at the proper place:—

(a)   Where a place of payment is specified in the bill and the bill is there presented.

(b)   Where no place of payment is specified, but the address of the drawee or acceptor is given in the bill, and the bill is there presented.

(c)   Where no place of payment is specified and no address given, and the bill is presented at the drawee's or acceptor's place of business if known, and if not, at his ordinary residence if known.

(d)   In any other case if presented to the drawee or acceptor wherever he can be found, or if presented at his last known place of business or residence.

(5)   Where a bill is presented at the proper place, and after the exercise of reasonable diligence no person authorised to pay or refuse payment can be found there, no further presentment to the drawee or acceptor is required.

(6)   Where a bill is drawn upon, or accepted by two or more persons who are not partners, and no place of payment is specified, presentment must be made to them all.

(7)   Where the drawee or acceptor of a bill is dead, and no place of payment is specified, presentment must be made to a personal representative, if such there be, and with the exercise of reasonable diligence he can be found.

(8)   Where authorised by agreement or usage a presentment through [a postal operator] is sufficient.

### 46   Excuses for delay or non-presentment for payment

(1)   Delay in making presentment for payment is excused when the delay is caused by circumstances beyond the control of the holder, and not imputable to his default, misconduct, or negligence. When the cause of delay ceases to operate presentment must be made with reasonable diligence.

(2)   Presentment for payment is dispensed with,—

(a)   Where, after the exercise of reasonable diligence presentment, as required by this Act, cannot be effected.

The fact that the holder has reason to believe that the bill will, on presentment, be dishonoured, does not dispense with the necessity for presentment.

(b)   Where the drawee is a fictitious person.

(c)   As regards the drawer where the drawee or acceptor is not bound, as between himself and the drawer, to accept or pay the bill, and the drawer has no reason to believe that the bill would be paid if presented.

(d)   As regards an indorser, where the bill was accepted or made for the accommodation of that indorser, and he has no reason to expect that the bill would be paid if presented.

(e)   By waiver of presentment, express or implied.

### 47   Dishonour by non-payment

(1)   A bill is dishonoured by non-payment (a) when it is duly presented for payment and payment is refused or cannot be obtained, or (b) when presentment is excused and the bill is overdue and unpaid.

(2)   Subject to the provisions of this Act, when a bill is dishonoured by non-payment, an immediate right of recourse against the drawer and indorsers accrues to the holder.

### 48   Notice of dishonour and effect of non-notice

Subject to the provisions of this Act, when a bill has been dishonoured by non-acceptance or by non-payment, notice of dishonour must be given to the drawer and each indorser, and any drawer or indorser to whom such notice is not given is discharged; Provided that—

(1)   Where a bill is dishonoured by non-acceptance, and notice of dishonour is not given, the rights of the holder in due course subsequent to the omission, shall not be prejudiced by the omission.

(2)   Where a bill is dishonoured by non-acceptance and due notice of dishonour is given, it shall not be necessary to give notice of a subsequent dishonour by non-payment unless the bill shall in the meantime have been accepted.

### 49   Rules as to notice of dishonour

Notice of dishonour in order to be valid and effectual must be given in accordance with the following rules:—

(1)   The notice must be given by or on behalf of the holder, or by or on behalf of an indorser who, at the time of giving it, is himself liable on the bill.

(2)   Notice of dishonour may be given by an agent either in his own name, or in the name of any party entitled to give notice whether that party be his principal or not.

(3)   Where the notice is given by or on behalf of the holder, it enures for the benefit of all subsequent holders and all prior indorsers who have a right of recourse against the party to whom it is given.

(4)   Where notice is given by or on behalf of an indorser entitled to give notice as herein-before provided, it enures for the benefit of the holder and all indorsers subsequent to the party to whom notice is given.

(5)   The notice may be given in writing or by personal communication, and may be given in any terms which sufficiently identify the bill, and intimate that the bill has been dishonoured by non-acceptance or non-payment.

(6)   The return of a dishonoured bill to the drawer or an indorser is, in point of form, deemed a sufficient notice of dishonour.

(7)   A written notice need not be signed, and an insufficient written notice may be supplemented and validated by verbal communication. A misdescription of the bill shall not vitiate the notice unless the party to whom the notice is given is in fact misled thereby.

(8)   Where notice of dishonour is required to be given to any person, it may be given either to the party himself, or to his agent in that behalf.

(9)   Where the drawer or indorser is dead, and the party giving notice knows it, the notice must be given to a personal representative if such there be, and with the exercise of reasonable diligence he can be found.

(10)   Where the drawer or indorser is bankrupt, notice may be given either to the party himself or to the trustee.

(11)   Where there are two or more drawers or indorsers who are not partners, notice must be given to each of them, unless one of them has authority to receive such notice for the others.

(12)   The notice may be given as soon as the bill is dishonoured and must be given within a reasonable time thereafter.

In the absence of special circumstances notice is not deemed to have been given within a reasonable time, unless—

(a)   where the person giving and the person to receive notice reside in the same place, the notice is given or sent off in time to reach the latter on the day after the dishonour of the bill.

(b)   where the person giving and the person to receive notice reside in different places, the notice is sent off on the day after the dishonour of the bill, if there be a post at a convenient hour on that day, and if there be no such post on that day then by the next post thereafter.

(13)   Where a bill when dishonoured is in the hands of an agent, he may either himself give notice to the parties liable on the bill, or he may give notice to his principal. If he gives notice to his principal, he must do so within the same time as if he were the holder, and the principal upon receipt of such notice has himself the same time for giving notice as if the agent had been an independent holder.

(14)   Where a party to a bill receives due notice of dishonour, he has after the receipt of such notice the same period of time for giving notice to antecedent parties that the holder has after the dishonour.

(15)   Where a notice of dishonour is duly addressed and posted, the sender is deemed to have given due notice of dishonour, notwithstanding any miscarriage by the [postal operator concerned].

**50   Excuses for non-notice and delay**

(1)   Delay in giving notice of dishonour is excused where the delay is caused by circumstances beyond the control of the party giving notice, and not imputable to his default, misconduct, or negligence. When the cause of delay ceases to operate the notice must be given with reasonable diligence.

(2)   Notice of dishonour is dispensed with—

(a)   When, after the exercise of reasonable diligence, notice as required by this Act cannot be given to or does not reach the drawer or indorser sought to be charged:

(b)   By waiver express or implied. Notice of dishonour may be waived before the time of giving notice has arrived, or after the omission to give due notice:

(c)   As regards the drawer in the following cases, namely, (1) where drawer and drawee are the same person, (2) where the drawee is a fictitious person or a person not having capacity to contract, (3) where the drawer is the person to whom the bill is presented for payment, (4) where the drawee or acceptor is as between himself and the drawer under no obligation to accept or pay the bill, (5) where the drawer has countermanded payment:

(d)   As regards the indorser in the following cases, namely, (1) where the drawee is a fictitious person or a person not having capacity to contract and the indorser was aware of the fact at the time he indorsed the bill, (2) where the indorser is the person to whom the bill is presented for payment, (3) where the bill was accepted or made for his accommodation.

**51   Noting or protest of bill**

(1)   Where an inland bill has been dishonoured it may, if the holder think fit, be noted for non-acceptance or non-payment, as the case may be; but it shall not be necessary to note or protest any such bill in order to preserve the recourse against the drawer or indorser.

(2)   Where a foreign bill, appearing on the face of it to be such, has been dishonoured by non-acceptance it must be duly protested for non-acceptance and where such a bill, which has not been previously dishonoured by non-acceptance, is dishonoured by non-payment it must be duly protested for non-payment. If it be not so protested the drawer and indorsers are discharged. Where a bill does not appear on the face of it to be a foreign bill, protest thereof in the case of dishonour is unnecessary.

(3)   A bill which has been protested for non-acceptance may be subsequently protested for non-payment.

(4)   Subject to the provisions of this Act, when a bill is noted or protested, [it may be noted on the day of its dishonour and must be noted not later than the next succeeding business day]. When a bill has been duly noted, the protest may be subsequently extended as of the date of the noting.

(5)   Where the acceptor of the bill becomes bankrupt or insolvent or suspends payment before it matures, the holder may cause the bill to be protested for better security against the drawer and indorsers.

(6)   A bill must be protested at the place where it is dishonoured: Provided that—

(a)   When a bill is presented through [a postal operator], and returned by post dishonoured, it may be protested at the place to which it is returned and on the day of its return if received during business hours, and if not received during business hours, then not later than the next business day:

(b)   When a bill drawn payable at the place of business or residence of some person other than the drawee, has been dishonoured by non-acceptance, it must be protested for non-payment at the place where it is expressed to be payable, and no further presentment for payment to, or demand on, the drawee is necessary.

(7)   A protest must contain a copy of the bill, and must be signed by the notary making it, and must specify—

(a)   The person at whose request the bill is protested:

(b)   The place and date of protest, the cause or reason for protesting the bill, the demand made, and the answer given, if any, or the fact that the drawee or acceptor could not be found.

[(7A)   In subsection (7) 'notary' includes a person who, for the purposes of the Legal Services Act 2007, is an authorised person in relation to any activity which constitutes a notarial activity (within the meaning of that Act).]

(8)   Where a bill is lost or destroyed, or is wrongly detained from the person entitled to hold it, protest may be made on a copy or written particulars thereof.

(9)   Protest is dispensed with by any circumstance which would dispense with notice of dishonour. Delay in noting or protesting is excused when the delay is caused by circumstances beyond the control of the holder, and not imputable to his default, misconduct, or negligence. When the cause of delay ceases to operate the bill must be noted or protested with reasonable diligence.

### 52   Duties of holder as regards drawee or acceptor

(1)   When a bill is accepted generally presentment for payment is not necessary in order to render the acceptor liable.

(2)   When by the terms of a qualified acceptance presentment for payment is required, the acceptor, in the absence of an express stipulation to that effect, is not discharged by the omission to present the bill for payment on the day that it matures.

(3)   In order to render the acceptor of a bill liable it is not necessary to protest it, or that notice of dishonour should be given to him.

(4)   [Subject to Part 4A (presentment by electronic means)] where the holder of a bill presents it for payment, he shall exhibit the bill to the person from whom he demands payment, and when a bill is paid the holder shall forthwith deliver it up to the party paying it.

*Liabilities of parties*

### 53   Funds in hands of drawee

(1)   [Does not apply to Scotland.]

(2)   In Scotland, where the drawee of a bill [other than a cheque] has in his hands funds available for the payment thereof, the bill operates as an assignment of the sum for which it is drawn in favour of the holder, from the time when the bill is presented to the drawee.

### 54   Liability of acceptor

The acceptor of a bill, by accepting it—

(1)   Engages that he will pay it according to the tenor of his acceptance:

(2)   Is precluded from denying to a holder in due course:

(a)   The existence of the drawer, the genuineness of his signature, and his capacity and authority to draw the bill;

(b)   In the case of a bill payable to drawer's order, the then capacity of the drawer to indorse, but not the genuineness or validity of his indorsement;

(c)   In the case of a bill payable to the order of a third person, the existence of the payee and his then capacity to indorse, but not the genuineness or validity of his indorsement.

### 55   Liability of drawer or indorser

(1)   The drawer of a bill by drawing it—

(a)   Engages that on due presentment it shall be accepted and paid according to its tenor, and that if it be dishonoured he will compensate the holder or any indorser who is compelled to pay it, provided that the requisite proceedings on dishonour be duly taken;

(b)   Is precluded from denying to a holder in due course the existence of the payee and his then capacity to indorse.

(2)   The indorser of a bill by indorsing it—

(a)   Engages that on due presentment it shall be accepted and paid according to its tenor, and that if it be dishonoured he will compensate the holder or a subsequent indorser who is compelled to pay it, provided that the requisite proceedings on dishonour be duly taken;

(b)   Is precluded from denying to a holder in due course the genuineness and regularity in all respects of the drawer's signature and all previous indorsements;

(c)   Is precluded from denying to his immediate or a subsequent indorsee that the bill was at the time of his indorsement a valid and subsisting bill, and that he had then a good title thereto.

### 56   Stranger signing bill liable as indorser
Where a person signs a bill otherwise than as drawer or acceptor, he thereby incurs the liabilities of an indorser to a holder in due course.

### 57   Measure of damages against parties to dishonoured bill
Where a bill is dishonoured, the measure of damages, which shall be deemed to be liquidated damages, shall be as follows:

(1)   The holder may recover from any party liable on the bill, and the drawer who has been compelled to pay the bill may recover from the acceptor, and an indorser who has been compelled to pay the bill may recover from the acceptor or from the drawer, or from a prior indorser—

(a)   The amount of the bill:

(b)   Interest thereon from the time of presentment for payment if the bill is payable on demand, and from the maturity of the bill in any other case:

(c)   The expenses of noting, or, when protest is necessary, and the protest has been extended, the expenses of protest.

[. . .]

(3)   Where by this Act interest may be recovered as damages, such interest may, if justice require it, be withheld wholly or in part, and where a bill is expressed to be payable with interest at a given rate, interest as damages may or may not be given at the same rate as interest proper.

### 58   Transferor by delivery and transferee
(1)   Where the holder of a bill payable to bearer negotiates it by delivery without indorsing it, he is called a 'transferor by delivery'.

(2)   A transferor by delivery is not liable on the instrument.

(3)   A transferor by delivery who negotiates a bill thereby warrants to his immediate transferee being a holder for value that the bill is what it purports to be, that he has a right to transfer it, and that at the time of the transfer he is not aware of any fact which renders it valueless.

*Discharge of bill*

### 59   Payment in due course
(1)   A bill is discharged by payment in due course by or on behalf of the drawee or acceptor.

'Payment in due course' means payment made at or after the maturity of the bill to the holder thereof in good faith and without notice that his title to the bill is defective.

(2)   Subject to the provisions herein-after contained, when a bill is paid by the drawer or an indorser it is not discharged; but

(a)   Where a bill payable to, or to the order of, a third party is paid by the drawer, the drawer may enforce payment thereof against the acceptor, but may not re-issue the bill.

(b)  Where a bill is paid by an indorser, or where a bill payable to drawer's order is paid by the drawer, the party paying it is remitted to his former rights as regards the acceptor or antecedent parties, and he may, if he thinks fit, strike out his own subsequent indorsements, and again negotiate the bill.

(3)  Where an accommodation bill is paid in due course by the party accommodated the bill is discharged.

## 60  Banker paying demand draft whereon indorsement is forged

When a bill payable to order on demand is drawn on a banker, and the banker on whom it is drawn pays the bill in good faith and in the ordinary course of business, it is not incumbent on the banker to show that the indorsement of the payee or any subsequent indorsement was made by or under the authority of the person whose indorsement it purports to be, and the banker is deemed to have paid the bill in due course, although such indorsement has been forged or made without authority.

## 61  Acceptor the holder at maturity

When the acceptor of a bill is or becomes the holder of it at or after its maturity, in his own right, the bill is discharged.

## 62  Express waiver

(1)  When the holder of a bill at or after its maturity absolutely and unconditionally renounces his rights against the acceptor the bill is discharged.

The renunciation must be in writing, unless the bill is delivered up to the acceptor.

(2)  The liabilities of any party to a bill may in like manner be renounced by the holder before, at, or after its maturity; but nothing in this section shall affect the rights of a holder in due course without notice of the renunciation.

## 63  Cancellation

(1)  Where a bill is intentionally cancelled by the holder or his agent, and the cancellation is apparent thereon, the bill is discharged.

(2)  In like manner any party liable on a bill may be discharged by the intentional cancellation of his signature by the holder or his agent. In such case any indorser who would have had a right of recourse against the party whose signature is cancelled, is also discharged.

(3)  A cancellation made unintentionally, or under a mistake, or without the authority of the holder is inoperative; but where a bill or any signature thereon appears to have been cancelled the burden of proof lies on the party who alleges that the cancellation was made unintentionally, or under a mistake, or without authority.

## 64  Alteration of bill

(1)  Where a bill or acceptance is materially altered without the assent of all parties liable on the bill, the bill is avoided except as against a party who has himself made, authorised, or assented to the alteration, and subsequent indorsers.

Provided that,

Where a bill has been materially altered, but the alteration is not apparent, and the bill is in the hands of a holder in due course, such holder may avail himself of the bill as if it had not been altered, and may enforce payment of it according to its original tenor.

(2)  In particular the following alterations are material, namely, any alteration of the date, the sum payable, the time of payment, the place of payment, and where a bill has been accepted generally, the addition of a place of payment without the acceptor's assent.

*Acceptance and payment for honour*

## 65  Acceptance for honour supra protest

(1)  Where a bill of exchange has been protested for dishonour by non-acceptance, or protested for better security, and is not overdue, any person, not being a party already liable thereon, may, with the consent of the holder, intervene and accept the bill supra protest, for the honour of any party liable thereon, or for the honour of the person for whose account the bill is drawn.

(2)  A bill may be accepted for honour for part only of the sum for which it is drawn.

(3)  An acceptance for honour supra protest in order to be valid must—

  (a)  be written on the bill, and indicate that it is an acceptance for honour;

  (b)  be signed by the acceptor for honour.

(4)  Where an acceptance for honour does not expressly state for whose honour it is made, it is deemed to be an acceptance for the honour of the drawer.

(5)  Where a bill payable after sight is accepted for honour, its maturity is calculated from the date of the noting for non-acceptance, and not from the date of the acceptance for honour.

## 66  Liability of acceptor for honour

(1)  The acceptor for honour of a bill by accepting it engages that he will, on due presentment, pay the bill according to the tenor of his acceptance, if it is not paid by the drawee, provided it has been duly presented for payment, and protested for non-payment, and that he receives notice of these facts.

(2)  The acceptor for honour is liable to the holder and to all parties to the bill subsequent to the party for whose honour he has accepted.

## 67  Presentment to acceptor for honour

(1)  Where a dishonoured bill has been accepted for honour supra protest, or contains a reference in case of need, it must be protested for non-payment before it is presented for payment to the acceptor for honour, or referee in case of need.

(2)  Where the address of the acceptor for honour is in the same place where the bill is protested for non-payment, the bill must be presented to him not later than the day following its maturity; and where the address of the acceptor for honour is in some place other than the place where it was protested for non-payment, the bill must be forwarded not later than the day following its maturity for presentment to him.

(3)  Delay in presentment or non-presentment is excused by any circumstances which would excuse delay in presentment for payment or non-presentment for payment.

(4)  When a bill of exchange is dishonoured by the acceptor for honour it must be protested for non-payment by him.

## 68  Payment for honour supra protest

(1)  Where a bill has been protested for non-payment any person may intervene and pay it supra protest for the honour of any party liable thereon, or for the honour of the person for whose account the bill is drawn.

(2)  Where two or more persons offer to pay a bill for the honour of different parties, the person whose payment will discharge most parties to the bill shall have the preference.

(3)  Payment for honour supra protest, in order to operate as such and not as a mere voluntary payment, must be attested by a notarial act of honour which may be appended to the protest or form an extension of it.

(4)  The notarial act of honour must be founded on a declaration made by the payer for honour, or his agent in that behalf, declaring his intention to pay the bill for honour, and for whose honour he pays.

(5)  Where a bill has been paid for honour, all parties subsequent to the party for whose honour it is paid are discharged, but the payer for honour is subrogated

for, and succeeds to both the rights and duties of, the holder as regards the party for whose honour he pays, and all parties liable to that party.

(6)   The payer for honour on paying to the holder the amount of the bill and the notarial expenses incidental to its dishonour is entitled to receive both the bill itself and the protest. If the holder do not on demand deliver them up he shall be liable to the payer for honour in damages.

(7)   Where the holder of a bill refuses to receive payment supra protest he shall lose his right of recourse against any party who would have been discharged by such payment.

*Lost instruments*

## 69   Holder's right to duplicate of lost bill
Where a bill has been lost before it is overdue, the person who was the holder of it may apply to the drawer to give him another bill of the same tenor, giving security to the drawer if required to indemnify him against all persons whatever in case the bill alleged to have been lost shall be found again.

If the drawer on request as aforesaid refuses to give such duplicate bill, he may be compelled to do so.

## 70   Action on lost bill
In any action or proceeding upon a bill, the court or a judge may order that the loss of the instrument shall not be set up, provided an indemnity be given to the satisfaction of the court or judge against the claims of any other person upon the instrument in question.

*Bill in a set*

## 71   Rules as to sets
(1)   Where a bill is drawn in a set, each part of the set being numbered and containing a reference to the other parts, the whole of the parts constitute one bill.

(2)   Where the holder of a set indorses two or more parts to different persons, he is liable to every such part, and every indorser subsequent to him is liable on the part he has himself indorsed as if the said parts were separate bills.

(3)   Where two or more parts of a set are negotiated to different holders in due course, the holder whose title first accrues is as between such holders deemed the true owner of the bill; but nothing in this sub-section shall affect the rights of a person who in due course accepts or pays the part first presented to him.

(4)   The acceptance may be written on any part, and it must be written on one part only.

If the drawee accepts more than one part, and such accepted parts get into the hands of different holders in due course, he is liable on every such part as if it were a separate bill.

(5)   When the acceptor of a bill drawn in a set pays it without requiring the part bearing the acceptance to be delivered up to him, and that part at maturity is outstanding in the hands of a holder in due course, he is liable to the holder thereof.

(6)   Subject to the preceding rules, where any one part of a bill drawn in a set is discharged by payment or otherwise, the whole bill is discharged.

*Conflict of laws*

## 72   Rules where laws conflict
Where a bill drawn in one country is negotiated, accepted, or payable in another, the rights, duties, and liabilities of the parties thereto are determined as follows:

(1)   The validity of a bill as regards requisites in form is determined by the law of the place of issue, and the validity as regards requisites in form of the supervening contracts, such as acceptance, or indorsement, or acceptance supra protest, is determined by the law of the place where such contract was made.

Provided that—

(a)   Where a bill is issued out of the United Kingdom it is not invalid by reason only that it is not stamped in accordance with the law of the place of issue:

(b)   Where a bill, issued out of the United Kingdom, conforms, as regards requisites in form, to the law of the United Kingdom, it may, for the purpose of enforcing payment thereof, be treated as valid as between all persons who negotiate, hold, or become parties to it in the United Kingdom.

(2)   Subject to the provisions of this Act, the interpretation of the drawing, indorsement, acceptance, or acceptance supra protest of a bill, is determined by the law of the place where such contract is made.

Provided that where an inland bill is indorsed in a foreign country the indorsement shall as regards the payer be interpreted according to the law of the United Kingdom.

(3)   The duties of the holder with respect to presentment for acceptance or payment and the necessity for or sufficiency of a protest or notice of dishonour, or otherwise, are determined by the law of the place where the act is done or the bill is dishonoured.

[. . .]

(5)   Where a bill is drawn in one country and is payable in another, the due date thereof is determined according to the law of the place where it is payable.


## PART III
## CHEQUES ON A BANKER

### 73   Cheque defined
A cheque is a bill of exchange drawn on a banker payable on demand. Except as otherwise provided in this Part, the provisions of this Act applicable to a bill of exchange payable on demand apply to a cheque.

### 74   Presentment of cheque for payment
Subject to the provisions of this Act—

(1)   Where a cheque is not presented for payment within a reasonable time of its issue, and the drawer or the person on whose account it is drawn had the right at the time of such presentment as between him and the banker to have the cheque paid and suffers actual damage through the delay, he is discharged to the extent of such damage, that is to say, to the extent to which such drawer or person is a creditor of such banker to a larger amount than he would have been had such cheque been paid.

(2)   In determining what is a reasonable time regard shall be had to the nature of the instrument, the usage of trade and of bankers, and the facts of the particular case.

(3)   The holder of such cheque as to which such drawer or person is discharged shall be a creditor, in lieu of such drawer or person, of such banker to the extent of such discharge, and entitled to recover the amount from him.

[. . .]

### 75   Revocation of banker's authority
The duty and authority of a banker to pay a cheque drawn on him by his customer are determined by—

(1)   Countermand of payment:

(2)   Notice of the customer's death.

[. . .]

*Crossed cheques*

## 76 General and special crossings defined

(1)   Where a cheque bears across its face an addition of—

(a)   The words 'and company' or any abbreviation thereof between two parallel transverse lines either with or without the words 'not negotiable'; or

(b)   Two parallel transverse lines simply, either with or without the words 'not negotiable';

that addition constitutes a crossing, and the cheque is crossed generally.

(2)   Where a cheque bears across its face an addition of the name of a banker, either with or without the words 'not negotiable', that addition constitutes a crossing, and the cheque is crossed specially and to that banker.

## 77 Crossing by drawer or after issue

(1)   A cheque may be crossed generally or specially by the drawer.

(2)   Where a cheque is uncrossed, the holder may cross it generally or specially.

(3)   Where a cheque is crossed generally, the holder may cross it specially.

(4)   Where a cheque is crossed generally or specially, the holder may add the words 'not negotiable'.

(5)   Where a cheque is crossed specially, the banker to whom it is crossed may again cross it specially to another banker for collection.

(6)   Where an uncrossed cheque, or a cheque crossed generally is sent to a banker for collection, he may cross it specially to himself.

## 78 Crossing a material part of cheque

A crossing authorised by this Act is a material part of the cheque; it shall not be lawful for any person to obliterate or, except as authorised by this Act, to add to or alter the crossing.

## 79 Duties of banker as to crossed cheques

(1)   Where a cheque is crossed specially to more than one banker except when crossed to an agent for collection being a banker, the banker on whom it is drawn shall refuse payment thereof.

(2)   Where the banker on whom a cheque is drawn which is so crossed nevertheless pays the same, or pays a cheque crossed generally otherwise than to a banker, or if crossed specially otherwise than to the banker to whom it is crossed, or his agent for collection being a banker, he is liable to the true owner of the cheque for any loss he may sustain owing to the cheque having been so paid.

Provided that where a cheque is presented for payment which does not at the time of presentment appear to be crossed, or to have had a crossing which had been obliterated, or to have been added to or altered otherwise than as authorised by this Act, the banker paying the cheque in good faith and without negligence shall not be responsible or incur any liability, nor shall the payment be questioned by reason of the cheque having been crossed, or of the crossing having been obliterated on having been added to or altered otherwise than as authorised by this Act, and of payment having been made otherwise than to a banker or to the banker to whom the cheque is or was crossed, or to his agent for collection being a banker as the case may be.

## 80 Protection to banker and drawer where cheque is crossed

Where the banker, on whom a crossed cheque [(including a cheque which under section 81A below or otherwise is not transferable)] is drawn in good faith and without negligence pays it, if crossed generally to a banker, and if crossed specially, to the banker to whom it is crossed, or his agent for collection being a banker, the banker paying the cheque, and, if the cheque has come into the hands of the payee, the drawer, shall respectively be entitled to the same rights and be placed in the same position as if payment of the cheque had been made to the true owner thereof.

### 81   Effect of crossing on holder

Where a person takes a crossed cheque which bears on it the words 'not negotiable', he shall not have and shall not be capable of giving a better title to the cheque than that which the person from whom he took it had.

### [81A   Non-transferable cheques

(1)   Where a cheque is crossed and bears across its face the words 'account payee' or 'a/c payee', either with or without the words 'only', the cheque shall not be transferable, but shall only be valid as between the parties thereto.

(2)   A banker is not to be treated for the purposes of section 80 above as having been negligent by reason only of his failure to concern himself with any purported indorsement of a cheque which under subsection (1) above or otherwise is not transferable.]

[. . .]

## PART IV
## PROMISSORY NOTES

### 83   Promissory note defined

(1)   A promissory note is an unconditional promise in writing made by one person to another signed by the maker, engaging to pay, on demand or at a fixed or determinable future time, a sum certain in money, to, or to the order of, a specified person or to bearer.

(2)   An instrument in the form of a note payable to maker's order is not a note within the meaning of this section unless and until it is indorsed by the maker.

(3)   A note is not invalid by reason only that it contains also a pledge of collateral security with authority to sell or dispose thereof.

(4)   A note which is, or on the face of it purports to be, both made and payable within the British Islands is an inland note. Any other note is a foreign note.

### 84   Delivery necessary

A promissory note is inchoate and incomplete until delivery thereof to the payee or bearer.

### 85   Joint and several notes

(1)   A promissory note may be made by two or more makers, and they may be liable thereon jointly, or jointly and severally according to its tenor.

(2)   Where a note runs 'I promise to pay' and is signed by two or more persons it is deemed to be their joint and several note.

### 86   Note payable on demand

(1)   Where a note payable on demand has been indorsed, it must be presented for payment within a reasonable time of the indorsement. If it be not so presented the indorser is discharged.

(2)   In determining what is a reasonable time, regard shall be had to the nature of the instrument, the usage of trade, and the facts of the particular case.

(3)   Where a note payable on demand is negotiated, it is not deemed to be overdue for the purpose of affecting the holder with defects of title of which he had no notice, by reason that it appears that a reasonable time for presenting it for payment has elapsed since its issue.

### 87   Presentment of note for payment

(1)   Where a promissory note is in the body of it made payable at a particular place, it must be presented for payment at that place in order to render the maker liable. In any other case, presentment for payment is not necessary in order to render the maker liable.

(2)   Presentment for payment is necessary in order to render the indorser of a note liable.

(3)   Where a note is in the body of it made payable at a particular place, presentment at that place is necessary in order to render an indorser liable; but when a place of payment is indicated by way of memorandum only, presentment at that place is sufficient to render the indorser liable, but a presentment to the maker elsewhere, if sufficient in other respects, shall also suffice.

*[(4)   This section is subject to Part 4A (presentment by electronic means).]*

### 88   Liability of maker
The maker of a promissory note by making it—
(1)   Engages that he will pay it according to its tenor;
(2)   Is precluded from denying to a holder in due course the existence of the payee and his then capacity to indorse.

### 89   Application of Part II to notes
(1)   Subject to the provisions in this part and, except as by this section provided, the provisions of this Act relating to bills of exchange apply, with the necessary modifications, to promissory notes.
(2)   In applying those provisions the maker of a note shall be deemed to correspond with the acceptor of a bill, and the first indorser of a note shall be deemed to correspond with the drawer of an accepted bill payable to drawer's order.
(3)   The following provisions as to bills do not apply to notes; namely, provisions relating to—
(a)   Presentment for acceptance;
(b)   Acceptance;
(c)   Acceptance supra protest;
(d)   Bills in a set.
(4)   Where a foreign note is dishonoured, protest thereof is unnecessary.


[PART 4A*
PRESENTMENT OF CHEQUES AND OTHER INSTRUMENTS BY
ELECTRONIC MEANS

### 89A   Presentment of instruments by electronic means
(1)   Presentment for payment of an instrument to which this section applies may be effected by provision of an electronic image of both faces of the instrument, instead of by presenting the physical instrument, if the person to whom presentment is made accepts the presentment as effective.
This is subject to regulations under subsection (2) and to section 89C.
(2)   The Treasury may by regulations prescribe circumstances in which subsection (1) does not apply.
(3)   Regulations under subsection (2) may in particular prescribe circumstances by reference to—
(a)   descriptions of instrument;
(b)   arrangements under which presentment is made;
(c)   descriptions of persons by or to whom presentment is made;
(d)   descriptions of persons receiving payment or on whose behalf payment is received.
(4)   Where presentment for payment is made under subsection (1)—
(a)   any requirement—
(i)   that the physical instrument must be exhibited, presented or delivered on or in connection with presentment or payment (including after presentment or payment or in connection with dishonour for non-payment), or
(ii)   as to the day, time or place on or at which presentment of the physical instrument may be or is to be made, and

*Part 4A comes into force on 31/07/2016.

(b)   any other requirement which is inconsistent with subsection (1),
does not apply.

(5)   Subsection (4) does not affect any requirement as to the latest time for presentment.

(6)   References in subsections (4) and (5) to a requirement are to a requirement or prohibition, whether imposed by or under any enactment, by a rule of law or by the instrument in question.

(7)   Where an instrument is presented for payment under this section—

(a)   any banker providing the electronic image,

(b)   any banker to whom it is provided, and

(c)   any banker making payment of the instrument as a result of provision of the electronic image,

are subject to the same duties in relation to collection and payment of the instrument as if the physical instrument had been presented.

This is subject to any provision made by or under this Part.

### 89B   Instruments to which section 89A applies

(1)   Subject to subsection (2), section 89A applies to—

(a)   a cheque, or

(b)   any other bill of exchange or any promissory note or other instrument—

(i)   which appears to be intended by the person creating it to enable a person to obtain payment from a banker indicated in it of the sum so mentioned,

(ii)   payment of which requires the instrument to be presented, and

(iii)   which, but for section 89A, could not be presented otherwise than by presenting the physical instrument.

(2)   Section 89A does not apply to any banknote (within the meaning given in section 208 of the Banking Act 2009).

(3)   The reference in subsection (1) to the person creating an instrument is—

(a)   in the case of a bill of exchange, a reference to the drawer;

(b)   in the case of a promissory note, a reference to the maker.

(4)   For the purposes of subsection (1)(b)(i) an indication may be by code or number and need not indicate that payment is intended to be obtained from the banker.

### 89C   Banker's obligation in relation to accepting physical instrument for presentment

Provision of an electronic image of an instrument does not constitute presentment of the instrument under section 89A if the arrangements between—

(a)   the banker authorised to collect payment of the instrument on behalf of a customer, and

(b)   that customer,

do not permit the customer to pay in the physical instrument but instead require an electronic image to be provided (whether to that banker or to any other person).

### 89D   Copies of instruments and evidence of payment

(1)   The Treasury may by regulations make provision for—

(a)   requiring a copy of an instrument paid as a result of presentment under section 89A to be provided, on request, to the creator of the instrument by the banker who paid the instrument;

(b)   a copy of an instrument provided in accordance with the regulations to be evidence of receipt by a person identified in accordance with the regulations of the sum payable by the instrument.

(2)   Regulations under subsection (1)(a) may in particular—

(a)   prescribe the manner and form in which a copy is to be provided;

(b)   require the copy to be certified to be a true copy of the electronic image provided to the banker making the payment on presentment under section 89A;

(c)    provide for the copy to be accompanied by prescribed information;

(d)    require any copy to be provided free of charge or permit charges to be made for the provision of copies in prescribed circumstances.

(3)    The reference in subsection (1)(a) to the creator of the instrument is—

(a)    in the case of a bill of exchange, a reference to the drawer;

(b)    in the case of a promissory note, a reference to the maker.

## 89E    Compensation in cases of presentment by electronic means

(1)    The Treasury may by regulations make provision for the responsible banker to compensate any person for any loss of a kind specified by the regulations which that person incurs in connection with electronic presentment or purported electronic presentment of an instrument.

(2)    In this section 'electronic presentment or purported electronic presentment of an instrument' includes—

(a)    presentment of an instrument to which section 89A applies under that section;

(b)    presentment of any other instrument by any means involving provision of an electronic image by which it may be presented for payment;

(c)    purported presentment for payment by any means involving provision of an electronic image of an instrument that may not be presented for payment in that way;

(d)    provision, in purported presentment for payment, of—

(i)    an electronic image that purports to be, but is not, an image of a physical instrument (including an image that has been altered electronically), or

(ii)    an electronic image of an instrument which has no legal effect; or

(e)    provision, in presentment or purported presentment for payment, of an electronic image which has been stolen.

(3)    In this section, the 'responsible banker', in relation to electronic presentment or purported electronic presentment of an instrument, means—

(a)    the banker who is authorised to collect payment of the instrument on a customer's behalf, or

(b)    if the holder of the instrument is a banker, that banker.

(4)    In this section—

(a)    references to an instrument include references to an instrument which has no legal effect (whether because it has been fraudulently altered or created, or because it has been discharged, or otherwise);

(b)    in relation to an electronic image which is not an image of a physical instrument, references to the instrument are to a purported instrument (of which it purports to be an image); and

(c)    in relation to an instrument which is not a bill of exchange or promissory note, references to the holder are to the payee or indorsee of the instrument who is in possession of it or, if it is payable to bearer, the person in possession of it.

(5)    Regulations under this section may in particular make provision for—

(a)    the responsible banker to be required to pay compensation irrespective of fault;

(b)    the amount of compensation to be reduced by virtue of anything done, or any failure to act, by the person to whom compensation is payable.

(6)    Nothing in this section or regulations under it is to be taken to—

(a)    prevent the responsible banker claiming a contribution from any other person, or

(b)    affect any remedy available to the responsible banker in contract or otherwise.

(7)    Except so far as regulations under this section provide expressly, nothing in this section or regulations under it is to be taken to affect any liability of the responsible banker which exists apart from this section or any such regulations.

**89F   Supplementary**

(1)   Regulations under this Part may—

(a)   include incidental, supplementary and consequential provision;

(b)   make transitory or transitional provision or savings;

(c)   make different provision for different cases or circumstances or for different purposes;

(d)   make provision subject to exceptions.

(2)   The power to make regulations under this Part is exercisable by statutory instrument.

(3)   An instrument containing—

(a)   regulations under section 89A or 89D, or

(b)   the first regulations to be made under section 89E, may not be made unless a draft of the instrument has been laid before, and approved by resolution of, each House of Parliament.

(4)   An instrument containing any other regulations under section 89E is subject to annulment in pursuance of a resolution of either House of Parliament.

(5)   For the purposes of this Part, a banker collects payment of an instrument on behalf of a customer by—

(a)   receiving payment of the instrument for the customer, or

(b)   receiving payment of the instrument for the banker (but not as holder), having—

(i)   credited the customer's account with the amount of the instrument, or

(ii)   otherwise given value to the customer in respect of the instrument.

(6)   Section 89E(4) applies for the purposes of subsection (5) in its application to section 89E.]

PART V
SUPPLEMENTARY

**90   Good faith**

A thing is deemed to be done in good faith, within the meaning of this Act, where it is in fact done honestly, whether it is done negligently or not.

**91   Signature**

(1)   Where, by this Act, any instrument or writing is required to be signed by any person, it is not necessary that he should sign it with his own hand, but it is sufficient if his signature is written thereon by some other person by or under his authority.

(2)   In the case of a corporation, where, by this Act, any instrument or writing is required to be signed, it is sufficient if the instrument or writing be sealed with the corporate seal.

But nothing in this section shall be construed as requiring the bill or note of a corporation to be under seal.

**92   Computation of time**

Where, by this Act, the time limited for doing any act or thing is less than three days, in reckoning time, non-business days are excluded.

'Non-business days' for the purposes of this Act mean—

(a)   [Saturday,] Sunday, Good Friday, Christmas Day;

(b)   A bank holiday under [the Banking and Financial Dealings Act 1971];

(c)   A day appointed by Royal proclamation as a public fast or thanksgiving day;

[(d)   A day declared by an order under section 2 of the Banking and Financial Dealings Act 1971 to be a non-business day.]

Any other day is a business day.

**93   When noting equivalent to protest**

For the purposes of this Act, where a bill or note is required to be protested within a specified time or before some further proceeding is taken, it is sufficient that the bill has been noted for protest before the expiration of the specified time or the taking of the proceeding; and the formal protest may be extended at any time thereafter as of the date of the noting.

### 94  Protest when notary not accessible

[(1)]  Where a dishonoured bill or note is authorised or required to be protested, and the services of a notary cannot be obtained at the place where the bill is dishonoured, any householder, or substantial resident of the place may, in the presence of two witnesses, give a certificate, signed by them, attesting to the dishonour of the bill, and the certificate shall in all respects operate as if it were a formal protest of the bill.

The form given in Schedule I to this Act may be used with necessary modifications, and if used shall be sufficient.

[(2)  In subsection (1) 'notary' includes a person who, for the purposes of the Legal Services Act 2007, is an authorised person in relation to any activity which constitutes a notarial activity (within the meaning of that Act).]

### 95  Dividend warrants may be crossed

The provisions of this Act as to crossed cheques shall apply to a warrant for payment of dividend.

[. . .]

### 97  Savings

(1)  The rules in bankruptcy relating to bills of exchange, promissory notes, and cheques, shall continue to apply thereto notwithstanding anything in this Act contained.

(2)  The rules of common law including the law merchant, save in so far as they are inconsistent with the express provisions of this Act, shall continue to apply to bills of exchange, promissory notes, and cheques.

(3)  Nothing in this Act or in any repeal effected thereby shall affect—

(a)  [. . .] any law or enactment for the time being in force relating to the revenue:

(b)  The provisions of the Companies Act, 1862, or Acts amending it, or any Act relating to joint stock banks or companies:

(c)  The provisions of any Act relating to or confirming the privileges of the Bank of England or the Bank of Ireland respectively:

(d)  The validity of any usage relating to dividend warrants, or the indorsements thereof.

### 98  Saving of summary diligence in Scotland

Nothing in this Act or in any repeal effected thereby shall extend or restrict, or in any way alter or affect the law and practice in Scotland in regard to summary diligence.

### 99  Construction with other Acts, etc

Where any Act or document refers to any enactment repealed by this Act, the Act or document shall be construed, and shall operate as if it referred to the corresponding provisions of this Act.

### 100  Parole evidence allowed in certain judicial proceedings in Scotland

In any judicial proceeding in Scotland, any fact relating to a bill of exchange, bank cheque, or promissory note, which is relevant to any question of liability thereon, may be proved by parole evidence: Provided that this enactment shall not in any way affect the existing law and practice whereby the party who is, according to the tenor of any bill of exchange, bank cheque, or promissory note, debtor to the holder in the amount thereof, may be required, as a condition of obtaining a sist of diligence, or suspension of a charge, or threatened charge, to make such consignation, or to find such caution as the court or judge before whom the cause is depending may require. [. . .]

## SCHEDULES

### FIRST SCHEDULE

Section 94

*Form of protest which may be used when the services of a notary cannot be obtained*

Know all men that I, *A. B.* [householder], of             in the county of             in the United Kingdom, at the request of *C. D.*, there being no notary public available, did on the             day of             188    at_____ demand payment [*or* acceptance] of the bill of exchange hereunder written, from *E. F.*, to which demand he made answer [state answer, if any] wherefore I now, in the presence of *G. H.* and *J. K.* do protest the said bill of exchange.

(Signed)    A. B. ⎫
G. H. ⎬  *Witnesses*
J. K.  ⎭

N.B.—The bill itself should be annexed, or a copy of the bill and all that is written thereon should be underwritten.

## FACTORS ACT 1889
### (52 & 53 Vict, c 45)

*Preliminary*

### 1  Definitions

For the purposes of this Act—

(1)   The expression 'mercantile agent' shall mean a mercantile agent having in the customary course of his business as such agent authority either to sell goods or to consign goods for the purpose of sale, or to buy goods, or to raise money on the security of goods:

(2)   A person shall be deemed to be in possession of goods or of the documents of title to goods, where the goods or documents are in the actual custody or are held by any other person subject to his control or for him or on his behalf:

(3)   The expression 'goods' shall include wares and merchandise:

(4)   The expression 'document of title' shall include any bill of lading, dock warrant, warehouse-keeper's certificate, and warrant or order for the delivery of goods, and any other document used in the ordinary course of business as proof of the possession or control of goods, or authorising or purporting to authorise, either by endorsement or by delivery, the possessor of the document to transfer or receive goods thereby represented:

(5)   The expression 'pledge' shall include any contract pledging, or giving a lien or security on, goods, whether in consideration of an original advance or of any further or continuing advance or of any pecuniary liability:

(6)   The expression 'person' shall include any body of persons corporate or unincorporated.

*Dispositions by mercantile agents*

### 2  Powers of mercantile agent with respect to disposition of goods

(1)   Where a mercantile agent is, with the consent of the owner, in possession of goods or of the documents of title to goods, any sale, pledge, or other disposition of the goods, made by him when acting in the ordinary course of business of a

mercantile agent, shall, subject to the provisions of this Act, be as valid as if he were expressly authorised by the owner of the goods to make the same; provided that the person taking under the disposition acts in good faith, and has not at the time of the disposition notice that the person making the disposition has not authority to make the same.

(2)   Where a mercantile agent has, with the consent of the owner, been in possession of goods or of the documents of title to goods, any sale, pledge, or other disposition, which would have been valid if the consent had continued, shall be valid notwithstanding the determination of the consent; provided that the person taking under the disposition has not at the time thereof notice that the consent has been determined.

(3)   Where a mercantile agent has obtained possession of any documents of title to goods by reason of his being or having been, with the consent of the owner, in possession of the goods represented thereby, or of any other documents of title to the goods, his possession of the first-mentioned documents shall, for the purposes of this Act, be deemed to be with the consent of the owner.

(4)   For the purposes of this Act the consent of the owner shall be presumed in the absence of evidence to the contrary.

*Dispositions by sellers and buyers of goods*

### 8   Disposition by seller remaining in possession

Where a person, having sold goods, continues, or is, in possession of the goods or of the documents of title to the goods, the delivery or transfer by that person, or by a mercantile agent acting for him, of the goods or documents of title under any sale, pledge, or other disposition thereof, or under any agreement for sale, pledge, or other disposition thereof, to any person receiving the same in good faith and without notice of the previous sale, shall have the same effect as if the person making the delivery or transfer were expressly authorised by the owner of the goods to make the same.

### 9   Disposition by buyer obtaining possession

Where a person, having bought or agreed to buy goods, obtains with the consent of the seller possession of the goods or the documents of title to the goods, the delivery or transfer, by that person or by a mercantile agent acting for him, of the goods or documents of title under any sale, pledge, or other disposition thereof, or under any agreement for sale, pledge, or other disposition thereof, to any person receiving the same in good faith and without notice of any lien or other right of the original seller in respect of the goods, shall have the same effect as if the person making the delivery or transfer were a mercantile agent in possession of the goods or documents of title with the consent of the owner.

[For the purposes of this section—

(i)   the buyer under a conditional sale agreement shall be deemed not to be a person who has bought or agreed to buy goods, and

(ii)   'conditional sale agreement' means an agreement for the sale of goods which is a consumer credit agreement within the meaning of the Consumer Credit Act 1974 under which the purchase price or part of it is payable by instalments, and the property in the goods is to remain in the seller (notwithstanding that the buyer is to be in possession of the goods) until such conditions as to the payment of instalments or otherwise as may be specified in the agreement are fulfilled.]

## PARTNERSHIP ACT 1890
### (53 & 54 Vict, c 39)

*Nature of partnership*

### 1  Definition of partnership
(1)  Partnership is the relation which subsists between persons carrying on a business in common with a view of profit.

(2)  But the relation between members of any company or association which is—

[(a)  Registered under the Companies Act 2006,] or

(b)  Formed or incorporated by or in pursuance of any other Act of Parliament or letters patent, or Royal Charter

[. . .]

is not a partnership within the meaning of this Act.

### 2  Rules for determining existence of partnership
In determining whether a partnership does or does not exist, regard shall be had to the following rules:

(1)  joint tenancy, tenancy in common, joint property, common property, or part ownership does not of itself create a partnership as to anything so held or owned, whether the tenants or owners do or do not share any profits made by the use thereof.

(2)  The sharing of gross returns does not of itself create a partnership, whether the persons sharing such returns have or have not a joint or common right or interest in any property from which or from the use of which the returns are derived.

(3)  The receipt by a person of a share of the profits of a business is prima facie evidence that he is a partner in the business, but the receipt of such a share, or of a payment contingent on or varying with the profits of a business, does not of itself make him a partner in the business; and in particular—

(a)  The receipt by a person of a debt or other liquidated amount by instalments, or otherwise out of the accruing profits of a business does not of itself make him a partner in the business or liable as such:

(b)  A contract for the remuneration of a servant or agent of a person engaged in a business by a share of the profits of the business does not of itself make the servant or agent a partner in the business or liable as such:

(c)  A person being the widow [, widower, surviving civil partner] or child of a deceased partner, and receiving by way of annuity a portion of the profits made in the business in which the deceased person was a partner, is not by reason only of such receipt a partner in the business or liable as such:

(d)  The advance of money by way of loan to a person engaged or about to engage in any business on a contract with that person that the lender shall receive a rate of interest varying with the profits, or shall receive a share of the profits arising from carrying on the business, does not of itself make the lender a partner with the person or persons carrying on the business or liable as such. Provided that the contract is in writing, and signed by or on behalf of all the parties thereto:

(e)  A person receiving by way of annuity or otherwise a portion of the profits of a business in consideration of the sale by him of the goodwill of the business is not by reason only of such receipt a partner in the business or liable as such.

### 3  Postponement of rights of person lending or selling in consideration of share of profits in case of insolvency
In the event of any person to whom money has been advanced by way of loan upon such a contract as is mentioned in the last foregoing section, or of any buyer

of a goodwill in consideration of a share of the profits of the business, being adjudged a bankrupt, entering into an arrangement to pay his creditors less than [100p] in the pound, or dying in insolvent circumstances, the lender of the loan shall not be entitled to recover anything in respect of the loan, and the seller of the goodwill shall not be entitled to recover anything in respect of the share of profits contracted for, until the claims of the other creditors of the borrower or buyer for valuable consideration in money or money's worth have been satisfied.

## 4  Meaning of firm

(1)  Persons who have entered into partnership with one another are for the purposes of this Act called collectively a firm, and the name under which their business is carried on is called the firm-name.

(2)  In Scotland a firm is a legal person distinct from the partners of whom it is composed, but an individual partner may be charged on a decree or diligence directed against the firm, and on payment of the debts is entitled to relief pro rata from the firm and its other members.

*Relations of partners to persons dealing with them*

## 5  Power of partner to bind the firm

Every partner is an agent of the firm and his other partners for the purpose of the business of the partnership; and the acts of every partner who does any act for carrying on in the usual way business of the kind carried on by the firm of which he is a member bind the firm and his partners, unless the partner so acting has in fact no authority to act for the firm in the particular matter, and the person with whom he is dealing either knows that he has no authority, or does not know or believe him to be a partner.

## 6  Partners bound by acts on behalf of firm

An act or instrument relating to the business of the firm and done or executed in the firm-name, or in any other manner showing an intention to bind the firm, by any person thereto authorised, whether a partner or not, is binding on the firm and all the partners.

Provided that this section shall not affect any general rule of law relating to the execution of deeds or negotiable instruments.

## 7  Partner using credit of firm for private purposes

Where one partner pledges the credit of the firm for a purpose apparently not connected with the firm's ordinary course of business, the firm is not bound, unless he is in fact specially authorised by the other partners; but this section does not affect any personal liability incurred by an individual partner.

## 8  Effect of notice that firm will not be bound by acts of partner

If it has been agreed between the partners that any restriction shall be placed on the power of any one or more of them to bind the firm, no act done in contravention of the agreement is binding on the firm with respect to persons having notice of the agreement.

## 9  Liability of partners

Every partner in a firm is liable jointly with the other partners, and in Scotland severally also, for all debts and obligations of the firm incurred while he is a partner; and after his death his estate is also severally liable in a due course of administration for such debts and obligations, so far as they remain unsatisfied, but subject in England or Ireland to the prior payment of his separate debts.

## 10  Liability of the firm for wrongs

Where, by any wrongful act or omission of any partner acting in the ordinary course of the business of the firm, or with the authority of his co-partners, loss or injury is caused to any person not being a partner in the firm, or any penalty is incurred, the firm is liable therefor to the same extent as the partner so acting or omitting to act.

## 11  Misapplication of money or property received for or in custody of the firm
In the following cases; namely—
    (a)  Where one partner acting within the scope of his apparent authority receives the money or property of a third person and misapplies it; and
    (b)  Where a firm in the course of its business receives money or property of a third person, and the money or property so received is misapplied by one or more of the partners while it is in the custody of the firm;
the firm is liable to make good the loss.

## 12  Liability for wrongs joint and several
Every partner is liable jointly with his co-partners and also severally for everything for which the firm while he is a partner therein becomes liable under either of the two last preceding sections.

## 13  Improper employment of trust-property for partnership purposes
If a partner, being a trustee, improperly employs trust property in the business or on the account of the partnership, no other partner is liable for the trust-property to the persons beneficially interested therein.
    Provided as follows:—
    (1)  This section shall not affect any liability incurred by any partner by reason of his having notice of a breach of trust; and
    (2)  Nothing in this section shall prevent trust money from being followed and recovered from the firm if still in its possession or under its control.

## 14  Persons liable by 'holding out'
    (1)  Every one who by words spoken or written or by conduct represents himself, or who knowingly suffers himself to be represented, as a partner in a particular firm, is liable as a partner to anyone who has on the faith of any such representation given credit to the firm, whether the representation has or has not been made or communicated to the person so giving credit by or with the knowledge of the apparent partner making the representation or suffering it to be made.
    (2)  Provided that where after a partner's death the partnership business is continued in the old firm-name, the continued use of that name or of the deceased partner's name as part thereof shall not of itself make his executors' or administrators' estate or effects liable for any partnership debts contracted after his death.

## 15  Admissions and representations of partners
An admission or representation made by any partner concerning the partnership affairs, and in the ordinary course of its business, is evidence against the firm.

## 16  Notice to acting partner to be notice to the firm
Notice to any partner who habitually acts in the partnership business of any matter relating to partnership affairs operates as a notice to the firm, except in the case of a fraud on the firm committed by or with the consent of that partner.

## 17  Liabilities of incoming and outgoing partners
    (1)  A person who is admitted as a partner into an existing firm does not thereby become liable to the creditors of the firm for anything done before he became a partner.
    (2)  A partner who retires from a firm does not thereby cease to be liable for partnership debts or obligations incurred before his retirement.
    (3)  A retiring partner may be discharged from any existing liabilities, by an agreement to that effect between himself and the members of the firm as newly constituted and the creditors, and this agreement may be either express or in-

ferred, as a fact from the course of dealing between the creditors and the firm as newly constituted.

**18   Revocation of continuing guaranty by change in firm**
A continuing guaranty or cautionary obligation given either to a firm or to a third person in respect of the transactions of a firm is, in the absence of agreement to the contrary, revoked as to future transactions by any change in the constitution of the firm to which, or of the firm in respect of the transactions of which, the guaranty or obligation was given.

*Relations of partners to one another*

**19   Variation by consent of terms of partnership**
The mutual rights and duties of partners, whether ascertained by agreement or defined by this Act, may be varied by the consent of all the partners, and such consent may be either express or inferred from a course of dealing.

**20   Partnership property**
   (1)   All property and rights and interests in property originally brought into the partnership stock or acquired, whether by purchase or otherwise, on account of the firm or for the purposes and in the course of the partnership business, are called in this Act partnership property, and must be held and applied by the partners exclusively for the purposes of the partnership and in accordance with the partnership agreement.
   (2)   Provided that the legal estate or interest in any land, or in Scotland [of . . .] any heritable estate, which belongs to the partnership shall devolve according to the nature and tenure thereof, and the general rules of law thereto applicable, but in trust, so far as necessary, for the persons beneficially interested in the land under this section.
   (3)   Where co-owners of an estate or interest in any land, or in Scotland of any heritable estate, not being itself partnership property, are partners as to profits made by the use of that land or estate, and purchase other land or estate out of the profits to be used in like manner, the land or estate so purchased belongs to them, in the absence of an agreement to the contrary, not as partners but as co-owners for the same respective estates and interests as are held by them in the land or estate first mentioned at the date of the purchase.

**21   Property bought with partnership money**
Unless the contrary intention appears, property bought with money belonging to the firm is deemed to have been bought on account of the firm.

**22 Conversion into personal estate of land held as partnership property**
Where land or any heritable interest therein has become partnership property, it shall, unless the contrary intention appears, be treated as between the partners (including the representatives of a deceased partner), and also as between the heirs of a deceased partner and his executors or administrators, as personal or moveable and not real or heritable estate.

**23**   *[Does not apply to Scotland]*

**24   Rules as to interests and duties of partners subject to special agreement**
The interests of partners in the partnership property and their rights and duties in relation to the partnership shall be determined, subject to any agreement express or implied between the partners, by the following rules:
   (1)   All the partners are entitled to share equally in the capital and profits of the business, and must contribute equally towards the losses whether of capital or otherwise sustained by the firm.
   (2)   The firm must indemnify every partner in respect of payments made and personal liabilities incurred by him—

(a)   In the ordinary and proper conduct of the business of the firm-, or,

(b)   In or about anything necessarily done for the preservation of the business or property of the firm.

(3)   A partner making, for the purpose of the partnership, any actual payment or advance beyond the amount of capital which he has agreed to subscribe, is entitled to interest at the rate of five per cent. per annum from the date of the payment or advance.

(4)   A partner is not entitled, before the ascertainment of profits, to interest on the capital subscribed by him.

(5)   Every partner may take part in the management of the partnership business.

(6)   No partner shall be entitled to remuneration for acting in the partnership business.

(7)   No person may be introduced as a partner without the consent of all existing partners.

(8)   Any difference arising as to ordinary matters connected with the partnership business may be decided by a majority of the partners, but no change may be made in the nature of the partnership business without the consent of all existing partners.

(9)   The partnership books are to be kept at the place of business of the partnership (or the principal place, if there is more than one), and every partner may, when he thinks fit, have access to and inspect and copy any of them.

## 25  Expulsion of partner

No majority of the partners can expel any partner unless a power to do so has been conferred by express agreement between the partners.

## 26  Retirement from partnership at will

(1)   Where no fixed term has been agreed upon for the duration of the partnership, any partner may determine the partnership at any time on giving notice of his intention so to do to all the other partners.

(2)   Where the partnership has originally been constituted by deed, a notice in writing, signed by the partner giving it, shall be sufficient for this purpose.

## 27  Where partnership for term is continued over, continuance on old terms presumed

(1)   Where a partnership entered into for a fixed term is continued after the term has expired, and without any express new agreement, the rights and duties of the partners remain the same as they were at the expiration of the term, so far as is consistent with the incidents of a partnership at will.

(2)   A continuance of the business by the partners or such of them as habitually acted therein during the term, without any settlement or liquidation of the partnership affairs, is presumed to be a continuance of the partnership.

## 28  Duty of partners to render accounts, &c

Partners are bound to render true accounts and full information of all things affecting the partnership to any partner or his legal representatives.

## 29  Accountability of partners for private profits

(1)   Every partner must account to the firm for any benefit derived by him without the consent of the other partners from any transaction concerning the partnership, or from any use by him of the partnership property name or business connexion.

(2)   This section applies also to transactions undertaken after a partnership has been dissolved by the death of a partner, and before the affairs thereof have been completely wound up, either by any surviving partner or by the representatives of the deceased partner.

## 30  Duty of partner not to compete with firm

If a partner, without the consent of the other partners, carries on any business of the same nature as and competing with that of the firm, he must account for and pay over to the firm all profits made by him in that business.

## 31   Rights of assignee of share in partnership

(1)   An assignment by any partner of his share in the partnership, either absolute or by way of mortgage or redeemable charge, does not, as against the other partners, entitle the assignee, during the continuance of the partnership, to interfere in the management or administration of the partnership business or affairs, or to require any accounts of the partnership transactions, or to inspect the partnership books, but entitles the assignee only to receive the share of profits to which the assigning partner would otherwise be entitled, and the assignee must accept the account of profits agreed to by the partners.

(2)   In the case of a dissolution of the partnership, whether as respects all the partners or as respects the assigning partner, the assignee is entitled to receive the share of the partnership assets to which the assigning partner is entitled as between himself and the other partners, and, for the purpose of ascertaining that share, to an account as from the date of the dissolution.

*Dissolution of partnership, and its consequences*

## 32   Dissolution by expiration or notice

Subject to any agreement between the partners a partnership is dissolved—

(a)   If entered into for a fixed term, by the expiration of that term:

(b)   If entered into for a single adventure or undertaking, by the termination of that adventure or undertaking:

(c)   If entered into for an undefined time, by any partner giving notice to the other or others of his intention to dissolve the partnership.

In the last-mentioned case the partnership is dissolved as from the date mentioned in the notice as the date of dissolution, or, if no date is so mentioned, as from the date of the communication of the notice.

## 33   Dissolution by bankruptcy, death, or charge

(1)   Subject to any agreement between the partners, every partnership is dissolved as regards all partners by the death or bankruptcy of any partner.

(2)   A partnership may, at the option of the other partners, be dissolved if any partner suffers his share of the partnership property to be charged under this Act for his separate debt.

## 34   Dissolution by illegality of partnership

A partnership is in every case dissolved by the happening of any event which makes it unlawful for the business of the firm to be carried on or for the members of the firm to carry it on in partnership.

## 35   Dissolution by the Court

On application by a partner the Court may decree a dissolution of the partnership in any of the following cases:

(a)   When a partner is found lunatic by inquisition, or in Scotland by cognition, or is shown to the satisfaction of the Court to be of permanently unsound mind, in either of which cases the application may be made as well on behalf of that partner by his committee or next friend or person having title to intervene as by any other partner:

(b)   When a partner, other than the partner suing, becomes in any other way permanently incapable of performing his part of the partnership contract:

(c)   When a partner, other than the partner suing, has been guilty of such conduct as, in the opinion of the Court, regard being had to the nature of the business, is calculated to prejudicially affect the carrying on of the business:

(d)   When a partner, other than the partner suing, wilfully or persistently commits a breach of the partnership agreement, or otherwise so conducts himself in matters relating to the partnership business that it is not reasonably practicable for the other partner or partners to carry on the business in partnership with him:

(e)    When the business of the partnership can only be carried on at a loss:

(f)    Whenever in any case circumstances have arisen which, in the opinion of the Court, render it just and equitable that the partnership be dissolved.

### 36   Rights of persons dealing with firm against apparent members of firm

(1)    Where a person deals with a firm after a change in its constitution he is entitled to treat all apparent members of the old firm as still being members of the firm until he has notice of the change.

(2)    An advertisement in the London Gazette as to a firm whose principal place of business is in England or Wales, in the Edinburgh Gazette as to a firm whose principal place of business is in Scotland, and in the [Belfast Gazette] as to a firm whose principal place of business is in Ireland, shall be notice as to persons who had not dealings with the firm before the date of the dissolution or change so advertised.

(3)    The estate of a partner who dies, or who becomes bankrupt, or of a partner who, not having been known to the person dealing with the firm to be a partner, retires from the firm, is not liable for partnership debts contracted after the date of the death, bankruptcy, or retirement respectively.

### 37   Right of partners to notify dissolution

On dissolution of a partnership or retirement of a partner any partner may publicly notify the same, and may require the other partner or partners to concur for that purpose in all necessary or proper acts, if any, which cannot be done without his or their concurrence.

### 38   Continuing authority of partners for purposes of winding up

After the dissolution of a partnership the authority of each partner to bind the firm, and the other rights and obligations of the partners, continue notwithstanding the dissolution so far as may be necessary to wind up the affairs of the partnership, and to complete transactions begun but unfinished at the time of the dissolution [, and in relation to any prosecution of the partnership by virtue of section 1 of the Partnerships (Prosecution) (Scotland) Act 2013], but not otherwise.

Provided that the firm is in no case bound by the acts of a partner who has become bankrupt; but this proviso does not affect the liability of any person who has after the bankruptcy represented himself or knowingly suffered himself to be represented as a partner of the bankrupt.

### 39   Rights of partners as to application of partnership property

On the dissolution of a partnership every partner is entitled, as against the other partners in the firm, and all persons claiming through them in respect of their interests as partners, to have the property of the partnership applied in payment of the debts and liabilities of the firm, and to have the surplus assets after such payment applied in payment of what may be due to the partners respectively after deducting what may be due from them as partners to the firm; and for that purpose any partner or his representatives may on the termination of the partnership apply to the Court to wind up the business and affairs of the firm.

### 40   Apportionment of premium where partnership prematurely dissolved

Where one partner has paid a premium to another on entering into a partnership for a fixed term, and the partnership is dissolved before the expiration of that term otherwise than by the death of a partner, the Court may order the repayment of the premium, or of such part thereof as it thinks just, having regard to the terms of the partnership contract and to the length of time during which the partnership has continued; unless

(a)   the dissolution is, in the judgment of the Court, wholly or chiefly due to the misconduct of the partner who paid the premium, or

(b)   the partnership has been dissolved by an agreement containing no provision for a return of any part of the premium.

### 41   Rights where partnership dissolved for fraud or misrepresentation

Where a partnership contract is rescinded on the ground of fraud or misrepresentation of one of the parties thereto, the party entitled to rescind is, without prejudice to any other right, entitled—

(a)   to a lien on, or right of retention of, the surplus of the partnership assets, after satisfying the partnership liabilities, for any sum of money paid by him for the purchase of a share in the partnership and for any capital contributed by him, and is

(b)   to stand in the place of the creditors of the firm for any payments made by him in respect of the partnership liabilities, and

(c)   to be indemnified by the person guilty of the fraud or making the representation against all the debts and liabilities of the firm.

### 42   Right of outgoing partner in certain cases to share in profits made after dissolution

(1)   Where any member of a firm has died or otherwise ceased to be a partner, and the surviving or continuing partners carry on the business of the firm with its capital or assets without any final settlement of accounts as between the firm and the outgoing partner or his estate, then, in the absence of any agreement to the contrary, the outgoing partner or his estate is entitled at the option of himself or his representatives to such share of the profits made since the dissolution as the Court may find to be attributable to the use of his share of the partnership assets, or to interest at the rate of five per cent. per annum on the amount of his share of the partnership assets.

(2)   Provided that where by the partnership contract an option is given to surviving or continuing partners to purchase the interest of a deceased or outgoing partner, and that option is duly exercised, the estate of the deceased partner, or the outgoing partner or his estate, as the case may be, is not entitled to any further or other share of profits; but if any partner assuming to act in exercise of the option does not in all material respects comply with the terms thereof, he is liable to account under the foregoing provisions of this section.

### 43   Retiring or deceased partner's share to be a debt

Subject to any agreement between the partners, the amount due from surviving or continuing partners to an outgoing partner or the representatives of a deceased partner in respect of the outgoing or deceased partner's share is a debt accruing at the date of the dissolution or death.

### 44   Rule for distribution of assets on final settlement of accounts

In settling accounts between the partners after a dissolution of partnership, the following rules shall, subject to any agreement, be observed:

(a)   Losses, including losses and deficiencies of capital, shall be paid first out of profits, next out of capital, and lastly, if necessary, by the partners individually in the proportion in which they were entitled to share profits:

(b)   The assets of the firm including the sums, if any, contributed by the partners to make up losses or deficiencies of capital, shall be applied in the following manner and order:

1   In paying the debts and liabilities of the firm to persons who are not partners therein:

2   In paying to each partner rateably what is due from the firm to him for advances as distinguished from capital:

3   In paying to each partner rateably what is due from the firm to him in respect of capital:

4   The ultimate residue, if any, shall be divided among the partners in the proportion in which the profits are divisible.

*Supplemental*

### 45   Definitions of 'court' and 'business'
In this Act, unless the contrary intention appears—

The expression 'court' includes every court and judge having jurisdiction in the case:

The expression 'business' includes every trade, occupation or profession.

### 46   Saving for rules of equity and common law
The rules of equity and of common law applicable to partnership shall continue in force except so far as they are inconsistent with the express provisions of this Act.

### 47   Provision as to bankruptcy in Scotland
(1)   In the application of this Act to Scotland the bankruptcy of a firm or of an individual shall mean sequestration under the Bankruptcy (Scotland) Acts, and also in the case of an individual the issue against him of a decree of cessio bonorum.

(2)   Nothing in this Act shall alter the rules of the law of Scotland relating to the bankruptcy of a firm or of the individual partners thereof.

[. . .]

### 50   Short title
This Act may be cited as the Partnership Act, 1890.

## FACTORS (SCOTLAND) ACT 1890
### (53 & 54 Vict, c 40)

### 1   Application of 52 & 53 Vict c 45 to Scotland
Subject to the following provisions, the Factors Act, 1889, shall apply to Scotland—

(1)   The expression 'lien' shall mean and include right of retention; the expression 'vendor's lien' shall mean and include any right of retention competent to the original owner or vendor; and the expression 'set off' shall mean and include compensation.

(2)   In the application of section five of the recited Act, a sale, pledge, or other disposition of goods shall not be valid unless made for valuable consideration.

# MARINE INSURANCE ACT 1906
## (6 Edw 7, c 41)

*Marine insurance*

### 1   Marine insurance defined

A contract of marine insurance is a contract whereby the insurer undertakes to indemnify the assured, in manner and to the extent thereby agreed, against marine losses, that is to say, the losses incident to marine adventure.

### 2   Mixed sea and land risks

(1)   A contract of marine insurance may, by its express terms, or by usage of trade, be extended so as to protect the assured against losses on inland waters or on any land risk which may be incidental to any sea voyage.

(2)   Where a ship in course of building, or the launch of a ship, or any adventure analogous to marine adventure, is covered by a policy in the form of a marine policy, the provisions of this Act, in so far as applicable, shall apply thereto; but, except as by this section provided, nothing in this Act shall alter or affect any rule of law applicable to any contract of insurance other than a contract of marine insurance as by this Act defined.

### 3   Marine adventure and maritime perils defined

(1)   Subject to the provisions of this Act, every lawful marine adventure may be the subject of marine insurance.

(2)   In particular there is a marine adventure where—

(a)   Any ship goods or other moveables are exposed to maritime perils. Such property is in this Act referred to as 'insurable property';

(b)   The earning or acquisition of any freight, passage money, commission, profit, or other pecuniary benefit, or the security for any advances, loan or disbursements, is endangered by the exposure of insurable property to maritime perils;

(c)   Any liability to a third party may be incurred by the owner of, or other person interested in or responsible for, insurable property, by reason of maritime perils.

'Maritime perils' means the perils consequent on, or incidental to, the navigation of the sea, that is to say, perils of the seas, fire, war perils, pirates, rovers, thieves, captures, seisures, restraints, and detainments of princes and peoples, jettisons, barratry, and any other perils, either of the like kind or which may be designated by the policy.

*Insurable interest*

### 4   Avoidance of wagering or gaming contracts

(1)   Every contract of marine insurance by way of gaming or wagering is void.

(2)   A contract of marine insurance is deemed to be a gaming or wagering contract—

(a)   Where the assured has not an insurable interest as defined by this Act, and the contract is entered into with no expectation of acquiring such an interest; or

(b)   Where the policy is made 'interest or no interest', or 'without further proof of interest than the policy itself', or 'without benefit of salvage to the insurer', or subject to any other like term:

Provided that, where there is no possibility of salvage, a policy may be effected without benefit of salvage to the insurer.

### 5   Insurable interest defined

(1)   Subject to the provisions of this Act, every person has an insurable interest who is interested in a marine adventure.

(2)   In particular a person is interested in a marine adventure where he stands in any legal or equitable relation to the adventure or to any insurable property at risk therein, in consequence of which he may benefit by the safety or due arrival of insurable property, or may be prejudiced by its loss, or damage thereto, or by the detention thereof, or may incur liability in respect thereof.

### 6   When interest must attach

(1)   The assured must be interested in the subject-matter insured at the time of the loss though he need not be interested when the insurance is effected:

Provided that where the subject-matter is insured 'lost or not lost', the assured may recover although he may not have acquired his interest until after the loss, unless at the time of effecting the contract of insurance the assured was aware of the loss, and the insurer was not.

(2)   Where the assured has no interest at the time of the loss, he cannot acquire interest by any act or election after he is aware of the loss.

### 7   Defeasible or contingent interest

(1)   A defeasible interest is insurable, as also is a contingent interest.

(2)   In particular, where the buyer of goods has insured them, he has an insurable interest, notwithstanding that he might, at his election, have rejected the goods, or have treated them as at the seller's risk, by reason of the latter's delay in making delivery or otherwise.

### 8   Partial interest

A partial interest of any nature is insurable.

### 9   Re-insurance

(1)   The insurer under a contract of marine insurance has an insurable interest in his risk, and may re-insure in respect of it.

(2)   Unless the policy otherwise provides, the original assured has no right or interest in respect of such re-insurance.

### 10   Bottomry

The lender of money on bottomry or respondentia has an insurable interest in respect of the loan.

### 11   Master's and seamen's wages

The master or any member of the crew of a ship has an insurable interest in respect of his wages.

### 12   Advance freight

In the case of advance freight, the person advancing the freight has an insurable interest, in so far as such freight is not repayable in case of loss.

### 13   Charges of insurance

The assured has an insurable interest in the charges of any insurance which he may effect.

### 14   Quantum of interest

(1)   Where the subject-matter insured is mortgaged, the mortgagor has an insurable interest in the full value thereof, and the mortgagee has an insurable interest in respect of any sum due or to become due under the mortgage.

(2)   A mortgagee, consignee, or other person having an interest in the subject-matter insured may insure on behalf and for the benefit of other persons interested as well as for his own benefit.

(3)   The owner of insurable property has an insurable interest in respect of the full value thereof, notwithstanding that some third person may have agreed, or be liable, to indemnify him in case of loss.

### 15   Assignment of interest

Where the assured assigns or otherwise parts with his interest in the subject-matter insured, he does not thereby transfer to the assignee his rights under the contract of insurance, unless there be an express or implied agreement with the assignee to that effect.

But the provisions of this section do not affect a transmission of interest by operation of law.

*Insurable value*

## 16  Measure of insurable value

Subject to any express provision or valuation in the policy, the insurable value of the subject-matter insured must be ascertained as follows:—

(1)  In insurance on ship, the insurable value is the value, at the commencement of the risk, of the ship, including her outfit, provisions and stores for the officers and crew, money advanced for seamen's wages, and other disbursements (if any) incurred to make the ship fit for the voyage or adventure contemplated by the policy, plus the charges of insurance upon the whole.

The insurable value, in the case of a steamship, includes also the machinery, boilers, and coals and engine stores if owned by the assured, and, in the case of a ship engaged in a special trade, the ordinary fittings requisite for that trade.

(2)  In insurance on freight, whether paid in advance or otherwise, the insurable value is the gross amount of freight at the risk of the assured, plus the charges of insurance.

(3)  In insurance on goods or merchandise, the insurable value is the prime cost of the property insured, plus the expenses of and incidental to shipping and the charges of insurance upon the whole.

(4)  In insurance on any other subject-matter, the insurable value is the amount at the risk of the assured when the policy attaches, plus the charges of insurance.

*Disclosure and representations*

## 17  Insurance is uberrimae fidei

A contract of marine insurance is a contract based upon the utmost good faith, and, if the utmost good faith is not observed by either party, the contract may be avoided by the other party.

## 18  Disclosure by assured

(1)  Subject to the provisions of this section, the assured must disclose to the insurer, before the contract is concluded, every material circumstance which is known to the assured, and the assured is deemed to know every circumstance which, in the ordinary course of business, ought to be known by him. If the assured fails to make such disclosure, the insurer may avoid the contract.

(2)  Every circumstance is material which would influence the judgment of a prudent insurer in fixing the premium, or determining whether he will take the risk.

(3)  In the absence of inquiry the following circumstances need not be disclosed, namely:—

(a)  Any circumstance which diminishes the risk;

(b)  Any circumstance which is known or presumed to be known to the insurer. The insurer is presumed to know matters of common notoriety or knowledge, and matters which an insurer in the ordinary course of his business, as such, ought to know;

(c)  Any circumstance as to which information is waived by the insurer;

(d)  Any circumstance which it is superfluous to disclose by reason of any express or implied warranty.

(4)  Whether any particular circumstance, which is not disclosed, be material or not is, in each case, a question of fact.

(5) The term 'circumstance' includes any communication made to, or information received by, the assured.

[(6) This section does not apply in relation to a contract of marine insurance if it is a consumer insurance contract within the meaning of the Consumer Insurance (Disclosure and Representations) Act 2012.]

## 19 Disclosure by agent effecting insurance

[(1)] Subject to the provisions of the preceding section as to circumstances which need not be disclosed, where an insurance is effected for the assured by an agent, the agent must disclose to the insurer—

(a) Every material circumstance which is known to himself, and an agent to insure is deemed to know every circumstance which in the ordinary course of business ought to be known by, or to have been communicated to, him; and

(b) Every material circumstance which the assured is bound to disclose, unless it come to his knowledge too late to communicate it to the agent.

[(2) This section does not apply in relation to a contract of marine insurance if it is a consumer insurance contract within the meaning of the Consumer Insurance (Disclosure and Representations) Act 2012.]

## 20 Representations pending negotiation of contract

(1) Every material representation made by the assured or his agent to the insurer during the negotiations for contract, and before the contract is concluded, must be true. If it be untrue the insurer may avoid the contract.

(2) A representation is material which would influence the judgment of a prudent insurer in fixing the premium, or determining whether he will take the risk.

(3) A representation may be either a representation as to a matter of fact, or as to a matter of expectation or belief.

(4) A representation as to matter of fact is true, if it be substantially correct, that is to say, if the difference between what is represented and what is actually correct would not be considered material by a prudent insurer.

(5) A representation as to a matter of expectation or belief is true if it be made in good faith.

(6) A representation may be withdrawn or corrected before the contract is concluded.

(7) Whether a particular representation be material or not is, in each case, a question of fact.

[(8) This section does not apply in relation to a contract of marine insurance if it is a consumer insurance contract within the meaning of the Consumer Insurance (Disclosure and Representations) Act 2012.]

## 21 When contract is deemed to be concluded

A contract of marine insurance is deemed to be concluded when the proposal of the assured is accepted by the insurer, whether the policy be then issued or not; and, for the purpose of showing when the proposal was accepted, reference may be made to the slip or covering note or other customary memorandum of the contract. [. . .]

*The policy*

## 22 Contract must be embodied in policy

Subject to the provisions of any statute, a contract of marine insurance is inadmissible in evidence unless it is embodied in a marine policy in accordance with this Act. The policy may be executed and issued either at the time when the contract is concluded, or afterwards.

## 23 What policy must specify

A marine policy must specify—

(1)   The name of the assured, or of some person who effects the insurance on his behalf.
[. . .]

### 24   Signature of insurer
(1)   A marine policy must be signed by or on behalf of the insurer, provided that in the case of a corporation the corporate seal may be sufficient, but nothing in this section shall be construed as requiring the subscription of a corporation to be under seal.

(2)   Where a policy is subscribed by or on behalf of two or more insurers, each subscription, unless the contrary be expressed, constitutes a distinct contract with the assured.

### 25   Voyage and time policies
(1)   Where the contract is to insure the subject-matter 'at and from', or from one place to another or others, the policy is called a 'voyage policy', and where the contract is to insure the subject-matter for a definite period of time the policy is called a 'time policy'. A contract for both voyage and time may be included in the same policy.
[. . .]

### 26   Designation of subject-matter
(1)   The subject-matter insured must be designated in a marine policy with reasonable certainty.

(2)   The nature and extent of the interest of the assured in the subject-matter insured need not be specified in the policy.

(3)   Where the policy designates the subject-matter insured in general terms, it shall be construed to apply to the interest intended by the assured to be covered.

(4)   In the application of this section regard shall be had to any usage regulating the designation of the subject-matter insured.

### 27   Valued policy
(1)   A policy may be either valued or unvalued.

(2)   A valued policy is a policy which specifies the agreed value of the subject-matter insured.

(3)   Subject to the provisions of this Act, and in the absence of fraud, the value fixed by the policy is, as between the insurer and the assured, conclusive of the insurable value of the subject intended to be insured, whether the loss be total or partial.

(4)   Unless the policy otherwise provides, the value fixed by the policy is not conclusive for the purpose of determining whether there has been a constructive total loss.

### 28   Unvalued policy
An unvalued policy is a policy which does not specify the value of the subject-matter insured, but, subject to the limit of the sum insured, leaves the insurable value to be subsequently ascertained, in the manner herein-before specified.

### 29   Floating policy by ship or ships
(1)   A floating policy is a policy which describes the insurance in general terms, and leaves the name of the ship or ships and other particulars to be defined by subsequent declaration.

(2)   The subsequent declaration or declarations may be made by indorsement on the policy, or in other customary manner.

(3)   Unless the policy otherwise provides, the declarations must be made in the order of dispatch or shipment. They must, in the case of goods, comprise all consignments within the terms of the policy, and the value of the goods or other property must be honestly stated, but an omission or erroneous declaration may be

rectified even after loss or arrival, provided the omission or declaration was made in good faith.

(4)   Unless the policy otherwise provides, where a declaration of value is not made until after notice of loss or arrival, the policy must be treated as an unvalued policy as regards the subject-matter of that declaration.

### 30   Construction of terms in policy

(1)   A policy may be in the form in the First Schedule to this Act.

(2)   Subject to the provisions of this Act, and unless the context of the policy otherwise requires, the terms and expressions mentioned in the First Schedule to this Act shall be construed as having the scope and meaning in that schedule assigned to them.

### 31   Premium to be arranged

(1)   Where an insurance is effected at a premium to be arranged, and no arrangement is made, a reasonable premium is payable.

(2)   Where an insurance is effected on the terms that an additional premium is to be arranged in a given event, and that event happens but no arrangement is made, then a reasonable additional premium is payable.

*Double insurance*

### 32   Double insurance

(1)   Where two or more policies are effected by or on behalf of the assured on the same adventure and interest or any part thereof, and the sums insured exceed the indemnity allowed by this Act, the assured is said to be over-insured by double insurance.

(2)   Where the assured is over-insured by double insurance—

(a)   The assured, unless the policy otherwise provides, may claim payment from the insurers in such order as he may think fit, provided that he is not entitled to receive any sum in excess of the indemnity allowed by this Act;

(b)   Where the policy under which the assured claims is a valued policy, the assured must give credit as against the valuation for any sum received by him under any other policy without regard to the actual value of the subject-matter insured;

(c)   Where the policy under which the assured claims is an unvalued policy he must give credit, as against the full insurable value, for any sum received by him under any other policy.

(d)   Where the assured receives any sum in excess of the indemnity allowed by this Act, he is deemed to hold such sum in trust for the insurers, according to their right of contribution among themselves.

*Warranties, etc*

### 33   Nature of warranty

(1)   A warranty, in the following sections relating to warranties, means a promissory warranty, that is to say, a warranty by which the assured undertakes that some particular thing shall or shall not be done, or that some condition shall be fulfilled, or whereby he affirms or negatives the existence of a particular state of facts.

(2)   A warranty may be express or implied.

(3)   A warranty, as above defined, is a condition which must be exactly complied with, whether it be material to the risk or not. If it be not so complied with, then, subject to any express provision in the policy, the insurer is discharged from liability as from the date of the breach of warranty, but without prejudice to any liability incurred by him before that date.

### 34   When breach of warranty excused

(1)   Non-compliance with a warranty is excused when, by reason of a change of circumstances, the warranty ceases to be applicable to the circumstances of the contract, or when compliance with the warranty is rendered unlawful by any subsequent law.

(2)   Where a warranty is broken, the assured cannot avail himself of the defence that the breach has been remedied, and the warranty complied with, before loss.

(3)   A breach of warranty may be waived by the insurer.

### 35   Express warranties

(1)   An express warranty may be in any form of words from which the intention to warrant is to be inferred.

(2)   An express warranty must be included in, or written upon, the policy, or must be contained in some document incorporated by reference into the policy.

(3)   An express warranty does not exclude an implied warranty, unless it be inconsistent therewith.

### 36   Warranty of neutrality

(1)   Where insurable property, whether ship or goods, is expressly warranted neutral, there is an implied condition that the property shall have a neutral character at the commencement of the risk, and that, so far as the assured can control the matter, its neutral character shall be preserved during the risk.

(2)   Where a ship is expressly warranted 'neutral' there is also an implied condition that, so far as the assured can control the matter, she shall be properly documented, that is to say, that she shall carry the necessary papers to establish her neutrality, and that she shall not falsify or suppress her papers, or use simulated papers. If any loss occurs through breach of this condition, the insurer may avoid the contract.

### 37   No implied warranty of nationality

There is no implied warranty as to the nationality of a ship, or that her nationality shall not be changed during the risk.

### 38   Warranty of good safety

Where the subject-matter insured is warranted 'well' or 'in good safety' on a particular day, it is sufficient if it be safe at any time during that day.

### 39   Warranty of seaworthiness of ship

(1)   In a voyage policy there is an implied warranty that at the commencement of the voyage the ship shall be seaworthy for the purpose of the particular adventure insured.

(2)   Where the policy attaches while the ship is in port, there is also an implied warranty that she shall, at the commencement of the risk, be reasonably fit to encounter the ordinary perils of the port.

(3)   Where the policy relates to a voyage which is performed in different stages, during which the ship requires different kinds of or further preparation or equipment, there is an implied warranty that at the commencement of each stage the ship is seaworthy in respect of such preparation or equipment for the purposes of that stage.

(4)   A ship is deemed to be seaworthy when she is reasonably fit in all respects to encounter the ordinary perils of the seas of the adventure insured.

(5)   In a time policy there is no implied warranty that the ship shall be seaworthy at any stage of the adventure, but where, with the privity of the assured, the ship is sent to sea in an unseaworthy state, the insurer is not liable for any loss attributable to unseaworthiness.

### 40   No implied warranty that goods are seaworthy

(1)   In a policy on goods or other moveables there is no implied warranty that the goods or moveables are seaworthy.

(2)   In a voyage policy on goods or other moveables there is an implied warranty that at the commencement of the voyage the ship is not only seaworthy as a ship, but also that she is reasonably fit to carry the goods or other moveables to the destination contemplated by the policy.

### 41   Warranty of legality
There is an implied warranty that the adventure insured is a lawful one, and that, so far as the assured can control the matter, the adventure shall be carried out in a lawful manner.

*The voyage*

### 42   Implied condition as to commencement of risk
(1)   Where the subject-matter is insured by a voyage policy 'at and from' or 'from' a particular place, it is not necessary that the ship should be at that place when the contract is concluded, but there is an implied condition that the adventure shall be commenced within a reasonable time, and that if the adventure be not so commenced the insurer may avoid the contract.

(2)   The implied condition may be negatived by showing that the delay was caused by circumstances known to the insurer before the contract was concluded, or by showing that he waived the condition.

### 43   Alteration of port of departure
Where the place of departure is specified by the policy, and the ship instead of sailing from that place sails from any other place, the risk does not attach.

### 44   Sailing for different destination
Where the destination is specified in the policy, and the ship, instead of sailing for that destination, sails for any other destination, the risk does not attach.

### 45   Change of voyage
(1)   Where, after the commencement of the risk, the destination of the ship is voluntarily changed from the destination contemplated by the policy, there is said to be a change of voyage.

(2)   Unless the policy otherwise provides, where there is a change of voyage, the insurer is discharged from liability as from the time of the change, that is to say, as from the time when the determination to change it is manifested; and it is immaterial that the ship may not have left the course of voyage contemplated by the policy when the loss occurs.

### 46   Deviation
(1)   Where a ship, without lawful excuse, deviates from the voyage contemplated by the policy, the insurer is discharged from liability as from the time of deviation, and it is immaterial that the ship may have regained her route before any loss occurs.

(2)   There is a deviation from the voyage contemplated by the policy—
   (a)   Where the course of the voyage is specifically designated by the policy, and that course is departed from; or
   (b)   Where the course of the voyage is not specifically designated by the policy, but the usual and customary course is departed from.

(3)   The intention to deviate is immaterial; there must be a deviation in fact to discharge the insurer from his liability under the contract.

### 47   Several ports of discharge
(1)   Where several ports of discharge are specified by the policy, the ship may proceed to all or any of them, but, in the absence of any usage or sufficient cause to the contrary, she must proceed to them, or such of them as she goes to, in the order designated by the policy. If she does not there is a deviation.

(2)   Where the policy is to 'ports of discharge', within a given area, which are

not named, the ship must, in the absence of any usage or sufficient cause to the contrary, proceed to them, or such of them as she goes to, in their geographical order. If she does not there is a deviation.

## 48  Delay in voyage

In the case of a voyage policy, the adventure insured must be prosecuted throughout its course with reasonable dispatch, and, if without lawful excuse it is not so prosecuted, the insurer is discharged from liability as from the time when the delay becomes unreasonable.

## 49  Excuses for deviation or delay

(1)  Deviation or delay in prosecuting the voyage contemplated by the policy is excused—

(a)  Where authorised by any special term in the policy; or

(b)  Where caused by circumstances beyond the control of the master and his employer; or

(c)  Where reasonably necessary in order to comply with an express or implied warranty; or

(d)  Where reasonably necessary for the safety of the ship or subject-matter insured; or

(e)  For the purpose of saving human life, or aiding a ship in distress where human life may be in danger; or

(f)  Where reasonably necessary for the purpose of obtaining medical or surgical aid for any person on board the ship; or

(g)  Where caused by the barratrous conduct of the master or crew, if barratry be one of the perils insured against.

(2)  When the cause excusing the deviation or delay ceases to operate, the ship must resume her course, and prosecute her voyage, with reasonable dispatch.

*Assignment of policy*

## 50  When and how policy is assignable

(1)  A marine policy is assignable unless it contains terms expressly prohibiting assignment. It may be assigned either before or after loss.

(2)  Where a marine policy has been assigned so as to pass the beneficial interest in such policy, the assignee of the policy is entitled to sue thereon in his own name; and the defendant is entitled to make any defence arising out of the contract which he would have been entitled to make if the action had been brought in the name of the person by or on behalf of whom the policy was effected.

(3)  A marine policy may be assigned by indorsement thereon or in other customary manner.

## 51  Assured who has no interest cannot assign

Where the assured has parted with or lost his interest in the subject-matter insured, and has not, before or at the time of so doing, expressly or impliedly agreed to assign the policy, any subsequent assignment of the policy is inoperative:

Provided that nothing in this section affects the assignment of a policy after loss.

*The premium*

## 52  When premium payable

Unless otherwise agreed, the duty of the assured or his agent to pay the premium, and the duty of the insurer to issue the policy to the assured or his agent, are concurrent conditions, and the insurer is not bound to issue the policy until payment or tender of the premium.

## 53  Policy effected through broker

(1)  Unless otherwise agreed, where a marine policy is effected on behalf of the assured by a broker, the broker is directly responsible to the insurer for the

premium, and the insurer is directly responsible to the assured for the amount which may be payable in respect of losses, or in respect of returnable premium.

(2)   Unless otherwise agreed, the broker has, as against the assured, a lien upon the policy for the amount of the premium and his charges in respect of effecting the policy; and, where he has dealt with the person who employs him as a principal, he has also a lien on the policy in respect of any balance on any insurance account which may be due to him from such person, unless when the debt was incurred he had reason to believe that such person was only an agent.

## 54   Effect of receipt on policy

Where a marine policy effected on behalf of the assured by a broker acknowledges the receipt of the premium, such acknowledgement is, in the absence of fraud, conclusive as between the insurer and the assured, but not as between the insurer and broker.

*Loss and abandonment*

## 55   Included and excluded losses

(1)   Subject to the provisions of this Act, and unless the policy otherwise provides, the insurer is liable for any loss proximately caused by a peril insured against, but, subject as aforesaid, he is not liable for any loss which is not proximately caused by a peril insured against.

(2)   In particular,—

(a)   The insurer is not liable for any loss attributable to the wilful misconduct of the assured, but, unless the policy otherwise provides, he is liable for any loss proximately caused by a peril insured against, even though the loss would not have happened but for the misconduct or negligence of the master or crew;

(b)   Unless the policy otherwise provides, the insurer on ship or goods is not liable for any loss proximately caused by delay, although the delay be caused by a peril insured against.

(c)   Unless the policy otherwise provides, the insurer is not liable for ordinary wear and tear, ordinary leakage and breakage, inherent vice or nature of the subject-matter insured, or for any loss proximately caused by rats or vermin, or for any injury to machinery not proximately caused by maritime perils.

## 56   Partial and total loss

(1)   A loss may be either total or partial. Any loss other than a total loss, as herein-after defined, is a partial loss.

(2)   A total loss may be either an actual total loss, or a constructive total loss.

(3)   Unless a different intention appears from the terms of the policy, an insurance against total loss includes a constructive, as well as an actual, total loss.

(4)   Where the assured brings an action for a total loss and the evidence proves only a partial loss, he may, unless the policy otherwise provides, recover for a partial loss.

(5)   Where goods reach their destination in specie, but by reason of obliteration of marks, or otherwise, they are incapable of identification, the loss, if any, is partial, and not total.

## 57   Actual total loss

(1)   Where the subject-matter insured is destroyed, or so damaged as to cease to be a thing of the kind insured, or where the assured is irretrievably deprived thereof, there is an actual total loss.

(2)   In the case of an actual total loss no notice of abandonment need be given.

## 58   Missing ship

Where the ship concerned in the adventure is missing, and after the lapse of a reasonable time no news of her has been received, an actual total loss may be presumed.

### 59   Effect of transhipment, etc

Where, by a peril insured against, the voyage is interrupted at any intermediate port or place, under such circumstances as, apart from any special stipulation in the contract of affreightment, to justify the master in landing and re-shipping the goods or other moveables, or in transhipping them, and sending them on to their destination, the liability of the insurer continues, notwithstanding the landing or transhipment.

### 60   Constructive total loss defined

(1)   Subject to any express provision in the policy, there is a constructive total loss where the subject-matter insured is reasonably abandoned on account of its total loss appearing to be unavoidable, or because it could not be preserved from actual total loss without an expenditure which would exceed its value when the expenditure had been incurred.

(2)   In particular, there is a constructive total loss—

(i)   Where the assured is deprived of the possession of his ship or goods by a peril insured against, and (a) it is unlikely that he can recover the ship or goods, as the case may be, or (b) the cost of recovering the ship or goods, as the case may be, would exceed their value when recovered; or

(ii)   In the case of damage to a ship, where she is so damaged by a peril insured against that the cost of repairing the damage would exceed the value of the ship when repaired.

In estimating the cost of repairs, no deduction is to be made in respect of general average contributions to those repairs payable by other interests, but account is to be taken of the expense of future salvage operations and of any future general average contributions to which the ship would be liable if repaired; or

(iii)   In the case of damage to goods, where the cost of repairing the damage and forwarding the goods to their destination would exceed their value on arrival.

### 61   Effect of constructive total loss

Where there is a constructive total loss the assured may either treat the loss as a partial loss, or abandon the subject-matter insured to the insurer and treat the loss as if it were an actual total loss.

### 62   Notice of abandonment

(1)   Subject to the provisions of this section, where the assured elects to abandon the subject-matter insured to the insurer, he must give notice of the abandonment. If he fails to do so the loss can only be treated as a partial loss.

(2)   Notice of abandonment may be given in writing, or by word of mouth, or partly in writing and partly by word of mouth, and may be given in terms which indicate the intention of the assured to abandon his insured interest in the subject-matter insured unconditionally to the insurer.

(3)   Notice of abandonment must be given with reasonable diligence after the receipt of reliable information of the loss, but where the information is of a doubtful character the assured is entitled to a reasonable time to make inquiry.

(4)   Where notice of abandonment is properly given, the rights of the assured are not prejudiced by the fact that the insurer refuses to accept the abandonment.

(5)   The acceptance of an abandonment may be either express or implied from the conduct of the insurer. The mere silence of the insurer after notice is not an acceptance.

(6)   Where a notice of abandonment is accepted the abandonment is irrevocable. The acceptance of the notice conclusively admits liability for the loss and the sufficiency of the notice.

(7)   Notice of abandonment is unnecessary where, at the time when the assured

receives information of the loss, there would be no possibility of benefit to the insurer if notice were given to him.

(8)   Notice of abandonment may be waived by the insurer.

(9)   Where an insurer has re-insured his risk, no notice of abandonment need be given by him.

### 63   Effect of abandonment

(1)   Where there is a valid abandonment the insurer is entitled to take over the interest of the assured in whatever may remain of the subject-matter insured, and all proprietary rights incidental thereto.

(2)   Upon the abandonment of a ship, the insurer thereof is entitled to any freight in course of being earned, and which is earned by her subsequent to the casualty causing the loss, less the expenses of earning it incurred after the casualty; and, where a ship is carrying the owner's goods, the insurer is entitled to a reasonable remuneration for the carriage of them subsequent to the casualty causing the loss.

*Partial losses (including salvage and general average and particular charges)*

### 64   Particular average loss

(1)   A particular average loss is a partial loss of the subject-matter insured, caused by a peril insured against, and which is not a general average loss.

(2)   Expenses incurred by or on behalf of the assured for the safety or preservation of the subject-matter insured, other than general average and salvage charges, are called particular charges. Particular charges are not included in particular average.

### 65   Salvage charges

(1)   Subject to any express provision in the policy, salvage charges incurred in preventing a loss by perils insured against may be recovered as a loss by those perils.

(2)   'Salvage charges' means the charges recoverable under maritime law by a salvor independently of contract. They do not include the expenses of services in the nature of salvage rendered by the assured or his agents, or any person employed for hire by them, for the purpose of averting a peril insured against. Such expenses, where properly incurred, may be recovered as particular charges or as a general average loss, according to the circumstances under which they were incurred.

### 66   General average loss

(1)   A general average loss is a loss caused by or directly consequential on a general average act. It includes a general average expenditure as well as a general average sacrifice.

(2)   There is a general average act where any extraordinary sacrifice or expenditure is voluntarily and reasonably made or incurred in the time of peril for the purpose of preserving the property imperilled in the common adventure.

(3)   Where there is a general average loss, the party on whom it falls is entitled, subject to the conditions imposed by maritime law, to a rateable contribution from the other parties interested, and such contribution is called a general average contribution.

(4)   Subject to any express provision in the policy, where the assured has incurred a general average expenditure, he may recover from the insurer in respect of the proportion of the loss which falls upon him; and, in the case of a general average sacrifice, he may recover from the insurer in respect of the whole loss without having enforced his right of contribution from the other parties liable to contribute.

(5)   Subject to any express provision in the policy, where the assured has paid,

or is liable to pay, a general average contribution in respect of the subject insured, he may recover therefor from the insurer.

(6) In the absence of express stipulation, the insurer is not liable for any general average loss or contribution where the loss was not incurred for the purpose of avoiding, or in connexion with the avoidance of, a peril insured against.

(7) Where ship, freight, and cargo, or any two of those interests, are owned by the same assured, the liability of the insurer in respect of general average losses or contributions is to be determined as if those subjects were owned by different persons.

## *Measure of indemnity*

### 67 Extent of liability of insurer for loss

(1) The sum which the assured can recover in respect of a loss on a policy by which he is insured, in the case of an unvalued policy to the full extent of the insurable value, or in the case of a valued policy to the full extent of the value fixed by the policy, is called the measure of indemnity.

(2) Where there is a loss recoverable under the policy, the insurer, or each insurer if there be more than one, is liable for such proportion of the measure of indemnity as the amount of his subscription bears to the value fixed by the policy in the case of a valued policy, or to the insurable value in the case of an unvalued policy.

### 68 Total loss

Subject to the provisions of this Act and to any express provision in the policy, where there is a total loss of the subject-matter insured,—

(1) If the policy be a valued policy, the measure of indemnity is the sum fixed by the policy.

(2) If the policy be an unvalued policy, the measure of indemnity is the insurable value of the subject-matter insured.

### 69 Partial loss of ship

Where a ship is damaged, but not totally lost, the measure of indemnity, subject to any express provision in the policy, is as follows:—

(1) Where the ship has been repaired, the assured is entitled to the reasonable cost of the repairs, less the customary deductions, but not exceeding the sum insured in respect of any one casualty.

(2) Where the ship has been only partially repaired, the assured is entitled to the reasonable cost of such repairs, computed as above, and also to be indemnified for the reasonable depreciation, if any, arising from the unrepaired damage, provided that the aggregate amount shall not exceed the cost of repairing the whole damage, computed as above.

(3) Where the ship has not been repaired, and has not been sold in her damaged state during the risk, the assured is entitled to be indemnified for the reasonable depreciation arising from the unrepaired damage, but not exceeding the reasonable cost of repairing such damage, computed as above.

### 70 Partial loss of freight

Subject to any express provision in the policy, where there is a partial loss of freight, the measure of indemnity is such proportion of the sum fixed by the policy in the case of a valued policy, or of the insurable value in the case of an unvalued policy, as the proportion of freight lost by the assured bears to the whole freight at the risk of the assured under the policy.

### 71 Partial loss of goods, merchandise, etc

Where there is a partial loss of goods, merchandise, or other moveables, the measure of indemnity, subject to any express provision in the policy, is as follows:—

(1)   Where part of the goods, merchandise, or other moveables insured by a valued policy is totally lost, the measure of indemnity is such proportion of the sum fixed by the policy as the insurable value of the part lost bears to the insurable value of the whole, ascertained as in the case of an unvalued policy.

(2)   Where part of the goods, merchandise, or other moveables insured by an unvalued policy is totally lost, the measure of indemnity is the insurable value of the part lost, ascertained as in the case of total loss.

(3)   Where the whole or any part of the goods or merchandise insured has been delivered damaged at its destination, the measure of indemnity is such proportion of the sum fixed by the policy in the case of a valued policy, or of the insurable value in the case of an unvalued policy, as the difference between the gross sound and damaged values at the place of arrival bears to the gross sound value.

(4)   'Gross value' means the wholesale price or, if there be no such price, the estimated value, with, in either case, freight, landing charges, and duty paid beforehand; provided that, in the case of goods or merchandise customarily sold in bond, the bonded price is deemed to be the gross value. 'Gross proceeds' means the actual price obtained at a sale where all charges on sale are paid by the sellers.

## 72   Apportionment of valuation

(1)   Where different species of property are insured under a single valuation, the valuation must be apportioned over the different species in proportion to their respective insurable values, as in the case of an unvalued policy. The insured value of any part of a species is such proportion of the total insured value of the same as the insurable value of the part bears to the insurable value of the whole, ascertained in both cases as provided by this Act.

(2)   Where a valuation has to be apportioned, and particulars of the prime cost of each separate species, quality, or description of goods cannot be ascertained, the division of the valuation may be made over the net arrived sound values of the different species, qualities, or descriptions of goods.

## 73   General average contributions and salvage charges

(1)   Subject to any express provision in the policy, where the assured has paid, or is liable for, any general average contribution, the measure of indemnity is the full amount of such contribution, if the subject-matter liable to contribution is insured for its full contributory value; but, if such subject-matter be not insured for its full contributory value, or if only part of it be insured, the indemnity payable by the insurer must be reduced in proportion to the under insurance, and where there has been a particular average loss which constitutes a deduction from the contributory value, and for which the insurer is liable, that amount must be deducted from the insured value in order to ascertain what the insurer is liable to contribute.

(2)   Where the insurer is liable for salvage charges the extent of his liability must be determined on the like principle.

## 74   Liabilities to third parties

Where the assured has effected an insurance in express terms against any liability to a third party, the measure of indemnity, subject to any express provision in the policy, is the amount paid or payable by him to such third party in respect of such liability.

## 75   General provisions as to measure of indemnity

(1)   Where there has been a loss in respect of any subject-matter not expressly provided for in the foregoing provisions of this Act, the measure of indemnity shall be ascertained, as nearly as may be, in accordance with those provisions, in so far as applicable to the particular case.

(2)   Nothing in the provisions of this Act relating to the measure of indemnity shall affect the rules relating to double insurance, or prohibit the insurer from dis-

proving interest wholly or in part, or from showing that at the time of the loss the whole or any part of the subject-matter insured was not at risk under the policy.

## 76 Particular average warranties

(1)   Where the subject-matter insured is warranted free from particular average, the assured cannot recover for a loss of part, other than a loss incurred by a general average sacrifice, unless the contract contained in the policy be apportionable; but, if the contract be apportionable, the assured may recover for a total loss of any apportionable part.

(2)   Where the subject-matter insured is warranted free from particular average, either wholly or under a certain percentage, the insurer is nevertheless liable for salvage charges, and for particular charges and other expenses properly incurred pursuant to the provisions of the suing and labouring clause in order to avert a loss insured against.

(3)   Unless the policy otherwise provides, where the subject-matter is warranted free from particular average under a specified percentage, a general average loss cannot be added to a particular average loss to make up the specified percentage.

(4)   For the purpose of ascertaining whether the specified percentage has been reached, regard shall be had only to the actual loss suffered by the subject-matter insured. Particular charges and the expenses of and incidental to ascertaining and proving the loss must be excluded.

## 77 Successive losses

(1)   Unless the policy otherwise provides, and subject to the provisions of this Act, the insurer is liable for successive losses, even though the total amount of such losses may exceed the sum insured.

(2)   Where, under the same policy, a partial loss, which has not been repaired or otherwise made good, is followed by a total loss, the assured can only recover in respect of the total loss:

Provided that nothing in this section shall affect the liability of the insurer under the suing and labouring clause.

## 78 Suing and labouring clause

(1)   Where the policy contains a suing and labouring clause, the engagement thereby entered into is deemed to be supplementary to the contract of insurance, and the assured may recover from the insurer any expenses properly incurred pursuant to the clause, notwithstanding that the insurer may have paid for a total loss, or that the subject-matter may have been warranted free from particular average, either wholly or under a certain percentage.

(2)   General average losses and contributions and salvage charges, as defined by this Act, are not recoverable under the suing and labouring clause.

(3)   Expenses incurred for the purpose of averting or diminishing any loss not covered by the policy are not recoverable under the suing and labouring clause.

(4)   It is the duty of the assured and his agents, in all cases, to take such measures as may be reasonable for the purpose of averting or minimising a loss.

*Rights of insurer on payment*

## 79 Right of subrogation

(1)   Where the insurer pays for a total loss, either of the whole, or in the case of goods of any apportionable part, of the subject-matter insured, he thereupon becomes entitled to take over the interest of the assured in whatever may remain of the subject-matter so paid for, and he is thereby subrogated to all the rights and remedies of the assured in and in respect of that subject-matter as from the time of the casualty causing the loss.

(2)   Subject to the foregoing provisions, where the insurer pays for a partial loss, he acquires no title to the subject-matter insured, or such part of it as may remain, but he is thereupon subrogated to all rights and remedies of the assured in

and in respect of the subject-matter insured as from the time of the casualty causing the loss, in so far as the assured has been indemnified, according to this Act,
by such payment for the loss.

## 80   Right of contribution

(1)   Where the assured is over-insured by double insurance, each insurer is
bound, as between himself and the other insurers, to contribute rateably to the loss
in proportion to the amount for which he is liable under his contract.

(2)   If any insurer pays more than his proportion of the loss, he is entitled to
maintain an action for contribution against the other insurers, and is entitled to the
like remedies as a surety who has paid more than his proportion of the debt.

## 81   Effect of under insurance

Where the assured is insured for an amount less than the insurable value or, in the
case of a valued policy, for an amount less than the policy valuation, he is deemed
to be his own insurer in respect of the uninsured balance.

*Return of premium*

## 82   Enforcement of return

Where the premium or a proportionate part thereof is, by this Act, declared to be
returnable,—

(a)   If already paid, it may be recovered by the assured from the insurer; and

(b)   If unpaid, it may be retained by the assured or his agent.

## 83   Return by agreement

Where the policy contains a stipulation for the return of the premium, or a proportionate part thereof, on the happening of a certain event, and that event happens,
the premium, or, as the case may be, the proportionate part thereof, is thereupon
returnable to the assured.

## 84   Return for failure of consideration

(1)   Where the consideration for the payment of the premium totally fails, and
there has been no fraud or illegality on the part of the assured or his agents, the
premium is thereupon returnable to the assured.

(2)   Where the consideration for the payment of the premium is apportionable
and there is a total failure of any apportionable part of the consideration, a proportionate part of the premium is, under the like conditions, thereupon returnable to
the assured.

(3)   In particular—

(a)   Where the policy is void, or is avoided by the insurer as from the
commencement of the risk, the premium is returnable, provided that there has
been no fraud or illegality on the part of the assured; but if the risk is not
apportionable, and has once attached, the premium is not returnable;

(b)   Where the subject-matter insured, or part thereof, has never been imperilled, the premium, or, as the case may be, a proportionate part thereof, is
returnable:

Provided that where the subject-matter has been insured 'lost or not lost' and
has arrived in safety at the time when the contract is concluded, the premium is
not returnable unless, at such time, the insurer knew of the safe arrival.

(c)   Where the assured has no insurable interest throughout the currency of
the risk, the premium is returnable, provided that this rule does not apply to a
policy effected by way of gaming or wagering;

(d)   Where the assured has a defeasible interest which is terminated during
the currency of the risk, the premium is not returnable;

(e)   Where the assured has over-insured under an unvalued policy, a
proportionate part of the premium is returnable;

(f)   Subject to the foregoing provisions, where the assured has over-insured by double insurance, a proportionate part of the several premiums is returnable:

Provided that, if the policies are effected at different times, and any earlier policy has at any time borne the entire risk, or if a claim has been paid on the policy in respect of the full sum insured thereby, no premium is returnable in respect of that policy, and when the double insurance is effected knowingly by the assured no premium is returnable.

*Mutual insurance*

## 85   Modification of Act in case of mutual insurance

(1)   Where two or more persons mutually agree to insure each other against marine losses there is said to be a mutual insurance.

(2)   The provisions of this Act relating to the premium do not apply to mutual insurance, but a guarantee, or such other arrangement as may be agreed upon, may be substituted for the premium.

(3)   The provisions of this Act, in so far as they may be modified by the agreement of the parties, may in the case of mutual insurance be modified by the terms of the policies issued by the association, or by the rules and regulations of the association.

(4)   Subject to the expectations mentioned in this section, the provisions of this Act apply to a mutual insurance.

*Supplemental*

## 86   Ratification by assured

Where a contract of marine insurance is in good faith effected by one person on behalf of another, the person on whose behalf it is effected may ratify the contract even after he is aware of a loss.

## 87   Implied obligations varied by agreement or usage

(1)   Where any right, duty, or liability would arise under a contract of marine insurance by implication of law, it may be negatived or varied by express agreement or by usage, if the usage be such as to bind both parties to the contract.

(2)   The provisions of this section extend to any right, duty, or liability declared by this Act which may be lawfully modified by agreement.

## 88   Reasonable time, etc, a question of fact

Where by this Act any reference is made to reasonable time, reasonable premium, or reasonable diligence, the question what is reasonable is a question of fact.

## 89   Slip as evidence

Where there is a duly stamped policy, reference may be made, as heretofore, to the slip or covering note, in any legal proceeding.

## 90   Interpretation of terms

In this Act, unless the context or subject-matter otherwise requires,—

'Action' includes counter-claim and set off:

'Freight' includes the profit derivable by a shipowner from the employment of his ship to carry his own goods or moveables, as well as freight payable by a third party, but does not include passage money:

'Moveables' means any moveable tangible property, other than the ship, and includes money, valuable securities, and other documents:

'Policy' means a marine policy.

## 91   Savings

(1)   Nothing in this Act, or in any repeal effected thereby, shall affect—

(a)   The provisions of the Stamp Act 1891, or any enactment for the time being in force relating to the revenue;

(b)   The provisions of the Companies Act 1862, or any enactment amending or substituted for the same;

(c)   The provisions of any statute not expressly repealed by this Act.

(2)   The rules of the common law including the law merchant, save in so far as they are inconsistent with the express provisions of this Act, shall continue to apply to contracts of marine insurance.

## 94   Short title

This Act may be cited as the Marine Insurance Act 1906.

## SCHEDULES

### SCHEDULE 1
### FORM OF POLICY

Section 30

BE IT KNOWN THAT .. .. .. as well in .. .. .. .. own name as for and in the name and names of all and every other person or persons to whom the same doth, may, or shall appertain, in part or in all doth make assurance and cause .. .. .. .. and them, and every of them, to be insured lost or not lost, at and from .. .. .. ..

Upon any kind of goods and merchandises, and also upon the body, tackle, apparel, ordnance, munition, artillery, boat, and other furniture, of and in the good ship or vessel called the .. .. .. .. whereof is master under God, for this present voyage, .. .. .. .. or whosoever else shall go for master in the said ship, or by whatsoever other name or names the said ship, or the master thereof, is or shall be named or called; beginning the adventure upon the said goods and merchandises from the loading thereof aboard the said ship, ... .. .. upon the said ship, .. .. .. .. etc and so shall continue and endure, during her abode there, upon the said ship, etc. And further, until the said ship, with all her ordnance, tackle, apparel, etc, and goods and merchandises whatsoever shall be arrived at .. .. .. .. upon the said ship, etc, until she hath moored at anchor for twenty-four hours in good safety; and upon the goods and merchandises, until the same be there discharged and safely landed. And it shall be lawful for the said ship, etc, in this voyage, to proceed and sail to and touch and stay at any ports or places whatsoever without prejudice to this insurance. The said ship, etc, goods and merchandises, etc, for so much as concerns the assured by agreement between the assured and assurers in this policy, are and shall be valued at .. .. .. ..

Touching the adventures and perils which we the assurers are contented to bear and do take upon us in this voyage: they are of the seas, men of war, fire, enemies, pirates, rovers, thieves, jettisons, letters of mart and countermart, surprisals, takings at sea, arrests, restraints, and detainments of all kings, princes, and people, of what nation, condition, or quality soever, barratry of the master and mariners, and of all other perils, losses, and misfortunes, that have or shall come to the hurt, detriment, or damage of the said goods and merchandises, and ship, etc, or any part thereof. And in case of any loss or misfortune it shall be lawful to the assured, their factors, servants and assigns, to sue, labour, and travel for, in and about the defence, safeguards, and recovery of the said goods and merchandises, and ship, etc, or any part thereof, without prejudice to this insurance; to the charges whereof we, the assurers, will contribute each one according to the rate and quantity of his sum herein assured. And it is especially declared and agreed that no acts of the insurer or insured in recovering, saving, or preserving the property insured shall be considered as a waiver, or acceptance of abandonment. And it is agreed by us, the insurers, that this writing or policy of assurance shall be of as much force and effect as the surest writing or policy of assurance heretofore made in Lombard Street, or in the Royal Exchange, or elsewhere in London. And so we, the assurers, are contented, and do hereby promise and bind ourselves, each one for his own part, our heirs, executors, and goods to the assured, their executors, administrators, and assigns, for the true performance of the premises, confessing ourselves paid the consideration due unto us for this assurance by the assured, at and after the rate of .. .. .. ..

IN WITNESS whereof we, the assurers, have subscribed our names and sums assured in London.

N.B.—Corn, fish, salt, fruit, flour, and seed are warranted free from average, unless general, or the ship be stranded—sugar, tobacco, hemp, flax, hides and skins are warranted free from average, under five pounds per cent, and all other goods, also the ship and freight, are warranted free from average, under three pounds per cent unless general, or the ship be stranded.

## *Rules for construction of policy*

*The following are the rules referred to by this Act for the construction of a policy in the above or other like form, where the context does not otherwise require:—*

1   Where the subject-matter is insured 'lost or not lost', and the loss has occurred before the contract is concluded, the risk attaches, unless at such time the assured was aware of the loss, and the insurer was not.

2   Where the subject-matter is insured 'from' a particular place, the risk does not attach until the ship starts on the voyage insured.

3   (a)   Where a ship is insured 'at and from' a particular place, and she is at that place in good safety when the contract is concluded, the risk attaches immediately.

(b)   If she be not at that place when the contract is concluded, the risk attaches as soon as she arrives there in good safety, and, unless the policy otherwise provides, it is immaterial that she is covered by another policy for a specified time after arrival.

(c)   Where chartered freight is insured 'at and from' a particular place, and the ship is at that place in good safety when the contract is concluded the risk attaches immediately. If she be not there when the contract is concluded, the risk attaches as soon as she arrives there in good safety.

(d)   Where freight, other than chartered freight, is payable without special conditions and is insured 'at and from' a particular place, the risk attaches pro rata as the goods or merchandise are shipped; provided that if there be cargo in readiness which belongs to the shipowner, or which some other person has contracted with him to ship, the risk attaches as soon as the ship is ready to receive such cargo.

4   Where goods or other moveables are insured 'from the loading thereof', the risk does not attach until such goods or moveables are actually on board, and the insurer is not liable for them while in transit from shore to ship.

5   Where the risk on goods or other moveables continues until they are 'safely landed', they must be landed in the customary manner and within a reasonable time after arrival at the port of discharge, and if they are not so landed the risk ceases.

6   In the absence of any further license or usage, the liberty to touch and stay 'at any port or place whatsoever' does not authorise the ship to depart from the course of her voyage from the port of departure to the port of destination.

7   The term 'perils of the seas' refers only to fortuitous accidents or casualties of the seas. It does not include the ordinary action of the winds and waves.

8   The term 'pirates' includes passengers who mutiny and rioters who attack the ship from the shore.

9   The term 'thieves' does not cover clandestine theft or a theft committed by anyone of the ship's company, whether crew or passengers.

10   The term 'arrests, etc, of kings, princes, and people' refers to political or

executive acts, and does not include a loss caused by riot or by ordinary judicial process.

11   The term 'barratry' includes every wrongful act wilfully committed by the master or crew to the prejudice of the owner, or, as the case may be, the charterer.

12   The term 'all other perils' includes only perils similar in kind to the perils specifically mentioned in the policy.

13   The term 'average unless general' means a partial loss of the subject-matter insured other than a general average loss, and does not include 'particular charges'.

14   Where the ship has stranded, the insurer is liable for the excepted losses, although the loss is not attributable to the stranding, provided that when the stranding takes place the risk has attached and, if the policy be on goods, that the damaged goods are on board.

15   The term 'ship' includes the hull, materials and outfit, stores and provisions for the officers and crew, and, in the case of vessels engaged in a special trade, the ordinary fittings requisite for the trade, and also, in the case of a steamship, the machinery, boilers, and coals and engine stores, if owned by the assured.

16   The term 'freight' includes the profit derivable by a shipowner from the employment of his ship to carry his own goods or moveables, as well as freight payable by a third party, but does not include passage money.

17   The term 'goods' means goods in the nature of merchandise, and does not include personal effects or provisions and stores for use on board.

In the absence of any usage to the contrary, deck cargo and living animals must be insured specifically, and not under the general denomination of goods.


## LIMITED PARTNERSHIPS ACT 1907
### (7 Edw 7, c 24)

### 3   Interpretation of terms

In the construction of this Act the following words and expressions shall have the meanings respectively assigned to them in this section, unless there be something in the subject or context repugnant to such construction:—

'Firm,' 'firm name,' and 'business' have the same meanings as in the Partnership Act 1890:

'General partner' shall mean any partner who is not a limited partner as defined by this Act.

### 4   Definition and constitution of limited partnership

(1)   [. . .] Limited partnerships may be formed in the manner and subject to the conditions by this Act provided.

(2)   A limited partnership [. . .] must consist of one or more persons called general partners, who shall be liable for all debts and obligations of the firm, and one or more persons to be called limited partners, who shall at the time of entering into such partnership contribute thereto a sum or sums as capital or property valued at a stated amount, and who shall not be liable for the debts or obligations of the firm beyond the amount so contributed.

(3)   A limited partner shall not during the continuance of the partnership, either directly or indirectly, draw out or receive back any part of his contribution, and if he does so draw out or receive back any such part shall be liable for the debts and obligations of the firm up to the amount so drawn out or received back.

(4)   A body corporate may be a limited partner.

### 5   Registration of limited partnership required

Every limited partnership must be registered as such in accordance with the provisions of this Act [. . .].

## 6 Modifications of general law in case of limited partnerships

(1)   A limited partner shall not take part in the management of the partnership business, and shall not have power to bind the firm:

Provided that a limited partner may by himself or his agent at any time inspect the books of the firm and examine into the state and prospects of the partnership business, and may advise with the partners thereon.

If a limited partner takes part in the management of the partnership business he shall be liable for all debts and obligations of the firm incurred while he so takes part in the management as though he were a general partner.

(2)   A limited partnership shall not be dissolved by the death or bankruptcy of a limited partner, and the lunacy of a limited partner shall not be a ground for dissolution of the partnership by the court unless the lunatic's share cannot be otherwise ascertained and realised.

(3)   In the event of the dissolution of a limited partnership its affairs shall be wound up by the general partners unless the court otherwise orders.

[. . .]

(5)   Subject to any agreement expressed or implied between the partners—

(a)   Any difference arising as to ordinary matters connected with the partnership business may be decided by a majority of the general partners;

(b)   A limited partner may, with the consent of the general partners, assign his share in the partnership, and upon such an assignment the assignee shall become a limited partner with all the rights of the assignor;

(c)   The other partners shall not be entitled to dissolve the partnership by reason of any limited partner suffering his share to be charged for his separate debt;

(d)   A person may be introduced as a partner without the consent of the existing limited partners;

(e)   A limited partner shall not be entitled to dissolve the partnership by notice.

## 7   Law as to private partnerships to apply where not excluded by this Act

Subject to the provisions of this Act, the Partnership Act 1890, and the rules of equity and of common law applicable to partnerships, except so far as they are inconsistent with the express provisions of the last-mentioned Act, shall apply to limited partnerships.

## [8   Duty to register

The registrar shall register a limited partnership if an application is made to the registrar in accordance with section 8A.]

## [8A   Application for registration

(1)   An application for registration must—

(a)   specify the firm name, complying with section 8B, under which the limited partnership is to be registered,

(b)   contain the details listed in subsection (2),

(c)   be signed or otherwise authenticated by or on behalf of each partner, and

(d)   be made to the registrar for the part of the United Kingdom in which the principal place of business of the limited partnership is to be situated.

(2)   The required details are—

(a)   the general nature of the partnership business,

(b)   the name of each general partner,

(c)   the name of each limited partner,

(d)   the amount of the capital contribution of each limited partner (and whether the contribution is paid in cash or in another specified form),

(e)   the address of the proposed principal place of business of the limited partnership, and

(f)    the term (if any) for which the limited partnership is to be entered into (beginning with the date of registration).]

## [8B    Name of limited partnership

(1)    This section sets out conditions which must be satisfied by the firm name of a limited partnership as specified in the application for registration.

(2)    The name must end with—

(a)    the words 'limited partnership' (upper or lower case, or any combination), or

(b)    the abbreviation 'LP' (upper or lower case, or any combination, with or without punctuation).

(3)    But if the principal place of business of a limited partnership is to be in Wales, its firm name may end with—

(a)    the words 'partneriaeth cyfyngedig' (upper or lower case, or any combination), or

(b)    the abbreviation 'PC' (upper or lower case, or any combination, with or without punctuation).]

## [8C    Certificate of registration

(1)    On registering a limited partnership the registrar shall issue a certificate of registration.

(2)    The certificate must be—

(a)    signed by the registrar, or

(b)    authenticated with the registrar's seal.

(3)    The certificate must state—

(a)    the firm name of the limited partnership given in the application for registration,

(b)    the limited partnership's registration number,

(c)    the date of registration, and

(d)    that the limited partnership is registered as a limited partnership under this Act.

(4)    The certificate is conclusive evidence that a limited partnership came into existence on the date of registration.]

## 9    Registration of changes in partnerships

(1)    If during the continuance of a limited partnership any change is made or occurs in—

(a)    the firm name,

(b)    the general nature of the business,

(c)    the principal place of business,

(d)    the partners or the name of any partner,

(e)    the term of character of the partnership,

(f)    the sum contributed by any limited partner,

(g)    the liability of any partner by reason of his becoming a limited instead of a general partner or a general instead of a limited partner,

a statement, signed by the firm, specifying the nature of the change, shall within seven days be sent by post or delivered to the registrar [. . .].

(2)    If default is made in compliance with the requirements of this section each of the general partners shall, on conviction under [the Magistrates' Courts Act 1952], be liable to a fine not exceeding one pound for each day during which the default continues.

## 10    Advertisement in Gazette of statement of general partner becoming a limited partner and of assignment of share of limited partner

(1)    Notice of any arrangement or transaction under which any person will cease to be a general partner in any firm, and will become a limited partner in that firm, or under which the share of a limited partner in a firm will be assigned to

any person, shall be forthwith advertised in the Gazette, and until notice of the arrangement or transaction is so advertised the arrangement or transaction shall, for the purposes of this Act, be deemed to be of no effect.

(2)   For the purposes of this section, the expression 'the Gazette' means—

In the case of a limited partnership registered in England, the London Gazette;

In the case of a limited partnership registered in Scotland, the Edinburgh Gazette;

In the case of a limited partnership registered in [Northern Ireland], the [Belfast] Gazette.

[. . .]

### 13   Registrar to file statement and issue certificate of registration

On receiving any statement made in pursuance of this Act the registrar shall cause the same to be filed, and he shall send by post to the firm from whom such statement shall have been received a certificate of the registration thereof.

### 14   Register and index to be kept

[. . .] the registrar shall keep [. . .] a register and an index of all the limited partnerships registered as aforesaid, and of all the statements registered in relation to such partnerships.

### [15   The registrar

(1)   The registrar of companies is the registrar of limited partnerships.

(2)   In this Act—

(a)   references to the registrar in relation to the registration of a limited partnership are to the registrar to whom the application for registration is to be made (see section 8A(1)(d));

(b)   references to registration in a particular part of the United Kingdom are to registration by the registrar for that part of the United Kingdom;

(c)   references to the registrar in relation to any other matter relating to a limited partnership are to the registrar for the part of the United Kingdom in which the partnership is registered.]

### 16   Inspection of statements registered

(1)   Any person may inspect the statements filed by the registrar [. . .]; and any person may require a certificate of the registration of any limited partnership, or a copy of or extract from any registered statement, to be certified by the registrar [. . .].

(2)   A certificate of registration, or a copy of or extract from any statement registered under this Act, if duly certified to be a true copy under the hand of the registrar [. . .] (whom it shall not be necessary to prove to be the registrar [. . .]) shall, in all legal proceedings, civil or criminal, and in all cases whatsoever be received in evidence.

## CONVEYANCING (SCOTLAND) ACT 1924
### (14 & 15 Geo 5, c 27)

**44 General Register of Inhibitions and Register of Adjudications to be combined; limitation of effect of entries therein**

(1) The General Register of Inhibitions and Interdictions and the Register of Adjudications shall be combined, and the Keeper thereof shall keep only one register for inhibitions, interdictions, adjudications, reductions, and notices of litigiosity, and such register shall be called the Register of Inhibitions and Adjudications; and a reference in any public, general or local Act to the General Register of Inhibitions or the Register of Adjudications shall be deemed to mean and include such Register of Inhibitions and Adjudications.

(2)(a) No action whether raised before or after the commencement of this Act relating to land or to a lease or to a heritable security, shall be deemed to have had or shall have the effect of making such land, lease or heritable security litigious, unless and until [—

(i)] a notice relative to such action in or as nearly as may be in the form of Schedule RR annexed to the Titles to Land Consolidation (Scotland) Act, 1868, shall have been or shall be registered in the Register of Inhibitions and Adjudications in the manner provided by section one hundred and fifty-nine of that Act [; or

(ii) a notice of an application under section 8 of the Law Reform (Miscellaneous Provisions)(Scotland) Act 1985 has been registered in the said register.]

(b) No decree in any action of adjudication of land or of a lease or of a heritable security, whether pronounced before or after the commencement of this Act, and no abbreviate of any such decree shall be deemed to have had or to have any effect in making such land, lease or heritable security litigious.

[(2A) A notice registered under subsection (2)(a)(i) of this section on or after the date on which section 67 of the Land Registration etc (Scotland) Act 2012 (asp 5) (warrant to place a caveat) comes into force shall not have any effect in rendering—

(a) any land or lease for which there is a title sheet in the Land Register of Scotland, or

(b) any heritable security the particulars of which are entered in a title sheet in that register,

litigious or in placing in bad faith any person acquiring such land, lease or heritable security.]

(3)(a) All inhibitions and all notices of litigiosity registered in terms of section one hundred and fifty-nine of the Titles to Land Consolidation (Scotland) Act, 1868, subsisting at the commencement of this Act shall prescribe and be of no effect on the lapse of five years after such commencement or at such earlier date as they would prescribe according to the present law and practice; and all [. . .] [, notices of litigiosity and notices of applications under section 8 of the Law Reform (Miscellaneous Provisions)(Scotland) Act 1985] which relate to land or to a lease or to a heritable security and which shall be first registered after the commencement of this Act, shall prescribe and be of no effect on the lapse of five years from the date on which the same shall respectively take effect: Provided that in no case shall litigiosity be pleadable or be founded on to any effect after the expiry of six months from and after final decree is pronounced in the action creating such litigiosity.

[(aa) all inhibitions shall cease to have effect on the lapse of five years from the date on which they take effect.]

(b) From and after the commencement of this Act interdiction, whether judicial or voluntary, shall be incompetent, and any interdiction which is legally operative at such commencement shall remain legally operative for not longer than the period of five years thereafter.

(4)  [. . .]

(c)  No deed, decree, instrument or writing granted or expede by a person whose estates have been sequestrated under the Bankruptcy (Scotland) Act, 1856, or the Bankruptcy (Scotland) Act, 1913 [or the Bankruptcy (Scotland) Act 1985], or the heirs, executors, successors or assignees of such person relative to any land or lease or heritable security belonging to such person at the date of such sequestration or subsequently acquired by him shall be challengeable or denied effect on the ground of such sequestration if such deed, decree, instrument or writing shall have been granted or expede, or shall come into operation at a date when the effect of recording [(a)] the abbreviate provided for under section forty-four of the said Act of 1913, as amended by this Act, shall have expired in terms of the said section as amended as aforesaid [; or (b) under subsection (1)(a) of section 14 of the Bankruptcy (Scotland) Act 1985 the certified copy of an order shall have expired by virtue of subsection (3) of that section], unless the trustee in such sequestration shall before the recording of such deed, decree, instrument or writing in the appropriate Register of Sasines have completed his title to such land, lease or heritable security by recording the same in such register [or have recorded a memorandum in such register [in the form provided by Schedule O to this Act]] Provided always, in the case of sequestrations awarded under the Bankruptcy (Scotland) Act, 1856, that the provisions of this section shall not apply to any deed, decree, instrument or writing dated within five years after the commencement of this Act.

(5)  The provisions of this section shall not affect the ranking of adjudgers inter se, or any real right obtained in virtue of a decree of adjudication, or in virtue of a decree pronounced in an action creating litigiosity, or by a trustee in bankruptcy, if such right has been completed by the recording in the appropriate Register of Sasines of any deed, decree, abbreviate, or instrument necessary to effect the completion of such right.

(6)  Section one hundred and fifty-nine of the Titles to Land Consolidation (Scotland) Act, 1868, and sections sixteen and seventeen of the Land Registers (Scotland) Act, 1868, [. . .] are hereby amended in accordance with this section, and section forty-two of the Conveyancing (Scotland) Act, 1874, and Schedule J thereto annexed, are hereby repealed.

## THIRD PARTIES (RIGHTS AGAINST INSURERS) ACT 1930
### (20 & 21 Geo 5, c 25)

### 1  Rights of third parties against insurers on bankruptcy &c of the insured

(1)  Where under any contract of insurance a person (hereinafter referred to as the insured) is insured against liabilities to third parties which he may incur, then—

(a)  in the event of the insured becoming bankrupt or making a composition or arrangement with his creditors; or

(b)  in the case of the insured being a company, in the event of a winding-up order being made, or a resolution for a voluntary winding-up being passed, with respect to the company, [or of the company entering administration,] or of a receiver or manager of the company's business or undertaking being duly appointed, or of possession being taken, by or on behalf of the holders of any debentures secured by a floating charge, of any property comprised in or subject to the charge [or of a voluntary arrangement proposed for the purposes of Part I of the Insolvency Act 1986 being approved under that Part];

if, either before or after that event, any such liability as aforesaid is incurred by the insured, his rights against the insurer under the contract in respect of the liability shall, notwithstanding anything in any Act or rule of law to the contrary, be transferred to and vest in the third party to whom the liability was so incurred.

(2)   Where [the estate of any person falls to be administered in accordance with an order under section 421 of the Insolvency Act 1986], then, if any debt provable in bankruptcy [(in Scotland, any claim accepted in the sequestration)] is owing by the deceased in respect of a liability against which he was insured under a contract of insurance as being a liability to a third party, the deceased debtor's rights against the insurer under the contract in respect of that liability shall, notwithstanding anything in [any such order], be transferred to and vest in the person to whom the debt is owing.

(3)   In so far as any contract of insurance made after the commencement of this Act in respect of any liability of the insured to third parties purports, whether directly or indirectly, to avoid the contract or to alter the rights of the parties thereunder upon the happening to the insured of any of the events specified in paragraph (a) or paragraph (b) of subsection (1) of this section or upon the [estate of any person falling to be administered in accordance with an order under section 421 of the Insolvency Act 1986], the contract shall be of no effect.

(4)   Upon a transfer under subsection (1) or subsection (2) of this section, the insurer shall, subject to the provisions of section three of this Act, be under the same liability to the third party as he would have been under to the insured, but—

(a)   if the liability of the insurer exceeds the liability of the insured to the third party, nothing in this Act shall affect the rights of the insured against the insurer in respect of the excess; and

(b)   if the liability of the insurer to the insured is less than the liability of the insured to the third party, nothing in this Act shall affect the rights of the third party against the insured in respect of the balance.

(5)   For the purposes of this Act, the expression 'liabilities to third parties', in relation to a person insured under any contract of insurance, shall not include any liability of that person in the capacity of insurer under some other contract of insurance.

(6)   This Act shall not apply—

(a)   where a company is wound up voluntarily merely for the purposes of reconstruction or of amalgamation with another company; or

(b)   to any case to which subsections (1) and (2) of section seven of the Workmen's Compensation Act 1925, applies.

## 2   Duty to give necessary information to third parties

(1)   In the event of any person becoming bankrupt or making a composition or arrangement with his creditors, or in the event of [the estate of any person falling to be administered in accordance with an order under section 421 of the Insolvency Act 1986], or in the event of a winding-up order being made, or a resolution for a voluntary winding-up being passed, with respect to any company [or of the company entering administration] or of a receiver or manager of the company's business or undertaking being duly appointed or of possession being taken by or on behalf of the holders of any debentures secured by a floating charge of any property comprised in or subject to the charge it shall be the duty of the bankrupt, debtor, personal representative of the deceased debtor or company, and, as the case may be, of the trustee in bankruptcy, trustee, liquidator, [administrator,] receiver, or manager, or person in possession of the property to give at the request of any person claiming that the bankrupt, debtor, deceased debtor, or company is under a liability to him such information as may reasonably be required by him for the purpose of ascertaining whether any rights have been transferred to and vested in him by this Act and for the purpose of enforcing such rights, if any, and any contract of insurance, in so far as it purports, whether directly or indirectly, to

avoid the contract or to alter the rights of the parties thereunder upon the giving of any such information in the events aforesaid or otherwise to prohibit or prevent the giving thereof in the said events shall be of no effect.

[(1A)   The reference in subsection (1) of this section to a trustee includes a reference to the supervisor of a [voluntary arrangement proposed for the purposes of, and approved under, Part I or Part VIII of the Insolvency Act 1986]].

(2)   If the information given to any person in pursuance of subsection (1) of this section discloses reasonable ground for supposing that there have or may have been transferred to him under this Act rights against any particular insurer, that insurer shall be subject to the same duty as is imposed by the said subsection on the persons therein mentioned.

(3)   The duty to give information imposed by this section shall include a duty to allow all contracts of insurance, receipts for premiums, and other relevant documents in the possession or power of the person on whom the duty is so imposed to be inspected and copies thereof to be taken.

### 3   Settlement between insurers and insured persons

Where the insured has become bankrupt or where in the case of the insured being a company, a winding-up order [or an administrative order] has been made or a resolution for a voluntary winding-up has been passed, with respect to the company, no agreement made between the insurer and the insured after liability has been incurred to a third party and after the commencement of the bankruptcy or winding-up [or the day of the making of the administration order], as the case may be, nor any waiver, assignment, or other disposition made by, or payment made to the insured after the commencement [or day] aforesaid shall be effective to defeat or affect the rights transferred to the third party under this Act, but those rights shall be the same as if no such agreement, waiver, assignment, disposition or payment had been made.

### [3A   Application to limited liability partnerships

(1)   This Act applies to limited liability partnerships as it applies to companies.

(2)   In its application to limited liability partnerships, references to a resolution for a voluntary winding-up being passed are references to a determination for a voluntary winding-up being made.]

### 4   Application to Scotland

In the application of this Act to Scotland—

[. . .]

(b)   any reference to [an estate falling to be administered in accordance with an order under section 421 of the Insolvency Act 1986], shall be deemed to include a reference to an award of sequestration of the estate of a deceased debtor, and a reference to an appointment of a judicial factor, under section [11A of the Judicial Factors (Scotland) Act 1889], on the insolvent estate of a deceased person.

### 5   Short title

This Act may be cited as the Third Parties (Rights against Insurers) Act 1930.

## CURRENCY AND BANK NOTES ACT 1954
### (2 & 3 Eliz 2, c 12)

### 1  Issue and recall of bank notes by Bank of England

(1)  The Bank of England may issue bank notes of such denominations as the Treasury may approve and shall not issue any other bank notes, and any bank notes issued under this section may be put into circulation in Scotland and Northern Ireland as well as in England and Wales.

(2)  All bank notes issued under this section shall be legal tender in England and Wales, and all such notes of denominations of less than five pounds shall be legal tender in Scotland and Northern Ireland.

(3)  Bank notes shall be payable only at the head office of the Bank of England unless expressly made payable also at some other place.

(4)  The holder of bank notes of any denominations shall be entitled, on a demand made by him during office hours at the head office of the Bank of England or, in the case of notes payable also at some place other than the head office, either at the head office or at that other place, to receive in exchange for the notes bank notes of such lower denominations, being bank notes which for the time being are legal tender in the United Kingdom or in England and Wales, as he may specify.

(5)  The Bank of England shall have power, on giving not less than one month's notice in the London, Edinburgh and Belfast Gazettes, to call in any bank notes on payment of the face value thereof, and any such notes with respect to which a notice has been given under this subsection shall on the expiration of the notice cease to be legal tender.

(6)  All bank notes which, immediately before the commencement of this Act, were legal tender in the United Kingdom, or were legal tender in England and Wales subject to the provisions of section six of the Bank of England Act 1833 (under which five-pound notes were not legal tender by the Bank of England), shall be deemed to have been issued under this section and shall be legal tender accordingly in the United Kingdom or, as the case may be, in England and Wales.

## CHEQUES ACT 1957
### (5 & 6 Eliz 2, c 36)

### 1  Protection of bankers paying unindorsed or irregularly indorsed cheques, etc

(1)  Where a banker in good faith and in the ordinary course of business pays a cheque drawn on him which is not indorsed or is irregularly indorsed, he does not in doing so, incur any liability by reason only of the absence of, or irregularly in indorsement, and he is deemed to have paid it in due course.

(2)  Where a banker in good faith and in the ordinary course of business pays any such instrument as the following namely—

(a)  a document issued by a customer of his which, though not a bill of exchange, is intended to enable a person to obtain payment from him of the sum mentioned in the document;

(b)  a draft payable on demand drawn by him upon himself, whether payable at the head office or some other office of his bank; he does not, in so doing, incur any liability by reason only of the absence of, or irregularity in, indorsement, and the payment discharges the instrument.

### 2  Rights of bankers collecting cheques not indorsed by holders

A banker who gives value for, or has a lien on, a cheque payable to order which the holder delivers to him for collection without indorsing it, has such (if any) rights as he would have had if, upon delivery, the holder had indorsed it in blank.

### 3 Unindorsed cheques as evidence of payment

[(1)] An unindorsed cheque which appears to have been paid by the banker on whom it is drawn is evidence of the receipt by the payee of the sum payable by the cheque.

[(2) For the purposes of subsection (1) above, a copy of a cheque to which that subsection applies is evidence of the cheque if—

(a) the copy is made by the banker in whose possession the cheque is after presentment and,

(b) it is certified by him to be a true copy of the original.]

### 4 Protection of bankers collecting payment of cheques, etc

(1) Where a banker, in good faith and without negligence—

(a) receives payment for a customer of an instrument to which this section applies; or

(b) having credited a customer's account with the amount of such an instrument, receives payment thereof for himself;

and the customer has no title, or a defective title, to the instrument, the banker does not incur any liability to the true owner of the instrument by reason only of having received payment thereof.

(2) This section applies to the following instruments, namely:—

(a) cheques [(including cheques which under section 81A(1) of the Bills of Exchange Act 1882 or otherwise are not transferable)];

(b) any document issued by a customer of a banker which, though not a bill of exchange, is intended to enable a person to obtain payment from that banker of the sum mentioned in the document;

(c) any document issued by a public officer is intended to enable a person to obtain payment from the Paymaster General or the Queen's and Lord Treasurer's Remembrancer of the sum mentioned in the document but is not a bill of exchange;

(d) any draft payable on demand drawn by a banker upon himself whether payable at the head office or some other office of his bank.

(3) A banker is not to be treated for the purposes of this section as having been negligent by reason only of his failure to concern himself with absence of, or irregularity in, indorsement of an instrument.

### 5 Application of certain provisions of Bills of Exchange Act, 1882, to instruments not being bills of exchange

The provisions of the Bills of Exchange Act, 1882, relating to crossed cheques shall, so far as applicable, have effect in relation to instruments (other than cheques) to which the last foregoing section applies as they have effect in relation to cheques.

### 6 Construction, saving and repeal

(1) This Act shall be construed as one with the Bills of Exchange Act, 1882.

(2) The foregoing provisions of this Act do not make negotiable any instrument which, apart from them, is not negotiable.

[. . .]

## HIRE-PURCHASE ACT 1964
### (1964, c 53)

[PART III
TITLE TO MOTOR VEHICLES ON HIRE-PURCHASE OR CONDITIONAL SALE

**27  Protection of purchasers of motor vehicles**

(1)  This section applies where a motor vehicle has been bailed or (in Scotland) hired under a hire-purchase agreement, or has been agreed to be sold under a conditional sale agreement, and, before the property in the vehicle has become vested in the debtor, he disposes of the vehicle to another person.

(2)  Where the disposition referred to in subsection (1) above is to a private purchaser, and he is a purchaser of the motor vehicle in good faith without notice of the hire-purchase or conditional sale agreement (the 'relevant agreement') that disposition shall have effect as if the creditor's title to the vehicle has been vested in the debtor immediately before that disposition.

(3)  Where the person to whom the disposition referred to in subsection (1) above is made (the 'original purchaser') is a trade or finance purchaser, then if the person who is the first private purchaser of the motor vehicle after that disposition (the 'first private purchaser') is a purchaser of the vehicle in good faith without notice of the relevant agreement, the disposition of the vehicle to the first private purchaser shall have effect as if the title of the creditor to the vehicle had been vested in the debtor immediately before he disposed of it to the original purchaser.

(4)  Where, in a case within subsection (3) above—

(a)  the disposition by which the first private purchaser becomes a purchaser of the motor vehicle in good faith without notice of the relevant agreement is itself a bailment or hiring under a hire-purchase agreement, and

(b)  the person who is the creditor in relation to that agreement disposes of the vehicle to the first private purchaser, or a person claiming under him, by transferring to him the property in the vehicle in pursuance of a provision in the agreement in that behalf, the disposition referred to in paragraph (b) above (whether or not the person to whom it is made is a purchaser in good faith without notice of the relevant agreement) shall as well as the disposition referred to in paragraph (a) above, have effect as mentioned in subsection (3) above.

(5)  The preceding provisions of this section apply—

(a)  notwithstanding anything in [section 21 of the Sale of Goods Act 1979] (sale of goods by a person not the owner), but

(b)  without prejudice to the provisions of the Factors Acts (as defined by [section 61(1) of the said Act of 1979]) or any other enactment enabling the apparent owner of goods to dispose of them as if he were the true owner.

(6)  Nothing in this section shall exonerate the debtor from any liability (whether criminal or civil) to which he would be subject apart from this section; and, in a case where the debtor disposes of the motor vehicle to a trade or finance purchaser, nothing in this section shall exonerate—

(a)  that trade or finance purchaser, or

(b)  any other trade or finance purchaser who becomes a purchaser of the vehicle and is not a person claiming under the first private purchaser,

from any liability (whether criminal or civil) to which he would be subject apart from this section.

**28  Presumptions relating to dealings with motor vehicles**

(1)  Where in any proceedings (whether criminal or civil) relating to a motor vehicle it is proved—

(a)  that the vehicle was bailed or (in Scotland) hired under a hire-purchase agreement, or was agreed to be sold under a conditional sale agreement, and

(b)  that a person (whether a party to the proceedings or not) became a private purchaser of the vehicle in good faith without notice of the hire-purchase or conditional sale agreement (the 'relevant agreement'), this section shall have effect for the purposes of the operation of section 27 of this Act in relation to those proceedings.

(2)   It shall be presumed for those purposes unless the contrary is proved, that the disposition of the vehicle to the person referred to in subsection (1)(b) above (the 'relevant purchaser') was made by the debtor.

(3)   If it is proved that that disposition was not made by the debtor, then it shall be presumed for those purposes, unless the contrary is proved—

(a)   that the debtor disposed of the vehicle to a private purchaser purchasing in good faith without notice of the relevant agreement, and

(b)   that the relevant purchaser is or was a person claiming under the person to whom the debtor so disposed of the vehicle.

(4)   If it is proved that the disposition of the vehicle to the relevant purchaser was not made by the debtor, and that the person to whom the debtor disposed of the vehicle (the 'original purchaser') was a trade or finance purchaser, then it shall be presumed for those purposes, unless the contrary is proved—

(a)   that the person who, after the disposition of the vehicle to the original purchaser, first became a private purchaser of the vehicle was a purchaser in good faith without notice of the relevant agreement, and

(b)   that the relevant purchaser is or was a person claiming under the original purchaser.

(5)   Without prejudice to any other method of proof, where in any proceedings a party thereto admits a fact, that fact shall, for the purposes of this section, be taken as against him to be proved in relation to those proceedings.

## 29   Interpretation of Part III

(1)   In this Part of this Act—

'conditional sale agreement' means an agreement for the sale of goods under which the purchase price or part of it is payable by instalments, and the property in the goods is to remain in the seller (notwithstanding that the buyer is to be in possession of the goods) until such conditions as to the payment of instalments or otherwise as may be specified in the agreement are fulfilled;

'creditor' means the person by whom goods are bailed or (in Scotland) hired under a hire-purchase agreement or as the case may be, the seller under a conditional sale agreement, or the person to whom his rights and duties have passed by assignment or operation of law;

'disposition' means any sale or contract of sale (including a conditional sale agreement), any bailment or (in Scotland) hiring under a hire-purchase agreement and any transfer of the property in goods in pursuance of a provision in that behalf contained in a hire-purchase agreement, and includes any transaction purporting to be a disposition (as so defined), and 'dispose of' shall be construed accordingly;

'hire-purchase agreement' means an agreement, other than a conditional sale agreement, under which—

(a)   goods are bailed or (in Scotland) hired in return for periodical payments by the person to whom they are bailed or hired, and

(b)   the property in the goods will pass to that person if the terms of the agreement are complied with and one or more of the following occurs—

(i)   the exercise of an option to purchase by that person,

(ii)   the doing of any other specified act by any party to the agreement,

(iii)   the happening of any other specified events; and

'motor vehicle' means a mechanically propelled vehicle intended or adapted for use on roads to which the public has access.

(2)   In this Part of this Act 'trade or finance purchaser' means a purchaser who, at the time of the disposition made to him, carries on a business which consists, wholly or partly—

(a)   of purchasing motor vehicles for the purpose of offering or exposing them for sale, or

(b)   of providing finance by purchasing motor vehicles for the purpose of bailing or (in Scotland) hiring them under hire-purchase agreements or agreeing to sell them under conditional sale agreements,

and 'private purchaser' means a purchaser who, at the time of the disposition made to him, does not carry on any such business.

(3)   For the purposes of this Part of this Act a person becomes a purchaser of a motor vehicle if, and at the time when, a disposition of the vehicle is made to him; and a person shall be taken to be a purchaser of a motor vehicle without notice of a hire-purchase agreement or conditional sale agreement if, at the time of the disposition made to him, he has no actual notice that the vehicle is or was the subject of any such agreement.

(4)   In this Part of this Act the 'debtor' in relation to a motor vehicle which has been bailed or hired under a hire-purchase agreement, or, as the case may be, agreed to be sold under a conditional sale agreement, means the person who at the material time (whether the agreement has before that time been terminated or not) either—

(a)   is the person to whom the vehicle is bailed or hired under that agreement, or

(b)   is, in relation to the agreement, the buyer,

including a person who at that time is, by virtue of section 130(4) of the Consumer Credit Act 1974 treated as a bailee or (in Scotland) a custodier of the vehicle.

(5)   In this Part of this Act any reference to the title of the creditor to a motor vehicle which has been bailed or (in Scotland) hired under a hire-purchase agreement or agreed to be sold under a conditional sale agreement, and is disposed of by the debtor, is a reference to such title (if any) to the vehicle as, immediately before that disposition, was vested in the person who then was the creditor in relation to the agreement.]

## CARRIAGE OF GOODS BY ROAD ACT 1965
### (1965, c 37)

**1   Convention to have force of law**

Subject to the following provisions of this Act, the provisions of the Convention on the Contract for the International Carriage of Goods by Road (in this Act referred to as 'the Convention'), as set out in the Schedule to this Act, shall have the force of law in the United Kingdom so far as they relate to the rights and liabilities of persons concerned in the carriage of goods by road under a contract to which the Convention applies.

**2   Designation of High Contracting Parties**

(1)   Her Majesty may by Order in Council from time to time certify who are the High Contracting Parties to the Convention and in respect of what territories they are respectively parties.

(2)   An Order in Council under this section shall, except so far as it has been superseded by a subsequent Order, be conclusive evidence of the matters so certified.

**3   Power of court to take account of other proceedings**

(1)   A court before which proceedings are brought to enforce a liability which is limited by article 23 in the Schedule to this Act may at any stage of the proceedings make any such order as appears to the court to be just and equitable in view of the provisions of the said article 23 and of any other proceedings which have

been, or are likely to be, commenced in the United Kingdom or elsewhere to enforce the liability in whole or in part.

(2) Without prejudice to the preceding subsection, a court before which proceedings are brought to enforce a liability which is limited by the said article 23 shall, where the liability is, or may be, partly enforceable in other proceedings in the United Kingdom or elsewhere, have jurisdiction to award an amount less than the court would have awarded if the limitation applied solely to the proceedings before the court, or to make any part of its award conditional on the result of any other proceedings.

## 4   Registration of foreign judgments

(1)   Subject to the next following subsection, Part I of the Foreign Judgments (Reciprocal Enforcement) Act 1933 (in this section referred to as 'the Act of 1933') shall apply whether or not it would otherwise have so applied, to any judgment which—

(a)   has been given in any such action as is referred to in paragraph 1 of article 31 in the Schedule to this Act, and

(b)   has been so given by any court or tribunal of a territory in respect of which one of the High Contracting Parties other than the United Kingdom, is a party to the Convention, and

(c)   has become enforceable in that territory.

(2)   In the application of Part I of the Act of 1933 in relation to any such judgment as is referred to in the preceding subsection, section 4 of that Act shall have effect with the omission of subsections (2) and (3).

(3)   The registration, in accordance with Part I of the Act of 1933, of any such judgment as is referred to in subsection (1) of this section shall constitute, in relation to that judgment compliance with the formalities for the purposes of paragraph 3 of article 31 in the Schedule to this Act.

## 5   Contribution between carriers

(1)   Where a carrier under a contract to which the Convention applies is liable in respect of any loss or damage for which compensation is payable under the Convention, nothing in [section 1 of the Civil Liability (Contribution) Act 1978] or section 3(2) of the Law Reform (Miscellaneous Provisions) (Scotland) Act 1940 shall confer on him any right to recover contribution in respect of that loss or damage from any other carrier who, in accordance with article 34 in the Schedule to this Act, is a party to the contract of carriage.

(2)   The preceding subsection shall be without prejudice to the operation of article 37 in the Schedule to this Act.

## 6   Actions against High Contracting Parties

Every High Contracting Party to the Convention shall, for the purpose of any proceedings brought in a court in the United Kingdom in accordance with the provisions of article 31 in the Schedule to this Act to enforce a claim in respect of carriage undertaken by that Party, be deemed to have submitted to the jurisdiction of that court, and accordingly rules of court may provide for the manner in which any such action is to be commenced and carried on; but nothing in this section shall authorise the issue of execution, or in Scotland the execution of diligence, against the property of any High Contracting Party.

## 7   Arbitrations

(1)   Any reference in the preceding provisions of this Act to a court includes a reference to an arbitration tribunal acting by virtue of article 33 in the Schedule to this Act.

(2)   For the purposes of article 32 in the Schedule to this Act, as it has effect (by virtue of the said article 33) in relation to arbitrations,—

[(a)   as respects England and Wales and Northern Ireland, the provisions of section 14(3) to (5) of the Arbitration Act 1996 (which determine the time at which an arbitration is commenced) apply;]

(c)   as respects Scotland, an arbitration shall be deemed to be commenced when one party to the arbitration serves on the other party or parties a notice requiring him or them to appoint an arbiter or to agree to the appointment of an arbiter or, where the arbitration agreement provides that the reference shall be to a person named or designated in the agreement, requiring him or them to submit the dispute to the person so named or designated.

## 8   Resolution of conflicts between Conventions on carriage of goods

(1)   If it appears to Her Majesty in Council that there is any conflict between the provisions of this Act (including the provisions of the Convention as set out in the Schedule to this Act) and any provisions relating to the carriage of goods for reward by land, sea or air contained in—

(a)   any other Convention which has been signed or ratified by or on behalf of Her Majesty's Government in the United Kingdom before the passing of this Act, or

(b)   any enactment of the Parliament of the United Kingdom giving effect to such a Convention,

Her Majesty may by Order in Council make such provision as may seem to her to be appropriate for resolving that conflict by amending or modifying this Act or any such enactment.

(2)   Any statutory instrument made by virtue of this section shall be subject to annulment in pursuance of a resolution of either House of Parliament.

## [8A   Amendments consequential on revision of Convention

(1)   If at any time it appears to Her Majesty in Council that Her Majesty's Government in the United Kingdom have agreed to any revision of the Convention, Her Majesty may by Order in Council make such amendment of—

[(a)   this Act; and]

(c)   section 5(1) of the Carriage by Air and Road Act 1979,

as appear to Her to be appropriate in consequence of the revision.

(2)   In the preceding subsection 'revision' means an omission from, addition to or alteration of the Convention and includes replacement of the Convention or part of it by another Convention.

(3)   An Order in Council under this section shall not be made unless a draft of the Order has been laid before Parliament and approved by a resolution of each House of Parliament. [. . .]

## 9   Application to British possessions, etc

Her Majesty may by Order in Council direct that this Act shall extend, subject to such exceptions, adaptations and modifications as may be specified in the Order, to—

(a)   the Isle of Man;

(b)   any of the Channel Islands;

(c)   any colony.

## 10   Application to Scotland

In its application to Scotland, the Schedule to this Act shall have effect as if—

(a)   any reference therein to a plaintiff included a reference to a pursuer;

(b)   any reference therein to a defendant included a reference to a defender; and

(c)   any reference to security for costs included a reference to caution for expenses.

## 11   [Applies to Northern Ireland]

## 12   Orders in Council

An Order in Council made under any of the preceding provisions of this Act may contain such transitional and supplementary provisions as appear to Her Majesty to be expedient and may be varied or revoked by a subsequent Order in Council made under that provision.

**13   Application to Crown**
This Act shall bind the Crown.

**14   Short title, interpretation and commencement**
(1)   This Act may be cited as the Carriage of Goods by Road Act 1965.
(2)   The persons who, for the purposes of this Act, are persons concerned in the carriage of goods by road under a contract to which the Convention applies are—
    (a)   the sender,
    (b)   the consignee,
    (c)   any carrier who, in accordance with article 34 in the Schedule to this Act or otherwise, is a party to the contract of carriage,
    (d)   any person for whom such a carrier is responsible by virtue of article 3 in the Schedule to this Act,
    (e)   any person to whom the rights and liabilities of any of the persons referred to in paragraphs (a) to (d) of this subsection have passed (whether by assignment or assignation or by operation of law).
(3)   Except in so far as the context otherwise requires, any reference in this Act to an enactment shall be construed as a reference to that enactment as amended or extended by or under any other enactment.
(4)   This Act shall come into operation on such day as Her Majesty may by Order in Council appoint; but nothing in this Act shall apply in relation to any contract for the carriage of goods by road made before the day so appointed.

## SCHEDULE
## CONVENTION ON THE CONTRACT FOR THE INTERNATIONAL CARRIAGE OF GOODS BY ROAD (CMR)
Section 1

### CHAPTER I
*Scope of application*

**Article 1**
1   This Convention shall apply to every contract for the carriage of goods by road in vehicles for reward, when the place of taking over of the goods and the place designated for delivery, as specified in the contract, are situated in two different countries, of which at least one is a contracting country, irrespective of the place of residence and the nationality of the parties.
2   For the purposes of this Convention, 'vehicles' means motor vehicles, articulated vehicles, trailers and semi-trailers as defined in article 4 of the Convention on Road Traffic dated 19th September 1949.
3   This Convention shall apply also where carriage coming within its scope is carried out by States or by governmental institutions or organisations.
4   This Convention shall not apply:
    (a)   to carriage performed under the terms of any international postal convention;
    (b)   to funeral consignments;
    (c)   to furniture removal.
5   The Contracting Parties agree not to vary any of the provisions of this Convention by special agreements between two or more of them, except to make it inapplicable to their frontier traffic or to authorise the use in transport operations entirely confined to their territory of consignment notes representing a title to the goods.

## Article 2

1  Where the vehicle containing the goods is carried over part of the journey by sea, rail, inland waterways or air, and except where the provisions of article 14 are applicable, the goods are not unloaded from the vehicle, this Convention shall nevertheless apply to the whole of the carriage. Provided that to the extent that it is proved that any loss, damage or delay in delivery of the goods which occurs during the carriage by the other means of transport was not caused by an act or omission of the carrier by road, but by some event which could only have occurred in the course of and by reason of the carriage by that other means of transport, the liability of the carrier by road shall be determined not by this Convention but in the manner in which the liability of the carrier by the other means of transport would have been determined if a contract for the carriage of the goods alone had been made by the sender with the carrier by the other means of transport in accordance with the conditions prescribed by law for the carriage of goods by that means of transport. If, however, there be no such prescribed conditions, the liability of the carrier by road shall be determined by this Convention.

2  If the carrier by road is also himself the carrier by the other means of transport, his liability shall also be determined in accordance with the provisions of paragraph 1 of this article, but as if, in his capacities as carrier by road and as carrier by the other means of transport, he were two separate persons.

## CHAPTER II
### Persons for whom the carrier is responsible

## Article 3

For the purposes of this Convention the carrier shall be responsible for the acts and omissions of his agents and servants and of any other persons of whose services he makes use for the performance of the carriage, when such agents, servants or other persons are acting within the scope of their employment, as if such acts or omissions were his own.

## CHAPTER III
### Conclusion and performance of the contract of carriage

## Article 4

The contract of carriage shall be confirmed by the making out of a consignment note. The absence, irregularity or loss of the consignment note shall not affect the existence or the validity of the contract of carriage which shall remain subject to the provisions of this Convention.

## Article 5

1  The consignment note shall be made out in three original copies signed by the sender and by the carrier. These signatures may be printed or replaced by the stamps of the sender and the carrier if the law of the country in which the consignment note has been made out so permits. The first copy shall be handed to the sender, the second shall accompany the goods and the third shall be retained by the carrier.

2  When the goods which are to be carried have to be loaded in different vehicles, or are of different kinds or are divided into different lots, the sender or the carrier shall have the right to require a separate consignment note to be made out for each vehicle used, or for each kind or lot of goods.

## Article 6

1  The consignment note shall contain the following particulars:
   (a)  the date of the consignment note and the place at which it is made out;
   (b)  the name and address of the sender;
   (c)  the name and address of the carrier;

(d)  the place and the date of taking over of the goods and the place designated for delivery;

(e)  the name and address of the consignee;

(f)  the description in common use of the nature of the goods and the method of packing, and, in the case of dangerous goods, their generally recognised description;

(g)  the number of packages and their special marks and numbers;

(h)  the gross weight of the goods or their quantity otherwise expressed;

(i)  charges relating to the carriage (carriage charges, supplementary charges, customs duties and other charges incurred from the making of the contract to the time of delivery);

(j)  the requisite instructions for Customs and other formalities;

(k)  a statement that the carriage is subject, notwithstanding any clause to the contrary, to the provisions of this Convention.

2  Where applicable, the consignment note shall also contain the following particulars:

(a)  a statement that transhipment is not allowed;

(b)  the charges which the sender undertakes to pay;

(c)  the amount of 'cash on delivery' charges;

(d)  a declaration of the value of the goods and the amount representing special interest on delivery;

(e)  the sender's instructions to the carrier regarding insurance of the goods;

(f)  the agreed time-limit within which the carriage is to be carried out;

(g)  a list of documents handed to the carrier.

3  The parties may enter in the consignment note any other particulars which they deem useful.

### Article 7

1  The sender shall be responsible for all expenses, loss and damage sustained by the carrier by reason of the inaccuracy or inadequacy of:

(a)  the particulars specified in article 6, paragraph 1, (b), (d), (e), (f), (g), (h) and (j);

(b)  the particulars specified in article 6, paragraph 2;

(c)  any other particulars or instructions given by him to enable the consignment note to be made out or for the purpose of their being entered therein.

2  If, at the request of the sender, the carrier enters in the consignment note the particulars referred to in paragraph 1 of this article, he shall be deemed, unless the contrary is proved to have done so on behalf of the sender.

3  If the consignment note does not contain the statement specified in article 6, paragraph 1(k), the carrier shall be liable for all expenses, loss and damage sustained through such omission by the person entitled to dispose of the goods.

### Article 8

1  On taking over the goods, the carrier shall check:

(a)  the accuracy of the statements in the consignment note as to the number of packages and their marks and numbers, and

(b)  the apparent condition of the goods and their packaging.

2  Where the carrier has no reasonable means of checking the accuracy of the statements referred to in paragraph 1(a) of this article, he shall enter his reservations in the consignment note together with the grounds on which they are based. He shall likewise specify the grounds for any reservations which he makes with regard to the apparent condition of the goods and their packaging. Such reservations shall not bind the sender unless he has expressly agreed to be bound by them in the consignment note.

3  The sender shall be entitled to require the carrier to check the gross weight of the goods or their quantity otherwise expressed. He may also require the contents

of the packages to be checked. The carrier shall be entitled to claim the cost of such checking. The result of the checks shall be entered in the consignment note.

### Article 9

1   The consignment note shall be prima facie evidence of the making of the contract of carriage, the conditions of the contract and the receipt of the goods by the carrier.

2   If the consignment note contains no specific reservations by the carrier, it shall be presumed, unless the contrary is proved, that the goods and their packaging appeared to be in good condition when the carrier took them over and that the number of packages, their marks and numbers corresponded with the statements in the consignment note.

### Article 10

The sender shall be liable to the carrier for damage to persons, equipment or other goods, and for any expenses due to defective packing of the goods, unless the defect was apparent or known to the carrier at the time when he took over the goods and he made no reservations concerning it.

### Article 11

1   For the purposes of the Customs or other formalities which have to be completed before delivery of the goods, the sender shall attach the necessary documents to the consignment note or place them at the disposal of the carrier and shall furnish him with all the information which he requires.

2   The carrier shall not be under any duty to enquire into either the accuracy or the adequacy of such documents and information. The sender shall be liable to the carrier for any damage caused by the absence, inadequacy or irregularity of such documents and information, except in the case of some wrongful act or neglect on the part of the carrier.

3   The liability of the carrier for the consequences arising from the loss or incorrect use of the documents specified in and accompanying the consignment note or deposited with the carrier shall be that of an agent, provided that the compensation payable by the carrier shall not exceed that payable in the event of loss of the goods.

### Article 12

1   The sender has a right to dispose of the goods, in particular by asking the carrier to stop the goods in transit, to change the place at which delivery is to take place or to deliver the goods to a consignee other than the consignee indicated in the consignment note.

2   This right shall cease to exist when the second copy of the consignment note is handed to the consignee or when the consignee exercises his right under article 13, paragraph 1; from that time onwards the carrier shall obey the orders of the consignee.

3   The consignee shall, however, have the right of disposal from the time when the consignment note is drawn up, if the sender makes an entry to that effect in the consignment note.

4   If in exercising his right of disposal the consignee has ordered the delivery of the goods to another person, that other person shall not be entitled to name other consignees.

5   The exercise of the right of disposal shall be subject to the following conditions:

(a)   that the sender or, in the case referred to in paragraph 3 of this article, the consignee who wishes to exercise the right produces the first copy of the consignment note on which the new instructions to the carrier have been entered and indemnifies the carrier against all expenses, loss and damage involved in carrying out such instructions;

(b)   that the carrying out of such instructions is possible at the time when the instructions reach the person who is to carry them out and does not either interfere with the normal working of the carrier's undertaking or prejudice the senders or consignees of other consignments;

(c)   that the instructions do not result in a division of the consignment.

6   When, by reason of the provisions of paragraph 5(b) of this article, the carrier cannot carry out the instructions which he receives he shall immediately notify the person who gave him such instructions.

7   A carrier who has not carried out the instructions given under the conditions provided for in this article, or who has carried them out without requiring the first copy of the consignment note to be produced, shall be liable to the person entitled to make a claim for any loss or damage caused thereby.

### Article 13

1   After arrival of the goods at the place designated for delivery, the consignee shall be entitled to require the carrier to deliver to him, against a receipt, the second copy of the consignment note and the goods. If the loss of the goods is established or if the goods have not arrived after the expiry of the period provided for in article 19, the consignee shall be entitled to enforce in his own name against the carrier any rights arising from the contract of carriage.

2   The consignee who avails himself of the rights granted to him under paragraph 1 of this article shall pay the charges shown to be due on the consignment note, but in the event of dispute on this matter the carrier shall not be required to deliver the goods unless security has been furnished by the consignee.

### Article 14

1   If for any reason it is or becomes impossible to carry out the contract in accordance with the terms laid down in the consignment note before the goods reach the place designated for delivery, the carrier shall ask for instructions from the person entitled to dispose of the goods in accordance with the provisions of article 12.

2   Nevertheless, if circumstances are such as to allow the carriage to be carried out under conditions differing from those laid down in the consignment note and if the carrier has been unable to obtain instructions in reasonable time from the person entitled to dispose of the goods in accordance with the provisions of article 12, he shall take such steps as seem to him to be in the best interests of the person entitled to dispose of the goods.

### Article 15

1   Where circumstances prevent delivery of the goods after their arrival at the place designated for delivery, the carrier shall ask the sender for his instructions. If the consignee refuses the goods the sender shall be entitled to dispose of them without being obliged to produce the first copy of the consignment note.

2   Even if he has refused the goods, the consignee may nevertheless require delivery so long as the carrier has not received instructions to the contrary from the sender.

3   When circumstances preventing delivery of the goods arise after the consignee, in exercise of his rights under article 12, paragraph 3, has given an order for the goods to be delivered to another person, paragraphs 1 and 2 of this article shall apply as if the consignee were the sender and that other person were the consignee.

### Article 16

1   The carrier shall be entitled to recover the cost of his request for instructions and any expenses entailed in carrying out such instructions, unless such expenses were caused by the wrongful act or neglect of the carrier.

2   In the cases referred to in article 14, paragraph 1, and in article 15, the carrier may immediately unload the goods for account of the person entitled to dispose of them and thereupon the carriage shall be deemed to be at an end. The carrier shall then hold the goods on behalf of the person so entitled. He may however entrust

them to a third party, and in that case he shall not be under any liability except for the exercise of reasonable care in the choice of such third party. The charges due under the consignment note and all other expenses shall remain chargeable against the goods.

3   The carrier may sell the goods, without awaiting instructions from the person entitled to dispose of them, if the goods are perishable or their condition warrants such a course, or when the storage expenses would be out of proportion to the value of the goods. He may also proceed to the sale of the goods in other cases if after the expiry of a reasonable period he has not received from the person entitled to dispose of the goods instructions to the contrary which he may reasonably be required to carry out.

4   If the goods have been sold pursuant to this article, the proceeds of sale, after deduction of the expenses chargeable against the goods, shall be placed at the disposal of the person entitled to dispose of the goods. If these charges exceed the proceeds of sale, the carrier shall be entitled to the difference.

5   The procedure in the case of sale shall be determined by the law or custom of the place where the goods are situated.

## CHAPTER IV
### *Liability of the carrier*

**Article 17**

1   The carrier shall be liable for the total or partial loss of the goods and for damage thereto occurring between the time when he takes over the goods and the time of delivery, as well as for any delay in delivery.

2   The carrier shall however be relieved of liability if the loss, damage or delay was caused by the wrongful act or neglect of the claimant, by the instructions of the claimant given otherwise than as the result of a wrongful act or neglect on the part of the carrier, by inherent vice of the goods or through circumstances which the carrier could not avoid and the consequences of which he was unable to prevent.

3   The carrier shall not be relieved of liability by reason of the defective condition of the vehicle used by him in order to perform the carriage, or by reason of the wrongful act or neglect of the person from whom he may have hired the vehicle or of the agents or servants of the latter.

4   Subject to article 18, paragraphs 2 to 5 the carrier shall be relieved of liability when the loss or damage arises from the special risks inherent in one or more of the following circumstances:

(a)   use of open unsheeted vehicles, when their use has been expressly agreed and specified in the consignment note;

(b)   the lack of, or defective condition of packing in the case of goods which, by their nature, are liable to wastage or to be damaged when not packed or when not properly packed;

(c)   handling, loading, stowage or unloading of the goods by the sender, the consignee or person acting on behalf of the sender or consignee;

(d)   the nature of certain kinds of goods which particularly exposes them to total or partial loss or to damage, especially through breakage, rust, decay, desiccation, leakage, normal wastage, or the action of moth or vermin;

(e)   insufficiency or inadequacy of marks or numbers on the packages;

(f)   the carriage of livestock.

5   Where under this article the carrier is not under any liability in respect of some of the factors causing the loss, damage or delay, he shall only be liable to the extent that those factors for which he is liable under this article have contributed to the loss, damage or delay.

## Article 18

1 The burden of proving that loss, damage or delay was due to one of the causes specified in article 17, paragraph 2, shall rest upon the carrier.

2 When the carrier establishes that in the circumstances of the case, the loss or damage could be attributed to one or more of the special risks referred to in article 17, paragraph 4, it shall be presumed that it was so caused. The claimant shall however be entitled to prove that the loss or damage was not, in fact, attributable either wholly or partly to one of these risks.

3 This presumption shall not apply in the circumstances set out in article 17, paragraph 4(a), if there has been an abnormal shortage, or a loss of any package.

4 If the carriage is performed in vehicles specially equipped to protect the goods from the effects of heat, cold, variations in temperature or the humidity of the air, the carrier shall not be entitled to claim the benefit of article 17, paragraph 4(d) unless he proves that all steps incumbent on him in the circumstances with respect to the choice, maintenance and use of such equipment were taken and that he complied with any special instructions issued to him.

5 The carrier shall not be entitled to claim the benefit of article 17, paragraph 4(f), unless he proves that all steps normally incumbent on him in the circumstances were taken and that he complied with any special instructions issued to him.

## Article 19

Delay in delivery shall be said to occur when the goods have not been delivered within the agreed time-limit or when, failing an agreed time-limit, the actual duration of the carriage having regard to the circumstances of the case, and in particular, in the case of partial loads, the time required for making up a complete load in the normal way, exceeds the time it would be reasonable to allow a diligent carrier.

## Article 20

1 The fact that the goods have not been delivered within thirty days following the expiry of the agreed time-limit, or if there is no agreed time-limit, within sixty days from the time when the carrier took over the goods, shall be conclusive evidence of the loss of the goods, and the person entitled to make a claim may thereupon treat them as lost.

2 The person so entitled may, on receipt of compensation for the missing goods, request in writing that he shall be notified immediately should the goods be recovered in the course of the year following the payment of compensation. He shall be given a written acknowledgement of such request.

3 Within the thirty days following receipt of such notification, the person entitled as aforesaid may require the goods to be delivered to him against payment of the charges shown to be due on the consignment note and also against refund of the compensation he received less any charges included therein but without prejudice to any claims to compensation for delay in delivery under article 23 and, where applicable, article 26.

4 In the absence of the request mentioned in paragraph 2 or of any instructions given within the period of thirty days specified in paragraph 3, or if the goods are not recovered until more than one year after the payment of compensation, the carrier shall be entitled to deal with them in accordance with the law of the place where the goods are situated.

## Article 21

Should the goods have been delivered to the consignee without collection of the 'cash on delivery' charge which should have been collected by the carrier under the terms of the contract of carriage, the carrier shall be liable to the sender for compensation not exceeding the amount of such charge without prejudice to his right of action against the consignee.

## Article 22

1   When the sender hands goods of a dangerous nature to the carrier, he shall inform the carrier of the exact nature of the danger and indicate, if necessary, the precautions to be taken. If this information has not been entered in the consignment note, the burden of proving, by some other means, that the carrier knew the exact nature of the danger constituted by the carriage of the said goods shall rest upon the sender or the consignee.

2   Goods of a dangerous nature which, in the circumstances referred to in paragraph 1 of this article, the carrier did not know were dangerous, may, at any time or place, be unloaded, destroyed or rendered harmless by the carrier without compensation; further, the sender shall be liable for all expenses, loss or damage arising out of their handing over for carriage or of their carriage.

## Article 23

1   When, under the provisions of this Convention, a carrier is liable for compensation in respect of total or partial loss of goods, such compensation shall be calculated by reference to the value of the goods at the place and time at which they were accepted for carriage.

2   The value of the goods shall be fixed according to the commodity exchange price or, if there is no such price, according to the current market price, or, if there is no commodity exchange price or current market price, by reference to the normal value of goods of the same kind and quality.

[3   Compensation shall not, however, exceed 8.33 units of account per kilogram of gross weight short.]

4   In addition, the carriage charges, Customs duties and other charges incurred in respect of the carriage of the goods shall be refunded in full in case of total loss and in proportion to the loss sustained in case of partial loss, but no further damages shall be payable.

5   In the case of delay, if the claimant proves that damage has resulted therefrom the carrier shall pay compensation for such damage not exceeding the carriage charges.

6   Higher compensation may only be claimed where the value of the goods or a special interest in delivery has been declared in accordance with articles 24 and 26.

[7   The unit of account mentioned in this Convention is the Special Drawing Right as defined by the International Monetary Fund. The amount mentioned in paragraph 3 of this article shall be converted into the national currency of the State of the Court seised of the case on the basis of the value of that currency on the date of judgment or the date agreed upon by the Parties.]

## Article 24

The sender may, against payment of a surcharge to be agreed upon, declare in the consignment note a value for the goods exceeding the limit laid down in article 23, paragraph 3, and in that case the amount of the declared value shall be substituted for that limit.

## Article 25

1   In case of damage, the carrier shall be liable for the amount by which the goods have diminished in value, calculated by reference to the value of the goods fixed in accordance with article 23, paragraphs 1, 2 and 4.

2   The compensation may not, however, exceed:

    (a)   if the whole consignment has been damaged, the amount payable in the case of total loss;

    (b)   if part only of the consignment has been damaged, the amount payable in the case of loss of the part affected.

## Article 26

1   The sender may, against payment of a surcharge to be agreed upon, fix the amount of a special interest in delivery in the case of loss or damage or of the

agreed time-limit being exceeded, by entering such amount in the consignment note.

2  If a declaration of a special interest in delivery has been made, compensation for the additional loss or damage proved may be claimed, up to the total amount of the interest declared, independently of the compensation provided for in articles 23, 24 and 25.

### Article 27

1  The claimant shall be entitled to claim interest on compensation payable. Such interest, calculated at five per centum per annum, shall accrue from the date on which the claim was sent in writing to the carrier or, if no such claim has been made, from the date on which legal proceedings were instituted.

2  When the amounts on which the calculation of the compensation is based are not expressed in the currency of the country in which payment is claimed, conversion shall be at the rate of exchange applicable on the day and at the place of payment of compensation.

### Article 28

1  In cases where, under the law applicable, loss, damage or delay arising out of carriage under this Convention gives rise to an extra-contractual claim, the carrier may avail himself of the provisions of this Convention which exclude his liability or which fix or limit the compensation due.

2  In cases where the extra-contractual liability for loss, damage or delay of one of the persons for whom the carrier is responsible under the terms of article 3 is in issue, such person may also avail himself of the provisions of this Convention which exclude the liability of the carrier or which fix or limit the compensation due.

### Article 29

1  The carrier shall not be entitled to avail himself of the provisions of this chapter which exclude or limit his liability or which shift the burden of proof if the damage was caused by his wilful misconduct or by such default on his part as, in accordance with the law of the court or tribunal seised of the case, is considered as equivalent to wilful misconduct.

2  The same provision shall apply if the wilful misconduct or default is committed by the agents or servants of the carrier or by any other persons of whose services he makes use for the performance of the carriage, when such agents, servants or other persons are acting within the scope of their employment. Furthermore, in such a case such agents, servants or other persons shall not be entitled to avail themselves, with regard to their personal liability, of the provisions of this chapter referred to in paragraph 1.

### CHAPTER V
*Claims and actions*

### Article 30

1  If the consignee takes delivery of the goods without duly checking their condition with the carrier or without sending him reservations giving a general indication of the loss or damage, not later than the time of delivery in the case of apparent loss or damage and within seven days of delivery, Sundays and public holidays excepted, in the case of loss or damage which is not apparent, the fact of his taking delivery shall be prima facie evidence that he has received the goods in the condition described in the consignment note. In the case of loss or damage which is not apparent the reservations referred to shall be made in writing.

2  When the condition of the goods has been duly checked by the consignee and the carrier, evidence contradicting the result of this checking shall only be admissible in the case of loss or damage which is not apparent and provided that

the consignee has duly sent reservations in writing to the carrier within seven days, Sundays and public holidays excepted, from the date of checking.

3   No compensation shall be payable for delay in delivery unless a reservation has been sent in writing to the carrier, within twenty-one days from the time that the goods were placed at the disposal of the consignee.

4   In calculating the time-limits provided for in this article the date of delivery, or the date of checking, or the date when the goods were placed at the disposal of the consignee, as the case may be, shall not be included.

5   The carrier and the consignee shall give each other every reasonable facility for making the requisite investigations and checks.

### Article 31

1   In legal proceedings arising out of carriage under this Convention, the plaintiff may bring an action in any court or tribunal of a contracting country designated by agreement between the parties and, in addition, in the courts or tribunals of a country within whose territory:

(a)   the defendant is ordinarily resident, or has his principal place of business, or the branch or agency through which the contract of carriage was made, or

(b)   the place where the goods were taken over by the carrier or the place designated for delivery is situated,

and in no other courts or tribunals.

2   Where in respect of a claim referred to in paragraph 1 of this article an action is pending before a court or tribunal competent under that paragraph, or where in respect of such a claim a judgment has been entered by such a court or tribunal no new action shall be started between the same parties on the same grounds unless the judgment of the court or tribunal before which the first action was brought is not enforceable in the country in which the fresh proceedings are brought.

3   When a judgment entered by a court or tribunal of a contracting country in any such action as is referred to in paragraph 1 of this article has become enforceable in that country, it shall also become enforceable in each of the other contracting States, as soon as the formalities required in the country concerned have been complied with. These formalities shall not permit the merits of the case to be reopened.

4   The provisions of paragraph 3 of this article shall apply to judgments after trial, judgments by default and settlements confirmed by an order of the court, but shall not apply to interim judgments or to awards of damages, in addition to costs against a plaintiff who wholly or partly fails in his action.

5   Security for costs shall not be required in proceedings arising out of carriage under this Convention from nationals of contracting countries resident or having their place of business in one of those countries.

### Article 32

1   The period of limitation for an action arising out of carriage under this Convention shall be one year. Nevertheless, in the case of wilful misconduct, or such default as in accordance with the law of the court or tribunal seised of the case, is considered as equivalent to wilful misconduct, the period of limitation shall be three years. The period of limitation shall begin to run:

(a)   in the case of partial loss, damage or delay in delivery, from the date of delivery;

(b)   in the case of total loss, from the thirtieth day after the expiry of the agreed time-limit or where there is no agreed time-limit from the sixtieth day from the date on which the goods were taken over by the carrier;

(c)   in all other cases, on the expiry of a period of three months after the making of the contract of carriage.

The day on which the period of limitation begins to run shall not be included in the period.

2   A written claim shall suspend the period of limitation until such date as the carrier rejects the claim by notification in writing and returns the documents attached thereto. If a part of the claim is admitted the period of limitation shall start to run again only in respect of that part of the claim still in dispute. The burden of proof of the receipt of the claim, or of the reply and of the return of the documents, shall rest with the party relying upon these facts. The running of the period of limitation shall not be suspended by further claims having the same object.

3   Subject to the provisions of paragraph 2 above, the extension of the period of limitation shall be governed by the law of the court or tribunal seised of the case. That law shall also govern the fresh accrual rights of action.

4   A right of action which has become barred by lapse of time may not be exercised by way of counter-claim or set-off.

### Article 33
The contract of carriage may contain a clause conferring competence on an arbitration tribunal if the clause conferring competence on the tribunal provides that the tribunal shall apply this Convention.

### CHAPTER VI
*Provisions relating to carriage performed by successive carriers*

### Article 34
If carriage governed by a single contract is performed by successive road carriers, each of them shall be responsible for the performance of the whole operation, the second carrier and each succeeding carrier becoming a party to the contract of carriage, under the terms of the consignment note, by reason of his acceptance of the goods and the consignment note.

### Article 35
1   A carrier accepting the goods from a previous carrier shall give the latter a dated and signed receipt. He shall enter his name and address on the second copy of the consignment note. Where applicable, he shall enter on the second copy of the consignment note and on the receipt reservations of the kind provided for in article 8, paragraph 2.

2   The provisions of article 9 shall apply to the relations between successive carriers.

### Article 36
Except in the case of a counter-claim or a set-off raised in an action concerning a claim based on the same contract of carriage, legal proceedings in respect of liability for loss, damage or delay may only be brought against the first carrier, the last carrier or the carrier who was performing that portion of the carriage during which the event causing the loss, damage or delay occurred; an action may be brought at the same time against several of these carriers.

### Article 37
A carrier who has paid compensation in compliance with the provisions of this Convention, shall be entitled to recover such compensation, together with interest thereon and all costs and expenses incurred by reason of the claim, from the other carriers who have taken part in the carriage, subject to the following provisions:

   (a)   the carrier responsible for the loss or damage shall be solely liable for the compensation whether paid by himself or by another carrier;

   (b)   when the loss or damage has been caused by the action of two or more carriers, each of them shall pay an amount proportionate to his share of liability; should it be impossible to apportion the liability, each carrier shall be liable in proportion to the share of the payment for the carriage which is due to him;

   (c)   if it cannot be ascertained to which carriers liability is attributable for the loss or damage, the amount of the compensation shall be apportioned between all the carriers as laid down in (b) above.

## Article 38
If one of the carriers is insolvent, the share of the compensation due from him and unpaid by him shall be divided among the other carriers in proportion to the share of the payment for the carriage due to them.

## Article 39
1   No carrier against whom a claim is made under articles 37 and 38 shall be entitled to dispute the validity of the payment made by the carrier making the claim if the amount of the compensation was determined by judicial authority after the first mentioned carrier had been given due notice of the proceedings and afforded an opportunity of entering an appearance.

2   A carrier wishing to take proceedings to enforce his right of recovery may make his claim before the competent court or tribunal of the country in which one of the carriers concerned is ordinarily resident, or has his principal place of business or the branch or agency through which the contract of carriage was made. All the carriers concerned may be made defendants in the same action.

3   The provisions of article 31, paragraphs 3 and 4 shall apply to judgments entered in the proceedings referred to in articles 37 and 38.

4   The provisions of article 32 shall apply to claims between carriers. The period of limitation shall, however, begin to run either on the date of the final judicial decision fixing the amount of compensation payable under the provisions of this Convention, or, if there is no such judicial decision, from the actual date of payment.

## Article 40
Carriers shall be free to agree among themselves on provisions other than those laid down in articles 37 and 38.

### CHAPTER VII
*Nullity of stipulations contrary to the Convention*

## Article 41
1   Subject to the provisions of article 40, any stipulation which would directly or indirectly derogate from the provisions of this Convention shall be null and void. The nullity of such a stipulation shall not involve the nullity of the other provisions of the contract.

2   In particular, a benefit of insurance in favour of the carrier or any other similar clause, or any clause shifting the burden of proof shall be null and void.

*[Chapter VIII deals with the coming into force of the Convention, the settlement of disputes between the high contracting parties and related matters.]*

## CARRIAGE OF GOODS BY SEA ACT 1971
### (1971, c 19)

**1  Application of Hague Rules as amended**

(1)  In this Act, 'the Rules' means the International Convention for the unification of certain rules of law relating to bills of lading signed at Brussels on 25th August 1924, as amended by the Protocol signed at Brussels on 23rd February 1968 [and by the protocol signed at Brussels on 21st December 1979].

(2)  The provisions of the Rules, as set out in the Schedule to this Act, shall have the force of law.

(3)  Without prejudice to subsection (2) above, the said provisions shall have effect (and have the force of law) in relation to and in connection with the carriage of goods by sea in ships where the port of shipment is a port in the United Kingdom, whether or not the carriage is between ports in two different States within the meaning of Article X of the Rules.

(4)  Subject to subsection (6) below, nothing in this section shall be taken as applying anything in the Rules to any contract for the carriage of goods by sea, unless the contract expressly or by implication provides for the issue of a bill of lading or any similar document of title.

[. . .]

(6)  Without prejudice to Article X(c) of the Rules, the Rules shall have the force of law in relation to—

(a)  any bill of lading if the contract contained in or evidenced by it expressly provides that the Rules shall govern the contract, and

(b)  any receipt which is a non-negotiable document marked as such if the contract contained in or evidenced by it is a contract for the carriage of goods by sea which expressly provides that the Rules are to govern the contract as if the receipt were a bill of lading, but subject, where paragraph (b) applies, to any necessary modifications and in particular with the omission in Article III of the Rules of the second sentence of paragraph 4 and of paragraph 7.

(7)  If and so far as the contract contained in or evidenced by a bill of lading or receipt within paragraph (a) or (b) of subsection (6) above applies to deck cargo or live animals, the Rules as given the force of law by that subsection shall have effect as if Article I(c) did not exclude deck cargo and live animals.

In this subsection 'deck cargo' means cargo which by the contract of carriage is stated as being carried on deck and is so carried.

**[1A  Conversion of special drawing rights into sterling**

(1)  For the purposes of Article IV of the Rules the value on a particular day of one special drawing right shall be treated as equal to such a sum in sterling as the International Monetary Fund have fixed as being the equivalent of one special drawing right—

(a)  for that day; or

(b)  if no sum has been so fixed for that day, for the last day before that day for which a sum has been so fixed.

(2)  A certificate given by or on behalf of the Treasury stating—

(a)  that a particular sum in sterling has been fixed as aforesaid for a particular day; or

(b)  that no sum has been so fixed for a particular day and that a particular sum in sterling has been so fixed for a day which is the last day for which a sum has been so fixed before the particular day,

shall be conclusive evidence of those matters for the purposes of subsection (1) above;

and a document purporting to be such a certificate shall in any proceedings be received in evidence and, unless the contrary is proved, be deemed to be such a certificate.

(3)  The Treasury may charge a reasonable fee for any certificate given in

pursuance of subsection (2) above, and any fee received by the Treasury by virtue of this subsection shall be paid into the Consolidated Fund.]

**2  Contracting States, etc**
(1)   If Her Majesty by Order in Council certifies to the following effect, that is to say, that for the purposes of the Rules—
(a)   a State specified in the Order is a contracting State, or is a contracting State in respect of any place or territory so specified; or
(b)   any place or territory specified in the Order forms part of a State so specified (whether a contracting State or not),
the Order shall, except so far as it has been superseded by a subsequent Order, be conclusive evidence of the matters so certified.
(2)   An Order in Council under this section may be varied or revoked by a subsequent Order in Council.

**3  Absolute warranty of seaworthiness not to be implied in contracts to which Rules apply**
There shall not be implied in any contract for the carriage of goods by sea to which the Rules apply by virtue of this Act any absolute undertaking by the carrier of the goods to provide a seaworthy ship.

**4  Application of Act to British possessions, etc**
(1)   Her Majesty may by Order in Council direct that this Act shall extend, subject to such exceptions, adaptations and modifications as may be specified in the Order, to all or any of the following territories, that is—
(a)   any colony (not being a colony for whose external relations a country other than the United Kingdom is responsible),
(b)   any country outside Her Majesty's dominions in which Her Majesty has jurisdiction in right of Her Majesty's Government of the United Kingdom.
(2)   An Order in Council under this section may contain such transitional and other consequential and incidental provisions as appear to Her Majesty to be expedient, including provisions amending or repealing any legislation about the carriage of goods by sea forming part of the law of any of the territories mentioned in paragraphs (a) and (b) above.
(3)   An Order in Council under this section may be varied or revoked by a subsequent Order in Council.

**5  Extension of application of Rules to carriage from ports in British possessions, etc**
(1)   Her Majesty may by Order in Council provide that section 1(3) of this Act shall have effect as if the reference therein to the United Kingdom included a reference to all or any of the following territories, that is—
(a)   the Isle of Man;
(b)   any of the Channel Islands specified in the Order;
(c)   any colony specified in the Order (not being a colony for whose external relations a country other than the United Kingdom is responsible);
[. . .]
(e)   any country specified in the Order, being a country outside Her Majesty's dominions in which Her Majesty has jurisdiction in right of Her Majesty's Government of the United Kingdom.
(2)   An Order in Council under this section may be varied or revoked by a subsequent Order in Council.

**6  Supplemental**
(1)   This Act may be cited as the Carriage of Goods by Sea Act 1971.
(2)   It is hereby declared that this Act extends to Northern Ireland.
(3)   The following enactments shall be repealed, that is—
(a)   the Carriage of Goods by Sea Act 1924,

(b)   section 12(4)(a) of the Nuclear Installations Act 1965,
and without prejudice to section [17(2)(a) of the Interpretation Act 1978], the reference to the said Act of 1924 in section 1(1)(i)(ii) of the Hovercraft Act 1968 shall include a reference to this Act.

[(4)   It is hereby declared that for the purposes of Article VIII of the Rules section 186 of the Merchant Shipping Act 1995 (which entirely exempts shipowners and others in certain circumstances for loss of, or damage to, goods) is a provision relating to limitation of liability.]

(5)   This Act shall come into force on such day as Her Majesty may by Order in Council appoint, and, for the purposes of the transition from the law in force immediately before the day appointed under this subsection to the provisions of this Act, the Order appointing the day may provide that those provisions shall have effect subject to such transitional provisions as may be contained in the Order.

## SCHEDULE

### THE HAGUE RULES AS AMENDED BY THE BRUSSELS PROTOCOL 1968

**Article I**
In these Rules the following words are employed, with the meanings set out below:—

(a)   'Carrier' includes the owner or the charterer who enters into a contract of carriage with a shipper.

(b)   'Contract of carriage' applies only to contracts of carriage covered by a bill of lading or any similar document of title, in so far as such document relates to the carriage of goods by sea, including any bill of lading or any similar document as aforesaid issued under or pursuant to a charter party from the moment at which such bill of lading or similar document of title regulates the relations between a carrier and a holder of the same.

(c)   'Goods' includes goods, wares, merchandise, and articles of every kind whatsoever except live animals and cargo which by the contract of carriage is stated as being carried on deck and is so carried.

(d)   'Ship' means any vessel used for the carriage of goods by sea.

(e)   'Carriage of goods' covers the period from the time when the goods are loaded on to the time they are discharged from the ship.

**Article II**
Subject to the provisions of Article VI, under every contract of carriage of goods by sea the carrier, in relation to the loading, handling, stowage, carriage, custody, care and discharge of such goods, shall be subject to the responsibilities and liabilities, and entitled to the rights and immunities hereinafter set forth.

**Article III**
(1)   The carrier shall be bound before and at the beginning of the voyage to exercise due diligence to—

(a)   Make the ship seaworthy.

(b)   Properly man, equip and supply the ship.

(c)   Make the holds, refrigerating and cool chambers, and all other parts of the ship in which goods are carried, fit and safe for their reception, carriage and preservation.

(2)   Subject to the provisions of Article IV, the carrier shall properly and carefully load, handle, stow, carry, keep, care for, and discharge the goods carried.

(3)   After receiving the goods into his charge the carrier or the master or agent of the carrier shall, on demand of the shipper, issue to the shipper a bill of lading showing among other things—

(a)   The leading marks necessary for identification of the goods as the same are furnished in writing by the shipper before the loading of such goods starts, provided such marks are stamped or otherwise shown clearly upon the goods if uncovered, or on the cases or coverings in which such goods are contained, in such a manner as should ordinarily remain legible until the end of the voyage.

(b)  Either the number of packages or pieces, or the quantity, or weight, as the case may be, as furnished in writing by the shipper.

(c)  The apparent order and condition of the goods.

Provided that no carrier, master or agent of the carrier shall be bound to state or show in the bill of lading any marks, number, quantity, or weight which he has reasonable ground for suspecting not accurately to represent the goods actually received, or which be has had no reasonable means of checking.

(4)  Such a bill of lading shall be prima facie evidence of the receipt by the carrier of the goods as therein described in accordance with paragraph 3(a), (b) and (c). However, proof to the contrary shall not be admissible when the bill of lading has been transferred to a third party acting in good faith.

(5)  The shipper shall be deemed to have guaranteed to the carrier the accuracy at the time of shipment of the marks, number, quantity and weight, as furnished by him, and the shipper shall indemnify the carrier against all loss, damages and expenses arising or resulting from inaccuracies in such particulars. The right of the carrier to such indemnity shall in no way limit his responsibility and liability under the contract of carriage to any person other than the shipper.

(6)  Unless notice of loss or damage and the general nature of such loss or damage be given in writing to the carrier or his agent at the port of discharge before or at the time of the removal of the goods into the custody of the person entitled to delivery thereof under the contract of carriage, or, if the loss or damage be not apparent, within three days, such removal shall be prima facie evidence of the delivery by the carrier of the goods as described in the bill of lading.

The notice in writing need not be given if the state of the goods has, at the time of their receipt, been the subject of joint survey or inspection.

Subject to paragraph 6bis the carrier and the ship shall in any event be discharged from all liability whatsoever in respect of the goods, unless suit is brought within one year of their delivery or of the date when they should have been delivered. This period may, however, be extended if the parties so agree after the cause of action has arisen.

In the case of any actual or apprehended loss or damage the carrier and the receiver shall give all reasonable facilities to each other for inspecting and tallying the goods.

(6bis)  An action for indemnity against a third person may be brought even after the expiration of the year provided for in the preceding paragraph if brought within the time allowed by the law of the court seised of the case. However, the time allowed shall be not less than three months, commencing from the day when the person bringing such action for indemnity has settled the claim or has been served with process in the action against himself.

(7)  After the goods are loaded the bill of lading to be issued by the carrier, master, or agent of the carrier, to the shipper shall, if the shipper so demands, be a 'shipped' bill of lading, provided that if the shipper shall have previously taken up any document of title to such goods, he shall surrender the same as against the issue of the 'shipped' bill of lading, but at the option of the carrier such document of title may be noted at the port of shipment by the carrier, master, or agent with the name or names of the ship or ships upon which the goods have been shipped and the date or dates of shipment, and when so noted if it shows the particulars mentioned in paragraph 3 of Article III, shall for the purpose of this article be deemed to constitute a 'shipped' bill of lading.

(8)  Any clause, covenant, or agreement in a contract of carriage relieving the carrier or the ship from liability for loss or damage to, or in connection with, goods arising from negligence, fault, or failure in the duties and obligations provided in

this article or lessening such liability otherwise than as provided in these Rules, shall be null and void and of no effect. A benefit of insurance in favour of the carrier or similar clause shall be deemed to be a clause relieving the carrier from liability.

## Article IV

(1)   Neither the carrier nor the ship shall be liable for loss or damage arising or resulting from unseaworthiness unless caused by want of due diligence on the part of the carrier to make the ship seaworthy, and to secure that the ship is properly manned, equipped and supplied, and to make the holds, refrigerating and cool chambers and all other parts of the ship in which goods are carried fit and safe for their reception, carriage and preservation in accordance with the provisions of paragraph 1 of Article III. Whenever loss or damage has resulted from unseaworthiness the burden of proving the exercise of due diligence shall be on the carrier or other person claiming exemption under this article.

(2)   Neither the carrier nor the ship shall be responsible for loss or damage arising or resulting from—

(a)   Act, neglect, or default of the master, mariner, pilot, or the servants of the carrier in the navigation or in the management of the ship.

(b)   Fire, unless caused by the actual fault or privity of the carrier.

(c)   Perils, dangers and accidents of the sea or other navigable waters.

(d)   Act of God.

(e)   Act of war.

(f)   Act of public enemies.

(g)   Arrest or restraint of princes, rulers or people, or seizure under legal process.

(h)   Quarantine restrictions.

(i)   Act or omission of the shipper or owner of the goods, his agent or representative.

(j)   Strikes or lockouts or stoppage or restraint of labour from whatever cause, whether partial or general.

(k)   Riots and civil commotions.

(l)   Saving or attempting to save life or property at sea.

(m)   Wastage in bulk or weight or any other loss or damage arising from inherent defect, quality or vice of the goods.

(n)   Insufficiency of packing.

(o)   Insufficiency or inadequacy of marks.

(p)   Latent defects not discoverable by due diligence.

(q)   Any other cause arising without the actual fault or privity of the carrier, or without the fault or neglect of the agents or servants of the carrier, but the burden of proof shall be on the person claiming the benefit of this exception to show that neither the actual fault or privity of the carrier nor the fault or neglect of the agents or servants of the carrier contributed to the loss or damage.

(3)   The shipper shall not be responsible for the loss or damage sustained by the carrier or the ship arising or resulting from any cause without the act, fault or neglect of the shipper, his agents or his servants.

(4)   Any deviation in saving or attempting to save life or property at sea or any reasonable deviation shall not be deemed to be an infringement or breach of these Rules or of the contract of carriage, and the carrier shall not be liable for any loss or damage resulting therefrom.

(5)(a)   Unless the nature and value of such goods have been declared by the shipper before shipment and inserted in the bill of lading, neither the carrier nor the ship shall in any event be or become liable for any loss or damage to or in connection with the goods in an amount exceeding [666.67 units of account] per package or unit or [2 units of account per kilogramme] of gross weight of the goods lost or damaged, whichever is the higher.

(b)   The total amount recoverable shall be calculated by reference to the value of such goods at the place and time at which the goods are discharged from the ship in accordance with the contract or should have been so discharged.

The value of the goods shall be fixed according to the commodity exchange price, or, if there be no such price, according to the current market price, or, if there be no commodity exchange price or current market price, by reference to the normal value of goods of the same kind and quality.

(c)   Where a container, pallet or similar article of transport is used to consolidate goods, the number of packages or units enumerated in the bill of lading as packed in such article of transport shall be deemed the number of packages or units for the purpose of this paragraph as far as these packages or units are concerned. Except as aforesaid such article of transport shall be considered the package or unit.

[(d)   The unit of account mentioned in this Article is the special drawing right as defined by the International Monetary Fund. The amounts mentioned in sub-paragraph (a) of this paragraph shall be converted into national currency on the basis of the value of that currency on a date to be determined by the law of the court seised of the case.]

(e)   Neither the carrier nor the ship shall be entitled to the benefit of the limitation of liability provided for in this paragraph if it is proved that the damage resulted from an act or omission of the carrier done with intent to cause damage, or recklessly and with knowledge that damage would probably result.

(f)   The declaration mentioned in sub-paragraph (a) of this paragraph, if embodied in the bill of lading, shall be prima facie evidence, but shall not be binding or conclusive on the carrier.

(g)   By agreement between the carrier, master or agent of the carrier and the shipper other maximum amounts than those mentioned in sub-paragraph (a) of this paragraph may be fixed, provided that no maximum amount so fixed shall be less than the appropriate maximum mentioned in that sub-paragraph.

(h)   Neither the carrier nor the ship shall be responsible in any event for loss or damage to, or in connection with, goods if the nature or value thereof has been knowingly mis-stated by the shipper in the bill of lading.

(6)   Goods of an inflammable, explosive or dangerous nature to the shipment whereof the carrier, master or agent of the carrier has not consented with knowledge of their nature and character, may at any time before discharge be landed at any place, or destroyed or rendered innocuous by the carrier without compensation and the shipper of such goods shall be liable for all damages and expenses directly or indirectly arising out of or resulting from such shipment. If any such goods shipped with such knowledge and consent shall become a danger to the ship or cargo, they may in like manner be landed at any place, or destroyed or rendered innocuous by the carrier without liability on the part of the carrier except to general average, if any.

## Article IV bis

(1)   The defences and limits of liability provided for in these Rules shall apply in any action against the carrier in respect of loss or damage to goods covered by a contract of carriage whether the action be founded in contract or in tort.

(2)   If such an action is brought against a servant or agent of the carrier (such servant or agent not being an independent contractor), such servant or agent shall be entitled to avail himself of the defences and limits of liability which the carrier is entitled to invoke under these Rules.

(3)   The aggregate of the amounts recoverable from the carrier, and such servants and agents, shall in no case exceed the limit provided for in these Rules.

(4)   Nevertheless, a servant or agent of the carrier shall not be entitled to avail himself of the provisions of this article, if it is proved that the damage resulted

from an act or omission of the servant or agent done with intent to cause damage or recklessly and with knowledge that damage would probably result.

### Article V
A carrier shall be at liberty to surrender in whole or in part all or any of his rights and immunities or to increase any of his responsibilities and obligations under these Rules, provided such surrender or increase shall be embodied in the bill of lading issued to the shipper. The provisions of the Rules shall not be applicable to charter parties, but if bills of lading are issued in the case of a ship under a charter party they shall comply with the terms of these Rules. Nothing in these Rules shall be held to prevent the insertion in a bill of lading of any lawful provisions regarding general average.

### Article VI
Notwithstanding the provisions of the preceding articles, a carrier, master or agent of the carrier and a shipper shall in regard to any particular goods be at liberty to enter into any agreement in any terms as to the responsibility and liability of the carrier for such goods, and as to the rights and immunities of the carrier in respect of such goods, or his obligation as to seaworthiness, so far as this stipulation is not contrary to public policy, or the care or diligence of his servants or agents in regard to the loading, handling, stowage, carriage, custody, care and discharge of the goods carried by sea, provided that in this case no bill of lading has been or shall be issued and that the terms agreed shall be embodied in a receipt which shall be a non-negotiable document and shall be marked as such.

Any agreement so entered into shall have full legal effect.

Provided that this article shall not apply to ordinary commercial shipment made in the ordinary course of trade, but only to other shipments where the character or condition of the property to be carried or the circumstances, terms and conditions under which the carriage is to be performed are such as reasonably to justify a special agreement.

### Article VII
Nothing herein contained shall prevent a carrier or a shipper from entering into any agreement, stipulation, condition, reservation or exemption as to the responsibility and liability of the carrier or the ship for the loss or damage to, or in connection with, the custody and care and handling of goods prior to the loading on, and subsequent to the discharge from, the ship on which the goods are carried by sea.

### Article VIII
The provisions of these Rules shall not affect the rights and obligations of the carrier under any statute for the time being in force relating to the limitation of the liability of owners of sea-going vessels.

### Article IX
These rules shall not affect the provisions of any international Convention or national law governing liability for nuclear damage.

### Article X
The provisions of these Rules shall apply to every bill of lading relating to the carriage of goods between ports in two different States if:
    (a)    the bill of lading is issued in a contracting State, or
    (b)    the carriage is from a port in a contracting State, or
    (c)    the contract contained in or evidenced by the bill of lading provides that these Rules or legislation of any State giving effect to them are to govern the contract, whatever may be the nationality of the ship, the carrier, the shipper, the consignee, or any other interested person.

*[The last two paragraphs of this article require contracting States to apply the Rules to*

*bills of lading mentioned in the article and authorise them to apply the Rules to other bills of lading.]*

*[Articles XI to XVI deal with the coming into force of the Convention, procedure for ratification, accession and denunciation and the right to call for a fresh conference to consider amendments to the Rules contained in the Convention.]*

## COINAGE ACT 1971
### (1971, c 24)

### 2 Legal tender

(1)   Gold coins shall be legal tender for payment of any amount, but shall not be legal tender if their weight has become less than that specified in Schedule 1 to this Act, or in the proclamation under which they are made, as the least current weight.

(1A)   Subject to any provision made by proclamation under section 3 of this Act, coins of cupro-nickel, silver or bronze shall be legal tender as follows—

(a)   coins of cupro-nickel or silver of denominations of more than 10 pence, for payment of any amount not exceeding £10;

(b)   coins of cupro-nickel or silver of denominations of not more than 10 pence, for payment of any amount not exceeding £5;

(c)   coins of bronze, for payment of any amount not exceeding 20 pence.

(1B)   Other coins, if made current by a proclamation under section 3 of this Act, shall be legal tender in accordance with the provision made by that proclamation or by any later proclamation made under that section.

(2)   References in [subsection (1A)] of this section to coins of any denomination include references to coins treated as being of such a denomination by virtue of a proclamation made in pursuance of section 15(5) of the Decimal Currency Act 1969; and silver coins of the Queen's Maundy money issued before 15th February 1971 shall be treated for the purposes of this section as being denominated in the same number of new pence as the number of pence in which they were denominated.

(3)   In this section 'coins' means coins made by the Mint in accordance with this Act and not called in by proclamation under section 3 of this Act.

## UNSOLICITED GOODS AND SERVICES ACT 1971
### (1971, c 30)

[. . .]

### 2 Demands and threats regarding payment

(1)   A person who, not having reasonable cause to believe there is a right to payment, in the course of any trade or business makes a demand for payment, or asserts a present or prospective right to payment, for what he knows are unsolicited goods sent (after the commencement of this Act) to another person with a view to his acquiring them [for the purposes of his trade or business], shall be guilty of an offence and on summary conviction shall be liable to a fine not exceeding [level 4 on the standard scale].

(2)   A person who, not having reasonable cause to believe there is a right to payment, in the course of any trade or business and with a view to obtaining any payment for what he knows are unsolicited goods sent as aforesaid—

(a)   threatens to bring any legal proceedings; or

(b)   places or causes to be placed the name of any person on a list of defaulters or debtors or threatens to do so; or

(c)   invokes or causes to be invoked any other collection procedure or threatens to do so, shall be guilty of an offence and shall be liable on summary conviction to a fine not exceeding [level 5 on the standard scale].

## 3  Directory entries

[(1)  A person ('the purchaser') shall not be liable to make any payment, and shall be entitled to recover any payment made by him, by way of charge for including or arranging for the inclusion in a directory of an entry relating to that person or his trade or business, unless—

(a)  there has been signed by the purchaser or on his behalf an order complying with this section,

(b)  there has been signed by the purchaser or on his behalf a note complying with this section of his agreement to the charge and before the note was signed, a copy of it was supplied, for retention by him, to him or a person acting on his behalf,

(c)  there has been transmitted by the purchaser or a person acting on his behalf an electronic communication which includes a statement that the purchaser agrees to the charge and the relevant condition is satisfied in relation to that communication, [or

(d)  the charge arises under a contract in relation to which the conditions in section 3B(1) (renewed and extended contracts) are met.]

(2)  A person shall be guilty of an offence punishable on summary conviction with a fine not exceeding [level 5 on the standard scale] if, in a case where a payment in respect of a charge would [. . .] be recoverable from him in accordance with the terms of subsection (1) above, he demands payment, or asserts a present or prospective right to payment, of the charge or any part of it, without knowing or having reasonable cause to believe [that—

(a)  the entry to which the charge relates was ordered in accordance with this section,

(b)  a proper note of the agreement has been duly signed, or

(c)  the requirements set out in subsection (1)(c) [or (d)] above have been met.]

(3)  For the purposes of [this section—

(a)]  an order for an entry in a directory must be made by means of an order form or other stationery belonging to the [purchaser, which may be sent electronically but which must bear his name and address (or one or more of his addresses)]; and

[b]  the note [of a person's agreement to a charge must—

(i)  specify the particulars set out in Part 1 of the Schedule to the Regulatory Reform (Unsolicited Goods and Services Act 1971) (Directory Entries and Demands for Payment) Order 2005, and

(ii)  give reasonable particulars of the entry in respect of which the charge would be payable].

[(3A)  In relation to an electronic communication which includes a statement that the purchaser agrees to a charge for including or arranging the inclusion in a directory of any entry, the relevant condition is that—

(a)  before the electronic communication was transmitted the information referred to in subsection (3B) below was communicated to the purchaser, and

(b)  the electronic communication can readily be produced and retained in a visible and legible form.

(3B)  that information is—

(a)  the following particulars—

(i)  the amount of the charge;

(ii)  the name of the directory or proposed directory;

(iii)  the name of the person producing the directory;

(iv)  the geographic address at which that person is established;

(v)  if the directory is or is to be available in printed form, the proposed date of publication of the directory or of the issue in which the entry is to be included;

(vi)  if the directory or the issue in which the entry is to be included is to be put on sale, the price at which it is to be offered for sale and the minimum number of copies which are to be available for sale;

(vii)  if the directory or the issue in which the entry is to be included is to be distributed free of charge (whether or not it is also to be put on sale), the minimum number of copies which are to be so distributed;

(viii)  if the directory is or is to be available in a form other than in printed form, adequate details of how it may be accessed; and

(b)  reasonable particulars of the entry in respect of which the charge would be payable.

(3C)  In this section 'electronic communication' has the same meaning as in the Electronic Communications Act 2000.]

[. . .]

### [3B  Renewed and extended contracts

(1)  The conditions referred to in section 3(1)(d) above are met in relation to a contract ('the new contract') if—

(a)  a person ('the purchaser') has entered into an earlier contract ('the earlier contract') for including or arranging for the inclusion in a particular issue or version of a directory ('the earlier directory') of an entry ('the earlier entry') relating to him or his trade or business;

(b)  the purchaser was liable to make a payment by way of a charge arising under the earlier contract for including or arranging for the inclusion of the earlier entry in the earlier directory;

(c)  the new contract is a contract for including or arranging for the inclusion in a later issue or version of a directory ('the later directory') of an entry ('the later entry') relating to the purchaser or his trade or business;

(d)  the form, content and distribution of the later directory is materially the same as the form, content and distribution of the earlier directory;

(e)  the form and content of the later entry is materially the same as the form and content of the earlier entry;

(f)  if the later directory is published other than in electronic form—

(i)  the earlier directory was the last, or the last but one, issue or version of the directory to be published before the later directory, and

(ii)  the date of publication of the later directory is not more than 13 months after the date of publication of the earlier directory;

(g)  if the later directory is published in electronic form, the first date on which the new contract requires the later entry to be published is not more than the relevant period after the last date on which the earlier contract required the earlier entry to be published;

(h)  if it was a term of the earlier contract that the purchaser renew or extend the contract—

(i)  before the start of the new contract the relevant publisher has given notice in writing to the purchaser containing the information set out in Part 3 of the Schedule to the Regulatory Reform (Unsolicited Goods and Services Act 1971) (Directory Entries and Demands for Payment) Order 2005; and

(ii)  the purchaser has not written to the relevant publisher withdrawing his agreement to the renewal or extension of the earlier contract within the period of 21 days starting when he receives the notice referred to in sub-paragraph (i); and

(i)  if the parties to the earlier contract and the new contract are different—

(i)  the parties to both contracts have entered into a novation agreement in respect of the earlier contract; or

(ii)  the relevant publisher has given the purchaser the information set out in Part 4 of the Schedule to the Regulatory Reform (Unsolicited Goods and Services Act 1971) (Directory Entries and Demands for Payment) Order 2005.

(2)   For the purposes of subsection (1)(d) and (e), the form, content or distribution of the later directory, or the form or content of the later entry, shall be taken to be materially the same as that of the earlier directory or the earlier entry (as the case may be), if a reasonable person in the position of the purchaser would—

(a)   view the two as being materially the same; or

(b)   view that of the later directory or the later entry as being an improvement on that of the earlier directory or the earlier entry.

(3)   For the purposes of subsection (1)(g) 'the relevant period' means the period of 13 months or (if shorter) the period of time between the first and last dates on which the earlier contract required the earlier entry to be published.

(4)   For the purposes of subsection (1)(h) and (i) 'the relevant publisher' is the person with whom the purchaser has entered into the new contract.

(5)   The information referred to in subsection (1)(i)(ii) must be given to the purchaser prior to the conclusion of the new contract.]

## 4   Unsolicited publications

(1)   A person shall be guilty of an offence if he sends or causes to be sent to another person any book, magazine or leaflet (or advertising material for any such publication) which he knows or ought reasonably to know is unsolicited and which describes or illustrates human sexual techniques.

(2)   A person found guilty of an offence under this section shall be liable on summary conviction to a fine not exceeding [level 5 on the standard scale].

(3)   A prosecution for an offence under this section shall not in England and Wales be instituted except by, or with the consent of, the Director of Public Prosecutions.

## 5   Offences by corporations

(1)   Where an offence under this Act which has been committed by a body corporate is proved to have been committed with the consent or connivance of, or to be attributable to any neglect on the part of, any director, manager, secretary, or other similar officer of the body corporate, or of any person who was purporting to act in any such capacity, he as well as the body corporate shall be guilty of that offence and shall be liable to be proceeded against and punished accordingly.

(2)   Where the affairs of a body corporate are managed by its members, this section shall apply in relation to the acts or defaults of a member in connection with his functions of management as if he were a director of the body corporate.

## 6   Interpretation

(1)   In this Act, unless the context or subject matter otherwise requires,—

'acquire' includes hire;

'send' includes deliver, and 'sender' shall be construed accordingly;

'unsolicited' means, in relation to goods sent to any person, that they are sent without any prior request made by him or on his behalf.

[(2)   For the purposes of this Act any invoice or similar document stating the amount of any payment shall be regarded as asserting a right to the payment unless it complies with the conditions set out in Part 2 of the Schedule to the Regulatory Reform (Unsolicited Goods and Services Act 1971) (Directory Entries and Demands for Payment) Order 2005.]

[(3)   Nothing in section 3 or 3B affects the rights of any consumer under the Consumer Contracts (Information, Cancellation and Additional Charges) Regulations 2013.]

## 7   Citation, commencement and extent

(1)   This Act may be cited as the Unsolicited Goods and Services Act 1971.

(2)   This Act shall come into force at the expiration of three months beginning with the day on which it is passed.

(3)   This Act does not extend to Northern Ireland.

## SUPPLY OF GOODS (IMPLIED TERMS) ACT 1973
### (1973, c 13)

### 8   Implied terms as to title

[(1)   In every [*relevant* hire-purchase agreement], other than one to which subsection (2) below applies, there is—

(a)   an implied term on the part of the creditor that he will have a right to sell the goods at the time when the property is to pass; and

(b)   an implied term that—

(i)   the goods are free, and will remain free until the time when the property is to pass, from any charge or encumbrance not disclosed or known to the person to whom the goods are bailed or (in Scotland) hired before the agreement is made, and

(ii)   that person will enjoy quiet possession of the goods except so far as it may be disturbed by any person entitled to the benefit of any charge or encumbrance so disclosed or known.

(2)   In a [*relevant* hire-purchase agreement], in the case of which there appears from the agreement or is to be inferred from the circumstances of the agreement an intention that the creditor should transfer only such title as he or a third person may have, there is—

(a)   an implied term that all charges or encumbrances known to the creditor and not known to the person to whom the goods are bailed or hired have been disclosed to that person before the agreement is made; and

(b)   an implied term that neither—

(i)   the creditor; nor

(ii)   in a case where the parties to the agreement intend that any title which may be transferred shall be only such title as a third person may have, that person; nor

(iii)   anyone claiming through or under the creditor or that third person otherwise than under a charge or encumbrance disclosed or known to the person to whom the goods are bailed or hired, before the agreement is made;

will disturb the quiet possession of the person to whom the goods are bailed or hired.

(3)   As regards England and Wales and Northern Ireland, the term implied by subsection (1)(a) above is a condition and the terms implied by subsections (1)(b), (2)(a) and (2)(b) above are warranties.]

### 9   Bailing or hiring by description

[(1)   Where under a [*relevant* hire-purchase agreement] goods are bailed or (in Scotland) hired by description, there is an implied term that the goods will correspond with the description, and if under the agreement the goods are bailed or hired by reference to a sample as well as a description, it is not sufficient that the bulk of the goods corresponds with the sample if the goods do not also correspond with the description.

(1A)   As regards England and Wales and Northern Ireland, the term implied by subsection (1) above is a condition.

(2)   Goods shall not be prevented from being bailed or hired by description by reason only that, being exposed for sale, bailment or hire, they are selected by the person to whom they are bailed or hired.]

### 10   Implied undertakings as to quality or fitness

[(1)   Except as provided by this section and section 11 below and subject to the provisions of any other enactment, including any enactment of the Parliament of

Northern Ireland or the Northern Ireland Assembly, there is no implied term as to the quality or fitness for any particular purpose of goods bailed or (in Scotland) hired under a [*relevant* hire-purchase agreement].

(2)   Where the creditor bails or hires goods under a [*relevant* hire-purchase agreement] in the course of a business, there is an implied term that the goods supplied under the agreement are of satisfactory quality.

(2A)   For the purposes of this Act, goods are of satisfactory quality if they meet the standard that a reasonable person would regard as satisfactory, taking account of any description of the goods, the price (if relevant) and all the other relevant circumstances.

(2B)   For the purposes of this Act, the quality of goods includes their state and condition and the following (among others) are in appropriate cases aspects of the quality of goods—

(a)   fitness for all the purposes for which goods of the kind in question are commonly supplied,

(b)   appearance and finish,

(c)   freedom from minor defects,

(d)   safety, and

(e)   durability.

(2C)   The term implied by subsection (2) above does not extend to any matter making the quality of goods unsatisfactory—

(a)   which is specifically drawn to the attention of the person to whom the goods are bailed or hired before the agreement is made,

(b)   where that person examines the goods before the agreement is made, which that examination ought to reveal, or

(c)   where the goods are bailed or hired by reference to a sample, which would have been apparent on a reasonable examination of the sample.

[. . .]

(3)   Where the creditor bails or hires goods under a [*relevant* hire-purchase agreement] in the course of a business and the person to whom the goods are bailed or hired, expressly or by implication, makes known—

(a)   to the creditor in the course of negotiations conducted by the creditor in relation to the making of the [*relevant* hire-purchase agreement], or

(b)   to a credit-broker in the course of negotiations conducted by that broker in relation to goods sold by him to the creditor before forming the subject matter of the [*relevant* hire-purchase agreement],

any particular purpose for which the goods are being bailed or hired, there is an implied term that the goods supplied under the agreement are reasonably fit for that purpose, whether or not that is a purpose for which such goods are commonly supplied, except where the circumstances show that the person to whom the goods are bailed or hired does not rely, or that it is unreasonable for him to rely, on the skill or judgment of the creditor or credit-broker.

(4)   An implied term as to quality or fitness for a particular purpose may be annexed to a [*relevant* hire-purchase agreement] by usage.

(5)   The preceding provisions of this section apply to a [*relevant* hire-purchase agreement] made by a person who in the course of a business is acting as agent for the creditor as they apply to an agreement made by the creditor in the course of a business, except where the creditor is not bailing or hiring in the course of a business and either the person to whom the goods are bailed or hired knows that fact or reasonable steps are taken to bring it to the notice of that person before the agreement is made.

(6)   In subsection (3) above and this subsection—

(a)   'credit-broker' means a person acting in the course of a business of credit brokerage;

(b)   'credit brokerage' means the effecting of introductions of individuals desiring to obtain credit—

(i)    to persons carrying on any business so far as it relates to the provision of credit, or

(ii)   to other persons engaged in credit brokerage.

(7)   As regards England and Wales and Northern Ireland, the terms implied by
subsections (2) and (3) above are conditions.

[. . .]

## 11   Samples

[(1)   Where under a [*relevant* hire-purchase agreement] goods are bailed or (in
Scotland) hired by reference to a sample, there is an implied term—

(a)    that the bulk will correspond with the sample in quality; and

(b)    that the person to whom the goods are bailed or hired will have a
reasonable opportunity of comparing the bulk with the sample; and

(c)    that the goods will be free from any defect, making their quality
unsatisfactory, which would not be apparent on reasonable examination of the
sample.

(2)   As regards England and Wales and Northern Ireland, the term implied by
subsection (1) above is a condition.]

## [12   Exclusion of implied terms

An express term does not negative a term implied by this Act unless inconsistent
with it.]

## [12A   Remedies for breach of [*relevant* hire-purchase agreement] as respects Scotland

(1)   Where in a [*relevant* hire-purchase agreement] the creditor is in breach of
any term of the agreement (express or implied), the person to whom the goods are
hired shall be entitled—

(a)    to claim damages, and

(b)    if the breach is material, to reject any goods delivered under the
agreement and treat it as repudiated.

[. . .]

(4)   This section applies to Scotland only.]

[. . .]
 [. . .]

## 15   Supplementary

[(1)   In sections 8 to 14 above and this section—

'business' includes a profession and the activities of any government department
(including a Northern Ireland department), [or local or public authority];

'buyer' and 'seller' includes a person to whom rights and duties under a conditional sale agreement have passed by assignment or operation of law;

'conditional sale agreement' means an agreement for the sale of goods under
which the purchase price or part of it is payable by instalments, and the property
in the goods is to remain in the seller (notwithstanding that the buyer is to be in
possession of the goods) until such conditions as to the payment of instalments or
otherwise as may be specified in the agreement are fulfilled;

['consumer sale' has the same meaning as in section 55 of the Sale of Goods Act
1979 (as set out in paragraph 11 of Schedule 1 to that Act)];

'creditor' means the person by whom the goods are bailed or (in Scotland) hired
under a hire-purchase agreement or the person to whom his rights and duties
under the agreement have passed by assignment or operation of law; and

'hire-purchase agreement' means an agreement, other than conditional sale
agreement, under which—

(a)    goods are bailed or (in Scotland) hired in return for periodical payments
by the person to whom they are bailed or hired, and

(b)   the property in the goods will pass to that person if the terms of the agreement are complied with and one or more of the following occurs—

(i)   the exercise of an option to purchase by that person,

(ii)   the doing of any other specified act by any party to the agreement,

(iii)   the happening of any other specified event.

[and a hire-purchase agreement is relevant if it is not a contract to which Chapter 2 of Part 1 of the Consumer Rights Act 2015 applies;]

[. . .]

(4)   Nothing in sections 8 to 13 above shall prejudice the operation of any other enactment including any enactment of the Parliament of Northern Ireland or the Northern Ireland Assembly or any rule of law whereby any term, other than one relating to quality or fitness, is to be implied in any [relevant hire-purchase agreement].]

## CONSUMER CREDIT ACT 1974
### (1974, c 39)

[. . .]

### PART II
### CREDIT AGREEMENTS, HIRE AGREEMENTS AND LINKED TRANSACTIONS

#### 8   Consumer credit agreements

(1)   A [consumer] credit agreement is an agreement between an individual ('the debtor') and any other person ('the creditor') by which the creditor provides the debtor with credit of any amount.

[. . .]

[(3)   A consumer credit agreement is a regulated credit agreement within the meaning of this Act if it—

(a)   is a regulated credit agreement for the purposes of Chapter 14A of Part 2 of the Regulated Activities Order; and

(b)   is not an agreement of the type described in Article 3(1)(b) of Directive 2014/17/EU of the European Parliament and of the Council of 4th February 2014 on credit agreements for consumers relating to residential immovable property.]

[(4)   Subsection (1) does not apply in relation to an agreement that is a green deal plan (see instead section 189B).]

#### 9   Meaning of credit

(1)   In this Act 'credit' includes a cash loan, and any other form of financial accommodation.

(2)   Where credit is provided otherwise than in sterling it shall be treated for the purposes of this Act as provided in sterling of an equivalent amount.

(3)   Without prejudice to the generality of subsection (1), the person by whom goods are bailed or (in Scotland) hired to an individual under a hire-purchase agreement shall be taken to provide him with fixed-sum credit to finance the transaction of an amount equal to the total price of the goods less the aggregate of the deposit (if any) and the total charge for credit.

(4)   For the purposes of this Act, an item entering into the total charge for credit shall not be treated as credit even though time is allowed for its payment.

#### 10   Running-account credit and fixed-sum credit

(1)   For the purposes of this Act—

(a)   running-account credit is a facility under a [consumer] credit agreement whereby the debtor is enabled to receive from time to time (whether in his own person, or by another person) from the creditor or a third party cash, goods and services (or any of them) to an amount or value such that, taking into account payments made by or to the credit of the debtor, the credit limit (if any) is not at any time exceeded; and

(b)   fixed-sum credit is any other facility under a [consumer] credit agreement whereby the debtor is enabled to receive credit (whether in one amount or by instalments).

(2)   In relation to running-account credit, 'credit limit' means, as respects any period, the maximum debit balance which, under the credit agreement, is allowed to stand on the account during that period, disregarding any term of the agreement allowing that maximum to be exceeded merely temporarily.

(3)   For the purposes of [any provision of this Act that specifies an amount of credit (except section 17(1)(a))], running-account credit shall be taken not to exceed the amount specified in [that provision] ('the specified amount') if—

(a)   the credit limit does not exceed the specified amount; or

(b)   whether or not there is a credit limit, and if there is, notwithstanding that it exceeds the specified amount,—

(i)   the debtor is not enabled to draw at any one time an amount which, so far as (having regard to section 9(4)) it represents credit, exceeds the specified amount, or

(ii)   the agreement provides that, if the debit balance rises above a given amount (not exceeding the specified amount), the rate of the total charge for credit increases or any other condition favouring the creditor or his associate comes into operation, or

(iii)   at the time the agreement is made it is probable, having regard to the terms of the agreement and any other relevant considerations, that the debit balance will not at any time rise above the specified amount.

## 11   Restricted-use credit and unrestricted-use credit

(1)   A restricted-use credit agreement is a regulated consumer credit agreement—

(a)   to finance a transaction between the debtor and the creditor, whether forming part of that agreement or not, or

(b)   to finance a transaction between the debtor and a person (the 'supplier') other than the creditor, or

(c)   to refinance any existing indebtedness of the debtor's, whether to the creditor or another person, and 'restricted-use credit' shall be construed accordingly.

(2)   An unrestricted-use credit agreement is a regulated consumer credit agreement not falling within subsection (1), and 'unrestricted-use credit' shall be construed accordingly.

(3)   An agreement does not fall within subsection (1) if the credit is in fact provided in such a way as to leave the debtor free to use it as he chooses, even though certain uses would contravene that or any other agreement.

(4)   An agreement may fall within subsection (1)(b) although the identity of the supplier is unknown at the time the agreement is made.

## 12   Debtor-creditor-supplier agreements

A debtor-creditor-supplier agreement is a regulated consumer credit agreement being—

(a)   a restricted-use credit agreement which falls within section 11(1)(a), or

(b)   a restricted-use credit agreement which falls within section 11(1)(b) and is made by the creditor under pre-existing arrangements, or in contemplation of future arrangements, between himself and the supplier, or

(c)   an unrestricted-use credit agreement which is made by the creditor under pre-existing arrangements between himself and a person (the 'supplier') other than the debtor in the knowledge that the credit is to be used to finance a transaction between the debtor and the supplier.

### 13  Debtor-creditor agreements

A debtor-creditor agreement is a regulated consumer credit agreement being—

(a)  a restricted-use credit agreement which falls within section 11(1)(b) but is not made by the creditor under pre-existing arrangements, or in contemplation of future arrangements, between himself and the supplier, or

(b)  a restricted-use credit agreement which falls within section 11(1)(c), or

(c)  an unrestricted-use credit agreement which is not made by the creditor under pre-existing arrangements between himself and a person (the 'supplier') other than the debtor in the knowledge that the credit is to be used to finance a transaction between the debtor and the supplier.

### 14  Credit-token agreements

(1)  A credit-token is a card, check, voucher, coupon, stamp, form, booklet or other document or thing given to an individual by a person carrying on a consumer credit business, who undertakes—

(a)  that on the production of it (whether or not some other action is also required) he will supply cash, goods and services (or any of them) on credit, or

(b)  that where, on the production of it to a third party (whether or not any other action is also required), the third party supplies cash, goods and services (or any of them), he will pay the third party for them (whether or not deducting any discount or commission), in return for payment to him by the individual.

(2)  A credit-token agreement is a regulated agreement for the provision of credit in connection with the use of a credit-token.

(3)  Without prejudice to the generality of section 9(1), the person who gives to an individual an undertaking falling within subsection (1)(b) shall be taken to provide him with credit drawn on whenever a third party supplies him with cash, goods or services.

(4)  For the purposes of subsection (1), use of an object to operate a machine provided by the person giving the object or a third party shall be treated as the production of the object to him.

### 15  Consumer hire agreements

(1)  A consumer hire agreement is an agreement made by a person with an individual (the 'hirer') for the bailment or (in Scotland) the hiring of goods to the hirer, being an agreement which—

(a)  is not a hire-purchase agreement, and

(b)  is capable of subsisting for more than three months, [. . .].

[(2)  A consumer hire agreement is a regulated agreement within the meaning of this Act if it is a regulated consumer hire agreement for the purposes of Chapter 14B of Part 2 of the Regulated Activities Order.]

[. . .]

### 17  Small agreements

(1)  A small agreement is—

(a)  a regulated consumer credit agreement for credit not exceeding [£50], other than a hire-purchase or conditional sale agreement; or

(b)  a regulated consumer hire agreement which does not require the hirer to make payments exceeding [£50],

being an agreement which is either unsecured or secured by a guarantee or indemnity only (whether or not the guarantee or indemnity is itself secured).

[(2)  For the purposes of paragraph (a) of subsection (1), running-account credit shall be taken not to exceed the amount specified in that paragraph if the credit limit does not exceed that amount.]

(3)  Where—

(a)  two or more small agreements are made at or about the same time between the same parties, and

(b)  it appears probable that they would instead have been made as a single

agreement but for the desire to avoid the operation of provisions of this Act which would have applied to that single agreement but, apart from this subsection, are not applicable to the small agreements,
this Act applies to the small agreements as if they were regulated agreements other than small agreements.

(4)  If, apart from this subsection, subsection (3) does not apply to any agreements but would apply if, for any party or parties to any of the agreements, there were substituted an associate of that party, or associates of each of those parties, as the case may be, then subsection (3) shall apply to the agreements.

## 18  Multiple agreements

(1)  This section applies to an agreement (a 'multiple agreement') if its terms are such as—

(a)  to place a part of it within one category of agreement mentioned in this Act, and another part of it within a different category of agreement so mentioned, or within a category of agreement not so mentioned, or

(b)  to place it, or a part of it, within two or more categories of agreement so mentioned.

(2)  Where a part of an agreement falls within subsection (1), that part shall be treated for the purposes of this Act as a separate agreement.

(3)  Where an agreement falls within subsection (1)(b), it shall be treated as an agreement in each of the categories in question, and this Act shall apply to it accordingly.

(4)  Where under subsection (2) a part of a multiple agreement is to be treated as a separate agreement, the multiple agreement shall (with any necessary modifications) be construed accordingly; and any sum payable under the multiple agreement, if not apportioned by the parties, shall for the purposes of proceedings in any court relating to the multiple agreement be apportioned by the court as may be requisite.

(5)  In the case of an agreement for running-account credit, a term of the agreement allowing the credit limit to be exceeded merely temporarily shall not be treated as a separate agreement or as providing fixed-sum credit in respect of the excess.

(6)  This Act does not apply to a multiple agreement so far as the agreement relates to goods if under the agreement payments are to be made in respect of the goods in the form of rent (other than a rentcharge) issuing out of land.

## 19  Linked transactions

(1)  A transaction entered into by the debtor or hirer, or a relative of his, with any other person ('the other party'), except one for the provision of security, is a linked transaction in relation to an actual or prospective regulated agreement (the 'principal agreement') of which it does not form part if—

(a)  the transaction is entered into in compliance with a term of the principal agreement; or

(b)  the principal agreement is a debtor-creditor-supplier agreement and the transaction is financed, or to be financed, by the principal agreement; or

(c)  the other party is a person mentioned in subsection (2), and a person so mentioned initiated the transaction by suggesting it to the debtor or hirer, or his relative, who enters into it—

(i)  to induce the creditor or owner to enter into the principal agreement, or

(ii)  for another purpose related to the principal agreement, or

(iii)  where the principal agreement is a restricted-use credit agreement, for a purpose related to a transaction financed, or to be financed, by the principal agreement.

(2)  The persons referred to in subsection (1)(c) are—

(a)   the creditor or owner, or his associate;

(b)   a person who, in the negotiation of the transaction, is represented by a credit-broker who is also a negotiator in antecedent negotiations for the principal agreement;

(c)   a person who, at the time the transaction is initiated, knows that the principal agreement has been made or contemplates that it might be made.

(3)   A linked transaction entered into before the making of the principal agreement has no effect until such time (if any) as that agreement is made.

(4)   Regulations may exclude linked transactions of the prescribed description from the operation of subsection (3).

### [20   Total charge for credit

In this Act, the 'total charge for credit' has the meaning given by the Regulated Activities Order for the purposes of Chapter 14A of Part 2 of that Order.]


## PART V
## ENTRY INTO CREDIT OR HIRE AGREEMENTS

### *Preliminary matters*

### 55   Disclosure of information

(1)   Regulations may require specified information to be disclosed in the prescribed manner to the debtor or hirer before a regulated agreement is made.

[(2)   If regulations under subsection (1) are not complied with, the agreement is enforceable against the debtor or hirer on an order of the court only (and for these purposes a retaking of goods or land to which the agreement relates is an enforcement of the agreement).]

[. . .]

### [55C   Copy of draft consumer credit agreement

(1)   Before a regulated consumer credit agreement, other than an excluded agreement, is made, the creditor must, if requested, give to the debtor without delay a copy of the prospective agreement (or such of its terms as have at that time been reduced to writing).

(2)   Subsection (1) does not apply if at the time the request is made, the creditor is unwilling to proceed with the agreement.

(3)   A breach of the duty imposed by subsection (1) is actionable as a breach of statutory duty.

(4)   For the purposes of this section an agreement is an excluded agreement if it is—

(a)   an agreement secured on land,

(b)   an agreement under which a person takes an article in pawn,

(c)   an agreement under which the creditor provides the debtor with credit which exceeds £60,260 [and which is not a residential renovation agreement], or

(d)   an agreement entered into by the debtor wholly or predominantly for the purposes of a business carried on, or intended to be carried on, by him.

[(5)   Article 60C(5) and (6) of the Regulated Activities Order applies for the purposes of subsection 4(d).]

### 56   Antecedent negotiations

(1)   In this Act 'antecedent negotiations' means any negotiations with the debtor or hirer—

(a)   conducted by the creditor or owner in relation to the making of any regulated agreement, or

(b)   conducted by a credit-broker in relation to goods sold or proposed to be sold by the credit-broker to the creditor before forming the subject-matter of a debtor-creditor-supplier agreement within section 12(a), or

(c)   conducted by the supplier in relation to a transaction financed or proposed to be financed by a debtor-creditor-supplier agreement within section 12(b) or (c), and 'negotiator' means the person by whom negotiations are so conducted with the debtor or hirer.

(2)   Negotiations with the debtor in a case falling within subsection (1)(b) or (c) shall be deemed to be conducted by the negotiator in the capacity of agent of the creditor as well as in his actual capacity.

(3)   An agreement is void if, and to the extent that, it purports in relation to an actual or prospective regulated agreement—

(a)   to provide that a person acting as, or on behalf of, a negotiator is to be treated as the agent of the debtor or hirer, or

(b)   to relieve a person from liability for acts or omissions of any person acting as, or on behalf of, a negotiator.

(4)   For the purposes of this Act, antecedent negotiations shall be taken to begin when the negotiator and the debtor or hirer first enter into communication (including communication by advertisement), and to include any representations made by the negotiator to the debtor or hirer and any other dealings between them.

## 57   Withdrawal from prospective agreement

(1)   The withdrawal of a party from a prospective regulated agreement shall operate to apply this Part to the agreement, any linked transaction and any other thing done in anticipation of the making of the agreement as it would apply if the agreement were made and then cancelled under section 69.

(2)   The giving to a party of a written or oral notice which, however expressed, indicates the intention of the other party to withdraw from a prospective regulated agreement operates as a withdrawal from it.

(3)   Each of the following shall be deemed to be the agent of the creditor or owner for the purpose of receiving a notice under subsection (2)—

(a)   a credit-broker or supplier who is the negotiator in antecedent negotiations, and

(b)   any person who, in the course of a business carried on by him, acts on behalf of the debtor or hirer in any negotiations for the agreement.

(4)   Where the agreement, if made, would not be a cancellable agreement, subsection (1) shall nevertheless apply as if the contrary were the case.

## 58   Opportunity for withdrawal from prospective land mortgage

(1)   Before sending to the debtor or hirer, for his signature, an unexecuted agreement in a case where the prospective regulated agreement is to be secured on land (the 'mortgaged land'), the creditor or owner shall give the debtor or hirer a copy of the unexecuted agreement which contains a notice in the prescribed form indicating the right of the debtor or hirer to withdraw from the prospective agreement, and how and when the right is exercisable, together with a copy of any other document referred to in the unexecuted agreement.

(2)   Subsection (1) does not apply to—

(a)   a restricted-use credit agreement to finance the purchase of the mortgaged land, or

(b)   an agreement for a bridging loan in connection with the purchase of the mortgaged land or other land.

## 59   Agreement to enter future agreement void

(1)   An agreement is void if, and to the extent that, it purports to bind a person to enter as debtor or hirer into a prospective regulated agreement.

(2)   Regulations may exclude from the operation of subsection (1) agreements such as are described in the regulations.

*Making the agreement*

### 60  Form and content of agreements

(1)  The [Treasury] shall make regulations as to the form and content of documents embodying regulated agreements, and the regulations shall contain such provisions as appear to [them] appropriate with a view to ensuring that the debtor or hirer is made aware of—

(a)   the rights and duties conferred or imposed on him by the agreement,

(b)   the amount and rate of the total charge for credit (in the case of a consumer credit agreement),

(c)   the protection and remedies available to him under this Act, and

(d)   any other matters which, in the opinion of the [Treasury], it is desirable for him to know about in connection with the agreement.

(2)   Regulations under subsection (1) may in particular—

(a)   require specified information to be included in the prescribed manner in documents, and other specified material to be excluded;

(b)   contain requirements to ensure that specified information is clearly brought to the attention of the debtor or hirer, and that one part of a document is not given insufficient or excessive prominence compared with another.

(3)  If, on an application made to the [FCA] by a person carrying on a consumer credit business or a consumer hire business, it appears to the [FCA] impracticable for the applicant to comply with any requirement of regulations under subsection (1) in a particular case, [it] may, by notice to the applicant direct that the requirement be waived or varied in relation to such agreements, and subject to such conditions (if any), as [it] may specify, and this Act and the regulations shall have effect accordingly.

(4)  The [FCA] shall give a notice under subsection (3) only if [it] is satisfied that to do so would not prejudice the interests of debtors or hirers.

[(5)   An application may be made under subsection (3) only if it relates to—

(a)   a consumer credit agreement secured on land,

(b)   a consumer credit agreement under which a person takes an article in pawn,

(c)   a consumer credit agreement under which the creditor provides the debtor with credit which exceeds £60,260 [and which is not a residential renovation agreement],

(d)   a consumer credit agreement entered into by the debtor wholly or predominantly for the purposes of a business carried on, or intended to be carried on, by him, or

(e)   a consumer hire agreement.

[(6)   Article 60C(5) and (6) of the Regulated Activities Order applies for the purposes of subsection (5)(d).]

### 61  Signing of agreement

(1)   A regulated agreement is not properly executed unless—

(a)   a document in the prescribed form itself containing all the prescribed terms and conforming to regulations under section 60(1) is signed in the prescribed manner both by the debtor or hirer and by or on behalf of the creditor or owner, and

(b)   the document embodies all the terms of the agreement, other than implied terms, and

(c)   the document is, when presented or sent to the debtor or hirer for signature, in such a state that all its terms are readily legible.

(2)   In addition, where the agreement is one to which section 58(1) applies, it is not properly executed unless—

(a)   the requirements of section 58(1) were complied with, and

(b)   the unexecuted agreement was sent, for his signature, to the debtor or hirer [by an appropriate method] not less than seven days after a copy of it was given to him under section 58(1), and

(c)    during the consideration period, the creditor or owner refrained from approaching the debtor or hirer (whether in person, by telephone or letter, or in any other way) except in response to a specific request made by the debtor or hirer after the beginning of the consideration period, and

(d)    no notice of withdrawal by the debtor or hirer was received by the creditor or owner before the sending of the unexecuted agreement.

(3)    In subsection (2)(c), 'the consideration period' means the period beginning with the giving of the copy under section 58(1) and ending—

(a)    at the expiry of seven days after the day on which the unexecuted agreement is sent, for his signature, to the debtor or hirer, or

(b)    on its return by the debtor or hirer after signature by him, whichever first occurs.

(4)    Where the debtor or hirer is a partnership or an unincorporated body of persons, subsection (1)(a) shall apply with the substitution for 'by the debtor or hirer' of 'by or on behalf of the debtor or hirer'.

## [61A    Duty to supply copy of executed consumer credit agreement

(1)    Where a regulated consumer credit agreement, other than an excluded agreement, has been made, the creditor must give a copy of the executed agreement, and any other document referred to in it, to the debtor.

(2)    Subsection (1) does not apply if—

(a)    a copy of the unexecuted agreement (and of any other document referred to in it) has already been given to the debtor, and

(b)    the unexecuted agreement is in identical terms to the executed agreement.

(3)    In a case referred to in subsection (2), the creditor must inform the debtor in writing—

(a)    that the agreement has been executed,

(b)    that the executed agreement is in identical terms to the unexecuted agreement a copy of which has already been given to the debtor, and

(c)    that the debtor has the right to receive a copy of the executed agreement if the debtor makes a request for it at any time before the end of the period referred to in section 66A(2).

(4)    Where a request is made under subsection (3)(c) the creditor must give a copy of the executed agreement to the debtor without delay.

(5)    If the requirements of this section are not observed, the agreement is not properly executed.

(6)    For the purposes of this section, an agreement is an excluded agreement if it is—

(a)    a cancellable agreement, or

(b)    an agreement—

(i)    secured on land,

(ii)    under which the creditor provides the debtor with credit which exceeds £60,260, or

(iii)    entered into by the debtor wholly or predominantly for the purposes of a business carried on, or intended to be carried on, by him,

unless the creditor or a credit intermediary has complied with or purported to comply with regulation 3(2) of the Consumer Credit (Disclosure of Information) Regulations 2010.

[(6A)    An agreement is not an excluded agreement by virtue of subsection (6)(b)(ii) if it is a residential renovation agreement.]

[(7)    Article 60C(5) and (6) of the Regulated Activities Order applies for the purposes of subsection (6)(b)(iii).

(8) In this section, 'credit intermediary' means a person who in the course of business—

    (a) carries on any of the activities specified in article 36A(1)(d) to (f) of the Regulated Activities Order for a consideration that is or includes a financial consideration, and

    (b) does not do so as a creditor.]]

### [61B Duty to supply copy of overdraft agreement

(1) Where an authorised business overdraft agreement or an authorised non-business overdraft agreement has been made, a document containing the terms of the agreement must be given to the debtor.

(2) The creditor must provide the document referred to in subsection (1) to the debtor before or at the time the agreement is made unless—

    (a) the creditor has provided the debtor with the information referred to in regulation 10(3) of the Consumer Credit (Disclosure of Information) Regulations 2010, in which case it [may] be provided after the agreement is made,

    (b) the creditor has provided the debtor with the information referred to in regulation 10(3)(c), (e), (f), (h) and (k) of those Regulations, in which case it must be provided immediately after the agreement is made, or

    (c) the agreement is an agreement of a description referred to in regulation 10(4)(b) of those Regulations, in which case it must be provided immediately after the agreement is made.

(3) If the requirements of this section are not observed, the agreement is enforceable against the debtor on an order of the court only (and for these purposes a retaking of goods or land to which the agreement relates is an enforcement of the agreement).]

### 62 Duty to supply copy of unexecuted agreement [: excluded agreement]

(1) If [in the case of a regulated agreement which is an excluded agreement] the unexecuted agreement is presented personally to the debtor or hirer for his signature, but on the occasion when he signs it the document does not become an executed agreement, a copy of it, and of any other document referred to in it, must be there and then delivered to him.

(2) If the unexecuted agreement is sent to the debtor or hirer for his signature, a copy of it, and of any other document referred to in it, must be sent to him at the same time.

(3) A regulated agreement [which is an excluded agreement] is not properly executed if the requirements of this section are not observed.

    [(4) In this section, 'excluded agreement' has the same meaning as in section 61A.]

### 63 Duty to supply copy of executed agreement [: excluded agreements]

(1) If [in the case of a regulated agreement which is an excluded agreement] the unexecuted agreement is presented personally to the debtor or hirer for his signature, and on the occasion when he signs it the document becomes an executed agreement, a copy of the executed agreement, and of any other document referred to in it, must be there and then delivered to him.

(2) A copy of the executed agreement, and of any other document referred to in it, must be given to the debtor or hirer within the seven days following the making of the agreement unless—

    (a) subsection (1) applies, or

    (b) the unexecuted agreement was sent to the debtor or hirer for his signature and, on the occasion of his signing it, the document became an executed agreement.

(3) In the case of a cancellable agreement, a copy under subsection (2) must be sent [by an appropriate method].

(4)   In the case of a credit-token agreement, a copy under subsection (2) need not be given within the seven days following the making of the agreement if it is given before or at the time when the credit-token is given to the debtor.

(5)   A regulated agreement [which is an excluded agreement] is not properly executed if the requirements of this section are not observed.

[(6)   In this section, 'excluded agreement' has the same meaning as in section 61A.]

### 64   Duty to give notice of cancellation rights

(1)   In the case of a cancellable agreement, a notice in the prescribed form indicating the right of the debtor or hirer to cancel the agreement, how and when that right is exercisable, and the name and address of a person to whom notice of cancellation may be given,—

(a)   must be included in every copy given to the debtor or hirer under section 62 or 63, and

(b)   except where section 63(2) applied, must also be sent [by an appropriate method] to the debtor or hirer within the seven days following the making of the agreement.

(2)   In the case of a credit-token agreement, a notice under subsection (1)(b) need not be sent [by an appropriate method] within the seven days following the making of the agreement if either—

(a)   it is sent [by an appropriate method] to the debtor or hirer before the credit-token is given to him, or

(b)   it is sent [by an appropriate method] to him together with the credit-token.

(3)   Regulations may provide that except where section 63(2) applied a notice sent under subsection (1)(b) shall be accompanied by a further copy of the executed agreement, and of any other document referred to in it.

(4)   Regulations may provide that subsection (1)(b) is not to apply in the case of agreements such as are described in the regulations, being agreements made by a particular person, if—

(a)   on an application by that person to the [FCA], the [FCA] has determined that, having regard to—

(i)   the manner in which antecedent negotiations for agreements with the applicant of that description are conducted, and

(ii)   the information provided to debtors or hirers before such agreements are made, the requirement imposed by subsection (1)(b) can be dispensed with without prejudicing the interests of debtors or hirers, and

(b)   any conditions imposed by the [FCA] in making the determination are complied with.

(5)   A cancellable agreement is not properly executed if the requirements of this section are not observed.

### 65   Consequences of improper execution

(1)   An improperly-executed regulated agreement is enforceable against the debtor or hirer on an order of the court only.

(2)   A retaking of goods or land to which a regulated agreement relates is an enforcement of the agreement.

### 66   Acceptance of credit-tokens

(1)   The debtor shall not be liable under a credit-token agreement for use made of the credit-token by any person unless the debtor had previously accepted the credit-token, or the use constituted an acceptance of it by him.

(2)   The debtor accepts a credit-token when—

(a)   it is signed, or

(b)   a receipt for it is signed, or

(c)   it is first used,

either by the debtor himself or by a person who, pursuant to the agreement, is authorised by him to use it.

[*Withdrawal from certain agreements*]

## [66A   Withdrawal from consumer credit agreement

(1)   The debtor under a regulated consumer credit agreement, other than an excluded agreement, may withdraw from the agreement, without giving any reason, in accordance with this section.

(2)   To withdraw from an agreement under this section the debtor must give oral or written notice of the withdrawal to the creditor before the end of the period of 14 days beginning with [the day after] the relevant day.

(3)   For the purposes of subsection (2) the relevant day is whichever is the latest of the following—

(a)   the day on which the agreement is made;

(b)   where the creditor is required to inform the debtor of the credit limit under the agreement, the day on which the creditor first does so;

(c)   in the case of an agreement to which section 61A (duty to supply copy of executed consumer credit agreement) applies, the day on which the debtor receives a copy of the agreement under that section or on which the debtor is informed as specified in subsection (3) of that section;

(d)   in the case of an agreement to which section 63 (duty to supply copy of executed agreement: excluded agreements) applies, the day on which the debtor receives a copy of the agreement under that section.

(4)   Where oral notice under this section is given to the creditor it must be given in a manner specified in the agreement.

(5)   Where written notice under this section is given by facsimile transmission or electronically—

(a)   it must be sent to the number or electronic address specified for the purpose in the agreement, and

(b)   where it is so sent, it is to be regarded as having been received by the creditor at the time it is sent (and section 176A does not apply).

(6)   Where written notice under this section is given in any other form—

(a)   it must be sent by post to, or left at, the postal address specified for the purpose in the agreement, and

(b)   where it is sent by post to that address, it is to be regarded as having been received by the creditor at the time of posting (and section 176 does not apply).

(7)   Subject as follows, where the debtor withdraws from a regulated consumer credit agreement under this section—

(a)   the agreement shall be treated as if it had never been entered into, and

(b)   where an ancillary service relating to the agreement is or is to be provided by the creditor, or by a third party on the basis of an agreement between the third party and the creditor, the ancillary service contract shall be treated as if it had never been entered into.

(8)   In the case referred to in subsection (7)(b) the creditor must without delay notify any third party of the fact that the debtor has withdrawn from the agreement.

(9)   Where the debtor withdraws from an agreement under this section—

(a)   the debtor must repay to the creditor any credit provided and the interest accrued on it (at the rate provided for under the agreement), but

(b)   the debtor is not liable to pay to the creditor any compensation, fees or charges except any non-returnable charges paid by the creditor to a public administrative body.

(10)   An amount payable under subsection (9) must be paid without undue delay and no later than the end of the period of 30 days beginning with the day

after the day on which the notice of withdrawal was given (and if not paid by the end of that period may be recovered by the creditor as a debt).

(11)   Where a regulated consumer credit agreement is a conditional sale, hire-purchase or credit-sale agreement and—

(a)   the debtor withdraws from the agreement under this section after the credit has been provided, and

(b)   the sum payable under subsection (9)(a) is paid in full by the debtor, title to the goods purchased or supplied under the agreement is to pass to the debtor on the same terms as would have applied had the debtor not withdrawn from the agreement.

(12)   In subsections (2), (4), (5), (6) and (9)(a) references to the creditor include a person specified by the creditor in the agreement.

(13)   In subsection (7)(b) the reference to an ancillary service means a service that relates to the provision of credit under the agreement and includes in particular an insurance or payment protection policy.

(14)   For the purposes of this section, an agreement is an excluded agreement if it is—

(a)   an agreement for credit exceeding £60,260 [, other than a residential renovation agreement],

(b)   an agreement secured on land,

(c)   a restricted-use credit agreement to finance the purchase of land, or

(d)   an agreement for a bridging loan in connection with the purchase of land.]

*Cancellation of certain agreements within cooling-off period*

## 67   Cancellable agreements

[(1)   Subject to subsection (2)] a regulated agreement may be cancelled by the debtor or hirer in accordance with this Part if the antecedent negotiations included oral representations made when in the presence of the debtor or hirer by an individual acting as, or on behalf of, the negotiator, unless—

(a)   the agreement is secured on land, or is a restricted-use credit agreement to finance the purchase of land or is an agreement for a bridging loan in connection with the purchase of land, or

(b)   the unexecuted agreement is signed by the debtor or hirer at premises at which any of the following is carrying on any business (whether on a permanent or temporary basis)—

(i)   the creditor or owner;

(ii)   any party to a linked transaction (other than the debtor or hirer or a relative of his);

(iii)   the negotiator in any antecedent negotiations.

[(2)   This section does not apply where section 66A applies.]

## 68   Cooling-off period

The debtor or hirer may serve notice of cancellation of a cancellable agreement between his signing of the unexecuted agreement and—

(a)   the end of the fifth day following the day on which he received a copy under section 63(2) or a notice under section 64(1)(b), or

(b)   if (by virtue of regulations made under section 64(4)) section 64(1)(b) does not apply, the end of the fourteenth day following the day on which he signed the unexecuted agreement.

## 69   Notice of cancellation

(1)   If within the period specified in section 68 the debtor or hirer under a cancellable agreement serves on—

(a)   the creditor or owner, or

(b)   the person specified in the notice under section 64(1), or

(c)    a person who (whether by virtue of subsection (6) or otherwise) is the agent of the creditor or owner, a notice (a 'notice of cancellation') which, however expressed and whether or not conforming to the notice given under section 64(1), indicates the intention of the debtor or hirer to withdraw from the agreement, the notice shall operate—

    (i)    to cancel the agreement, and any linked transaction, and

    (ii)    to withdraw any offer by the debtor or hirer, or his relative, to enter into a linked transaction.

(2)    In the case of a debtor-creditor-supplier agreement for restricted-use credit financing—

    (a)    the doing of work or supply of goods to meet an emergency, or

    (b)    the supply of goods which, before service of the notice of cancellation, had by the act of the debtor or his relative become incorporated in any land or thing not comprised in the agreement or any linked transaction,

subsection (1) shall apply with the substitution of the following for paragraph (i)—

'(i)    to cancel only such provisions of the agreement and any linked transaction as—

    (aa)    relate to the provision of credit, or

    (bb)    require the debtor to pay an item in the total charge for credit, or

    (cc)    subject the debtor to any obligation other than to pay for the doing of the said work, or the supply of the said goods.'

(3)    Except so far as is otherwise provided, references in this Act to the cancellation of an agreement or transaction do not include a case within subsection (2).

(4)    Except as otherwise provided by or under this Act, an agreement or transaction cancelled under subsection (1) shall be treated as if it had never been entered into.

(5)    Regulations may exclude linked transactions of the prescribed description from subsection (1)(i) or (ii).

(6)    Each of the following shall be deemed to be the agent of the creditor or owner for the purpose of receiving a notice of cancellation—

    (a)    a credit-broker or supplier who is the negotiator in antecedent negotiations, and

    (b)    any person who, in the course of a business carried on by him, acts on behalf of the debtor or hirer in any negotiations for the agreement.

[(7)    Whether or not it is actually received by him, a notice of cancellation sent to a person shall be deemed to be served on him—

    (a)    in the case of a notice sent by post, at the time of posting, and

    (b)    in the case of a notice transmitted in the form of an electronic communication in accordance with section 17A(1), at the time of the transmission.]

## 70    Cancellation: recovery of money paid by debtor or hirer

(1)    On the cancellation of a regulated agreement, and of any linked transaction,—

    (a)    any sum paid by the debtor or hirer, or his relative, under or in contemplation of the agreement or transaction, including any item in the total charge for credit, shall become repayable, and

    (b)    any sum, including any item in the total charge for credit, which but for the cancellation is, or would or might become, payable by the debtor or hirer, or his relative, under the agreement or transaction shall cease to be, or shall not become, so payable, and

    (c)    in the case of a debtor-creditor-supplier agreement falling within section 12(b), any sum paid on the debtor's behalf by the creditor to the supplier shall become repayable to the creditor.

(2)    If, under the terms of a cancelled agreement or transaction, the debtor or hirer, or his relative, is in possession of any goods, he shall have a lien on them for

any sum repayable to him under subsection (1) in respect of that agreement or transaction, or any other linked transaction.

(3)   A sum repayable under subsection (1) is repayable by the person to whom it was originally paid, but in the case of a debtor-creditor-supplier agreement falling within section 12(b) the creditor and the supplier shall be under a joint and several liability to repay sums paid by the debtor, or his relative, under the agreement or under a linked transaction falling within section 19(1)(b) and accordingly, in such a case, the creditor shall be entitled, in accordance with rules of court, to have the supplier made a party to any proceedings brought against the creditor to recover any such sums.

(4)   Subject to any agreement between them, the creditor shall be entitled to be indemnified by the supplier for loss suffered by the creditor in satisfying his liability under subsection (3), including costs reasonably incurred by him in defending proceedings instituted by the debtor.

(5)   Subsection (1) does not apply to any sum which, if not paid by a debtor, would be payable by virtue of section 71, and applies to a sum paid or payable by a debtor for the issue of a credit-token only where the credit-token has been returned to the creditor or surrendered to a supplier.

(6)   If the total charge for credit includes an item in respect of a fee or commission charged by a credit-broker, the amount repayable under subsection (1) in respect of that item shall be the excess over [£5] of the fee or commission.

(7)   If the total charge for credit includes any sum payable or paid by the debtor to a credit-broker otherwise than in respect of a fee or commission charged by him, that sum shall for the purposes of subsection (6) be treated as if it were such a fee or commission.

(8)   So far only as is necessary to give effect to section 69(2), this section applies to an agreement or transaction within that subsection as it applies to a cancelled agreement or transaction.

### 71   Cancellation: repayment of credit

(1)   Notwithstanding the cancellation of a regulated consumer credit agreement, other than a debtor-creditor-supplier agreement for restricted-use credit, the agreement shall continue in force so far as it relates to repayment of credit and payment of interest.

(2)   If, following the cancellation of a regulated consumer credit agreement, the debtor repays the whole or a portion of the credit—

(a)   before the expiry of one month following service of the notice of cancellation, or

(b)   in the case of a credit repayable by instalments, before the date on which the first instalment is due,

no interest shall be payable on the amount repaid.

(3)   If the whole of a credit repayable by instalments is not repaid on or before the date specified in subsection (2)(b), the debtor shall not be liable to repay any of the credit except on receipt of a request in writing in the prescribed form, signed by or on behalf of the creditor, stating the amounts of the remaining instalments (recalculated by the creditor as nearly as may be in accordance with the agreement and without extending the repayment period), but excluding any sum other than principal and interest.

(4)   Repayment of a credit, or payment of interest, under a cancelled agreement shall be treated as duly made if it is made to any person on whom, under section 69, a notice of cancellation could have been served, other than a person referred to in section 69(6)(b).

### 72   Cancellation: return of goods

(1)   This section applies where any agreement or transaction relating to goods, being—

(a)   a restricted-use debtor-creditor-supplier agreement, a consumer hire agreement, or a linked transaction to which the debtor or hirer under any regulated agreement is a party, or

(b)   a linked transaction to which a relative of the debtor or hirer under any regulated agreement is a party,

is cancelled after the debtor or hirer (in a case within paragraph (a)) or the relative (in a case within paragraph (b)) has acquired possession of the goods by virtue of the agreement or transaction.

(2)   In this section—

(a)   'the possessor' means the person who has acquired possession of the goods as mentioned in subsection (1),

(b)   'the other party' means the person from whom the possessor acquired possession, and

(c)   'the pre-cancellation period' means the period beginning when the possessor acquired possession and ending with the cancellation.

(3)   The possessor shall be treated as having been under a duty throughout the pre-cancellation period—

(a)   to retain possession of the goods, and

(b)   to take reasonable care of them.

(4)   On the cancellation, the possessor shall be under a duty, subject to any lien to restore the goods to the other party in accordance with this section, and meanwhile to retain possession of the goods and take reasonable care of them.

(5)   The possessor shall not be under any duty to deliver the goods except at his own premises and in pursuance of a request in writing signed by or on behalf of the other party and served on the possessor either before, or at the time when, the goods are collected from those premises.

(6)   If the possessor—

(a)   delivers the goods (whether at his own premises or elsewhere) to any person on whom, under section 69, a notice of cancellation could have been served (other than a person referred to in section 69(6)(b)), or

(b)   sends the goods at his own expense to such a person, he shall be discharged from any duty to retain the goods or deliver them to any person.

(7)   Where the possessor delivers the goods as mentioned in subsection (6)(a), his obligation to take care of the goods shall cease; and if he sends the goods as mentioned in subsection (6)(b), he shall be under a duty to take reasonable care to see that they are received by the other party and not damaged in transit, but in other respects his duty to take care of the goods shall cease.

(8)   Where, at any time during the period of 21 days following the cancellation, the possessor receives such a request as is mentioned in subsection (5), and unreasonably refuses or unreasonably fails to comply with it, his duty to take reasonable care of the goods shall continue until he delivers or sends the goods as mentioned in subsection (6), but if within that period he does not receive such a request his duty to take reasonable care of the goods shall cease at the end of that period.

(9)   The preceding provisions of this section do not apply to—

(a)   perishable goods, or

(b)   goods which by their nature are consumed by use and which, before the cancellation, were so consumed, or

(c)   goods supplied to meet an emergency, or

(d)   goods which, before the cancellation, had become incorporated in any land or thing not comprised in the cancelled agreement or a linked transaction.

(10)   Where the address of the possessor is specified in the executed agreement, references in this section to his own premises are to that address and no other.

(11)   Breach of a duty imposed by this section is actionable as a breach of statutory duty.

**73  Cancellation: goods given in part-exchange**

(1)  This section applies on the cancellation of a regulated agreement where, in antecedent negotiations, the negotiator agreed to take goods in part-exchange (the 'part-exchange goods') and those goods have been delivered to him.

(2)  Unless, before the end of the period of ten days beginning with the date of cancellation, the part-exchange goods are returned to the debtor or hirer in a condition substantially as good as when they were delivered to the negotiator, the debtor or hirer shall be entitled to recover from the negotiator a sum equal to the part-exchange allowance (as defined in subsection (7)(b)).

(3)  In the case of a debtor-creditor-supplier agreement within section 12(b), the negotiator and the creditor shall be under a joint and several liability to pay to the debtor a sum recoverable under subsection (2).

(4)  Subject to any agreement between them, the creditor shall be entitled to be indemnified by the negotiator for loss suffered by the creditor in satisfying his liability under subsection (3), including costs reasonably incurred by him in defending proceedings instituted by the debtor.

(5)  During the period of ten days beginning with the date of cancellation, the debtor or hirer, if he is in possession of goods to which the cancelled agreement relates, shall have a lien on them for—

(a)  delivery of the part-exchange goods, in a condition substantially as good as when they were delivered to the negotiator; or

(b)  a sum equal to the part-exchange allowance;

and if the lien continues to the end of that period it shall thereafter subsist only as a lien for a sum equal to the part-exchange allowance.

(6)  Where the debtor or hirer recovers from the negotiator or creditor, or both of them jointly, a sum equal to the part-exchange allowance, then, if the title of the debtor or hirer to the part-exchange goods has not vested in the negotiator, it shall so vest on the recovery of that sum.

(7)  For the purposes of this section—

(a)  the negotiator shall be treated as having agreed to take goods in part-exchange if, in pursuance of the antecedent negotiations, he either purchased or agreed to purchase those goods or accepted or agreed to accept them as part of the consideration for the cancelled agreement, and

(b)  the part-exchange allowance shall be the sum agreed as such in the antecedent negotiations or, if no such agreement was arrived at, such sum as it would have been reasonable to allow in respect of the part-exchange goods if no notice of cancellation had been served.

(8)  In an action brought against the creditor for a sum recoverable under subsection (2), he shall be entitled, in accordance with rules of court, to have the negotiator made a party to the proceedings.

*Exclusion of certain agreements from Part V*

**74  Exclusion of certain agreements from Part V**

[(1)  Except as provided in subsections (1A) to (2), this Part does not apply to—

(a)  a non-commercial agreement,

(b)  a debtor-creditor agreement enabling the debtor to overdraw on a current account,

(c)  a debtor-creditor agreement to finance the making of such payments arising on, or connected with, the death of a person as may be prescribed, or

(d)  a small debtor-creditor-supplier agreement for restricted-use credit.

(1A)  Section 56 (antecedent negotiations) applies to a non-commercial agreement.

(1B)  Where an agreement that falls within subsection (1)(b) is an authorised business overdraft agreement the following provisions apply—

[. . .]
(b)    section 56 (antecedent negotiations);
(c)    section 60 (regulations on form and content of agreements);
(d)    section 61B (duty to supply copy of overdraft agreement).

(1C)   Where an agreement that falls within subsection (1)(b) is an authorised non-business overdraft agreement the following provisions apply—
(a)    section 55 (regulations on disclosure of information);
[. . .]
(c)    section 55C (copy of draft consumer credit agreement);
(d)    section 56 (antecedent negotiations);
(e)    section 60 (regulations on form and content of agreements);
(f)    section 61B (duty to supply copy of overdraft agreement).

(1D)   Where an agreement that falls within subsection (1)(b) would be an authorised non-business overdraft agreement but for the fact that the credit is not repayable on demand or within three months the following provisions apply—
(a)    section 55 (regulations on disclosure of information);
[. . .]
(d)    section 55C (copy of draft consumer credit agreement);
(e)    section 56 (antecedent negotiations);
(f)    section 60 (regulations on form and content of agreements);
(g)    section 61 (signing of agreement);
(h)    section 61A (duty to supply copy of executed agreement);
(i)    section 66A (withdrawal from consumer credit agreement).

(1E)   In the case of an agreement that falls within subsection (1)(b) but does not fall within subsection (1B), (1C) or (1D), section 56 (antecedent negotiations) applies.

(1F)   The following provisions apply to a debtor-creditor agreement to finance the making of such payments arising on, or connected with, the death of a person as may be prescribed—
(a)    section 55 (regulations on disclosure of information);
[. . .]
(d)    section 55C (copy of draft consumer credit agreement);
(e)    section 56 (antecedent negotiations);
(f)    section 60 (regulations on form and content of agreements);
(g)    section 61 (signing of agreement);
(h)    section 61A (duty to supply copy of executed agreement);
(i)    section 66A (withdrawal from consumer credit agreement).]

[(2)   The following provisions apply to a small debtor-creditor-supplier agreement for restricted-use credit—
(a)    section 55 (regulations on disclosure of information);
(b)    section 56 (antecedent negotiations);
(c)    section 66A (withdrawal from consumer credit agreement).]

[(2A)   In the case of an agreement to which Part 2 or 3 of the Consumer Contracts (Information, Cancellation and Additional Charges) Regulations 2013 applies, the reference in subsection (2) to a small agreement is to be read as if in section 17(1)(a) and (b) '£42' were substituted for '£50'.]

(3)   [Subsection (1)(c) applies] only where the [FCA] so determines, and such a determination—
(a)    may be made subject to such conditions as the [FCA] thinks fit, and
(b)    shall be made only if the [FCA] is of opinion that it is not against the interests of debtors.
[. . .]

(4)   If any term of an agreement falling within subsection [(1)(d)] is expressed in writing, regulations under section 60(1) shall apply to that term (subject to section 60(3)) as if the agreement were a regulated agreement not falling within subsection [(1)(d)].

[. . .]

## PART VI
## MATTERS ARISING DURING CURRENCY OF CREDIT OR HIRE AGREEMENTS

**75   Liability of creditor for breaches by supplier**

(1)   If the debtor under a debtor-creditor-supplier agreement falling within section 12(b) or (c) has, in relation to a transaction financed by the agreement, any claim against the supplier in respect of a misrepresentation or breach of contract, he shall have a like claim against the creditor, who, with the supplier, shall accordingly be jointly and severally liable to the debtor.

(2)   Subject to any agreement between them, the creditor shall be entitled to be indemnified by the supplier for loss suffered by the creditor in satisfying his liability under subsection (1), including costs reasonably incurred by him in defending proceedings instituted by the debtor.

(3)   Subsection (1) does not apply to a claim—

(a)   under a non-commercial agreement,

(b)   so far as the claim relates to any single item to which the supplier has attached a cash price not exceeding [£100] or more than [£30,000] [, or

[(c)   under a debtor-creditor-supplier agreement for running-account credit—

(i)   which provides for the making of payments by the debtor in relation to specified periods which, in the case of an agreement which is not secured on land, do not exceed three months, and

(ii)   which requires that the number of payments to be made by the debtor in repayments of the whole amount of the credit provided in each such period shall not exceed one.]

(4)   This section applies notwithstanding that the debtor, in entering into the transaction, exceeded the credit limit or otherwise contravened any term of the agreement.

(5)   In an action brought against the creditor under subsection (1) he shall be entitled, in accordance with rules of court, to have the supplier made a party to the proceedings.

**[75A   Further provision for liability of creditor for breaches by supplier**

(1)   If the debtor under a linked credit agreement has a claim against the supplier in respect of a breach of contract the debtor may pursue that claim against the creditor where any of the conditions in subsection (2) are met.

(2)   The conditions in subsection (1) are—

(a)   that the supplier cannot be traced,

(b)   that the debtor has contacted the supplier but the supplier has not responded,

(c)   that the supplier is insolvent, or

(d)   that the debtor has taken reasonable steps to pursue his claim against the supplier but has not obtained satisfaction for his claim.

(3)   The steps referred to in subsection (2)(d) need not include litigation.

(4)   For the purposes of subsection (2)(d) a debtor is to be deemed to have obtained satisfaction where he has accepted a replacement product or service or other compensation from the supplier in settlement of his claim.

(5)   In this section 'linked credit agreement' means a regulated consumer credit agreement which serves exclusively to finance an agreement for the supply of specific goods or the provision of a specific service and where—

(a)   the creditor uses the services of the supplier in connection with the preparation or making of the credit agreement, or

(b)   the specific goods or provision of a specific service are explicitly specified in the credit agreement.

(6)   This section does not apply where—

(a)   the cash value of the goods or service is £30, 000 or less,

(b)  the linked credit agreement is for credit which exceeds £60,260 [and is not a residential renovation agreement], or

(c)  the linked credit agreement is entered into by the debtor wholly or predominantly for the purposes of a business carried on, or intended to be carried on, by him.

[(7)  Article 60C(5) and (6) of the Regulated Activities Order applies for the purposes of subsection (6)(c).]]

[(8)  This section does not apply to an agreement secured on land.]

## 76  Duty to give notice before taking certain action

(1)  The creditor or owner is not entitled to enforce a term of a regulated agreement by—

(a)  demanding earlier payment of any sum, or

(b)  recovering possession of any goods or land, or

(c)  treating any right conferred on the debtor or hirer by the agreement as terminated, restricted or deferred,

except by or after giving the debtor or hirer not less than seven days' notice of his intention to do so.

(2)  Subsection (1) applies only where—

(a)  a period for the duration of the agreement is specified in the agreement, and

(b)  that period has not ended when the creditor or owner does an act mentioned in subsection (1),

but so applies notwithstanding that, under the agreement, any party is entitled to terminate it before the end of the period so specified.

(3)  A notice under subsection (1) is ineffective if not in the prescribed form.

(4)  Subsection (1) does not prevent a creditor from treating the right to draw on any credit as restricted or deferred and taking such steps as may be necessary to make the restriction or deferment effective.

(5)  Regulations may provide that subsection (1) is not to apply to agreements described by the regulations.

(6)  Subsection (1) does not apply to a right of enforcement arising by reason of any breach by the debtor or hirer of the regulated agreement.

## 77  Duty to give information to debtor under fixed-sum credit agreement

(1)  The creditor under a regulated agreement for fixed-sum credit, within the prescribed period after receiving a request in writing to that effect from the debtor and payment of a fee of [£1], shall give the debtor a copy of the executed agreement (if any) and of any other document referred to in it, together with a statement signed by or on behalf of the creditor showing, according to the information to which it is practicable for him to refer,—

(a)  the total sum paid under the agreement by the debtor;

(b)  the total sum which has become payable under the agreement by the debtor but remains unpaid, and the various amounts comprised in that total sum, with the date when each became due; and

(c)  the total sum which is to become payable under the agreement by the debtor, and the various amounts comprised in that total sum, with the date, or mode of determining the date, when each becomes due.

(2)  If the creditor possesses insufficient information to enable him to ascertain the amounts and dates mentioned in subsection (1)(c), he shall be taken to comply with that paragraph if his statement under subsection (1) gives the basis on which, under the regulated agreement, they would fall to be ascertained.

[(2A)  Subsection (2B) applies if the regulated agreement is a green deal plan [. . .].

(2B)  The duty imposed on the creditor by subsection (1) may be discharged by another person acting on the creditor's behalf.]

(3)  Subsection (1) does not apply to—

(a)   an agreement under which no sum is, or will or may become, payable by the debtor, or

(b)   a request made less than one month after a previous request under that subsection relating to the same agreement was complied with.

(4)   If the creditor under an agreement fails to comply with subsection (1)—

(a)   he is not entitled, while the default continues, to enforce the agreement [. . .]

(5)   This section does not apply to a non-commercial agreement.

**[77A   Statements to be provided in relation to fixed-sum credit agreements**

[(1)   The creditor under a regulated agreement for fixed-sum credit must give the debtor statements under this section.

(1A)   The statements must relate to consecutive periods.

(1B)   The first such period must begin with either—

(a)   the day on which the agreement is made, or

(b)   the day the first movement occurs on the debtor's account with the creditor relating to the agreement.

(1C)   No such period may exceed a year.

(1D)   For the purposes of subsection (1C), a period of a year which expires on a non-working day may be regarded as expiring on the next working day.

(1E)   Each statement under this section must be given to the debtor before the end of the period of thirty days beginning with the day after the end of the period to which the statement relates.]

(2)   Regulations may make provision about the form and content of statements under this section.

[(2A)   Subsection (2B) applies if the regulated agreement is a green deal plan [. . .].

(2B)   Any duty imposed on the creditor by this section may be discharged by another person acting on the creditor's behalf.]

(3)   The debtor shall have no liability to pay any sum in connection with the preparation or the giving to him of a statement under this section.

(4)   The creditor is not required to give the debtor any statement under this section once the following conditions are satisfied—

(a)   that there is no sum payable under the agreement by the debtor; and

(b)   that there is no sum which will or may become so payable.

(5)   Subsection (6) applies if at a time before the conditions mentioned in subsection (4) are satisfied the creditor fails to give the debtor—

(a)   a statement under this section within the period mentioned in subsection [(1E)].

[. . .]

(6)   Where this subsection applies in relation to a failure to give a statement under this section to the debtor—

(a)   the creditor shall not be entitled to enforce the agreement during the period of non-compliance;

(b)   the debtor shall have no liability to pay any sum of interest to the extent calculated by reference to the period of non-compliance or to any part of it; and

(c)   the debtor shall have no liability to pay any default sum which (apart from this paragraph)—

(i)   would have become payable during the period of non-compliance; or

(ii)   would have become payable after the end of that period in connection with a breach of the agreement which occurs during that period (whether or not the breach continues after the end of that period).

(7)   In this section 'the period of non-compliance' means, in relation to a failure to give a statement under this section to the debtor, the period which—

(a)   begins immediately after the end of the period mentioned in [. . .] subsection (5); and

(b)   ends at the end of the day on which the statement is given to the debtor or on which the conditions mentioned in subsection (4) are satisfied, whichever is earlier.

(8)   This section does not apply in relation to a non-commercial agreement or to a small agreement.]

[(9)   This section does not apply where the holder of a current account over-draws on the account without a pre-arranged overdraft or exceeds a pre-arranged overdraft limit.]

### [77B   Fixed-sum credit agreement: statement of account to be provided on request

(1)   This section applies to a regulated consumer credit agreement—

    (a)   which is for fixed-sum credit,

    (b)   which is of fixed duration,

    (c)   where the credit is repayable in instalments by the debtor, and

    (d)   which is not an excluded agreement.

(2)   Upon a request from the debtor, the creditor must as soon as reasonably practicable give to the debtor a statement in writing which complies with subsections (3) to (5).

(3)   The statement must include a table showing the details of each instalment owing under the agreement as at the date of the request.

(4)   Details to be provided under subsection (3) must include—

    (a)   the date on which the instalment is due,

    (b)   the amount of the instalment,

    (c)   any conditions relating to payment of the instalment, and

    (d)   a breakdown of the instalment showing how much of it is made up of capital repayment, interest payment and other charges.

(5)   Where the rate of interest is variable or the charges under the agreement may be varied, the statement must also indicate clearly and concisely that the information in the table is valid only until the rate of interest or charges are varied.

(6)   The debtor may make a request under subsection (2) at any time that the agreement is in force unless a previous request has been made less than a month before and has been complied with.

(7)   The debtor shall have no liability to pay any sum in connection with the preparation or the giving of a statement under this section.

[(7A)   Subsection (7B) applies if the regulated agreement is a green deal plan [. . .].

(7B)   The duty imposed on the creditor by this section may be discharged by another person acting on the creditor's behalf.]

(8)   A breach of the duty imposed by this section is actionable as a breach of statutory duty.

(9)   For the purposes of this section, an agreement is an excluded agreement if it is—

    (a)   an agreement secured on land,

    (b)   an agreement under which a person takes an article in pawn,

    (c)   an agreement under which the creditor provides the debtor with credit which exceeds £60,260 [and which is not a residential renovation agreement], or

    (d)   an agreement entered into by the debtor wholly or predominantly for the purpose of a business carried on, or intended to be carried on, by him.

[(10)   Article 60C(5) and (6) of the Regulated Activities Order applies for the purposes of subsection (9)(d).]]

### 78   Duty to give information to debtor under running-account credit agreement

(1)   The creditor under a regulated agreement for running-account credit, within the prescribed period after receiving a request in writing to that effect from the debtor and payment of a fee of [£1], shall give the debtor a copy of the ex-

ecuted agreement (if any) and of any other document referred to in it, together with a statement signed by or on behalf of the creditor showing, according to the information to which it is practicable for him to refer,—

(a)   the state of the account, and

(b)   the amount, if any, currently payable under the agreement by the debtor to the creditor, and

(c)   the amounts and due dates of any payments which, if the debtor does not draw further on the account, will later become payable under the agreement by the debtor to the creditor.

(2)   If the creditor possesses insufficient information to enable him to ascertain the amounts and dates mentioned in subsection (1)(c), he shall be taken to comply with that paragraph if his statement under subsection (1) gives the basis on which, under the regulated agreement, they would fall to be ascertained.

(3)   Subsection (1) does not apply to—

(a)   an agreement under which no sum is, or will or may become, payable by the debtor, or

(b)   a request made less than one month after a previous request under that subsection relating to the same agreement was complied with.

(4)   Where running-account credit is provided under a regulated agreement, the creditor shall give the debtor statements in the prescribed form, and with the prescribed contents—

(a)   showing according to the information to which it is practicable for him to refer, the state of the account at regular intervals of not more than twelve months, and

(b)   where the agreement provides, in relation to specified periods, for the making of payments by the debtor, or the charging against him of interest or any other sum, showing according to the information to which it is practicable for him to refer the state of the account at the end of each of those periods during which there is any movement in the account.

[(4A)   Regulations may require a statement under subsection (4) to contain also information in the prescribed terms about the consequences of the debtor—

(a)   failing to make payments as required by the agreement; or

(b)   only making payments of a prescribed description in prescribed circumstances.]

(5)   A statement under subsection (4) shall be given within the prescribed period after the end of the period to which the statement relates.

(6)   If the creditor under an agreement fails to comply with subsection (1)—

(a)   he is not entitled, while the default continues, to enforce the agreement [. . .]

(7)   This section does not apply to a non-commercial agreement, and subsections [(4) to (5)] do not apply to a small agreement.

## [78A   Duty to give information to debtor on change of rate of interest

(1)   Where the rate of interest charged under a regulated consumer credit agreement, other than an excluded agreement, is to be varied, the creditor must inform the debtor in writing of the matters mentioned in subsection (3) before the variation can take effect.

(2)   But subsection (1) does not apply where—

(a)   the agreement provides that the creditor is to inform the debtor in writing periodically of the matters mentioned in subsection (3) in relation to any variation, at such times as may be provided for in the agreement,

(b)   the agreement provides that the rate of interest is to vary according to a reference rate,

(c)   the reference rate is publicly available,

(d)   information about the reference rate is available on the premises of the creditor, and

(e) the variation of the rate of interest results from a change to the reference rate.

(3) The matters referred to in subsections (1) and (2)(a) are—

(a) the variation in the rate of interest,

(b) the amount of any payments that are to be made after the variation has effect, if different, expressed as a sum of money where practicable, and

(c) if the number or frequency of payments changes as a result of the variation, the new number or frequency.

(4) In the case of an agreement mentioned in subsection (5) this section applies as follows—

(a) the obligation in subsection (1) only applies if the rate of interest increases, and

(b) subsection (3) is to be read as if paragraphs (b) and (c) were omitted.

(5) The agreements referred to in subsection (4) are—

(a) an authorised business overdraft agreement,

(b) an authorised non-business overdraft agreement, or

(c) an agreement which would be an authorised non-business overdraft agreement but for the fact that the credit is not repayable on demand or within three months.

(6) For the purposes of this section an agreement is an excluded agreement if it is—

(a) a debtor-creditor agreement arising where the holder of a current account overdraws on the account without a pre-arranged overdraft or exceeds a pre-arranged overdraft limit, or

(b) an agreement secured on land.]

## 79 Duty to give hirer information

(1) The owner under a regulated consumer hire agreement, within the prescribed period after receiving a request in writing to that effect from the hirer and payment of a fee of [£1], shall give to the hirer a copy of the executed agreement and of any other document referred to in it, together with a statement signed by or on behalf of the owner showing, according to the information to which it is practicable for him to refer, the total sum which has become payable under the agreement by the hirer but remains unpaid and the various amounts comprised in that total sum, with the date when each became due.

(2) Subsection (1) does not apply to—

(a) an agreement under which no sum is, or will or may become, payable by the hirer, or

(b) a request made less than one month after a previous request under that subsection relating to the same agreement was complied with.

(3) If the owner under an agreement fails to comply with subsection (1)—

(a) he is not entitled, while the default continues, to enforce the agreement [. . .]

(4) This section does not apply to a non-commercial agreement.

## 80 Debtor or hirer to give information about goods

(1) Where a regulated agreement, other than a non-commercial agreement, requires the debtor or hirer to keep goods to which the agreement relates in his possession or control, he shall, within seven working days after he has received a request in writing to that effect from the creditor or owner, tell the creditor or owner where the goods are.

(2) If the debtor or hirer fails to comply with subsection (1), and the default continues for 14 days, he commits an offence.

[. . .]

## 82 Variation of agreements

(1) Where, under a power contained in a regulated agreement, the creditor or

owner varies the agreement, the variation shall not take effect before notice of it is given to the debtor or hirer in the prescribed manner.

[(1A)   Subsection (1) does not apply to a variation in the rate of interest charged under an agreement not secured on land (see section 78A).

(1B)   Subsection (1) does not apply to a variation in the rate of interest charged under an agreement secured on land if—

(a)   the agreement falls within subsection (1D), and

(b)   the variation is a reduction in the rate.

(1C)   Subsection (1) does not apply to a variation in any other charge under an agreement if—

(a)   the agreement falls within subsection (1D), and

(b)   the variation is a reduction in the charge.

(1D)   The agreements referred to in subsections (1B) and (1C) are—

(a)   an authorised business overdraft agreement,

(b)   an authorised non-business overdraft agreement, or

(c)   an agreement which would be an authorised non-business overdraft agreement but for the fact that the credit is not repayable on demand or within three months.

(1E)   Subsection (1) does not apply to a debtor-creditor agreement arising where the holder of a current account overdraws on the account without a pre-arranged overdraft or exceeds a pre-arranged overdraft limit.]

(2)   Where an agreement (a 'modifying agreement') varies or supplements an earlier agreement, the modifying agreement shall for the purposes of this Act be treated as—

(a)   revoking the earlier agreement, and

(b)   containing provisions reproducing the combined effect of the two agreements, and obligations outstanding in relation to the earlier agreement shall accordingly be treated as outstanding instead in relation to the modifying agreement.

[(2A)   Subsection (2) does not apply if [the earlier agreement or] the modifying agreement is an exempt agreement [. . .].]

[(2B)   Subsection (2) does not apply if the modifying agreement varies—

(a)   the amount of the repayment to be made under the earlier agreement, or

(b)   the duration of the agreement,

as a result of the discharge of part of the debtor's indebtedness under the earlier agreement by virtue of section 94(3).]

(3)   If the earlier agreement is a regulated agreement but (apart from this subsection) the modifying agreement is not then, [unless the modifying agreement is—

(a)   for running account credit; or

(b)   an exempt agreement [. . .], it shall be treated as a regulated agreement.]

(4)   If the earlier agreement is a regulated agreement for running-account credit, and by the modifying agreement the creditor allows the credit limit to be exceeded but intends the excess to be merely temporary, Part V (except section 56) shall not apply to the modifying agreement.

(5)   If—

(a)   the earlier agreement is a cancellable agreement, and

(b)   the modifying agreement is made within the period applicable under section 68 to the earlier agreement,

then, whether or not the modifying agreement would, apart from this subsection, be a cancellable agreement, it shall be treated as a cancellable agreement in respect of which a notice may be served under section 68 not later than the end of the period applicable under that section to the earlier agreement.

[(5A)   Subsection (5) does not apply where the modifying agreement is an exempt agreement [. . .].]

(6)   Except under subsection (5), a modifying agreement shall not be treated as a cancellable agreement.

[(6A)   If—

(a)   the earlier agreement is an agreement to which section 66A (right of withdrawal) applies, and

(b)   the modifying agreement is made within the period during which the debtor may give notice of withdrawal from the earlier agreement (see section 66A(2)),

then, whether or not the modifying agreement would, apart from this subsection, be an agreement to which section 66A applies, it shall be treated as such an agreement in respect of which notice may be given under subsection (2) of that section within the period referred to in paragraph (b) above.

(6B)   Except as provided for under subsection (6A) section 66A does not apply to a modifying agreement.]

(7)   This section does not apply to a non-commercial agreement.

[(8)   In this section, an 'exempt agreement' means an agreement which is an exempt agreement for the purposes of Chapter 14A of Part 2 of the Regulated Activities Order by virtue of article 60C(2) (regulated mortgage contracts and regulated home purchase plans) or article 60D (exemption relating to the purchase of land for non-residential purposes) of that Order.]

[. . .]

### 83   Liability for misuse of credit facilities

(1)   The debtor under a regulated consumer credit agreement shall not be liable to the creditor for any loss arising from use of the credit facility by another person not acting, or to be treated as acting, as the debtor's agent.

(2)   This section does not apply to a non-commercial agreement, or to any loss in so far as it arises from misuse of an instrument to which section 4 of the Cheques Act 1957 applies.

### 84   Misuse of credit-tokens

(1)   Section 83 does not prevent the debtor under a credit-token agreement from being made liable to the extent of [£50] (or the credit limit if lower) for loss to the creditor arising from use of the credit-token by other persons during a period beginning when the credit-token ceases to be in the possession of any authorised person and ending when the credit-token is once more in the possession of an authorised person.

(2)   Section 83 does not prevent the debtor under a credit-token agreement from being made liable to any extent for loss to the creditor from use of the credit-token by a person who acquired possession of it with the debtor's consent.

(3)   Subsections (1) and (2) shall not apply to any use of the credit-token after the creditor has been given oral or written notice that it is lost or stolen, or is for any other reason liable to misuse.

[(3A)   Subsections (1) and (2) shall not apply to any use, in connection with a distance contract (other than an excepted contract), of a card which is a credit-token.

(3B)   In subsection (3A), 'distance contract' and 'excepted contract' have the meanings given in the Consumer Protection (Distance Selling) Regulations 2000.

(3C)   Subsections (1) and (2) shall not apply to any use, in connection with a distance contract within the meaning of the Financial Services (Distance Marketing) Regulations 2004, of a card which is a credit-token.

(3D)   In subsection (3C), 'distance contract' and 'excepted contract' have the meanings given in the Financial Services (Distance Marketing) Regulations 2004.]

(4)   Subsections (1) and (2) shall not apply unless there are contained in the credit-token agreement in the prescribed manner particulars of the name, address

and telephone number of a person stated to be the person to whom notice is to be given under subsection (3).

(5)   Notice under subsection (3) takes effect when received, but where it is given orally, and the agreement so requires, it shall be treated as not taking effect if not confirmed in writing within seven days.

(6)   Any sum paid by the debtor for the issue of the credit-token to the extent (if any) that it has not been previously offset by use made of the credit-token, shall be treated as paid towards satisfaction of any liability under subsection (1) or (2).

(7)   The debtor, the creditor, and any person authorised by the debtor to use the credit-token, shall be authorised persons for the purposes of subsection (1).

(8)   Where two or more credit-tokens are given under one credit-token agreement, the preceding provisions of this section apply to each credit-token separately.

### 85   Duty on issue of new credit-tokens

(1)   Whenever, in connection with a credit-token agreement, a credit-token (other than the first) is given by the creditor to the debtor, the creditor shall give the debtor a copy of the executed agreement (if any) and of any other document referred to in it.

(2)   If the creditor fails to comply with this section—

(a)   he is not entitled, while the default continues, to enforce the agreement [. . .]

(3)   This section does not apply to a small agreement.

### 86   Death of debtor or hirer

(1)   The creditor or owner under a regulated agreement is not entitled, by reason of the death of the debtor or hirer, to do an act specified in paragraphs (a) to (e) of section 87(1) if at the death the agreement is fully secured.

(2)   If at the death of the debtor or hirer a regulated agreement is only partly secured or is unsecured, the creditor or owner is entitled, by reason of the death of the debtor or hirer, to do an act specified in paragraphs (a) to (e) of section 87(1) on an order of the court only.

(3)   This section applies in relation to the termination of an agreement only where—

(a)   a period for its duration is specified in the agreement, and

(b)   that period has not ended when the creditor or owner purports to terminate the agreement,

but so applies notwithstanding that, under the agreement, any party is entitled to terminate it before the end of the period so specified.

(4)   The section does not prevent the creditor from treating the right to draw on any credit as restricted or deferred, and taking such steps as may be necessary to make the restriction or deferment effective.

(5)   This section does not affect the operation of any agreement providing for payment of sums—

(a)   due under the regulated agreement, or

(b)   becoming due under it on the death of the debtor or hirer,

out of the proceeds of a policy of assurance on his life.

(6)   For the purposes of this section an act is done by reason of the death of the debtor or hirer if it is done under a power conferred by the agreement which is—

(a)   exercisable on his death, or

(b)   exercisable at will and exercised at any time after his death.

PART VII
DEFAULT AND TERMINATION

*[Information sheets*

### [86A [FCA] to prepare information sheets on arrears and default
(1) The [FCA shall prepare and issue], an arrears information sheet and a default information sheet.

(2) The arrears information sheet shall include information to help debtors and hirers who receive notices under section 86B or 86C.

(3) The default information sheet shall include information to help debtors and hirers who receive default notices.

(4) Regulations may make provision about the information to be included in an information sheet.

(5) An information sheet takes effect for the purposes of this Part at the end of the period of three months beginning with the day on which [it is issued] [or on such later date as the FCA may specify in relation to the information sheet].

[(6) If the FCA revises an information sheet after it has been issued, it shall issue the revised information sheet.]

(7) A revised information sheet takes effect for the purposes of this Part at the end of the period of three months beginning with the day on which [it is issued] [or on such later date as the FCA may specify in relation to the information sheet].]

*[Sums in arrears and default sums*

### [86B Notice of sums in arrears under fixed-sum credit agreements etc
(1) This section applies where at any time the following conditions are satisfied—

(a) that the debtor or hirer under an applicable agreement is required to have made at least two payments under the agreement before that time;

(b) that the total sum paid under the agreement by him is less than the total sum which he is required to have paid before that time;

(c) that the amount of the shortfall is no less than the sum of the last two payments which he is required to have made before that time;

(d) that the creditor or owner is not already under a duty to give him notices under this section in relation to the agreement; and

(e) if a judgment has been given in relation to the agreement before that time, that there is no sum still to be paid under the judgment by the debtor or hirer.

(2) The creditor or owner—

(a) shall, within the period of 14 days beginning with the day on which the conditions mentioned in subsection (1) are satisfied, give the debtor or hirer a notice under this section; and

(b) after the giving of that notice, shall give him further notices under this section at intervals of not more than six months.

(3) The duty of the creditor or owner to give the debtor or hirer notices under this section shall cease when either of the conditions mentioned in subsection (4) is satisfied; but if either of those conditions is satisfied before the notice required by subsection (2)(a) is given, the duty shall not cease until that notice is given.

(4) The conditions referred to in subsection (3) are—

(a) that the debtor or hirer ceases to be in arrears;

(b) that a judgment is given in relation to the agreement under which a sum is required to be paid by the debtor or hirer.

(5) For the purposes of subsection (4)(a) the debtor or hirer ceases to be in arrears when—

(a)    no [payments], which he has ever failed to [make] under the agreement when required, [are] still owing;

(b)    no default sum, which has ever become payable under the agreement in connection with his failure to pay any sum under the agreement when required, is still owing;

(c)    no sum of interest, which has ever become payable under the agreement in connection with such a default sum, is still owing; and

(d)    no other sum of interest, which has ever become payable under the agreement in connection with his failure to pay any sum under the agreement when required, is still owing.

(6)    A notice under this section shall include a copy of the current arrears information sheet under section 86A.

(7)    The debtor or hirer shall have no liability to pay any sum in connection with the preparation or the giving to him of a notice under this section.

(8)    Regulations may make provision about the form and content of notices under this section.

(9)    In the case of an applicable agreement under which the debtor or hirer must make all payments he is required to make at intervals of one week or less, this section shall have effect as if in subsection (1)(a) and (c) for 'two' there were substituted 'four'.

(10)    If an agreement mentioned in subsection (9) was made before the beginning of the relevant period, only amounts resulting from failures by the debtor or hirer to make payments he is required to have made during that period shall be taken into account in determining any shortfall for the purposes of subsection (1)(c).

(11)    In subsection (10) 'relevant period' means the period of 20 weeks ending with the day on which the debtor or hirer is required to have made the most recent payment under the agreement.

[(12)    In this section 'applicable agreement' means an agreement which falls within subsection (12A) or (12B).

(12A)    An agreement falls within this subsection if—
    (a)    it is a regulated agreement for fixed-sum credit; and
    (b)    it is not—
        (i)    a non-commercial agreement;
        (ii)    a small agreement; or
        (iii)    a green deal plan [. . .].

(12B)    An agreement falls within this subsection if—
    (a)    it is a regulated consumer hire agreement; and
    (b)    it is neither a non-commercial agreement nor a small agreement.]

[(13)    In this section—
    (a)    'payments' in relation to an applicable agreement which is a regulated agreement for fixed-sum credit means payments to be made at predetermined intervals provided for under the terms of the agreement; and
    (b)    'payments' in relation to an applicable agreement which is a regulated consumer hire agreement means any payments to be made by the hirer in relation to any period in consideration of the bailment or hiring to him of goods under the agreement.]]

### [86C    Notice of sums in arrears under running-account credit agreements

(1)    This section applies where at any time the following conditions are satisfied—
    (a)    that the debtor under an applicable agreement is required to have made at least two payments under the agreement before that time;
    (b)    that the last two payments which he is required to have made before that time have not been made;

(c)    that the creditor has not already been required to give a notice under this section in relation to either of those payments; and

(d)    if a judgment has been given in relation to the agreement before that time, that there is no sum still to be paid under the judgment by the debtor.

(2)    The creditor shall, no later than the end of the period within which he is next required to give a statement under section 78(4) in relation to the agreement, give the debtor a notice under this section.

(3)    The notice shall include a copy of the current arrears information sheet under section 86A.

(4)    The notice may be incorporated in a statement or other notice which the creditor gives the debtor in relation to the agreement by virtue of another provision of this Act.

(5)    The debtor shall have no liability to pay any sum in connection with the preparation or the giving to him of the notice.

(6)    Regulations may make provision about the form and content of notices under this section.

(7)    In this section 'applicable agreement' means an agreement which—

(a)    is a regulated agreement for running-account credit; and

(b)    is neither a non-commercial agreement nor a small agreement.

[(8)    In this section 'payments' means payments to be made at predetermined intervals provided for under the terms of the agreement.]]

**[86D    Failure to give notice of sums in arrears**

(1)    This section applies where the creditor or owner under an agreement is under a duty to give the debtor or hirer notices under section 86B but fails to give him such a notice—

(a)    within the period mentioned in subsection (2)(a) of that section; or

(b)    within the period of six months beginning with the day after the day on which such a notice was last given to him.

(2)    This section also applies where the creditor under an agreement is under a duty to give the debtor a notice under section 86C but fails to do so before the end of the period mentioned in subsection (2) of that section.

(3)    The creditor or owner shall not be entitled to enforce the agreement during the period of non-compliance.

(4)    The debtor or hirer shall have no liability to pay—

(a)    any sum of interest to the extent calculated by reference to the period of non-compliance or to any part of it; or

(b)    any default sum which (apart from this paragraph)—

(i)    would have become payable during the period of non-compliance; or

(ii)    would have become payable after the end of that period in connection with a breach of the agreement which occurs during that period (whether or not the breach continues after the end of that period).

(5)    In this section 'the period of non-compliance' means, in relation to a failure to give a notice under section 86B or 86C to the debtor or hirer, the period which—

(a)    begins immediately after the end of the period mentioned in (as the case may be) subsection (1)(a) or (b) or (2); and

(b)    ends at the end of the day mentioned in subsection (6).

(6)    That day is—

(a)    in the case of a failure to give a notice under section 86B as mentioned in subsection (1)(a) of this section, the day on which the notice is given to the debtor or hirer;

(b)    in the case of a failure to give a notice under that section as mentioned in subsection (1)(b) of this section, the earlier of the following—

(i)    the day on which the notice is given to the debtor or hirer;

(ii)    the day on which the condition mentioned in subsection (4)(a) of that section is satisfied;

(c)   in the case of a failure to give a notice under section 86C, the day on which the notice is given to the debtor.]

**[86E   Notice of default sums**

(1)   This section applies where a default sum becomes payable under a regulated agreement by the debtor or hirer.

(2)   The creditor or owner shall, within the prescribed period after the default sum becomes payable, give the debtor or hirer a notice under this section.

(3)   The notice under this section may be incorporated in a statement or other notice which the creditor or owner gives the debtor or hirer in relation to the agreement by virtue of another provision of this Act.

(4)   The debtor or hirer shall have no liability to pay interest in connection with the default sum to the extent that the interest is calculated by reference to a period occurring before the 29th day after the day on which the debtor or hirer is given the notice under this section.

(5)   If the creditor or owner fails to give the debtor or hirer the notice under this section within the period mentioned in subsection (2), he shall not be entitled to enforce the agreement until the notice is given to the debtor or hirer.

(6)   The debtor or hirer shall have no liability to pay any sum in connection with the preparation or the giving to him of the notice under this section.

(7)   Regulations may—

(a)   provide that this section does not apply in relation to a default sum which is less than a prescribed amount;

(b)   make provision about the form and content of notices under this section.

(8)   This section does not apply in relation to a non-commercial agreement or to a small agreement.]

**[86F   Interest on default sums**

(1)   This section applies where a default sum becomes payable under a regulated agreement by the debtor or hirer.

(2)   The debtor or hirer shall only be liable to pay interest in connection with the default sum if the interest is simple interest.]]

*Default notices*

**87   Need for default notice**

(1)   Service of a notice on the debtor or hirer in accordance with section 88 (a 'default notice') is necessary before the creditor or owner can become entitled, by reason of any breach by the debtor or hirer of a regulated agreement,—

(a)   to terminate the agreement, or

(b)   to demand earlier payment of any sum, or

(c)   to recover possession of any goods or land, or

(d)   to treat any right conferred on the debtor or hirer by the agreement as terminated, restricted or deferred, or

(e)   to enforce any security.

(2)   Subsection (1) does not prevent the creditor from treating the right to draw upon any credit as restricted or deferred, and taking such steps as may be necessary to make the restriction or deferment effective.

(3)   The doing of an act by which a floating charge becomes fixed is not enforcement of a security.

(4)   Regulations may provide that section (1) is not to apply to agreements described by the regulations.

[(5)   Subsection (1)(d) does not apply in a case referred to in section 98A(4) (termination or suspension of debtor's right to draw on credit under open-end agreement).]

**88   Contents and effect of default notice**

(1)   The default notice must be in the prescribed form and specify—

(a)   the nature of the alleged breach;

(b)   if the breach is capable of remedy, what action is required to remedy it and the date before which that action is to be taken;

(c)   if the breach is not capable of remedy, the sum (if any) required to be paid as compensation for the breach, and the date before which it is to be paid.

(2)   A date specified under subsection (1) must not be less than [14] days after the date of service of the default notice, and the creditor or owner shall not take action such as is mentioned in section 87(1) before the date so specified or (if no requirement is made under subsection (1)) before those [14] days have elapsed.

(3)   The default notice must not treat as a breach failure to comply with a provision of the agreement which becomes operative only on breach of some other provision, but if the breach of that other provision is not duly remedied or compensation demanded under subsection (1) is not duly paid, or (where no requirement is made under subsection (1)) if the [14] days mentioned in subsection (2) have elapsed, the creditor or owner may treat the failure as a breach and section 87(1) shall not apply to it.

(4)   The default notice must contain information in the prescribed terms about the consequences of failure to comply with it [and any other prescribed matters relating to the agreement].

[(4A)   The default notice must also include a copy of the current default information sheet under section 86A.]

(5)   A default notice making a requirement under subsection (1) may include a provision for the taking of action such as is mentioned in section 87(1) at any time after the restriction imposed by subsection (2) will cease, together with a statement that the provision will be ineffective if the breach is duly remedied or the compensation duly paid.

### 89   Compliance with default notice
If before the date specified for that purpose in the default notice the debtor or hirer takes the action specified under section 88(1)(b) or (c) the breach shall be treated as not having occurred.

*Further restriction of remedies for default*

### 90   Retaking of protected hire-purchase etc goods
(1)   At any time when—

(a)   the debtor is in breach of a regulated hire-purchase or a regulated conditional sale agreement relating to goods, and

(b)   the debtor has paid to the creditor one-third or more of the total price of the goods, and

(c)   the property in the goods remains in the creditor,

the creditor is not entitled to recover possession of the goods from the debtor except on an order of the court.

(2)   Where under a hire-purchase or conditional sale agreement the creditor is required to carry out any installation and the agreement specifies, as part of the total price, the amount to be paid in respect of the installation (the 'installation charge') the reference in subsection (1)(b) to one-third of the total price shall be construed as a reference to the aggregate of the installation charge and one-third of the remainder of the total price.

(3)   In a case where—

(a)   subsection (1)(a) is satisfied, but not subsection (1)(b), and

(b)   subsection (1)(b) was satisfied on a previous occasion in relation to an earlier agreement, being a regulated hire-purchase or regulated conditional sale agreement, between the same parties, and relating to any of the goods comprised in the later agreement (whether or not other goods were also included),

subsection (1) shall apply to the later agreement with the omission of paragraph (b).

(4)   If the later agreement is a modifying agreement, subsection (3) shall apply with the substitution, for the second reference to the later agreement, of a reference to the modifying agreement.

(5)   Subsection (1) shall not apply, or shall cease to apply, to an agreement if the debtor has terminated, or terminates, the agreement.

(6)   Where subsection (1) applies to an agreement at the death of the debtor, it shall continue to apply (in relation to the possessor of the goods) until the grant of probate or administration, or (in Scotland) confirmation (on which the personal representative would fall to be treated as the debtor).

(7)   Goods falling within this section are in this Act referred to as 'protected goods'.

## 91   Consequences of breach of s 90

If goods are recovered by the creditor in contravention of section 90—

(a)   the regulated agreement, if not previously terminated, shall terminate, and

(b)   the debtor shall be released from all liability under the agreement, and shall be entitled to recover from the creditor all sums paid by the debtor under the agreement.

## 92   Recovery of possession of goods or land

(1)   Except under an order of the court, the creditor or owner shall not be entitled to enter any premises to take possession of goods subject to a regulated hire-purchase agreement, regulated conditional sale agreement or regulated consumer hire agreement.

(2)   At any time when the debtor is in breach of a regulated conditional sale agreement relating to land, the creditor is entitled to recover possession of the land from the debtor, or any person claiming under him, on an order of the court only.

(3)   An entry in contravention of subsection (1) or (2) is actionable as a breach of statutory duty.

## 93   Interest not to be increased on default

The debtor under a regulated consumer credit agreement shall not be obliged to pay interest on sums which, in breach of the agreement, are unpaid by him at a rate—

(a)   where the total charge for credit includes an item in respect of interest, exceeding the rate of that interest, or

(b)   in any other case, exceeding what would be the rate of the total charge for credit if any items included in the total charge for credit by virtue of [rules made by the FCA under paragraph (2)(d) of article 60M of the Regulated Activities Order] were disregarded.

## [93A   Summary diligence not competent in Scotland

Summary diligence shall not be competent in Scotland to enforce payment of a debt due under a regulated agreement or under any security related thereto.]

*Early payment by debtor*

## 94   Right to complete payments ahead of time

(1)   The debtor under a regulated consumer credit agreement is entitled at any time, by notice to the creditor and the payment to the creditor of all amounts payable by the debtor to him under the agreement [and any amount which the creditor claims under section 95A(2)] [or section 95B(2)] (less any rebate allowable under section 95), to discharge the debtor's indebtedness under the agreement.

(2)   A notice under subsection (1) may embody the exercise by the debtor of any option to purchase goods conferred on him by the agreement, and deal with any other matter arising on, or in relation to, the termination of the agreement.

[(3)   The debtor under a regulated consumer credit agreement, other than an agreement secured on land, is entitled at any time to discharge part of his indebtedness by taking the steps in subsection (4).

(4) The steps referred to in subsection (3) are as follows—

(a) he provides notice to the creditor,

(b) he pays to the creditor some of the amount payable by him to the creditor under the agreement before the time fixed by the agreement, and

(c) he makes the payment—

(i) before the end of the period of 28 days beginning with the day following that on which notice under paragraph (a) was received by the creditor, or

(ii) on or before any later date specified in the notice.

(5) Where a debtor takes the steps in subsection (4) his indebtedness shall be discharged by an amount equal to the sum of the amount paid and any rebate allowable under section 95 less any amount which the creditor claims under section 95A(2) [or section 95B(2)].

(6) A notice—

(a) under subsection (1), other than a notice relating to a regulated consumer credit agreement secured on land, or

(b) under subsection (4)(a),

need not be in writing.]

## 95 Rebate on early settlement

(1) Regulations may provide for the allowance of a rebate of charges for credit to the debtor under a regulated consumer credit agreement where, under section 94, on refinancing, on breach of the agreement, or for any other reason, his indebtedness is discharged [or is discharged in part] or becomes payable before the time fixed by the agreement, or any sum becomes payable by him before the time so fixed.

(2) Regulations under subsection (1) may provide for calculation of the rebate by reference to any sums paid or payable by the debtor or his relative under or in connection with the agreement (whether to the creditor or some other person), including sums under linked transactions and other items in the total charge for credit.

## [95A Compensatory amount

(1) This section applies where—

(a) a regulated consumer credit agreement, other than an agreement secured on land, provides for the rate of interest on the credit to be fixed for a period of time, and

(b) under section 94 the debtor discharges all or part of his indebtedness during that period.

(2) The creditor may claim an amount equal to the cost which the creditor has incurred as a result only of the debtor's indebtedness being discharged during that period if—

(a) the amount of the payment under section 94 exceeds £8,000 or, where more than one such payment is made in any 12 month period, the total of those payments exceeds £8,000,

(b) the agreement is not a debtor-creditor agreement enabling the debtor to overdraw on a current account, and

(c) the amount of the payment under section 94 is not paid from the proceeds of a contract of payment protection insurance.

(3) The amount in subsection (2)—

(a) must be fair,

(b) must be objectively justified, and

(c) must not exceed whichever is the higher of—

(i) the relevant percentage of the amount of the payment under section 94, and

(ii) the total amount of interest that would have been paid by the debtor under the agreement in the period from the date on which the debtor makes the payment under section 94 to the date fixed by the agreement for the discharge of the indebtedness of the debtor.

(4) In subsection (3)(c)(i) 'relevant percentage' means—

(a) 1%, where the period from the date on which the debtor makes the payment under section 94 to the date fixed by the agreement for the discharge of the indebtedness of the debtor is more than one year, or

(b) 0.5%, where that period is equal to or less than one year.]

### [95B  Compensatory amount: green deal finance

(1) This section applies where—

(a) a regulated consumer credit agreement provides for the rate of interest on the credit to be fixed for a period of time ('the fixed rate period'),

(b) the agreement is a green deal plan [. . .] which is of a duration specified for the purposes of this section in regulations, and

(c) under section 94 the debtor discharges all or part of his indebtedness during the fixed rate period.

(2) The creditor may claim an amount equal to the cost which the creditor has incurred as a result only of the debtor's indebtedness being discharged during the fixed rate period if—

(a) the amount of the payment under section 94 is not paid from the proceeds of a contract of payment protection insurance, and

(b) such other conditions as may be specified for the purposes of this section in regulations are satisfied.

(3) The amount in subsection (2)—

(a)    must be fair,

(b)    must be objectively justified,

(c)    must be calculated by the creditor in accordance with provision made for the purposes of this section in regulations, and

(d)    must not exceed the total amount of interest that would have been paid by the debtor under the agreement in the period from the date on which the debtor makes the payment under section 94 to the date fixed by the agreement for the discharge of the indebtedness of the debtor.

(4) If a creditor could claim under either section 95A or this section, the creditor may choose under which section to claim.]

### 96  Effect on linked transactions

(1) Where for any reason the indebtedness of the debtor under a regulated consumer credit agreement is discharged before the time fixed by the agreement, he, and any relative of his, shall at the same time be discharged from any liability under a linked transaction, other than a debt which has already become payable.

(2) Subsection (1) does not apply to a linked transaction which is itself an agreement providing the debtor or his relative with credit.

(3) Regulations may exclude linked transactions of the prescribed description from the operation of subsection (1).

### 97  Duty to give information

(1) The creditor under a regulated consumer credit agreement, within the prescribed period after he has received a request [. . .] to that effect from the debtor, shall give the debtor a statement in the prescribed form indicating, according to the information to which it is practicable for him to refer, the amount of the payment required to discharge the debtor's indebtedness under the agreement, together with the prescribed particulars showing how the amount is arrived at.

(2) Subsection (1) does not apply to a request made less than one month after a previous request under that subsection relating to the same agreement was complied with.

[(2A)   A request under subsection (1) need not be in writing unless the agreement is secured on land.]

(3)   If the creditor fails to comply with subsection (1)—

(a)   he is not entitled, while the default continues, to enforce the agreement [. . .]

### [97A   Duty to give information on partial repayment

(1)   Where a debtor under a regulated consumer credit agreement—

(a)   makes a payment by virtue of which part of his indebtedness is discharged under section 94, and

(b)   at the same time or subsequently requests the creditor to give him a statement concerning the effect of the payment on the debtor's indebtedness,

the creditor must give the statement to the debtor before the end of the period of seven working days beginning with the day following that on which the creditor receives the request.

(2)   The statement shall be in writing and shall contain the following particulars—

(a)   a description of the agreement sufficient to identify it,

(b)   the name, postal address and, where appropriate, any other address of the creditor and the debtor,

(c)   where the creditor is claiming an amount under section 95A(2) [or section 95B(2)], that amount and the method used to determine it,

(d)   the amount of any rebate to which the debtor is entitled—

(i)   under the agreement, or

(ii)   by virtue of section 95 where that is higher,

(e)   where the amount of the rebate mentioned in paragraph (d)(ii) is given, a statement indicating that this amount has been calculated having regard to the Consumer Credit (Early Settlement) Regulations 2004,

(f)   where the debtor is not entitled to any rebate, a statement to this effect,

(g)   any change to—

(i)   the number, timing or amount of repayments to be made under the agreement, or

(ii)   the duration of the agreement,

which results from the partial discharge of the indebtedness of the debtor, and

(h)   the amount of the debtor's indebtedness remaining under the agreement at the date the creditor gives the statement.]

*Termination of agreements*

### 98   Duty to give notice of termination (non-default cases)

(1)   The creditor or owner is not entitled to terminate a regulated agreement except by or after giving the debtor or hirer not less than seven days' notice of the termination.

(2)   Subsection (1) applies only where—

(a)   a period for the duration of the agreement is specified in the agreement, and

(b)   that period has not ended when the creditor or owner does an act mentioned in subsection (1),

but so applies notwithstanding that, under the agreement, any party is entitled to terminate it before the end of the period so specified.

(3)   A notice under subsection (1) is ineffective if not in the prescribed form.

(4)   Subsection (1) does not prevent a creditor from treating the right to draw on any credit as restricted or deferred and taking such steps as may be necessary to make the restriction or deferment effective.

(5)   Regulations may provide that subsection (1) is not to apply to agreements described by the regulations.

(6)  Subsection (1) does not apply to the termination of a regulated agreement by reason of any breach by the debtor or hirer of the agreement.

## [98A  Termination etc of open-end consumer credit agreements

(1)  The debtor under a regulated open-end consumer credit agreement, other than an excluded agreement, may by notice terminate the agreement, free of charge, at any time, subject to any period of notice not exceeding one month provided for by the agreement.

(2)  Notice under subsection (1) need not be in writing unless the creditor so requires.

(3)  Where a regulated open-end consumer credit agreement, other than an excluded agreement, provides for termination of the agreement by the creditor—

  (a)  the termination must be by notice served on the debtor, and

  (b)  the termination may not take effect until after the end of the period of two months, or such longer period as the agreement may provide, beginning with the day after the day on which notice is served.

(4)  Where a regulated open-end consumer credit agreement, other than an excluded agreement, provides for termination or suspension by the creditor of the debtor's right to draw on credit—

  (a)  to terminate or suspend the right to draw on credit the creditor must serve a notice on the debtor before the termination or suspension or, if that is not practicable, immediately afterwards,

  (b)  the notice must give reasons for the termination or suspension, and

  (c)  the reasons must be objectively justified.

(5)  Subsection (4)(a) and (b) does not apply where giving the notice—

  (a)  is prohibited by an EU obligation, or

  (b)  would, or would be likely to, prejudice—

    (i)  the prevention or detection of crime,

    (ii)  the apprehension or prosecution of offenders, or

    (iii)  the administration of justice.

(6)  An objectively justified reason under subsection (4)(c) may, for example, relate to—

  (a)  the unauthorised or fraudulent use of credit, or

  (b)  a significantly increased risk of the debtor being unable to fulfil his obligation to repay the credit.

(7)  Subsections (1) and (3) do not affect any right to terminate an agreement for breach of contract.

(8)  For the purposes of this section an agreement is an excluded agreement if it is—

  (a)  an authorised non-business overdraft agreement,

  (b)  an authorised business overdraft agreement,

  (c)  a debtor-creditor agreement arising where the holder of a current account overdraws on the account without a pre-arranged overdraft or exceeds a pre-arranged overdraft limit, or

  (d)  an agreement secured on land.]

## 99  Right to terminate hire-purchase etc agreements

(1)  At any time before the final payment by the debtor under a regulated hire-purchase or regulated conditional sale agreement falls due, the debtor shall be entitled to terminate the agreement by giving notice to any person entitled or authorised to receive the sums payable under the agreement.

(2)  Termination of an agreement under subsection (1) does not affect any liability under the agreement which has accrued before the termination.

(3)  Subsection (1) does not apply to a conditional sale agreement relating to land after the title to the land has passed to the debtor.

(4)  In the case of a conditional sale agreement relating to goods, where the property in the goods, having become vested in the debtor, is transferred to a

person who does not become the debtor under the agreement, the debtor shall not thereafter be entitled to terminate the agreement under subsection (1).

(5)   Subject to subsection (4), where a debtor under a conditional sale agreement relating to goods terminates the agreement under this section after the property in the goods has become vested in him, the property in the goods shall thereupon vest in the person (the 'previous owner') in whom it was vested immediately before it became vested in the debtor:

Provided that if the previous owner has died, or any other event has occurred whereby that property, if vested in him immediately before that event, would thereupon have vested in some other person, the property shall be treated as having devolved as if it had been vested in the previous owner immediately before his death or immediately before that event, as the case may be.

## 100   Liability of debtor on termination of hire-purchase etc agreement

(1)   Where a regulated hire-purchase or regulated conditional sale agreement is terminated under section 99 the debtor shall be liable, unless the agreement provides for a smaller payment, or does not provide for any payment, to pay to the creditor the amount (if any) by which one-half of the total price exceeds the aggregate of the sums paid and the sums due in respect of the total price immediately before the termination.

(2)   Where under a hire-purchase or conditional sale agreement the creditor is required to carry out any installation and the agreement specifies, as part of the total price, the amount to be paid in respect of the installation (the 'installation charge') the reference in subsection (1) to one-half of the total price shall be construed as a reference to the aggregate of the installation charge and one-half of the remainder of the total price.

(3)   If in any action the court is satisfied that a sum less than the amount specified in subsection (1) would be equal to the loss sustained by the creditor in consequence of the termination of the agreement by the debtor, the court may make an order for the payment of that sum in lieu of the amount specified in subsection (1).

(4)   If the debtor has contravened an obligation to take reasonable care of the goods or land, the amount arrived at under subsection (1) shall be increased by the sum required to recompense the creditor for that contravention, and subsection (2) shall have effect accordingly.

(5)   Where the debtor, on the termination of the agreement, wrongfully retains possession of goods to which the agreement relates, then, in any action brought by the creditor to recover possession of the goods from the debtor, the court, unless it is satisfied that having regard to the circumstances it would not be just to do so, shall order the goods to be delivered to the creditor without giving the debtor an option to pay the value of the goods.

## 101   Right to terminate hire agreement

(1)   The hirer under a regulated consumer hire agreement is entitled to terminate the agreement by giving notice to any person entitled or authorised to receive the sums payable under the agreement.

(2)   Termination of an agreement under subsection (1) does not affect any liability under the agreement which has accrued before the termination.

(3)   A notice under subsection (1) shall not expire earlier than eighteen months after the making of the agreement, but apart from that the minimum period of notice to be given under subsection (1), unless the agreement provides for a shorter period, is as follows.

(4)   If the agreement provides for the making of payments by the hirer to the owner at equal intervals, the minimum period of notice is the length of one interval or three months, whichever is less.

(5)   If the agreement provides for the making of such payments at differing in-

tervals, the minimum period of notice is the length of the shortest interval or three months, whichever is less.

(6)   In any other case, the minimum period of notice is three months.

(7)   This section does not apply to—

(a)   any agreement which provides for the making by the hirer of payments which in total (and without breach of the agreement) exceed [£1,500] in any year, or

(b)   any agreement where—

(i)   goods are bailed or (in Scotland) hired to the hirer for the purposes of a business carried on by him, or the hirer holds himself out as requiring the goods for those purposes, and

(ii)   the goods are selected by the hirer, and acquired by the owner for the purposes of the agreement at the request of the hirer from any person other than the owner's associate, or

(c)   any agreement where the hirer requires, or holds himself out as requiring, the goods for the purpose of bailing or hiring them to other persons in the course of a business carried on by him.

(8)   If, on an application made to the [FCA] by a person carrying on a consumer hire business, it appears to the [FCA] that it would be in the interest of hirers to do so, [it] may [. . .] direct that [, subject to such conditions (if any) as it may specify, this section shall not apply to consumer hire agreements made by the applicant; and this Act shall have effect accordingly].

[(8A)   If it appears to the [FCA] that it would be in the interest of hirers to do so, it may [. . .] direct that, subject to such conditions (if any) as it may specify, this section shall not apply to a consumer hire agreement if the agreement falls within a specified description; and this Act shall have effect accordingly.]

(9)   In the case of a modifying agreement, subsection (3) shall apply with the substitution for 'the making of the agreement' of 'the making of the original agreement'.

## 102   Agency for receiving notice of rescission

(1)   Where the debtor or hirer under a regulated agreement claims to have a right to rescind the agreement, each of the following shall be deemed to be the agent of the creditor or owner for the purpose of receiving any notice rescinding the agreement which is served by the debtor or hirer—

(a)   a credit-broker or supplier who was the negotiator in antecedent negotiations, and

(b)   any person who, in the course of a business carried on by him, acted on behalf of the debtor or hirer in any negotiations for the agreement.

(2)   In subsection (1) 'rescind' does not include—

(a)   service of a notice of cancellation, or

(b)   termination of an agreement under section 99 or 101 or by the exercise of a right or power in that behalf expressly conferred by the agreement.

## 103   Termination statements

(1)   If an individual (the 'customer') serves on any person (the 'trader') a notice—

(a)   stating that—

(i)   the customer was the debtor or hirer under a regulated agreement described in the notice, and the trader was the creditor or owner under the agreement, and

(ii)   the customer has discharged his indebtedness to the trader under the agreement, and

(iii)   the agreement has ceased to have any operation; and

(b)   requiring the trader to give the customer a notice, signed by or on behalf of the trader, confirming that those statements are correct, the trader shall, within the prescribed period after receiving the notice, either comply with it or serve on the customer a counter-notice stating that, as the case may be, he disputes the correctness of the notice or asserts that the customer is not indebted to him under the agreement.

(2) Where the trader disputes the correctness of the notice he shall give particulars of the way in which he alleges it to be wrong.

(3) Subsection (1) does not apply in relation to any agreement if the trader has previously complied with that subsection on the service of a notice under it with respect to that agreement.

(4) Subsection (1) does not apply to a non-commercial agreement.

[. . .]

[(6) A breach of the duty imposed by subsection (1) is actionable as a breach of statutory duty.]

## 104 Goods not to be treated as subject to landlord's hypothec in Scotland

Goods comprised in a hire-purchase agreement or goods comprised in a conditional sale agreement which have not become vested in the debtor shall not be treated in Scotland as subject to the landlord's hypothec—

(a) during the period between the service of a default notice in respect of the goods and the date on which the notice expires or is earlier complied with; or

(b) if the agreement is enforceable on an order of the court only, during the period between the commencement and termination of an action by the creditor to enforce the agreement.

PART VIII
SECURITY

*General*

## 105 Form and content of securities

(1) Any security provided in relation to a regulated agreement shall be expressed in writing.

(2) Regulations may prescribe the form and content of documents ('security instruments') to be made in compliance with subsection (1).

(3) Regulations under subsection (2) may in particular—

(a) require specified information to be included in the prescribed manner in documents, and other specified material to be excluded;

(b) contain requirements to ensure that specified information is clearly brought to the attention of the surety, and that one part of a document is not given insufficient or excessive prominence compared with another.

(4) A security instrument is not properly executed unless—

(a) a document in the prescribed form, itself containing all the prescribed terms and conforming to regulations under subsection (2), is signed in the prescribed manner by or on behalf of the surety, and

(b) the document embodies all the terms of the security, other than implied terms, and

(c) the document, when presented or sent for the purpose of being signed by or on behalf of the surety, is in such state that its terms are readily legible, and

(d) when the document is presented or sent for the purpose of being signed by or on behalf of the surety there is also presented or sent a copy of the document.

(5) A security instrument is not properly executed unless—

(a) where the security is provided after, or at the time when, the regulated agreement is made, a copy of the executed agreement, together with a copy of any other document referred to in it, is given to the surety at the time the security is provided, or

(b)   where the security is provided before the regulated agreement is made, a copy of the executed agreement, together with a copy of any other document referred to in it, is given to the surety within seven days after the regulated agreement is made.

(6)   Subsection (1) does not apply to a security provided by the debtor or hirer.

(7)   If—

(a)   in contravention of subsection (1) a security is not expressed in writing, or

(b)   a security instrument is improperly executed,

the security, so far as provided in relation to a regulated agreement, is enforceable against the surety on an order of the court only.

(8)   If an application for an order under subsection (7) is dismissed (except on technical grounds only) section 106 (ineffective securities) shall apply to the security.

(9)   Regulations under section 60(1) shall include provision requiring documents embodying regulated agreements also to embody any security provided in relation to a regulated agreement by the debtor or hirer.

## 106   Ineffective securities

Where, under any provision of this Act, this section is applied to any security provided in relation to a regulated agreement, then, subject to section 177 (saving for registered charges)—

(a)   the security, so far as it is so provided, shall be treated as never having effect;

(b)   any property lodged with the creditor or owner solely for the purposes of the security as so provided shall be returned by him forthwith;

(c)   the creditor or owner shall take any necessary action to remove or cancel an entry in any register, so far as the entry relates to the security as so provided; and

(d)   any amount received by the creditor or owner on realisation of the security shall, so far as it is referable to the agreement, be repaid to the surety.

## 107   Duty to give information to surety under fixed-sum credit agreement

(1)   The creditor under a regulated agreement for fixed-sum credit in relation to which security is provided, within the prescribed period after receiving a request in writing to that effect from the surety and payment of a fee of [£1], shall give to the surety (if a different person from the debtor)—

(a)   a copy of the executed agreement (if any) and of any other document referred to in it;

(b)   a copy of the security instrument (if any); and

(c)   a statement signed by or on behalf of the creditor showing, according to the information to which it is practicable for him to refer,—

(i)   the total sum paid under the agreement by the debtor,

(ii)   the total sum which has become payable under the agreement by the debtor but remains unpaid, and the various amounts comprised in that total sum, with the date when each became due, and

(iii)   the total sum which is to become payable under the agreement by the debtor, and the various amounts comprised in that total sum, with the date, or mode of determining the date, when each becomes due.

(2)   If the creditor possesses insufficient information to enable him to ascertain the amounts and dates mentioned in subsection (1)(c)(iii), he shall be taken to comply with that sub-paragraph if his statement under subsection (1)(c) gives the basis on which, under the regulated agreement, they would fall to be ascertained.

(3)   Subsection (1) does not apply to—

(a)   an agreement under which no sum is, or will or may become, payable by the debtor, or

(b)   a request made less than one month after a previous request under that subsection relating to the same agreement was complied with.

(4)   If the creditor under an agreement fails to comply with subsection (1)—

(a)   he is not entitled, while the default continues, to enforce the security, so far as provided in relation to the agreement [. . .]

(5)   This section does not apply to a non-commercial agreement.

## 108   Duty to give information to surety under running-account credit agreement

(1)   The creditor under a regulated agreement for running-account credit in relation to which security is provided, within the prescribed period after receiving a request in writing to that effect from the surety and payment of a fee of [£1], shall give to the surety (if a different person from the debtor)—

(a)   a copy of the executed agreement (if any) and of any other document referred to in it;

(b)   a copy of the security instrument (if any); and

(c)   a statement signed by or on behalf of the creditor showing, according to the information to which it is practicable for him to refer,—

(i)   the state of the account, and

(ii)   the amount if any, currently payable under the agreement by the debtor to the creditor, and

(iii)   the amounts and due dates of any payments which, if the debtor does not draw further on the account, will later become payable under the agreement by the debtor to the creditor.

(2)   If the creditor possesses insufficient information to enable him to ascertain the amounts and dates mentioned in subsection (1)(c)(iii), he shall be taken to comply with that sub-paragraph if his statement under subsection (1)(c) gives the basis on which, under the regulated agreement, they would fall to be ascertained.

(3)   Subsection (1) does not apply to—

(a)   an agreement under which no sum is, or will or may become, payable by the debtor, or

(b)   a request made less than one month after a previous request under that subsection relating to the same agreement was complied with.

(4)   If the creditor under an agreement fails to comply with subsection (1)—

(a)   he is not entitled, while the default continues, to enforce the security, so far as provided in relation to the agreement [. . .]

(5)   This section does not apply to a non-commercial agreement.

## 109   Duty to give information to surety under consumer hire agreement

(1)   The owner under a regulated consumer hire agreement in relation to which security is provided, within the prescribed period after receiving a request in writing to that effect from the surety and payment of a fee of [£1], shall give to the surety (if a different person from the hirer)—

(a)   a copy of the executed agreement and of any other document referred to in it;

(b)   a copy of the security instrument (if any); and

(c)   a statement signed by or on behalf of the owner showing, according to the information to which it is practicable for him to refer, the total sum which has become payable under the agreement by the hirer but remains unpaid and the various amounts comprised in that total sum, with the date when each became due.

(2)   Subsection (1) does not apply to—

(a)   an agreement under which no sum is, or will or may become, payable by the hirer, or

(b)    a request made less than one month after a previous request under that subsection relating to the same agreement was complied with.

(3)    If the owner under an agreement fails to comply with subsection (1)—

(a)    he is not entitled, while the default continues, to enforce the security, so far as provided in relation to the agreement [. . .]

(4)    This section does not apply to a non-commercial agreement.

### 110    Duty to give information to debtor or hirer

(1)    The creditor or owner under a regulated agreement, within the prescribed period after receiving a request in writing to that effect from the debtor or hirer and payment of a fee of [£1], shall give the debtor or hirer a copy of any security instrument executed in relation to the agreement after the making of the agreement.

(2)    Subsection (1) does not apply to—

(a)    a non-commercial agreement, or

(b)    an agreement under which no sum is, or will or may become, payable by the debtor or hirer, or

(c)    a request made less than one month after a previous request under subsection (1) relating to the same agreement was complied with.

(3)    If the creditor or owner under an agreement fails to comply with subsection (1)—

(a)    he is not entitled, while the default continues, to enforce the security (so far as provided in relation to the agreement) [. . .]

### 111    Duty to give surety copy of default etc notice

(1)    When a default notice or a notice under section 76(1) or 98(1) is served on a debtor or hirer, a copy of the notice shall be served by the creditor or owner on any surety (if a different person from the debtor or hirer).

(2)    If the creditor or owner fails to comply with subsection (1) in the case of any surety, the security is enforceable against the surety (in respect of the breach or other matter to which the notice relates) on an order of the court only.

[. . .]

### 113    Act not to be evaded by use of security

(1)    Where a security is provided in relation to an actual or prospective regulated agreement, the security shall not be enforced so as to benefit the creditor or owner, directly or indirectly, to an extent greater (whether as respects the amount of any payment or the time or manner of its being made) than would be the case if the security were not provided and any obligations of the debtor or hirer, or his relative, under or in relation to the agreement were carried out to the extent (if any) to which they would be enforced under this Act.

(2)    In accordance with subsection (1), where a regulated agreement is enforceable on an order of the court or the [FCA] only, any security provided in relation to the agreement is enforceable (so far as provided in relation to the agreement) where such an order has been made in relation to the agreement, but not otherwise.

(3)    Where—

(a)    a regulated agreement is cancelled under section 69(1) or becomes subject to section 69(2), or

(b)    a regulated agreement is terminated under section 91, or

(c)    in relation to any agreement an application for an order under section [65(1) or 124(1) or a notice under section 28A of the Financial Services and Markets Act 2000] is dismissed (except on technical grounds only), or

(d)    a declaration is made by the court under section 142(1) (refusal of enforcement order) as respects any regulated agreement,

section 106 shall apply to any security provided in relation to the agreement.

(4)   Where subsection (3)(d) applies and the declaration relates to a part only of the regulated agreement, section 106 shall apply to the security only so far as it concerns that part.

(5)   In the case of a cancelled agreement, the duty imposed on the debtor or hirer by section 71 or 72 shall not be enforceable before the creditor or owner has discharged any duty imposed on him by section 106 (as applied by subsection (3)(a)).

(6)   If the security is provided in relation to a prospective agreement or transaction, the security shall be enforceable in relation to the agreement or transaction only after the time (if any) when the agreement is made; and until that time the person providing the security shall be entitled, by notice to the creditor or owner, to require that section 106 shall thereupon apply to the security.

(7)   Where an indemnity [or guarantee] is given in a case where the debtor or hirer is a minor, or [an indemnity is given in a case where he] is otherwise not of full capacity, the reference in subsection (1) to the extent to which his obligations would be enforced shall be read in relation to the indemnity [or guarantee] as a reference to the extent to which [those obligations] would be enforced if he were of full capacity.

(8)   Subsections (1) and (3) also apply where a security is provided in relation to an actual or prospective linked transaction, and in that case—

(a)   references to the agreement shall be read as references to the linked transaction, and

(b)   references to the creditor or owner shall be read as references to any person (other than the debtor or hirer, or his relative) who is a party, or prospective party, to the linked transaction.

*Pledges*

### 114   Pawn-receipts

(1)   At the time he receives the article, a person who takes any article in pawn under a regulated agreement shall give to the person from whom he receives it a receipt in the prescribed form (a 'pawn-receipt').

(2)   A person who takes any article in pawn from an individual whom he knows to be, or who appears to be and is, a minor commits an offence.

(3)   This section and sections [117] to 122 do not apply to—

(a)   a pledge of documents of title [or of bearer bonds], or

(b)   a non-commercial agreement.

[. . .]

### 116   Redemption period

(1)   A pawn is redeemable at any time within six months after it was taken.

(2)   Subject to subsection (1), the period within which a pawn is redeemable shall be the same as the period fixed by the parties for the duration of the credit secured by the pledge, or such longer period as they may agree.

(3)   If the pawn is not redeemed by the end of the period laid down by subsections (1) and (2) (the 'redemption period'), it nevertheless remains redeemable until it is realised by the pawnee under section 121 except where under section 120(1)(a) the property in it passes to the pawnee.

(4)   No special charge shall be made for redemption of a pawn after the end of the redemption period, and charges in respect of the safe keeping of the pawn shall not be at a higher rate after the end of the redemption period than before.

### 117   Redemption procedure

(1)   On surrender of the pawn-receipt, and payment of the amount owing, at any time when the pawn is redeemable, the pawnee shall deliver the pawn to the bearer of the pawn-receipt.

(2)   Subsection (1) does not apply if the pawnee knows or has reasonable cause to suspect that the bearer of the pawn-receipt is neither the owner of the pawn nor authorised by the owner to redeem it.

(3)   The pawnee is not liable to any person in tort or delict for delivering the pawn where subsection (1) applies, or refusing to deliver it where the person demanding delivery does not comply with subsection (1) or, by reason of subsection (2), subsection (1) does not apply.

### 118   Loss etc of pawn-receipt

(1)   A person (the 'claimant') who is not in possession of the pawn-receipt but claims to be the owner of the pawn, or to be otherwise entitled or authorised to redeem it, may do so at any time when it is redeemable by tendering to the pawnee in place of the pawn-receipt—

(a)   a statutory declaration made by the claimant in the prescribed form, and with the prescribed contents, or

(b)   where the pawn is security for fixed-sum credit not exceeding [£75] or running-account credit on which the credit limit does not exceed [£75], and the pawnee agrees, a statement in writing in the prescribed form, and with the prescribed contents, signed by the claimant.

(2)   On compliance by the claimant with subsection (1), section 117 shall apply as if the declaration or statement were the pawn-receipt, and the pawn-receipt itself shall become inoperative for the purposes of section 117.

### 119   Unreasonable refusal to deliver pawn

(1)   If a person who has taken a pawn under a regulated agreement refuses without reasonable cause to allow the pawn to be redeemed, he commits an offence.

(2)   On the conviction in England and Wales of a pawnee under subsection (1) where the offence does not amount to theft, [section 148 of the Powers of Criminal Courts (Sentencing) Act 2000 (restitution orders)] shall apply as if the pawnee had been convicted of stealing the pawn.

(3)   On the conviction in Northern Ireland of a pawnee under subsection (1) where the offence does not amount to theft, section 27 (orders for restitution) of the Theft Act (Northern Ireland) 1969, and any provision of the Theft Act (Northern Ireland) 1969 relating to that section, shall apply as if the pawnee had been convicted of stealing the pawn.

### 120   Consequence of failure to redeem

(1)   If at the end of the redemption period the pawn has not been redeemed—

(a)   notwithstanding anything in section 113, the property in the pawn passes to the pawnee where—

[(i)   the redemption period is six months,

(ii)   the pawn is security for fixed-sum credit not exceeding £75 or running-account credit on which the credit limit does not exceed £75, and

(iii)   the pawn was not immediately before the making of the regulated consumer credit agreement a pawn under another regulated consumer credit agreement in respect of which the debtor has discharged his indebtedness in part under section 94(3); or]

(b)   in any other case the pawn becomes realisable by the pawnee.

(2)   Where the debtor or hirer is entitled to apply to the court for a time order under section 129, subsection (1) shall apply with the substitution, for 'at the end of the redemption period' of 'after the expiry of five days following the end of the redemption period'.

### 121   Realisation of pawn

(1)   When a pawn has become realisable by him, the pawnee may sell it, after giving to the pawnor (except in such cases as may be prescribed) not less than the

prescribed period of notice of the intention to sell, indicating in the notice the asking price and such other particulars as may be prescribed.

(2)   Within the prescribed period after the sale takes place, the pawnee shall give the pawnor the prescribed information in writing as to the sale, its proceeds and expenses.

(3)   Where the net proceeds of sale are not less than the sum which, if the pawn had been redeemed on the date of the sale, would have been payable for its redemption, the debt secured by the pawn is discharged and any surplus shall be paid by the pawnee to the pawnor.

(4)   Where subsection (3) does not apply, the debt shall be treated as from the date of sale as equal to the amount by which the net proceeds of sale fall short of the sum which would have been payable for the redemption of the pawn on that date.

(5)   In this section the 'net proceeds of sale' is the amount realised (the 'gross amount') less the expenses (if any) of the sale.

(6)   If the pawnor alleges that the gross amount is less than the true market value of the pawn on the date of sale, it is for the pawnee to prove that he and any agents employed by him in the sale used reasonable care to ensure that the true market value was obtained, and if he fails to do so subsections (3) and (4) shall have effect as if the reference in subsection (5) to the gross amount were a reference to the true market value.

(7)   If the pawnor alleges that the expenses of the sale were unreasonably high, it is for the pawnee to prove that they were reasonable, and if he fails to do so subsections (3) and (4) shall have effect as if the reference in subsection (5) to expenses were a reference to reasonable expenses.

## 122   Order in Scotland to deliver pawn

(1)   As respects Scotland where—
    (a)   a pawn is either—
        (i)   an article which has been stolen, or
        (ii)   an article which has been obtained by fraud, and a person is convicted of any offence in relation to the theft or, as the case may be, the fraud; or
    (b)   a person is convicted of an offence under section 119(1), the court by which that person is so convicted may order delivery of the pawn to the owner or the person otherwise entitled thereto.

(2)   A court making an order under subsection (1)(a) for delivery of a pawn may make the order subject to such conditions as to payment of the debt secured by the pawn as it thinks fit.

*Negotiable instruments*

## 123   Restrictions on taking and negotiating instruments

(1)   A creditor or owner shall not take a negotiable instrument, other than a bank note or cheque, in discharge of any sum payable—
    (a)   by the debtor or hirer under a regulated agreement, or
    (b)   by any person as surety in relation to the agreement.

(2)   The creditor or owner shall not negotiate a cheque taken by him in discharge of a sum payable as mentioned in subsection (1) except to a banker (within the meaning of the Bills of Exchange Act 1882).

(3)   The creditor or owner shall not take a negotiable instrument as security for the discharge of any sum payable as mentioned in subsection (1).

(4)   A person takes a negotiable instrument as security for the discharge of a sum if the sum is intended to be paid in some other way, and the negotiable instrument is to be presented for payment only if the sum is not paid in that way.

(5)   This section does not apply where the regulated agreement is a non-commercial agreement.

(6)   The [Treasury] may by order provide that this section shall not apply

where the regulated agreement has a connection with a country outside the United Kingdom.

### 124 Consequences of breach of s 123

(1) After any contravention of section 123 has occurred in relation to a sum payable as mentioned in section 123(1)(a), the agreement under which the sum is payable is enforceable against the debtor or hirer on an order of the court only.

(2) After any contravention of section 123 has occurred in relation to a sum payable by any surety, the security is enforceable on an order of the court only.

(3) Where an application for an order under subsection (2) is dismissed (except on technical grounds only) section 106 shall apply to the security.

### 125 Holders in due course

(1) A person who takes a negotiable instrument in contravention of section 123(1) or (3) is not a holder in due course, and is not entitled to enforce the instrument.

(2) Where a person negotiates a cheque in contravention of section 123(2), his doing so constitutes a defect in his title within the meaning of the Bills of Exchange Act 1882.

(3) If a person mentioned in section 123(1)(a) and (b) ('the protected person') becomes liable to a holder in due course of an instrument taken from the protected person in contravention of section 123(1) or (3), or taken from the protected person and negotiated in contravention of section 123(2), the creditor or owner shall indemnify the protected person in respect of that liability.

(4) Nothing in this Act affects the rights of the holder in due course of any negotiable instrument.

*Land mortgages*

### 126 Enforcement of land mortgages

[(1)] A land mortgage securing a regulated agreement [or a regulated mortgage contract (within the meaning of the Regulated Activities Order)] is enforceable (so far as provided in relation to the agreement) on an order of the court only.

[(2) Subject to section 140A(5) (unfair relationships between creditors and debtors), for the purposes of subsection (1) and Part 9 (judicial control), a regulated mortgage contract which would, but for article 60C(2) of the Financial Services and Markets Act 2000 (Regulated Activities) Order 2001, be a regulated agreement is to be treated as if it were a regulated agreement.]

### PART IX
### JUDICIAL CONTROL

*Enforcement of certain regulated agreements and securities*

### 127 Enforcement orders in cases of infringement

(1) In the case of an application for an enforcement order under—

[(za) section 55(2) (disclosure of information), or]

[(zb) section 61B(3) (duty to supply copy of overdraft agreement), or]

  (a) section 65(1) (improperly executed agreements), or

  (b) section 105(7)(a) or (b) (improperly executed security instruments), or

  (c) section 111(2) (failure to serve copy of notice on surety), or

  (d) section 124(1) or (2) (taking of negotiable instrument in contravention of section 123),

the court shall dismiss the application if, but [. . .] only if, it considers it just to do so having regard to—

     (i) prejudice caused to any person by the contravention in question, and the degree of culpability for it; and

(ii) the powers conferred on the court by subsection (2) and sections 135 and 136.

(2) If it appears to the court just to do so, it may in an enforcement order reduce or discharge any sum payable by the debtor or hirer, or any surety, so as to compensate him for prejudice suffered as a result of the contravention in question.
[. . .]

### 128 Enforcement orders on death of debtor or hirer

The court shall make an order under section 86(2) if, but only if, the creditor or owner proves that he has been unable to satisfy himself that the present and future obligations of the debtor or hirer under the agreement are likely to be discharged.

*Extension of time*

### 129 Time orders

(1) [Subject to subsection (3) below,] if it appears to the court just to do so—

(a) on an application for an enforcement order; or

(b) on an application made by a debtor or hirer under this paragraph after service on him of—

(i) a default notice, or

(ii) a notice under section 76(1) or 98(1); or

[(ba) on an application made by a debtor or hirer under this paragraph after he has been given a notice under section 86B or 86C; or]

(c) in an action brought by a creditor or owner to enforce a regulated agreement or any security, or recover possession of any goods or land to which a regulated agreement relates,

the court may make an order under this section (a 'time order').

(2) A time order shall provide for one or both of the following, as the court considers just—

(a) the payment by the debtor or hirer or any surety of any sum owed under a regulated agreement or a security by such instalments, payable at such times, as the court having regard to the means of the debtor or hirer and any surety, considers reasonable;

(b) the remedying by the debtor or hirer of any breach of a regulated agreement (other than non-payment of money) within such period as the court may specify.

[(3) Where in Scotland a time to pay direction or a time order has been made in relation to a debt, it shall not thereafter be competent to make a time order in relation to the same debt.]

### [129A Debtor or hirer to give notice of intent etc to creditor or owner

(1) A debtor or hirer may make an application under section 129(1)(ba) in relation to a regulated agreement only if—

(a) following his being given the notice under section 86B or 86C, he gave a notice within subsection (2) to the creditor or owner; and

(b) a period of at least 14 days has elapsed after the day on which he gave that notice to the creditor or owner.

(2) A notice is within this subsection if it—

(a) indicates that the debtor or hirer intends to make the application;

(b) indicates that he wants to make a proposal to the creditor or owner in relation to his making of payments under the agreement; and

(c) gives details of that proposal.]

### 130 Supplemental provisions about time orders

(1) Where in accordance with rules of court an offer to pay any sum by instalments is made by the debtor or hirer and accepted by the creditor or owner, the court may in accordance with rules of court make a time order under section 129(2)(a) giving effect to the offer without hearing evidence of means.

(2)   In the case of a hire-purchase or conditional sale agreement only, a time order under section 129(2)(a) may deal with sums which, although not payable by the debtor at the time the order is made, would if the agreement continued in force become payable under it subsequently.

(3)   A time order under section 129(2)(a) shall not be made where the regulated agreement is secured by a pledge if, by virtue of regulations made under section 76(5), 87(4) or 98(5), service of a notice is not necessary for enforcement of the pledge.

(4)   Where, following the making of a time order in relation to a regulated hire-purchase or conditional sale agreement or a regulated consumer hire agreement, the debtor or hirer is in possession of the goods, he shall be treated (except in the case of a debtor to whom the creditor's title has passed) as a bailee or (in Scotland) a custodier of the goods under the terms of the agreement, notwithstanding that the agreement has been terminated.

(5)   Without prejudice to anything done by the creditor or owner before the commencement of the period specified in a time order made under section 129(2)(b) ('the relevant period'),—

(a)   he shall not while the relevant period subsists take in relation to the agreement any action such as is mentioned in section 87(1);

(b)   where—

(i) a provision of the agreement ('the secondary provision') becomes operative only on breach of another provision of the agreement ('the primary provision'), and

(ii) the time order provides for the remedying of such a breach of the primary provision within the relevant period,

he shall not treat the secondary provision as operative before the end of that period;

(c)   if while the relevant period subsists the breach to which the order relates is remedied it shall be treated as not having occurred.

(6)   On the application of any person affected by a time order, the court may vary or revoke the order.

*[Interest*

**[130A   Interest payable on judgment debts etc**

(1)   If the creditor or owner under a regulated agreement wants to be able to recover from the debtor or hirer post-judgment interest in connection with a sum that is required to be paid under a judgment given in relation to the agreement (the 'judgment sum'), he—

(a)   after the giving of that judgment, shall give the debtor or hirer a notice under this section (the 'first required notice'); and

(b)   after the giving of the first required notice, shall give the debtor or hirer further notices under this section at intervals of not more than six months.

(2)   The debtor or hirer shall have no liability to pay post-judgment interest in connection with the judgment sum to the extent that the interest is calculated by reference to a period occurring before the day on which he is given the first required notice.

(3)   If the creditor or owner fails to give the debtor or hirer a notice under this section within the period of six months beginning with the day after the day on which such a notice was last given to the debtor or hirer, the debtor or hirer shall have no liability to pay post-judgment interest in connection with the judgment sum to the extent that the interest is calculated by reference to the whole or to a part of the period which—

(a)   begins immediately after the end of that period of six months; and

(b)   ends at the end of the day on which the notice is given to the debtor or hirer.

(4)   The debtor or hirer shall have no liability to pay any sum in connection with the preparation or the giving to him of a notice under this section.

(5)   A notice under this section may be incorporated in a statement or other notice which the creditor or owner gives the debtor or hirer in relation to the agreement by virtue of another provision of this Act.

(6)   Regulations may make provision about the form and content of notices under this section.

(7)   This section does not apply in relation to post-judgment interest which is required to be paid by virtue of any of the following—

(a)   section 4 of the Administration of Justice (Scotland) Act 1972;

(b)   Article 127 of the Judgments Enforcement (Northern Ireland) Order 1981;

(c)   section 74 of the County Courts Act 1984.

(8)   This section does not apply in relation to a non-commercial agreement or to a small agreement.

(9)   In this section 'post-judgment interest' means interest to the extent calculated by reference to a period occurring after the giving of the judgment under which the judgment sum is required to be paid.]]

### Protection of property pending proceedings

#### 131   Protection orders

The court, on application of the creditor or owner under a regulated agreement, may make such orders as it thinks just for protecting any property of the creditor or owner, or property subject to any security, from damage or depreciation pending the determination of any proceedings under this Act, including orders restricting or prohibiting use of the property or giving directions as to its custody.

### Hire and hire-purchase etc agreements

#### 132   Financial relief for hirer

(1)   Where the owner under a regulated consumer hire agreement recovers possession of goods to which the agreement relates otherwise than by action, the hirer may apply to the court for an order that—

(a)   the whole or part of any sum paid by the hirer to the owner in respect of the goods shall be repaid, and

(b)   the obligation to pay the whole or part of any sum owed by the hirer to the owner in respect of the goods shall cease,

and if it appears to the court just to do so, having regard to the extent of the enjoyment of the goods by the hirer, the court shall grant the application in full or in part.

(2)   Where in proceedings relating to a regulated consumer hire agreement the court makes an order for the delivery to the owner of goods to which the agreement relates the court may include in the order the like provision as may be made in an order under subsection (1).

#### 133   Hire-purchase etc agreements: special powers of court

(1)   If, in relation to a regulated hire-purchase or conditional sale agreement, it appears to the court just to do so—

(a)   on an application for an enforcement order or time order; or

(b)   in an action brought by the creditor to recover possession of goods to which the agreement relates,

the court may—

(i)   make an order (a 'return order') for the return to the creditor of goods to which the agreement relates;

(ii)   make an order (a 'transfer order') for the transfer to the debtor of the creditor's title to certain goods to which the agreement relates ('the transferred goods'), and the return to the creditor of the remainder of the goods.

(2)   In determining for the purposes of this section how much of the total price has been paid ('the paid-up sum'), the court may—

(a)   treat any sum paid by the debtor, or owed by the creditor, in relation to the goods as part of the paid-up sum;

(b)   deduct any sum owed by the debtor in relation to the goods (otherwise than as part of the total price) from the paid-up sum,

and make corresponding reductions in amounts so owed.

(3)   Where a transfer order is made, the transferred goods shall be such of the goods to which the agreement relates as the court thinks just; but a transfer order shall be made only where the paid-up sum exceeds the part of the total price referable to the transferred goods by an amount equal to at least one-third of the unpaid balance of the total price.

(4)   Notwithstanding the making of a return order or transfer order, the debtor may at any time before the goods enter the possession of the creditor, on payment of the balance of the total price and the fulfilment of any other necessary conditions, claim the goods ordered to be returned to the creditor.

(5)   When, in pursuance of a time order or under this section, the total price of goods under a regulated hire-purchase agreement or regulated conditional sale agreement is paid and any other necessary conditions are fulfilled, the creditor's title to the goods vests in the debtor.

(6)   If, in contravention of a return order or transfer order, any goods to which the order relates are not returned to the creditor, the court, on the application of the creditor, may—

(a)   revoke so much of the order as relates to those goods, and

(b)   order the debtor to pay the creditor the unpaid portion of so much of the total price as is referable to those goods.

(7)   For the purposes of this section, the part of the total price referable to any goods is the part assigned to those goods by the agreement or (if no such assignment is made) the part determined by the court to be reasonable.

### 134   Evidence of adverse detention in hire-purchase etc cases

(1)   Where goods are comprised in a regulated hire-purchase agreement, regulated conditional sale agreement or regulated consumer hire agreement, and the creditor or owner—

(a)   brings an action or makes an application to enforce a right to recover possession of the goods from the debtor or hirer, and

(b)   proves that a demand for the delivery of the goods was included in the default notice under section 88(5), or that, after the right to recover possession of the goods accrued but before the action was begun or the application was made, he made a request in writing to the debtor or hirer to surrender the goods,

then, for the purposes of the claim of the creditor or owner to recover possession of the goods, the possession of them by the debtor or hirer shall be deemed to be adverse to the creditor or owner.

(2)   In subsection (1) 'the debtor or hirer' includes a person in possession of the goods at any time between the debtor's or hirer's death and the grant of probate or administration, or (in Scotland) confirmation.

(3)   Nothing in this section affects a claim for damages for conversion or (in Scotland) for delict.

*Supplemental provisions as to orders*

### 135   Power to impose conditions, or suspend operation of order

(1)   If it considers it just to do so, the court may in an order made by it in relation to a regulated agreement include provisions—

(a)   making the operation of any term of the order conditional on the doing of specified acts by any party to the proceedings;

(b)   suspending the operation of any term of the order either—

    (i)   until such time as the court subsequently directs, or

    (ii)   until the occurrence of a specified act or omission.

(2)   The court shall not suspend the operation of a term requiring the delivery up of goods by any person unless satisfied that the goods are in his possession or control.

(3)   In the case of a consumer hire agreement, the court shall not so use its powers under subsection (1)(b) as to extend the period for which, under the terms of the agreement, the hirer is entitled to possession of the goods to which the agreement relates.

(4)   On the application of any person affected by a provision included under subsection (1), the court may vary the provision.

### 136   Power to vary agreements and securities

(1)   The court may in an order made by it under this Act include such provision as it considers just for amending any agreement or security in consequence of a term of the order.

[. . .]

*[Unfair relationships*

### [140A   Unfair relationships between creditors and debtors

(1)   The court may make an order under section 140B in connection with a credit agreement if it determines that the relationship between the creditor and the debtor arising out of the agreement (or the agreement taken with any related agreement) is unfair to the debtor because of one or more of the following—

    (a)   any of the terms of the agreement or of any related agreement;

    (b)   the way in which the creditor has exercised or enforced any of his rights under the agreement or any related agreement;

    (c)   any other thing done (or not done) by, or on behalf of, the creditor (either before or after the making of the agreement or any related agreement).

(2)   In deciding whether to make a determination under this section the court shall have regard to all matters it thinks relevant (including matters relating to the creditor and matters relating to the debtor).

(3)   For the purposes of this section the court shall (except to the extent that it is not appropriate to do so) treat anything done (or not done) by, or on behalf of, or in relation to, an associate or a former associate of the creditor as if done (or not done) by, or on behalf of, or in relation to, the creditor.

(4)   A determination may be made under this section in relation to a relationship notwithstanding that the relationship may have ended.

(5)   An order under section 140B shall not be made in connection with a credit agreement which is an exempt agreement [for the purposes of Chapter 14A of Part 2 of the Regulated Activities Order by virtue of article 60C(2) of that Order (regulated mortgage contracts and regulated home purchase plans)].]

### [140B   Powers of court in relation to unfair relationships

(1)   An order under this section in connection with a credit agreement may do one or more of the following—

    (a)   require the creditor, or any associate or former associate of his, to repay (in whole or in part) any sum paid by the debtor or by a surety by virtue of the agreement or any related agreement (whether paid to the creditor, the associate or the former associate or to any other person);

    (b)   require the creditor, or any associate or former associate of his, to do or not to do (or to cease doing) anything specified in the order in connection with the agreement or any related agreement;

    (c)   reduce or discharge any sum payable by the debtor or by a surety by virtue of the agreement or any related agreement;

(d)   direct the return to a surety of any property provided by him for the purposes of a security;

(e)   otherwise set aside (in whole or in part) any duty imposed on the debtor or on a surety by virtue of the agreement or any related agreement;

(f)   alter the terms of the agreement or of any related agreement;

(g)   direct accounts to be taken, or (in Scotland) an accounting to be made, between any persons.

(2)   An order under this section may be made in connection with a credit agreement only—

(a)   on an application made by the debtor or by a surety;

(b)   at the instance of the debtor or a surety in any proceedings in any court to which the debtor and the creditor are parties, being proceedings to enforce the agreement or any related agreement; or

(c)   at the instance of the debtor or a surety in any other proceedings in any court where the amount paid or payable under the agreement or any related agreement is relevant.

(3)   An order under this section may be made notwithstanding that its effect is to place on the creditor, or any associate or former associate of his, a burden in respect of an advantage enjoyed by another person.

(4)   An application under subsection (2)(a) may only be made—

(a)   in England and Wales, to the county court;

(b)   in Scotland, to the sheriff court;

(c)   in Northern Ireland, to the High Court (subject to subsection (6)).

(5)   In Scotland such an application may be made in the sheriff court for the district in which the debtor or surety resides or carries on business.

(6)   In Northern Ireland such an application may be made to the county court if the credit agreement is an agreement under which the creditor provides the debtor with—

(a)   fixed-sum credit not exceeding £15,000; or

(b)   running-account credit on which the credit limit does not exceed £15,000.

(7)   Without prejudice to any provision which may be made by rules of court made in relation to county courts in Northern Ireland, such rules may provide that an application made by virtue of subsection (6) may be made in the county court for the division in which the debtor or surety resides or carries on business.

(8)   A party to any proceedings mentioned in subsection (2) shall be entitled, in accordance with rules of court, to have any person who might be the subject of an order under this section made a party to the proceedings.

(9)   If, in any such proceedings, the debtor or a surety alleges that the relationship between the creditor and the debtor is unfair to the debtor, it is for the creditor to prove to the contrary.]

### [140C   Interpretation of ss 140A and 140B

(1)   In this section and in sections 140A and 140B 'credit agreement' means any agreement between an individual (the 'debtor') and any other person (the 'creditor') by which the creditor provides the debtor with credit of any amount.

(2)   References in this section and in sections 140A and 140B to the creditor or to the debtor under a credit agreement include—

(a)   references to the person to whom his rights and duties under the agreement have passed by assignment or operation of law;

(b)   where two or more persons are the creditor or the debtor, references to any one or more of those persons.

(3)   The definition of 'court' in section 189(1) does not apply for the purposes of sections 140A and 140B.

(4)   References in sections 140A and 140B to an agreement related to a credit agreement (the 'main agreement') are references to—

(a)   a credit agreement consolidated by the main agreement;

(b)  a linked transaction in relation to the main agreement or to a credit agreement within paragraph (a);

(c)  a security provided in relation to the main agreement, to a credit agreement within paragraph (a) or to a linked transaction within paragraph (b).

(5)  In the case of a credit agreement which is not a regulated consumer credit agreement, for the purposes of subsection (4) a transaction shall be treated as being a linked transaction in relation to that agreement if it would have been such a transaction had that agreement been a regulated consumer credit agreement.

(6)  For the purposes of this section and section 140B the definitions of 'security' and 'surety' in section 189(1) apply (with any appropriate changes) in relation to—

(a)  a credit agreement which is not a consumer credit agreement as if it were a consumer credit agreement; and

(b)  a transaction which is a linked transaction by virtue of subsection (5).

(7)  For the purposes of this section a credit agreement (the 'earlier agreement') is consolidated by another credit agreement (the 'later agreement') if—

(a)  the later agreement is entered into by the debtor (in whole or in part) for purposes connected with debts owed by virtue of the earlier agreement; and

(b)  at any time prior to the later agreement being entered into the parties to the earlier agreement included—

(i)  the debtor under the later agreement; and

(ii)  the creditor under the later agreement or an associate or a former associate of his.

(8)  Further, if the later agreement is itself consolidated by another credit agreement (whether by virtue of this subsection or subsection (7)), then the earlier agreement is consolidated by that other agreement as well.]

[. . .]

*Miscellaneous*

## 141  Jurisdiction and parties

(1)  In England and Wales the county court shall have jurisdiction to hear and determine—

(a)  any action by the creditor or owner to enforce a regulated agreement or any security relating to it;

(b)  any action to enforce any linked transaction against the debtor or hirer or his relative,

and such an action shall not be brought in any other court.

(2)  Where an action or application is brought in the High Court which, by virtue of this Act, ought to have been brought in the county court it shall not be treated as improperly brought, but shall be transferred to the county court.

[(3)  In Scotland the sheriff court shall have jurisdiction to hear and determine any action referred to in subsection (1) and such an action shall not be brought in any other court.

(3A)  Subject to subsection (3B) an action which is brought in the sheriff court by virtue of subsection (3) shall be brought only in one of the following courts, namely—

(a)  the court for the place where the debtor or hirer is domiciled (within the meaning of section 41 or 42 of the Civil Jurisdiction and Judgments Act 1982);

(b)  the court for the place where the debtor or hirer carries on business; and

(c)  where the purpose of the action is to assert, declare or determine proprietary or possessory rights, or rights of security, in or over moveable property, or to obtain authority to dispose of moveable property, the court for the place where the property is situated.

(3B)  Subsection (3A) shall not apply—

(a)  where rule 3 of Schedule 8 to the said Act of 1982 applies; or

(b)   where the jurisdiction of another court has been prorogated by an agreement entered into after the dispute has arisen.]

(4)   In Northern Ireland the county court shall have jurisdiction to hear and determine any action or application falling within subsection (1).

(5)   Except as may be provided by rules of court, all the parties to a regulated agreement, and any surety, shall be made parties to any proceedings relating to the agreement.

### 142   Power to declare rights of parties

(1)   Where under any provision of this Act a thing can be done by a creditor or owner on an enforcement order only, and either—

(a)   the court dismisses (except on technical grounds only) an application for an enforcement order, or

(b)   where no such application has been made or such an application has been dismissed on technical grounds only an interested party applies to the court for a declaration under this subsection,

the court may if it thinks just make a declaration that the creditor or owner is not entitled to do that thing, and thereafter no application for an enforcement order in respect of it shall be entertained.

(2)   Where—

(a)   a regulated agreement or linked transaction is cancelled under section 69(1), or becomes subject to section 69(2), or

(b)   a regulated agreement is terminated under section 91, and an interested party applies to the court for a declaration under this subsection, the court may make a declaration to that effect.

**143, 144**   [*Apply to Northern Ireland*]

## PART X
## ANCILLARY CREDIT BUSINESSES

### *Definitions*

### 145   Types of ancillary credit business

(1)   An ancillary credit business is any business so far as it comprises or relates to—

(a)   credit brokerage,
(b)   debt-adjusting,
(c)   debt-counselling,
(d)   debt-collecting,
[(da)  debt administration;
(db)   the provision of credit information services, or]
(e)   the operation of a credit reference agency.

[(2)   'Credit brokerage' means the carrying on of an activity of the kind specified by article 36A(1)(a) to (c) of the Regulated Activities Order (credit broking), disregarding the effect of paragraph (2) of that article.]

[. . .]

[(5)   'Debt adjusting' means the carrying on of an activity of the kind specified by article 39D of that Order (debt adjusting).

(6)   'Debt-counselling' means the carrying on of an activity of the kind specified by article 39E of that Order (debt-counselling).

(7)   'Debt-collecting' means the carrying on of an activity of the kind specified by article 39F of that Order (debt-collecting).

(7A)   'Debt administration' means the carrying on of an activity of the kind specified by article 39G of that Order (debt administration), disregarding the effect of paragraph (3) of that article.

(7B)   A person ('P') provides credit information services if P carries on, by way of business, an activity of the kind specified by article 89A(1) or (2) of that Order (providing credit information services).

(8)   A person ('P') operates a credit reference agency if P carries on, by way of business, an activity of the kind specified by article 89B of that Order (providing credit references).]

[. . .]

### 153   Definition of canvassing off trade premises (agreements for ancillary credit services)

(1)   An individual (the 'canvasser') canvasses off trade premises the services of a person carrying on an ancillary credit business if he solicits the entry of another individual (the 'consumer') into an agreement for the provision to the consumer of those services by making oral representations to the consumer, or any other individual, during a visit by the canvasser to any place (not excluded by subsection (2)) where the consumer, or that other individual as the case may be, is, being a visit—

(a)   carried out for the purpose of making such oral representations to individuals who are at that place, but

(b)   not carried out in response to a request made on a previous occasion.

(2)   A place is excluded from subsection (1) if it is a place where (whether on a permanent or temporary basis)—

(a)   the ancillary credit business is carried on, or

(b)   any business is carried on by the canvasser or the person whose employee or agent the canvasser is, or by the consumer.

### 154   Prohibition of canvassing certain ancillary credit services off trade premises

It is an offence to canvass off trade premises the services of a person carrying on a business of credit-brokerage, debt-adjusting [, debt-counselling or the provision of credit information services].

### 155   Right to recover brokerage fees

(1)   [Subject to subsection (2A)] the excess over [£5] of a fee or commission for his services charged by a credit-broker to an individual to whom this subsection applies shall cease to be payable or, as the case may be, shall be recoverable by the individual if the introduction does not result in his entering into a relevant agreement within the six months following the introduction (disregarding any agreement which is cancelled under section 69(1) or becomes subject to section 69(2)).

(2)   Subsection (1) applies to an individual who sought an introduction for a purpose which would have been fulfilled by his entry into—

(a)   a regulated agreement, or

(b)   in the case of an individual [desiring to obtain credit to finance the acquisition or provision of a dwelling occupied or to be occupied by that individual or a relative of that individual], an agreement for credit secured on land,

[(c)   a credit agreement which is an exempt agreement for the purposes of Chapter 14A of Part 2 of the Regulated Activities Order, or

(d)   an agreement which is not a regulated credit agreement or a regulated consumer hire agreement but which would be such an agreement if the law applicable to the agreement were the law of a part of the United Kingdom.]

[(2A)   But subsection (1) does not apply where—

(a)   the fee or commission relates to the effecting of an introduction of a kind mentioned in [article 36E of the Regulated Activities Order (activities in relation to certain agreements relating to land)]; and

(b)   the person charging that fee or commission is an authorised person or an appointed representative, within the meaning of the Financial Services and Markets Act 2000.]

(3)   An agreement is a relevant agreement for the purposes of subsection (1) in relation to an individual if it is an agreement such as is referred to in subsection (2) in relation to that individual.

(4)   In the case of an individual desiring to obtain credit under a consumer credit agreement, any sum payable or paid by him to a credit-broker otherwise than as a fee or commission for the credit-broker's services shall for the purposes of subsection (1) be treated as such a fee or commission if it enters, or would enter, into the total charge for credit.

[. . .]

## Credit reference agencies

### 157   Duty to disclose name etc of agency

[(A1)   Where a creditor under a prospective regulated agreement, other than an excluded agreement, decides not to proceed with it on the basis of information obtained by the creditor from a credit reference agency, the creditor must, when informing the debtor of the decision—

(a)   inform the debtor that this decision has been reached on the basis of information from a credit reference agency, and

(b)   provide the debtor with the particulars of the agency including its name, address and telephone number.]

(1)   [In any other case,] a creditor, owner or negotiator, within the prescribed period after receiving a request in writing to that effect from the debtor or hirer, shall give him notice of the name and address of any credit reference agency from which the creditor, owner or negotiator has, during the antecedent negotiations, applied for information about his financial standing.

(2)   Subsection (1) does not apply to a request received more than 28 days after the termination of the antecedent negotiations, whether on the making of the regulated agreement or otherwise.

[(2A)   A creditor is not required to disclose information under this section if such disclosure—

(a)   contravenes the Data Protection Act 1998,

(b)   is prohibited by any EU obligation,

(c)   would create or be likely to create a serious risk that any person would be subject to violence or intimidation, or

(d)   would, or would be likely to, prejudice—

(i)   the prevention or detection of crime,

(ii)   the apprehension or prosecution of offenders, or

(iii)   the administration of justice.]

(3)   If the creditor, owner or negotiator fails to comply with subsection [(A1) or] (1) he commits an offence.

[(4)   For the purposes of subsection (A1) an agreement is an excluded agreement if it is—

(a)   a consumer hire agreement, or

(b)   an agreement secured on land.]

### 158   Duty of agency to disclose filed information

(1)   A credit reference agency, within the prescribed period after receiving,—

(a)   [a request in writing to that effect from a consumer], and

(b)   such particulars as the agency may reasonably require to enable them to identify the file, and

(c)   a fee of [£2],

shall give the consumer a copy of the file relating to [it] kept by the agency.

(2)   When giving a copy of the file under subsection (1), the agency shall also give the consumer a statement in the prescribed form of [the consumer's] rights under section 159.

(3)   If the agency does not keep a file relating to [the consumer] it shall give the consumer notice of that fact, but need not return any money paid.

(4)   If the agency contravenes any provision of this section it commits an offence.

[(4A)   In this section 'consumer' means—

(a)   a partnership consisting of two or three persons not all of whom are bodies corporate; or

(b)   an unincorporated body of persons which does not consist entirely of bodies corporate and is not a partnership.]

(5)   In this Act 'file', in relation to an individual, means all the information about him kept by a credit reference agency, regardless of how the information is stored, and 'copy of the file', as respects information not in plain English, means a transcript reduced into plain English.

### 159   Correction of wrong information

[(1)   Any individual (the 'objector') given—

(a)   information under section 7 of the Data Protection Act 1998 by a credit reference agency, or

(b)   information under section 158,

who considers that an entry in his file is incorrect, and that if it is not corrected he is likely to be prejudiced, may give notice to the agency requiring it either to remove the entry from the file or amend it.]

(2)   Within 28 days after receiving a notice under subsection (1), the agency shall by notice inform the [objector] that it has—

(a)   removed the entry from the file, or

(b)   amended the entry, or

(c)   taken no action,

and if the notice states that the agency has amended the entry it shall include a copy of the file so far as it comprises the amended entry.

(3)   Within 28 days after receiving a notice under subsection (2), or where no such notice was given, within 28 days after the expiry of the period mentioned in subsection (2), the [objector] may, unless he has been informed by the agency that it has removed the entry from his file, serve a further notice on the agency requiring it to add to the file an accompanying notice of correction (not exceeding 200 words) drawn up by the [objector], and include a copy of it when furnishing information included in or based on that entry.

(4)   Within 28 days after receiving a notice under subsection (3), the agency, unless it intends to apply to the [the relevant authority] under subsection (5), shall by notice inform the [objector] that it has received the notice under subsection (3) and intends to comply with it.

(5)   If—

(a)   the [objector] has not received a notice under subsection (4) within the time required, or

(b)   it appears to the agency that it would be improper for it to publish a notice of correction because it is incorrect, or unjustly defames any person, or is frivolous or scandalous, or is for any other reason unsuitable, the [objector] or, as the case may be, the agency may, in the prescribed manner and on payment of [the prescribed fee], apply to [the relevant authority], who may make such order on the application as he thinks fit.

(6)   If a person to whom an order under this section is directed fails to comply with it within the period specified in the order he commits an offence.

[(7)  The Information Commissioner may vary or revoke any order made by him under this section.

(8)  In this section 'the relevant authority' means—

(a)  where the objector is a partnership or other unincorporated body of persons, the [FCA], and

(b)  in any other case, the Information Commissioner.]

### 160  Alternative procedure for business consumers

(1)  The [FCA], on an application made by a credit reference agency, may direct that this section shall apply to the agency if [it] is satisfied—

(a)  that compliance with section 158 in the case of consumers who carry on a business would adversely affect the service provided to its customers by the agency, and

(b)  that, having regard to the methods employed by the agency and to any other relevant factors, it is probable that consumers carrying on a business would not be prejudiced by the making of the direction.

(2)  Where an agency to which this section applies receives a request, particulars and a fee under section 158(1) from a consumer who carries on a business and section 158(3) does not apply, the agency, instead of complying with section 158, may elect to deal with the matter under the following subsections.

(3)  Instead of giving the consumer a copy of the file, the agency shall within the prescribed period give notice to the consumer that it is proceeding under this section, and by notice give the consumer such information included in or based on entries in the file as the [FCA] may direct, together with a statement in the prescribed form of the consumer's rights under subsections (4) and (5).

(4)  If within 28 days after receiving the information given [to the consumer] under subsection (3), or such longer period as the [FCA] may allow, the consumer—

(a)  gives notice to the [FCA] that [the consumer] is dissatisfied with the information, and

(b)  satisfies the [FCA] that [the consumer] has taken such steps in relation to the agency as may be reasonable with a view to removing the cause of [the consumer's] dissatisfaction, and

(c)  pays the [FCA] [the prescribed fee],

the [FCA] may direct the agency to give the [FCA] a copy of the file, and the [FCA] may disclose to the consumer such of the information on the file as the [FCA] thinks fit.

(5)  Section 159 applies with any necessary modifications to information given to the consumer under this section as it applies to information given under section 158.

(6)  If an agency making an election under subsection (2) fails to comply with subsection (3) or (4) it commits an offence.

[(7)  In this section 'consumer' has the same meaning as in section 158.]

[. . .]

## PART XI
## ENFORCEMENT OF ACT

### 161  Enforcement authorities

(1)  The following authorities ('enforcement authorities') have a duty to enforce this Act and regulations made under it—

[. . .]

(b)  in Great Britain, the local weights and measures authority,

(c)  in Northern Ireland, the Department of Commerce for Northern Ireland.

[(1A)  Subsection (1) does not limit any function of the FCA in relation to the enforcement of this Act or regulations made under it.]

*[(1B)   For the investigatory powers available to a local weights and measures authority or the Department of Enterprise, Trade and Investment in Northern Ireland for the purposes of the duty in subsection (1), see Schedule 5 to the Consumer Rights Act 2015.]*
[. . .]
(3)   Every local weights and measures authority shall, whenever the [FCA] requires, report to [it] in such form and with such particulars as [it] requires on the exercise of their functions under this Act.
[. . .]

[. . .]

### 166   Notification of convictions and judgments to [FCA]
Where a person is convicted of an offence or has a judgment given against him by or before any court in the United Kingdom and it appears to the court—
(a)   having regard to the functions of the [FCA under the Financial Services and Markets Act 2000 or] this Act, that the conviction or judgment should be brought to the [FCA's] attention, and
(b)   that it may not be brought to [its] attention unless arrangements for that purpose are made by the court,
the court may make such arrangements notwithstanding that the proceedings have been finally disposed of.

### 167   Penalties
(1)   An offence under a provision of this Act specified in column 1 of Schedule 1 is triable in the mode or modes indicated in column 3, and on conviction is punishable as indicated in column 4 (where a period of time indicates the maximum term of imprisonment, and a monetary amount indicates the maximum fine, for the offence in question).
[. . .]

### 168   Defences
(1)   In any proceedings for an offence under this Act it is a defence for the person charged to prove—
(a)   that his act or omission was due to a mistake, or to reliance on information supplied to him, or to an act or omission by another person, or to an accident or some other cause beyond his control, and
(b)   that he took all reasonable precautions and exercised all due diligence to avoid such an act or omission by himself or any person under his control.
(2)   If in any case the defence provided by subsection (1) involves the allegation that the act or omission was due to an act or omission by another person or to reliance on information supplied by another person, the person charged shall not, without leave of the court, be entitled to rely on that defence unless, within a period ending seven clear days before the hearing, he has served on the prosecutor a notice giving such information identifying or assisting in the identification of that other person as was then in his possession.

### 169   Offences by bodies corporate
Where at any time a body corporate commits an offence under this Act with the consent or connivance of, or because of neglect by, any individual, the individual commits the like offence if at that time—
(a)   he is a director, manager, secretary or similar officer of the body corporate, or
(b)   he is purporting to act as such an officer, or
(c)   the body corporate is managed by its members of whom he is one.

### 170   No further sanctions for breach of Act
(1)   A breach of any requirement made (otherwise than by any court) by or under this Act shall incur no civil or criminal sanction as being such a breach, except to the extent (if any) expressly provided by or under this Act [or by or

under the Financial Services and Markets Act 2000 by virtue of an order made under section 107 of the Financial Services Act 2012].

(2)   In exercising [its] functions under this Act the [FCA] may take account of any matter appearing to [it] to constitute a breach of a requirement made by or under this Act, whether or not any sanction for that breach is provided by or under this Act and, if it is so provided, whether or not proceedings have been brought in respect of the breach.

(3)   Subsection (1) does not prevent the grant of an injunction, or the making of an order of certiorari, mandamus or prohibition or as respects Scotland the grant of an interdict or of an order under [section 45 of the Court of Session Act 1988] (order for specific performance of statutory duty).

### 171   Onus of proof in various proceedings

(1)   If an agreement contains a term signifying that in the opinion of the parties section 10(3)(b)(iii) does not apply to the agreement, it shall be taken not to apply unless the contrary is proved.

(2)   It shall be assumed in any proceedings, unless the contrary is proved, that when a person initiated a transaction as mentioned in section 19(1)(c) he knew the principal agreement had been made, or contemplated that it might be made.

[. . .]

(4)   In proceedings brought by the creditor under a credit-token agreement—

(a)   it is for the creditor to prove that the credit-token was lawfully supplied to the debtor, and was accepted by him, and

(b)   if the debtor alleges that any use made of the credit-token was not authorised by him, it is for the creditor to prove either—

(i)   that the use was so authorised, or

(ii)   that the use occurred before the creditor had been given notice under section 84(3).

(5)   In proceedings under section 50(1) in respect of a document received by a minor at any school or other educational establishment for minors, it is for the person sending it to him at that establishment to prove that he did not know or suspect it to be such an establishment.

(6)   In proceedings under section 119(1) it is for the pawnee to prove that he had reasonable cause to refuse to allow the pawn to be redeemed.

[. . .]

### 172   Statements by creditor or owner to be binding

(1)   A statement by a creditor or owner is binding on him if given under—

section 77(1),
section 78(1),
section 79(1),
section 97(1),
section 107(1)(c),
section 108(1)(c), or
section 109(1)(c).

(2)   Where a trader—

(a)   gives a customer a notice in compliance with section 103(1)(b), or

(b)   gives a customer a notice under section 103(1) asserting that the customer is not indebted to him under an agreement,

the notice is binding on the trader.

(3)   Where in proceedings before any court—

(a)   it is sought to reply on a statement or notice given as mentioned in subsection (1) or (2), and

(b)   the statement or notice is shown to be incorrect, the court may direct such relief (if any) to be given to the creditor or owner from the operation of subsection (1) or (2) as appears to the court to be just.

### 173  Contracting-out forbidden

(1)   A term contained in a regulated agreement or linked transaction, or in any other agreement relating to an actual or prospective regulated agreement or linked transaction, is void if, and to the extent that, it is inconsistent with a provision for the protection of the debtor or hirer or his relative or any surety contained in this Act or in any regulation made under this Act.

(2)   Where a provision specifies the duty or liability of the debtor or hirer or his relative or any surety in certain circumstances, a term is inconsistent with that provision if it purports to impose, directly or indirectly, an additional duty or liability on him in those circumstances.

(3)   Notwithstanding subsection (1), a provision of this Act under which a thing may be done in relation to any person on an order of the court or the [FCA] only shall not be taken to prevent its being done at any time with that person's consent given at that time, but the refusal of such consent shall not give rise to any liability.

PART XII

SUPPLEMENTAL

[. . .]

### [174A  Powers to require provision of information or documents etc

(1)   Every power conferred on a relevant authority by or under this Act (however expressed) to require the provision or production of information or documents includes the power—

(a)   to require information to be provided or produced in such form as the authority may specify, including, in relation to information recorded otherwise than in a legible form, in a legible form;

(b)   to take copies of, or extracts from, any documents provided or produced by virtue of the exercise of the power;

(c)   to require the person who is required to provide or produce any information or document by virtue of the exercise of the power—

(i)   to state, to the best of his knowledge and belief, where the information or document is;

(ii)   to give an explanation of the information or document;

(iii)   to secure that any information provided or produced, whether in a document or otherwise, is verified in such manner as may be specified by the authority;

(iv)   to secure that any document provided or produced is authenticated in such manner as may be so specified;

(d)   to specify a time at or by which a requirement imposed by virtue of paragraph (c) must be complied with.

(2)   Every power conferred on a relevant authority by or under this Act (however expressed) to inspect or to seize documents at any premises includes the power to take copies of, or extracts from, any documents inspected or seized by virtue of the exercise of the power.

(3)   But a relevant authority has no power under this Act—

(a)   to require another person to provide or to produce,

(b)   to seize from another person, or

(c)   to require another person to give access to premises for the purposes of the inspection of,

any information or document which the other person would be entitled to refuse to provide or produce in proceedings in the High Court on the grounds of legal professional privilege or (in Scotland) in proceedings in the Court of Session on the grounds of confidentiality of communications.

(4)   In subsection (3) 'communications' means—

(a)   communications between a professional legal adviser and his client;

(b)  communications made in connection with or in contemplation of legal proceedings and for the purposes of those proceedings.

[(5)  In this section, 'relevant authority' means an enforcement authority or an officer of an enforcement authority.]]

### 175  Duty of persons deemed to be agents

Where under this Act a person is deemed to receive a notice or payment as agent of the creditor or owner under a regulated agreement, he shall be deemed to be under a contractual duty to the creditor or owner to transmit the notice, or remit the payment, to him forthwith.

### 176  Service of documents

(1)  A document to be served under this Act by one person ('the server') on another person ('the subject') is to be treated as properly served on the subject if dealt with as mentioned in the following subsections.

(2)  The document may be delivered or sent [by an appropriate method] to the subject, or addressed to him by name and left at his proper address.

(3)  For the purposes of this Act, a document sent by post to, or left at, the address last known to the server as the address of a person shall be treated as sent by post to, or left at, his proper address.

(4)  Where the document is to be served on the subject as being the person having any interest in land, and it is not practicable after reasonable inquiry to ascertain the subject's name or address, the document may be served by—

(a)  addressing it to the subject by the description of the person having that interest in the land (naming it), and

(b)  delivering the document to some responsible person on the land or affixing it, or a copy of it, in a conspicuous position on the land.

(5)  Where a document to be served on the subject as being a debtor, hirer or surety, or as having any other capacity relevant for the purposes of this Act, is served at any time on another person who—

(a)  is the person last known to the server as having that capacity, but

(b)  before that time had ceased to have it, the document shall be treated as having been served at that time on the subject.

(6)  Anything done to a document in relation to a person who (whether to the knowledge of the server or not) has died shall be treated for the purposes of subsection (5) as service of the document on that person if it would have been so treated had he not died.

[(7)  The following enactments shall not be construed as authorising service on the Public Trustee (in England and Wales) or the Probate Judge (in Northern Ireland) of any document which is to be served under this Act—

section 9 of the Administration of Estates Act 1925;

section 3 of the Administration of Estates Act (Northern Ireland) 1955.]

(8)  References in the preceding subsections to the serving of a document on a person include the giving of the document to that person.

### [176A  Electronic transmission of documents

(1)  A document is transmitted in accordance with this subsection if—

(a)  the person to whom it is transmitted agrees that it may be delivered to him by being transmitted to a particular electronic address in a particular electronic form,

(b)  it is transmitted to that address in that form, and

(c)  the form in which the document is transmitted is such that any information in the document which is addressed to the person to whom the document is transmitted is capable of being stored for future reference for an appropriate period in a way which allows the information to be reproduced without change.

(2)  A document transmitted in accordance with subsection (1) shall, unless the

contrary is proved, be treated for the purposes of this Act, except section 69, as having been delivered on the working day immediately following the day on which it is transmitted.

(3)   In this section, 'electronic address' includes any number or address used for the purposes of receiving electronic communications.]

### 177   Saving for registered charges

(1)   Nothing in this Act affects the rights of a creditor in a heritable security who—

(a)   became the creditor under a transfer for value without notice of any defect in the title arising (apart from this section) by virtue of this Act; or

(b)   derives title from such a creditor.

(2)   Nothing in this Act affects the operation of section 41 of the Conveyancing (Scotland) Act 1924 (protection of purchasers), or of that section as applied to standard securities by section 32 of the Conveyancing and Feudal Reform (Scotland) Act 1970.

(3)   Subsection (1) does not apply to a creditor carrying on [a consumer credit business, a consumer hire business or a business of debt-collecting or debt administration].

(4)   Where, by virtue of subsection (1), a land mortgage is enforced which apart from this section would be treated as never having effect, the original creditor or owner shall be liable to indemnify the debtor or hirer against any loss thereby suffered by him.

(5)   [Substitutes subsections (1) to (3) for Scotland.]

(6)   [Applies to Northern Ireland.]

### 178   Local Acts

The [Treasury] or the Department of Commerce for Northern Ireland may by order make such amendments or repeals of any provision of any local Act as appears to the [Treasury] or, as the case may be, the Department, necessary or expedient in consequence of the replacement by this Act of the enactments relating to pawnbrokers and moneylenders.

*Regulations, orders, etc*

### 179   Power to prescribe form etc of secondary documents

(1)   Regulations may be made as to the form and content of credit-cards, trading-checks, receipts, vouchers and other documents or things issued by creditors, owners or suppliers under or in connection with regulated agreements or by other persons in connection with linked transactions, and may in particular—

(a)   require specified information to be included in the prescribed manner in documents, and other specified material to be excluded;

(b)   contain requirements to ensure that specified information is clearly brought to the attention of the debtor or hirer, or his relative, and that one part of a document is not given insufficient or excessive prominence compared with another.

(2)   If a person issues any document or thing in contravention of regulations under subsection (1) then, as from the time of the contravention but without prejudice to anything done before it, this Act shall apply as if the regulated agreement had been improperly executed by reason of a contravention of regulations under section 60(1).

### 180   Power to prescribe form etc of copies

(1)   Regulations may be made as to the form and content of documents to be issued as copies of any executed agreement, security instrument or other document referred to in this Act, and may in particular—

(a)   require specified information to be included in the prescribed manner in any copy, and contain requirements to ensure that such information is clearly brought to the attention of a reader of the copy;

(b)   authorise the omission from a copy of certain material contained in the original, or the inclusion of such material in condensed form.

(2)   A duty imposed by any provision of this Act [. . .] to supply a copy of any document—

(a)   is not satisfied unless the copy supplied is in the prescribed form and conforms to the prescribed requirements;

(b)   is not infringed by the omission of any material, or its inclusion in condensed form, if that is authorised by regulations;

and references in this Act to copies shall be construed accordingly.

(3)   Regulations may provide that a duty imposed by this Act to supply a copy of a document referred to in an unexecuted agreement or an executed agreement shall not apply to documents of a kind specified in the regulations.

### 181   Power to alter monetary limits etc

(1)   The [Treasury] may by order made by statutory instrument amend, or further amend, any of the following provisions of this Act so as to reduce or increase a sum mentioned in that provision, namely, sections [. . .], 17(1), [. . .] [. . .], 70(6), 75(3)(b), 77(1), 78(1), 79(1), 84(1), 101(7)(a), 107(1), 108(1), 109(1), 110(1), [. . .] [. . .], 140B(6), 155(1) and 158(1).

(2)   An order under subsection (1) amending section [. . .], 17(1), [. . .] [. . .], 75(3)(b) [. . . or 140B(6)] shall be of no effect unless a draft of the order has been laid before and approved by each House of Parliament.

### 182   Regulations and orders

(1)   Any power of the [Treasury] to make regulations or orders under this Act, except the power conferred by sections [. . .] 181 and 192 shall be exercisable by statutory instrument subject to annulment in pursuance of a resolution of either House of Parliament.

[. . .]

(2)   Where a power to make regulations or orders is exercisable by the [Treasury] by virtue of this Act, regulations or orders made in the exercise of that power may—

(a)   make different provision in relation to different cases or classes of case, and

(b)   exclude certain cases or classes of case, and

(c)   contain such transitional provision as the [Treasury] thinks fit.

(3)   Regulations may provide that specified expressions, when used as described by the regulations, are to be given the prescribed meaning, notwithstanding that another meaning is intended by the person using them.

(4)   Any power conferred on the [Treasury] by this Act to make orders includes power to vary or revoke an order so made.

### 183   Determinations etc by [FCA]

[(1)   The [FCA] may vary or revoke any determination made, or direction given, by it under this Act.

[. . .]

*Interpretation*

### 184   Associates

[(1)   A person is an associate of an individual if that person is—

(a)   the individual's husband or wife or civil partner,

(b)   a relative of—

(i)   the individual, or

(ii)   the individual's husband or wife or civil partner, or

(c)   the husband or wife or civil partner of a relative of—

(i)   the individual, or

(ii)  the individual's husband or wife or civil partner.]

(2)   A person is an associate of any person with whom he is in partnership, and of the husband or wife [or civil partner] or a relative of any individual with whom he is in partnership.

(3)   A body corporate is an associate of another body corporate—

(a)   if the same person is a controller of both, or a person is a controller of one and persons who are his associates, or he and persons who are his associates, are controllers of the other; or

(b)   if a group of two or more persons is a controller of each company, and the groups either consist of the same persons or could be regarded as consisting of the same persons by treating (in one or more cases) a member of either group as replaced by a person of whom he is an associate.

(4)   A body corporate is an associate of another person if that person is a con-troller of it or if that person and persons who are his associates together are controllers of it.

(5)   In this section 'relative' means brother, sister, uncle, aunt, nephew, niece, lineal ancestor or lineal descendant, references to a husband or wife include a former husband or wife and a reputed husband or wife, [and references to a civil partner include a former civil partner] [and a reputed civil partner]; and for the purposes of this subsection a relationship shall be established as if any illegitimate child, step-child or adopted child of a person [were the legitimate child of the re-lationship in question].

### 185   Agreement with more than one debtor or hirer

(1)   Where an actual or prosective regulated agreement has two or more debtors or hirers (not being a partnership or an unincorporated body of persons)—

(a)   anything required by or under this Act to be done to or in relation to the debtor or hirer shall be done to or in relation to each of them; and

(b)   anything done under this Act by or on behalf of one of them shall have effect as if done by or on behalf of all of them.

[. . .]

[(2)   Notwithstanding subsection (1)(a), where credit is provided under an agreement to two or more debtors jointly, in performing his duties—

(a)   in the case of fixed-sum credit, under section 77A, or

(b)   in the case of running-account credit, under section 78(4),

the creditor need not give statements to any debtor who has signed and given to him a notice (a 'dispensing notice') authorising him not to comply in the debtor's case with section 77A or (as the case may be) 78(4).

(2A)   A dispensing notice given by a debtor is operative from when it is given to the creditor until it is revoked by a further notice given to the creditor by the debtor.

(2B)   But subsection (2) does not apply if (apart from this subsection) dispen-sing notices would be operative in relation to all of the debtors to whom the credit is provided.

(2C)   Any dispensing notices operative in relation to an agreement shall cease to have effect if any of the debtors dies.

(2D)   A dispensing notice which is operative in relation to an agreement shall be operative also in relation to any subsequent agreement which, in relation to the earlier agreement, is a modifying agreement.]

(3)   Subsection (1)(b) does not apply for the purposes of section 61(1)(a) [. . .].

(4)   Where a regulated agreement has two or more debtors or hirers (not being a partnership or an unincorporated body of persons), section 86 applies to the death of any of them.

(5)   An agreement for the provision of credit, or the bailment or (in Scotland) the hiring of goods, to two or more persons jointly where—

(a)   one or more of those persons is an individual, and

(b)   one or more of them is [not an individual],

is a consumer credit agreement or consumer hire agreement if it would have been one had they all been individuals; and [each person within paragraph (b)] shall accordingly be included among the debtors or hirers under the agreement.

(6)   Where subsection (5) applies, references in this Act to the signing of any document by the debtor or hirer shall be construed in relation to a body corporate [within paragraph (b) of that subsection] as referring to a signing on behalf of the body corporate.

## 186   Agreement with more than one creditor or owner

Where an actual or prospective regulated agreement has two or more creditors or owners, anything required by or under this Act to be done to, or in relation to, or by, the creditor or owner shall be effective if done to, or in relation to, or by, any one of them.

## 187   Arrangements between creditor and supplier

(1)   A consumer credit agreement shall be treated as entered into under pre-existing arrangements between a creditor and a supplier if it is entered into in accordance with, or in furtherance of, arrangements previously made between persons mentioned in subsection (4)(a), (b) or (c).

(2)   A consumer credit agreement shall be treated as entered into in contemplation of future arrangements between a creditor and a supplier if it is entered into in the expectation that arrangements will subsequently be made between persons mentioned in subsection (4)(a), (b) or (c) for the supply of cash, goods and services (or any of them) to be financed by the consumer credit agreement.

(3)   Arrangements shall be disregarded for the purposes of subsection (1) or (2) if—

(a)   they are arrangements for the making, in specified circumstances, of payments to the supplier by the creditor, and

(b)   the creditor holds himself out as willing to make, in such circumstances, payments of the kind to suppliers generally.

[(3A)   Arrangements shall also be disregarded for the purposes of subsections (1) and (2) if they are arrangements for the electronic transfer of funds from a current account at a bank within the meaning of the Bankers' Books Evidence Act 1879.]

(4)   The persons referred to in subsections (1) and (2) are—

(a)   the creditor and the supplier;

(b)   one of them and an associate of the other's;

(c)   an associate of one and an associate of the other's.

(5)   Where the creditor is an associate of the supplier's, the consumer credit agreement shall be treated, unless the contrary is proved, as entered into under pre-existing arrangements between the creditor and the supplier.

## [187A   Definition of 'default sum'

(1)   In this Act 'default sum' means, in relation to the debtor or hirer under a regulated agreement, a sum (other than a sum of interest) which is payable by him under the agreement in connection with a breach of the agreement by him.

(2)   But a sum is not a default sum in relation to the debtor or hirer simply because, as a consequence of his breach of the agreement, he is required to pay it earlier than he would otherwise have had to.]

## 188   Examples of use of new terminology

(1)   Schedule 2 shall have effect for illustrating the use of terminology employed in this Act.

(2)   The examples given in Schedule 2 are not exhaustive.

(3)   In the case of conflict between Schedule 2 and any other provision of this Act, that other provision shall prevail.

(4)  The [Treasury] may by order amend Schedule 2 by adding further examples or in any other way.

## 189  Definitions

(1)  In this Act, unless the context otherwise requires—

'advertisement' includes every form of advertising, whether in a publication, by television or radio, by display of notices, signs, labels, showcards or goods, by distribution of samples, circulars, catalogues, price lists or other material, by exhibition of pictures, models or films, or in any other way, and references to the publishing of advertisements shall be construed accordingly;

[. . .]

'ancillary credit business' has the meaning given by section 145(1);

'antecedent negotiations' has the meaning given by section 56;

[. . .]

['appropriate method' means—

(a)   post, or

(b)   transmission in the form of an electronic communication [in accordance with section 176A(1)].]

'assignment', in relation to Scotland, means assignation;

'associate' shall be construed in accordance with section 184;

['authorised business overdraft agreement' means a debtor-creditor agreement which provides authorisation in advance for the debtor to overdraw on a current account, where the agreement is entered into by the debtor wholly or predominantly for the purposes of the debtor's business (see subsection (2A));

'authorised non-business overdraft agreement' means a debtor-creditor agreement which provides authorisation in advance for the debtor to overdraw on a current account where—

(a)   the credit must be repaid on demand or within three months, and

(b)   the agreement is not entered into by the debtor wholly or predominantly for the purposes of the debtor's business (see subsection (2A));]

[. . .]

'bill of sale' has the meaning given by section 4 of the Bills of Sale Act 1878 or, for Northern Ireland, by section 4 of the Bills of Sale (Ireland) Act 1879;

['building society' means a building society within the meaning of the Building Societies Act 1986;]

'business' includes profession or trade, and references to a business apply subject to subsection (2);

'cancellable agreement' means a regulated agreement which, by virtue of section 67, may be cancelled by the debtor or hirer;

'canvass' shall be construed in accordance with sections 48 and 153;

'cash' includes money in any form;

'charity' means as respects England and Wales a charity registered under [the Charities Act [2011]] or an exempt charity (within the meaning of that Act), and as respects Northern Ireland an institution or other organisation established for charitable purposes only ('organisation' including any persons administering a trust and 'charitable' being construed in the same way as if it were contained in the Income Tax Acts) [, and as respects Scotland a body entered in the Scottish Charity Register];

'conditional sale agreement' means an agreement for the sale of goods or land under which the purchase price or part of it is payable by instalments, and the property in the goods or land is to remain in the seller (notwithstanding that the buyer is to be in possession of the goods or land) until such conditions as to the payment of instalments or otherwise as may be specified in the agreement are fulfilled;

'consumer credit agreement' has the meaning given by section 8, and includes a consumer credit agreement which is cancelled under section 69(1), or becomes subject to section 69(2), so far as the agreement remains in force;

['consumer credit business' means any business being carried on by a person so far as it comprises or relates to—

    (a)   the provision of credit by him, or

    (b)   otherwise his being a creditor,

under regulated consumer credit agreements];

'consumer hire agreement' has the meaning given by section 15;

['consumer hire business' means any business being carried on by a person so far as it comprises or relates to—

    (a)   the bailment or (in Scotland) the hiring of goods by him, or

    (b)   otherwise his being an owner,

under regulated consumer hire agreements;]

'controller', in relation to a body corporate, means a person—

    (a)   in accordance with whose directions or instructions the directors of the body corporate or of another body corporate which is its controller (or any of them) are accustomed to act, or

    (b)   who, either alone or with any associate or associates, is entitled to exercise, or control the exercise of, one third or more of the voting power at any general meeting of the body corporate or of another body corporate which is its controller;

'copy' shall be construed in accordance with section 180;

[. . .]

'court' means in relation to England and Wales the county court, in relation to Scotland the sheriff court and in relation to Northern Ireland the High Court or the county court;

'credit' shall be construed in accordance with section 9;

'credit-broker' means a person carrying on a business of credit-brokerage;

'credit-brokerage' has the meaning given by section 145(2);

['credit information services' [is to be read in accordance with] section 145(7B);]

['credit intermediary' has the meaning given by section 160A;]

'credit limit' has the meaning given by section 10(2);

'creditor' means [(except in relation to green deal plans: see instead section 189B(2))] the person providing credit under a consumer credit agreement or the person to whom his rights and duties under the agreement have passed by assignment or operation of law, and in relation to a prospective consumer credit agreement, includes the prospective creditor;

'credit reference agency' [is to be read in accordance with] section 145(8);

'credit-sale agreement' means an agreement for the sale of goods, under which the purchase price or part of it is payable by instalments, but which is not a conditional sale agreement;

'credit-token' has the meaning given by section 14(1);

'credit-token agreement' means a regulated agreement for the provision of credit in connection with the use of a credit-token;

'debt-adjusting' has the meaning given by section 145(5);

['debt administration' has the meaning given by section 145(7A);]

'debt-collecting' has the meaning given by section 145(7);

'debt-counselling' has the meaning given by section 145(6);

'debtor' means [(except in relation to green deal plans: see instead section 189B(3))] the individual receiving credit under a consumer credit agreement or the person to whom his rights and duties under the agreement have passed by assignment or operation of law, and in relation to a prospective consumer credit agreement includes the prospective debtor;

'debtor-creditor agreement' has the meaning given by section 13;

'debtor-creditor-supplier agreement' has the meaning given by section 12;

'default notice' has the meaning given by section 87(1);

['default sum' has the meaning given by section 187A;]

'deposit' means [. . .] any sum payable by a debtor or hirer by way of deposit or downpayment, or credited or to be credited to him on account of any deposit or downpayment, whether the sum is to be or has been paid to the creditor or owner or any other person, or is to be or has been discharged by a payment of money or a transfer or delivery of goods or by any other means;

['documents' includes information recorded in any form;]

[. . .]

'electric line' has the meaning given by [the Electricity Act 1989] or, for Northern Ireland the Electricity Supply (Northern Ireland) Order 1972;

['electronic communication' means an electronic communication within the meaning of the Electronic Communications Act 2000 (c 7).]

'embodies' and related words shall be construed in accordance with subsection (4);

'enforcement authority' has the meaning given by section 161(1);

'enforcement order' means an order under section 65(1), 105(7)(a) or (b), 111(2) or 124(1) or (2);

'executed agreement' means a document, signed by or on behalf of the parties, embodying the terms of a regulated agreement, or such of them as have been reduced to writing;

[. . .]

['FCA' means the Financial Conduct Authority;]

'finance' means to finance wholly or partly, and 'financed' and 'refinanced' shall be construed accordingly;

'file' and 'copy of the file' have the meanings given by section 158(5);

'fixed-sum credit' has the meaning given by section 10(1)(b);

'friendly society' means a society registered [or treated as registered under the Friendly Societies Act 1974 or the Friendly Societies Act 1992];

'future arrangements' shall be construed in accordance with section 187;

[. . .]

'give' means deliver or send [by an appropriate method] to;

'goods' has the meaning given by [section 61(1) of the Sale of Goods Act 1979];

['green deal plan' has the meaning given by section 1 of the Energy Act 2011;]

[. . .]

'High Court' means Her Majesty's High Court of Justice, or the Court of Session in Scotland or the High Court of Justice in Northern Ireland;

'hire-purchase agreement' means an agreement, other than a conditional sale agreement, under which—

(a)   goods are bailed or (in Scotland) hired in return for periodical payments by the person to whom they are bailed or hired, and

(b)   the property in the goods will pass to that person if the terms of the agreement are complied with and one or more of the following occurs—

(i)   the exercise of an option to purchase by that person,

(ii)   the doing of any other specified act by any party to the agreement,

(iii)   the happening of any other specified event;

'hirer' means the individual to whom goods are bailed or (in Scotland) hired under a consumer hire agreement, or the person to whom his rights and duties under the agreement have passed by assignment or operation of law, and in relation to a prospective consumer hire agreement includes the prospective hirer;

['individual' includes—

(a)   a partnership consisting of two or three persons not all of whom are bodies corporate; and

(b)   an unincorporated body of persons which does not consist entirely of bodies corporate and is not a partnership.]

'installation' means—

(a)    the installing of any electric line or any gas or water pipe,

(b)    the fixing of goods to the premises where they are to be used, and the alteration of premises to enable goods to be used on them,

(c)    where it is reasonably necessary that goods should be constructed or erected on the premises where they are to be used, any work carried out for the purpose of constructing or erecting them on those premises;

[. . .]

'judgment' includes an order or decree made by any court;

'land' includes an interest in land, and in relation to Scotland includes heritable subjects of whatever description;

'land improvement company' means an improvement company as defined by section 7 of the improvement of Land Act 1899;

'land mortgage' includes any security charged on land;

[. . .]

'linked transaction' has the meaning given by section 19(1);

'local authority', in relation to England [. . .], means [. . .] a county council, a London borough council, a district council, the Common Council of the City of London, or the Council of the Isles of Scilly, [in relation to Wales means a county council or a county borough council,] and in relation to Scotland, means a [council constituted under section 2 of the Local Government etc (Scotland) Act 1994], and, in relation to Northern Ireland, means a district council;

'modifying agreement' has the meaning given by section 82(2);

'mortgage', in relation to Scotland, includes any heritable security;

'multiple agreement' has the meaning given by section 18(1);

'negotiator' has the meaning given by section 56(1);

'non-commercial agreement' means a consumer credit agreement or a consumer hire agreement not made by the creditor or owner in the course of a business carried on by him;

'notice' means notice in writing;

'notice of cancellation' has the meaning given by section 69(1);

[. . .]

['open-end' in relation to a consumer credit agreement, means of no fixed duration;]

'owner' means a person who bails or (in Scotland) hires out goods under a consumer hire agreement or the person to whom his rights and duties under the agreement have passed by assignment or operation of law, and in relation to a prospective consumer hire agreement, includes the prospective bailor or person from whom the goods are to be hired;

'pawn' means any article subject to a pledge;

'pawn-receipt' has the meaning given by section 114;

'pawnee' and 'pawnor' include any person to whom the rights and duties of the original pawnee or the original pawnor, as the case may be, have passed by assignment or operation of law;

'payment' includes tender;

[. . .]

'pledge' means the pawnee's rights over an article taken in pawn;

'prescribed' means prescribed by regulations made by the Secretary of State;

'pre-existing arrangements' shall be construed in accordance with section 187;

'principal agreement' has the meaning given by section 19(1);

'protected goods' has the meaning given by section 90(7);

[. . .]

'redemption period' has the meaning given by section 116(3);

[. . .]

['regulated agreement' means a consumer credit agreement which is a regulated agreement (within the meaning of section 8(3)) or a consumer hire agreement which is a regulated agreement (within the meaning of section 15(2));]

['Regulated Activities Order' means the Financial Services and Markets Act 2000 (Regulated Activities) Order 2001;]

'regulations' means regulations made by the [Treasury];

'relative', except in section 184, means a person who is an associate by virtue of section 184(1);

'representation' includes any condition or warranty, and any other statement or undertaking, whether oral or in writing;

['residential renovation agreement' means a consumer credit agreement—

(a)   which is unsecured; and

(b)   the purpose of which is the renovation of residential property, as described in Article 2(2a) of Directive 2008/48/EC of the European Parliament and of the Council of 23rd April 2008 on credit agreements for consumers.]

'restricted-use credit agreement' and 'restricted-use credit' have the meanings given by section 11(1);

'rules of court', in relation to Northern Ireland means, in relation to the High Court, rules made under section 7 of the Northern Ireland Act 1962, and, in relation to any other court, rules made by the authority having for the time being power to make rules regulating the practice and procedure in that court;

'running-account credit' shall be construed in accordance with section 10;

'security', in relation to an actual or prospective consumer credit agreement or consumer hire agreement, or any linked transaction, means a mortgage, charge, pledge, bond, debenture, indemnity, guarantee, bill, note or other right provided by the debtor or hirer, or at his request (express or implied), to secure the carrying out of the obligations of the debtor or hirer under the agreement;

'security instrument' has the meaning given by section 105(2);

'serve on' means deliver or send [by an appropriate method] to;

'signed' shall be construed in accordance with subsection (3);

'small agreement' has the meaning given by section 17(1), and 'small' in relation to an agreement within any category shall be construed accordingly;

[. . .]

[. . .]

'supplier' has the meaning given by section 11(1)(b) or 12(c) or 13(c) or, in relation to an agreement falling within section 11(1)(a), means the creditor, and includes a person to whom the rights and duties of a supplier (as so defined) have passed by assignment or operation of law, or (in relation to a prospective agreement) the prospective supplier;

'surety' means the person by whom any security is provided, or the person to whom his rights and duties in relation to the security have passed by assignment or operation of law;

'technical grounds' shall be construed in accordance with subsection (5);

'time order' has the meaning given by section 129(1);

['total charge for credit' has the meaning given by section 20];

'total price' means the total sum payable by the debtor under a hire-purchase agreement or a conditional sale agreement, including any sum payable on the exercise of an option to purchase, but excluding any sum payable as a penalty or as compensation or damages for a breach of the agreement;

[. . .]

'unexecuted agreement' means a document embodying the terms of a prospective regulated agreement, or such of them as it is intended to reduce to writing;

[. . .]

'unrestricted-use credit agreement' and 'unrestricted-use credit' have the meanings given by section 11(2);

'working day' means any day other than—

(a)   Saturday or Sunday,

(b)   Christmas Day or Good Friday,

(c)    a bank holiday within the meaning given by section 1 of the Banking and Financial Dealings Act 1971.

[(1A)    In sections [. . .], 70(4), 73(4) and 75(2) [. . .] 'costs', in relation to proceedings in Scotland, means expenses.]

(2)    A person is not to be treated as carrying on a particular type of business merely because occasionally he enters into transactions belonging to a business of that type.

[(2A)    For the purpose of the definitions of 'authorised business overdraft agreement' and 'authorised non-business overdraft agreement' [article 60C(5) and (6) of the Regulated Activities Order applies.]]

(3)    Any provision of this Act requiring a document to be signed is complied with by a body corporate if the document is sealed by that body.

This subsection does not apply to Scotland.

(4)    A document embodies a provision if the provision is set out either in the document itself or in another document referred to in it.

(5)    An application dismissed by the court [. . .] shall, if the court [. . .] so certifies, be taken to be dismissed on technical grounds only.

(6)    Except in so far as the context otherwise requires, any reference in this Act to an enactment shall be construed as a reference to that enactment as amended by or under any other enactment, including this Act.

(7)    In this Act, except where otherwise indicated—

(a)    a reference to a numbered Part, section or Schedule is a reference to the Part or section of, or the Schedule to, this Act so numbered, and

(b)    a reference in a section to a numbered subsection is a reference to the subsection of that section so numbered, and

(c)    a reference in a section, subsection or Schedule to a numbered paragraph is a reference to the paragraph of that section, subsection or Schedule so numbered.

[. . .]

**191**    [*Applies to Northern Ireland*]

### 193    Short title and extent

(1)    This Act may be cited as the Consumer Credit Act 1974.

(2)    This Act extends to Northern Ireland.

## SCHEDULES

[. . .]

## SCHEDULE 1. PROSECUTION AND PUNISHMENT OF OFFENCES

**Section 167**

| 1<br>Section | 2<br>Offence | 3<br>Mode of prosecution | 4<br>Imprisonment or fine |
|---|---|---|---|
| [. . .] | [. . .] | [. . .] | [. . .] |
| 49(1) | Canvassing debtor-creditor agreements off trade premises. | (a) Summarily. | [£400] |
|  |  | (b) On indictment. | 1 year or a fine or both. |
| 49(2) | Soliciting debtor-creditor agreements during visits made in response to previous oral requests. | (a) Summarily. | [£400] |
|  |  | (b) On indictment. | 1 year or a fine or both. |
| 50(1) | Sending circulars to minors. | (a) Summarily. | [£400] |
|  |  | (b) On indictment. | 1 year or a fine or both. |
| [. . .] |  | [. . .] | [. . .] |
| [. . .] |  | [. . .] | [. . .] |
| 79(3) | Failure of owner under consumer hire agreement to supply copies of documents etc. | Summarily. | [Level 4 on the standard scale.] |
| 80(2) | Failure to tell creditor or owner whereabouts of goods. | Summarily. | [Level 3 on the standard scale.] |
| [. . .] |  | [. . .] | [. . .] |
| 114(2) | Taking pledges from minors. | (a) Summarily. | [£400] |
|  |  | (b) On indictment. | 1 year or a fine or both. |
| [. . .] |  | [. . .] | [. . .] |
| 119(1) | Unreasonable refusal to allow pawn to be redeemed. | Summarily. | [Level 4 on the standard scale.] |
| 154 | Canvassing ancillary credit services of trade premises. | (a) Summarily. | [£200] |
|  |  | (b) On indictment. | 1 year or a fine or both. |
| 157(3) | Refusal to give name etc of credit reference agency. | Summarily. | [Level 4 on the standard scale.] |
| 158(4) | Failure of credit reference agency to disclose filed information. | Summarily. | [Level 4 on the standard scale.] |
| 159(6) | Failure of credit reference agency to correct information. | Summarily. | [Level 4 on the standard scale.] |
| 160(6) | Failure of credit reference agency to comply with section 160(3) or (4). | Summarily. | [Level 4 on the standard scale.] |
| [. . .] |  | [. . .] | [. . .] |

SCHEDULE 2
EXAMPLES OF USE OF NEW TERMINOLOGY

Section 188(1)

PART I
LIST OF TERMS

| Term | Defined in section | Illustrated by examples(s) |
|---|---|---|
| Advertisement ... ... ... ... ... ... ... ... | 189(1) | 2 |
| [. . .] | | |
| Antecedent negotiations ... ... ... ... ... | 56 | 1, 2, 3, 4 |
| Cancellable agreement ... ... ... ... ... ... | 67 | 4 |
| Consumer credit agreement ... ... ... ... | 8 | 5, 6, 7, 15, 19, 21 |
| Consumer hire agreement ... ... ... ... ... | 15 | 20, 24 |
| Credit ... ... ... ... ... ... ... ... ... ... | 9 | 16, 19, 21 |
| Credit-broker ... ... ... ... ... ... ... ... | 189(1) | 2 |
| Credit limit ... ... ... ... ... ... ... ... | 10(2) | 6, 7, 19, 22, 23 |
| Creditor ... ... ... ... ... ... ... ... ... | 189(1) | 1, 2, 3, 4 |
| Credit-sale agreement ... ... ... ... ... ... | 189(1) | 5 |
| Credit-token ... ... ... ... ... ... ... ... | 14 | 3, 14, 16 |
| Credit-token agreement ... ... ... ... ... | 14 | 3, 14, 16, 22 |
| Debtor-creditor agreement ... ... ... ... ... | 13 | 8, 16, 17, 18 |
| Debtor-creditor-supplier agreement ... ... | 12 | 8, 16 |
| Fixed-sum credit ... ... ... ... ... ... ... | 10 | 9, 10, 17, 23 |
| Hire-purchase agreement ... ... ... ... ... | 189(1) | 10 |
| Individual ... ... ... ... ... ... ... ... ... | 189(1) | 19, 24 |
| Linked transaction ... ... ... ... ... ... ... | 19 | 11 |
| Modifying agreement ... ... ... ... ... ... | 82(2) | 24 |
| Multiple agreement ... ... ... ... ... ... | 18 | 16, 18 |
| Negotiator ... ... ... ... ... ... ... ... ... | 56(1) | 1, 2, 3, 4 |
| [. . .] | | |
| Pre-existing arrangements ... ... ... ... ... | 187 | 8, 21 |
| Restricted-use credit ... ... ... ... ... ... | 11 | 10, 12, 13, 14, 16 |
| Running-account credit ... ... ... ... ... | 10 | 15, 16, 18, 23 |
| Small agreement ... ... ... ... ... ... ... | 17 | 16, 17, 22 |
| Supplier ... ... ... ... ... ... ... ... ... | 189(1) | 3, 14 |
| Total charge for credit ... ... ... ... ... ... | 20 | 5, 10 |
| Total price ... ... ... ... ... ... ... ... ... | 189(1) | 10 |
| Unrestricted-use credit ... ... ... ... ... ... | 11 | 8, 12, 16, 17, 18 |

PART II
EXAMPLES

*Example 1*

*Facts*  Correspondence passes between an employee of a money-lending company (writing on behalf of the company) and an individual about the terms on which the company would grant him a loan under a regulated agreement.

*Analysis*  The correspondence constitutes antecedent negotiations falling within section 56(1)(a), the money-lending company being both creditor and negotiator.

*Example 2*

*Facts*  Representations are made about goods in a poster displayed by a shopkeeper near the goods, the goods being selected by a customer who has read the poster and then sold by the shopkeeper to a finance company introduced by him (with whom he has a business relationship). The goods are disposed of by the finance company to the customer under a regulated hire-purchase agreement.

*Analysis* The representations in the poster constitute antecedent negotiations falling within section 56(1)(b), the shopkeeper being the credit-broker and negotiator and the finance company being the creditor. The poster is an advertisement and the shopkeeper is the advertiser.

## Example 3

*Facts* Discussions take place between a shopkeeper and a customer about goods the customer wishes to buy using a credit-card issued by the D Bank under a regulated agreement.

*Analysis* The discussions constitute antecedent negotiations falling within section 56(1)(c), the shopkeeper being the supplier and negotiator and the D Bank the creditor. The credit-card is a credit-token as defined in section 14(1), and the regulated agreement under which it was issued is a credit-token agreement as defined in section 14(2).

## Example 4

*Facts* Discussions take place and correspondence passes between a second-hand car dealer and a customer about a car, which is then sold by the dealer to the customer under a regulated conditional sale agreement. Subsequently, on a revocation of that agreement by consent, the car is resold by the dealer to a finance company introduced by him (with whom he has a business relationship), who in turn dispose of it to the same customer under a regulated hire-purchase agreement.

*Analysis* The discussions and correspondence constitute antecedent negotiations in relation both to the conditional sale agreement and the hire-purchase agreement. They fall under section 56(1)(a) in relation to the conditional sale agreement, the dealer being the creditor and the negotiator. In relation to the hire-purchase agreement they fall within section 56(1)(b), the dealer continuing to be treated as the negotiator but the finance company now being the creditor. Both agreements are cancellable if the discussions took place when the individual conducting the negotiations (whether the 'negotiator' or his employee or agent) was in the presence of the debtor, unless the unexecuted agreement was signed by the debtor at trade premises (as defined in section 67(b)). If the discussions all took place by telephone however, or the unexecuted agreement was signed by the debtor on trade premises (as so defined) the agreements are not cancellable.

## Example 5

*Facts* E agrees to sell to F (an individual) an item of furniture in return for 24 monthly instalments of £10 payable in arrear. The property in the goods passes to F immediately.

*Analysis* This is a credit-sale agreement (see definition of 'credit-sale agreement' in section 189(1)). The credit provided amounts to £240 less the amount which [constitutes the total charge for credit (within the meaning given by section 20)]. (This amount is required to be deducted by section 9(4).) Accordingly the agreement falls within section 8(2) and is a consumer credit agreement.

## Example 6

*Facts* The G Bank grants H (an individual) an unlimited over-draft, with an increased rate of interest on so much of any debit balance as exceeds £2,000.

*Analysis* Although the overdraft purports to be unlimited, the stipulation for increased interest above £2,000 brings the agreement within section 10(3)(b)(ii) and it is a consumer credit agreement.

## Example 7

*Facts* J is an individual who owns a small shop which usually carries a stock worth about £1,000. K makes a stocking agreement under which he undertakes to provide on short-term credit the stock needed from time to time by J without any specified limit.

*Analysis* Although the agreement appears to provide unlimited credit, it is probable, having regard to the stock usually carried by J, that his indebtedness to K will not at any time rise above £5,000. Accordingly the agreement falls within section 10(3)(b)(iii) and is a consumer credit agreement.

## Example 8

*Facts* U, a moneylender, lends £500 to V (an individual) knowing he intends to use it to buy office equipment from W. W introduced V to U, it being his practice to introduce customers needing finance to him. Sometimes U gives W a commission for this and sometimes not. U pays the £500 direct to V.

*Analysis* Although this appears to fall under section 11(1)(b), it is excluded by section 11(3) and is therefore (by section 11(2)) an unrestricted-use credit agreement. Whether it is a debtor-creditor agreement (by section 13(c)) or a debtor-creditor-supplier agreement (by section 12(c)) depends on whether the previous dealings between U and W amount to 'pre-existing arrangements', that is whether the agreement can be taken to have been entered into 'in accordance with, or in furtherance of' arrangements previously made between U and W, as laid down in section 187(1).

## Example 9

*Facts* A agrees to lend B (an individual) £4,500 in nine monthly instalments of £500.

*Analysis* This is a cash loan and is a form of credit (see section 9 and definition of 'cash' in section 189(1)). Accordingly it falls within section 10(1)(b) and is fixed-sum credit amounting to £4,500.

## Example 10

*Facts* C (in England) agrees to bail goods to D (an individual) in return for periodical payments. The agreement provides for the property in the goods to pass to D on payment of a total of £7,500 and the exercise by D of an option to purchase. The sum of £7,500 includes a down-payment of £1,000. It also includes an amount which, according to regulations made under section 20(1), constitutes a total charge for credit of £1,500.

*Analysis* This is a hire-purchase agreement with a deposit of £1,000 and a total price of £7,500 (see definitions of 'hire-purchase agreement', 'deposit' and 'total price' in section 189(1)). By section 9(3), it is taken to provide credit amounting to £7,500 − (£1,500 + £1,000), which equals £5,000. Under section 8(2), the agreement is therefore a consumer credit agreement, and under sections 9(3) and 11(1) it is a restricted-use credit agreement for fixed-sum credit. A similar result would follow if the agreement by C had been a hiring agreement in Scotland.

## Example 11

*Facts* X (an individual) borrows £500 from Y (Finance). As a condition of the granting of the loan X is required—

(a)   to execute a second mortgage on his house in favour of Y (Finance), and

(b)   to take out a policy of insurance on his life with Y (Insurances).

In accordance with the loan agreement, the policy is charged to Y (Finance) as collateral security for the loan. The two companies are associates within the meaning of section 184(3).

*Analysis* The second mortgage is a transaction for the provision of security and accordingly does not fall within section 19(1), but the taking out of the insurance policy is a linked transaction falling within section 19(1)(a). The charging of the policy is a separate transaction (made between different parties) for the provision of security and again is excluded from section 19(1). The only linked transaction is therefore the taking out of the insurance policy. If X had not been required by the loan agreement to take out the policy, but it had been done at the suggestion of Y (Finance) to induce them to enter into the loan agreement, it would have been a linked transaction under section 19(1)(c)(i) by virtue of section 19(2)(a).

## Example 12

*Facts*   The N Bank agrees to lend O (an individual) £2,000 to buy a car from P. To make sure the loan is used as intended, the N Bank stipulates that the money must be paid by it direct to P.

*Analysis*   The agreement is a consumer credit agreement by virtue of section 8(2). Since it falls within section 11(1)(b), it is a restricted-use credit agreement, P being the supplier. If the N Bank had not stipulated for direct payment to the supplier, section 11(3) would have operated and made the agreement into one for unrestricted-use credit.

## Example 13

*Facts*   Q, a debt-adjuster, agrees to pay off debts owed by R (an individual) to various moneylenders. For this purpose the agreement provides for the making of a loan by Q to R in return for R's agreeing to repay the loan by instalments with interest. The loan money is not paid over to R but retained by Q and used to pay off the money lenders.

*Analysis*   This is an agreement to refinance existing indebtedness of the debtor's, and if the loan by Q does not exceed £5,000 is a restricted-use credit agreement falling within section 11(1)(c).

## Example 14

*Facts*   On payment of £1, S issues to T (an individual) a trading check under which T can spend up to £20 at any shop which has agreed, or in future agrees, to accept S's trading checks.

*Analysis*   The trading check is a credit-token falling within section 14(1)(b). The credit-token agreement is a restricted-use credit agreement within section 11(1)(b), any shop in which the credit-token is used being the 'supplier'. The fact that further shops may be added after the issue of the credit-token is irrelevant in view of section 11(4).

## Example 15

*Facts*   A retailer L agrees with M (an individual) to open an account in M's name and, in return for M's promise to pay a specified minimum sum into the account each month and to pay a monthly charge for credit, agrees to allow to be debited to the account, in respect of purchases made by M from L, such sums as will not increase the debit balance at any time beyond the credit limit, defined in the agreement as a given multiple of the specified minimum sum.

*Analysis*   This agreement provides credit falling within the definition of running-account credit in section 10(1)(a). Provided the credit limit is not over £5,000, the agreement falls within section 8(2) and is a consumer credit agreement for running-account credit.

## Example 16

*Facts*   Under an unsecured agreement, A (Credit), an associate of the A Bank, issues to B (an individual) a credit-card for use in obtaining cash on credit from A (Credit), to be paid by branches of the A Bank (acting as agent of A (Credit)), or goods or cash from suppliers or banks who have agreed to honour credit-cards issued by A (Credit). The credit limit is £30.

*Analysis*   This is a credit-token agreement falling within section 14(1)(a) and (b). It is a regulated consumer credit agreement for running-account credit. Since the credit limit does not exceed £30, the agreement is a small agreement. So far as the agreement relates to goods it is a debtor-creditor-supplier agreement within section 12(b), since it provides restricted-use credit under section 11(1)(b). So far as it relates to cash it is a debtor-creditor agreement within section 13(c) and the credit it provides is unrestricted-use credit. This is therefore a multiple agreement. In that the whole agreement falls within several of the categories of agreement mentioned in this Act, it is, by section 18(3), to be treated as an agreement in each of those categories. So far as it is a debtor-creditor-supplier agreement providing restricted-use credit it is, by section 18(2), to be treated as a separate agreement; and similarly so far as it is a debtor-creditor agreement providing unrestricted-use credit. (See also Example 22.)

### Example 17

*Facts*   The manager of the C Bank agrees orally with D (an individual) to open a current account in D's name. Nothing is said about overdraft facilities. After main-taining the account in credit for some weeks, D draws a cheque in favour of E for an amount exceeding D's credit balance by £20. E presents the cheque and the Bank pay it.

*Analysis*   In drawing the cheque D, by implication, requests the Bank to grant him an overdraft of £20 on its usual terms as to interest and other charges. In deciding to honour the cheque, the Bank by implication accept the offer. This con-stitutes a regulated small consumer credit agreement for unrestricted-use, fixed sum credit. It is a debtor-creditor agreement, and falls within section 74(1)(b) [. . .] (Compare Example 18.)

### Example 18

*Facts*   F (an individual) has had a current account with the G Bank for many years. Although usually in credit, the account has been allowed by the Bank to become overdrawn from time to time. The maximum such overdraft has been is about £1,000. No explicit agreement has ever been made about overdraft facilities. Now, with a credit balance of £500, F draws a cheque for £1,300.

*Analysis*   It might well be held that the agreement with F (express or implied) under which the Bank operate his account includes an implied term giving him the right to overdraft facilities up to say £1,000. If so, the agreement is a regulated consumer credit agreement for unrestricted-use, running-account credit. It is a debtor-creditor agreement, and falls within section 74(1)(b) [. . .]. It is also a mul-tiple agreement, part of which (i.e. the part not dealing with the overdraft), as referred to in section 18(1)(a), falls within a category of agreement not mentioned in this Act. (Compare Example 17.)

### Example 19

*Facts*   H (a finance house) agrees with J (a partnership of individuals) to open an unsecured loan account in J's name on which the debit balance is not to exceed £7,000 (having regard to payments into the account made from time to time by J). Interest is to be payable in advance on this sum, with provision for yearly adjust-ments. H is entitled to debit the account with interest, a 'setting-up' charge, and other charges. Before J has an opportunity to draw on the account it is initially debited with £2,250 for advance interest and other charges.

*Analysis*   This is a personal running-account credit agreement (see sections 8(1) and 10(1)(a), and definition of 'individual' in section 189(1)). By section 10(2) the credit limit is £7,000. By section 9(4) however the initial debit of £2,250, and any other charges later debited to the account by H, are not to be treated as credit even though time is allowed for their payment. Effect is given to this by section 10(3). Although the credit limit of £7,000 exceeds the amount (£5,000) specified in section 8(2) as the maximum for a consumer credit agreement, so that the agreement is not within section 10(3)(a), it is caught by section 10(3)(b)(i). At the beginning J can effectively draw (as credit) no more than £4,750, so the agreement is a consumer credit agreement.

### Example 20

*Facts*   K (in England) agrees with L (an individual) to bail goods to L for a period of three years certain at £2,000 a year, payable quarterly. The agreement contains no provision for the passing of the property in the goods to L.

*Analysis*   This is not a hire-purchase agreement (see paragraph (b) of the definition of that term in section 189(1)), and is capable of subsisting for more than three months. Paragraphs (a) and (b) of section 15(1) are therefore satisfied, but paragraph (c) is not. The payments by L must exceed £5,000 if he conforms to the agreement. It is true that under section 101 L has a right to terminate the agreement on giving K three months' notice expiring not earlier than eighteen months after the making of the agreement, but that section applies only where the agreement is a regulated consumer hire agreement apart from the section (see subsection (1)). So the agreement is not a consumer hire agreement, though it would be if the hire charge were say £1,500 a year, or there were a 'break' clause in it operable by either party before the hire charges exceeded £5,000. A similar result would follow if the agreement by K had been a hiring agreement in Scotland.

### Example 21

*Facts*   The P Bank decides to issue cheque cards to its customers under a scheme whereby the bank undertakes to honour cheques of up to £30 in every case where the payee has taken the cheque in reliance on the cheque card, whether the customer has funds in his account or not. The P Bank writes to the major retailers advising them of this scheme and also publicises it by advertising. The Bank issues a cheque card to Q (an individual), who uses it to pay by cheque for goods costing £20 bought by Q from R, a major retailer. At the time, Q has £500 in his account at the P Bank.

*Analysis*   The agreement under which the cheque card is issued to Q is a consumer credit agreement even though at all relevant times Q has more than £30 in his account. This is because Q is free to draw out his whole balance and then use the cheque card, in which case the Bank has bound itself to honour the cheque. In other words the cheque card agreement provides Q with credit, whether he avails himself of it or not. Since the amount of the credit is not subject to any express limit, the cheque card can be used any number of times. It may be presumed however that section 10(3)(b)(iii) will apply. The agreement is an unrestricted-use debtor-creditor agreement (by section 13(c)). Although the P Bank wrote to R informing R of the P Bank's willingness to honour any cheque taken by R in reliance on a cheque card, this does not constitute pre-existing arrangements as mentioned in section 13(c) because section 187(3) operates to prevent it. The agreement is not a credit-token agreement within section 14(1)(b) because payment by the P Bank to R, would be a payment of the cheque and not a payment for the goods.

### Example 22

*Facts*   The facts are as in Example 16. On one occasion B uses the credit-card in a way which increases his debit balance with A (Credit) to £40. A (Credit) writes to B agreeing to allow the excess on that occasion only, but stating that it must be paid off within one month.

*Analysis*   In exceeding his credit limit B, by implication, requests A (Credit) to allow him a temporary excess (compare Example 17). A (Credit) is thus faced by B's action with the choice of treating it as a breach of contract or granting his implied request. He does the latter. If he had done the former, B would be treated as taking credit to which he was not entitled (see section 14(3)) and, subject to the terms of his contract with A (Credit), would be liable to damages for breach of contract. As it is, the agreement to allow the excess varies the original credit-token agreement by adding a new term. Under section 10(2), the new term is to be disregarded in arriving at the credit limit, so that the credit-token agreement at no time ceases to be a small agreement. By section 82(2) the later agreement is deemed to revoke the original agreement and contain provisions reproducing the combined effect of the two agreements. By section 82(4), this later agreement is exempted from Part V (except section 56).

### Example 23

*Facts* Under an oral agreement made on 10th January, X (an individual) has an overdraft on his current account at the Y bank with a credit limit of £100. On 15th February, when his overdraft stands at £90, X draws a cheque for £25. It is the first time that X has exceeded his credit limit, and on 16th February the bank honours the cheque.

*Analysis* The agreement of 10th January is a consumer credit agreement for running-account credit. The agreement of 15th–16th February varies the earlier agreement by adding a term allowing the credit limit to be exceeded merely temporarily. By section 82(2) the later agreement is deemed to revoke the earlier agreement and reproduce the combined effect of the two agreements. By section 82(4), Part V of this Act (except section 56) does not apply to the later agreement. By section 18(5), a term allowing a merely temporary excess over the credit limit is not to be treated as a separate agreement, or as providing fixed-sum credit. The whole of the £115 owed to the bank by X on 16th February is therefore running-account credit.

### Example 24

*Facts* On 1st March 1975 Z (in England) enters into an agreement with A (an unincorporated body of persons) to bail to A equipment consisting of two components (component P and component Q). The agreement is not a hire-purchase agreement and is for a fixed term of 3 years, so paragraphs (a) and (b) of section 15(1) are both satisfied. The rental is payable monthly at a rate of £2,400 a year, but the agreement provides that this is to be reduced to £1,200 a year for the remainder of the agreement if at any time during its currency A returns component Q to the owner Z. On 5th May 1976 A is incorporated as A Ltd, taking over A's assets and liabilities. On 1st March 1977, A Ltd returns component Q. On 1st January 1978, Z and A Ltd agree to extend the earlier agreement by one year, increasing the rental for the final year by £250 to £1,450.

*Analysis* When entered into on 1st March 1975, the agreement is a consumer hire agreement. A falls within the definition of 'individual' in section 189(1) and if A returns component Q before 1st May 1976 the total rental will not exceed £5,000 (see section 15(1)(c)). When this date is passed without component Q having been returned it is obvious that the total rental must now exceed £5,000. Does this mean that the agreement then ceases to be a consumer hire agreement? The answer is no, because there has been no change in the terms of the agreement, and without such a change the agreement cannot move from one category to the other. Similarly, the fact that A's rights and duties under the agreement pass to a body corporate on 5th May 1976 does not cause the agreement to cease to be a consumer hire agreement (see definition of 'hirer' in section 189(1)).

The effect of the modifying agreement of 1st January 1978 is governed by section 82(2), which requires it to be treated as containing provisions reproducing the combined effect of the two actual agreements, that is to say as providing that—

(a)   obligations outstanding on 1st January 1978 are to be treated as outstanding under the modifying agreement;

(b)   the modifying agreement applies at the old rate of hire for the months of January and February 1978, and

(c)   for the year beginning 1st March 1978 A Ltd will be the bailee of component P at a rental of £1,450.

The total rental under the modifying agreement is £1,850. Accordingly the modifying agreement is a regulated agreement. Even if the total rental under the modifying agreement exceeded £5,000 it would still be regulated because of the provisions of section 82(3).

## UNFAIR CONTRACT TERMS ACT 1977
### (1977, c 50)

### PART II
### AMENDMENT OF LAW FOR SCOTLAND

### 15   Scope of Part II

(1)   This Part of this Act [. . .] is subject to Part III of this Act and does not affect the validity of any discharge or indemnity given by a person in consideration of the receipt by him of compensation in settlement of any claim which he has.

(2)   Subject to subsection (3) below, sections 16 [and 17] of this Act apply to any contract only to the extent that the contract—

(a)   relates to the transfer of the ownership or possession of goods from one person to another (with or without work having been done on them);

(b)   constitutes a contract of service or apprenticeship;

(c)   relates to services of whatever kind, including (without prejudice to the foregoing generality) carriage, deposit and pledge, care and custody, mandate, agency, loan and services relating to the use of land;

(d)   relates to the liability of an occupier of land to persons entering upon or using that land;

(e)   relates to a grant of any right or permission to enter upon or use land not amounting to an estate or interest in the land.

(3)   Notwithstanding anything in subsection (2) above, sections 16 [and 17]—

(a)   do not apply to any contract to the extent that the contract—

(i)   is a contract of insurance (including a contract to pay an annuity on human life);

(ii)   relates to the formation, constitution or dissolution of any body corporate or unincorporated association or partnership;

(b)   apply to—

a contract of marine salvage or towage;

a charter party of a ship or hovercraft;

a contract for the carriage of goods by ship or hovercraft; or

a contract to which subsection (4) below relates,

only to the extent that—

(i)   both parties deal or hold themselves out as dealing in the course of a business (and then only in so far as the contract purports to exclude or restrict liability for breach of duty in respect of death or personal injury);
[. . .]

(4)   This subsection relates to a contract in pursuance of which goods are carried by ship or hovercraft and which either—

(a)   specifies ship or hovercraft as the means of carriage over part of the journey to be covered; or

(b)   makes no provision as to the means of carriage and does not exclude ship or hovercraft as that means,

in so far as the contract operates for and in relation to the carriage of the goods by that means.

**16  Liability for breach of duty**

(1)  [Subject to subsection (1A) below,] where a term of a contract [, or a pro-vision of a notice given to persons generally or to particular persons,] purports to exclude or restrict liability for breach of duty arising in the course of any business or from the occupation of any premises used for business purposes of the occu-pier, that term [or provision]—

(a)  shall be void in any case where such exclusion or restriction is in respect of death or personal injury;

(b)  shall, in any other case, have no effect if it was not fair and reasonable to incorporate the term in the contract [or, as the case may be, if it is not fair and reasonable to allow reliance on the provision].

[(1A)  Nothing in paragraph (b) of subsection (1) above shall be taken as imply-ing that a provision of a notice has effect in circumstances where, apart from that paragraph, it would not have effect.]

(2)  Subsection (1)(a) above does not affect the validity of any discharge and indemnity given by a person, on or in connection with an award to him of com-pensation for pneumoconiosis attributable to employment in the coal industry, in respect of any further claim arising from his contracting that disease.

(3)  Where under subsection (1) above a term of a contract [or a provision of a notice] is void or has no effect, the fact that a person agreed to, or was aware of, the term [or provision] shall not of itself be sufficient evidence that he knowingly and voluntarily assumed any risk.

[(4)  *This section does not apply to*—

(a)  *a term in a consumer contract, or*

(b)  *a notice to the extent that it is a consumer notice,*

(but see the provision made about such contracts and notices in sections 62 and 65 of the Consumer Rights Act 2015).]

**17  Control of unreasonable exemptions in [. . .] standard form contracts**

(1)  Any term of a contract which is [. . .] a standard form contract shall have no effect for the purpose of enabling a party to the contract—

(a)  who is in breach of a contractual obligation, to exclude or restrict any liability of his to the [. . .] customer in respect of the breach;

(b)  in respect of a contractual obligation, to render no performance, or to render a performance substantially different from that which the [. . .] customer reasonably expected from the contract;

if it was not fair and reasonable to incorporate the term in the contract.

(2)  In this section 'customer' means a party to a standard form contract who deals on the basis of written standard terms of business of the other party to the contract who himself deals in the course of a business.

[(3)  *This section does not apply to a term in a consumer contract (but see the provision made about such contracts in section 62 of the Consumer Rights Act 2015).]*

[. . .]

**20  Obligations implied by law in sale and hire-purchase contracts**

(1)  Any term of a contract which purports to exclude or restrict liability for breach of the obligations arising from—

(a)  section 12 of the Sale of Goods Act [1979] (seller's implied undertakings as to title etc);

(b)  section 8 of the Supply of Goods (Implied Terms) Act 1973 (implied terms as to title in hire-purchase agreements),

shall be void.

[(1A)  *Any term of a contract which purports to exclude or restrict liability for breach of the obligations arising from*—

(a)  *section 13, 14 or 15 of the 1979 Act (seller's implied undertakings as to conformity of goods with description or sample, or as to their quality or fitness for a particular purpose);*

(b) *section 9, 10 or 11 of the 1973 Act (the corresponding things in relation to hire purchase),*

shall have effect only if it was fair and reasonable to incorporate the term in the contract.

(1B) *This section does not apply to a consumer contract (but see the provision made about such contracts in section 31 of the Consumer Rights Act 2015).]*

*[. . .]*

## 21 Obligations implied by law in other contracts for the supply of goods

(1) Any term of a contract to which this section applies purporting to exclude or restrict liability for breach of an obligation *[such as is referred to in subsection (3) below shall have no effect if it was not fair and reasonable to incorporate the term in the contract.]*

(2) This section applies to any contract to the extent that it relates to any such matter as is referred to in section 15(2)(a) of this Act, but does not apply to—

(a) a contract of sale of goods or a hire-purchase agreement; or

(b) a charterparty of a ship or hovercraft *[. . .]*

(3) An obligation referred to in this subsection is an obligation incurred under a contract in the course of a business and arising by implication of law from the nature of the contract which relates—

(a) to the correspondence of goods with description or sample, or to the quality or fitness of goods for any particular purpose; or

(b) to any right to transfer ownership or possession of goods, or to the enjoyment of quiet possession of goods.

[(3A) Notwithstanding anything in the foregoing provisions of this section, any term of a contract which purports to exclude or restrict liability for breach of the obligations arising under section 11B of the Supply of Goods and Services Act 1982 (implied terms about title, freedom from encumbrances and quiet possession in certain contracts for the transfer of property in goods) shall be void.]

[(3B) *This section does not apply to a consumer contract (but see the provision made about such contracts in section 31 of the Consumer Rights Act 2015).]*

*[. . .]*

*[. . .]*

## 23 Evasion by means of secondary contract

Any term of any contract shall be void which purports to exclude or restrict, or has the effect of excluding or restricting—

(a) the exercise, by a party to any other contract, of any right or remedy which arises in respect of that other contract in consequence of breach of duty, or of obligation, liability for which could not by virtue of the provisions of this Part of this Act be excluded or restricted by a term of that other contract;

(b) the application of the provisions of this Part of this Act in respect of that or any other contract.

## 24 The 'reasonableness' test

(1) In determining for the purposes of this Part of this Act whether it was fair and reasonable to incorporate a term in a contract, regard shall be had only to the circumstances which were, or ought reasonably to have been, known to or in the contemplation of the parties to the contract at the time the contract was made.

(2) In determining for the purposes of section 20 or 21 of this Act whether it was fair and reasonable to incorporate a term in a contract, regard shall be had in particular to the matters specified in Schedule 2 to this Act; but this sub-section shall not prevent a court or arbiter from holding in accordance with any rule of law, that a term which purports to exclude or restrict any relevant liability is not a term of the contract.

[(2A) In determining for the purposes of this Part of this Act whether it is fair and reasonable to allow reliance on a provision of a notice (not being a notice having contractual effect), regard shall be had to all the circumstances obtaining when the liability arose or (but for the provision) would have arisen.]

(3)   Where a term in a contract [or a provision of a notice] purports to restrict liability to a specified sum of money, and the question arises for the purposes of this Part of this Act whether it was fair and reasonable to incorporate the term in the contract [or whether it is fair and reasonable to allow reliance on the provision], then, without prejudice to subsection (2) above [in the case of a term in a contract], regard shall be had in particular to—

(a)   the resources which the party seeking to rely on that term [or provision] could expect to be available to him for the purpose of meeting the liability should it arise;

(b)   how far it was open to that party to cover himself by insurance.

(4)   The onus of proving that it was fair and reasonable to incorporate a term in a contract [or that it is fair and reasonable to allow reliance on a provision of a notice] shall lie on the party so contending.

## 25   Interpretation of Part II

(1)   In this Part of this Act—

'breach of duty' means the breach—

(a)   of any obligation, arising from the express or implied terms of a contract, to take reasonable care or exercise reasonable skill in the performance of the contract;

(b)   of any common law duty to take reasonable care or exercise reasonable skill;

(c)   of the duty of reasonable care imposed by section 2(1) of the Occupiers' Liability (Scotland) Act 1960;

'business' includes a profession and the activities of any government department or local or public authority;

[. . .]

['consumer contract' has the same meaning as in the Consumer Rights Act 2015 (see section 61);

'consumer notice' has the same meaning as in the Consumer Rights Act 2015 (see section 61);]

'goods' has the same meaning as in the Sale of Goods Act [1979];

'hire-purchase agreement' has the same meaning as in section 189(1) of the Consumer Credit Act 1974;

['notice' includes an announcement, whether or not in writing, and any other communication or pretended communication;]

'personal injury' includes any disease and any impairment of physical or mental condition.

[. . .]

(2)   In relation to any breach of duty or obligation, it is immaterial for any purpose of this Part of this Act whether the act or omission giving rise to that breach was inadvertent or intentional or whether liability for it arises directly or vicariously.

(3)   In this Part of this Act, any reference to excluding or restricting any liability includes—

(a)   making the liability or its enforcement subject to any restrictive or onerous conditions;

(b)   excluding or restricting any right or remedy in respect of the liability, or subjecting a person to any prejudice in consequence of his pursuing any such right or remedy;

(c)   excluding or restricting any rule of evidence or procedure;

[. . .]

but does not include an agreement to submit any question to arbitration.

(5)   In section 15 [, 16, 20 and] 21 of this Act, any reference to excluding or

restricting liability for breach of any obligation or duty shall include a reference to excluding or restricting the obligation or duty itself.

## PART III
## PROVISIONS APPLYING TO WHOLE OF UNITED KINGDOM

### 26  International supply contracts

(1)  The limits imposed by this Act on the extent to which a person may exclude or restrict liability by reference to a contract term do not apply to liability arising under such a contract as is described in subsection (3) below.

(2)  The terms of such a contract are not subject to any requirement of reasonableness under section 3 [. . .]: and nothing in Part II of this Act should require the incorporation of the terms of such a contract to be fair and reasonable for them to have effect.

(3)  Subject to subsection (4), that description of contract is one whose characteristics are the following—

(a)  either it is a contract of sale of goods or it is one under or in pursuance of which the possession of ownership of goods passes, and

(b)  it is made by parties whose places of business (or, if they have none, habitual residences) are in the territories of different States (the Channel Islands and the Isle of Man being treated for this purpose as different States from the United Kingdom).

(4)  A contract falls within subsection (3) above only if either—

(a)  the goods in question are, at the time of the conclusion of the contract, in the course of carriage, or will be carried, from the territory of one State to the territory of another; or

(b)  the acts constituting the offer and acceptance have been done in the territories of different States; or

(c)  the contract provides for the goods to be delivered to the territory of a state other than that within whose territory those acts were done.

### 27  Choice of law clauses

(1)  Where the [law applicable to] a contract is the law of any part of the United Kingdom only by choice of the parties (and apart from that choice would be the law of some country outside the United Kingdom) sections 2 to 7 and 16 to 21 of this Act do not operate as part [of the law applicable to the contract].

(2)  This Act has effect notwithstanding any contract term which applies or purports to apply the law of some country outside the United Kingdom, where [. . .]—

(a)  the term appears to the court, or arbitrator or arbiter to have been imposed wholly or mainly for the purpose of enabling the party imposing it to evade the operation of this Act; [. . .]

### 29  Saving for other relevant legislation

(1)  Nothing in this Act removes or restricts the effect of, or prevents reliance upon, any contractual provision which—

(a)  is authorised or required by the express terms or necessary implication of an enactment; or

(b)  being made with a view to compliance with an international agreement to which the United Kingdom is a party, does not operate more restrictively than is contemplated by the agreement.

(2)  A contract term is to be taken—

(a)  for the purposes of Part I of this Act, as satisfying the requirement of reasonableness; and

(b)  for those of Part II, to have been fair and reasonable to incorporate,

if it is incorporated or approved by, or incorporated pursuant to a decision or ruling of, a competent authority acting in the exercise of any statutory jurisdiction or function and is not a term in a contract to which the competent authority is itself a party.

(3)   In this section—

'competent authority' means any court, arbitrator or arbiter, government department or public authority;

'enactment' means any legislation (including subordinate legislation) of the United Kingdom or Northern Ireland and any instrument having effect by virtue of such legislation; and

'statutory' means conferred by an enactment.

. . .

## SCHEDULE 2
### 'GUIDELINES' FOR APPLICATION OF REASONABLENESS TEST

*Sections 11(2) and 24(2)*

The matters to which regard is to be had in particular for the purposes of sections *[6(1A), 7(1A) and (4),]* 20 and 21 are any of the following which appear to be relevant—

(a)   the strength of the bargaining positions of the parties relative to each other, taking into account (among other things) alternative means by which the customer's requirements could have been met;

(b)   whether the customer received an inducement to agree to the terms, or in accepting it had an opportunity of entering into a similar contract with other persons, but without having to accept similar terms;

(c)   whether the customer knew or ought reasonably to have known of the existence and extent of the term (having regard, among other things, to any customs of the trade and any previous course of dealing between the parties);

(d)   where the term excludes or restricts any relevant liability if some condition is not complied with, whether it was reasonable at the time of the contract to expect that compliance with that condition would be practicable;

(e)   whether the goods were manufactured, processed or adapted to the special order of the customer.

### SALE OF GOODS ACT 1979
### (1979, c 54)

## PART I
### CONTRACTS TO WHICH ACT APPLIES

**1   Contracts to which Act applies**

(1)   This Act applies to contracts of sale of goods made on or after (but not to those made before) 1 January 1894.

(2)   In relation to contracts made on certain dates, this Act applies subject to the modification of certain of its sections as mentioned in Schedule 1 below.

(3)   Any such modification is indicated in the section concerned by a reference to Schedule 1 below.

(4)   Accordingly, where a section does not contain such a reference, this Act applies in relation to the contract concerned without such modification of the section.

*[(5)   Certain sections or subsections of this Act do not apply to a contract to which Chapter 2 of Part 1 of the Consumer Rights Act 2015 applies.*

*(6)   Where that is the case it is indicated in the section concerned.]*

## PART II
## FORMATION OF THE CONTRACT

*Contract of sale*

**2  Contract of sale**

(1)  A contract of sale of goods is a contract by which the seller transfers or agrees to transfer the property in goods to the buyer for a money consideration, called the price.

(2)  There may be a contract of sale between one part owner and another.

(3)  A contract of sale may be absolute or conditional.

(4)  Where under a contract of sale the property in the goods is transferred from the seller to the buyer the contract is called a sale.

(5)  Where under a contract of sale the transfer of the property in the goods is to take place at a future time or subject to some condition later to be fulfilled the contract is called an agreement to sell.

(6)  An agreement to sell becomes a sale when the time elapses or the conditions are fulfilled subject to which the property in the goods is to be transferred.

**3  Capacity to buy and sell**

(1)  Capacity to buy and sell is regulated by the general law concerning capacity to contract and to transfer and acquire property.

(2)  Where necessaries are sold and delivered [. . .] to a person who by reason of mental incapacity or drunkenness is incompetent to contract, he must pay a reasonable price for them.

(3)  In subsection (2) above 'necessaries' means goods suitable to the condition in life of the [. . .] person concerned and to his actual requirements at the time of the sale and delivery.

*Formalities of contract*

**4  How contract of sale is made**

(1)  Subject to this and any other Act, a contract of sale may be made in writing (either with or without seal), or by word of mouth, or partly in writing and partly by word of mouth, or may be implied from the conduct of the parties.

(2)  Nothing in this section affects the law relating to corporations.

*Subject matter of contract*

**5  Existing or future goods**

(1)  The goods which form the subject of a contract of sale may be either existing goods, owned or possessed by the seller, or goods to be manufactured or acquired by him after the making of the contract of sale, in this Act called future goods.

(2)  There may be a contract for the sale of goods the acquisition of which by the seller depends on a contingency which may or may not happen.

(3)  Where by a contract of sale the seller purports to effect a present sale of future goods, the contract operates as an agreement to sell the goods.

**6  Goods which have perished**

Where there is a contract for the sale of specific goods, and the goods without the knowledge of the seller have perished at the time when a contract is made, the contract is void.

**7  Goods perishing before sale but after agreement to sell**

Where there is an agreement to sell specific goods and subsequently the goods, without any fault on the part of the seller or buyer, perish before the risk passes to the buyer, the agreement is avoided.

*The price*

## 8  Ascertainment of price

(1)   The price in a contract of sale may be fixed by the contract, or may be left to be fixed in a manner agreed by the contract, or may be determined by the course of dealing between the parties.

(2)   Where the price is not determined as mentioned in subsection (1) above the buyer must pay a reasonable price.

(3)   What is a reasonable price is a question of fact dependent on the circumstances of each particular case.

## 9  Agreement to sell at valuation

(1)   Where there is an agreement to sell goods on the terms that the price is to be fixed by the valuation of a third party, and he cannot or does not make the valuation, the agreement is avoided; but if the goods or any part of them have been delivered to and appropriated by the buyer he must pay a reasonable price for them.

(2)   Where the third party is prevented from making the valuation by the fault of the seller or buyer, the party not at fault may maintain an action for damages against the party at fault.

*[Implied terms etc]*

## 10  Stipulations about time

(1)   Unless a different intention appears from the terms of the contract, stipulations as to time of payment are not of the essence of a contract of sale.

(2)   Whether any other stipulation as to time is or is not of the essence of the contract depends on the terms of the contract.

(3)   In a contract of sale 'month' prima facie means calendar month.

## 11  [*Does not apply to Scotland.*]

## 12  Implied terms about title, etc

(1)   In a contract of sale, other than one to which subsection (3) below applies, there is an implied [term] on the part of the seller that in the case of a sale he has a right to sell the goods, and in the case of an agreement to sell he will have such a right at the time when the property is to pass.

(2)   In a contract of sale, other than one to which subsection (3) below applies, there is also an implied [term] that—

(a)   the goods are free, and will remain free until the time when the property is to pass, from any charge or encumbrance not disclosed or known to the buyer before the contract is made, and

(b)   the buyer will enjoy quiet possession of the goods except so far as it may be disturbed by the owner or other person entitled to the benefit of any charge or encumbrance so disclosed or known.

(3)   This subsection applies to a contract of sale in the case of which there appears from the contract or is to be inferred from its circumstances an intention that the seller should transfer only such title as he or a third person may have.

(4)   In a contract to which subsection (3) above applies there is an implied [term] that all charges or encumbrances known to the seller and not known to the buyer have been disclosed to the buyer before the contract is made.

(5)   In a contract to which subsection (3) above applies there is also an implied [term] that none of the following will disturb the buyer's quiet possession of the goods, namely—

(a)   the seller;

(b)   in a case where the parties to the contract intend that the seller should transfer only such title as a third person may have, that person;

(c)   anyone claiming through or under the seller or that third person otherwise than under a charge or encumbrance disclosed or known to the buyer before the contract is made.

[(5A)   As regards England and Wales and Northern Ireland, the term implied by subsection (1) above is a condition and the terms implied by subsections (2), (4) and (5) above are warranties.]

(6)   Paragraph 3 of Schedule 1 below applies in relation to a contract made before 18 May 1973.

[(7)   *This section does not apply to a contract to which Chapter 2 of Part 1 of the Consumer Rights Act 2015 applies (but see the provision made about such contracts in section 17 of that Act).*]

## 13   Sale by description

(1)   Where there is a contract for the sale of goods by description, there is an implied [term] that the goods will correspond with the description.

[(1A)   As regards England and Wales and Northern Ireland, the term implied by subsection (1) above is a condition.]

(2)   If the sale is by sample as well as by description it is not sufficient that the bulk of the goods corresponds with the sample if the goods do not also correspond with the description.

(3)   A sale of goods is not prevented from being a sale by description by reason only that, being exposed for sale or hire, they are selected by the buyer.

(4)   Paragraph 4 of Schedule 1 below applies in relation to a contract made before 18 May 1973.

[(5)   *This section does not apply to a contract to which Chapter 2 of Part 1 of the Consumer Rights Act 2015 applies (but see the provision made about such contracts in section 11 of that Act).*]

## 14   Implied terms about quality or fitness

(1)   Except as provided by this section and section 15 below and subject to any other enactment, there is no implied [term] about the quality or fitness for any particular purpose of goods supplied under a contract of sale.

[(2)   Where the seller sells goods in the course of a business, there is an implied term that the goods supplied under the contract are of satisfactory quality.

(2A)   For the purposes of this Act, goods are of satisfactory quality if they meet the standard that a reasonable person would regard as satisfactory, taking account of any description of the goods, the price (if relevant) and all the other relevant circumstances.

(2B)   For the purposes of this Act, the quality of goods includes their state and condition and the following (among others) are in appropriate cases aspects of the quality of goods—

(a)   fitness for all the purposes for which goods of the kind in question are commonly supplied,

(b)   appearance and finish,

(c)   freedom from minor defects,

(d)   safety, and

(e)   durability.

(2C)   The term implied by subsection (2) above does not extend to any matter making the quality of goods unsatisfactory—

(a)   which is specifically drawn to the buyer's attention before the contract is made,

(b)   where the buyer examines the goods before the contract is made, which that examination ought to reveal, or

(c)   in the case of a contract for sale by sample, which would have been apparent on a reasonable examination of the sample.]

[. . .]

(3)   Where the seller sells goods in the course of a business and the buyer, expressly or by implication, makes known—

(a)    to the seller, or

(b)    where the purchase price or part of it is payable by instalments and the goods were previously sold by a credit-broker to the seller, to that credit-broker,

any particular purpose for which the goods are being bought,

there is an implied [term] that the goods supplied under the contract are reason-ably fit for that purpose, whether or not that is a purpose for which such goods are commonly supplied, except where the circumstances show that the buyer does not rely, or that it is unreasonable for him to rely, on the skill or judgment of the seller or credit-broker.

(4)    An implied [term] about quality or fitness for a particular purpose may be annexed to a contract of sale by usage.

(5)    The preceding provisions of this section apply to a sale by a person who in the course of a business is acting as agent for another as they apply to a sale by a principal in the course of a business, except where that other is not selling in the course of a business and either the buyer knows that fact or reasonable steps are taken to bring it to the notice of the buyer before the contract is made.

[(6)    As regards England and Wales and Northern Ireland, the terms implied by subsections (2) and (3) above are conditions.]

(7)    Paragraph 5 of Schedule 1 below applies in relation to a contract made on or after 18 May 1973 and before the appointed day, and paragraph 6 in relation to one made before 18 May 1973.

(8)    In subsection (7) above and paragraph 5 of Schedule 1 below references to the appointed day are to the day appointed for the purposes of those provisions by an order of the Secretary of State made by statutory instrument.

[(9)    This section does not apply to a contract to which Chapter 2 of Part 1 of the Consumer Rights Act 2015 applies (but see the provision made about such contracts in sections 9, 10 and 18 of that Act).]

*Sale by sample*

## 15    Sale by sample

(1)    A contract of sale is a contract for sale by sample where there is an express or implied term to that effect in the contract.

(2)    In the case of a contract for sale by sample there is an implied [term]—

(a)    that the bulk will correspond with the sample in quality;

[. . .]

(c)    that the goods will be free from any defect, making their quality unsatisfactory, which would not be apparent on reasonable examination of the sample.

[(3)    As regards England and Wales and Northern Ireland, the term implied by subsection (2) above is a condition.]

(4)    Paragraph 7 of Schedule 1 below applies in relation to a contract made before 18 May 1973.

[(5)    This section does not apply to a contract to which Chapter 2 of Part 1 of the Consumer Rights Act 2015 applies (but see the provision made about such contracts in sections 13 and 18 of that Act).]

*Miscellaneous*

## 15A    [*Does not apply to Scotland.*]

## [15B    Remedies for breach of contract as respects Scotland

(1)    Where in a contract of sale the seller is in breach of any term of the contract (express or implied), the buyer shall be entitled—

(a)    to claim damages, and

(b)    if the breach is material, to reject any goods delivered under the contract and treat it as repudiated.

[(1A)   *Subsection (1) does not apply to a contract to which Chapter 2 of Part 1 of the Consumer Rights Act 2015 applies (but see the provision made about such contracts in sections 19 to 22 of that Act).]*
[. . .]
(3)   This section applies to Scotland only.]

## PART III
## EFFECTS OF THE CONTRACT

*Transfer of property as between seller and buyer*

### 16   Goods must be ascertained
[Subject to section 20A below] where there is a contract for the sale of unascertained goods no property in the goods is transferred to the buyer unless and until the goods are ascertained.

### 17   Property passes when intended to pass
(1)   Where there is a contract for the sale of specific or ascertained goods the property in them is transferred to the buyer at such time as the parties to the contract intend it to be transferred.

(2)   For the purpose of ascertaining the intention of the parties regard shall be had to the terms of the contract, the conduct of the parties and the circumstances of the case.

### 18   Rules for ascertaining intention
Unless a different intention appears, the following are rules for ascertaining the intention of the parties as to the time at which the property in the goods is to pass to the buyer.

*Rule 1.*—Where there is an unconditional contract for the sale of specific goods in a deliverable state the property in the goods passes to the buyer when the contract is made, and it is immaterial whether the time of payment or the time of delivery, or both, be postponed.

*Rule 2.*—Where there is a contract for the sale of specific goods and the seller is bound to do something to the goods for the purpose of putting them into a deliverable state, the property does not pass until the thing is done and the buyer has notice that it has been done.

*Rule 3.*—Where there is a contract for the sale of specific goods in a deliverable state but the seller is bound to weigh, measure, test, or do some other act or thing with reference to the goods for the purpose of ascertaining the price, the property does not pass until the act or thing is done and the buyer has notice that it has been done.

*Rule 4.*—When goods are delivered to the buyer on approval or on sale or return or other similar terms the property in the goods passes to the buyer:—

(a)   when he signifies his approval or acceptance to the seller or does any other act adopting the transaction;

(b)   if he does not signify his approval or acceptance to the seller but retains the goods without giving notice of rejection, then, if a time has been fixed for the return of the goods, on the expiration of that time, and, if no time has been fixed, on the expiration of a reasonable time.

*Rule 5.*—(1)   Where there is a contract for the sale of unascertained or future goods by description, and goods of that description and in a deliverable state are unconditionally appropriated to the contract, either by the seller with the assent of the buyer or by the buyer with the assent of the seller, the property in the goods then passes to the buyer; and the assent may be express or implied, and may be given either before or after the appropriation is made.

(2)   Where, in pursuance of the contract, the seller delivers the goods to the buyer or to a carrier or other bailee or custodier (whether named by the buyer or

not) for the purpose of transmission to the buyer, and does not reserve the right of disposal, he is to be taken to have unconditionally appropriated the goods to the contract.

[(3)   Where there is a contract for the sale of a specified quantity of unascertained goods in a deliverable state forming part of a bulk which is identified either in the contract or by subsequent agreement between the parties and the bulk is reduced to (or to less than) that quantity, then, if the buyer under that contract is the only buyer to whom goods are then due out of the bulk—

(a)   the remaining goods are to be taken as appropriated to that contract at the time when the bulk is so reduced; and

(b)   the property in those goods then passes to that buyer.

(4)   Paragraph (3) above applies also (with the necessary modifications) where a bulk is reduced to (or to less than) the aggregate of the quantities due to a single buyer under separate contracts relating to that bulk and he is the only buyer to whom goods are then due out of that bulk.]

## 19   Reservation of right of disposal

(1)   Where there is a contract for the sale of specific goods or where goods are subsequently appropriated to the contract, the seller may, by the terms of the contract or appropriation, reserve the right of disposal of the goods until certain conditions are fulfilled; and in such a case, notwithstanding the delivery of the goods to the buyer, or to a carrier or other bailee or custodier for the purpose of transmission to the buyer, the property in the goods does not pass to the buyer until the conditions imposed by the seller are fulfilled.

(2)   Where goods are shipped, and by the bill of lading the goods are deliverable to the order of the seller or his agent, the seller is prima facie to be taken to reserve the right of disposal.

(3)   Where the seller of goods draws on the buyer for the price, and transmits the bill of exchange and bill of lading to the buyer together to secure acceptance or payment of the bill of exchange, the buyer is bound to return the bill of lading if he does not honour the bill of exchange, and if he wrongfully retains the bill of lading the property in the goods does not pass to him.

## 20   [Passing of risk]

(1)   Unless otherwise agreed, the goods remain at the seller's risk until the property in them is transferred to the buyer, but when the property in them is transferred to the buyer the goods are at the buyer's risk whether delivery has been made or not.

(2)   But where delivery has been delayed through the fault of either buyer or seller the goods are at the risk of the party at fault as regards any loss which might not have occurred but for such fault.

(3)   Nothing in this section affects the duties or liabilities of either seller or buyer as a bailee or custodier of the goods of the other party.

[(4)   *This section does not apply to a contract to which Chapter 2 of Part 1 of the Consumer Rights Act 2015 applies (but see the provision made about such contracts in section 29 of that Act).*]

## [20A   Undivided shares in goods forming part of a bulk

(1)   This section applies to a contract for the sale of a specified quantity of unascertained goods if the following conditions are met—

(a)   the goods or some of them form part of a bulk which is identified either in the contract or by subsequent agreement between the parties; and

(b)   the buyer has paid the price for some or all of the goods which are the subject of the contract and which form part of the bulk.

(2)   Where this section applies, then (unless the parties agree otherwise), as soon as the conditions specified in paragraphs (a) and (b) of subsection (1) above are met or at such later time as the parties may agree—

(a)   property in an undivided share in the bulk is transferred to the buyer; and

(b)   the buyer becomes an owner in common of the bulk.

(3)   Subject to subsection (4) below, for the purposes of this section, the undivided share of a buyer in a bulk at any time shall be such share as the quantity of goods paid for and due to the buyer out of the bulk bears to the quantity of goods in the bulk at that time.

(4)   Where the aggregate of the undivided shares of buyers in a bulk determined under subsection (3) above would at any time exceed the whole of the bulk at that time, the undivided share in the bulk of each buyer shall be reduced proportionately so that the aggregate of the undivided shares is equal to the whole bulk.

(5)   Where a buyer has paid the price for only some of the goods due to him out of a bulk, any delivery to the buyer out of the bulk shall, for the purposes of this section, be ascribed in the first place to the goods in respect of which payment has been made.

(6)   For the purpose of this section payment of part of the price for any goods shall be treated as payment for a corresponding part of the goods.]

### [20B   Deemed consent by co-owner to dealings in bulk goods

(1)   A person who has become an owner in common of a bulk by virtue of section 20A above shall be deemed to have consented to—

(a)   any delivery of goods out of the bulk to any other owner in common of the bulk, being goods which are due to him under his contract;

(b)   any dealing with or removal, delivery or disposal of goods in the bulk by any other person who is an owner in common of the bulk in so far as the goods fall within that co-owner's undivided share in the bulk at the time of the removal, dealing, delivery or disposal.

(2)   No cause of action shall accrue to anyone against a person by reason of that person having acted in accordance with paragraph (a) or (b) of subsection (1) above in reliance on any consent deemed to have been given under that subsection.

(3)   Nothing in this section or section 20A above shall—

(a)   impose an obligation on a buyer of goods out of a bulk to compensate any other buyer of goods out of that bulk for any shortfall in the goods received by that other buyer;

(b)   affects any contractual arrangement between buyers of goods out of a bulk for adjustments between themselves; or

(c)   affect the rights of any buyer under his contract.]

*Transfer of title*

### 21   Sale by person not the owner

(1)   Subject to this Act, where goods are sold by a person who is not their owner, and who does not sell them under the authority or with the consent of the owner, the buyer acquires no better title to the goods than the seller had, unless the owner of the goods is by his conduct precluded from denying the seller's authority to sell.

(2)   Nothing in this Act affects—

(a)   the provisions of the Factors Acts or any enactment enabling the apparent owner of goods to dispose of them as if he were their true owner;

(b)   the validity of any contract of sale under any special common law or statutory power of sale or under the order of a court of competent jurisdiction.

### 22   [*Does not apply to Scotland.*]

### 23   Sale under voidable title

When the seller of goods has a voidable title to them, but his title has not been avoided at the time of the sale, the buyer acquires a good title to the goods, provided he buys them in good faith and without notice of the seller's defect of title.

### 24  Seller in possession after sale
Where a person having sold goods continues or is in possession of the goods, or of the documents of title to the goods, the delivery or transfer by that person, or by a mercantile agent acting for him, of the goods or documents of title under any sale, pledge, or other disposition thereof, to any person receiving the same in good faith and without notice of the previous sale, has the same effect as if the person making the delivery or transfer were expressly authorised by the owner of the goods to make the same.

### 25  Buyer in possession after sale
(1)   Where a person having bought or agreed to buy goods obtains, with the consent of the seller, possession of the goods or the documents of title to the goods, the delivery or transfer by that person, or by a mercantile agent acting for him, of the goods or documents of title, under any sale, pledge, or other disposition thereof, to any person receiving the same in good faith and without notice of any lien or other right of the original seller in respect of the goods, has the same effect as if the person making the delivery or transfer were a mercantile agent in possession of the goods or documents of title with the consent of the owner.

(2)   For the purposes of subsection (1) above—

(a)   the buyer under a conditional sale agreement is to be taken not to be a person who has bought or agreed to buy goods, and

(b)   'conditional sale agreement' means an agreement for the sale of goods which is a consumer credit agreement within the meaning of the Consumer Credit Act 1974 under which the purchase price or part of it is payable by instalments, and the property in the goods is to remain in the seller (notwithstanding that the buyer is to be in possession of the goods) until such conditions as to the payment of instalments or otherwise as may be specified in the agreement are fulfilled.

(3)   Paragraph 9 of Schedule 1 below applies in relation to a contract under which a person buys or agrees to buy goods and which is made before the appointed day.

(4)   In subsection (3) above and paragraph 9 of Schedule 1 below references to the appointed day are to the day appointed for the purposes of those provisions by an order of the Secretary of State made by statutory instrument.

### 26  Supplementary to sections 24 and 25
In sections 24 and 25 above 'mercantile agent' means a mercantile agent having in the customary course of his business as such agent authority either—

(a)   to sell goods, or
(b)   to consign goods for the purpose of sale, or
(c)   to buy goods, or
(d)   to raise money on the security of goods.

PART IV
## PERFORMANCE OF THE CONTRACT

### 27  Duties of seller and buyer
It is the duty of the seller to deliver the goods, and of the buyer to accept and pay for them, in accordance with the terms of the contract of sale.

### 28  Payment and delivery are concurrent conditions
Unless otherwise agreed, delivery of the goods and payment of the price are concurrent conditions, that is to say, the seller must be ready and willing to give possession of the goods to the buyer in exchange for the price and the buyer must be ready and willing to pay the price in exchange for possession of the goods.

## 29  Rules about delivery

(1)  Whether it is for the buyer to take possession of the goods or for the seller to send them to the buyer is a question depending in each case on the contract, express or implied, between the parties.

(2)  Apart from any such contract, express or implied, the place of delivery is the seller's place of business if he has one, and if not, his residence; except that, if the contract is for the sale of specific goods, which to the knowledge of the parties when the contract is made are in some other place, then that place is the place of delivery.

(3)  Where under the contract of sale the seller is bound to send the goods to the buyer, but no time for sending them is fixed, the seller is bound to send them within a reasonable time.

[(3A)  Subsection (3) does not apply to a contract to which Chapter 2 of Part 1 of the Consumer Rights Act 2015 applies (but see the provision made about such contracts in section 28 of that Act).]

(4)  Where the goods at the time of sale are in the possession of a third person, there is no delivery by seller to buyer unless and until the third person acknowledges to the buyer that he holds the goods on his behalf; but nothing in this section affects the operation of the issue or transfer of any document of title to goods.

(5)  Demand or tender of delivery may be treated as ineffectual unless made at a reasonable hour, and what is a reasonable hour is a question of fact.

(6)  Unless otherwise agreed, the expenses of and incidental to putting the goods into a deliverable state must be borne by the seller.

## 30  Delivery of wrong quantity

(1)  Where the seller delivers to the buyer a quantity of goods less than he contracted to sell, the buyer may reject them, but if the buyer accepts the goods so delivered he must pay for them at the contract rate.

(2)  Where the seller delivers to the buyer a quantity of goods larger than he contracted to sell, the buyer may accept the goods included in the contract and reject the rest, or he may reject the whole.

. . .

[(2C)  Subsections (2A) and (2B) above do not apply to Scotland.

(2D)  Where the seller delivers a quantity of goods—

(a)  less than he contracted to sell, the buyer shall not be entitled to reject the goods under subsection (1) above,

(b)  larger than he contracted to sell, the buyer shall not be entitled to reject the whole under subsection (2) above,

unless the shortfall or excess is material.

(2E)  Subsection (2D) above applies to Scotland only.]

(3)  Where the seller delivers to the buyer a quantity of goods larger than he contracted to sell and the buyer accepts the whole of the goods so delivered he must pay for them at the contract rate.

[. . .]

(5)  This section is subject to any usage of trade, special agreement, or course of dealing between the parties.

[(6)  This section does not apply to a contract to which Chapter 2 of Part 1 of the Consumer Rights Act 2015 applies (but see the provision made about such contracts in section 25 of that Act).]

## 31  Instalment deliveries

(1)  Unless otherwise agreed, the buyer of goods is not bound to accept delivery of them by instalments.

(2)  Where there is a contract for the sale of goods to be delivered by stated instalments, which are to be separately paid for, and the seller makes defective deliveries in respect of one or more instalments, or the buyer neglects or refuses to

take delivery of or pay for one or more instalments, it is a question in each case depending on the terms of the contract and the circumstances of the case whether the breach of contract is a repudiation of the whole contract or whether it is a severable breach giving rise to a claim for compensation but not to a right to treat the whole contract as repudiated.

*[(3) This section does not apply to a contract to which Chapter 2 of Part 1 of the Consumer Rights Act 2015 applies (but see the provision made about such contracts in section 26 of that Act).]*

### 32 Delivery to carrier

(1) Where, in pursuance of a contract of sale, the seller is authorised or required to send the goods to the buyer, delivery of the goods to a carrier (whether named by the buyer or not) for the purpose of transmission to the buyer is prima facie deemed to be delivery of the goods to the buyer.

(2) Unless otherwise authorised by the buyer, the seller must make such contact with the carrier on behalf of the buyer as may be reasonable having regard to the nature of the goods and the other circumstances of the case; and if the seller omits to do so, and the goods are lost or damaged in course of transit, the buyer may decline to treat the delivery to the carrier as a delivery to himself or may hold the seller responsible in damages.

(3) Unless otherwise agreed, where goods are sent by the seller to the buyer by a route involving sea transit, under circumstances in which it is usual to insure, the seller must give such notice to the buyer as may enable him to insure them during their sea transit, and if the seller fails to do so, the goods are at his risk during such sea transit.

*[(4) This section does not apply to a contract to which Chapter 2 of Part 1 of the Consumer Rights Act 2015 applies (but see the provision made about such contracts in section 29 of that Act).]*

### 33 Risk where goods are delivered at distant place

*[(1)]* Where the seller of goods agrees to deliver them at his own risk at a place other than that where they are when sold, the buyer must nevertheless (unless otherwise agreed) take any risk of deterioration in the goods necessarily incident to the course of transit.

*[(2) This section does not apply to a contract to which Chapter 2 of Part 1 of the Consumer Rights Act 2015 applies (but see the provision made about such contracts in section 29 of that Act).]*

### 34 Buyer's right of examining the goods

*[(1)]* [Unless otherwise agreed, when the seller tenders delivery of goods to the buyer, he is bound on request to afford the buyer a reasonable opportunity of examining the goods for the purpose of ascertaining whether they are in conformity with the contract and, in the case of a contract for sale by sample, of comparing the bulk with the sample.]

*[(2) Nothing in this section affects the operation of section 22 (time limit for short-term right to reject) of the Consumer Rights Act 2015.]*

### 35 Acceptance

(1) The buyer is deemed to have accepted the goods [subject to subsection (2) below—

    (a)   when he intimates to the seller that he has accepted them, or

    (b)   when the goods have been delivered to him and he does any act in relation to them which is inconsistent with the ownership of the seller.

(2) Where goods are delivered to the buyer, and he has not previously examined them, he is not deemed to have accepted them under subsection (1) above until he has had a reasonable opportunity of examining them for the purpose—

(a)    of ascertaining whether they are in conformity with the contract, and

(b)    in the case of a contract for sale by sample, of comparing the bulk with the sample.

*[. . .]*

(4)    The buyer is also deemed to have accepted the goods when after the lapse of a reasonable time he retains the goods without intimating to the seller that he has rejected them.

(5)    The questions that are material in determining for the purposes of subsection (4) above whether a reasonable time has elapsed include whether the buyer has had a reasonable opportunity of examining the goods for the purpose mentioned in subsection (2) above.

(6)    The buyer is not by virtue of this section deemed to have accepted the goods merely because—

(a)    he asks for, or agrees to, their repair by or under an arrangement with the seller, or

(b)    the goods are delivered to another under a sub-sale or other disposition.

(7)    Where the contract is for the sale of goods making one or more commercial units, a buyer accepting any goods included in a unit is deemed to have accepted all the goods making the unit; and in this subsection 'commercial unit' means a unit division of which would materially impair the value of the goods or the character of the unit.

(8)]    Paragraph 10 of Schedule 1 below applies in relation to a contract made before 22 April 1967 or (in the application of this Act to Northern Ireland) 28 July 1967.

*[(9)    This section does not apply to a contract to which Chapter 2 of Part 1 of the Consumer Rights Act 2015 applies (but see the provision made about such contracts in section 21 of that Act).]*

## [35A    Right of partial rejection

(1)    If the buyer—

(a)    has the right to reject the goods by reason of a breach on the part of the seller that affects some or all of them, but

(b)    accepts some of the goods, including, where there are any goods unaffected by the breach, all such goods,

he does not by accepting them lose his right to reject the rest.

(2)    In the case of a buyer having the right to reject an instalment of goods, subsection (1) above applies as if references to the goods were references to the goods comprised in the instalment.

(3)    For the purposes of subsection (1) above, goods are affected by a breach if by reason of the breach they are not in conformity with the contract.

(4)    This section applies unless a contrary intention appears in, or is to be implied from, the contract.]

*[(5)    This section does not apply to a contract to which Chapter 2 of Part 1 of the Consumer Rights Act 2015 applies (but see the provision made about such contracts in section 21 of that Act).]*

## 36    Buyer not bound to return rejected goods

*[(1)]*    Unless otherwise agreed, where goods are delivered to the buyer, and he refuses to accept them, having the right to do so, he is not bound to return them to the seller, but it is sufficient if he intimates to the seller that he refuses to accept them.

*[(2)    This section does not apply to a contract to which Chapter 2 of Part 1 of the Consumer Rights Act 2015 applies (but see the provision made about such contracts in section 20 of that Act).]*

## 37    Buyer's liability for not taking delivery of goods

(1)    When the seller is ready and willing to deliver the goods, and requests the

buyer to take delivery, and the buyer does not within a reasonable time after such request take delivery of the goods, he is liable to the seller for any loss occasioned by his neglect or refusal to take delivery, and also for a reasonable charge for the care and custody of the goods.

(2)  Nothing in this section affects the rights of the seller where the neglect or refusal of the buyer to take delivery amounts to a repudiation of the contract.

## PART V
## RIGHTS OF UNPAID SELLER AGAINST THE GOODS

### *Preliminary*

### 38  Unpaid seller defined

(1)  The seller of goods is an unpaid seller within the meaning of this Act—

(a)   when the whole of the price has not been paid or tendered;

(b)   when a bill of exchange or other negotiable instrument has been received as conditional payment, and the condition on which it was received has not been fulfilled by reason of the dishonour of the instrument or otherwise.

(2)  In this Part of this Act 'seller' includes any person who is in the position of a seller, as, for instance, an agent of the seller to whom the bill of lading has been indorsed, or a consignor or agent who has himself paid (or is directly responsible for) the price.

### 39  Unpaid seller's rights

(1)  Subject to this and any other Act, notwithstanding that the property in the goods may have passed to the buyer, the unpaid seller of goods, as such, has by implication of law—

(a)   a lien on the goods or right to retain them for the price while he is in possession of them;

(b)   in the case of the insolvency of the buyer, a right of stopping the goods in transit after he has parted with the possession of them;

(c)   a right of re-sale as limited by this Act.

(2)  Where the property in goods has not passed to the buyer, the unpaid seller has (in addition to his other remedies) a right of withholding delivery similar to and coextensive with his rights of lien or retention and stoppage in transit where the property has passed to the buyer.

[. . .]

### *Unpaid seller's lien*

### 41  Seller's lien

(1)  Subject to this Act, the unpaid seller of goods who is in possession of them is entitled to retain possession of them until payment or tender of the price in the following cases:—

(a)   where the goods have been sold without any stipulation as to credit;

(b)   where the goods have been sold on credit but the term of credit has expired;

(c)   where the buyer becomes insolvent.

(2)  The seller may exercise his lien or right of retention notwithstanding that he is in possession of the goods as agent or bailee or custodier for the buyer.

### 42  Part delivery

Where an unpaid seller has made part delivery of the goods, he may exercise his lien or right of retention on the remainder, unless such part delivery has been made under such circumstances as to show an agreement to waive the lien or right of retention.

### 43  Termination of lien

(1)   The unpaid seller of goods loses his lien or right of retention in respect of them—

(a)   when he delivers the goods to a carrier or other bailee or custodier for the purpose of transmission to the buyer without reserving the right of disposal of the goods;

(b)   when the buyer or his agent lawfully obtains possession of the goods;

(c)   by waiver of the lien or right of retention.

(2)   An unpaid seller of goods who has a lien or right of retention in respect of them does not lose his lien or right of retention by reason only that he has obtained judgment or decree for the price of the goods.

*Stoppage in transit*

### 44  Right of stoppage in transit

Subject to this Act, when the buyer of goods becomes insolvent the unpaid seller who has parted with the possession of the goods has the right of stopping them in transit, that is to say, he may resume possession of the goods as long as they are in course of transit, and may retain them until payment or tender of the price.

### 45  Duration of transit

(1)   Goods are deemed to be in course of transit from the time when they are delivered to a carrier or other bailee or custodier for the purpose of transmission to the buyer, until the buyer or his agent in that behalf takes delivery of them from the carrier or other bailee or custodier.

(2)   If the buyer or his agent in that behalf obtains delivery of the goods before their arrival at the appointed destination, the transit is at an end.

(3)   If, after the arrival of the goods at the appointed destination, the carrier or other bailee or custodier acknowledges to the buyer or his agent that he holds the goods on his behalf and continues in possession of them as bailee or custodier for the buyer or his agent, the transit is at an end, and it is immaterial that a further destination for the goods may have been indicated by the buyer.

(4)   If the goods are rejected by the buyer, and the carrier or other bailee or custodier continues in possession of them, the transit is not deemed to be at an end, even if the seller has refused to receive them back.

(5)   When goods are delivered to a ship chartered by the buyer it is a question depending on the circumstances of the particular case whether they are in the possession of the master as a carrier or as agent to the buyer.

(6)   Where the carrier or other bailee or custodier wrongfully refuses to deliver the goods to the buyer or his agent in that behalf, the transit is deemed to be at an end.

(7)   Where part delivery of the goods has been made to the buyer or his agent in that behalf, the remainder of the goods may be stopped in transit, unless such part delivery has been made under such circumstances as to show an agreement to give up possession of the whole of the goods.

### 46  How stoppage in transit is effected

(1)   The unpaid seller may exercise his right of stoppage in transit either by taking actual possession of the goods or by giving notice of his claim to the carrier or other bailee or custodier in whose possession the goods are.

(2)   The notice may be given either to the person in actual possession of the goods or to his principal.

(3)   If given to the principal, the notice is ineffective unless given at such time and under such circumstances that the principal, by the exercise of reasonable diligence, may communicate it to his servant or agent in time to prevent a delivery to the buyer.

(4)   When notice of stoppage in transit is given by the seller to the carrier or

other bailee or custodier in possession of the goods, he must re-deliver the goods to, or according to the directions of, the seller; and the expenses of the re-delivery must be borne by the seller.

*Re-sale etc by buyer*

**47   Effect of sub-sale etc by buyer**
(1)   Subject to this Act, the unpaid seller's right of lien or retention or stoppage in transit is not affected by any sale or other disposition of the goods which the buyer may have made, unless the seller has assented to it.

(2)   Where a document of title to goods has been lawfully transferred to any person as buyer or owner of the goods, and that person transfers the document to a person who takes it in good faith and for valuable consideration, then—
    (a)   if the last-mentioned transfer was by way of sale the unpaid seller's right of lien or retention or stoppage in transit is defeated; and
    (b)   if the last-mentioned transfer was made by way of pledge or other disposition for value, the unpaid seller's right of lien or retention of stoppage in transit can only be exercised subject to the rights of the transferee.

*Rescission: and re-sale by seller*

**48   Rescission: and re-sale by seller**
(1)   Subject to this section, a contract of sale is not rescinded by the mere exercise by an unpaid seller of his right of lien or retention or stoppage in transit.

(2)   Where an unpaid seller who has exercised his right of lien or retention or stoppage in transit re-sells the goods, the buyer acquires a good title to them as against the original buyer.

(3)   Where the goods are of a perishable nature, or where the unpaid seller gives notice to the buyer of his intention to re-sell, and the buyer does not within a reasonable time pay or tender the price, the unpaid seller may re-sell the goods and recover from the original buyer damages for any loss occasioned by his breach of contract.

(4)   Where the seller expressly reserves the right of re-sale in case the buyer should make default, and on the buyer making default re-sells the goods, the original contract of sale is rescinded but without prejudice to any claim the seller may have for damages.

*[. . .]*

PART VI
ACTIONS FOR BREACH OF THE CONTRACT

*Seller's remedies*

**49   Action for price**
(1)   Where, under a contract of sale, the property in the goods has passed to the buyer and he wrongfully neglects or refuses to pay for the goods according to the terms of the contract, the seller may maintain an action against him for the price of the goods.

(2)   Where, under a contract of sale, the price is payable on a day certain irrespective of delivery and the buyer wrongfully neglects or refuses to pay such price, the seller may maintain an action for the price, although the property in goods has not passed and the goods have not been appropriated to the contract.

(3)   Nothing in this section prejudices the right of the seller in Scotland to recover interest on the price from the date of tender of the goods, or from the date on which the price was payable, as the case may be.

## 50   Damages for non-acceptance

(1)   Where the buyer wrongfully neglects or refuses to accept and pay for the goods, the seller may maintain an action against him for damages for non-acceptance.

(2)   The measure of damages is the estimated loss directly and naturally resulting in the ordinary course of events, from the buyer's breach of contract.

(3)   Where there is an available market for the goods in question the measure of damages is prima facie to be ascertained by the difference between the contract price and the market or current price at the time or times when the goods ought to have been accepted or (if no time was fixed for acceptance) at the time of the refusal to accept.

*Buyer's remedies*

## 51   Damages for non-delivery

(1)   Where the seller wrongfully neglects or refuses to deliver the goods to the buyer, the buyer may maintain an action against the seller for damages for non-delivery.

(2)   The measure of damages is the estimated loss directly and naturally resulting, in the ordinary course of events, from the seller's breach of contract.

(3)   Where there is an available market for the goods in question the measure of damages is prima facie to be ascertained by the difference between the contract price and the market or current price of the goods at the time or times when they ought to have been delivered or (if no time was fixed) at the time of the refusal to deliver.

[(4)   *This section does not apply to a contract to which Chapter 2 of Part 1 of the Consumer Rights Act 2015 applies (but see the provision made about such contracts in section 19 of that Act).]*

## 52   Specific performance

(1)   If any action for breach of contract to deliver specific or ascertained goods the court may, if it thinks fit, on the plaintiff's application, by its judgment or decree direct that the contract shall be performed specifically, without giving the defendant the option of retaining the goods on payment of damages.

(2)   The plaintiff's application may be made at any time before judgment or decree.

(3)   The judgment or decree may be unconditional, or on such terms and conditions as to damages, payment of the price and otherwise as seem just to the court.

(4)   The provisions of this section shall be deemed to be supplementary to, and not in derogation of, the right of specific implement in Scotland.

[(5)   *This section does not apply to a contract to which Chapter 2 of Part 1 of the Consumer Rights Act 2015 applies (but see the provision made about such contracts in section 19 of that Act).]*

## 53   [*Does not apply to Scotland.*]

## [53A   Measure of damages as respects Scotland

(1)   The measure of damages for the seller's breach of contract is the estimated loss directly and naturally resulting, in the ordinary course of events, from the breach.

(2)   Where the seller's breach consists of the delivery of goods which are not of the quality required by the contract and the buyer retains the goods, such loss as aforesaid is prima facie the difference between the value of the goods at the time of delivery to the buyer and the value they would have had if they had fulfilled the contract.

*[(2A)   This section does not apply to a contract to which Chapter 2 of Part 1 of the Consumer Rights Act 2015 applies (but see the provision made about such contracts in section 19 of that Act).]*

(3)   This section applies to Scotland only.]

*Interest, etc*

### 54   Interest, etc

*[(1)]*   Nothing in this Act affects the right of the buyer or the seller to recover interest or special damages in any case where by law interest or special damages may be recoverable, or to recover money paid where the consideration for the payment of it has failed.

*[(2)   This section does not apply to a contract to which Chapter 2 of Part 1 of the Consumer Rights Act 2015 applies (but see the provision made about such contracts in section 19 of that Act.]*

## PART VII
## SUPPLEMENTARY

### 55   Exclusion of implied terms

(1)   Where a right, duty or liability would arise under a contract of sale of goods by implication of law, it may (subject to the Unfair Contract Terms Act 1977) be negatived or varied by express agreement, or by the course of dealing between the parties, or by such usage as binds both parties to the contract.

*[(1A)   Subsection (1) does not apply to a contract to which Chapter 2 of Part 1 of the Consumer Rights Act 2015 applies (but see the provision made about such contracts in section 31 of that Act).]*

(2)   An express [term] does not negative a [term] implied by this Act unless inconsistent with it.

(3)   Paragraph 11 of Schedule 1 below applies in relation to a contract made on or after 18 May 1973 and before 1 February 1978, and paragraph 12 in relation to one made before 18 May 1973.

### 56   Conflict of laws

Paragraph 13 of Schedule 1 below applies in relation to a contract made on or after 18 May 1973 and before 1 February 1978, so as to make provision about conflict of laws in relation to such a contract.

### 57   Auction sales

(1)   Where goods are put up for sale by auction in lots, each lot is prima facie deemed to be the subject of a separate contract of sale.

(2)   A sale by auction is complete when the auctioneer announces its completion by the fall of the hammer, or in other customary manner; and until the announcement is made any bidder may retract his bid.

(3)   A sale by auction may be notified to be subject to a reserve or upset price, and a right to bid may also be reserved expressly by or on behalf of the seller.

(4)   Where a sale by auction is not notified to be subject to a right to bid by or on behalf of the seller, it is not lawful for the seller to bid himself or to employ any person to bid at the sale, or for the auctioneer knowingly to take any bid from the seller or any such person.

(5)   A sale contravening subsection (4) above may be treated as fraudulent by the buyer.

(6)   Where, in respect of a sale by auction, a right to bid is expressly reserved (but not otherwise) the seller or any one person on his behalf may bid at the auction.

### 58   Payment into court in Scotland

*[(1)]*   In Scotland where a buyer has elected to accept goods which he might

have rejected, and to treat a breach of contract as only giving rise to a claim for damages, he may, in an action by the seller for the price, be required, in the discretion of the court before which the action depends, to consign or pay into court the price of the goods, or part of the price, or to give other reasonable security for its due payment.

[(2)   This section does not apply to a contract to which Chapter 2 of Part 1 of the *Consumer Rights Act 2015* applies (but see the provision made about such contracts in section 27 of that Act).]

### 59   Reasonable time a question of fact
Where a reference is made in this Act to a reasonable time the question what is a reasonable time is a question of fact.

### 60   Rights etc enforceable by action
Where a right, duty or liability is declared by this Act, it may (unless otherwise provided by this Act) be enforced by action.

### 61   Interpretation
(1)   In this Act, unless the context or subject matter otherwise requires,—
'action' includes counterclaim and set-off, and in Scotland condescendence and claim and compensation;
['bulk' means a mass or collection of goods of the same kind which—
  (a)   is contained in a defined space or area; and
  (b)   is such that any goods in the bulk are interchangeable with any other goods therein of the same number or quantity;]
'business' includes a profession and the activities of any government department (including a Northern Ireland department) or local or public authority;
'buyer' means a person who buys or agrees to buy goods;
[. . .]
'contract of sale' includes an agreement to sell as well as a sale;
'credit-broker' means a person acting in the course of a business of credit brokerage carried on by him, that is a business of effecting introductions of individuals desiring to obtain credit—
  (a)   to persons carrying on any business so far as it relates to the provision of credit, or
  (b)   to other persons engaged in credit brokerage;
'defendant' includes in Scotland defender, respondent, and claimant in a multiplepoinding;
'delivery' means voluntary transfer of possession from one person to another; [except that in relation to sections 20A and 20B above it includes such appropriation of goods to the contract as results in property in the goods being transferred to the buyer;]
'document of title to goods' has the same meaning as it has in the Factors Acts;
'Factors Acts' means the Factors Act 1889, the Factors (Scotland) Act 1890, and any enactment amending or substituted for the same;
'fault' means wrongful act or default;
'future goods' means goods to be manufactured or acquired by the seller after the making of the contract of sale;
'goods' includes all personal chattels other than things in action and money, and in Scotland all corporeal moveables except money; and in particular 'goods' includes emblements, industrial growing crops, and things attached to or forming part of the land which are agreed to be severed before sale or under the contract of sale; [and includes an undivided share in goods;]
'plaintiff' includes pursuer, complainer, claimant in a multiplepoinding and defendant or defender counter-claiming;
[. . .]

'property' means the general property in goods, and not merely a special property;

[. . .]

'sale' includes a bargain and sale as well as a sale and delivery;

'seller' means a person who sells or agrees to sell goods;

'specific goods' means goods identified and agreed on at the time a contract of sale is made; [and includes an undivided share, specified as a fraction or percentage, of goods identified and agreed on as aforesaid;]

'warranty' (as regards England and Wales and Northern Ireland) means an agreement with reference to goods which are the subject of a contract of sale, but collateral to the main purpose of such contract, the breach of which gives rise to a claim for damages, but not to a right to reject the goods and treat the contract as repudiated.

[. . .]

(3)   A thing is deemed to be done in good faith within the meaning of this Act when it is in fact done honestly, whether it is done negligently or not.

(4)   A person is deemed to be insolvent within the meaning of this Act if he has either ceased to pay his debts in the ordinary course of business or he cannot pay his debts as they become due, [. . .]

(5)   Goods are in a deliverable state within the meaning of this Act when they are in such a state that the buyer would under the contract be bound to take delivery of them.

[. . .]

(6)   As regards the definition of 'business' in subsection (1) above, paragraph 14 of Schedule 1 below applies in relation to a contract made on or after 18 May 1973 and before 1 February 1978, and paragraph 15 in relation to one made before 18 May 1973,

## 62   Savings: rules of law etc

(1)   The rules in bankruptcy relating to contracts of sale apply to those contracts, notwithstanding anything in this Act.

(2)   The rules of the common law, including the law merchant, except in so far as they are inconsistent with the provisions of *[legislation including this Act and the Consumer Rights Act 2015]*, and in particular the rules relating to the law of principal and agent and the effect of fraud, misrepresentation, duress or coercion, mistake, or other invalidating cause, apply to contracts for the sale of goods.

(3)   Nothing in this Act or the Sale of Goods Act 1893 affects the enactments relating to bills of sale, or any enactment relating to the sale of goods which is not expressly repealed or amended by this Act or that.

(4)   The provisions of this Act about contracts of sale do not apply to a transaction in the form of a contract of sale which is intended to operate by way of mortgage, pledge, charge, or other security.

(5)   Nothing in this Act prejudices or affects the landlord's right of hypothec [. . .] in Scotland.

## 64   Short title and commencement

(1)   This Act may be cited as the Sale of Goods Act 1979.

(2)   This Act comes into force on 1 January 1980.

## SUPPLY OF GOODS AND SERVICES ACT 1982
### (1982, c 29)

[PART IA
SUPPLY OF GOODS AS RESPECTS SCOTLAND

*Contracts for the transfer of property in goods*

**11A   The contracts concerned**

(1)   In this Act in its application to Scotland a [*'relevant* contract for the transfer of goods'] means a contract under which one person transfers or agrees to transfer to another the property in goods, other than an excepted contract [*, and other than a contract to which Chapter 2 of Part 1 of the Consumer Rights Act 2015 applies*].

(2)   For the purposes of this section an excepted contract means any of the following—

(a)   a contract of sale of goods;

(b)   a hire-purchase agreement;

[. . .]

(d)   a transfer or agreement to transfer for which there is no consideration;

(e)   a contract intended to operate by way of mortgage, pledge, charge or other security.

(3)   For the purposes of this Act in its application to Scotland a contract is a [*relevant* contract for the transfer of goods] whether or not services are also provided or to be provided under the contract, and (subject to subsection (2) above) whatever is the nature of the consideration for the transfer or agreement to transfer.

**11B   Implied terms about title, etc**

(1)   In a [*relevant* contract for the transfer of goods], other than one to which subsection (3) below applies, there is an implied term on the part of the transferor that in the case of a transfer of the property in the goods he has a right to transfer the property and in the case of an agreement to transfer the property in the goods he will have such a right at the time when the property is to be transferred.

(2)   In a [*relevant* contract for the transfer of goods], other than one to which subsection (3) below applies, there is also an implied term that—

(a)   the goods are free, and will remain free until the time when the property is to be transferred, from any charge or encumbrance not disclosed or known to the transferee before the contract is made, and

(b)   the transferee will enjoy quiet possession of the goods except so far as it may be disturbed by the owner or other person entitled to the benefit of any charge or encumbrance so disclosed or known.

(3)   This subsection applies to a [*relevant* contract for the transfer of goods] in the case of which there appears from the contract or is to be inferred from its circumstances an intention that the transferor should transfer only such title as he or a third person may have.

(4)   In a contract to which subsection (3) above applies there is an implied term that all charges or encumbrances known to the transferor and not known to the transferee have been disclosed to the transferee before the contract is made.

(5)   In a contract to which subsection (3) above applies there is also an implied term that none of the following will disturb the transferee's quiet possession of the goods, namely—

(a)   the transferor;

(b)   in a case where the parties to the contract intend that the transferor should transfer only such title as a third person may have, that person;

(c)   anyone claiming through or under the transferor or that third person otherwise than under a charge or encumbrance disclosed or known to the transferee before the contract is made.

(6)   [amends Unfair Contract Terms Act 1977]

**11C   Implied terms where transfer is by description**

(1)   This section applies where, under a [relevant contract for the transfer of goods], the transferor transfers or agrees to transfer the property in the goods by description.

(2)   In such a case there is an implied term that the goods will correspond with the description.

(3)   If the transferor transfers or agrees to transfer the property in the goods by reference to a sample as well as by description it is not sufficient that the bulk of the goods corresponds with the sample if the goods do not also correspond with the description.

(4)   A contract is not prevented from falling within subsection (1) above by reason only that, being exposed for supply, the goods are selected by the transferee.

**11D   Implied terms about quality or fitness**

(1)   Except as provided by this section and section 11E below and subject to the provisions of any other enactment, there is no implied term about the quality or fitness for any particular purpose of goods supplied under a [relevant contract for the transfer of goods].

(2)   Where, under such a contract, the transferor transfers the property in goods in the course of a business, there is an implied term that the goods supplied under the contract are of satisfactory quality.

(3)   For the purposes of this section and section 11E below, goods are of satisfactory quality if they meet the standard that a reasonable person would regard as satisfactory, taking account of any description of the goods, the price (if relevant) and all the other relevant circumstances.

[. . .]

(4)   The term implied by subsection (2) above does not extend to any matter making the quality of goods unsatisfactory—

(a)   which is specifically drawn to the transferee's attention before the contract is made,

(b)   where the transferee examines the goods before the contract is made, which that examination ought to reveal, or

(c)   where the property in the goods is, or is to be, transferred by reference to a sample, which would have been apparent on a reasonable examination of the sample.

(5)   Subsection (6) below applies where, under a [relevant contract for the transfer of goods], the transferor transfers the property in goods in the course of a business and the transferee, expressly or by implication, makes known—

(a)   to the transferor, or

(b)   where the consideration or part of the consideration for the transfer is a sum payable by instalments and the goods were previously sold by a credit-broker to the transferor, to that credit-broker,

any particular purpose for which the goods are being acquired.

(6)   In that case there is (subject to subsection (7) below) an implied term that the goods supplied under the contract are reasonably fit for the purpose, whether or not that is a purpose for which such goods are commonly supplied.

(7)   Subsection (6) above does not apply where the circumstances show that the transferee does not rely, or that it is unreasonable for him to rely, on the skill or judgment of the transferor or credit-broker.

(8)   An implied term about quality or fitness for a particular purpose may be annexed by usage to a [relevant contract for the transfer of goods].

(9)   The preceding provisions of this section apply to a transfer by a person who in the course of a business is acting as agent for another as they apply to a transfer by a principal in the course of a business, except where that other is not

transferring in the course of a business and either the transferee knows that fact or reasonable steps are taken to bring it to the transferee's notice before the contract concerned is made.
  *[. . .]*

**11E   Implied terms where transfer is by sample**
  (1)   This section applies where, under a [*relevant* contract for the transfer of goods], the transferor transfers or agrees to transfer the property in the goods by reference to a sample.
  (2)   In such a case there is an implied term—
    (a)   that the bulk will correspond with the sample in quality;
    (b)   that the transferee will have a reasonable opportunity of comparing the bulk with the sample; and
    (c)   that the goods will be free from any defect, making their quality unsatisfactory, which would not be apparent on reasonable examination of the sample.
  (3)   For the purposes of this section a transferor transfers or agrees to transfer the property in goods by reference to a sample where there is an express or implied term to that effect in the contract concerned.

**11F   Remedies for breach of contract**
  (1)   Where in a [*relevant* contract for the transfer of goods] a transferor is in breach of any term of the contract (express or implied), the other party to the contract (in this section referred to as 'the transferee') shall be entitled—
    (a)   to claim damages; and
    (b)   if the breach is material, to reject any goods delivered under the contract and treat it as repudiated.
  *[. . .]*


*Contracts for the hire of goods*

**11G   The contracts concerned**
  (1)   In this Act in its application to Scotland a '[*relevant* contract for the hire of goods'] means a contract under which one person ('the supplier') hires or agrees to hire goods to another, other than [a hire-purchase agreement] *[and other than a contract to which Chapter 2 of Part 1 of the Consumer Rights Act 2015 applies]*.
  *[. . .]*
  (3)   For the purposes of this Act in its application to Scotland a contract is a [*relevant* contract for the hire of goods] whether or not services are also provided or to be provided under the contract, and [. . .] whatever is the nature of the consideration for the hire or agreement to hire.

**11H   Implied terms about right to transfer possession etc**
  (1)   In a [*relevant* contract for the hire of goods] there is an implied term on the part of the supplier that—
    (a)   in the case of a hire, he has a right to transfer possession of the goods by way of hire for the period of the hire; and
    (b)   in the case of an agreement to hire, he will have such a right at the time of commencement of the period of the hire.
  (2)   In a [*relevant* contract for the hire of goods] there is also an implied term that the person to whom the goods are hired will enjoy quiet possession of the goods for the period of the hire except so far as the possession may be disturbed by the owner or other person entitled to the benefit of any charge or encumbrance disclosed or known to the person to whom the goods are hired before the contract is made.
  (3)   The preceding provisions of this section do not affect the right of the supplier to repossess the goods under an express or implied term of the contract.

**11I   Implied terms where hire is by description**

(1)   This section applies where, under a [*relevant* contract for the hire of goods], the supplier hires or agrees to hire the goods by description.

(2)   In such a case there is an implied term that the goods will correspond with the description.

(3)   If under the contract the supplier hires or agrees to hire the goods by reference to a sample as well as by description it is not sufficient that the bulk of the goods corresponds with the sample if the goods do not also correspond with the description.

(4)   A contract is not prevented from falling within subsection (1) above by reason only that, being exposed for supply, the goods are selected by the person to whom the goods are hired.

**11J   Implied terms about quality or fitness**

(1)   Except as provided by this section and section 11K below and subject to the provisions of any other enactment, there is no implied term about the quality or fitness for any particular purpose of goods hired under a [*relevant* contract for the hire of goods].

(2)   Where, under such a contract, the supplier hires goods in the course of a business, there is an implied term that the goods supplied under the contract are of satisfactory quality.

(3)   For the purposes of this section and section 11K below, goods are of satisfactory quality if they meet the standard that a reasonable person would regard as satisfactory, taking account of any description of the goods, the consideration for the hire (if relevant) and all the other relevant circumstances.

[. . .]

(4)   The term implied by subsection (2) above does not extend to any matter making the quality of goods unsatisfactory—

    (a)   which is specifically drawn to the attention of the person to whom the goods are hired before the contract is made, or

    (b)   where that person examines the goods before the contract is made, which that examination ought to reveal; or

    (c)   where the goods are hired by reference to a sample, which would have been apparent on reasonable examination of the sample.

(5)   Subsection (6) below applies where, under a [*relevant* contract for the hire of goods], the supplier hires goods in the course of a business and the person to whom the goods are hired, expressly or by implication, makes known—

    (a)   to the supplier in the course of negotiations conducted by him in relation to the making of the contract; or

    (b)   to a credit-broker in the course of negotiations conducted by that broker in relation to goods sold by him to the supplier before forming the subject matter of the contract,

any particular purpose for which the goods are being hired.

(6)   In that case there is (subject to subsection (7) below) an implied term that the goods supplied under the contract are reasonably fit for that purpose, whether or not that is a purpose for which such goods are commonly supplied.

(7)   Subsection (6) above does not apply where the circumstances show that the person to whom the goods are hired does not rely, or that it is unreasonable for him to rely, on the skill or judgment of the hirer or credit-broker.

(8)   An implied term about quality or fitness for a particular purpose may be annexed by usage to a contract for the hire of goods.

(9)   The preceding provisions of this section apply to a hire by a person who in the course of a business is acting as agent for another as they apply to a hire by a principal in the course of a business, except where that other is not hiring in the course of a business and either the person to whom the goods are hired knows

that fact or reasonable steps are taken to bring it to that person's notice before the contract concerned is made.

[. . .]

## 11K  Implied terms where hire is by sample

(1)  This section applies where, under a [relevant contract for the hire of goods], the supplier hires or agrees to hire the goods by reference to a sample.

(2)  In such a case there is an implied term—

(a)  that the bulk will correspond with the sample in quality; and

(b)  that the person to whom the goods are hired will have a reasonable opportunity of comparing the bulk with the sample; and

(c)  that the goods will be free from any defect, making their quality unsatisfactory, which would not be apparent on reasonable examination of the sample.

(3)  For the purposes of this section a supplier hires or agrees to hire goods by reference to a sample where there is an express or implied term to that effect in the contract concerned.

*Exclusion of implied terms, etc*

## 11L  Exclusion of implied terms etc

(1)  Where a right, duty or liability would arise under a [relevant contract for the transfer of goods] or a [relevant contract for the hire of goods] by implication of law, it may (subject to subsection (2) below and the 1977 Act) be negatived or varied by express agreement, or by the course of dealing between the parties, or by such usage as binds both parties to the contract.

(2)  An express term does not negative a term implied by the preceding provisions of this Part of this Act unless inconsistent with it.

(3)  Nothing in the preceding provisions of this Part of this Act prejudices the operation of any other enactment or any rule of law whereby any term (other than one relating to quality or fitness) is to be implied in a [relevant contract for the transfer of goods] or a [relevant contract for the hire of goods].]

[. . .]

## BANKRUPTCY (SCOTLAND) ACT 1985
### (1985, c 66)

## 1  Accountant in Bankruptcy

[(1)  The Accountant in Bankruptcy shall be appointed by the Scottish Ministers.

[(1A)  The Accountant in Bankruptcy shall be an officer of the court.]

(2)  The Scottish Ministers may appoint a member of the staff of the Accountant in Bankruptcy to be Depute Accountant in Bankruptcy to exercise all of the functions of the Accountant in Bankruptcy at any time when the Accountant in Bankruptcy is unable to do so.]

## [1A  Supervisory functions of the Accountant in Bankruptcy

(1)  The Accountant in Bankruptcy shall have the following general functions in the administration of sequestration and personal insolvency—

(a)  the supervision of the performance by—

(i)  interim trustees (not being the Accountant in Bankruptcy);

(ii)  [trustees (not being the Accountant in Bankruptcy)];

[(iia)  trustees under protected trust deeds;]

[. . .]

(iii)  commissioners,
of the functions conferred on them by this Act or any other enactment
(including an enactment contained in subordinate legislation) or any rule of
law and the investigation of any complaints made against them;
    [(aa)  the determination of debtor applications;]
    (b)  the maintenance of a register (in this Act referred to as the 'register of
insolvencies'), in such form as may be prescribed by [regulations made by the
Scottish Minister], which shall contain particulars of—
        [(ai)  persons who are the subject of notices under section 4A(1) and 4B(1),]
        (i)  estates which have been sequestrated;
        (ii)  trust deeds which have been sent to him for registration [. . .];
    [(iia)  bankruptcy restrictions orders, [and interim bankruptcy restrictions
orders];]
    [. . .]
    [(iii)  the winding up and receivership of business associations which the
Court of Session has jurisdiction to wind up];
    [(iv)  any other document as may be specified in regulations made under
this subsection or any other enactment.]
    (c)  the preparation of an annual report which shall be presented to the
Secretary of State and the Court of Session and shall contain—
        (i)  statistical information relating to the state of all sequestrations [and the
winding up and receiverships of business associations] of which particulars
have been registered in the register of insolvencies during the year to which
the report relates;
        (ii)  particulars of trust deeds registered as protected trust deeds in that
year; and
        (iii)  particulars of the performance of the Accountant in Bankruptcy's
functions under this Act;
    (d)  such other functions as may from time to time be conferred on him by
the Secretary of State [; and
    (e)  in this subsection 'business association' has the meaning given in Section
C2 of Part II of Schedule 5 to the Scotland Act 1998].
    (2)  If it appears to the Accountant in Bankruptcy that a person mentioned in
paragraph (a) of subsection (1) above has failed without reasonable excuse to perform a duty imposed on him by any provision of this Act or by any other enactment (including an enactment contained in subordinate legislation) or by any rule
of law, he shall report the matter to the [sheriff who], after hearing that person on
the matter, may remove him from office or censure him or make such other order
as the circumstances of the case may require.
    (3)  Where the Accountant in Bankruptcy has reasonable grounds to suspect
that an offence has been committed—
    (a)  by a person mentioned in paragraph (a) of subsection (1) above in the
performance of his functions under this Act or any other enactment (including
an enactment contained in subordinate legislation) or any rule of law; or
    (b)  in relation to a sequestration, by the debtor in respect of his assets, his
dealings with them or his conduct in relation to his business or financial affairs;
or
    (c)  in relation to a sequestration, by a person other than the debtor in that
person's dealings with the debtor, the interim trustee or the [. . .] trustee in
respect of the debtor's assets, business or financial affairs,
he shall report the matter to the Lord Advocate.
    (4)  The Accountant in Bankruptcy shall—
    (a)  make the register of insolvencies, at all reasonable times, available for
inspection; and
    (b)  provide any person, on request, with a certified copy of any entry in the
register.]

[(5)  Regulations under subsection (1)(b) may in particular prescribe circumstances where information need not be included in the register of insolvencies, if in the opinion of the Accountant in Bankruptcy inclusion of the information would be likely to jeopardise the safety or welfare of any person.]

**[1B  Performance of certain functions of the Accountant in Bankruptcy**
(1)  The functions of the Accountant in Bankruptcy, other than functions conferred by section 1A of this Act, may be carried out on his behalf by any member of his staff authorised by him to do so.
(2)  Without prejudice to subsection (1) above, the Accountant in Bankruptcy may appoint on such terms and conditions as he considers appropriate such persons as he considers fit to perform on his behalf any of his functions in respect of the sequestration of the estate of any debtor.
(3)  A person appointed under subsection (2) above shall comply with such general or specific directions as the Accountant in Bankruptcy may from time to time give to such person as to the performance of his functions in relation to any sequestration.
(4)  The Accountant in Bankruptcy may pay to a person appointed under subsection (2) above such fee as he may consider appropriate.]

**[1C  Directions**
(1)  The Secretary of State may, after consultation with the Lord President of the Court of Session, give to the Accountant in Bankruptcy general directions as to the performance of his functions under this Act.
(2)  Directions under this section may be given in respect of all cases or any class or description of cases, but may not be given in respect of any particular case.
(3)  The Accountant in Bankruptcy shall comply with any directions given to him under this section.]

**[1D  Conduct of proceedings in the sheriff court**
(1)  A person authorised by the Accountant in Bankruptcy may conduct civil proceedings in the sheriff court in relation to a function of the Accountant in Bankruptcy (including the functions listed in section 1A).
(2)  In subsection (1), 'civil proceedings' are proceedings which are not in respect of an offence.]

**2  Appointment and functions of [the trustee in the sequestration]**
[(1)  Where the [sheriff] awards sequestration of the debtor's estate and the petition for the sequestration—
    (a)  nominates a person to be [the] trustee;
    (b)  states that the person satisfies the conditions mentioned in subsection (3) below; and
    (c)  has annexed to it a copy of the undertaking mentioned in subsection (3)(c) below,
the [sheriff] may, if it appears to the [sheriff] that the person satisfies those conditions and if no interim trustee has been appointed in pursuance of subsection (5) below, appoint that person to be [the] trustee in the sequestration.
[(1A)  Subject to subsection [(1D)] below, where the Accountant in Bankruptcy awards sequestration of the debtor's estate and the debtor application—
    (a)  nominates a person to be the trustee;
    (b)  states that the person satisfies the conditions mentioned in subsection (3) below; and
    (c)  has annexed to it a copy of the undertaking mentioned in subsection (3)(c) below,
the Accountant in Bankruptcy may, if it appears to him that the person satisfies those conditions, appoint that person to be the trustee in the sequestration.
(1B)  Where the Accountant in Bankruptcy awards sequestration of the debtor's estate and does not appoint a person to be the trustee in pursuance of subsection

(1A) above, the Accountant in Bankruptcy shall be deemed to be appointed to be the trustee in the sequestration.

[. . .]

[(1D)   The Accountant in Bankruptcy is not to make an appointment under subsection (1A) where—

(a)   the debtor application is made by a debtor to whom section 5(2ZA) applies, and

(b)   the Accountant in Bankruptcy awards sequestration of the debtor's estate.]

(2)   Where the [sheriff] awards sequestration of the debtor's estate and—

(a)   [he] does not appoint a person to be [the] trustee in pursuance of subsection (1) above; and

(b)   no interim trustee has been appointed in pursuance of subsection (5) below,

the [sheriff] shall appoint the Accountant in Bankruptcy to be [the] trustee in the sequestration.

[(2A)   Where the sheriff awards sequestration of the debtor's estate and an interim trustee has been appointed in pursuance of subsection (5) below, the sheriff may appoint—

(a)   the interim trustee; or

(b)   subject to subsection (2B) below, such other person as may be nominated by the petitioner,

to be the trustee in the sequestration.

(2B)   A person nominated under subsection (2A)(b) above may be appointed to be the trustee in the sequestration only if—

(a)   it appears to the sheriff that the person satisfies the conditions mentioned in subsection (3) below; and

(b)   a copy of the undertaking mentioned in subsection (3)(c) below has been lodged with the sheriff.

(2C)   Where the sheriff does not appoint a person to be trustee in pursuance of subsection (2A) above, the sheriff shall appoint the Accountant in Bankruptcy to be the trustee in the sequestration.]

(3)   The conditions referred to in subsection (1) above are that the person—

[. . .]

(b)   is qualified to act as an insolvency practitioner; and

(c)   has given an undertaking, in writing, that he will act [as the trustee [in the sequestration]].

[. . .]

(5)   Where a petition for sequestration is presented by a creditor or a trustee acting under a trust deed, the [sheriff] may appoint an interim trustee before sequestration is awarded—

(a)   if the debtor consents; or

(b)   if the trustee acting under the trust deed or any creditor shows cause.

(6)   For the purposes of the appointment of an interim trustee under subsection (5) above—

(a)   where a person is nominated as mentioned in subsection (1)(a) above and the provisions of that subsection apply, the [sheriff] may appoint that person; and

(b)   where such a person is not appointed, the [sheriff] shall appoint the Accountant in Bankruptcy.

[(6A)   The interim trustee's general function shall be to safeguard the debtor's estate pending the determination of the petition for sequestration.

(6B)   Whether or not the interim trustee is still acting in the sequestration, the interim trustee shall supply the Accountant in Bankruptcy with such information as the Accountant in Bankruptcy considers necessary to enable him to discharge his functions under this Act.]

(7) Where—

[(a) a trustee is appointed in a sequestration where the petition was presented by a creditor or the trustee acting under a trust deed; or

(b) an interim trustee is appointed in pursuance of subsection (5) above,

he] shall, as soon as practicable, notify the debtor of his appointment.]

[(8) The trustee must at the same time as notifying the debtor under subsection (7)(a) or (b), send to the debtor, for signature by the debtor, a statement of undertakings in the form prescribed.]


**3 [Functions of the trustee]**

(1) In every sequestration there shall be a [. . .] trustee whose general functions shall be—

(a) to recover, manage and realise the debtor's estate, whether situated in Scotland or elsewhere;

(b) to distribute the estate among the debtor's creditors according to their respective entitlements;

(c) to ascertain the reasons for the debtor's insolvency and the circumstances surrounding it;

(d) to ascertain the state of the debtor's liabilities and assets;

(e) to maintain a sederunt book during his term of office for the purpose of providing an accurate record of the sequestration process;

(f) to keep regular accounts of his intromissions with the debtor's estate, such accounts being available for inspection at all reasonable times by the commissioners (if any), the creditors and the debtor; and

(g) whether or not he is still acting in the sequestration, to supply the Accountant in Bankruptcy with such information as the Accountant in Bankruptcy considers necessary to enable him to discharge his functions under this Act.

(2) A [. . .] trustee in performing his functions under this Act shall have regard to advice offered to him by the commissioners (if any).

(3) If the [. . .] trustee has reasonable grounds to suspect that an offence has been committed in relation to a sequestration—

(a) by the debtor in respect of his assets, his dealings with them or his conduct in relation to his business or financial affairs; or

(b) by a person other than the debtor in that person's dealings with the debtor, the interim trustee or the [. . .] trustee in respect of the debtor's assets, business or financial affairs,

he shall report the matter to the Accountant in Bankruptcy.

[(3A) If the trustee has reasonable grounds to believe that any behaviour on the part of the debtor is of a kind that would result in a sheriff granting, under section 56B(1) of this Act, an application for a bankruptcy restrictions order, he shall report the matter to the Accountant in Bankruptcy.]

(4) A report under subsection (3) [or (3A)] above shall be absolutely privileged.

[(5) Paragraph (g) of subsection (1) above and [subsections (3) and (3A)] above shall not apply in any case where the [. . .] trustee is the Accountant in Bankruptcy.]

[(6) [Where the Accountant in Bankruptcy is the trustee, the Accountant in Bankruptcy] may apply to the sheriff for directions in relation to any particular matter arising in the sequestration.]

[(7) Where the debtor, a creditor or any other person having an interest is dissatisfied with any act, omission or decision of the [. . .] trustee, he may apply to the sheriff and, on such an application being made, the sheriff may confirm, annul or modify any act or decision of the [. . .] trustee or may give him directions or make such order as he thinks fit.]

[(8) The trustee shall comply with the requirements of subsections (1)(a) to (d) and (2) above only in so far as, in his view, it would be of financial benefit to the estate of the debtor and in the interests of the creditors to do so.]

### [3A   Application to Accountant in Bankruptcy for a direction

(1)   This section applies where the Accountant in Bankruptcy is not the trustee.

(2)   The trustee may apply to the Accountant in Bankruptcy for a direction in relation to any particular matter arising in the sequestration.

(3)   The Accountant in Bankruptcy may, before giving a direction on any particular matter under this section, refer the matter to the sheriff by making an application for a direction in relation to that matter.

(4)   The trustee may apply to the Accountant in Bankruptcy for a review of a direction given by the Accountant in Bankruptcy under this section.

(5)   An application for a review under subsection (4) may not be made—

(a)   by an interim trustee,

(b)   after the expiry of the period of 14 days beginning with the day on which notice of the direction by the Accountant in Bankruptcy is given to the trustee, or

(c)   in relation to a matter on which the Accountant in Bankruptcy has applied to the sheriff for a direction under subsection (3).

(6)   If an application for a review under subsection (4) is made, the Accountant in Bankruptcy must—

(a)   take into account any representations made by the trustee, the debtor, any creditor and any other person having an interest before the expiry of the period of 21 days beginning with the day on which the application is made, and

(b)   confirm, amend or revoke the direction before the expiry of the period of 28 days beginning with the day on which the application is made.

(7)   The trustee may appeal to the sheriff against a decision by the Accountant in Bankruptcy under subsection (6)(b) before the expiry of the period of 14 days beginning with the day of the decision.]

### 4   Commissioners

In any sequestration [. . .] commissioners, whose general functions shall be to supervise the intromissions of the [. . .] trustee with the sequestrated estate and to advise him, may be elected in accordance with section 30 of this Act.


*Moratorium on diligence*

### 4A   Notice of intention to apply: debtor application etc

(1)   A person may give written notice to the Accountant in Bankruptcy of the person's intention—

(a)   to make a debtor application for sequestration under section 5,

(b)   to seek to fulfil the conditions required in order for a trust deed granted by or on behalf of that person to be granted the status of protected trust deed,

(c)   to apply for the approval of a debt payment programme in accordance with section 2 of the Debt Arrangement and Attachment (Scotland) Act 2002 (asp 17).

(2)   A person may not give a notice if that person has given a notice under subsection (1) in the immediately preceding period of 12 months.

(3)   The Accountant in Bankruptcy must, without delay after receipt of a notice under subsection (1), enter in the registers mentioned in subsection (4)—

(a)   the name of the person who gave the notice, and

(b)   such other information as the Accountant in Bankruptcy considers appropriate in relation to that person.

(4)   The registers are—

(a)   the register of insolvencies, and

(b)   the register of debt payment programmes established and maintained in accordance with section 7 of the Debt Arrangement and Attachment (Scotland) Act 2002 (the 'DAS register').

**4B   Notice of intention to apply: sequestration of estate under section 6**

(1)   A person may give written notice to the Accountant in Bankruptcy of the person's intention to make a debtor application under section 6.

(2)   A person may not give a notice in respect of an estate mentioned in section 6 if any person has given a notice under subsection (1) in respect of the same estate in the immediately preceding period of 12 months.

(3)   The Accountant in Bankruptcy must, without delay after receipt of a notice under subsection (1), enter in the register of insolvencies—

(a)   the name of the person who is the subject of the notice, and

(b)   such other information as the Accountant in Bankruptcy considers appropriate in relation to that person.

**4C   Moratorium on diligence**

(1)   This section applies where a person gives notice to the Accountant in Bankruptcy in accordance with section 4A(1) or 4B(1).

(2)   A moratorium on diligence applies in relation to the person who is the subject of the notice for the moratorium period determined in accordance with section 4D.

(3)   While a moratorium on diligence applies in relation to the person it is not competent—

(a)   to serve a charge for payment in respect of any debt owed by the person,

(b)   to commence or execute any diligence to enforce payment of any debt owed by the person,

(c)   to found on any debt owed by the person in presenting, or concurring in the presentation of, a petition for sequestration of the person's estate, or

(d)   in the case where an arrestment mentioned in subsection (1) of section 73J of the Debtors (Scotland) Act 1987 (c 18) has been granted in respect of funds due to the person, to release funds to the creditor under subsection (2) of that section.

(4)   The moratorium period applying in relation to the person is to be disregarded for the purposes of determining the period mentioned in section 73J(3) of the Debtors (Scotland) Act 1987 (c 18).

(5)   Despite subsection (3)(b), it is competent to—

(a)   auction an article which has been attached in accordance with the Debt Arrangement and Attachment (Scotland) Act 2002 (asp 17) where—

(i)   notice has been given to the debtor under section 27(4) of that Act, or

(ii)   the article has been removed, or notice of removal has been given, under section 53 of that Act,

(b)   implement a decree of furthcoming,

(c)   implement a decree or order for sale of a ship (or a share of it) or cargo,

(d)   execute an earnings arrestment, a current maintenance arrestment or a conjoined arrestment order which came into effect before the day on which the moratorium period in relation to the person begins.

**4D   Period of moratorium**

(1)   The moratorium period applying in relation to the person is the period which—

(a)   begins on the day on which an entry is made in the register of insolvencies under section 4A(3) or 4B(3), and

(b)   ends on—

(i)   the day which is 6 weeks after that day,

(ii)   such earlier day as is mentioned in subsection (2), or

(iii)   if subsection (3), (5) or (7) applies, such later day as is determined in accordance with subsection (4), (6) or (8).

(2)  The earlier day is the day on which, in relation to the person who is the subject of the moratorium—

(a)  an entry is made in the register of insolvencies recording the award of sequestration of the estate,

(b)  an entry is made in the register of insolvencies recording that a trust deed granted by the person has been granted or refused protected status,

(c)  an entry is made in the DAS register recording the approval of a debt payment programme in accordance with section 2 of the Debt Arrangement and Attachment (Scotland) Act 2002, or

(d)  written notice is given to the Accountant in Bankruptcy—

(i)  by the person withdrawing the notice given under section 4A(1), or

(ii)  by or on behalf of the person withdrawing the notice given under section 4B(1).

(3)  This subsection applies if, on the day which is 6 weeks after the day on which the moratorium began under subsection (1)(a)—

(a)  a person has made a debtor application for sequestration of the estate of the person who is the subject of the moratorium,

(b)  the moratorium has not ended in accordance with subsection (2)(a), and

(c)  no decision has been made by the Accountant in Bankruptcy under section 15(3C)(b).

(4)  Where subsection (3) applies, the moratorium period ends on—

(a)  the day on which an entry is made in the register of insolvencies recording the award of sequestration of the estate,

(b)  in the case of refusal to award sequestration—

(i)  the day of the expiry of the period applying by virtue of section 15(3B) where no application for review is made under section 15(3A), or

(ii)  the day on which a decision is made by the Accountant in Bankruptcy under section 15(3C)(b) where an application for review is made, or

(c)  the day on which written notice is given to the Accountant in Bankruptcy—

(i)  by the person withdrawing the notice given under section 4A(1), or

(ii)  by or on behalf of the person withdrawing the notice given under section 4B(1).

(5)  This subsection applies if, on the day which is 6 weeks after the day on which the moratorium began under subsection (1)(a)—

(a)  an entry has been made in the register of insolvencies recording an application for a trust deed granted by or on behalf of the person who is the subject of the moratorium to be granted the status of protected trust deed, and

(b)  the moratorium has not ended in accordance with subsection (2)(b).

(6)  Where subsection (5) applies, the moratorium period ends on—

(a)  the day on which an entry is made in the register of insolvencies recording that the trust deed granted by or on behalf of the person has been granted the status of protected trust deed,

(b)  where such an entry is not made, the day which is 13 weeks after the day on which the moratorium began under subsection (1)(a), or

(c)  the day on which written notice is given to the Accountant in Bankruptcy by the person withdrawing the notice given under section 4A(1).

(7)  This subsection applies if, on the day which is 6 weeks after the day on which the moratorium began under subsection (1)(a)—

(a)  the person who is the subject of the moratorium has applied for approval of a debt payment programme under section 2 of the Debt Arrangement and Attachment (Scotland) Act 2002,

(b)  the moratorium has not ended in accordance with subsection (2)(c), and

(c)  the application has not been determined.

(8)  Where subsection (7) applies, the moratorium period ends on—

(a)  the day on which an entry is made in the DAS register recording the approval of the debt payment programme in accordance with section 2 of the Debt Arrangement and Attachment (Scotland) Act 2002,

(b) in the case of a rejection of a debt payment programme, the day on which an entry is made in the DAS register recording the rejection, or

(c) the day on which written notice is given to the Accountant in Bankruptcy by the person withdrawing the notice given under section 4A(1).]

*Petitions for sequestration*

## 5 Sequestration of the estate of living or deceased debtor

(1) The estate of a debtor may be sequestrated in accordance with the provisions of this Act.

[(2) The sequestration of the estate of a living debtor shall be—

(a) by debtor application made by the debtor, if [subsection [(2ZA) or] (2B)] below applies to the debtor; or

(b) on the petition of—

(i) subject to subsection (2D) below, a qualified creditor or qualified creditors, if the debtor is apparently insolvent;

(ii) a temporary administrator;

(iii) a member State liquidator appointed in main proceedings; or

(iv) the trustee acting under a trust deed if, and only if, one or more of the conditions in subsection (2C) below is satisfied.]

[(2ZA) This subsection applies to the debtor where—

(a) the debtor—

(i) has been assessed by the common financial tool as requiring to make no debtor's contribution, or

(ii) has been in receipt of a prescribed payment for a period of at least 6 months ending with the day on which the application is made,

(b) the total amount of the debtor's debts (including interest) at the date the debtor application is made is—

(i) not less than £1500 or such other sum as may be prescribed, and

(ii) no more than £17000 or such other sum as may be prescribed,

(c) the total value of the debtor's assets (leaving out of account any liabilities) on the date the debtor application is made does not exceed £2000 or such other amount as may be prescribed,

(d) the value of a single asset of the debtor does not exceed £1000 or such other amount as may be prescribed,

(e) the debtor does not own land,

(f) within the prescribed period, the debtor has been granted a certificate for sequestration of the debtor's estate in accordance with section 5B,

(g) in the period of 10 years ending on the day before the day on which the debtor application is made or such other period as may be prescribed no award of sequestration has been made against the debtor in pursuance of an application made by the debtor by virtue of this subsection, and

(h) in the period of 5 years ending on the day before the day on which the debtor application is made no award of sequestration has been made against the debtor in pursuance of—

(i) an application made by the debtor other than by virtue of this subsection, or

(ii) a petition.

(2ZB) For the purposes of subsection (2ZA)(c) and (d)—

(a) any property of the debtor is not to be regarded as an asset if, under any provision of this or any other enactment, it would be excluded from vesting in the Accountant in Bankruptcy as trustee,

(b) if the debtor reasonably requires the use of a vehicle, any vehicle owned by the debtor the value of which does not exceed £3000 or such other amount as may be prescribed is not to be regarded as an asset,

(c)    any other property of the debtor that is of a prescribed type is not to be regarded as an asset.

(2ZC)    For the purposes of subsection (2ZA)(c) and (d), the Scottish Ministers may by regulations make provision about how the value of the debtor's assets is to be determined.

(2ZD)    The Scottish Ministers may by regulations modify subsection (2ZA).

(2ZE)    Schedule A1 to this Act makes further provision about the application of certain provisions of this Act in relation to a debtor to whom subsection (2ZA) applies.]

[. . .]

(2B)    This subsection applies to the debtor where—

(a)    the total amount of his debts (including interest) at the date [the debtor application is made] is not less than [£3,000 or such sum as may be prescribed];

(b)    an award of sequestration has not been made against him in the period of 5 years ending on the day before the date [the debtor application is made]; and

[(ba)    the debtor has obtained the advice of a money adviser in accordance with section 5C(1),]

[(bb)    the debtor has given a statement of undertakings (including an undertaking to pay to the trustee after the award of sequestration of the debtor's estate an amount determined using the common financial tool),]

(c)    the debtor [. . .]—

(i)    is apparently insolvent; [. . .]

[(ia)    is unable to pay his debts and each of the conditions in section 5A of this Act is met;]

[(ib)    has, within the prescribed period, been granted a certificate for sequestration of the debtor's estate in accordance with section 5B of this Act,] [or]

(ii)    has granted a trust deed [which is not a protected trust deed by reason of the creditors objecting, or not agreeing, in accordance with regulations under paragraph 5 of Schedule 5 to this Act, to the trust deed, and for the purposes of this paragraph a debtor shall not be apparently insolvent by reason only that he has granted a trust deed or that he has given notice to his creditors as mentioned in paragraph (b) of section 7(1) of this Act.]

(2C)    The conditions mentioned in subsection [(2)(b)(iv)] above are—

(a)    that the debtor has failed to comply—

(i)    with any obligation imposed on him under the trust deed with which he could reasonably have complied; or

(ii)    with any instruction or requirement reasonably given to or made of him by the trustee for the purposes of the trust deed; or

(b)    that the trustee avers in his petition that it would be in the best interests of the creditors that an award of sequestration be made.

(2D)    No petition may be presented under subsection (2)(b)(i) above unless the qualified creditor has provided, by such time prior to the presentation of the petition as may be prescribed, the debtor with a debt advice and information package.

(2E)    In subsection (2D) above, 'debt advice and information package' means the debt advice and information package referred to in section 10(5) of the Debt Arrangement and Attachment (Scotland) Act 2002 (asp 17).]

[(2F)    In subsection (2B)(c)(ib) above, 'the prescribed period' means such period, ending immediately before the debtor application is made, as may be prescribed under section 5B(5)(c) of this Act.]

[(3)    The sequestration of the estate of a deceased debtor is—

(a)    by debtor application made by the executor, or a person entitled to be appointed as executor, on the estate,

(b)    on the petition of a qualified creditor, or qualified creditors, of the deceased debtor,

(c)    on the petition of a temporary administrator,

(d)    on the petition of a member State liquidator appointed in main proceedings, or

(e)    on the petition of a trustee acting under a trust deed.]

(4)    In this Act 'qualified creditor' means a creditor who, at the date of the presentation of the petition [or, as the case may be, the date the debtor application is made], is a creditor of the debtor in respect of liquid or illiquid debts (other than contingent or future debts [or amounts payable under a confiscation order]), whether secured or unsecured, which amount (or of one such debt which amounts) to not less than [£3,000] or such sum as may be prescribed; and 'qualified creditors' means creditors who at the said date are creditors of the debtor in respect of such debts as aforesaid amounting in aggregate to not less than [£3,000] or such sum as may be prescribed [; and in the foregoing provisions of this subsection 'confiscation order' [means a confiscation order under Part 2, 3, or 4 of the Proceeds of Crime Act 2002].

[(4A)    In this Act, 'trust deed' means [—

(a)]    a voluntary trust deed granted by or on behalf of the debtor whereby his estate (other than such of his estate as would not, under [any provision of this or any other enactment], vest in the [. . .] trustee if his estate were sequestrated) is conveyed to the trustee for the benefit of his creditors generally[; and

(b)    any other trust deed which would fall within paragraph (a) but for—

(i)    the exclusion from the estate conveyed to the trustee of the whole or part of the debtor's dwellinghouse, where a secured creditor holds a security over it; and

(ii)    the fact that the debtor's estate is not conveyed to the trustee for the benefit of creditors generally because the secured creditor has, at the debtor's request, agreed before the trust deed is granted not to claim under the trust deed for any of the debt in respect of which the security is held.

(4AA)    In subsection (4A)(b) above 'debtor's dwellinghouse' means a dwellinghouse (including any yard, garden, outbuilding or other pertinents) which, on the day immediately preceding the date the trust deed was granted—

(a)    the debtor (whether alone or in common with any other person)—

(i)    owned; or

(ii)    leased under a long lease (long lease having the same meaning as in section [9(2) of the Land Registration etc (Scotland) Act 2012 (asp 5))]; and

(b)    was the sole or main residence of the debtor.

(4AB)    For the purposes of subsection (4AA)(b) above, a dwellinghouse may be a sole or main residence irrespective of whether it is used, to any extent, by the debtor for the purposes of any profession, trade or business.]

(4B)    A debtor application shall—

(a)    be made to the Accountant in Bankruptcy; [. . .]

[(4BA)    A debtor application must—

(a)    include a declaration by the money adviser who provided the advice referred to in section 5C(1) that such advice has been given, and

(b)    specify the name and address of the money adviser.]

[. . .]

(5)    Paragraphs 1(1) and (3), 2(1)(a) and (2) and 6 of Schedule 1 to this Act shall apply in order to ascertain the amount of the debt or debts for the purposes of subsection (4) above as they apply in order to ascertain the amount which a creditor is entitled to claim, but as if for any reference to the date of sequestration there were substituted a reference to the date of presentation of the petition [or, as the case may be, the date the debtor application is made].

(6)    The petitioner shall [on the day the petition for sequestration is presented under this section, send a copy of the petition] to the Accountant in Bankruptcy.

[(6A)    In the case of a debtor application, the debtor shall send a statement of assets and liabilities to the Accountant in Bankruptcy along with the application.]

[(6B)   In the case of a debtor application, the debtor must send a statement of undertakings to the Accountant in Bankruptcy along with the application.]

(7)   Where, after a petition for sequestration has been presented but before the sequestration has been awarded, the debtor dies then—
   [. . .]
   (b)   if the petitioner is a creditor, the proceedings shall continue in accordance with this Act so far as circumstances will permit.

[(7A)   Where, after a debtor application is made but before the sequestration is awarded, the debtor dies, then the application shall fall.]

(8)   Where, after a petition for sequestration has been presented under this section but before the sequestration has been awarded, a creditor who—
   (a)   is the petitioner [. . .]; or
   (b)   has lodged answers to the petition,
withdraws or dies, there may be sisted in the place of—
      (i)   the creditor mentioned in paragraph (a) above, any creditor who was a qualified creditor at the date when the petition was presented and who remains so qualified at the date of the sist;
      (ii)   the creditor mentioned in paragraph (b) above, any other creditor.

[(8A)   Where, after a debtor application is made but before the sequestration is awarded, a creditor who concurs in the application withdraws or dies, any other creditor who was a qualified creditor at the date the debtor application was made and who remains so qualified may notify the Accountant in Bankruptcy that he concurs in the application in place of the creditor who has withdrawn or died.]

[(9)   If the debtor—
   [. . .]
   (b)   fails to disclose any material fact in [a statement of assets and liabilities sent to the Accountant in Bankruptcy in accordance with subsection (6A)]; or
   (c)   makes a material misstatement in such statement of assets and liabilities, he shall be guilty of an offence and liable on summary conviction to a fine not exceeding level 5 on the standard scale or to imprisonment for a term not exceeding 3 months or to both such fine and imprisonment.

(10)   In any proceedings for an offence under subsection (9) above, it shall be a defence for the accused to show that he had a reasonable excuse for—
   [. . .]
   (b)   failing to disclose a material fact; or
   (c)   making a material misstatement.]

[. . .]


**[5B   Certificate for sequestration**
   (1)   A certificate for sequestration of a debtor's estate is a certificate granted by [a money adviser] certifying that the debtor is unable to pay debts as they become due.
   (2)   A certificate may be granted only on the application of the debtor.
   (3)   [A money adviser] must grant a certificate if, and only if, the debtor can demonstrate that the debtor is unable to pay debts as they become due.
   [. . .]
   (5)   The Scottish Ministers may by regulations—
      [. . .]
   (b)   make provision about certification by [a money adviser], including—
      (i)   the form and manner in which a certification must be made;
      (ii)   the fee, if any, which [a money adviser] is entitled to charge for or in connection with granting a certificate;
   (c)   prescribe a period for the purpose of section 5(2B)(c)(ib) of this Act;
      [. . .]]]

## [5C Money advice

(1) An application for the sequestration of a living debtor's estate may not be made unless the debtor has obtained from a money adviser—

(a) advice on the debtor's financial circumstances,

(b) advice on the effect of the proposed sequestration of the debtor's estate,

(c) advice on the preparation of the application, and

(d) advice on such other matters as may be prescribed.

(2) In this Act, 'money adviser' means a person who—

(a) is not an associate of the debtor, and

(b) is of a prescribed description or falls within a prescribed class.]

## [5D Assessment of debtor's contribution

(1) The Scottish Ministers may by regulations specify a method (the 'common financial tool') to be used to assess an appropriate amount of a living debtor's income to be paid to a trustee after the sequestration of the debtor's estate (the 'debtor's contribution').

(2) Regulations under subsection (1) may in particular—

(a) prescribe a method for assessing a debtor's financial circumstances (including the debtor's assets, income, liabilities and expenditure),

(b) prescribe a method for determining a reasonable amount of expenditure for a debtor after the sequestration of the debtor's estate,

(c) prescribe the proportion of a debtor's income that is to constitute the debtor's contribution,

(d) prescribe that a method determined by another person is to be used (with or without modification in accordance with regulations made under subsection (1)) as the common financial tool.

(3) The common financial tool must ensure that the amount of reasonable expenditure for a debtor is not less than the total amount of any income received by the debtor by way of guaranteed minimum pension (within the meaning of the Pension Schemes Act 1993 (c 48)).

(4) The common financial tool must ensure that an amount is allowed for—

(a) aliment for the debtor,

(b) the debtor's relevant obligations.

(5) The 'debtor's relevant obligations' are—

(a) any obligation of aliment owed by the debtor ('obligation of aliment' having the same meaning as in the Family Law (Scotland) Act 1985 (c 37)),

(b) any obligation of the debtor to make a periodical allowance to a former spouse or former civil partner, and

(c) any obligation of the debtor to pay child support maintenance under the Child Support Act 1991 (c 48).

(6) The amount allowed for the debtor's relevant obligations referred to in paragraphs (a) and (b) of subsection (5) need not be sufficient for compliance with a subsisting order or agreement as regards the aliment or periodical allowance.]

## 6 Sequestration of other estates

(1) Subject to subsection (2) below, the estate belonging to or held for or jointly by the members of any of the following entities may be sequestrated—

(a) a trust in respect of debts incurred by it;

(b) a partnership, including a dissolved partnership;

(c) a body corporate or an unincorporated body;

(d) a limited partnership (including a dissolved partnership) within the meaning of the Limited Partnerships Act 1907.

(2) It shall not be competent to sequestrate the estate of any of the following entities—

(a) a company registered under the [Companies Act 2006]; or

[(aa) a limited liability partnership,]

(b)   an entity in respect of which an enactment provides, expressly or by implication, that sequestration is incompetent.

(3)   The sequestration of a trust estate in respect of debts incurred by the trust shall be [. . .]—

[(a)   by debtor application made by a majority of trustees, with the concurrence of a qualified creditor or qualified creditors; or

(b)   on the petition of—

(i)   a temporary administrator;

(ii)   a member State liquidator appointed in main proceedings; or

(iii)   a qualified creditor or qualified creditors, if the trustees as such are apparently insolvent.]

(4)   The sequestration of the estate of a partnership shall be [. . .]—

[(za)   by a debtor application made by the partnership where the partner is apparently insolvent,]

[(a)   by debtor application made by the partnership with the concurrence of a qualified creditor or qualified creditors; or

(b)   on the petition of—

(i)   a temporary administrator;

(ii)   a member State liquidator appointed in main proceedings;

(iii)   a trustee acting under a trust deed; or

(iv)   a qualified creditor or qualified creditors, if the partnership is apparently insolvent.]

[(4A)   For the purposes of an application under subsection (4)(za), section 7(3)(a) is to be read as if—

(a)   the word 'either' were omitted, and

(b)   the words 'or if any of the partners is apparently insolvent for a debt of the partnership' were omitted.]

(5)   A petition under [subsection (4)(b)] above may be combined with a petition for the sequestration of the estate of any of the partners as an individual where that individual is apparently insolvent.

(6)   The sequestration of the estate of a body corporate or of an unincorporated body shall be—

[(a)   by debtor application made by a person authorised to act on behalf of the body, with the concurrence of a qualified creditor or qualified creditors; or

(b)   on the petition of—

(i)   a temporary administrator;

(ii)   a member State liquidator appointed in main proceedings; or

(iii)   a qualified creditor or qualified creditors, if the body is apparently insolvent.]

(7)   The application of this Act to the sequestration of the estate of a limited partnership shall be subject to such modifications as may be prescribed.

(8)   Subsections (6) [, (6A), (8) and (8A) [(but not (9) or (10))]] of section 5 of this Act shall apply for the purposes of this section as they apply for the purposes of that section.

#### [6A   Petition for sequestration of estate: provision of information

(1)   A petitioner for sequestration of a debtor's estate shall, insofar as it is within the petitioner's knowledge, state in the petition—

(a)   whether or not the debtor's centre of main interests is situated—

(i)   in the United Kingdom; or

(ii)   in another member State; and

(b)   whether or not the debtor possesses an establishment—

(i)   in the United Kingdom; or

(ii)   in any other member State.

(2)   If, to the petitioner's knowledge, there is a member State liquidator appointed in main proceedings in relation to the debtor, the petitioner shall, as soon

as reasonably practicable, send a copy of the petition to that member State liquidator.]

**[6B   Debtor application: provision of information**
(1)   Where a debtor application is made, the debtor shall state in the application [, other than an application under section 5(3)(a),]—
    (a)   whether or not the debtor's centre of main interests is situated—
        (i)   in the United Kingdom; or
        (ii)   in another member State; and
    (b)   whether or not the debtor possesses an establishment—
        (i)   in the United Kingdom; or
        (ii)   in any other member State.
(2)   If, to the debtor's knowledge, there is a member State liquidator appointed in main proceedings in relation to the debtor, the debtor shall, as soon as reasonably practicable, send a copy of the debtor application to that member State liquidator.]
[(2A)   Where a debtor application is made by an executor under section 5(3)(a) the executor must—
    (a)   state in the application whether or not the debtor's centre of main interests was situated in the United Kingdom or in another member State, and
    (b)   state in the application whether or not the debtor possessed an establishment in the United Kingdom or in another member State.]

**7   Meaning of apparent insolvency**
(1)   A debtor's apparent insolvency shall be constituted (or, where he is already apparently insolvent, constituted anew) whenever—
    (a)   his estate is sequestrated, or he is adjudged bankrupt in England or Wales or Northern Ireland; or
    (b)   [not being a person whose property is for the time being affected by a restraint order or subject to a confiscation, or charging, order,] he gives written notice to his creditors that he has ceased to pay his debts in the ordinary course of business; or
    [(ba)   he becomes subject to main proceedings in a member State other than the United Kingdom.]
    [(c)   the debtor grants a trust deed,
    (ca)   following the service on the debtor of a duly executed charge for payment of a debt, the days of charge expire without payment (unless the circumstances are shown to be such as are mentioned in subsection (1A)),
    (cb)   a decree of adjudication of any part of the debtor's estate is granted, either for payment or in security (unless the circumstances are shown to be such as are mentioned in subsection (1A)),
    (cc)   a debt constituted by a decree or document of debt (as defined in section 10 of the Debt Arrangement and Attachment (Scotland) Act 2002) is being paid by the debtor under a debt payment programme under Part 1 of that Act and the programme is revoked (unless the circumstances are shown to be such as are mentioned in subsection (1A)),]
    [. . .]
unless it is shown that at the time any such circumstance occurred, the debtor was able and willing to pay his debts as they became due [or that but for his property being affected by a restraint order or subject to a confiscation, or charging, order he would be able to do so]; or
    (d)   a creditor of the debtor, in respect of a liquid debt which amounts (or liquid debts which in aggregate amount) to not less than £750 or such sum as may be prescribed, has served on the debtor, by personal service by an officer of court, a demand in the prescribed form requiring him either to pay the debt (or debts) or to find security for its (or their) payment, and within 3 weeks after the date of service of the demand the debtor has not—

(i)  complied with the demand; or

(ii)  intimated to the creditor, by recorded delivery, that he denies that there is a debt or that the sum claimed by the creditor as the debt is immediately payable.

[In paragraph (d) above, 'liquid debt' does not include a sum payable under a confiscation order; and in the foregoing provisions of this subsection—

'charging order' has the meaning assigned by [section 78(2) of the Criminal Justice Act 1988 or by section 27(2) of the Drug Trafficking Act 1994];

[. . .] 'restraint order' means a confiscation order or a restraint order under Part 2, 3, or 4 of the Proceeds of Crime Act 2002.]

[(1A)  The circumstances are—

(a)  that, at the time of the occurrence, the debtor was able and willing to pay the debtor's debts as they became due, or

(b)  that, but for the debtor's property being affected by a restraint order or being subject to a confiscation order or charging order, the debtor would at that time have been able to pay those debts as they became due.]

(2)  A debtor's apparent insolvency shall continue, if constituted under—

(a)  subsection (1)(a) above, until his discharge; [. . .]

(b)  subsection (1)(b), (c) or (d) above, until he becomes able to pay his debts and pays them as they become due [; or

(c)  subsection (i)(ba), when main proceedings have ended.]

(3)  The apparent insolvency of—

(a)  a partnership shall be constituted [(or, as the case may be, again constituted)] either in accordance with the foregoing provisions of this section or if any of the partners is apparently insolvent for a debt of the partnership;

(b)  an unincorporated body shall be constituted [(or, as the case may be, again constituted)] if a person representing the body is apparently insolvent, or a person holding property of the body in a fiduciary capacity is apparently insolvent, for a debt of the body.

(4)  Notwithstanding subsection (2) of section 6 of this Act, the apparent insolvency of an entity such as is mentioned in paragraph (a) or (b) of that subsection may be constituted (or as the case may be constituted anew) under subsection (1) above; and any reference in the foregoing provisions of this section to a debtor shall, except where the context otherwise requires, be construed as including a reference to such an entity.

## 8  Further provisions relating to presentation of petitions

(1)  Subject to subsection (2) below, a petition for the sequestration of a debtor's estate (other than a deceased debtor's estate) may be presented—

[(a)  at any time by—

[. . .]

(ii)  a trustee under a trust deed;

(iii)  a temporary administrator; or

(iv)  a member State liquidator appointed in main proceedings;]

(b)  by a qualified creditor or qualified creditors, only if the apparent insolvency founded on in the petition was constituted within 4 months before the petition is presented.

[(2)  A petition for the sequestration of the estate of a limited partnership may be presented—

(a)  by a qualified creditor or qualified creditors only if the apparent insolvency founded on in the petition was constituted within 4 months (or such other period as may be prescribed) before the date of presentation of the petition, or

(b)  at any time by—

(i)  a temporary administrator,

(ii)  a member State liquidator appointed in main proceedings, or

(iii)  a trustee acting under a trust deed.]

(3)  A petition for the sequestration of the estate of a deceased debtor may be presented—

[(a)  at any time by—

[. . .]

(ii)  a person entitled to be appointed as executor of the estate;

(iii)  a trustee acting under a trust deed;

(iv)  a temporary administrator; or

(v)  a member State liquidator appointed in main proceedings;]

(b)  by a qualified creditor or qualified creditors of the deceased debtor—

(i)  in a case where the apparent insolvency of the debtor was constituted within 4 months before his death, at any time;

(ii)  in any other case (whether or not apparent insolvency has been constituted), not earlier than 6 months after the debtor's death.

[. . .]

(5)  The presentation of [. . .] a petition for sequestration shall bar the effect of any enactment or rule of law relating to the limitation of actions in any part of the United Kingdom.

(6)  Where before sequestration is awarded it becomes apparent that a petitioning [. . .] creditor was ineligible so to petition [. . .] he shall withdraw, or as the case may be withdraw from, the petition but another creditor may be sisted in his place.

## [8A  Further provisions relating to debtor applications

(1)  Subject to [subsections (2) and (2A)] below, a debtor application may be made at any time.

[(2)  A debtor application made in relation to the estate of a limited partnership may be made—

(a)  at any time, or

(b)  within such time as may be prescribed.]

[(2A)  Any intromission by an executor with the deceased debtor's estate after the period mentioned in subsection (2B) is deemed an intromission without a title unless, within that period, the executor—

(a)  makes a debtor application under section 5(3)(a), or

(b)  petitions for the appointment of a judicial factor to administer the estate.

(2B)  The period referred to in subsection (2A) is the period of 12 months following the day on which the executor knew or ought to have known that the estate was absolutely insolvent and likely to remain so.]

(3)  The making of, or the concurring in, a debtor application shall bar the effect of any enactment or rule of law relating to the limitation of actions.

(4)  Where, before sequestration is awarded, it becomes apparent that a creditor concurring in a debtor application was ineligible to so concur the Accountant in Bankruptcy shall withdraw him from the application but another creditor may concur in the place of the ineligible creditor and that other creditor shall notify the Accountant in Bankruptcy of that fact.]

## 9  Jurisdiction

(1)  [Where a petition is presented for the sequestration of an estate,] the [sheriff] shall have jurisdiction in respect of the sequestration of the estate of a living debtor or of a deceased debtor if the debtor had an established place of business in [the sheriffdom], or was habitually resident there, at the relevant time.

[(1A)  The Accountant in Bankruptcy may determine a debtor application for the sequestration of the estate of a living [or deceased] debtor if the debtor had an established place of business in Scotland, or was habitually resident there, at the relevant time.]

(2) [Where a petition is presented for the sequestration of an estate,] the [sheriff] shall have jurisdiction in respect of the sequestration of the estate of any entity which may be sequestrated by virtue of section 6 of this Act, if the entity—

(a)   had an established place of business in [the sheriffdom] at the relevant time; or

(b)   was constituted or formed under Scots law, and at any time carried on business in [the sheriffdom].

[(2A)   The Accountant in Bankruptcy may determine a debtor application for the sequestration of the estate of any entity which may be sequestrated by virtue of section 6 of this Act, if the entity—

(a)   had an established place of business in Scotland at the relevant time; or

(b)   was constituted or formed under Scots law, and at any time carried on business in Scotland.]

(3)   Notwithstanding that the partner of a firm, whether alive or deceased, does not fall within subsection (1) above, the [sheriff] shall have jurisdiction in respect of the sequestration of his estate if a petition has been presented for the sequestration of the estate of the firm of which he is, or was at the relevant time before his decease, a partner and the process of that sequestration is still current.

[(3A)   Any proceedings under this Act which—

(a)   relate to—

(i)   a debtor application; or

(ii)   the sequestration of a debtor's estate awarded following such an application; and

(b)   may be brought before a sheriff,

shall be brought before the sheriff who would, under subsection (1) or (2) above, have had jurisdiction in respect of a petition for sequestration of the debtor's estate.]

[. . .]

(5)   In this section 'the relevant time' means at any time in the year immediately preceding the date of presentation of the petition [, the date the debtor application is made] or the date of death, as the case may be.

[(6)   This section is subject to Article 3 of the EC Regulation.]

### [10   Duty to notify existence of concurrent proceedings for sequestration or analogous remedy

(1)   If, in the course of sequestration proceedings (referred to in this section and in section 10A of this Act as the 'instant proceedings')—

(a)   a petitioner for sequestration;

(b)   the debtor; or

(c)   a creditor concurring in a debtor application,

is, or becomes, aware of any of the circumstances mentioned in subsection (2) below, he shall as soon as possible take the action mentioned in subsection (3) below.

(2)   Those circumstances are that, notwithstanding the instant proceedings—

(a)   a petition for sequestration of the debtor's estate is before a sheriff or such sequestration has been awarded;

(b)   a debtor application has been made in relation to the debtor's estate or sequestration has been awarded by virtue of such an application;

(c)   a petition for the appointment of a judicial factor on the debtor's estate is before a court or such a judicial factor has been appointed;

(d)   a petition is before a court for the winding up of the debtor under Part

IV or V of the Insolvency Act 1986 (c 45) or section 372 of the Financial Services and Markets Act 2000 (c 8); or

(e)   an application for an analogous remedy in respect of the debtor's estate is proceeding or such an analogous remedy is in force.

(3)   The action referred to in subsection (1) above is—

(a)   in a case where the instant proceedings are by petition for sequestration, to notify the sheriff to whom that petition was presented; and

(b)   in a case where the instant proceedings are by debtor application, to notify the Accountant in Bankruptcy,

of the circumstance referred to in subsection (2) above.

[(3A)   The Accountant in Bankruptcy must grant a recall of an award of sequestration if—

(a)   sequestration has been awarded by virtue of a debtor application, and

(b)   the sheriff directs the Accountant in Bankruptcy to dismiss the debtor application.

(3B)   The effect of the recall of an award of sequestration is, so far as practicable, to restore the debtor and any other person affected by the sequestration to the position the debtor or, as the case may be, the other person would have been in if the sequestration had not been awarded.

(3C)   A recall of an award of sequestration does not—

(a)   affect the interruption of prescription caused by—

(i)   the presentation of the petition for sequestration,

(ii)   the making of the debtor application, or

(iii)   the submission of a claim under section 22 or 48,

(b)   invalidate any transaction entered into before such recall by the interim trustee, or by the trustee, with a person acting in good faith, or

(c)   affect a bankruptcy restrictions order which has not been annulled under section 56J(1)(a).

(3D)   Without delay after granting a recall of an award of sequestration under subsection (3A), the Accountant in Bankruptcy must send a certified copy of the decision to the Keeper of the Register of Inhibitions for recording in that register.]

(4)   If a petitioner fails to comply with subsection (1) above, he may be made liable for the expenses of presenting the petition for sequestration.

(5)   If a creditor concurring in a debtor application fails to comply with subsection (1) above, he may be made liable for the expenses of making the debtor application.

(6)   If a debtor fails to comply with subsection (1) above, he shall be guilty of an offence and liable, on summary conviction, to a fine not exceeding level 5 on the standard scale.

(7)   In this section and in section 10A of this Act 'analogous remedy' means [. . .] an individual voluntary arrangement or bankruptcy order under the Insolvency Act 1986 (c 45) or an administration order under section 112 of the County Courts Act 1984 (c 28) in England and Wales or under any enactment having the like effect in Northern Ireland or a remedy analogous to any of the aforesaid remedies, or to sequestration, in any other country (including England, Wales and Northern Ireland).]

### [10A   Powers in relation to concurrent proceedings for sequestration or analogous remedy

(1)   Where, in the course of instant proceedings which are by petition, any of the circumstances mentioned in paragraphs (a) to (d) of section 10(2) of this Act exists, the sheriff to whom the petition in the instant proceedings was presented may, on his own motion or at the instance of the debtor or any creditor or other person having an interest, allow that petition to proceed or may sist or dismiss it.

(2)   Without prejudice to subsection (1) above, where, in the course of instant proceedings which are by petition, any of the circumstances mentioned in para-

graphs (a), (c) or (d) of section 10(2) of this Act exists, the Court of Session may, on its own motion or on the application of the debtor or any creditor or other person having an interest, direct the sheriff before whom the petition in the instant proceedings is pending, or the sheriff before whom the other petition is pending, to sist or dismiss the petition in the instant proceedings or, as the case may be, the other petition, or may order the petitions to be heard together.

(3)   Without prejudice to subsection (1) above, where, in the course of instant proceedings which are by petition, the circumstance mentioned in paragraph (b) of section 10(2) of this Act exists, the sheriff to whom the petition in the instant proceedings was presented may, on his own motion or at the instance of the debtor or any creditor or other person having an interest, direct the Accountant in Bankruptcy to dismiss the debtor application.

(4)   Where, in the course of instant proceedings which are by debtor application, any of the circumstances mentioned in paragraphs (a) to (d) of section 10(2) of this Act exists, the Accountant in Bankruptcy may dismiss the debtor application in the instant proceedings.

(5)   Where, in respect of the same estate—

   (a)   a petition for sequestration is pending before a sheriff; and

   (b)   an application for an analogous remedy is proceeding or an analogous remedy is in force,

the sheriff, on his own motion or at the instance of the debtor or any creditor or other person having an interest, may allow the petition for sequestration to proceed or may sist or dismiss it.

(6)   Where, in respect of the same estate—

   (a)   a debtor application has been made and has not been determined; and

   (b)   an application for an analogous remedy is proceeding or an analogous remedy is in force,

the Accountant in Bankruptcy may proceed to determine the application or may dismiss it.]

## 11   Creditor's oath

(1)   Every creditor, being a petitioner for sequestration, a creditor who concurs in a [debtor application] or a qualified creditor who becomes sisted under subsection (8)(i) of section 5 of this Act or under that subsection as applied by section 6(8) of this Act, shall produce an oath in the prescribed form made by him or on his behalf.

(2)   The oath may be made—

   (a)   in the United Kingdom, before any person entitled to administer an oath there;

   (b)   outwith the United Kingdom, before a British diplomatic or consular officer or any person authorised to administer an oath or affirmation under the law of the place where the oath is made.

(3)   The identity of the person making the oath and the identity of the person before whom the oath is made and their authority to make and to administer the oath respectively shall be presumed to be correctly stated, and any seal or signature on the oath shall be presumed to be authentic, unless the contrary is established.

(4)   If the oath contains any error or has omitted any fact, the [sheriff to whom] the petition for sequestration was presented [or, in the case of a creditor concurring in a debtor application, the Accountant in Bankruptcy] may, at any time before sequestration is awarded, allow another oath to be produced rectifying the original oath; and this section shall apply to the making of that other oath as it applies to the making of the original oath.

(5)   Every creditor must produce along with the oath an account or voucher (according to the nature of the debt) which constitutes *prima facie* evidence of the debt; and a petitioning creditor shall in addition produce such evidence as is available to him to show the apparent insolvency of the debtor.

*Award of sequestration and appointment and resignation of interim trustee*

## [11A  Debtor application: incomplete application

(1)  This section applies where a debtor application is made and the Accountant in Bankruptcy considers that—

(a)  the application is incomplete,

(b)  further information is required in relation to the application,

(c)  further evidence is required to substantiate any fact relevant to the application, or

(d)  any fee or charge applicable to the application is outstanding.

(2)  The Accountant in Bankruptcy must specify by notice in writing to the debtor—

(a)  any further information which is to be provided,

(b)  any further evidence which is to be provided, and

(c)  any fee or charge to be paid.

(3)  Any information, evidence, fee or charge to be provided or paid under subsection (2) must be provided or paid within 21 days or such longer period as may be specified by the Accountant in Bankruptcy.

(4)  The Accountant in Bankruptcy may refuse to award sequestration if, after the expiry of the period referred to in subsection (3), the Accountant in Bankruptcy considers that—

(a)  the application remains incomplete,

(b)  the debtor has provided insufficient information or evidence under subsection (2)(a) or (b), or

(c)  any fee or charge applicable to the application remains outstanding.

## 11B  Refusal of debtor application: inappropriate application

(1)  This section applies where a debtor application is made and the Accountant in Bankruptcy considers that an award of sequestration may not be appropriate in the circumstances of the case.

(2)  The Accountant in Bankruptcy must specify by notice in writing to the debtor—

(a)  the reason why the Accountant in Bankruptcy considers the application may not be appropriate, and

(b)  any further information which is to be provided within 21 days or such longer period as may be specified by the Accountant in Bankruptcy.

(3)  The Accountant in Bankruptcy may refuse to award sequestration if, after the expiry of the period referred to in subsection (2), the Accountant in Bankruptcy remains of the view that an award of sequestration would be inappropriate in the circumstances of the case.]

## 12  When sequestration is awarded

[(1)  Where a [debtor application [, other than an application under section 5(3)(a),] is made [and sections 11A and 11B do not apply], the Accountant in Bankruptcy shall award sequestration forthwith if he is satisfied—

(a)  that the application has been made in accordance with the provisions of this Act and any provisions made under this Act;]

(b)  that [subsection] (2B) of section 5 of this Act applies to the debtor; and

(c)  that the provisions of [subsection (6A)] of that section have been complied with.

[. . .]

[(1B)  Where a debtor application is made under section 5(3)(a) the Accountant in Bankruptcy must award sequestration forthwith if the Accountant is satisfied—

(a)  that the application has been made in accordance with the provisions of this Act and any provision made under this Act, and

(b)  that the provisions of subsection (6A) of section 5 have been complied with.]

(2)   Where a petition for sequestration of a debtor's estate is presented by a creditor or a trustee acting under a trust deed, the [sheriff to whom] the petition is presented shall grant warrant to cite the debtor to appear before [him] on such date as shall be specified in the warrant, being a date not less than 6 nor more than 14 days after the date of citation, to show cause why sequestration should not be awarded.

[(3)   Where, on a petition for sequestration presented by a creditor or a trustee acting under a trust deed, the [sheriff] is satisfied—

(a)   that, if the debtor has not appeared, proper citation has been made of the debtor;

(b)   that the petition has been presented in accordance with the provisions of this Act;

(c)   that the provisions of subsection (6) of section 5 of this Act have been complied with;

(d)   that, in the case of a petition by a creditor, the requirements of this Act relating to apparent insolvency have been fulfilled; and

[(e)   that, in the case of a petition by a trustee—

(i)   one or more of the conditions in section 5(2C)(a) applies, or

(ii)   the petition includes an averment in accordance with section 5(2C)(b),]

[he] shall, subject to [subsections (3A) to (3C)] below, award sequestration forthwith.

[(3A)   Sequestration shall not be awarded in pursuance of subsection (3) above if—

(a)   cause is shown why sequestration cannot competently be awarded; or

(b)   the debtor forthwith pays or satisfies, or produces written evidence of the payment or satisfaction of [. . .]—

(i)   the debt in respect of which he became apparently insolvent; and

(ii)   any other debt due by him to the petitioner and any creditor concurring in the petition.

(3B)   Where the sheriff is satisfied that the debtor shall, before the expiry of the period of 42 days beginning with the day on which the debtor appears before the sheriff, pay or satisfy—

(a)   the debt in respect of which the debtor became apparently insolvent; and

(b)   any other debt due by the debtor to the petitioner and any creditor concurring in the petition,

the sheriff may continue the petition for a period of no more than 42 days.

(3C)   Where the sheriff is satisfied—

(a)   that a debt payment programme (within the meaning of Part 1 of the Debt Arrangement and Attachment (Scotland) Act 2002 (asp 17)) relating to—

(i)   the debt in respect of which the debtor became apparently insolvent; and

(ii)   any other debt due by the debtor to the petitioner and any creditor concurring in the petition,

has been applied for and has not yet been approved or rejected; or

(b)   that such a debt payment programme will be applied for,

the sheriff may continue the petition for such period as he thinks fit.]

[(4)   In this Act 'the date of sequestration' means—

(a)   where [a debtor application is made], the date on which sequestration is awarded;

(b)   where the petition for sequestration is presented by a creditor or a trustee acting under a trust deed [and sequestration is awarded]—

(i)   the date on which the [sheriff] grants warrant under subsection (2) above to cite the debtor; or

(ii)   where more than one such warrant is granted, the date on which the first such warrant is granted.]

**[13   Resignation, removal etc of interim trustee**

[(A1)   This section applies where an interim trustee is appointed under section 2(5) of this Act and the petition for sequestration has not been determined.]

(1)   Where, under section 1A(2) of this Act, the [sheriff] removes from office an interim trustee, the [sheriff] shall, on the application of the Accountant in Bankruptcy, appoint a new interim trustee.

(2)   Without prejudice to section 1A(2) of this Act or to subsection (1) above, where the [sheriff] is satisfied that an interim trustee—

(a)   is unable to act [for any reason mentioned in subsection (2A) below or] by, under or by virtue of [any other] provision of this Act [. . .]; or

(b)   has so conducted himself that he should no longer continue to act [. . .], the [sheriff], on the application of the debtor, a creditor or the Accountant in Bankruptcy, shall remove from office the interim trustee and appoint a new interim trustee.

[(2A)   the reasons referred to in subsection (2)(a) above are that the interim trustee—

(a)   is incapable within the meaning of section 1(6) of the Adults with Incapacity (Scotland) Act 2000 (asp 4); or

(b)   has some other incapacity by virtue of which he is unable to act as interim trustee.]

(3)   An interim trustee (not being the Accountant in Bankruptcy) may apply to the [sheriff] for authority to resign office; and if the [sheriff] is satisfied that the grounds mentioned in paragraph (a) or (b) of subsection (2) above apply in relation to the interim trustee, [the sheriff] shall grant the application.

(4)   Where, following an application under subsection (3) above, the interim trustee resigns office, the [sheriff] shall appoint a new interim trustee.

(5)   Where the interim trustee has died, the [sheriff], on the application of the debtor, a creditor or the Accountant in Bankruptcy, shall appoint a new interim trustee.

(6)   No one (other than the Accountant in Bankruptcy) shall act as interim trustee in a sequestration if he would, by virtue of section 24(2) of this Act, be [ineligible to be elected as replacement] trustee in that sequestration; but where an interim trustee is, by virtue of this subsection, prohibited from so acting, he shall forthwith make an application under subsection (3) above.

(7)   Subsections (1) and (2) of section 2 of this Act shall apply as regards the appointment of an interim trustee under this section as if for any reference to—

(a)   the [sheriff] awarding sequestration of the debtor's estate, there was substituted a reference to the [sheriff] appointing a new interim trustee; and

(b)   the petition for sequestration there was substituted a reference to the application under this section for the appointment of a new interim trustee.]

**[13A   Termination of interim trustee's functions where not appointed as trustee**

(1)   This section applies where an interim trustee (not being the Accountant in Bankruptcy) is appointed under section 2(5) of this Act and the sheriff—

(a)   awards sequestration and appoints another person as trustee under subsection (2A) or (2C) of section 2 of this Act; or

(b)   refuses to award sequestration.

(2)   Where the sheriff awards sequestration and appoints another person as trustee, the interim trustee shall hand over to the trustee everything in his possession which relates to the sequestration and shall thereupon cease to act in the sequestration.

(3)   The sheriff may make such order in relation to liability for the outlays and remuneration of the interim trustee as may be appropriate.

(4) Within 3 months of the sheriff awarding or, as the case may be, refusing to award sequestration, the interim trustee shall—

    (a) submit to the Accountant in Bankruptcy—

        (i) his accounts of his intromissions (if any) with the debtor's estate; and

        (ii) a claim for outlays reasonably incurred, and for remuneration for work reasonably undertaken, by him; and

    (b) send a copy of his accounts and the claim to—

        (i) the debtor;

        (ii) the petitioner; and

        (iii) in a case where sequestration is awarded, the trustee and all creditors known to the interim trustee.

(5) On a submission being made to him under subsection (4)(a) above, the Accountant in Bankruptcy shall—

    (a) audit the accounts;

    (b) issue a determination fixing the amount of the outlays and remuneration payable to the interim trustee;

    (c) send a copy of the determination to—

        (i) the interim trustee; and

        (ii) the persons mentioned in subsection (4)(b) above; and

    (d) where a trustee (not being the Accountant in Bankruptcy) has been appointed in the sequestration, send a copy of the audited accounts and of the determination to the trustee [. . .].

[. . .]

(7) The interim trustee or any person mentioned in subsection (4)(b) above may, within 14 days after the issuing of the determination under subsection (5)(b) above, appeal to the sheriff against the determination.

(8) On receiving a copy of the Accountant in Bankruptcy's determination sent under subsection (5)(c)(i) above the interim trustee may apply to him for a certificate of discharge.

(9) The interim trustee shall send notice of an application under subsection (8) above to the persons mentioned in subsection (4)(b) above and shall inform them—

    (a) that they may make written representations relating to the application to the Accountant in Bankruptcy within the period of 14 days after such notification; and

    (b) of the effect mentioned in subsection (16) below.

(10) On the expiry of the period mentioned in subsection (9)(a) above the Accountant in Bankruptcy, after considering any representations duly made to him, shall—

    (a) grant or refuse to grant the certificate of discharge; and

    (b) notify the persons mentioned in subsection (4)(b) above accordingly.

[(10A) The interim trustee or any person mentioned in subsection (4)(b) may apply to the Accountant in Bankruptcy for a review of a determination under subsection (10).

(10B) An application under subsection (10A) must be made before the expiry of the period of 14 days beginning with the day on which the determination is issued under subsection (10).

(10C) If an application under subsection (10A) is made, the Accountant in Bankruptcy must—

    (a) take into account any representations made by an interested person before the expiry of the period of 21 days beginning with the day on which the application is made, and

    (b) confirm, amend or revoke the determination under subsection (10) before the expiry of the period of 28 days beginning with the day on which the application is made.]

[(11) The interim trustee or any person mentioned in subsection (4)(b) may appeal to the sheriff against a decision by the Accountant in Bankruptcy under subsection (10C)(b) before the expiry of the period of 14 days beginning with the day of the decision.]

(12)  If, following an appeal under subsection (11) above, the sheriff determines that a certificate of discharge which has been refused should be granted he shall order the Accountant in Bankruptcy to grant it.

(13)  If, following an appeal under subsection (11) above, the sheriff determines that a certificate of discharge which has been granted should have been refused he shall revoke the certificate.

(14)  The sheriff clerk shall send a copy of the decree of the sheriff following an appeal under subsection (11) above to the Accountant in Bankruptcy.

(15)  The decision of the sheriff in an appeal under subsection (7) or (11) above shall be final.

(16)  The grant of a certificate of discharge under this section by the Accountant in Bankruptcy shall have the effect of discharging the interim trustee from all liability (other than any liability arising from fraud) to the debtor, to the petitioner or to the creditors in respect of any act or omission of the interim trustee in exercising the functions conferred on him by this Act.]

**[13B  Termination of Accountant in Bankruptcy's functions as interim trustee where not appointed as trustee**

(1)  This section applies where the Accountant in Bankruptcy is appointed as interim trustee under section 2(5) of this Act and the sheriff—

(a)  awards sequestration and appoints another person as trustee under section 2(2A) of this Act; or

(b)  refuses to award sequestration.

(2)  Where the sheriff awards sequestration and appoints another person as trustee, the Accountant in Bankruptcy shall hand over to the trustee everything in his possession which relates to the sequestration and shall thereupon cease to act in the sequestration.

(3)  The sheriff may make such order in relation to liability for the outlays and remuneration of the Accountant in Bankruptcy as may be appropriate.

(4)  Within 3 months of the sheriff awarding or, as the case may be, refusing to award sequestration, the Accountant in Bankruptcy shall—

(a)  send to the debtor and the petitioner—

(i)  his accounts of his intromissions (if any) with the debtor's estate;

(ii)  a determination of his fees and outlays calculated in accordance with regulations made under section 69A of this Act; and

(iii)  the notice mentioned in subsection (5) below; and

(b)  in a case where sequestration is awarded, send a copy of his accounts, the [determination] and the notice to all creditors known to him.

(5)  The notice referred to in subsection (4)(a)(iii) above is a notice in writing stating—

(a)  that the Accountant in Bankruptcy has commenced procedure under this Act leading to discharge in respect of his actings as interim trustee;

[(aa)  that an application for a review may be made under subsection (6A)];

(b)  that an appeal may be made to the sheriff under subsection (7) below; and

[(c)  that, in the circumstances mentioned in subsection (9), the Accountant in Bankruptcy is discharged from any liability incurred while acting as interim trustee.]

[. . .]

[(6A)  The debtor, the petitioner or any creditor may apply to the Accountant in Bankruptcy for a review of the discharge of the Accountant in Bankruptcy in respect of the Accountant in Bankruptcy's actings as interim trustee.

(6B)  An application under subsection (6A) must be made before the expiry of the period of 14 days beginning with the day on which notice is sent under subsection (4)(a)(iii) or (b).

(6C)   If an application for a review under subsection (6A) is made, the Accountant in Bankruptcy must—

(a)   take into account any representations made by an interested person before the expiry of the period of 21 days beginning with the day on which the application is made, and

(b)   confirm or revoke the discharge before the expiry of the period of 28 days beginning with the day on which the application is made.]

[(7)   The debtor, the petitioner or any creditor may appeal to the sheriff against—

(a)   the determination of the Accountant in Bankruptcy mentioned in subsection (4)(a)(ii) before the expiry of the period of 14 days beginning with the day on which notice is sent under subsection (4)(a)(iii) or (b),

(b)   a decision by the Accountant in Bankruptcy under subsection (6C)(b) before the expiry of the period of 14 days beginning with the day of the decision.

(7A)   The sheriff clerk must, following an appeal, send a copy of the decree to the Accountant in Bankruptcy.]

(8)   The decision of the sheriff in an appeal under subsection (7) above shall be final.

(9)   Where—

(a)   the requirements of this section have been complied with; and

(b)   no appeal is made to the sheriff under subsection (7) above or such an appeal is made but is refused as regards the discharge of the Accountant in Bankruptcy,

the Accountant in Bankruptcy shall be discharged from all liability (other than any liability arising from fraud) to the debtor, to the petitioner or to the creditors in respect of any act or omission of the Accountant in Bankruptcy in exercising the functions of interim trustee conferred on him by this Act.]

**14   Registration of [warrant or determination of debtor application]**

(1)   The [sheriff clerk] shall forthwith after the [sheriff grants warrant under section 12(2)] send—

(a)   a certified copy of the [order of the sheriff granting warrant under [that section]] to the keeper of the register of inhibitions and adjudications for recording in that register;

(b)   a copy of the order to the Accountant in Bankruptcy.

[. . .]

[(1A)   Where the Accountant in Bankruptcy awards sequestration on a debtor application he shall forthwith after the date of sequestration send a certified copy of his determination of the application to the keeper of the register of inhibitions for recording in that register.]

(2)   Recording under subsection (1)(a) [or (1A)] above shall have the effect as from the date of sequestration of an inhibition and of a citation in an adjudication of the debtor's heritable estate at the instance of the creditors who subsequently have claims in the sequestration accepted under section 49 of this Act.

(3)   The effect mentioned in subsection (2) above shall expire—

(a)   on the recording under section 15(5)(a) or 17(8)(a) of [. . .] this Act of a certified copy of an order; or

[. . .]

[(ab)   on the recording under section 10A(3D), 17D(6) or 17E(8) of a certified copy of a decision,]

(b)   subject to subsection (4) below, if the effect has not expired by virtue of [paragraphs (a) and (aa)] above, at the end of the period of 3 years beginning with the date of sequestration.

[(4)   The trustee may, if not discharged, send a memorandum in a form pre-scribed by the Court of Session by act of sederunt to the Keeper of the Register of Inhibitions for recording in that register before the expiry of—

(a)   the period of 3 years mentioned in subsection (3)(b), or

(b)   a period for which the effect mentioned in subsection (2) has been renewed by virtue of subsection (4A).

(4A)   The recording of a memorandum sent in accordance with subsection (4) renews the effect mentioned in subsection (2) for a period of 3 years beginning with the expiry of—

(a)   the period mentioned in subsection (3)(b), or

(b)   as the case may be, the period mentioned in subsection (4)(b).

(4B)   The trustee may, if appointed or reappointed under section 58B, send a memorandum in a form prescribed by the Court of Session by act of sederunt to the Keeper of the Register of Inhibitions for recording in that register before the expiry of that appointment.

(4C)   The recording of a memorandum sent in accordance with subsection (4B) imposes the effect mentioned in subsection (2) for a period of 3 years beginning with the day of notification in accordance with section 58C(1).]

[. . .]

## 15   Further provisions relating to award of sequestration

[. . .]

(2)   The [sheriff] may at any time after sequestration has been awarded, on application being made to [him and subject to subsection (2A) below], transfer the sequestration [. . .] to any other sheriff.

[(2A)   The debtor may, with leave of the sheriff, appeal to the sheriff principal against a transfer under subsection (2) above.]

(3)   Where the [sheriff] makes an order refusing to award sequestration, the petitioner [. . .] may appeal against the order within 14 days of the date of making of the order.

[(3A)   If, following a debtor application, the Accountant in Bankruptcy refuses to award sequestration, the debtor or a creditor concurring in the application may apply to the Accountant in Bankruptcy for a review of the refusal.

(3B)   An application under subsection (3A) must be made before the expiry of the period of 14 days beginning with the day on which the Accountant in Bank-ruptcy refuses to award sequestration.

(3C)   If an application under subsection (3A) is made, the Accountant in Bank-ruptcy must—

(a)   take into account any representations made by an interested person before the expiry of the period of 21 days beginning with the day on which the application is made, and

(b)   confirm the refusal or award sequestration before the expiry of the period of 28 days beginning with the day on which the application is made.

(3D)   If the Accountant in Bankruptcy confirms the refusal to award seques-tration under subsection (3C)(b), the debtor or a creditor concurring in the applica-tion may, before the expiry of the period of 14 days beginning with the day of that confirmation, appeal to the sheriff.]

(4)   Without prejudice to any right to bring an action of reduction of an award of sequestration, such an award shall not be subject to review otherwise than by recall under sections [10A(3A), 16, 17, 17D and 17E] of this Act.

(5)   Where a petition for sequestration is presented by a creditor or a trustee acting under a trust deed, the [sheriff clerk] shall—

(a)   on the final determination or abandonment of any appeal under sub-section (3) above in relation to the petition, or if there is no such appeal on the expiry of the 14 days mentioned in that subsection, send a certified copy of an

order refusing to award sequestration to the keeper of the register of inhibitions
and adjudications for recording in that register;
  [(b)  forthwith send a copy of the order refusing or awarding sequestration—
        (i)  to the Accountant in Bankruptcy; and
        (ii) where the debtor is taking part in a debt payment programme under
  Part 1 of the Debt Arrangement and Attachment (Scotland) Act 2002, to the
  DAS Administrator (as defined in regulation 2(1) of the Debt Arrangement
  Scheme (Scotland) Regulations 2011).]
  . . .
  (7)   Where sequestration has been awarded, the process of sequestration shall
not fall asleep.
  (8)   Where a debtor learns, whether before or after the date of sequestration,
that he may derive benefit from another estate, he shall as soon as practicable after
that date inform—
    (a)  the [. . .] trustee of that fact; and
    (b)  the person who is administering that other estate of the sequestration.
  (9)   If the debtor fails to comply with subsection (8) above, he shall be guilty of
an offence and liable, on summary conviction, to a fine not exceeding level 5 on
the standard scale.

### 16   Petitions for recall of sequestration

  (1)   A petition for recall of an award of sequestration may be presented to the
[sheriff] by—
    (a)  the debtor, any creditor or any other person having an interest (not-
withstanding that he was a petitioner, or concurred in the [debtor application],
for the sequestration);
    (b)  the [. . .] trustee, or the Accountant in Bankruptcy.
  [(1A)  A petition for recall of an award of sequestration may not be presented
to the sheriff if the only ground is that the debtor has paid or is able to pay the
debtor's debts in full.
  (1B)   Subsection (1A) does not apply where—
    (a)  sequestration was awarded following a petition of a qualified creditor or
qualified creditors, and
    (b)  a petition for recall of the award of sequestration includes the ground
that the debtor was not apparently insolvent.]
  (2)   The petitioner shall serve upon the debtor, any person who was a petitioner, or concurred in the [debtor application], for the sequestration, the [. . .]
trustee and the Accountant in Bankruptcy, a copy of the petition along with a
notice stating that the recipient of the notice may lodge answers to the petition
within 14 days of the service of the notice.
  [(3)   On service of a copy of the petition under subsection (2), the Accountant in
Bankruptcy must enter particulars of the petition in the register of insolvencies.]
  (4)   Subject to [sections 41(1)(b) and 41A(1)(b)] of this Act, a petition under this
section may be presented [at any time.] [. . .]
  (5)   Notwithstanding that a petition has been presented under this section, the
proceedings in the sequestration shall continue (subject to section 17(6) of this Act)
as if that petition had not been presented until the recall is granted.
  (6)   Where—
    (a)  a petitioner under this section; or
    (b)  a person who has lodged answers to the petition,
withdraws or dies, any person entitled to present or, as the case may be, lodge
answers to a petition under this section may be sisted in his place.

### 17   [Recall of sequestration by sheriff]

  (1)   The [sheriff] may recall an award of sequestration if [he] is satisfied that in

all the circumstances of the case (including those arising after the date of the award of sequestration) it is appropriate to do so and, without prejudice to the foregoing generality, may recall the award if [he] is satisfied that—

(a)   the debtor has paid his debts in full [. . .];

(b)   a majority in value of the creditors reside in a country other than Scotland and that it is more appropriate for the debtor's estate to be administered in that other country; or

(c)   one or more other awards of sequestration of the estate or analogous remedies (as defined in [section 10(7)] of this Act) have been granted.

(2)   Where one or more [other] awards of sequestration of the debtor's estate have been granted, the [sheriff] may, after such intimation as [he] considers necessary, recall an award whether or not the one in respect of which the petition for recall was presented.

[(2A)   Where the sheriff intends to recall an award of sequestration on the ground that the debtor has paid the debtor's debts in full, the order recalling the award may not—

(a)   be made before the payment in full of the outlays and remuneration of the interim trustee and the trustee,

(b)   be subject to any conditions which are to be fulfilled before the order takes effect.]

(3)   On recalling an award of sequestration, the [sheriff]—

(a)   shall make provision for the payment of the outlays and remuneration of [any] interim trustee and [the] trustee by directing that such payment shall be made out of the debtor's estate or by requiring any person who was a party to the petition for sequestration [or, as the case may be, the debtor application,] to pay the whole or any part of the said outlays and remuneration;

(b)   without prejudice to subsection (7) below, may direct that payment of the expenses of a creditor who was a petitioner, or concurred in the [debtor application], for sequestration shall be made out of the debtor's estate;

(c)   may make any further order that [he] considers necessary or reasonable in all the circumstances of the case.

(4)   Subject to subsection (5) below, the effect of the recall of an award of sequestration shall be, so far as practicable, to restore the debtor and any other person affected by the sequestration to the position he would have been in if the sequestration had not been awarded.

(5)   A recall of an award of sequestration shall not—

(a)   affect the interruption of prescription caused by the presentation of the petition for sequestration [, the making of the debtor application] or the submission of a claim under section 22 or 48 of this Act;

(b)   invalidate any transaction entered into before such recall by the interim trustee or [the] trustee with a person acting in good faith;

[(c)   affect a bankruptcy restrictions order which has not been annulled under section 56J(1)(a) of this Act.]

(6)   Where the [sheriff] considers that it is inappropriate to recall or to refuse to recall an award of sequestration forthwith, [he] may order that the proceedings in the sequestration shall continue but shall be subject to such conditions as [he] may think fit.

(7)   The [sheriff] may make such order in relation to the expenses in a petition for recall as [he] thinks fit.

(8)   The [sheriff clerk] shall send—

(a)   a certified copy of any order recalling an award of sequestration to the keeper of the register of inhibitions and adjudications for recording in that register; and

(b)   a copy of any order recalling or refusing to recall an award of sequestration, or of any order under section 41(1)(b)(ii) [or 41A(1)(b)(ii)] of this Act, to—

(i)   the Accountant in Bankruptcy; and

(ii)   [if the Accountant in Bankruptcy is not the trustee in sequestration, the trustee in sequestration] [. . .]

## [17A   Application to Accountant in Bankruptcy for recall of sequestration

(1)   An application for recall of an award of sequestration may be made to the Accountant in Bankruptcy on the ground that the debtor has paid or is able to pay the debtor's debts in full.

(2)   An application may be made by—

(a)   the debtor,

(b)   any creditor (whether or not a person who was a petitioner for, or concurred in a debtor application for, the sequestration),

(c)   the trustee (where the Accountant in Bankruptcy is not the trustee), or

(d)   any other person having an interest (whether or not a person who was a petitioner for the sequestration).

(3)   The person making an application must, at the same time as applying to the Accountant in Bankruptcy, give to the persons mentioned in subsection (4)—

(a)   a copy of the application, and

(b)   a notice informing the recipient that the person has a right to make representations to the Accountant in Bankruptcy in relation to the application before the expiry of the period of 21 days beginning with the day on which the notice is given.

(4)   The persons are—

(a)   the debtor,

(b)   any person who was a petitioner for, or concurred in a debtor application for, the sequestration,

(c)   the trustee.

(5)   Despite an application being made, the proceedings in the sequestration are to continue as if the application had not been made until a recall of an award of sequestration is granted under section 17D(1) (subject to any conditions imposed under section 17D(5)).

(6)   Where the applicant withdraws the application or dies, the Accountant in Bankruptcy may continue the application by substituting any person mentioned in subsection (2) for the applicant.

## 17B   Application under section 17A: further procedure

(1)   This section applies where an application is made under section 17A.

(2)   The trustee must prepare a statement on the debtor's affairs, so far as within the knowledge of the trustee.

(3)   The trustee must submit the statement to the Accountant in Bankruptcy—

(a)   at the same time as the trustee makes the application under section 17A, or

(b)   where the application is made by another person, before the expiry of the period of 21 days beginning with the day on which the notice is given under section 17A(3)(b).

(4)   The statement must—

(a)   indicate whether the debtor has agreed to—

(i)   the interim trustee's claim for outlays reasonably incurred and for remuneration for work reasonably undertaken by the interim trustee (including any outlays and remuneration which are yet to be incurred), and

(ii)   the trustee's claim for outlays reasonably incurred and for remuneration for work reasonably undertaken by the trustee (including any outlays and remuneration which are yet to be incurred),

(b)   state whether or not the debtor's debts have been paid in full (including the payment of the outlays and remuneration of the interim trustee and the trustee), (c)　where the debtor's debts have not been so paid—

    (i)　provide details of any debt which has not been paid, and

    (ii)　indicate whether, in the opinion of the trustee, the debtor's assets are likely to be sufficient to pay the debts in full (including the payment of the outlays and remuneration of the interim trustee and the trustee) before the day which is 8 weeks after the day on which the statement is submitted, and

(d)　provide details of any distribution of the debtor's estate.

(5)　The trustee must notify every creditor known to the trustee that an application has been made—

(a)　where the application is made by the trustee, before the expiry of the period of 7 days beginning with the day on which the application is made,

(b)　where the application is made by another person, before the expiry of the period of 7 days beginning with the day on which the notice is given under section 17A(3)(b).

(6)　If a creditor has not previously submitted a claim under section 22 or 48, the creditor must, in order to be included in the statement made by the trustee, submit a claim.

(7)　A claim must be submitted—

(a)　in accordance with section 22(2) and (3), and

(b)　before the expiry of the period of 14 days beginning with the day on which notice is given under subsection (5).

(8)　If any creditor submits a claim in accordance with subsection (7), the trustee must update and resubmit the statement before the expiry of the period of 7 days beginning with the expiry of the period mentioned in subsection (7)(b).

(9)　The trustee must update and resubmit the statement if—

(a)　the statement previously submitted did not state in accordance with subsection (4)(b) that the debtor's debts have been paid in full, and

(b)　before the day on which the application is determined by the Accountant in Bankruptcy, the trustee is able to make that statement.

## 17C　Determination of outlays and remuneration

(1)　This section applies where—

(a)　the Accountant in Bankruptcy receives an application under section 17A, and

(b)　the statement submitted by the trustee under section 17B indicates that the amount of the outlays and remuneration of the trustee is not agreed.

(2)　The trustee must provide to the Accountant in Bankruptcy—

(a)　at the same time as submitting the statement under section 17B—

    (i)　the trustee's accounts of the trustee's intromissions with the debtor's estate for audit, and

    (ii)　details of the trustee's claim for outlays reasonably incurred and for remuneration for work reasonably undertaken by the trustee (including any outlays and remuneration which are yet to be incurred), and

(b)　such other information in relation to that claim as may be reasonably requested by the Accountant in Bankruptcy.

(3)　The Accountant in Bankruptcy must before the expiry of the period of 28 days beginning with the expiry of the period mentioned in section 17B(8) issue a determination fixing the amount of the outlays and the remuneration payable to the trustee.

(4)　The Accountant in Bankruptcy may before the expiry of the period mentioned in subsection (3) determine the expenses reasonably incurred by a creditor who was a petitioner or, as the case may be, concurred in a debtor application for sequestration.

(5)　Subsections (4) and (5) of section 53 apply to the Accountant in Bankruptcy for the purpose of making a determination in accordance with subsection (3) as they apply to the commissioners or the Accountant in Bankruptcy for the purpose of fixing an amount under that section.

**17D   Recall of sequestration by Accountant in Bankruptcy**

(1)   The Accountant in Bankruptcy may grant a recall of an award of sequestration if—

(a)   the trustee has notified the Accountant in Bankruptcy in the statement submitted under section 17B that the debtor's debts have been paid in full (including the payment of the outlays and remuneration of the interim trustee and the trustee), and

(b)   the Accountant in Bankruptcy is satisfied that in all the circumstances of the case, it is appropriate to do so.

(2)   The Accountant in Bankruptcy may not grant a recall of an award of sequestration after—

(a)   where no appeal is made under section 17G(5)(a), the day which is 8 weeks after the day on which the statement was first submitted under section 17B(3), or

(b)   where such an appeal is made, such later day which is 14 days after the day on which the appeal is finally determined or abandoned.

(3)   The effect of the recall of an award of sequestration is, so far as practicable, to restore the debtor and any other person affected by the sequestration to the position the debtor or, as the case may be, the other person would have been in if the sequestration had not been awarded.

(4)   A recall of an award of sequestration is not to—

(a)   affect the interruption of prescription caused by—

(i)   the presentation of the petition for sequestration,

(ii)   the making of the debtor application, or

(iii)   the submission of a claim under section 22 or 48,

(b)   invalidate any transaction entered into before such recall by the interim trustee, or by the trustee, with a person acting in good faith, or

(c)   affect a bankruptcy restrictions order which has not been annulled under section 56J(1)(a).

(5)   If the Accountant in Bankruptcy does not grant a recall of an award of sequestration under subsection (1) the sequestration is to continue but is to be subject to such conditions as the Accountant in Bankruptcy thinks fit.

(6)   Without delay after granting a recall of an award of sequestration under subsection (1), the Accountant in Bankruptcy must send a certified copy of the decision to the Keeper of the Register of Inhibitions for recording in that register.

**17E   Recall where Accountant in Bankruptcy the trustee**

(1)   This section applies where the Accountant in Bankruptcy—

(a)   is the trustee, and

(b)   considers that recall of an award of sequestration should be granted on the ground that the debtor has paid or is able to pay the debtor's debts in full (including the payment of the outlays and remuneration of the interim trustee and the trustee).

(2)   The Accountant in Bankruptcy must notify the debtor and every creditor known to the Accountant in Bankruptcy that the Accountant in Bankruptcy considers that subsection (1) applies.

(3)   If a creditor has not previously submitted a claim under section 22 or 48, the creditor must, in order for the creditor's claim to a dividend out of the debtor's estate to be considered, submit a claim.

(4)   A claim must be submitted—

(a)   in accordance with section 22(2) and (3), and

(b)   before the expiry of the period of 14 days beginning with the day on which notice is given under subsection (2).

(5) Before granting a recall of an award of sequestration the Accountant in Bankruptcy must—

(a) take into account any representations made by an interested person before the expiry of the period of 21 days beginning with the day on which the notice is given under subsection (2), and

(b) make a determination of the Accountant in Bankruptcy's fees and outlays calculated in accordance with regulations made under section 69A.

(6) The Accountant in Bankruptcy may grant a recall of an award of sequestration if the Accountant in Bankruptcy is satisfied that—

(a) the debtor has paid the debtor's debts in full (including the payment of the outlays and remuneration of the interim trustee and the trustee),

(b) those debts were paid in full before the expiry of the period of 8 weeks beginning with the expiry of the period mentioned in subsection (5)(a), and

(c) in all the circumstances of the case, it is appropriate to do so.

(7) Subsections (2) and (3) of section 17D apply in relation to a recall of an award of sequestration granted under subsection (6) as they apply in relation to a recall of an award of sequestration granted under that section.

(8) Without delay after granting a recall of an award of sequestration under subsection (6), the Accountant in Bankruptcy must send a certified copy of the decision to the Keeper of the Register of Inhibitions for recording in that register.

**17F Reference to sheriff**

(1) The Accountant in Bankruptcy may, at any time before deciding under section 17D(1) whether to grant an application for recall of an award of sequestration, remit to the sheriff an application made under section 17A.

(2) The Accountant in Bankruptcy may, at any time before deciding under section 17E(6) whether to grant a recall of an award of sequestration, remit the case to the sheriff.

(3) If an application is remitted to the sheriff under subsection (1) or (2), the sheriff may dispose of the application or the case in accordance with section 17 as if it were a petition presented by the Accountant in Bankruptcy under section 16.

**17G Recall of sequestration by Accountant in Bankruptcy: review and appeal**

(1) A person mentioned in subsection (2) may apply to the Accountant in Bankruptcy for a review of—

(a) a decision of the Accountant in Bankruptcy under section 17D(1) or 17E(6) to grant or refuse to grant a recall of an award of sequestration,

(b) a determination of the Accountant in Bankruptcy under section 17C(4).

(2) The persons are—

(a) the debtor,

(b) any creditor,

(c) the trustee,

(d) any other person having an interest.

(3) An application under subsection (1) must be made before the expiry of the period of 14 days beginning with the day on which the decision or, as the case may be, the determination or requirement is made.

(4) If an application under subsection (1) is made, the Accountant in Bankruptcy must—

(a) take into account any representations made by an interested person before the expiry of the period of 21 days beginning with the day on which the application is made, and

(b) confirm, amend or revoke the decision, determination or requirement before the expiry of the period of 28 days beginning with the day on which the application is made.

(5) A person mentioned in subsection (2) may, before the expiry of the period of 14 days beginning with the day on which the decision, determination or requirement is made, appeal to the sheriff against—

(a) a determination of the Accountant in Bankruptcy under section 17C(3) or 17E(5)(b),

(b) a decision of the Accountant in Bankruptcy under subsection (4)(b),

(6) Any decision of the sheriff on an appeal relating to a determination of the Accountant in Bankruptcy under section 17C(3) or 17E(5)(b) is final.

(7) In upholding an appeal relating to a decision under section 17C(1) or the sheriff may quash the decision of the Accountant in Bankruptcy and remit the case, together with reasons for the sheriff's decision, to the Accountant in Bankruptcy.]

*[Initial stages of sequestration]*

## 18 Interim preservation of estate

(1) The interim trustee may [, in pursuance of the function conferred on him by section 2(6A) of this Act,] give general or particular directions to the debtor relating to the management of the debtor's estate.

(2) In exercising the [function] conferred on him by section [2(6A)] of this Act, an interim trustee may—

(a) require the debtor to deliver up to him any money or valuables, or any document relating to the debtor's business or financial affairs, belonging to or in the possession of the debtor or under his control;

(b) place in safe custody anything mentioned in paragraph (a) above;

(c) require the debtor to deliver up to him any perishable goods belonging to the debtor or under his control and may arrange for the sale or disposal of such goods;

(d) make or cause to be made an inventory or valuation of any property belonging to the debtor;

(e) require the debtor to implement any transaction entered into by the debtor;

(f) effect or maintain insurance policies in respect of the business or property of the debtor;

[. . .]

[(h) carry on any business of the debtor or borrow money in so far as it is necessary for the interim trustee to do so to safeguard the debtor's estate].

[(2A) Section 43 of this Act applies to an interim trustee as it applies to a trustee.]

(3) The [sheriff], on the application of the interim trustee, may—

[. . .]

(b) on cause shown, grant a warrant authorising the interim trustee to enter the house where the debtor resides or his business premises and to search for and take possession of anything mentioned in paragraphs (a) and (c) of subsection (2) above, if need be by opening shut and lock-fast places; or

(c) make such other order to safeguard the debtor's estate as [he] thinks appropriate.

[(3A) Where the Accountant in Bankruptcy is the interim trustee, the debtor may apply to the Accountant in Bankruptcy for a review of a direction under subsection (1) on the ground that the direction is unreasonable.

(3B) If an application under subsection (3A) is made, the Accountant in Bankruptcy must—

(a) take into account any representations made by an interested person before the expiry of the period of 21 days beginning with the day on which the application is made, and

(b) confirm, amend or revoke the direction (whether or not substituting a new direction) before the expiry of the period of 28 days beginning with the day on which the application is made.

(3C)   The sheriff may, on an application by the debtor made before the expiry of the period of 14 days beginning with the day on which the Accountant in Bankruptcy makes a decision under subsection (3B)(b)—

(a)   set aside a direction under subsection (1) or (3B)(b) if the sheriff considers it to be unreasonable, and

(b)   in any event, give such directions to the debtor regarding the management of the debtor's estate as the sheriff considers appropriate.

(3D)   The debtor must comply with a direction—

(a)   under subsection (1) pending a decision by the Accountant in Bankruptcy under subsection (3B)(b),

(b)   under subsection (3B)(b) pending the final determination of any appeal (subject to any interim order of the sheriff).]

(4)   [Where the Accountant in Bankruptcy is not the interim trustee,] the [sheriff], on an application by the debtor on the grounds that a direction under subsection (1) above is unreasonable, may—

(a)   if [he] considers the direction to be unreasonable, set aside the direction; and

(b)   in any event, give such directions to the debtor regarding the management of his estate as [he] considers appropriate;

but, subject to any interim order of the [sheriff], the debtor shall comply with the direction appealed against pending the final determination of the appeal.

(5)   The debtor shall be guilty of an offence if—

(a)   he fails without reasonable excuse to comply with—

(i)   a direction under subsection (1) [, (3B)(b), (3C)(b)] or (4)(b) above; or

(ii)   a requirement under subsection 2(a), (c) or (e) above; or

(b)   he obstructs the interim trustee where the interim trustee is acting in pursuance of subsection (3)(b) above.

(6)   A person convicted of an offence under subsection (5) above shall be liable—

(a)   on summary conviction to a fine not exceeding the statutory maximum or—

(i)   to imprisonment for a term not exceeding 3 months; or

(ii)   if he has previously been convicted of an offence inferring dishonest appropriation of property or an attempt at such appropriation, to imprisonment for a term not exceeding 6 months,

or (in the case of either sub-paragraph) to both such fine and such imprisonment; or

(b)   on conviction on indictment to a fine or to imprisonment for a term not exceeding 2 years or to both.

## 19   [Statement of assets and liabilities etc

(1)   Where the [debtor has made a debtor application] he shall, not later than 7 days after the appointment of the [trustee under section 2 of this Act] (where he is not the Accountant in Bankruptcy), send to the [. . .] trustee such statement of assets and liabilities as was [sent to the Accountant in Bankruptcy in pursuance of section 5(6A)] of this Act.

(2)   Where the petitioner for sequestration is a creditor or a trustee acting under a trust deed, the debtor shall, not later than 7 days after having been notified by the [. . .] trustee as mentioned in section [2(7)(a)] of this Act, send to the [. . .] trustee a statement of assets and liabilities.

(3)   If the debtor—

[. . .]

(b)   fails to disclose any material fact in [a statement of assets and liabilities sent to the trustee in accordance with subsection (1) or (2)]; or

(c)   makes a material misstatement in such statement of assets and liabilities,
he shall be guilty of an offence and liable on summary conviction to a fine not
exceeding level 5 on the standard scale or to imprisonment for a term not exceeding 3 months or to both such fine and imprisonment.

(4)   In any proceedings for an offence under subsection (3) above, it shall be a
defence for the accused to show that he had a reasonable excuse for—
[. . .]
(b)   failing to disclose a material fact; or
(c)   making a material misstatement.]

## 20   Trustee's duties on receipt of list of assets and liabilities

[(1)   When the [. . .] trustee has received the statement of assets and liabilities,
he shall, as soon as practicable, prepare a statement of the debtor's affairs so far as
within the knowledge of the [. . .] trustee and [if], in his opinion, the debtor's assets
are unlikely to be sufficient to pay any dividend whatsoever in respect of the debts
mentioned in paragraphs (e) to (h) of section 51(1) of this Act [the trustee is so to
indicate in the statement of the debtor's affairs].]

(2)   The [. . .] trustee shall, not later than 4 days before the date fixed for the
statutory meeting, [or, where the trustee does not intend to hold such a meeting,
not later than 60 days after the date on which sequestration is awarded,] send to
the Accountant in Bankruptcy—
(a)   [a statement] of assets and liabilities [(unless the statement has already
been received by the Accountant in Bankruptcy by virtue of section 5(6A) of this
Act)]; and
(b)   [subject to subsection (2A) below] a copy of the [. . .] statement of the
debtor's affairs; and
(c)   written comments by the [. . .] trustee indicating what in his opinion are
the causes of the insolvency and to what extent the conduct of the debtor may
have contributed to the insolvency.

[(2A)   The trustee need not send a statement of the debtor's affairs to the
Accountant in Bankruptcy in accordance with subsection (2)(b) above if the trustee
has sent a copy of the inventory and valuation to the Accountant in Bankruptcy in
accordance with section 38(1)(c) of this Act.]

(3)   The written comments made under subsection (2)(c) above shall be absolutely privileged.
[. . .]
[(5A)   Subsections (2) and (3) above do not apply in any case where the
Accountant in Bankruptcy is the [. . .] trustee.]

## [20A   Statutory meeting

A meeting of creditors called by the [. . .] trustee under section [. . .] 21A of this
Act shall, in this Act, be referred to as 'the statutory meeting'.]

*[Statutory meeting of creditors and trustee vote]*

[. . .]

## [21A   Calling of statutory meeting [. . .]

(1)   Subject to subsections (5) and (6) below, [. . .] the statutory meeting may be
held at such time and place as the [. . .] trustee may determine.

(2)   Not later than 60 days after the date [on which sequestration is awarded],
or such longer period as the sheriff may on cause shown allow, the [. . .] trustee
shall give notice to every creditor known to him of whether he intends to call the
statutory meeting.

(3)   A notice given under subsection (2) above shall—
(a)   be accompanied by a copy of the [. . .] trustee's statement of the debtor's
affairs; and

(b)    where the [. . .] trustee is notifying his intention not to hold the statutory meeting, inform creditors—
    (i)   of the effect of subsections (4) and (5) below.
    [. . .]
(4)    Within 7 days of the giving of notice under subsection (2) above, any creditor may request the [. . .] trustee to call the statutory meeting.

(5)    Where a request or requests under subsection (4) above are made by not less than one quarter in value of the debtor's creditors, the [. . .] trustee shall call the statutory meeting not later than 28 days, or such other period as the sheriff may on cause shown allow, after the giving of notice under subsection (2) above.

(6)    Where the [. . .] trustee gives notice under subsection (2) above that he intends to call the statutory meeting, such meeting shall be called not later than 28 days after the giving of such notice.

(7)    Not less than 7 days before the date fixed for the statutory meeting, the [. . .] trustee shall notify every creditor known to him of the date, time and place of the meeting, and shall in such notice invite the submission of such claims as have not already been submitted and inform them of his duties under section 23(3) of this Act.

(8)    The creditors may continue the statutory meeting to a date not later than 7 days after the end of the period mentioned in subsection (6) above or such longer period as the sheriff may on cause shown allow.]
    [. . .]

### [21B   Procedure where no statutory meeting called

(1)    Where the [. . .] trustee does not call the statutory meeting and the period mentioned in section 21A(4) of this Act has expired, he shall—
    (a)    forthwith make a report to the [Accountant in Bankruptcy] on the circumstances of the sequestration.
    [. . .]
[(1A)    This section does not apply in any case where the Accountant in Bankruptcy is the trustee.]
    [. . .]

### 22   Submission of claims for voting purposes at statutory meeting

(1)    For the purposes of voting at the statutory meeting, a creditor shall submit a claim in accordance with this section to the [. . .] trustee at or before the meeting.

(2)    A creditor shall submit a claim under this section by producing to the [. . .] trustee—
    (a)    a statement of claim in the prescribed form; and
    (b)    an account or voucher (according to the nature of the debt) which constitutes *prima facie* evidence of the debt:
Provided that the [. . .] trustee may dispense with any requirement under this subsection in respect of any debt or any class of debt.

(3)    Where a creditor neither resides nor has a place of business in the United Kingdom, the [. . .] trustee—
    (a)    shall, if he knows where the creditor resides or has a place of business and if no notification has been given to that creditor under section [21A(2)] of this Act, write to him informing him that he may submit a claim under this section;
    (b)    may allow the creditor to submit an informal claim in writing.

(4)    A creditor who has produced a statement of claim in accordance with subsection (2) above may at any time before the statutory meeting produce in place of that statement of claim another such statement of claim specifying a different amount for his claim.

(5)    If a creditor produces under this section a statement of claim, account, voucher or other evidence which is false—
    (a)    the creditor shall be guilty of an offence unless he shows that he neither

knew nor had reason to believe that the statement of claim, account, voucher or
other evidence was false;

    (b)   the debtor shall be guilty of an offence if he—

        (i)   knew or became aware that the statement of claim, account, voucher or
other evidence was false; and

        (ii)   failed as soon as practicable after acquiring such knowledge to report
it to the [. . .] trustee [. . .].

(6)   A creditor may, in such circumstances as may be prescribed, state the
amount of his claim in foreign currency.

(7)   The [. . .] trustee shall, on production of any document to him under this
section, initial the document and keep a record of it stating the date when it was
produced to him, and, if requested by the sender, shall return it (if it is not a statement of claim) to him.

(8)   The submission of a claim under this section shall bar the effect of any
enactment or rule of law relating to the limitation of actions in any part of the
United Kingdom.

(9)   Schedule 1 to this Act shall have effect for determining the amount in
respect of which a creditor shall be entitled to claim.

(10)   A person convicted of an offence under subsection (5) above shall be
liable—

    (a)   on summary conviction to a fine not exceeding the statutory maximum
or—

        (i)   to imprisonment for a term not exceeding 3 months; or

        (ii)   if he has previously been convicted of an offence inferring dishonest
appropriation of property or an attempt at such appropriation, to imprisonment for a term not exceeding 6 months,

or (in the case of either sub-paragraph) to both such fine and such imprisonment; or

    (b)   on conviction on indictment to a fine or to imprisonment for a term not
exceeding 2 years or to both.

## [23  Proceedings at statutory meeting before trustee vote]

(1)   At the commencement of the statutory meeting, the chairman shall be the
[. . .] trustee who as chairman shall—

    (a)   for the purposes of subsection (2) below, accept or reject in whole or in
part the claim of each creditor, and, if the amount of a claim is stated in foreign
currency, he shall convert that amount into sterling, in such manner as may be
prescribed, at the rate of exchange prevailing at the close of business on the date
of sequestration;

    (b)   invite the creditors thereupon to elect one of their number as chairman in
his place and shall preside over the election:

Provided that if a chairman is not elected in pursuance of this paragraph, the
[. . .] trustee shall remain the chairman throughout the meeting; and

    (c)   arrange for a record to be made of the proceedings at the meeting.

(2)   The acceptance of a claim in whole or in part under subsection (1) above
shall, subject to section 24(3) of this Act, determine the entitlement of a creditor to
vote at the statutory meeting.

(3)   On the conclusion of the proceedings under subsection (1) above, the [. . .]
trustee—

    [(a)   shall make available for inspection—

        (i)   the statement of assets and liabilities; and

        (ii)   his statement of the debtor's affairs prepared under section 20(1) of
this Act;]; and

    (b)   shall answer to the best of his ability any questions, and shall consider
any representations, put to him by the creditors relating to the debtor's assets,
business or financial affairs or his conduct in relation thereto;

[(c)  after considering any such representations as are mentioned in paragraph (b), shall, if in the interim trustee's opinion the debtor's assets are unlikely to be sufficient to pay any dividend whatsoever in respect of the debts mentioned in paragraphs (e) to (h) of section 51(1), so indicate,] and

[(d)  shall determine whether it is necessary to revise his statement of the debtor's affairs and, if he determines that it is necessary to revise the statement, he shall do so either at, or as soon as possible after, the statutory meeting.]

[. . .]

[(5)  Where the [. . .] trustee has revised his statement of the debtor's affairs, he shall, as soon as possible after the statutory meeting, send a copy of the revised statement to every creditor known to him.]

[. . .]

## 24  [Trustee vote]

[(1)  At the statutory meeting, the creditors shall, at the conclusion of the proceedings under section 23(3) of this Act, proceed to [a vote at which they shall—

(a)  confirm the appointment of the trustee appointed under section 2 of this Act (referred to in this section and in sections 25 to 27 of this Act as the 'original trustee'); or

(b)  elect another person as the trustee in the sequestration (referred to in this section and in sections 13 and 25 to 29 of this Act as the 'replacement trustee'), such a vote being referred to in this Act as a 'trustee vote'].]

(2)  None of the following persons shall be eligible for election as [replacement] trustee, nor shall anyone who becomes such a person after having been elected as [replacement] trustee be qualified to continue to act as [. . .] trustee—

(a)  the debtor;

(b)  a person who is not qualified to act as an insolvency practitioner or who, though qualified to act as an insolvency practitioner, is not qualified to act as such in relation to the debtor;

(c)  a person who holds an interest opposed to the general interests of the creditors;

[. . .]

[(e)  a person who has not given an undertaking, in writing, to act as [. . .] trustee;

(f)  the Accountant in Bankruptcy.]

(3)  The following persons shall not be entitled to vote in the [trustee vote]—

(a)  anyone acquiring a debt due by the debtor, otherwise than by succession, after the date of sequestration;

(b)  any creditor to the extent that his debt is a postponed debt.

[(3A)  In any case where the Accountant in Bankruptcy is the [original] trustee, if—

(a)  no creditor entitled to vote in the [trustee vote] attends the statutory meeting; or

(b)  no [replacement] trustee is elected, the Accountant in Bankruptcy shall forthwith report the proceedings at the statutory meeting to the sheriff and [shall continue to act as the trustee].]

[. . .]

(4)  [In any case where the Accountant in Bankruptcy is not the [original] trustee] if no creditor entitled to vote in the [trustee vote] attends the statutory meeting or if no [replacement] trustee is elected, the [original] trustee shall forthwith—

(a)  so notify the Accountant in Bankruptcy; and

(b)  report the proceedings at the statutory meeting to the sheriff [and he shall continue to act as the trustee].

[. . .]

**[25  Appointment of replacement trustee**

(1)  This section applies where a replacement trustee is elected by virtue of a trustee vote.

(2)  On the election of the replacement trustee, the original trustee must immediately make a report of the proceedings at the statutory meeting—

(a)  where the original trustee was not the Accountant in Bankruptcy, to the Accountant in Bankruptcy,

(b)  where the original trustee was the Accountant in Bankruptcy, to the sheriff.

(3)  The debtor, a creditor, the original trustee, the replacement trustee or the Accountant in Bankruptcy may object to any matter connected with the election—

(a)  in the case of an objection by a person other than the Accountant in Bankruptcy, by applying to the Accountant in Bankruptcy, or

(b)  in the case of an objection by the Accountant in Bankruptcy, by making a summary application to the sheriff.

(4)  An objection under subsection (3) must—

(a)  specify the grounds on which the objection is taken, and

(b)  be made before the expiry of the period of 4 days beginning with the day of the statutory meeting.

(5)  If there is no timeous objection under subsection (3), the Accountant in Bankruptcy must without delay declare the elected person to be the trustee in the sequestration.

(6)  No expense in objecting under this section is to fall on the debtor's estate.


**25A  Applications to Accountant in Bankruptcy: procedure**

(1)  This section applies where an application is made to the Accountant in Bankruptcy under section 25(3)(a).

(2)  The Accountant in Bankruptcy must—

(a)  without delay give the original trustee, the replacement trustee, the objector and any other interested person an opportunity to make written submissions on the application, and

(b)  make a decision.

(3)  If the Accountant in Bankruptcy decides—

(a)  to reject the objection in the application, the Accountant in Bankruptcy must without delay declare the elected person to be the trustee in the sequestration,

(b)  to sustain the objection in the application, the Accountant in Bankruptcy must order the original trustee to arrange a new meeting at which a new trustee vote must be held.

(4)  Sections 23 to 25B apply in relation to a meeting arranged by virtue of subsection (3)(b).

(5)  The original trustee, the replacement trustee, the objector and any other interested person may apply to the Accountant in Bankruptcy for a review of a decision under subsection (2)(b).

(6)  An application under subsection (5) must be made before the expiry of the period of 14 days beginning with the day on which notice of the decision is given.

(7)  If an application for a review under subsection (5) is made, the Accountant in Bankruptcy must—

(a)  take into account any representations made by an interested person before the expiry of the period of 21 days beginning with the day on which the application is made, and

(b)  confirm, amend or revoke the decision before the expiry of the period of 28 days beginning with the day on which the application is made.

(8)  The trustee, the objector and any other interested person may by summary application appeal to the sheriff against a decision by the Accountant in Bank-

ruptcy under subsection (7)(b), before the expiry of the period of 14 days beginning with the day of the decision.

(9)   No expense in objecting under this section is to fall on the debtor's estate.

### 25B   Applications and appeals to sheriff: procedure

(1)   This section applies where there is—

(a)   an application by the Accountant in Bankruptcy under section 25(3)(b), or

(b)   an appeal under section 25A(8).

(2)   The sheriff must—

(a)   without delay give the parties an opportunity to be heard on the application, and

(b)   make a decision.

(3)   If the sheriff decides—

(a)   to reject an objection to the appointment of an elected person, the sheriff must without delay declare the elected person to be the trustee in the sequestration and make an order appointing the elected person to be the trustee in the sequestration,

(b)   to sustain an objection to the appointment of an elected person, the sheriff must order the original trustee to arrange a new meeting at which a new trustee vote must be held.

(4)   Sections 23 to 25B apply in relation to a meeting arranged by virtue of subsection (3)(b).

(5)   Any declaration, appointment or decision of the sheriff under this section is final.]

### 26   [Provisions relating to termination of original trustee's functions]

[(A1)   This section applies where a replacement trustee is appointed under section 25 of this Act.]

(1)   [The original trustee shall, on the appointment of the replacement trustee,] hand over to him everything in his possession which relates to the sequestration (including [the statement of assets and liabilities, and a copy] of the statement [of the debtor's affairs prepared under section 20(1) (as revised under section 23(3)(d) if so revised)], and of the written comments sent under section 20(2)(c) of this Act) and shall thereupon cease to act in the sequestration.

(2)   Within 3 months of the [appointment of the replacement trustee, the original] trustee shall—

(a)   submit to the Accountant in Bankruptcy—

(i)   his accounts of his intromissions (if any) with the debtor's estate; and

(ii)   a claim for outlays reasonably incurred, and for remuneration for work reasonably undertaken, by him; and

(b)   send to the [replacement] trustee [. . .], a copy of what is submitted to the Accountant in Bankruptcy under paragraph (a) above.

[(2A)   Where the original trustee was appointed under section 2(5) of this Act as the interim trustee in the sequestration, his accounts and the claim referred to in subsection (2)(a) above shall include accounts and a claim for the period of his appointment as interim trustee.]

(3)   On a submission being made to him under subsection (2) above, the Accountant in Bankruptcy—

(a)   shall—

(i)   audit the accounts; and

(ii)   issue a determination fixing the amount of the outlays and remuneration payable to the [original] trustee; and

(b)   shall send a copy of—

(i)   the said determination to the [original] trustee [. . .]; and

(ii)   the [original] trustee's audited accounts and of the said determination to the [replacement] trustee [. . .].

(4)   The [original] trustee, the [replacement] trustee, the debtor or any creditor may appeal to the sheriff against a determination under subsection (3)(a)(ii) above within 14 days of its issue [and the decision of the sheriff on such an appeal shall be final].
   [. . .]
   [(5A)   This section does not apply in any case where the Accountant in Bankruptcy is the [original] trustee.]

**[26A   Accountant in Bankruptcy to account for intromissions**
   (1)   This section applies in any case where the Accountant in Bankruptcy was the [original] trustee and some other person [is appointed as replacement trustee under section 25 of this Act].
   (2)   The Accountant in Bankruptcy shall, on [the appointment of the replacement trustee], hand over to the [replacement] trustee everything in his possession which relates to the sequestration and which he obtained in his capacity as [original] trustee (including the statement of assets and liabilities); and thereupon he shall cease to act as [. . .] trustee.
   (3)   The Accountant in Bankruptcy shall, not later than 3 months after the [appointment of the replacement trustee], supply to the [replacement] trustee—
      (a)   his accounts of his intromissions (if any) as [original] trustee with the debtor's estate;
      (b)   a determination of his fees and outlays calculated in accordance with regulations made under section 69A of this Act; and
      (c)   a copy of the notice mentioned in subsection (4)(b) below.
   (4)   The Accountant in Bankruptcy shall send to the debtor and to all creditors known to him—
      (a)   a copy of the determination mentioned in subsection (3)(b) above; and
      (b)   a notice in writing stating—
         (i)   that the Accountant in Bankruptcy has commenced the procedure under this Act leading to discharge in respect of his actings as [. . .] trustee;
         (ii)   that the accounts of his intromissions (if any) with the debtor's estate are available for inspection at such address as the Accountant in Bankruptcy may determine;
         [(iia)   that an application for a review may be made under subsection (4A);]
         (iii)   that an appeal may be made to the sheriff under subsection (5) below; and
         (iv)   the effect of subsection (7) below.
   [(4A)   The replacement trustee, the debtor or any creditor may apply to the Accountant in Bankruptcy for a review of the discharge of the Accountant in Bankruptcy in respect of the Accountant in Bankruptcy's actings as trustee.
   (4B)   An application under subsection (4A) must be made before the expiry of the period of 14 days beginning with the day on which notice is sent under subsection (4)(b).
   (4C)   If an application under subsection (4A) is made, the Accountant in Bankruptcy must—
      (a)   take into account any representations made by an interested person before the expiry of the period of 21 days beginning with the day on which the application is made, and
      (b)   confirm or revoke the discharge before the expiry of the period of 28 days beginning with the day on which the application is made.]
   [(5)   The replacement trustee, the debtor or any creditor may appeal to the sheriff against—
      (a)   the determination of the Accountant in Bankruptcy mentioned in subsection (3)(b) before the expiry of the period of 14 days beginning with the day on which notice is sent under subsection (4)(b),
      (b)   a decision by the Accountant in Bankruptcy under subsection (4C)(b)

before the expiry of the period of 14 days beginning with the day on which the decision is made.]

[(6)   The decision of the sheriff on an appeal under subsection (5) is final.]

(7)   Where—

(a)   the requirements of this section have been complied with; and

(b)   no appeal is made to the sheriff under subsection (5) above or such an appeal is made but is refused as regards the discharge of the Accountant in Bankruptcy,

the Accountant in Bankruptcy shall be discharged from all liability (other than any liability arising from fraud) to the creditors or to the debtor in respect of any act or omission of the Accountant in Bankruptcy in exercising the functions of [. . .] trustee in the sequestration.

[. . .]]


**27   [Discharge of original trustee]**

(1)   On receiving a copy of the Accountant in Bankruptcy's determination sent under subsection (3)(b)(i) of section 26 of this Act the [original] trustee may apply to him for a certificate of discharge.

(2)   The [original] trustee shall send notice of an application under subsection (1) above to the debtor [, to all creditors known to the original trustee] and to the [replacement] trustee and shall inform the debtor—

(a)   that he, the [replacement] trustee or any creditor may make written representations relating to the application to the Accountant in Bankruptcy within a period of 14 days after such notification;

(b)   that the audited accounts of his intromissions (if any) with the debtor's estate are available for inspection at the office of the [original] trustee and that a copy of those accounts has been sent to the [replacement] trustee [. . .]; and

(c)   of the effect mentioned in subsection (5) below.

(3)   On the expiry of the period mentioned in subsection (2)(a) above the Accountant in Bankruptcy, after considering any representations duly made to him, shall—

(a)   grant or refuse to grant the certificate of discharge; and

(b)   notify (in addition to the [original] trustee) the debtor, the [replacement] trustee, and all creditors who have made such representations, accordingly.

[(3A)   The original trustee, the replacement trustee, the debtor or any creditor who has made representations may apply to the Accountant in Bankruptcy for a review of a determination under subsection (3).

(3B)   An application under subsection (3A) must be made before the expiry of the period of 14 days beginning with the day on which the determination is issued under subsection (3).

(3C)   If an application under subsection (3A) is made, the Accountant in Bankruptcy must—

(a)   take into account any representations made by an interested person before the expiry of the period of 21 days beginning with the day on which the application is made, and

(b)   confirm, amend or revoke the determination under subsection (3) (whether or not granting a certificate of discharge) before the expiry of the period of 28 days beginning with the day on which the application is made.]

(4)   The [original] trustee, the [replacement] trustee, the debtor or any creditor who has made representations [by virtue of] subsection (2)(a) above may, within 14 days after the [day of the decision under subsection (3C)(b)], appeal therefrom to the sheriff and if the sheriff determines that a certificate of discharge which has been refused should be granted he shall order the Accountant in Bankruptcy to grant it; and the sheriff clerk shall send a copy of the decree of the sheriff to the Accountant in Bankruptcy.

[(4A) The decision of the sheriff in an appeal under subsection (4) above shall be final.]

(5) The grant of a certificate of discharge under this section by the Accountant in Bankruptcy shall have the effect of discharging the [original] trustee from all liability (other than any liability arising from fraud) to the creditors or to the debtor in respect of any act or omission of the [original] trustee in exercising the functions conferred on him by this Act.

[. . .]

[(7A) This section does not apply in any case where the Accountant in Bankruptcy is the [original] trustee.]

## Replacement of [. . .] trustee

### 28  Resignation and death of [. . .] trustee

[(1) The [. . .] trustee may apply to the [Accountant in Bankruptcy] for authority to resign office and, where the [Accountant in Bankruptcy] is satisfied that [the trustee—

    (a)   is unable to act (whether by, under or by virtue of a provision of this Act or from any other cause whatsoever); or

    (b)   has so conducted himself that he should no longer continue to act,

the Accountant in Bankruptcy] shall grant the application.]

[(1A) The [Accountant in Bankruptcy] may make the granting of an application under subsection (1) above subject to the election of a new [. . .] trustee and to such conditions as he thinks appropriate in all the circumstances of the case.]

(2) Where the [Accountant in Bankruptcy] grants an application under [. . .] subsection (1) above—

    (a)   except where paragraph (b) below applies, the commissioners, or if there are no commissioners, the Accountant in Bankruptcy, shall call a meeting of the creditors, to be held not more than 28 days after the [. . .] trustee has resigned, for the election by them of a new [. . .] trustee;

    (b)   if the application has been granted subject to the election of a new [. . .] trustee, the resigning [. . .] trustee shall himself call a meeting of the creditors, to be held not more than 28 days after the granting of the application, for the purpose referred to in paragraph (a) above.

(3) Where the commissioners become, or if there are no commissioners, the Accountant in Bankruptcy becomes, aware that the [. . .] trustee has died, they or as the case may be the Accountant in Bankruptcy shall as soon as practicable after becoming so aware call a meeting of creditors for the election by the creditors of a new [. . .] trustee.

(4) The foregoing provisions of this Act relating to the election [of a replacement trustee and the appointment of that] trustee shall, subject to any necessary modifications, apply in relation to the election and [appointment] of a new [. . .] trustee in pursuance of subsection (1), [(1A)], (2) or (3) above.

[(5) Where no new trustee is elected in pursuance of subsection (2) or (3) the Accountant in Bankruptcy may appoint as the trustee in the sequestration—

    (a)   a person who applies to the Accountant in Bankruptcy within the period of 14 days beginning with the day of the meeting arranged under subsection (2) or (3), or

    (b)   any other person as may be determined by the Accountant in Bankruptcy and who consents to the appointment.

(5A) A person may not be appointed under subsection (5) if the person is ineligible for election as a replacement trustee under section 24(2).

(5B) If, after the expiry of the period mentioned in subsection (5)(a), the Accountant in Bankruptcy determines that no person is to be appointed under subsection (5), the Accountant in Bankruptcy is deemed to be the trustee in the sequestration.]

(6)  The new [. . .] trustee may require—

(a)  delivery to him of all documents relating to the sequestration in the possession of the former trustee or his representatives, except the former trustee's accounts of which he shall be entitled to delivery of only a copy;

(b)  the former trustee or his representatives to submit the trustee's accounts for audit to the commissioners or, if there are no commissioners, to the Accountant in Bankruptcy, and the commissioners or the Accountant in Bankruptcy shall issue a determination fixing the amount of the outlays and remuneration payable to the trustee or representatives in accordance with section 53 of this Act.

(7)  The former trustee or his representatives, the new [. . .] trustee, the debtor or any creditor may appeal against a determination issued under subsection (6)(b) above within 14 days after it is issued—

(a)  where it is a determination of the commissioners, to the Accountant in Bankruptcy; and

(b)  where it is a determination of the Accountant in Bankruptcy, to the sheriff; and the determination of the Accountant in Bankruptcy under paragraph (a) above shall be appealable to the sheriff.

[(8)  The decision of the sheriff on an appeal under subsection (7) above shall be final.]

**[28A  Replacement of trustee acting in more than one sequestration**

(1)  This section applies where a trustee acting as such in two or more sequestrations—

(a)  dies,

(b)  ceases to be qualified to continue to act as trustee by virtue of section 24(2), or

(c)  becomes subject to the circumstances mentioned in subsection (2).

(2)  The circumstances are that—

(a)  there is a conflict of interest affecting the trustee, or

(b)  there is a change in the personal circumstances of the trustee,

which prevents, or makes it impracticable for, the trustee to carry out the trustee's functions.

(3)  The Accountant in Bankruptcy may in a case where subsection (1)(b) or (c) applies, determine that the trustee is removed from office in each sequestration in which the trustee has ceased to be qualified.

(4)  The Accountant in Bankruptcy may appoint as the trustee in each sequestration in which the former trustee was acting a person—

(a)  determined by the Accountant in Bankruptcy, and

(b)  who consents to the appointment.

(5)  A person may not be appointed under subsection (4) if the person is ineligible for election as a replacement trustee under section 24(2).

(6)  If, in relation to any sequestration, the Accountant in Bankruptcy determines that no person is to be appointed under subsection (4), the Accountant in Bankruptcy is deemed to be the trustee in that sequestration.

(7)  A determination or appointment under this section may be made—

(a)  on the application of any person having an interest, or

(b)  without an application, where the Accountant in Bankruptcy proposes to make a determination or appointment of the Accountant in Bankruptcy's own accord.

(8)  The applicant must notify all interested persons where an application is made under subsection (7)(a).

(9)  The Accountant in Bankruptcy must notify all interested persons where the Accountant in Bankruptcy proposes to make a determination or appointment by virtue of subsection (7)(b).

(10)  A notice under subsection (8) or (9) must inform the recipient that the

person has a right to make representations to the Accountant in Bankruptcy in relation to the application or the proposed determination or appointment before the expiry of the period of 14 days beginning with the day on which the notice is given.

(11)   Before making a determination or appointment under this section, the Accountant in Bankruptcy must take into account any representations made by an interested person.

(12)   The Accountant in Bankruptcy must notify any determination or appointment under this section to—

(a)   the former trustee (or in the case where the former trustee has died, the former trustee's representatives),

(b)   the debtor,

(c)   the trustee appointed under this section (where the trustee appointed is not the Accountant in Bankruptcy),

(d)   each sheriff who awarded sequestration or to whom sequestration was transferred under section 15(2) of this Act.

(13)   The trustee appointed under this section—

(a)   must notify the determination or appointment under this section to every creditor known to the trustee,

(b)   may require—

(i)   delivery of all documents relating to each sequestration in which the former trustee was acting which are in the possession of the former trustee or the former trustee's representatives (other than the former trustee's accounts),

(ii)   delivery of a copy of the former trustee's accounts,

(iii)   the former trustee or the former trustee's representatives to submit the trustee's accounts for audit to the commissioners or, if there are no commissioners, to the Accountant in Bankruptcy.

(14)   Where the trustee appointed under this section requires submission of the accounts in accordance with subsection (13)(b)(iii), the commissioners or, as the case may be, the Accountant in Bankruptcy must issue a determination fixing the amount of the outlays and remuneration payable to the former trustee or the former trustee's representatives in accordance with section 53.

**28B   Determination etc under section 28A: review**

(1)   The persons mentioned in subsections (12)(a) and (b) and (13)(a) of section 28A may apply to the Accountant in Bankruptcy for a review by the Accountant in Bankruptcy of any determination or appointment under that section.

(2)   An application under subsection (1) must be made before the expiry of the period of 14 days beginning with the day on which notice of the determination or appointment is given.

(3)   If an application under subsection (1) is made, the Accountant in Bankruptcy must—

(a)   take into account any representations made by an interested person before the expiry of the period of 21 days beginning with the day on which the application is made, and

(b)   confirm, amend or revoke the determination or appointment before the expiry of the period of 28 days beginning with the day on which the application is made.

(4)   The persons mentioned in subsections (12)(a) and (b) and (13)(a) of section 28A may appeal to the sheriff against a decision by the Accountant in Bankruptcy under subsection (3)(b) before the expiry of the period of 14 days beginning with the day of the decision.

(5)   The Accountant in Bankruptcy may refer a case to the court for a direction before—

(a)   making any determination or appointment under section 28A, or

(b)   undertaking any review under this section.

(6)   An appeal under subsection (4) and a referral under subsection (5) must be made—

(a)   by a single petition to the Court of Session, where the appeal relates to two or more sequestrations and the sequestrations are, by virtue of section 9, in different sheriffdoms, and

(b)   in any other case to the sheriff.]

## 29   Removal of [. . .] trustee and trustee not acting

(1)   The [. . .] trustee may be removed from office—

(a)   by the creditors (other than any such person as is mentioned in section 24(3) of this Act) at a meeting called for the purpose if they also elect forthwith a new [. . .] trustee; or

[(b)   by order made by the Accountant in Bankruptcy, if the Accountant in Bankruptcy is satisfied that there are reasons to do so on the basis of circumstances other than those mentioned in subsection (9).]

[(1A)   An order removing a trustee in accordance with subsection (1)(b) may be made—

(a)   on the application of—

(i)   the commissioners, or

(ii)   a person representing not less than one quarter in value of the creditors, or

(b)   in any other case, where the Accountant in Bankruptcy is satisfied that there are reasons to do so on the basis of circumstances other than those mentioned in subsection (9).]

[(2)   The Accountant in Bankruptcy must—

(a)   order an application by a person mentioned in subsection (1A)(a) to be served on the trustee,

(b)   enter particulars of the application in the register of insolvencies, and

(c)   before deciding whether or not to make an order under subsection (1)(b), give the trustee the opportunity to make representations.]

[(3)   The Accountant in Bankruptcy may in ordering, or instead of ordering, the removal of the trustee from office under subsection (1)(b), make such further or other order as the Accountant in Bankruptcy thinks fit.

(3A)   The trustee, the commissioners or any creditor may apply to the Accountant in Bankruptcy for a review of any decision of the Accountant in Bankruptcy under subsection (1)(b) or (3).

(3B)   An application under subsection (3A) must be made before the expiry of the period of 14 days beginning with the day on which the decision is given.

(3C)   If an application for a review under subsection (3A) is made, the Accountant in Bankruptcy must—

(a)   take into account any representations made by an interested person before the expiry of the period of 21 days beginning with the day on which the application is made, and

(b)   confirm, amend or revoke the decision before the expiry of the period of 28 days beginning with the day on which the application is made.]

[(4)   The trustee, the commissioners or any creditor may appeal to the sheriff against any decision of the Accountant in Bankruptcy under subsection (3C)(b) before the end of the period of 14 days beginning with the date of the decision.]

(5)   If the [. . .] trustee has been removed from office under subsection (1)(b) above or under section [1A(2)] of this Act or following [a review under subsection (3A) or] an appeal under subsection (4) above, the commissioners or, if there are no commissioners, the Accountant in Bankruptcy shall call a meeting of creditors, to be held not more than 28 days after such removal, for the election by them of a new [. . .] trustee.

[(6)   If the Accountant in Bankruptcy is satisfied that any of the circumstances mentioned in subsection (9) apply, the Accountant in Bankruptcy may—

(a)    declare the office of trustee to have become or to be vacant, and

(b)    make any necessary order to enable the sequestration of the estate to proceed or to safeguard the estate pending the election of a new trustee.

(6A)    The declaration of the office of trustee as vacant and any necessary order in accordance with subsection (6) may be made—

    (a)    on the application of—

        (i)    the commissioners,

        (ii)    the debtor, or

        (iii)    a creditor, or

(b)    in any other case, where the Accountant in Bankruptcy is satisfied that there are reasons to do so on the basis of the circumstances mentioned in subsection (9).

(6B)    The Accountant in Bankruptcy must order such intimation of an application by a person mentioned in subsection (6A)(a) as the Accountant in Bankruptcy considers necessary.

(6C)    If the Accountant in Bankruptcy makes a declaration under subsection (6A), the commissioners, or if there are no commissioners the Accountant in Bankruptcy, must call a meeting of creditors for the election of a new trustee by the creditors.

(6D)    A meeting called under subsection (6C) must be held before the end of the period of 28 days beginning with the date of the declaration under subsection (6A).

(6E)    The trustee, the debtor, the commissioners or any creditor may apply to the Accountant in Bankruptcy for a review of any declaration or any order made by the Accountant in Bankruptcy under subsection (6).

(6F)    An application under subsection (6E) must be made before the expiry of the period of 14 days beginning with the day on which the declaration is made.

(6G)    If an application for a review under subsection (6E) is made, the Accountant in Bankruptcy must—

(a)    take into account any representations made by an interested person before the expiry of the period of 21 days beginning with the day on which the application is made, and

(b)    confirm, amend or revoke the declaration or order before the expiry of the period of 28 days beginning with the day on which the application is made.

(6H)    The trustee, the debtor, the commissioners or any creditor may appeal to the sheriff against any decision of the Accountant in Bankruptcy under subsection (6G)(b) before the end of the period of 14 days beginning with the date of the decision.

(6I)    The Accountant in Bankruptcy may refer a case to the sheriff for a direction before—

(a)    making any order under subsection (1)(b) or (3),

(b)    making any declaration or any order under subsection (6), or

(c)    undertaking any review under this section.

(6J)    An application for a review under subsection (3A) or (6E) may not be made in relation to a matter on which the Accountant in Bankruptcy has applied to the sheriff for a direction under subsection (6I).]

(7)    The foregoing provisions of this Act relating to the election [of a replacement trustee and the appointment of that] trustee shall, subject to any necessary modifications, apply in relation to the election and [appointment] of a new [. . .] trustee in pursuance of subsection (5) or [(6C)] above.

(8)    Subsections (5) to [(8)] of section 28 of this Act shall apply for the purposes of this section as they apply for the purposes of that section.

(9)    The circumstances to which this subsection applies are that the [. . .] trustee—

(a)    is unable to act (whether by, under or by virtue of a provision of this Act or from any other cause whatsoever other than death); or

(b)   has so conducted himself that he should no longer continue to act in the sequestration.

[(10)   This section does not apply in any case where the Accountant in Bankruptcy is the trustee [and is without prejudice to the powers under section 1A(2)].]

*Election, resignation and removal of commissioners*

## 30   Election, resignation and removal of commissioners

(1)   At the statutory meeting or any subsequent meeting of creditors, the creditors (other than any such person as is mentioned in section 24(3) of this Act) may, from among the creditors or their mandatories, elect one or more commissioners (or new or additional commissioners); but not more than 5 commissioners shall hold office in any sequestration at any one time.

(2)   None of the following persons shall be eligible for election as a commissioner, nor shall anyone who becomes such a person after having been elected as a commissioner be entitled to continue to act as a commissioner—

(a)   any person mentioned in paragraph (a) or (c) of section 24(2) of this Act as not being eligible for election;

(b)   a person who is an associate of the debtor or of the [. . .] trustee.

(3)   A commissioner may resign office at any time.

(4)   Without prejudice to section [1A(2)] of this Act, a commissioner may be removed from office—

(a)   if he is a mandatory of a creditor, by the creditor recalling the mandate and intimating in writing its recall to the [. . .] trustee;

(b)   by the creditors (other than any such person as is mentioned in section 24(3) of this Act) at a meeting called for the purpose.

[(c)   by order of the sheriff if the sheriff is satisfied that the commissioner is no longer acting in the interests of the efficient conduct of the sequestration.]

[(5)   An order under subsection (4)(c) may be made on the application of—

(a)   the Accountant in Bankruptcy,

(b)   a person representing not less than one quarter in value of the creditors, or

(c)   the trustee.

(6)   The sheriff must—

(a)   order an application by a person mentioned in subsection (5) to be served on the commissioner,

(b)   order that the application is intimated to every creditor who has given a mandate to the commissioner, and

(c)   before deciding whether or not to make an order under subsection (4)(c), give the commissioner the opportunity to make representations.

(7)   On an application under subsection (4)(c), the sheriff may, in ordering the removal of the commissioner from office, make such further order as the sheriff thinks fit or may, instead of removing the commissioner from office, make such other order as the sheriff thinks fit.

(8)   The trustee, the Accountant in Bankruptcy, any commissioner or any creditor may appeal against the decision of the sheriff on an application under subsection (4)(c) within 14 days after the date of that decision.]

*[Vesting of estate in trustee]*

## 31   Vesting of estate at date of sequestration

(1)   Subject to section 33 of this Act [and section 91(3) of the Pensions Act 1995], the whole estate of the debtor shall [by virtue of the trustee's appointment] vest [in the trustee] as at the date of sequestration [. . .] for the benefit of the creditors.

[. . .]

[(1A)   It shall not be competent for—

(a)   the trustee; or

(b)   any person deriving title from the trustee,
to complete title to any heritable estate in Scotland vested in the trustee by virtue
of his appointment before the expiry of the period mentioned in subsection (1B)
below.

(1B)   That period is the period of 28 days (or such other period as may be prescribed) beginning with the day on which—

(a)   the certified copy of the order of the sheriff granting warrant is recorded
under subsection (1)(a) of section 14 of this Act; or

(b)   the certified copy of the determination of the Accountant in Bankruptcy
awarding sequestration is recorded under subsection (1A) of that section,
in the register of inhibitions.]

(2)   The exercise by the [. . .] trustee of any power conferred on him by this Act
in respect of any heritable estate vested in him by virtue of [his appointment] shall
not be challengeable on the ground of any prior inhibition [. . .].

(3)   Where the debtor has an uncompleted title to any heritable estate in Scotland, the [. . .] trustee may complete title thereto either in his own name or in the
name of the debtor, but completion of title in the name of the debtor shall not vali-
date by accretion any unperfected right in favour of any person other than the
[. . .] trustee.

(4)   Any moveable property, in respect of which but for this subsection—

(a)   delivery or possession; or

(b)   intimation of its assignation,
would be required in order to complete title to it, shall vest in the [. . .] trustee by
virtue of [his appointment] as if at the date of sequestration the [. . .] trustee had
taken delivery or possession of the property or had made intimation of its assignation to him, as the case may be.

(5)   Any non-vested contingent interest which the debtor has shall vest in the
[. . .] trustee as if an assignation of that interest had been executed by the debtor
and intimation thereof made at the date of sequestration.

[(5A)   Any non-vested contingent interest vested in the trustee by virtue of subsection (5) above shall, where it remains so vested in the trustee on the date [which
is 4 years after the date of sequestration], be reinvested in the debtor as if an assignation of that interest had been executed by the trustee and intimation thereof
made at that date.]

(6)   Any person claiming a right to any estate claimed by the [. . .] trustee may
apply to the [sheriff] for the estate to be excluded from such vesting, a copy of the
application being served on the [. . .] trustee; and the [sheriff] shall grant the application if [he] is satisfied that the estate should not be so vested.

(7)   Where any successor of a deceased debtor whose estate has been sequestrated has made up title to, or is in possession of, any part of that estate, the
[sheriff] may, on the application of the [. . .] trustee, order the successor to convey
such estate to him.

(8)   In subsection (1) above [, subject to section 31A of this Act,] the 'whole
estate of the debtor' means [subject to subsection (9) below] [and to sections
71(10B) and 78(3B)]* his whole estate at the date of sequestration, wherever situated, including—

(a)   any income or estate vesting in the debtor on that date;

[(aa)   any property of the debtor, title to which has not been completed by
another person deriving right from the debtor;]

(b)   the capacity to exercise and to take proceedings for exercising, all such
powers in, over, or in respect of any property as might have been exercised by
the debtor for his own benefit as at, or on, the date of sequestration or might be
exercised on a relevant date (within the meaning of section 32(10) of this Act).

* There is now no statutory basis for the words which should follow, namely, 'of the Social Security
Administration Act 1992', but these words are necessary to give meaning to the provisions!

[(9)   Subject to subsection (10) below, the 'whole estate of the debtor' does not include any interest of the debtor as tenant under any of the following tenancies—

(a)   a tenancy which is an assured tenancy within the meaning of Part II of the Housing (Scotland) Act 1988, or

(b)   a protected tenancy within the meaning of the Rent (Scotland) Act 1984 in respect of which, by virtue of any provision of Part VIII of that Act, no premium can lawfully be required as a condition of the assignation, or

(c)   a Scottish secure tenancy within the meaning of the Housing (Scotland) Act 2001 (asp 10).

(10)   On the date on which the [. . .] trustee serves notice to that effect on the debtor, the interest of this debtor as tenant under any of the tenancies referred to in subsection (9) above shall form part of his estate and vest in the [. . .] trustee as if it had vested in him under section 32(6) of this Act.]

### [31ZA   Proceedings under EC Regulation: modified definition of 'estate'

In the application of this Act to insolvency proceedings under the EC Regulation, a reference to 'estate' is a reference to estate which may be dealt with in those proceedings.]

### [31A   Property subject to restraint order

(1)   This section applies where—

(a)   property is excluded from the debtor's estate by virtue of section 420(2)(a) of the Proceeds of Crime Act 2002 (property subject to a restraint order),

(b)   an order under section 50, 128, 198 of that Act has not been made in respect of the property, and

(c)   the restraint order is discharged.

(2)   On the discharge of the restraint order the property vests in the [. . .] trustee as part of the debtor's estate.

(3)   But subsection (2) does not apply to the proceeds of property realised by a management receiver under section 49(2)(d) or 197(2)(d) of that Act (realisation of property to meet receiver's remuneration and expenses).]

### [31B   Property in respect of which receivership or administration order is made

(1)   This section applies where—

(a)   property is excluded from the debtor's estate by virtue of section 420(2)(b), (c) or (d) of the Proceeds of Crime Act 2002 (property in respect of which an order for the appointment of a receiver or administrator under certain provisions of that Act is in force),

(b)   a confiscation order is made under section 6, 92 or 156 of that Act,

(c)   the amount payable under the confiscation order is fully paid, and

(d)   any of the property remains in the hands of the receiver or administrator (as the case may be).

(2)   The property vests in the [. . .] trustee as part of the debtor's estate.]

### [31C   Property subject to certain orders where confiscation order discharged or quashed

(1)   This section applies where—

(a)   property is excluded from the debtor's estate by virtue of section 420(2)(a), (b), (c) or (d) of the Proceeds of Crime Act 2002 (property in respect of which a restraint order or an order for the appointment of a receiver or administrator under that Act is in force),

(b)   a confiscation order is made under section 6, 92 or 156 of that Act, and

(c)   the confiscation order is discharged under section 30, 114 or 180 of that Act (as the case may be) or quashed under that Act or in pursuance of any enactment relating to appeals against conviction or sentence.

(2)  Any property in the hands of a receiver appointed under Part 2 or 4 of that Act or an administrator appointed under Part 3 of that Act vests in the [. . .] trustee as part of the debtor's estate.

(3)  But subsection (2) does not apply to the proceeds of property realised by a management receiver under section 49(2)(d) or 197(2)(d) of that Act (realisation of property to meet receiver's remuneration and expenses).]

## 32  Vesting of estate, and dealings of debtor, after sequestration

(1)  Subject to [sections 32A to 32H] below, any income of whatever nature received by the debtor on a relevant date, other than income arising from the estate which is vested in the [. . .] trustee, shall vest in the debtor.

[. . .]

(5)  Diligence [(which, for the purposes of this section, includes the making of a deduction from earnings order under the Child Support Act 1991)] in respect of a debt or obligation of which the debtor would be discharged under section 55 of this Act were he discharged under section 54 [, 54A or 54C] thereof shall not be competent against income vesting in him under subsection (1) above.

[(5A)  Where the trustee knows, or becomes aware, of any estate vested in the trustee under section 31 or this section which comprises funds held by a bank, the trustee must serve a notice on the bank—

(a)  informing the bank of the sequestration, and

(b)  specifying reasonable detail in order to allow the bank to identify the debtor and the funds held.

(5B)  A notice under subsection (5A)—

(a)  must be in writing and may be sent—

(i)  by first class post or by using a registered or recorded delivery postal service to the bank,

(ii)  in some other manner (including by electronic means) which the trustee reasonably considers likely to cause it to be delivered to the bank on the same or next day,

(b)  is deemed to have been received the day after it is sent.]

(6)  Without prejudice to subsection (1) above, any estate, wherever situated, which—

(a)  is acquired by the debtor on a relevant date; and

(b)  would have vested in the [. . .] trustee if it had been part of the debtor's estate on the date of sequestration,

shall vest in the [. . .] trustee for the benefit of the creditors as at the date of acquisition; and any person who holds any such estate shall, on production to him of a copy of the [order] certified by the sheriff clerk [or, as the case may be, by the Accountant in Bankruptcy appointing the trustee], convey or deliver the estate to the [. . .] trustee:

Provided that—

(i)  if such a person has in good faith and without knowledge of the sequestration conveyed the estate to the debtor or to anyone on the instructions of the debtor, he shall incur no liability to the [. . .] trustee except to account for any proceeds of the conveyance which are in his hands; and

[(ia) the trustee is not entitled by virtue of this subsection to any remedy against a bank in respect of a banking transaction entered into before the receipt by the bank of a notice under subsection (5A) (whether or not the bank is aware of the sequestration),]

(ii)  this subsection shall be without prejudice to any right [. . .] acquired in the estate in good faith and for value.

(7)  The debtor shall immediately notify the [. . .] trustee of any assets acquired by him on a relevant date or of any other substantial change in his financial circumstances; and, if the debtor fails to comply with this subsection, he shall be guilty of an offence and liable on summary conviction to a fine not exceeding level

5 on the standard scale or to imprisonment for a term not exceeding 3 months or to both.

(8)   Subject to subsection (9) [and (9C)] below, any dealing of or with the debtor relating to his estate vested in the [. . .] trustee under [this section or] section 31 of this Act shall be of no effect in a question with the [. . .] trustee.

(9)   Subsection (8) above shall not apply where the person seeking to uphold the dealing establishes—
    (a)   that the [. . .] trustee—
        (i)   has abandoned to the debtor the property to which the dealing relates;
        (ii)  has expressly or impliedly authorised the dealing; or
        (iii) is otherwise personally barred from challenging the dealing, or
    (b)   that the dealing is—
        (i)   the performance of an obligation undertaken before the date of sequestration by a person obliged to the debtor in the obligation;
        (ii)  the purchase from the debtor of goods for which the purchaser has given value to the debtor or is willing to give value to the [. . .] trustee; or
        [. . .]
        [(iv) one which satisfies the conditions mentioned in subsection (9ZA) below.]
and that the person dealing with the debtor was, at the time when the dealing occurred, unaware of the sequestration and had at that time no reason to believe that the debtor's estate had been sequestrated or was the subject of sequestration proceedings.

[(9ZA)   The conditions are that—
    (a)   the dealing constitutes—
        (i)   the transfer of incorporeal moveable property; or
        (ii)  the creation, transfer, variation or extinguishing of a real right in heritable property,
for which the person dealing with the debtor has given adequate consideration to the debtor, or is willing to give adequate consideration to the trustee;
    (b)   the dealing requires the delivery of a deed; and
    (c)   the delivery occurs during the period beginning with the date of sequestration and ending on the day which falls 7 days after the day on which—
        (i)   the certified copy of the order of the sheriff granting warrant is recorded under subsection (1)(a) of section 14 of this Act; or
        (ii)  the certified copy of the determination of the Accountant in Bankruptcy awarding sequestration is recorded under subsection (1A) of that section,
in the register of inhibitions.

(9A)   Where the trustee has abandoned to the debtor any heritable property, notice in such form as may be prescribed given to the debtor by the trustee shall be sufficient evidence that the property is vested in the debtor.

(9B)   Where the trustee gives notice under subsection (9A) above, he shall, as soon as reasonably practicable after giving the notice, record a certified copy of it in the register of inhibitions.]

[(9C)   Subsection (8) does not apply where the dealing is a banking transaction entered into before the receipt by the bank of a notice under subsection (5A) (whether or not the bank is aware of the sequestration).]

(10)   In this section 'a relevant date' means a date after the date of sequestration and before the date [which is 4 years after the date of sequestration].

[(11)   In this section 'bank' has the same meaning as 'appropriate bank or institution' in section 73(1).]

## [32A   Debtor contribution order

(1)   The Accountant in Bankruptcy must make an order fixing the debtor's contribution (a 'debtor contribution order')—

(a)   in the case of a debtor application, at the same time as awarding sequestration of the debtor's estate,

(b)   in the case of an award of sequestration following a petition under section 5(2)(b), after considering initial proposals for the debtor's contribution provided by the trustee.

(2)   In a case referred to in subsection (1)(b), the trustee must send initial proposals for the debtor's contribution before the end of the period of 6 weeks beginning with the date of award of sequestration.

(3)   In making a debtor contribution order, the Accountant in Bankruptcy must use the common financial tool to assess the debtor's contribution.

(4)   A debtor contribution order may fix the amount of the debtor's contribution as zero.

(5)   A debtor contribution order may be made irrespective of sections 11 and 12 of the Welfare Reform and Pensions Act 1999 (c 30).

(6)   A debtor contribution order may provide that a third person is to pay to the trustee a specified proportion of money due to the debtor by way of income.

(7)   Where a third person pays a sum of money to the trustee in accordance with subsection (6), the third person is discharged from any liability to the debtor to the extent of the sum so paid.

(8)   The Accountant in Bankruptcy must, immediately following the making of a debtor contribution order, give written notice of the order to—

(a)   the debtor,

(b)   the trustee, and

(c)   any third person mentioned in the order.

(9)   A debtor contribution order must not take effect on a date before the expiry of the period of 14 days beginning with the day of notification of the order.

**32B   Debtor contribution order: payment period and intervals**

(1)   A debtor contribution order must contain provision requiring the debtor to pay the debtor's contribution (if not zero)—

(a)   during the payment period, and

(b)   at regular intervals determined by the person making or varying the order.

(2)   In subsection (1)(a), 'payment period' means—

(a)   the period of 48 months beginning with the date of the first payment,

(b)   such shorter period as is determined by the person making or varying the order, or

(c)   such longer period as is—

(i)   determined by the trustee where there is a period during which the debtor did not pay an amount required under the debtor contribution order, or

(ii)   agreed by the debtor and the trustee.

(3)   The person making or varying the order may determine a shorter period under subsection (2)(b) only if, in the opinion of that person, the value of—

(a)   the debtor's contribution during the shorter period, and

(b)   any other estate of the debtor taken possession of by the trustee,

would be sufficient to allow a distribution of the debtor's estate to meet in full all of the debts mentioned in section 51.

(4)   The Accountant in Bankruptcy must, when making an order under section 32A—

(a)   determine the date of the first payment, or

(b)   in a case where the debtor's contribution is fixed as zero, determine the date which is to be deemed as the date of the first payment under the order.

**32C   Debtor contribution order: review and appeal**

(1)   The debtor, the trustee or any other interested person may apply to the

Accountant in Bankruptcy for a review of a debtor contribution order made by the Accountant in Bankruptcy under section 32A.

(2)　An application under subsection (1) must be made before the expiry of the period of 14 days beginning with the day on which the debtor contribution order is made.

(3)　If an application under subsection (1) is made, the debtor contribution order is suspended until the determination of that review by the Accountant in Bankruptcy.

(4)　If an application for a review under subsection (1) is made, the Accountant in Bankruptcy must—

(a)　take into account any representations made by an interested person before the expiry of the period of 21 days beginning with the day on which the application is made, and

(b)　confirm, amend or revoke the debtor contribution order before the expiry of the period of 28 days beginning with the day on which the application is made.

(5)　The trustee or the debtor may appeal to the sheriff against any decision of the Accountant in Bankruptcy under subsection (4)(b) before the expiry of the period of 14 days beginning with the date of the decision.

### 32D　Effect of debtor contribution order

(1)　The debtor must pay to the trustee any debtor's contribution which is not zero as—

(a)　fixed by the Accountant in Bankruptcy in making the debtor contribution order, or

(b)　varied in accordance with section 32F.

(2)　The requirement to pay the debtor's contribution applies irrespective of the debtor's discharge.

(3)　If the value of the debtor's estate and income when taken possession of by the trustee is sufficient to allow a distribution of the debtor's estate to meet in full all of the debts mentioned in section 51, any debtor contribution order ceases to have effect.

### 32E　Deductions from debtor's earnings and other income

(1)　Subsections (2) to (6) apply where under a debtor contribution order—

(a)　the debtor is required to pay to the trustee an amount from the debtor's earnings or other income, or

(b)　in accordance with section 32A(6), a third person is required to pay to the trustee money otherwise due to the debtor by way of income.

(2)　The debtor must give the person mentioned in subsection (3) an instruction to make—

(a)　deductions of specified amounts from the debtor's earnings or other income, and

(b)　payments to the trustee of the amounts so deducted.

(3)　The person mentioned is—

(a)　in the case of an amount to be paid from the debtor's earnings from employment, the person by whom the debtor is employed,

(b)　in the case of an amount to be paid from other earnings or income of the debtor, a third person who is required to pay the earnings or income to the debtor, and

(c)　in the case mentioned in subsection (1)(b), the third person who is required to pay the income to the trustee.

(4)　The trustee may give the person mentioned in subsection (3) an instruction of the type mentioned in subsection (2) if—

(a)　the debtor fails to comply with the requirements imposed by that subsection, and

(b)   the debtor fails to pay the debtor's contribution in respect of 2 payment intervals applying by virtue of the debtor contribution order.

(5)   A person mentioned in subsection (3) must comply with an instruction provided in accordance with subsection (2) or (4).

(6)   Where the person by whom the debtor is employed or another third person pays a sum of money to the trustee in accordance with this section, that person is discharged from any liability to the debtor to the extent of the sum so paid.

(7)   The Scottish Ministers may by regulations make provision about instructions to be provided under this section, including in particular—

(a)   the form in which an instruction must be made,

(b)   the manner in which an instruction provided in accordance with subsection (2) or (4) affects the recipient of that instruction, and

(c)   the consequence of any failure of a recipient of an instruction provided in accordance with subsection (2) or (4) to comply with the duty imposed by subsection (5).

**32F   Variation and removal of debtor contribution order by trustee**

(1)   The trustee may vary or quash a debtor contribution order—

(a)   on the application of the debtor, following any change in the debtor's circumstances,

(b)   if the trustee considers it to be appropriate, following any change in the debtor's circumstances, or

(c)   if the trustee considers it to be appropriate when—

(i)   sending a report to the Accountant in Bankruptcy under section 54(4), or

(ii)   granting a discharge under section 54A(2).

(2)   In deciding whether to vary or quash a debtor contribution order, the trustee must use the common financial tool to assess the debtor's contribution.

(3)   A decision by the trustee under subsection (1)(b) must not take effect on a day before the end of the period of 14 days beginning with the day on which the decision is made.

(4)   The trustee must notify in writing the persons mentioned in subsection (5) immediately following—

(a)   any variation or quashing of a debtor contribution order,

(b)   any refusal of an application.

(5)   The persons are—

(a)   the debtor,

(b)   the Accountant in Bankruptcy (if the trustee is not the Accountant in Bankruptcy),

(c)   any third person required to make a payment under the debtor contribution order or under section 32E(5), and

(d)   any other interested person.

**32G   Payment break**

(1)   The trustee may, on the application of the debtor, extend the payment period of a debtor contribution order by granting a payment break.

(2)   A 'payment break' is a period not exceeding 6 months during which payments under the debtor contribution order are deferred.

(3)   A debtor may apply for a payment break if—

(a)   there has been a reduction of at least 50% in the debtor's disposable income (as determined using the common financial tool) as a result of any of the circumstances mentioned in subsection (4) arising in relation to the debtor, and

(b)   the debtor has not previously applied for a payment break in relation to a debtor contribution order applying after the sequestration of the debtor's estate.

(4)   The circumstances are—

(a)   a period of unemployment or change in employment,

(b)   a period of leave from employment because of the birth or adoption of a child or the need to care for a dependant,

(c)   a period of illness of the debtor,

(d)   a divorce or dissolution of civil partnership,

(e)   a separation from a person to whom the debtor is married or is the civil partner,

(f)   the death of a person who, along with the debtor, cared for a dependant of the debtor.

(5)   An application for a payment break must specify the period during which the debtor wishes payments to be deferred.

(6)   If, in the opinion of the trustee, a payment break is fair and reasonable, the trustee may grant a payment break on such conditions and for such period as the trustee thinks fit.

(7)   The trustee must notify in writing the grant of a payment break to—

(a)   the debtor,

(b)   the Accountant in Bankruptcy (if the trustee is not the Accountant in Bankruptcy), and

(c)   any third person required to make a payment under the debtor contribution order.

(8)   If the trustee decides not to grant a payment break, the trustee must notify the debtor of that decision and of the reasons.

(9)   The payment period in a debtor contribution order is deemed to be varied by the addition to the period of any payment break granted under this section.

### 32H   Sections 32F and 32G: review and appeal

(1)   The debtor or any other interested person may apply to the Accountant in Bankruptcy for a review of a decision by the trustee under section 32F or 32G.

(2)   An application under subsection (1) must be made before the expiry of the period of 14 days beginning with the day on which the decision is made.

(3)   If an application under subsection (1) relates to a decision by the trustee under section 32F(1)(b), the decision is suspended until the determination of that review by the Accountant in Bankruptcy.

(4)   If an application for a review under subsection (1) is made, the Accountant in Bankruptcy must—

(a)   take into account any representations made by an interested person before the expiry of the period of 21 days beginning with the day on which the application is made, and

(b)   confirm, amend or revoke the decision before the expiry of the period of 28 days beginning with the day on which the application is made.

(5)   The trustee or the debtor may appeal to the sheriff against any decision of the Accountant in Bankruptcy under subsection (4)(b) before the expiry of the period of 14 days beginning with the date of the decision.]

### 33   Limitations on vesting

(1)   The following property of the debtor shall not vest in the [. . .] trustee—

(a)   [any property kept outwith a dwellinghouse in respect of which attachment is, by virtue of section 11(1) of the Debt Arrangement and Attachment (Scotland) Act 2002 (asp 17), incompetent];

[(aa)   any property kept in a dwellinghouse which is not a non-essential asset for the purposes of Part 3 of that Act;]

(b)   property held on trust by the debtor for any other person.

(2)   The vesting of a debtor's estate in a [. . .] trustee shall not affect the right of hypothec of a landlord.

(3)   Sections 31 and 32 of this Act are without prejudice to the right of any secured creditor which is preferable to the rights of the [. . .] trustee.

*Safeguarding of interests of creditors of insolvent persons*

## 34  Gratuitous alienations

(1)  Where this subsection applies, an alienation by a debtor shall be challenge-able by—

(a)  any creditor who is a creditor by virtue of a debt incurred on or before the date of sequestration, or before the granting of the trust deed or the debtor's death, as the case may be; or

(b)  the [. . .] trustee, the trustee acting under the trust deed or the judicial factor, as the case may be.

(2)  Subsection (1) above applies where—

(a)  by the alienation, whether before or after the coming into force of this section, any of the debtor's property has been transferred or any claim or right of the debtor has been discharged or renounced; and

(b)  any of the following has occurred—

(i)  his estate has been sequestrated (other than, in the case of a natural person, after his death); or

(ii)  he has granted a trust deed which has become a protected trust deed; or

(iii)  he has died and within 12 months after his death, his estate has been sequestrated; or

(iv)  he has died and within the said 12 months, a judicial factor has been appointed under section 11A of the Judicial Factors (Scotland) Act 1889 to administer his estate and the estate was absolutely insolvent at the date of death; and

(c)  the alienation took place on a relevant day.

(3)  For the purposes of paragraph (c) of subsection (2) above, the day on which an alienation took place shall be the day on which the alienation became com-pletely effectual; and in that paragraph 'relevant day' means, if the alienation has the effect of favouring—

(a)  a person who is an associate of the debtor, a day not earlier than 5 years before the date of sequestration, the granting of the trust deed or the debtor's death, as the case may be; or

(b)  any other person, a day not earlier than 2 years before the said date.

(4)  On a challenge being brought under subsection (1) above, the court shall grant decree of reduction or for such restoration of property to the debtor's estate or other redress as may be appropriate, but the court shall not grant such a decree if the person seeking to uphold the alienation establishes—

(a)  that immediately, or at any other time, after the alienation the debtor's assets were greater than his liabilities, or

(b)  that the alienation was made for adequate consideration; or

(c)  that the alienation—

(i)  was a birthday, Christmas or other conventional gift; or

(ii)  was a gift made, for a charitable purpose, to a person who is not an associate of the debtor,

which having regard to all the circumstances, it was reasonable for the debtor to make:

Provided that this subsection shall be without prejudice to any right [. . .] acquired in good faith and for value from or through the transferee in the alienation.

(5)  In subsection (4) above, 'charitable purpose' means any charitable, bene-volent or philanthropic purpose whether or not it is charitable within the meaning of any rule of law.

(6)  For the purposes of the foregoing provisions of this section, an alienation in implementation of a prior obligation shall be deemed to be one for which there was no consideration or no adequate consideration to the extent that the prior obli-gation was undertaken for no consideration or no adequate consideration.

(7)   This section is without prejudice to the operation of section 2 of the Married Women's Policies of Assurance (Scotland) Act 1880 (policy of assurance may be effected in trust for spouse, future spouse and children) [including the operation of that section as applied by section 132 of the Civil Partnership Act 2004].

(8)   A [. . .] trustee, the trustee acting under a protected trust deed and a judicial factor appointed under section 11A of the Judicial Factors (Scotland) Act 1889 shall have the same right as a creditor has under any rule of law to challenge an alienation of a debtor made for no consideration or for no adequate consideration.

[. . .]

## 35   Recalling of order for payment of capital sum on divorce

(1)   This section applies where—

(a)   a court has made an order, whether before or after the coming into force of this section, under section 5 of the Divorce (Scotland) Act 1976 or section 8(2) of the Family Law (Scotland) Act 1985, for the payment by a debtor of a capital sum or [a court has, under the said section 8(2), made an order for the transfer of property by him or made a pension sharing order];

(b)   on the date of the making of the order the debtor was absolutely insolvent or was rendered so by implementation of the order; and

(c)   within 5 years after the making of the order—

(i)   the debtor's estate has been sequestrated other than after his death; or

(ii)   he has granted a trust deed which has (whether or not within the 5 years) become a protected trust deed; or

(iii)   he has died and, within 12 months after his death, his estate has been sequestrated; or

(iv)   he has died and, within the said 12 months, a judicial factor has been appointed under section 11A of the Judicial Factors (Scotland) Act 1889 to administer his estate.

(2)   Where this section applies, the court, on an application brought by the [. . .] trustee, the trustee acting under the trust deed or the judicial factor, may make an order for recall of the order made under the said section 5 or 8(2) and for the repayment to the applicant of the whole or part of any sum already paid, or as the case may be for the return to the applicant of all or part of any property already transferred, under that order, or, where such property has been sold, for payment to the applicant of all or part of the proceeds of sale:

Provided that before making an order under this subsection the court shall have regard to all the circumstances including, without prejudice to the generality of this proviso, the financial, and other, circumstances (in so far as made known to the court) of the person against whom the order would be made.

[. . .]

## 36   Unfair preferences

(1)   Subject to subsection (2) below, subsection (4) below applies to a transaction entered into by a debtor, whether before or after the coming into force of this section, which has the effect of creating a preference in favour of a creditor to the prejudice of the general body of creditors, being a preference created not earlier than 6 months before—

(a)   the date of sequestration of the debtor's estate (if, in the case of a natural person, a date within his lifetime); or

(b)   the granting by him of a trust deed which has become a protected trust deed; or

(c)   his death where, within 12 months after his death—

(i)   his estate has been sequestrated, or

(ii)   a judicial factor has been appointed under section 11A of the Judicial Factors (Scotland) Act 1889 to administer his estate and his estate was absolutely insolvent at the date of death.

(2)   Subsection (4) below shall not apply to any of the following transactions—

(a)   a transaction in the ordinary course of trade or business;

(b)   a payment in cash for a debt which when it was paid had become payable unless the transaction was collusive with the purpose of prejudicing the general body of creditors;

(c)   a transaction whereby the parties thereto undertake reciprocal obligations (whether the performance by the parties of their respective obligations occurs at the same time or at different times) unless the transaction was collusive as aforesaid;

(d)   the granting of a mandate by a debtor authorising an arrestee to pay over the arrested funds or part thereof to the arrester where—

(i)   there has been a decree for payment or a warrant for summary diligence; and

(ii)   the decree or warrant has been preceded by an arrestment on the dependence of the action or followed by an arrestment in execution.

(3)   For the purposes of subsection (1) above, the day on which a preference was created shall be the day on which the preference became completely effectual.

(4)   A transaction to which this subsection applies shall be challengeable by—

(a)   any creditor who is a creditor by virtue of a debt incurred on or before the date of sequestration, the granting of the protected trust deed or the debtor's death, as the case may be; or

(b)   the [. . .] trustee, the trustee acting under the protected trust deed, or the judicial factor, as the case may be.

(5)   On a challenge being brought under subsection (4) above, the court, if satisfied that the transaction challenged is a transaction to which this section applies, shall grant decree of reduction or for such restoration of property to the debtor's estate or other redress as may be appropriate:

Provided that this subsection shall be without prejudice to any right [. . .] acquired in good faith and for value from or through the creditor in whose favour the preference was created.

(6)   A [. . .] trustee, the trustee acting under a protected trust deed and a judicial factor appointed under section 11A of the Judicial Factors (Scotland) Act 1889 shall have the same right as a creditor has under any rule of law to challenge a preference created by a debtor.

[. . .]

## [36A   Recovery of excessive pension contributions

(1)   Where a debtor's estate has been sequestrated and he—

(a)   has rights under an approved pension arrangement, or

(b)   has excluded rights under an unapproved pension arrangement, the [. . .] trustee may apply to the court for an order under this section.

(2)   If the court is satisfied—

(a)   that the rights under the arrangement are to any extent, and whether directly or indirectly, the fruits of relevant contributions, and

(b)   that the making of any of the relevant contributions ('the excessive contributions') has unfairly prejudiced the debtor's creditors,

the court may make such order as it thinks fit for restoring the position to what it would have been had the excessive contributions not been made.

(3)   Subsection (4) applies where the court is satisfied that the value of the rights under the arrangement is, as a result of rights of the debtor under the arrangement or any other pension arrangement having at any time become subject to a debit under section 29(1)(a) of the Welfare Reform and Pensions Act 1999 (debits giving effect to pension-sharing), less than it would otherwise have been.

(4)   Where this subsection applies—

(a)   any relevant contributions which were represented by the rights which became subject to the debit shall, for the purposes of subsection (2), be taken to be contributions of which the rights under the arrangement are the fruits, and

(b)   where the relevant contributions represented by the rights under the arrangement (including those so represented by virtue of paragraph (a)) are not all excessive contributions, relevant contributions which are represented by the rights under the arrangement otherwise than by virtue of paragraph (a) shall be treated as excessive contributions before any which are so represented by virtue of that paragraph.

(5)   In subsections (2) to (4) 'relevant contributions' means contributions to the arrangement or any other pension arrangement—

(a)   which the debtor has at any time made on his own behalf, or

(b)   which have at any time been made on his behalf.

(6)   The court shall, in determining whether it is satisfied under subsection (2)(b), consider in particular—

(a)   whether any of the contributions were made for the purpose of putting assets beyond the reach of the debtor's creditors or any of them, and

(b)   whether the total amount of any contributions—

(i)   made by or on behalf of the debtor to pension arrangements, and

(ii)   represented (whether directly or indirectly) by rights under approved pension arrangements or excluded rights under unapproved pension arrangements,

is an amount which is excessive in view of the debtor's circumstances when those contributions were made.

(7)   For the purposes of this section and sections 36B and 36C ('the recovery provisions'), rights of a debtor under an unapproved pension arrangement are excluded rights if they are rights which are excluded from his estate by virtue of regulations under section 12 of the Welfare Reform and Pensions Act 1999.

(8)   In the recovery provisions—

'approved pension arrangement' has the same meaning as in section 11 of the Welfare Reform and Pensions Act 1999;

'unapproved pension arrangement' has the same meaning as in section 12 of that Act.]

## [36B   Orders under section 36A

(1)   Without prejudice to the generality of section 36A(2) an order under section 36A may include provision—

(a)   requiring the person responsible for the arrangement to pay an amount to the [. . .] trustee,

(b)   adjusting the liabilities of the arrangement in respect of the debtor,

(c)   adjusting any liabilities of the arrangement in respect of any other person that derive, directly or indirectly, from rights of the debtor under the arrangement,

(d)   for the recovery by the person responsible for the arrangement (whether by deduction from any amount which that person is ordered to pay or otherwise) of costs incurred by that person in complying in the debtor's case with any requirement under section 36C(1) or in giving effect to the order.

(2)   In subsection (1), references to adjusting the liabilities of the arrangement in respect of a person include (in particular) reducing the amount of any benefit or future benefit to which that person is entitled under the arrangement.

(3)   In subsection (1)(c), the reference to liabilities of the arrangement does not include liabilities in respect of a person which result from giving effect to an order or provision falling within section 28(1) of the Welfare Reform and Pensions Act 1999 (pension sharing orders and agreements).

(4)   The maximum amount which the person responsible for an arrangement may be required to pay by an order under section 36A is the lesser of—

(a)   the amount of the excessive contributions, and

(b)   the value of the debtor's rights under the arrangement (if the arrangement is an approved pension arrangement) or of his excluded rights under the
arrangement (if the arrangement is an unapproved pension arrangement).

(5)   An order under section 36A which requires the person responsible for an
arrangement to pay an amount ('the restoration amount') to the [. . .] trustee must
provide for the liabilities of the arrangement to be correspondingly reduced.

(6)   For the purposes of subsection (5), liabilities are correspondingly reduced if
the difference between—

(a)   the amount of the liabilities immediately before the reduction, and

(b)   the amount of the liabilities immediately after the reduction, is equal to
the restoration amount.

(7)   An order under section 36A in respect of an arrangement—

(a)   shall be binding on the person responsible for the arrangement; and

(b)   overrides provisions of the arrangement to the extent that they conflict
with the provisions of the order.]

## [36C   Orders under section 36A: supplementary

(1)   The person responsible for—

(a)   an approved pension arrangement under which a debtor has rights,

(b)   an unapproved pension arrangement under which a debtor has excluded
rights, or

(c)   a pension arrangement under which a debtor has at any time had rights,
shall, on the [. . .] trustee making a written request, provide the [. . .] trustee with
such information about the arrangement and rights as the [. . .] trustee may
reasonably require for, or in connection with, the making of applications under
section 36A.

(2)   Nothing in—

(a)   any provision of section 159 of the Pensions Schemes Act 1993 or section
91 of the Pensions Act 1995 (which prevent assignation and the making of orders
that restrain a person from receiving anything which he is prevented from
assigning),

(b)   any provision of any enactment (whether passed or made before or after
the passing of the Welfare Reform and Pensions Act 1999) corresponding to any
of the provisions mentioned in paragraph (a), or

(c)   any provision of the arrangement in question corresponding to any of
those provisions, applies to a court exercising its powers under section 36A.

(3)   Where any sum is required by an order under section 36A to be paid to the
[. . .] trustee, that sum shall be comprised in the debtor's estate.

(4)   Regulations may, for the purposes of the recovery provisions, make provision about the calculation and verification of—

(a)   any such value as is mentioned in section 36B(4)(b);

(b)   any such amounts as are mentioned in section 36B(6)(a) and (b).

(5)   The power conferred by subsection (4) includes power to provide for calculation or verification—

(a)   in such manner as may, in the particular case, be approved by a
prescribed person; or

(b)   in accordance with guidance from time to time prepared by a prescribed
person. [. . .]

(6)   References in the recovery provisions to the person responsible for a
pension arrangement are to—

(a)   the trustees, managers or provider of the arrangement, or

(b)   the person having functions in relation to the arrangement corresponding
to those of a trustee, manager or provider.

(7)   In this section and sections 36A and 36B—

'the recovery provisions' means this section and sections 36A and 36B;

'regulations' means regulations made by the Secretary of State.

(8)  Regulations under the recovery provisions may contain such incidental, supplemental and transitional provisions as appear to the Secretary of State necessary or expedient.]

**[36D  Recovery of excessive contributions in pension-sharing cases**

(1)  For the purposes of section 34 of this Act, a pension-sharing transaction shall be taken—

(a)  to be a transaction, entered into by the transferor with the transferee, by which the appropriate amount is transferred by the transferor to the transferee; and

(b)  to be capable of being an alienation challengeable under that section only so far as it is a transfer of so much of the appropriate amount as is recoverable.

(2)  For the purposes of section 35 of this Act, a pension-sharing transaction shall be taken—

(a)  to be a pension sharing order made by the court under section 8(2) of the Family Law (Scotland) Act 1985; and

(b)  to be an order capable of being recalled under that section only so far as it is a payment or transfer of so much of the appropriate amount as is recoverable.

(3)  For the purposes of section 36 of this Act, a pension-sharing transaction shall be taken—

(a)  to be something (namely a transfer of the appropriate amount to the transferee) done by the transferor; and

(b)  to be capable of being an unfair preference given to the transferee only so far as it is a transfer of so much of the appropriate amount as is recoverable.

(4)  Where—

(a)  an alienation is challenged under section 34;

(b)  an application is made under section 35 for the recall of an order made in divorce proceedings; or

(c)  a transaction is challenged under section 36,

if any question arises as to whether, or the extent to which, the appropriate amount in the case of a pension-sharing transaction is recoverable, the question shall be determined in accordance with subsections (5) to (9).

(5)  The court shall first determine the extent (if any) to which the transferor's rights under the shared arrangement at the time of the transaction appear to have been (whether directly or indirectly) the fruits of contributions ('personal contributions')—

(a)  which the transferor has at any time made on his own behalf, or

(b)  which have at any time been made on the transferor's behalf,

to the shared arrangement or any other pension arrangement.

(6)  Where it appears that those rights were to any extent the fruits of personal contributions, the court shall then determine the extent (if any) to which those rights appear to have been the fruits of personal contributions whose making has unfairly prejudiced the transferor's creditors ('the unfair contributions').

(7)  If it appears to the court that the extent to which those rights were the fruits of the unfair contributions is such that the transfer of the appropriate amount could have been made out of rights under the shared arrangement which were not the fruits of the unfair contributions, then the appropriate amount is not recoverable.

(8)  If it appears to the court that the transfer could not have been wholly so made, then the appropriate amount is recoverable to the extent to which it appears to the court that the transfer could not have been so made.

(9)  In making the determination mentioned in subsection (6) the court shall consider in particular—

(a) whether any of the personal contributions were made for the purpose of putting assets beyond the reach of the transferor's creditors or any of them; and

(b) whether the total amount of any personal contributions represented, at the time the pension sharing arrangement was made, by rights under pension arrangements is an amount which is excessive in view of the transferor's circumstances when those contributions were made.

(10) In this section and sections 36E and 36F—

'appropriate amount', in relation to a pension-sharing transaction, means the appropriate amount in relation to that transaction for the purposes of section 29(1) of the Welfare Reform and Pensions Act 1999 (creation of pension credits and debits);

'pension-sharing transaction' means an order or provision falling within section 28(1) of the Welfare Reform and Pensions Act 1999 (orders and agreements which activate pension-sharing);

'shared arrangement', in relation to a pension-sharing transaction, means the pension arrangement to which the transaction relates;

'transferee', in relation to a pension-sharing transaction, means the person for whose benefit the transaction is made;

'transferor', in relation to a pension-sharing transaction, means the person to whose rights the transaction relates.]

**[36E  Recovery orders**

(1) In this section and section 36F of this Act, 'recovery order' means—

(a) a decree granted under section 34(4) of this Act;

(b) an order made under section 35(2) of this Act;

(c) a decree granted under section 36(5) of this Act,

in any proceedings to which section 36D of this Act applies.

(2) Without prejudice to the generality of section 34(4), 35(2) or 36(5) a recovery order may include provision—

(a) requiring the person responsible for a pension arrangement in which the transferee has acquired rights derived directly or indirectly from the pension-sharing transaction to pay an amount to the [. . .] trustee,

(b) adjusting the liabilities of the pension arrangement in respect of the transferee,

(c) adjusting any liabilities of the pension arrangement in respect of any other person that derive, directly or indirectly, from rights of the transferee under the arrangement,

(d) for the recovery by the person responsible for the pension arrangement (whether by deduction from any amount which that person is ordered to pay or otherwise) of costs incurred by that person in complying in the debtor's case with any requirement under section 36F(1) or in giving effect to the order.

(3) In subsection (2), references to adjusting the liabilities of a pension arrangement in respect of a person include (in particular) reducing the amount of any benefit or future benefit to which that person is entitled under the arrangement.

(4) The maximum amount which the person responsible for an arrangement may be required to pay by a recovery order is the smallest of—

(a) so much of the appropriate amount as, in accordance with section 36D of this Act, is recoverable,

(b) so much (if any) of the amount of the unfair contributions (within the meaning given by section 36D(6)) as is not recoverable by way of an order under section 36A of this Act containing provision such as is mentioned in section 36B(1)(a), and

(c) the value of the debtor's rights under the arrangement acquired by the transferee as a consequence of the transfer of the appropriate amount.

(5) A recovery order which requires the person responsible for an arrangement to pay an amount ('the restoration amount') to the [. . .] trustee must provide for the liabilities of the arrangement to be correspondingly reduced.

(6) For the purposes of subsection (5), liabilities are correspondingly reduced if the difference between—

(a) the amount of the liabilities immediately before the reduction, and

(b) the amount of the liabilities immediately after the reduction is equal to the restoration amount.

(7) A recovery order in respect of an arrangement—

(a) shall be binding on the person responsible for the arrangement, and

(b) overrides provisions of the arrangement to the extent that they conflict with the provisions of the order.]

## [36F Recovery orders: supplementary

(1) The person responsible for a pension arrangement under which the transferee has, at any time, acquired rights by virtue of the transfer of the appropriate amount shall, on the [. . .] trustee making a written request, provide the trustee with such information about the arrangement and the rights under it of the transferor and transferee as the [. . .] trustee may reasonably require for, or in connection with, the making of an application for a recovery order.

(2) Nothing in—

(a) any provision of section 159 of the Pension Schemes Act 1993 or section 91 of the Pensions Act 1995 (which prevent assignation and the making of orders which restrain a person from receiving anything which he is prevented from assigning),

(b) any provision of any enactment (whether passed or made before or after the passing of the Welfare Reform and Pensions Act 1999) corresponding to any of the provisions mentioned in paragraph (a), or

(c) any provision of the arrangement in question corresponding to any of those provisions, applies to a court exercising its power to make a recovery order.

(3) Regulations may, for the purposes of the recovery provisions, make provision about the calculation and verification of—

(a) any such value as is mentioned in section 36E(4)(c);

(b) any such amounts as are mentioned in section 36E(6)(a) and (b).

(4) The power conferred by subsection (3) includes power to provide for calculation or verification—

(a) in such manner as may, in the particular case, be approved by a prescribed person; or

(b) in accordance with guidance from time to time prepared by a prescribed person. [. . .]

(5) References in the recovery provisions to the person responsible for a pension arrangement are to—

(a) the trustees, managers or provider of the arrangement, or

(b) the person having functions in relation to the arrangement corresponding to those of a trustee, manager or provider.

(6) In this section—

'prescribed' means prescribed by regulations;

'the recovery provisions' means this section and sections 34, 35, 36 and 36E of this Act;

'regulations' means regulations made by the Secretary of State.

(7) Regulations under the recovery provisions may—

(a) make different provision for different cases;

(b) contain such incidental, supplemental and transitional provisions as appear to the Secretary of State necessary or expedient.

(8) Regulations under the recovery provisions shall be made by statutory in-

strument subject to annulment in pursuance of a resolution of either House of Parliament.]

*Effect of sequestration on diligence*

## 37 Effect of sequestration on diligence

(1) The order of the [sheriff or, as the case may be, the determination of the debtor application by the Accountant in Bankruptcy] awarding sequestration shall as from the date of sequestration have the effect, in relation to diligence done (whether before or after the date of sequestration) in respect of any part of the debtor's estate, of—

    (a)  a decree of adjudication of the heritable estate of the debtor for payment of his debts which has been duly recorded in the register of inhibitions and adjudications on that date; and

    (b)  an arrestment in execution and decree of furthcoming, an arrestment in execution and warrant of sale, and [an attachment],

in favour of the creditors according to their respective entitlements.

(2) [Where an] inhibition on the estate of the debtor [. . .] takes effect within the period of 60 days before the date of sequestration [. . .] any relevant right of challenge shall, at the date of sequestration, vest in the [. . .] trustee as shall any right of the inhibitor to receive payment for the discharge of the inhibition:

Provided that this subsection shall neither entitle the trustee to receive any payment made to the inhibitor before the date of sequestration nor affect the validity of anything done before that date in consideration of such payment.

(3) In subsection (2) above, 'any relevant right of challenge' means any right to challenge a deed voluntarily granted by the debtor if it is a right which vested in the inhibitor by virtue of the inhibition.

(4) No arrestment [, money attachment, interim attachment] or [attachment] of the estate of the debtor (including any estate vesting in the [. . .] trustee under section 32(6) of this Act) executed—

    (a)  within the period of 60 days before the date of sequestration and whether or not subsisting at that date; or

    (b)  on or after the date of sequestration,

shall be effectual to create a preference for the arrester or [attacher]; and the estate so arrested or [attached or any funds released under section 73J(2) of the Debtors (Scotland) Act 1987 (c 18) (automatic release of funds)], or the proceeds of sale thereof, shall be handed over to the [. . .] trustee.

(5) An arrester or [attacher] whose arrestment [, money attachment, interim attachment] or [attachment] is executed within the said period of 60 days shall be entitled to payment, out of the arrested or [attached] estate or out of the proceeds of the sale thereof, of the expenses incurred—

    (a)  in obtaining

      [(i)  warrant for interim attachment; or

      (ii)]  the extract of the decree or other document on which the arrestment [, money attachment] or [attachment] proceeded;

    (b)  in executing the arrestment [, money attachment, interim attachment] or [attachment]; and

    (c)  in taking any further action in respect of the diligence.

[(5A) Nothing in subsection (4) or (5) above shall apply to an earnings arrestment, a current maintenance arrestment, a conjoined arrestment order or a deduction from earnings order under the Child Support Act 1991.]

[. . .]

(6) No poinding of the ground in respect of the estate of the debtor (including any estate vesting in the [. . .] trustee under section 32(6) of this Act) executed within the period of 60 days before the date of sequestration or on or after that date shall be effectual in a question with the [. . .] trustee, except for the interest on

the debt of a secured creditor, being interest for the current half-yearly term and arrears of interest for one year immediately before the commencement of that term.

(7) The foregoing provisions of this section shall apply to the estate of a deceased debtor which—

(a) has been sequestrated; or

(b) was absolutely insolvent at the date of death and in respect of which a judicial factor has been appointed under section 11A of the Judicial Factors (Scotland) Act 1889,

within 12 months after his death, but as if for any reference to the date of sequestration and the debtor there were substituted respectively a reference to the date of the deceased's death and to the deceased debtor.

(8) It shall be incompetent on or after the date of sequestration for any creditor to raise or insist in an adjudication against the estate of a debtor (including any estate vesting in the permanent trustee under section 32(6) of this Act) or to be confirmed as executor-creditor on the estate.

[(8A) A notice of land attachment registered—

(a) on or after the date of sequestration against land forming part of the heritable estate of the debtor (including any estate vesting in the trustee by virtue of section 32(6) of this Act); or

(b) before that date in relation to which, by that date, no land attachment is created,

shall be of no effect.

(8B) Subject to subsections (8C) to (8F) below, it shall not be competent for a creditor to insist in a land attachment—

(a) created over heritable estate of the debtor before the beginning of the period of six months mentioned in subsection (5B) above; and

(b) which subsists on the date of sequestration.

(8C) Where, in execution of a warrant for sale, a contract to sell the land has been concluded—

(a) the trustee shall concur in and ratify the deed implementing that contract; and

(b) the appointed person shall account for and pay to the trustee any balance of the proceeds of sale which would, but for the sequestration, be due to the debtor after disbursing those proceeds in accordance with section 116 of the Bankruptcy and Diligence etc (Scotland) Act 2007 (asp 3) (disbursement of proceeds of sale of attached land).

(8D) Subsection (8C) above shall not apply where the deed implementing the contract is not registered before the expiry of the period of 28 days beginning with the day on which—

(a) the certified copy of the order of the sheriff granting warrant is recorded under subsection (1)(a) of section 14 of this Act; or

(b) the certified copy of the determination of the Accountant in Bankruptcy awarding sequestration is recorded under subsection (1A) of that section, in the register of inhibitions.

(8E) Where a decree of foreclosure has been granted but an extract of it has not registered, the creditor may proceed to complete title to the land by so registering that extract provided that the extract is registered before the expiry of the period mentioned in subsection (8D) above.

(8F) The Scottish Ministers may—

(a) prescribe such other period for the period mentioned in subsection (8D) above; and

(b) prescribe different periods for the purposes of that subsection and subsection (8E) above,

as they think fit.]

(9) Where—

(a)    a deceased debtor's estate is sequestrated; or

(b)    a judicial factor is appointed under section 11A of the Judicial Factors (Scotland) Act 1889 to administer his estate (in a case where the estate is absolutely insolvent),

within 12 months after the debtor's death, no confirmation as executor-creditor on that estate at any time after the debtor's death shall be effectual in a question with the [. . .] trustee or the judicial factor; but the executor-creditor shall be entitled out of that estate, or out of the proceeds of sale thereof, to the expenses incurred by him in obtaining the confirmation.

[(10)    Expressions used in subsections (5B), (5C) and (8A) to (8F) above which are also used in Chapter 2 of Part 4 of the Bankruptcy and Diligence etc (Scotland) Act 2007 (asp 3) have the same meanings in those subsections as they have in that Chapter.]

*[Administration of estate by trustee]*

## 38    Taking possession of estate by [. . .] trustee

(1)    The [. . .] trustee shall—

(a)    as soon as may be after his [appointment], for the purpose of recovering the debtor's estate under section 3(1)(a) of this Act, and subject to section 40 of this Act, take possession of the debtor's whole estate so far as vesting in the [. . .] trustee under sections 31 and 32 of this Act and any document in the debtor's possession or control relating to his assets or his business or financial affairs;

(b)    make up and maintain an inventory and valuation of the estate [. . .]; and

(c)    forthwith thereafter send a copy of any such inventory and valuation to the Accountant in Bankruptcy.

(2)    The [. . .] trustee shall be entitled to have access to all documents relating to the assets or the business or financial affairs of the debtor sent by or on behalf of the debtor to a third party and in that third party's hands and to make copies of any such documents.

(3)    If any person obstructs a [. . .] trustee who is exercising, or attempting to exercise, a power conferred by subsection (2) above, the sheriff, on the application of the [. . .] trustee, may order that person to cease so to obstruct the [. . .] trustee.

(4)    The [. . .] trustee may require delivery to him of any title deed or other document of the debtor, notwithstanding that a right of lien is claimed over the title deed or document; but this subsection is without prejudice to any preference of the holder of the lien.

## 39    Management and realisation of estate

(1)    As soon as may be after his [appointment], the [. . .] trustee shall consult [. . .] with the Accountant in Bankruptcy concerning the exercise of his functions under section 3(1)(a) of this Act; and, subject to [subsections (1A), (6) and (9)] below, the [. . .] trustee shall comply with any general or specific directions given to him, as the case may be—

(a)    by the creditors;

(b)    on the application under this subsection of the commissioners, by the [sheriff]; or

(c)    [. . .] by the Accountant in Bankruptcy,

as to the exercise by him of such functions.

[(1A)    Subsection (1) above does not apply in any case where the Accountant in Bankruptcy is the trustee.]

(2)    The [. . .] trustee may [. . .] do any of the following things [. . .]—

(a)    carry on [or close down] any business of the debtor;

(b)    bring, defend or continue any legal proceedings relating to the estate of the debtor;

(c)    create a security over any part of the estate;

(d)    where any right, option or other power forms part of the debtor's estate, make payments or incur liabilities with a view to obtaining, for the benefit of the creditors, any property which is the subject of the right, option or power;

[(e)   borrow money in so far as it is necessary for the trustee to do so to safeguard the debtor's estate;

(f)   effect or maintain insurance policies in respect of the business or property of the debtor.]

(3)   Any sale of the debtor's estate by the [. . .] trustee may be by either public sale or private bargain.

(4)   The following rules shall apply to the sale of any part of the debtor's heritable estate over which a heritable security is held by a creditor or creditors if the rights of the secured creditor or creditors are preferable to those of the [. . .] trustee—

(a)   the [. . .] trustee may sell that part only with the concurrence of every such creditor unless he obtains a sufficiently high price to discharge every such security;

(b)   subject to paragraph (c) below, the following acts shall be precluded—

(i)   the taking of steps by a creditor to enforce his security over that part after the [. . .] trustee has intimated to the creditor that he intends to sell it;

(ii)   the commencement by the [. . .] trustee of the procedure for the sale of that part after a creditor has intimated to the [. . .] trustee that he intends to commence the procedure for its sale;

(c)   where the [. . .] trustee or a creditor has given intimation under paragraph (b) above, but has unduly delayed in proceeding with the sale, then, if authorised by the [sheriff] in the case of intimation under—

(i)   sub-paragraph (i) of that paragraph, any creditor to whom intimation has been given may enforce his security; or

(ii)   sub-paragraph (ii) of that paragraph,

the [. . .] trustee may sell that part.

(5)   The function of the [. . .] trustee under section 3(1)(a) of this Act to realise the debtor's estate shall include the function of selling, with or without recourse against the estate, debts owing to the estate.

(6)   The [. . .] trustee may sell any perishable goods without complying with any directions given to him under subsection (1)(a) or (c) above if the [. . .] trustee considers that compliance with such directions would adversely affect the sale.

(7)   The validity of the title of any purchaser shall not be challengeable on the ground that there has been a failure to comply with a requirement of this section.

(8)   It shall be incompetent for the [. . .] trustee or an associate of his or for any commissioner, to purchase any of the debtor's estate in pursuance of this section.

[(9)   The trustee—

(a)   shall comply with the requirements of subsection (4) of this section; and

(b)   may do anything permitted by this section,

only in so far as, in his view, it would be of financial benefit to the estate of the debtor and in the interests of the creditors to do so.]

## [39A   Debtor's home ceasing to form part of sequestrated estate

(1)   This section applies where a debtor's sequestrated estate includes any right or interest in the debtor's family home.

(2)   At the end of the period of 3 years beginning with the date of sequestration the right or interest mentioned in subsection (1) above shall—

(a)   cease to form part of the debtor's sequestrated estate; and

(b)   be reinvested in the debtor (without disposition, conveyance, assignation or other transfer).

(3)   Subsection (2) above shall not apply if, during the period mentioned in that subsection—

(a)   the trustee disposes of or otherwise realises the right or interest mentioned in subsection (1) above;

(b)   the trustee concludes missives for sale of the right or interest;

(c)   the trustee sends a memorandum to the keeper of the register of inhibitions under section 14(4) of this Act;

(d)   the trustee [completes title in the Land Register of Scotland or, as the case may be, the Register of Sasines] in relation to the right or interest mentioned in subsection (1) above;

(e)   the trustee commences proceedings—

(i)   to obtain the authority of the sheriff under section 40(1)(b) of this Act to sell or dispose of the right or interest;

(ii)   in an action for division and sale of the family home; or

(iii)   in an action for the purpose of obtaining vacant possession of the family home;

(f)   the trustee and the debtor enter into an agreement such as is mentioned in subsection (5) below.

[(g)   the trustee has commenced an action under section 34 of this Act in respect of any right or interest mentioned in subsection (1) above or the trustee has not known about the facts giving rise to a right of action under section 34 of this Act, provided the trustee commences such an action reasonably soon after the trustee becomes aware of such right.]

(4)   The Scottish Ministers may, by regulations, modify paragraphs (a) to (f) of subsection (3) above so as to—

(a)   add or remove a matter; or

(b)   vary any such matter,

referred to in that subsection.

(5)   The agreement referred to in subsection (3)(f) above is an agreement that the debtor shall incur a specified liability to his estate (with or without interest from the date of the agreement) in consideration of which the right or interest mentioned in subsection (1) above shall—

(a)   cease to form part of the debtor's sequestrated estate; and

(b)   be reinvested in the debtor (without disposition, conveyance, assignation or other transfer).

(6)   If the debtor does not inform the trustee or the Accountant in Bankruptcy of his right or interest in the family home before the end of the period of 3 months beginning with the date of sequestration, the period of 3 years mentioned in subsection (2) above—

(a)   shall not begin with the date of sequestration; but

(b)   shall begin with the date on which the trustee [. . .] becomes aware of the debtor's right or interest.

(7)   The sheriff may, on the application of the trustee, substitute for the period of 3 years mentioned in subsection (2) above a longer period—

(a)   in prescribed circumstances; and

(b)   in such other circumstances as the sheriff thinks appropriate.

(8)   The Scottish Ministers may, by regulations—

(a)   make provision for this section to have effect with the substitution, in such circumstances as the regulations may prescribe, of a shorter period for the period of 3 years mentioned in subsection (2) above;

(b)   prescribe circumstances in which this section does not apply;

(c)   prescribe circumstances in which a sheriff may disapply this section;

(d)   make provision requiring the trustee to give notice that this section applies or does not apply;

(e)   make provision about compensation;

(f)   make such provision as they consider necessary or expedient in consequence of regulations made under paragraphs (a) to (e) above.

(9) In this section, 'family home' has the same meaning as in section 40 of this Act.]

**40 Power of [. . .] trustee in relation to the debtor's family home**

(1) Before the [. . .] trustee [or the trustee acting under the trust deed] sells or disposes of any right or interest in the debtor's family home he shall—

(a) obtain the relevant consent; or

(b) where he is unable to do so, obtain the authority of the [sheriff] in accordance with subsection (2) [or, as the case may be, subsection (3)] below.

(2) Where the [. . .] trustee [or the trustee acting under the trust deed] requires to obtain the authority of the [sheriff] in terms of subsection (1)(b) above, the [sheriff], after having regard to all the circumstances of the case, including—

(a) the needs and financial resources of the debtor's spouse or former spouse;

[(aa) the needs and financial resources of the debtor's civil partner or former civil partner;]

(b) the needs and financial resources of any child of the family;

(c) the interests of the creditors;

(d) the length of the period during which (whether before or after the relevant date) the family home was used as a residence by any of the persons referred to in [paragraphs (a) to (b)] above,

may refuse to grant the application or may postpone the granting of the application for such period (not exceeding [3 years]) as [he] may consider reasonable in the circumstances or may grant the application subject to such conditions as [he] may prescribe.

(3) Subsection (2) above shall apply—

(a) to an action for division and sale of the debtor's family home; or

(b) to an action for the purpose of obtaining vacant possession of the debtor's family home,

brought by the [. . .] trustee [or the trustee acting under the trust deed] as it applies to an application under subsection (1)(b) above and, for the purposes of this subsection, any reference in the said subsection (2) to that granting of the application shall be construed as a reference to the granting of decree in the action.

[(3A) Before commencing proceedings to obtain the authority of the sheriff under [subsection (2) or (3)] the trustee, or the trustee acting under the trust deed, must give notice of the proceedings to the local authority in whose area the home is situated.

(3B) Notice under subsection (3A) must be given in such form and manner as may be prescribed by the Scottish Ministers.]

(4) In this section—

(a) 'family home' means any property in which, at the relevant date, the debtor had (whether alone or in common with any other person) a right or interest, being property which was occupied at that date as a residence by the debtor and his spouse [or civil partner] or by the debtor's spouse [or civil partner] or former spouse [or civil partner] (in any case with or without a child of the family) or by the debtor with a child of the family;

(b) 'child of the family' includes any child or grandchild of either the debtor or his spouse [or civil partner] or former spouse [or civil partner], and any person who has been brought up or accepted by either the debtor or his spouse [or civil partner] or former spouse [or civil partner] as if he or she were a child of the debtor, spouse [or civil partner] or former spouse [or civil partner] whatever the age of such a child, grandchild or person may be;

[(ba) 'local authority' means a council constituted under section 2 of the Local Government (Scotland) Act 1994 (c 39);]

(c) 'relevant consent' means in relation to the sale or disposal of any right or interest in a family home—

(i)   in a case where the family home is occupied by the debtor's spouse [or civil partner] or former spouse [or civil partner], the consent of the spouse [or civil partner], or, as the case may be, the former spouse [or civil partner], whether or not the family home is also occupied by the debtor;

(ii)   where sub-paragraph (i) above does not apply, in a case where the family home is occupied by the debtor with a child of the family, the consent of the debtor; and

(d)   'relevant date' means the day immediately preceding the date of sequestration [or, as the case may be, the day immediately preceding the date the trust deed was granted].

**41   Protection of rights of spouse against arrangements intended to defeat them**

(1)   If a debtor's sequestrated estate includes a matrimonial home of which the debtor, immediately before the date [the order is made appointing] the [. . .] trustee (or, if more than one such [trustee is appointed] in the sequestration, of the first [order making such an appointment]) was an entitled spouse and the other spouse is a non-entitled spouse—

(a)   the [. . .] trustee shall, where he—

(i)   is aware that the entitled spouse is married to the non-entitled spouse; and

(ii)   knows where the non-entitled spouse is residing,

inform the non-entitled spouse, within the period of 14 days beginning with that date, of the fact that sequestration of the entitled spouse's estate has been awarded, of the right of petition which exists under section 16 of this Act and of the effect of paragraph (b) below; and

(b)   the [sheriff], on the petition under section 16 of this Act of the non-entitled spouse presented either within the period of 40 days beginning with that date or within the period of 10 weeks beginning with the date [of the award] of sequestration may—

(i)   under section 17 of this Act recall the sequestration; or

(ii)   make such order as [he] thinks appropriate to protect the occupancy rights of the non-entitled spouse;

if [he] is satisfied that the purpose of the petition for sequestration [or, as the case may be, the debtor application] was wholly or mainly to defeat the occupancy rights of the non-entitled spouse.

(2)   In subsection (1) above—

'entitled spouse' and 'non-entitled spouse' have the same meanings as in section 6 of the Matrimonial Homes (Family Protection) (Scotland) Act 1981;

'matrimonial home' has the meaning assigned by section 22 of that Act as amended by the Law Reform (Miscellaneous Provisions) (Scotland) Act 1985; and

'occupancy rights' has the meaning assigned by section 1(4) of the said Act of 1981.

**[41A   Protection of rights of civil partner against arrangements intended to defeat them**

(1)   If a debtor's sequestrated estate includes a family home of which the debtor, immediately before the date [the order is made appointing] the permanent trustee (or, if more than one [trustee is appointed] in the sequestration, of the first [order making such an appointment]) was an entitled partner and the other partner in the civil partnership is a non-entitled partner—

(a)   the [. . .] trustee shall, where he—

(i)   is aware that the entitled partner is in civil partnership with the non-entitled partner; and

(ii)   knows where the non-entitled partner is residing,

inform the non-entitled partner, within the period of 14 days beginning with that date, of the fact that sequestration of the entitled partner's estate has been awarded, of the right of petition which exists under section 16 of this Act and of the effect of paragraph (b) below; and

(b) the [sheriff], on the petition under section 16 of this Act of the non-entitled partner presented either within the period of 40 days beginning with that date or within the period of 10 weeks beginning with the date [of the award] of sequestration may—

(i) under section 17 of this Act recall the sequestration; or

(ii) make such order as [he] thinks appropriate to protect the occupancy rights of the non-entitled partner,

if [he] is satisfied that the purpose of the petition for sequestration [or, as the case may be, the debtor application] was wholly or mainly to defeat the occupancy rights of the non-entitled partner.

(2) In subsection (1) above—

'entitled partner' and 'non-entitled partner' have the same meanings as in section 101 of the Civil Partnership Act 2004;

'family home' has the meaning assigned by section 135 of the 2004 Act; and 'occupancy rights' means the rights conferred by subsection (1) of that section 101.]

## 42 Contractual powers of [. . .] trustee

(1) Subject to subsections (2) and (3) below, the [. . .] trustee may adopt any contract entered into by the debtor before the date of sequestration where he considers that its adoption would be beneficial to the administration of the debtor's estate, except where the adoption is precluded by the express or implied terms of the contract, or may refuse to adopt any such contract.

[(2) The trustee must, within 28 days from the receipt by the trustee of a request in writing from any party to a contract entered into by the debtor, adopt or refuse to adopt the contract.

(2A) The period mentioned in subsection (2) may be extended—

(a) in a case where the Accountant in Bankruptcy is the trustee, by the sheriff on the application of the Accountant in Bankruptcy,

(b) in any other case, by the Accountant in Bankruptcy on the application of the trustee.

(2B) The trustee may, before the expiry of the period of 14 days beginning with the day of the decision, apply to the Accountant in Bankruptcy for a review of a decision of the Accountant in Bankruptcy under subsection (2A)(b).

(2C) If an application for a review under subsection (2B) is made, the Accountant in Bankruptcy must—

(a) take into account any representations made by an interested person before the expiry of the period of 21 days beginning with the day on which the application is made, and

(b) confirm, amend or revoke the decision before the expiry of the period of 28 days beginning with the day on which the application is made.

(2D) The trustee may appeal to the sheriff against a decision by the Accountant in Bankruptcy under subsection (2C)(b), before the expiry of the period of 14 days beginning with the day of the decision.

(2E) The Accountant in Bankruptcy may refer a case to the sheriff for a direction before—

(a) making a decision under subsection (2A)(b), or

(b) undertaking any review under this section.

(2F) An application for a review under subsection (2B) may not be made in relation to a matter on which the Accountant in Bankruptcy has applied to the sheriff for a direction under subsection (2E).]

(3) If the [. . .] trustee does not reply in writing to the request under subsection (2) above within the said period of 28 days or longer period, as the case may be, he shall be deemed to have refused to adopt the contract.

(4)   The [. . .] trustee may enter into any contract where he considers that this would be beneficial for the administration of the debtor's estate.

### 43   Money received by [. . .] trustee
(1)   Subject to [subsections (1A) and (2)] below, all money received by the [. . .] trustee in the exercise of his functions shall be deposited by him in the name of the debtor's estate in an [interest-bearing account in an] appropriate bank or institution.
[(1A)   In any case where the Accountant in Bankruptcy is the trustee, subject to subsection (2) below, all money received by the Accountant in Bankruptcy in the exercise of his functions as trustee shall be deposited by him in an interest-bearing account in the name of the debtor's estate or in the name of the Scottish Ministers in an appropriate bank or institution.]
(2)   The [. . .] trustee may at any time retain in his hands a sum not exceeding £200 or such other sum as may be prescribed.

### [43A   Debtor's requirement to give account of state of affairs
(1)   This section applies to a debtor who—
    (a)   has not been discharged under this Act; or
    [(b)   is subject to a debtor contribution order.]
(2)   The trustee shall, at the end of—
    (a)   the period of 6 months beginning with the date of sequestration; and
    (b)   each subsequent period of 6 months,
require the debtor to give an account in writing, in such form as may be prescribed, of his current state of affairs.]

### [43B   Financial education
(1)   The trustee must notify a living debtor that the debtor is required to undertake a prescribed course of financial education (a 'financial education course') specified by the trustee if, in the opinion of the trustee—
    (a)   any of the circumstances mentioned in subsection (2) apply, and
    (b)   undertaking the course would be appropriate for the debtor.
(2)   The circumstances are—
    (a)   in the period of 5 years ending on the date on which the sequestration of the debtor's estate was awarded—
        (i)   the debtor's estate was sequestrated,
        (ii)   the debtor granted a protected trust deed,
        (iii)   an analogous remedy (within the meaning of section 10(7)) was in force in respect of the debtor, or
        (iv)   the debtor participated in a debt management programme under which the debtor made regular payments (including in particular a programme approved in accordance with section 2 of the Debt Arrangement and Attachment (Scotland) Act 2002 (asp 17)),
    (b)   the debtor is subject to, or under investigation with a view to an application being made for, a bankruptcy restrictions order,
    (c)   the trustee considers that the pattern of the debtor's behaviour, whether before or after the award of sequestration, is such that the debtor would benefit from a financial education course,
    (d)   the debtor agrees to undertake a financial education course.
(3)   The trustee must decide whether to issue a notification under subsection (1)—
    (a)   before the end of the period of 6 months beginning with the date of award of sequestration, and
    (b)   in a case where section 54F applies, as soon as reasonably practicable after the trustee ascertains the whereabouts of the debtor or the debtor makes contact with the trustee.

(4)   A debtor must not be required to undertake or, as the case may be, complete the financial education course specified by the trustee if, in the opinion of the trustee—

(a)   the debtor is unable to participate in the course as a result of the debtor's health (including by reason of disability or physical or mental illness), or

(b)   the debtor has completed a financial education course in the period of 5 years ending on the date on which the sequestration of the debtor's estate was awarded.

(5)   Regulations under subsection (1) may in particular—

(a)   prescribe the content, format and method of delivery of a course,

(b)   prescribe different courses for different circumstances,

(c)   make provision for particular courses to be specified by a trustee where particular circumstances in subsection (2) apply.]

*Examination of debtor*

### 44   Private examination

(1)   The [. . .] trustee may request—

(a)   the debtor to appear before him and to give information relating to his assets, his dealings with them or his conduct in relation to his business or financial affairs; or

(b)   the debtor's spouse [or civil partner] or any other person who the [. . .] trustee believes can give such information (in this Act such spouse [, civil partner] or other person being referred to as a 'relevant person'), to give that information.

and, if he considers it necessary, the [. . .] trustee may apply to the sheriff for an order to be made under subsection (2) below.

(2)   Subject to section 46(2) of this Act, on application to him under subsection (1) above the sheriff may make an order requiring the debtor or a relevant person to attend for private examination before him on a date (being not earlier than 8 days nor later than 16 days after the date of the order) and at a time specified in the order.

(3)   A person who fails without reasonable excuse to comply with an order made under subsection (2) above shall be guilty of an offence and liable on summary conviction to a fine not exceeding level 5 on the standard scale or to imprisonment for a term not exceeding 3 months or to both.

(4)   Where the debtor is an entity whose estate may be sequestrated by virtue of section 6(1) of this Act, the references in this section and in sections 45 to 47 of this Act to the debtor shall be construed, unless the context otherwise requires, as references to a person representing the entity.

### 45   Public examination

(1)   Not less than 8 weeks before the end of the first accounting period, the [. . .] trustee—

(a)   may; or

(b)   if requested to do so by the Accountant in Bankruptcy or the commissioners (if any) or one quarter in value of the creditors, shall,

apply to the sheriff for an order for the public examination before the sheriff of the debtor or of a relevant person relating to the debtor's assets, his dealings with them or his conduct in relation to his business or financial affairs:

Provided that, on cause shown, such application may be made by the [. . .] trustee at any time.

(2)   Subject to section 46(2) of this Act, the sheriff, on an application under subsection (1) above, shall make an order requiring the debtor or relevant person to attend for examination before him in open court on a date (being not earlier than 8 days nor later than 16 days after the date of the order) and at a time specified in the order.

(3)   On the sheriff making an order under subsection (2) above, the [. . .] trustee shall—

(a)   [send to the Accountant in Bankruptcy] a notice in such form and containing such particulars as may be prescribed; and

(b)   send a copy of the said notice—

(i)   to every creditor known to the [. . .] trustee; and

(ii)   where the order is in respect of a relevant person, to the debtor, and inform the creditor and, where applicable, the debtor that he may participate in the examination.

[(3A)   The Accountant in Bankruptcy must enter particulars of the notice sent under subsection (3)(a) in the register of insolvencies.]

(4)   A person who fails without reasonable excuse to comply with an order made under subsection (2) above shall be guilty of an offence and liable on summary conviction to a fine not exceeding level 5 on the standard scale or to imprisonment for a term not exceeding 3 months or to both.

### 46   Provisions ancillary to sections 44 and 45

(1)   If the debtor or relevant person is residing—

(a)   in Scotland, the sheriff may, on the application of the [. . .] trustee, grant a warrant which may be executed by a messenger-at-arms or sheriff officer anywhere in Scotland [to apprehend]; or

(b)   in any other part of the United Kingdom, [. . .] the sheriff may, on the application of the [. . .] trustee, [grant a warrant for the arrest of],

[. . .] the debtor or relevant person and [. . .] have him taken to the place of the examination:

Provided that a warrant under [this subsection shall not be granted] unless the [sheriff] is satisfied that it is necessary to do so to secure the attendance of the debtor or relevant person at the examination.

(2)   If the debtor or a relevant person is for any good reason prevented from attending for examination, the sheriff may, without prejudice to subsection (3) below, grant a commission to take his examination (the commissioner being in this section and section 47 below referred to as an 'examining commissioner').

(3)   The sheriff or the examining commissioner may at any time adjourn the examination to such day as the sheriff or the examining commissioner may fix.

(4)   The sheriff or the examining commissioner may order the debtor or a relevant person to produce for inspection any document in his custody or control relating to the debtor's assets, his dealings with them or his conduct in relation to his business or financial affairs, and to deliver the document or a copy thereof to the [. . .] trustee for further examination by him.

### 47   Conduct of examination

(1)   The examination, whether before the sheriff or an examining commissioner, shall be taken on oath.

(2)   At the examination—

(a)   the [. . .] trustee or a solicitor or counsel acting on his behalf and, in the case of public examination, any creditor may question the debtor or a relevant person; and

(b)   the debtor may question a relevant person,

as to any matter relating to the debtor's assets, his dealings with them or his conduct in relation to his business or financial affairs.

(3)   The debtor or a relevant person shall be required to answer any question relating to the debtor's assets, his dealings with them or his conduct in relation to his business or financial affairs and shall not be excused from answering any such question on the ground that the answer may incriminate or tend to incriminate him or on the ground of confidentiality:

Provided that—

(a)   a statement made by the debtor or a relevant person in answer to such a question shall not be admissible in evidence in any subsequent criminal proceedings against the person making the statement, except where the proceedings are in respect of a charge of perjury relating to the statement;

(b)   a person subject to examination shall not be required to disclose any information which he has received from a person who is not called for examination if the information is confidential between them.

(4)   [The rules relating to the recording of evidence in ordinary causes specified in the First Schedule to the Sheriff Courts (Scotland) Act 1907] shall apply in relation to the recording of evidence at the examination before the sheriff or the examining commissioner.

[. . .]

[(6)   The trustee must send a copy of the record of the examination to the Accountant in Bankruptcy.]

(7)   A relevant person shall be entitled to fees or allowances in respect of his attendance at the examination as if he were a witness in an ordinary civil cause in the sheriff court:

Provided that, if the sheriff thinks that it is appropriate in all the circumstances, he may disallow or restrict the entitlement to such fees or allowances.

*Submission and adjudication of claims*

## 48   [Submission of claims to permanent trustee]

(1)   Subject to [subsections (1A) and (2)] below and subsections (8) and (9) of section 52 of this Act, a creditor in order to obtain an adjudication as to his entitlement—

(a)   to vote at a meeting of creditors other than the statutory meeting; or

(b)   (so far as funds are available), to a dividend out of the debtor's estate in respect of any accounting period,

shall submit a claim in accordance with this section to the [. . .] trustee respectively—

(i)   at or before the meeting; or

[(ii)   in accordance with subsection (1A).]

[(1A   A creditor must, in order to obtain an adjudication as to the creditor's entitlement (so far as funds are available) to a dividend out of the debtor's estate, submit a claim to the trustee not later than the relevant day.

(1B)   The 'relevant day', in relation to a creditor, means—

(a)   where a notice is given to the creditor under section 21A(2), the day which is 120 days after the day on which the notice is given, or

(b)   where no notice is given to the creditor under that section, the day which is 120 days after the day on which the trustee gives notice to that creditor inviting the submission of claims.

(1C)   If a creditor submits a claim to the trustee after the relevant day, the trustee may, in respect of any accounting period, provide an adjudication as to the creditor's entitlement (so far as funds are available) to a dividend out of the debtor's estate if—

(a)   the claim is submitted not later than 8 weeks before the end of the accounting period, and

(b)   there were exceptional circumstances which prevented the claim from being submitted before the relevant day.]

(2)   A claim submitted by a creditor—

(a)   under section 22 of this Act and accepted in whole or in part by the [. . .] trustee for the purpose of voting at the statutory meeting; or

(b)   under this section [which has not been rejected in whole],

shall be deemed to have been re-submitted for the purpose of obtaining an adjudication as to his entitlement both to vote at any subsequent meeting and (so far as funds are available) to a dividend in respect of an accounting period, or, as the case may be, any subsequent accounting period.

(3) Subsections (2) and (3) of section 22 of this Act shall apply for the purposes of this section but as if in the proviso to subsection (2) for the words 'interim trustee' there should be substituted the words '[. . .] trustee with the consent of the commissioners, if any', and for any other reference to the interim trustee there were substituted a reference to a permanent trustee.

(4) A creditor who has submitted a claim under this section (or under section 22 of this Act, a statement of claim which has been deemed re-submitted as mentioned in subsection (2) above) may at any time submit a further claim under this section specifying a different amount for his claim:

Provided that a secured creditor shall not be entitled to produce a further claim specifying a different value for the security at any time after the [. . .] trustee requires the creditor to discharge, or convey or assign, the security under paragraph 5(2) of Schedule 1 to this Act.

(5) The [. . .] trustee, for the purpose of satisfying himself as to the validity or amount of a claim submitted by a creditor under this section, may require—

(a) the creditor to produce further evidence; or

(b) any other person who he believes can produce relevant evidence, to produce such evidence,

and, if the creditor or other person refuses or delays to do so, the [. . .] trustee may apply to the sheriff for an order requiring the creditor or other person to attend for his private examination before the sheriff.

(6) Sections 44(2) and (3) and 47(1) of this Act shall apply, subject to any necessary modifications, to the examination of the creditor or other person as they apply to the examination of a relevant person; and references in this subsection and subsection (5) above to a creditor in a case where the creditor is an entity mentioned in section 6(1) of this Act shall be construed, unless the context otherwise requires, as references to a person representing the entity.

(7) Subsections (5) to (10) of section 22 of this Act shall apply for the purposes of this section but as if—

[. . .]

[(b) in subsection (7) the words 'and keep a record of it stating the date when it was produced to him' were repealed.]

(8) At any private examination under subsection (5) above, a solicitor or counsel may act on behalf of the [. . .] trustee or he may appear himself.

## 49 Adjudication of claims

(1) At the commencement of every meeting of creditors (other than the statutory meeting), the [. . .] trustee shall, for the purposes of section 50 of this Act so far as it relates to voting at that meeting, accept or reject the claim of each creditor.

(2) Where funds are available for payment of a dividend out of the debtor's estate in respect of an accounting period, the [. . .] trustee for the purpose of determining who is entitled to such a dividend shall, not later than 4 weeks before the end of the period, accept or reject every claim submitted or deemed to have been re-submitted to him under this Act; and shall at the same time make a decision on any matter requiring to be specified under paragraph (a) or (b) of subsection (5) below.

[(2A) On accepting or rejecting, under subsection (2) above, every claim submitted or deemed to have been re-submitted, the trustee shall, as soon as is reasonably practicable, send a list of every claim so accepted or rejected (including the amount of each claim and whether he has accepted or rejected it) to—

(a) the debtor; and

(b) every creditor known to the trustee.]

(3) If the amount of a claim is stated in foreign currency the [. . .] trustee in

adjudicating on the claim under subsection (1) or (2) above shall convert the amount into sterling, in such manner as may be prescribed, at the rate of exchange prevailing at the close of business on the date of sequestration.

(4) Where the [. . .] trustee rejects a claim, he shall forthwith notify the creditor giving reasons for the rejection.

(5) Where the [. . .] trustee accepts or rejects a claim, he shall record [. . .] his decision on the claim specifying—

(a) the amount of the claim accepted by him,

(b) the category of debt, and the value of any security, as decided by him, and

(c) if he is rejecting the claim, his reasons therefor.

[(6) The debtor or any creditor may apply to the Accountant in Bankruptcy for a review of—

(a) the acceptance or rejection of any claim, or

(b) a decision in respect of any matter requiring to be specified under subsection (5)(a) or (b).]

[(6A) The debtor may make an application under subsection (6) only if the debtor satisfies the Accountant in Bankruptcy that the debtor has, or is likely to have, a pecuniary interest in the outcome of the review.

(6B) An application under subsection (6) must be made—

(a) in the case of a review relating to an acceptance or rejection under subsection (1), before the expiry of the period of 14 days beginning with the day of that decision, and

(b) in the case of a review relating to an acceptance or rejection under subsection (2), before the expiry of the period of 28 days beginning with the day of that decision.

(6C) If an application under subsection (6) is made, the Accountant in Bankruptcy must—

(a) take into account any representations made by an interested person before the expiry of the period of 21 days beginning with the day on which the application is made, and

(b) confirm, amend or revoke the decision before the expiry of the period of 28 days beginning with the day on which the application is made.

(6D) The debtor or any creditor may appeal to the sheriff against a decision by the Accountant in Bankruptcy under subsection (6C)(b) before the expiry of the period of 14 days beginning with the day of the decision.

(6E) The debtor may appeal under subsection (6D) only if the debtor satisfies the sheriff that the debtor has, or is likely to have, a pecuniary interest in the outcome of the appeal.]

(7) Any reference in this section to the acceptance or rejection of a claim shall be construed as a reference to the acceptance or rejection of the claim in whole or in part.

*Entitlement to vote and draw dividend*

## 50 Entitlement to vote and draw dividend

[(1)] A creditor who has had his claim accepted in whole or in part by the [. . .] trustee or [on review or appeal under] section 49 of this Act shall be entitled—

(a) subject to sections 29(1)(a) and 30(1) and (4)(b) of this Act, in a case where the acceptance is under (or on appeal arising from) subsection (1) of the said section 49, to vote on any matter at the meeting of creditors for the purpose of voting at which the claim is accepted; and

(b) in a case where the acceptance is under (or on appeal arising from) subsection (2) of the said section 49, to payment out of the debtor's estate of a dividend in respect of the accounting period for the purposes of which the claim is accepted; but such entitlement to payment shall arise only in so far as that estate has funds available to make that payment, having regard to section 51 of this Act.

[(2)   No vote shall be cast by virtue of a debt more than once on any resolution put to a meeting of creditors.

(3)   Where a creditor—

(a)   is entitled to vote under this section;

(b)   has lodged his claim in one or more sets of other proceedings; and

(c)   votes (either in person or by proxy) on a resolution put to the meeting, only the creditor's vote shall be counted.

(4)   Where—

(a)   a creditor has lodged his claim in more than one set of other proceedings; and

(b)   more than one member State liquidator seeks to vote by virtue of that claim,

the entitlement to vote by virtue of that claim is exercisable by the member State liquidator in main proceedings, whether or not the creditor has lodged his claim in the main proceedings.

(5)   For the purposes of subsections (3) and (4) above, 'other proceedings' means main proceedings, secondary proceedings or territorial proceedings in a member State other than the United Kingdom.]

*Distribution of debtor's estate*

## 51   Order of priority in distribution

(1)   The funds of the debtor's estate shall be distributed by the [. . .] trustee to meet the following debts in the order in which they are mentioned—

(a)   the outlays and remuneration of the interim trustee in the administration of the debtor's estate;

(b)   the outlays and remuneration of the [. . .] trustee in the administration of the debtor's estate;

(c)   where the debtor is a deceased debtor, deathbed and funeral expenses reasonably incurred and expenses reasonably incurred in administering the deceased's estate;

(d)   the expenses reasonably incurred by a creditor who is a petitioner, or concurs in [a debtor application], for sequestration;

[(e)   ordinary preferred debts (excluding any interest which has accrued thereon to the date of sequestration);

(ea)   secondary preferred debts (excluding any interest which has accrued thereon to the date of sequestration);]

(f)   ordinary debts, that is to say a debt which is neither a secured debt nor a debt mentioned in any other paragraph of this subsection;

(g)   interest at the rate specified in subsection (7) below on—

(i)   the [ordinary] preferred debts;

[(ia)   the secondary preferred debts;]

(ii)   the ordinary debts,

between the date of sequestration and the date of payment of the debt;

(h)   any postponed debt.

(2)   In this Act—

[(a)   'preferred debt' means a debt listed in Part I of Schedule 3 to this Act,

(b)   'ordinary preferred debt' means a debt within any of paragraphs 4 to 6B of Part I of Schedule 3 to this Act,

(c)   'secondary preferred debt' means a debt within paragraph 6C or 6D of Part 1 of Schedule 3 to this Act, and

Part II of that Schedule shall have effect for the interpretation of Part I.]

(3)   In this Act 'postponed debt' means—

(a)   a loan made to the debtor, in consideration of a share of the profits in his business, which is postponed under section 3 of the Partnership Act 1890 to the claims of other creditors;

(b)   a loan made to the debtor by the debtor's spouse [or civil partner];

(c)   a creditor's right to anything vesting in the [. . .] trustee by virtue of a successful challenge under section 34 of this Act or to the proceeds of sale of such a thing.

(4)   Any debt falling within any of paragraphs (c) to (h) of subsection (1) above shall have the same priority as any other debt falling within the same paragraph and, where the funds of the estate are inadequate to enable the debts mentioned in the paragraph to be paid in full, they shall abate in equal proportions.

(5)   Any surplus remaining, after all the debts mentioned in this section have been paid in full, shall be made over to the debtor or to his successors or assignees; and in this subsection 'surplus' includes any kind of estate but does not include any unclaimed dividend.

[(5A)   Subsection (5) above is subject to Article 35 of the EC Regulation (surplus in secondary proceedings to be transferred to main proceedings).]

(6)   Nothing in this section shall affect—

(a)   the right of a secured creditor which is preferable to the rights of the [. . .] trustee; or

(b)   any preference of the holder of a lien over a title deed or other document which has been delivered to the [. . .] trustee in accordance with a requirement under section 38(4) of this Act.

(7)   The rate of interest referred to in paragraph (g) of subsection (1) above shall be whichever is the greater of—

(a)   the prescribed rate at the date of sequestration; and

(b)   the rate applicable to that debt apart from the sequestration.

## 52   Estate to be distributed in respect of accounting periods

[(1)   The [. . .] trustee shall make up accounts of his intromissions with the debtor's estate in respect of each accounting period.

(2)   In this Act 'accounting period' shall be construed as follows—

(a)   [subject to subsection (2ZA) below,] the first accounting period shall be the period of 6 months [or such shorter period as may be agreed or determined in accordance with subsection (2ZB), either period] beginning with the date [on which sequestration is awarded]; and

(b)   any subsequent accounting period shall be the period of 6 months beginning with the end of the last accounting period; except that—

(i)   in a case where the Accountant in Bankruptcy is not the [. . .] trustee, the [. . .] trustee and the commissioners or, if there are no commissioners, the Accountant in Bankruptcy agree; or

(ii)   in a case where the Accountant in Bankruptcy is the [. . .] trustee, he determines,

that the accounting period shall be such other period beginning with the end of the last accounting period as may be agreed or, as the case may be determined, it shall be that other period.]

[(2ZA)   Where the trustee was appointed under section 2(5) of this Act as interim trustee in the sequestration, the first accounting period shall be the period beginning with the date of his appointment as interim trustee and ending on the date 12 months after the date on which sequestration is awarded [or such shorter period as may be agreed or determined in accordance with subsection (2ZB)].]

[(2ZB)   This subsection applies where the trustee considers that the funds of the debtor's estate are sufficient to pay a dividend in accordance with subsection (3) in respect of—

(a)    in the case where the trustee is the Accountant in Bankruptcy, a shorter period of not less than 6 months determined by the Accountant in Bankruptcy,

(b)    in any other case, a shorter period of not less than 6 months agreed—

(i)    between the trustee and the commissioners, or

(ii)   if there are no commissioners, between the trustee and the Accountant in Bankruptcy.]

[(2A)    An agreement or determination under subsection (2)(b)(i) or (ii) above—

(a)    may be made in respect of one or more than one accounting period;

(b)    may be made before the beginning of the accounting period in relation to which it has effect and, in any event, shall not have effect unless made before the day on which such accounting period would, but for the agreement or determination, have ended;

(c)    may provide for different accounting periods to be of different durations, [. . .].]

(3)    Subject to the following provisions of this section, the [. . .] trustee shall, if the funds of the debtor's estate are sufficient and after making allowance for future contingencies, pay under section 53(7) of this Act a dividend out of the estate to the creditors in respect of each accounting period.

(4)    The [. . .] trustee may pay—

(a)    the debts mentioned in subsection (1)(a) to (d) of section 51 of this Act, other than his own remuneration, at any time;

(b)    the preferred debts at any time but only with the consent of the commissioners or, if there are no commissioners, of the Accountant in Bankruptcy.

(5)    If the [. . .] trustee—

(a)    is not ready to pay a dividend in respect of an accounting period; or

(b)    considers it would be inappropriate to pay such a dividend because the expense of doing so would be disproportionate to the amount of the dividend, he may, with the consent of the commissioners, or if there are no commissioners of the Accountant in Bankruptcy, postpone such payment to a date not later than the time for payment of a dividend in respect of the next accounting period.

[. . .]

(7)    Where [a review or appeal is made under section 49] of this Act against the acceptance or rejection of a creditor's claim, the [. . .] trustee shall, at the time of payment of dividends and until the [review or appeal] is determined, set aside an amount which would be sufficient, if the determination in the [review or appeal] were to provide for the claim being accepted in full, to pay a dividend in respect of that claim.

(8)    Where a creditor—

(a)    has failed to produce evidence in support of his claim earlier than 8 weeks before the end of an accounting period on being required by the [. . .] trustee to do so under section 48(5) of this Act; and

(b)    has given a reason for such failure which is acceptable to the [. . .] trustee, the [. . .] trustee shall set aside, for such time as is reasonable to enable him to produce that evidence or any other evidence that will enable the [. . .] trustee to be satisfied under the said section 48(5), an amount which would be sufficient, if the claim were accepted in full, to pay a dividend in respect of that claim.

(9)    Where a creditor submits a claim to the [. . .] trustee later than 8 weeks before the end of an accounting period but more than 8 weeks before the end of a subsequent accounting period in respect of which, after making allowance for contingencies, funds are available for the payment of a dividend, the [. . .] trustee shall, if he accepts the claim in whole or in part, pay to the creditor—

(a)    the same dividend or dividends as has or have already been paid to creditors of the same class in respect of any accounting period or periods; and

(b)    whatever dividend may be payable to him in respect of the said subsequent accounting period:

Provided that paragraph (a) above shall be without prejudice to any dividend which has already been paid.

[(10) In the declaration of and payment of a dividend, no payments shall be made more than once by virtue of the same debt.

(11) Any dividend paid in respect of a claim should be paid to the creditor.]

### 53 Procedure after end of accounting period

(1) Within 2 weeks after the end of an accounting period, the [. . .] trustee shall in respect of that period submit to the commissioners or, if there are no commissioners, to the Accountant in Bankruptcy—

(a) his accounts of his intromissions with the debtor's estate for audit and, where funds are available after making allowance for contingencies, a scheme of division of the divisible funds; and

(b) a claim for the outlays reasonably incurred by him and for his remuneration;

and, where the said documents are submitted to the commissioners, he shall send a copy of them to the Accountant in Bankruptcy.

[(2) Subject to subsection (2A) below, all accounts in respect of legal services incurred by the [. . .] trustee shall, before payment thereof by him, be submitted for taxation to the auditor of the court before which the sequestration is pending.]

[(2A) Where—

(a) any such account has been agreed between the [. . .] trustee and the person entitled to payment in respect of that account (in this subsection referred to as 'the payee');

(b) the [. . .] trustee is not an associate of the payee; and

(c) the commissioners [or, if there are no commissioners, the Accountant in Bankruptcy, have determined that the account need not] be submitted for taxation, the [. . .] trustee may pay such account without submitting it for taxation.]

(3) Within 6 weeks after the end of an accounting period—

(a) the commissioners or, as the case may be, the Accountant in Bankruptcy—

(i) [may] audit the accounts; and

(ii) [shall] issue a determination fixing the amount of the outlays and the remuneration payable to the [. . .] trustee; and

(b) the [. . .] trustee shall make the audited accounts, scheme of division and the said determination available for inspection by the debtor and the creditors.

(4) The basis for fixing the amount of the remuneration payable to the [. . .] trustee may be a commission calculated by reference to the value of the debtor's estate which has been realised by the [. . .] trustee, but there shall in any event be taken into account—

(a) the work which, having regard to that value, was reasonably undertaken by him; and

(b) the extent of his responsibilities in administering the debtor's estate.

(5) In fixing the amount of such remuneration in respect of [any] accounting period, the commissioners or, as the case may be, the Accountant in Bankruptcy may take into account any adjustment which the commissioners or the Accountant in Bankruptcy may wish to make in the amount of the remuneration fixed in respect of any earlier accounting period.

(6) Not later than 8 weeks after the end of an accounting period, the [. . .] trustee, the debtor [(subject to subsection (6A) below)] or any creditor may appeal against a determination issued under subsection (3)(a)(ii) above—

(a) where it is a determination of the commissioners, to the Accountant in Bankruptcy; and

(b) where it is a determination of the Accountant in Bankruptcy, to the sheriff;

and the determination of the Accountant in Bankruptcy under paragraph (a) above shall be appealable to the sheriff [and the decision of the sheriff on [an appeal against a determination under paragraph (a) or, as the case may be, an appeal under paragraph (b)] shall be final].

[(6A)   A debtor may appeal under subsection [(6)(a) or (b)] above if, and only if, he satisfies the Accountant in Bankruptcy or, as the case may be, the sheriff that he has, or is likely to have, a pecuniary interest in the outcome of the appeal.

(6B)   Before—
(a)   a debtor; or
(b)   a creditor,
appeals under subsection (6) above, he must give notice to the trustee of his intention to appeal.]

(7)   On the expiry of the period within which an appeal may be taken under subsection (6) above or, if an appeal is so taken, on the final determination of the last such appeal, the [. . .] trustee shall pay to the creditors their dividends in accordance with the scheme of division.

(8)   Any dividend—
(a)   allocated to a creditor which is not cashed or uplifted; or
(b)   dependent on a claim in respect of which an amount has been set aside under subsection (7) or (8) of section 52 of this Act,
shall be deposited by the [. . .] trustee in an appropriate bank or institution.

(9)   If a creditor's claim is revalued, the [. . .] trustee may—
(a)   in paying any dividend to that creditor, make such adjustment to it as he considers necessary to take account of that revaluation; or
(b)   require the creditor to repay to him the whole or part of a dividend already paid to him.
[. . .]

### [53A   Modification of procedure under section 53 where Accountant in Bankruptcy is trustee

(1)   In any case where the Accountant in Bankruptcy is the trustee, section 53 of this Act shall have effect subject to the following modifications.

(2)   For subsections (1) to (7) of that section, there shall be substituted—

'(1)   At the end of each accounting period, the Accountant in Bankruptcy shall prepare accounts of his intromissions with the debtor's estate and he shall make a determination of his fees and outlays calculated in accordance with regulations made under section 69A of this Act.

(2)   Such accounts and determination shall be available for inspection by the debtor and the creditors not later than 6 weeks after the end of the accounting period to which they relate.

(3)   In making a determination as mentioned in subsection (1) above, the Accountant in Bankruptcy may take into account any adjustment which he may wish to make in the amount of his remuneration fixed in respect of any earlier accounting period.

(4)   Not later than 8 weeks after the end of an accounting period, the debtor (subject to subsection (5) below) or any creditor may appeal to the sheriff against the determination of the Accountant in Bankruptcy; and the decision of the sheriff on such an appeal shall be final.

(5)   A debtor may appeal under subsection (4) above if, and only if, he satisfies the sheriff that he has, or is likely to have, a pecuniary interest in the outcome of the appeal.

(6)   Before—
(a)   a debtor; or
(b)   any creditor,
appeals under subsection (4) above, he must give notice to the Accountant in Bankruptcy of his intention to appeal.

(7)   On the expiry of the period within which an appeal may be made under

subsection (4) above, the Accountant in Bankruptcy shall pay to the creditors their dividends in accordance with the scheme of division.'

(3)   In subsection (10) for the words 'the audited' there shall be substituted the word 'his'.]

*Discharge of debtor*

## [54   Discharge where Accountant in Bankruptcy not the trustee

(1)   This section applies where the Accountant in Bankruptcy is not the trustee.

(2)   The Accountant in Bankruptcy may discharge the debtor at any time after the date which is 12 months after the date on which sequestration is awarded by granting a certificate of discharge in the prescribed form.

(3)   Before deciding whether to discharge the debtor under subsection (2), the Accountant in Bankruptcy must—

(a)   consider the report provided by the trustee under subsection (4), and

(b)   take into account any representations received during the period mentioned in subsection (6)(b).

(4)   The trustee must prepare and send a report to the Accountant in Bankruptcy—

(a)   without delay after the date which is 10 months after the date on which sequestration is awarded, and

(b)   if the debtor is not otherwise discharged, before sending to the Accountant in Bankruptcy the documentation referred to in section 57(1)(b).

(5)   The report must include—

(a)   information about—

(i)   the debtor's assets, liabilities, financial affairs and business affairs,

(ii)   the debtor's conduct in relation to those assets, liabilities, financial affairs and business affairs,

(iii)   the sequestration, and

(iv)   the debtor's conduct in the course of the sequestration,

(b)   a statement of whether, in the opinion of the trustee, the debtor has as at the date of the report—

(i)   complied with any debtor contribution order,

(ii)   co-operated with the trustee in accordance with section 64,

(iii)   complied with the statement of undertakings,

(iv)   made a full and fair surrender of the debtor's estate,

(v)   made a full disclosure of all claims which the debtor is entitled to make against other persons, and

(vi)   delivered to the trustee every document under the debtor's control relating to the debtor's estate, business or financial affairs, and

(c)   a statement of whether the trustee has, as at the date that the report is sent to the Accountant in Bankruptcy, carried out all of the trustee's functions in accordance with section 3.

(6)   The trustee must, at the same time as sending a report to the Accountant in Bankruptcy under this section, give to the debtor and every creditor known to the trustee—

(a)   a copy of the report, and

(b)   a notice informing the recipient that the person has a right to make representations to the Accountant in Bankruptcy in relation to the report before the expiry of the period of 28 days beginning with the day on which the notice is given.

(7)   A discharge under this section must not take effect before the end of the period of 14 days beginning with the day of notification of the decision.

## 54A   Discharge where Accountant in Bankruptcy the trustee

(1)   This section applies where the Accountant in Bankruptcy is the trustee.

(2)   The Accountant in Bankruptcy may discharge the debtor at any time after

the date which is 12 months after the date on which sequestration is awarded by granting a certificate of discharge in the prescribed form.

(3) The Accountant in Bankruptcy must, as soon as is practicable after the date which is 12 months after the date on which sequestration is awarded—

(a)  decide whether to discharge the debtor under subsection (2),

(b)  notify the debtor and every creditor known to the Accountant in Bankruptcy of that decision, and

(c)  send a report to those persons.

(4) The report must give an account of—

(a)  the debtor's assets, liabilities, financial affairs and business affairs,

(b)  the debtor's conduct in relation to those assets, liabilities, financial affairs and business affairs,

(c)  the sequestration, and

(d)  the debtor's conduct in the course of the sequestration, including compliance with the statement of undertakings.

(5) Subsection (6) applies where—

(a)  the Accountant in Bankruptcy refuses to discharge the debtor under subsection (2), and

(b)  the debtor is not otherwise discharged.

(6) The Accountant in Bankruptcy must, as soon as is practicable after the date which is 12 months after the date of the refusal—

(a)  decide whether to discharge or refuse to discharge the debtor under subsection (2),

(b)  notify the debtor and every creditor known to the Accountant in Bankruptcy of that decision, and

(c)  send a report giving an account of the matters mentioned in subsection (4) to those persons.

(7) A discharge under this section must not take effect before the end of the period of 14 days beginning with the day of notification of the decision.

**54B  Discharge of debtor: review and appeal**

(1) The trustee or the debtor may apply to the Accountant in Bankruptcy for a review of a decision under section 54(2) or 54A(2) to refuse to discharge the debtor.

(2) Any creditor may apply to the Accountant in Bankruptcy for a review of a decision under section 54(2) or 54A(2) to discharge the debtor.

(3) An application under subsection (1) or (2) must be made before the end of the period of 14 days beginning with the day of notification of the decision under section 54(2) or, as the case may be, 54A(2).

(4) If an application for a review under subsection (2) is made, the discharge is suspended until the determination of that review by the Accountant in Bankruptcy.

(5) If an application for a review under subsection (1) or (2) is made, the Accountant in Bankruptcy must—

(a)  take into account any representations made by an interested person before the expiry of the period of 21 days beginning with the day on which the application is made, and

(b)  confirm or revoke the decision before the expiry of the period of 28 days beginning with the day on which the application is made.

(6) The debtor, the trustee or any creditor may appeal to the sheriff against any decision of the Accountant in Bankruptcy under subsection (5)(b) before the end of the period of 14 days beginning with the date of the decision.]

**[54C  Debtor to whom section 5(2ZA) applies: discharge**

(1) Where section 5(2ZA) applies to a debtor, the debtor is discharged on the date which is 6 months after the date on which sequestration is awarded.

(2) A debtor may, following a discharge, apply to the Accountant in Bankruptcy for a certificate of discharge in the prescribed form.]

### [54D Deferral of discharge where debtor cannot be traced

(1) Subsection (2) applies where—

(a) the trustee, having made reasonable inquiries, is unable to ascertain the whereabouts of the debtor, and

(b) as a result is unable to carry out the trustee's functions in accordance with section 3.

(2) The trustee must—

(a) notify the debtor by sending to the last known address of the debtor a deferral notice in the prescribed form,

(b) give a deferral notice to every creditor known to the trustee, and

(c) where the trustee is not the Accountant in Bankruptcy, apply in the prescribed form to the Accountant in Bankruptcy for a deferral.

(3) A deferral application under subsection (2)(c) must be made by the trustee—

(a) no earlier than the date which is 8 months after the date on which sequestration is awarded, and

(b) no later than the date which is 10 months after the date on which sequestration is awarded.

(4) After receiving a deferral application, the Accountant in Bankruptcy must—

(a) take into account any representations made by an interested person before the expiry of the period of 14 days beginning with the day on which the application is made, and

(b) if satisfied of the matters mentioned in subsection (5), issue a certificate deferring indefinitely the discharge of the debtor.

(5) The matters are—

(a) that the trustee is unable to ascertain the whereabouts of the debtor, and

(b) it would not be reasonably practicable for the trustee to continue to search for the debtor.

(6) Where the Accountant in Bankruptcy is the trustee and has given a deferral notice in accordance with subsection (2)(b), the Accountant in Bankruptcy must—

(a) take into account any representations made by an interested person before the expiry of the period of 14 days beginning with the day on which the deferral notice is given, and

(b) if satisfied that it would not be reasonably practicable to continue to search for the debtor, issue a certificate deferring indefinitely the discharge of the debtor.

(7) Where a certificate is issued under subsection (4)(b) or (6)(b), the Accountant in Bankruptcy must make an appropriate entry in the register of insolvencies.

### 54E Debtor not traced: new trustee

(1) This section applies where a certificate is issued under section 54D(4)(b).

(2) The trustee may apply to the Accountant in Bankruptcy in the prescribed form for authority to resign office.

(3) An application under subsection (2) must include details of every creditor known to the trustee.

(4) An application under subsection (2) may not be made—

(a) if after the certificate is issued the trustee ascertains the whereabouts of the debtor or the debtor makes contact with the trustee,

(b) after the date which is 6 months after the date on which the certificate is awarded.

(5)   Where an application is made under subsection (2), the Accountant in Bankruptcy must issue to the trustee who made the application a notice in the prescribed form granting the application.

(6)   Where a notice is issued under subsection (5)—

(a)   the Accountant in Bankruptcy is deemed to be the trustee,

(b)   the Accountant in Bankruptcy must notify every creditor known to the Accountant in Bankruptcy that the Accountant in Bankruptcy is deemed to be the trustee,

(c)   the former trustee is not entitled to recover outlays and remuneration payable in accordance with section 53 other than by a claim in the final distribution of the debtor's estate, and

(d)   subsections (6) to (8) of section 28 apply in relation to the appointment of the Accountant in Bankruptcy as the new trustee as they apply in relation to the appointment of a new trustee under that section.

### 54F   Debtor not traced: subsequent debtor contact

(1)   This section applies where—

(a)   a certificate is issued under section 54D(4)(b) or (6)(b), and

(b)   the trustee ascertains the whereabouts of the debtor or the debtor makes contact with the trustee.

(2)   Where the Accountant in Bankruptcy is the trustee, the Accountant in Bankruptcy may discharge the debtor at any time after the date which is 12 months after the date on which—

(a)   the whereabouts of the debtor were ascertained, or

(b)   the debtor made contact with the trustee.

(3)   Where the Accountant in Bankruptcy is not the trustee, the trustee must prepare and send a report to the Accountant in Bankruptcy without delay after the date which is 10 months after the earlier of the date on which—

(a)   the whereabouts of the debtor were ascertained by the trustee, or

(b)   the debtor made contact with the trustee.

(4)   If the trustee sends a report to the Accountant in Bankruptcy under subsection (3)—

(a)   the report must include the matters included in a report sent to the Accountant in Bankruptcy in accordance with subsection (5) of section 54, and

(b)   subsection (6) of that section applies to the report as it applies to a report sent in accordance with subsection (4) of that section.

(5)   After receiving a report under subsection (3), the Accountant in Bankruptcy may discharge the debtor by granting a certificate of discharge in the prescribed form.

(6)   Before deciding whether to discharge the debtor under subsection (5), the Accountant in Bankruptcy must—

(a)   consider the report prepared by the trustee under subsection (3), and

(b)   take into account any representations received during the period mentioned in subsection (6) of section 54 (as applied in accordance with subsection (4)).

(7)   A discharge under subsection (2) or (5) must not take effect on a date before the end of the period of 14 days beginning with the day of notification of the decision.

(8)   A discharge under subsection (2) or (5) is deemed for the purposes of section 55 to have been given under section 54(2).

### 54G   Subsequent debtor contact: review and appeal

(1)   The debtor may apply to the Accountant in Bankruptcy for a review of a decision under section 54F(2) or (5) to refuse to discharge the debtor.

(2)   Any creditor may apply to the Accountant in Bankruptcy for a review of a decision under section 54F(2) or (5) to discharge the debtor.

(3)   An application under subsection (1) or (2) must be made before the end

of the period of 14 days beginning with the day of notification of the decision under section 54F(2) or, as the case may be, 54F(5).

(4) If an application for a review under subsection (2) is made, the discharge is suspended until the determination of that review by the Accountant in Bankruptcy.

(5) If an application for a review under subsection (1) or (2) is made, the Accountant in Bankruptcy must—

(a) take into account any representations made by an interested person before the expiry of the period of 21 days beginning with the day on which the application is made, and

(b) confirm or revoke the decision before the expiry of the period of 28 days beginning with the day on which the application is made.

(6) The debtor, the trustee or any creditor may appeal to the sheriff against any decision of the Accountant in Bankruptcy under subsection (5)(b) before the end of the period of 14 days beginning with the date of the decision.]

**55 [Effect of discharge under section 54, 54A or 54C]**

(1) Subject to [subsections (2) and (3)] below, on the debtor's discharge under section 54 [, 54A or 54C] of this Act, the debtor shall be discharged within the United Kingdom of all debts and obligations contracted by him, or for which he was liable, at the date of sequestration.

(2) The debtor shall not be discharged by virtue of subsection (1) above from—

(a) any liability to pay a fine or other penalty due to the Crown;

[(aa) any liability to pay a fine imposed in a [justice of the peace court (or a district court)];

(ab) any liability under a compensation order within the meaning of section 249 of the Criminal Procedure (Scotland) Act 1995;]

(b) any liability to forfeiture of a sum of money deposited in court under [section 24(6) of the Criminal Procedure (Scotland) Act 1995 (c 46)];

(c) any liability incurred by reason of fraud or breach of trust;

(d) any obligation to pay aliment or any sum of an alimentary nature under any enactment or rule of law or any periodical allowance payable on divorce by virtue of a court order or under an obligation, not being—

(i) aliment or a periodical allowance which could be included in the amount of a creditor's claim under paragraph 2 of Schedule 1 to this Act; [or

(ii) child support maintenance within the meaning of the Child Support Act 1991 which was unpaid in respect of any period before the date of sequestration of—(aa) any person by whom it was due to be paid; or (bb) any employer by whom it was, or was due to be, deducted under section 31(5) of that Act].

(e) the obligation imposed on him by section 64 of this Act.

[(2A) In subsection (2)(a) above the reference to a fine or other penalty due to the Crown includes a reference to a confiscation order made under Part 2, 3 or 4 of the Proceeds of Crime Act 2002.]

[(3) The discharge of the debtor under the said section 54 [, 54A or 54C] shall not affect any right of a secured creditor—

[. . .]

(b) for an obligation in respect of which the debtor has been discharged to enforce his security in respect of the obligation.]

[(4) Nothing in this section affects regulations in relation to which section 73B of the Education (Scotland) Act 1980 (c 44) (regulations relating to student loans) applies.]

**[55A   Discharge under section 54C: condition**

(1) This section applies where a debtor is discharged under section 54C.

(2) During the relevant period the debtor must comply with the condition in

subsection (3) before the debtor, either alone or jointly with another person, obtains credit—

(a)   to the extent of £2000 (or such other sum as may be prescribed) or more, or

(b)   of any amount where, at the time of obtaining credit, the debtor has debts amounting to £1000 (or such other sum as may be prescribed) or more.

(3)   The condition is that the debtor must inform the person who is providing credit to the debtor (or, as the case may be, jointly to the debtor and another person) that the debtor is required to comply with the conditions in this section.

(4)   During the relevant period, the debtor must not engage (whether directly or indirectly) in a business under a name other than that to which the discharge relates unless the debtor complies with the condition in subsection (5).

(5)   The condition is that the debtor must inform any person with whom the debtor enters into any business transaction of the name of the business to which the discharge relates.

(6)   In this section, 'relevant period' means the period of 6 months beginning with the date of discharge.

### 55B   Section 55A: sanctions

(1)   If a debtor fails to comply with the requirement imposed by subsection (2) or (4) of section 55A, that section applies in relation to the debtor as if the relevant period were the period of 12 months beginning with the date of discharge of the debtor.

(2)   If a debtor fails to comply with the requirement imposed by subsection (2) or (4) of section 55A during the period when the section applies in relation to the debtor by virtue of subsection (1), the debtor commits an offence.

(3)   A debtor who is guilty of an offence under subsection (2) is liable on summary conviction to—

(a)   a fine not exceeding the statutory maximum,

(b)   imprisonment for—

(i)   a term not exceeding 3 months, or

(ii)   a term not exceeding 6 months, if the person has previously been convicted of an offence inferring dishonest appropriation of property or an attempt at such appropriation, or

(c)   both such fine and imprisonment.

(4)   A debtor who is guilty of an offence under subsection (2) is liable on conviction on indictment to—

(a)   a fine,

(b)   imprisonment for a term not exceeding 2 years, or

(c)   both such fine and imprisonment.]

[. . .]

*[Bankruptcy restrictions orders and undertakings]*

### [56A   Bankruptcy restrictions order

(1)   Where sequestration of a living debtor's estate is awarded, an order (to be known as a 'bankruptcy restrictions order') in respect of the debtor may be made by the—

(a)   Accountant in Bankruptcy, or

(b)   the sheriff.

(2)   A bankruptcy restrictions order may be made by the sheriff only on the application of the Accountant in Bankruptcy.

(3)   The Accountant in Bankruptcy must notify the debtor where the Accountant in Bankruptcy proposes to make a bankruptcy restrictions order.

(4)   A notice under subsection (3) must inform the debtor that the debtor has a

right to make representations to the Accountant in Bankruptcy in relation to the proposed bankruptcy restrictions order.

(5) Before making a bankruptcy restrictions order the Accountant in Bankruptcy must take into account any representations made by the debtor.]

[. . .]

## [56B Grounds for making order

[(1) A bankruptcy restrictions order must be made if the Accountant in Bankruptcy, or as the case may be, the sheriff thinks it appropriate having regard to the conduct of the debtor (whether before or after the date of sequestration).]

(2) The [Accountant in Bankruptcy, or as the case may be, the] sheriff shall, in particular, take into account any of the following kinds of behaviour on the part of the debtor—

(a) failing to keep records which account for a loss of property by the debtor, or by a business carried on by him, where the loss occurred in the period beginning 2 years before the date of presentation of the petition for sequestration or, as the case may be, the date the debtor application was made and ending with the date of the application for a bankruptcy restrictions order;

(b) failing to produce records of that kind on demand by—

(i) the Accountant in Bankruptcy;

(ii) the interim trustee; or

(iii) the trustee;

[(ba) failing to supply accurate information to an authorised person for the purpose of the granting under section 5B of a certificate for sequestration of the debtor's estate,]

(c) making a gratuitous alienation or any other alienation for no consideration or for no adequate consideration which a creditor has, under any rule of law, right to challenge;

(d) creating an unfair preference or any other preference which a creditor has, under any rule of law, right to challenge;

(e) making an excessive pension contribution;

(f) failing to supply goods or services which were wholly or partly paid for which gave rise to a claim submitted by a creditor under section 22 or 48 of this Act;

(g) trading at a time before the date of sequestration when the debtor knew or ought to have known that he was to be unable to meet his debts;

(h) incurring, before the date of sequestration, a debt which the debtor had no reasonable expectation of being able to pay;

(j) failing to account satisfactorily to—

(i) the sheriff;

(ii) the Accountant in Bankruptcy;

(iii) the interim trustee; or

(iv) the trustee,

for a loss of property or for an insufficiency of property to meet his debts;

(k) carrying on any gambling, speculation or extravagance which may have materially contributed to or increased the extent of his debts or which took place between the date of presentation of the petition for sequestration or, as the case may be, the date the debtor application was made and the date on which sequestration is awarded;

(l) neglect of business affairs of a kind which may have materially contributed to or increased the extent of his debts;

(m) fraud or breach of trust;

(n) failing to co-operate with—

(i) the Accountant in Bankruptcy;

(ii) the interim trustee; or

(iii) the trustee.

(3) The [Accountant in Bankruptcy, or as the case may be, the] sheriff shall also, in particular, consider whether the debtor—

(a) has previously been sequestrated; and

(b) remained undischarged from that sequestration at any time during the period of 5 years ending with the date of the sequestration to which the application relates.

(4) For the purposes of subsection (2) above—

'excessive pension contribution' shall be construed in accordance with section 36A of this Act; and

'gratuitous alienation' means an alienation challengeable under section 34(1) of this Act.]

### [56C  Application of section 67(9)

(1) Where the sheriff thinks it appropriate, the sheriff may specify in the bankruptcy restrictions order that subsection (9) of section 67 of this Act shall apply to the debtor during the period he is subject to the order as if he were a debtor within the meaning of subsection (10)(a) of that section.

(2) For the purposes of subsection (1) above, section 67(10) of this Act shall have effect as if, for paragraph (c) of that subsection, there were substituted—

'(c) the relevant information about the status of the debtor is the information that—

(i) he is subject to a bankruptcy restrictions order; or

(ii) where his estate has been sequestrated and he has not been discharged, that fact.'.]

### [56D  Timing of application for order

(1) An application for a bankruptcy restrictions order must be made, subject to subsection (2) below, within the period beginning with the date of sequestration and ending with the date on which the debtor's discharge becomes effective.

(2) An application may be made after the end of the period referred to in subsection (1) above only with the permission of the sheriff.]

### [56E  Duration of order and application for annulment

(1) A bankruptcy restrictions order—

(a) shall come into force when it is made; and

(b) shall cease to have effect at the end of the date specified in the order.

[(2) The date specified in a bankruptcy restrictions order under subsection (1)(b)—

(a) in the case of an order made by the Accountant in Bankruptcy—

(i) must not be before the end of the period of 2 years beginning with the date on which the order is made, but

(ii) must be before the end of the period of 5 years beginning with that date, and

(b) in the case of an order made by the sheriff must not be—

(i) before the end of the period of 5 years beginning with the date on which the order is made, or

(ii) after the end of the period of 15 years beginning with that date.]

(3) On an application by the debtor the [person mentioned in subsection (4)] may—

(a) annul a bankruptcy restrictions order; or

(b) vary such an order, including providing for such an order to cease to have effect at the end of a date earlier than the date specified in the order under subsection (1)(b) above.]

[(4) The person is—

(a) in the case of a bankruptcy restrictions order made by the Accountant in Bankruptcy, the Accountant in Bankruptcy, and

(b)   in the case of a bankruptcy restrictions order made by the sheriff, the sheriff.

(5)   If an application under subsection (3) is made to the Accountant in Bankruptcy, the Accountant in Bankruptcy must—

(a)   take into account any representations made by an interested person before the expiry of the period of 21 days beginning with the day on which the application is made, and

(b)   confirm, amend or revoke the decision before the expiry of the period of 28 days beginning with the day on which the application is made.

(6)   The debtor may appeal to the sheriff against any decision of the Accountant in Bankruptcy under subsection (5)(b) before the end of the period of 14 days beginning with the date of the decision.

(7)   The sheriff may—

(a)   in determining such an appeal, or

(b)   otherwise on an application by the Accountant in Bankruptcy,

make an order providing that the debtor may not make another application under subsection (3) for such period as may be specified in the order.]

## [56F   Interim bankruptcy restrictions order

[(1)   Subsection (2) applies at any time—

(a)   after the Accountant in Bankruptcy notifies the debtor under section 56A(3) that the Accountant in Bankruptcy proposes to make a bankruptcy restrictions order, and

(b)   before the Accountant in Bankruptcy decides whether to make the order.

(2)   The Accountant in Bankruptcy may make an interim bankruptcy restrictions order if the Accountant in Bankruptcy thinks that—

(a)   there are *prima facie* grounds to suggest that a bankruptcy restrictions order will be made, and

(b)   it is in the public interest to make an interim bankruptcy restrictions order.

(2A)   Subsection (2B) applies at any time between—

(a)   the making of an application to the sheriff for a bankruptcy restrictions order, and

(b)   the determination of the application.

(2B)   The sheriff may, on the application of the Accountant in Bankruptcy, make an interim bankruptcy restrictions order if the sheriff thinks that—

(a)   there are *prima facie* grounds to suggest that the application for the bankruptcy restrictions order will be successful, and

(b)   it is in the public interest to make an interim bankruptcy restrictions order.]

[. . .]

(4)   An interim order—

(a)   shall have the same effect as a bankruptcy restrictions order; and

(b)   shall come into force when it is made.

[(5)   An interim order ceases to have effect—

(a)   in the case of an interim order made by the Accountant in Bankruptcy, on the Accountant in Bankruptcy deciding whether or not to make a bankruptcy restrictions order,

(b)   in the case of an interim order made by the sheriff, on the determination of the application for the bankruptcy restrictions order, or

(c)   if the sheriff discharges the interim order, on the application of the Accountant in Bankruptcy or of the debtor.]

(6)   Where a bankruptcy restrictions order is made in respect of a debtor who is subject to an interim order, section 56E(2) of this Act shall have effect in relation to the bankruptcy restrictions order as if the reference to the date on which the order is made were a reference to the date on which the interim order was made.]

[. . .]

### [56] Effect of recall of sequestration

(1)   Where an award of sequestration of a debtor's estate is recalled under section 17(1) of this Act—

(a)   the sheriff may annul any bankruptcy restrictions order, [or interim bankruptcy restrictions order] which is in force in respect of the debtor [and];

(b)   no new bankruptcy restrictions order or interim order may be made in respect of the debtor;

[. . .]

(2)   Where the sheriff refuses to annul a bankruptcy restrictions order, [or interim bankruptcy restrictions order] under subsection (1)(a) above the debtor may, no later than 28 days after the date on which the award of sequestration is recalled, appeal to the sheriff principal against such a refusal.

(3)   The decision of the sheriff principal on an appeal under subsection (2) above is final.]

[(4)   Where an award of sequestration of a debtor's estate is recalled under section 17D(1) or 17E(6)—

(a)   the Accountant in Bankruptcy may annul any bankruptcy restrictions order or interim bankruptcy restrictions order which is in force in respect of the debtor, and

(b)   no new bankruptcy restrictions order or interim bankruptcy restrictions order may be made in respect of the debtor.

(5)   Where the Accountant in Bankruptcy refuses to annul a bankruptcy restrictions order or interim bankruptcy restrictions order under subsection (4) the debtor may apply to the Accountant in Bankruptcy for a review of such a refusal.

(6)   An application under subsection (5) must be made before the end of the period of 14 days beginning with the day on which the award of sequestration is recalled.

(7)   If an application under subsection (5) is made, the Accountant in Bankruptcy must—

(a)   take into account any representations made by an interested person before the expiry of the period of 21 days beginning with the day on which the application is made, and

(b)   confirm the refusal or annul the order before the expiry of the period of 28 days beginning with the day on which the application is made.

(8)   The debtor may appeal to the sheriff against any decision of the Accountant in Bankruptcy under subsection (7)(b) before the end of the period of 14 days beginning with the date of the decision.

(9)   The decision of the sheriff on an appeal under subsection (8) is final.]

[. . .]

*Discharge of [. . .] trustee*

### 57   Discharge of [. . .] trustee

(1)   After the [. . .] trustee has made a final division of the debtor's estate and has inserted his final audited accounts in the sederunt book, he—

[(a)   must pay to the Accountant in Bankruptcy any unclaimed dividends and unapplied balances,]

(b)   shall thereafter send to the Accountant in Bankruptcy the sederunt book [in the format specified by subsection (1A) and] a copy of the audited accounts [. . .]; and

(c)   may at the same time as sending the said documents apply to the Accountant in Bankruptcy for a certificate of discharge.

[(1A)   The trustee must send an electronic version of the sederunt book in such format as the Accountant in Bankruptcy may from time to time direct.]

[(1B) The Accountant in Bankruptcy must deposit any unclaimed dividends and any unapplied balances paid to the Accountant in Bankruptcy under subsection (1)(a) in an appropriate bank or institution.]

(2) The [. . .] trustee shall send notice of an application under subsection (1)(c) above to the debtor and to all the creditors known to the [. . .] trustee and shall inform the debtor and such creditors—

(a) that they may make written representations relating to the application to the Accountant in Bankruptcy within a period of 14 days after such notification;

(b) that the sederunt book is available for inspection [following a request made to the Accountant in Bankruptcy] and contains the audited accounts of, and scheme of division in, the sequestration; and

(c) of the effect mentioned in subsection (5) below.

(3) On the expiry of the period mentioned in subsection (2)(a) above, the Accountant in Bankruptcy, after examining the documents sent to him and considering any representations duly made to him, shall—

(a) grant or refuse to grant the certificate of discharge; and

(b) notify (in addition to the [. . .] trustee) the debtor and all creditors who have made such representations accordingly.

(4) The [. . .] trustee, the debtor or any creditor who has made representations under subsection (2)(a) above, may within 14 days after the issuing of the determination under subsection (3) above, appeal therefrom to the sheriff and if the sheriff determines that a certificate of discharge which has been refused should be granted he shall order the Accountant in Bankruptcy to grant it; and the sheriff clerk shall send a copy of the decree of the sheriff to the Accountant in Bankruptcy.

[(4A) The decision of the sheriff on an appeal under subsection (4) above shall be final.]

(5) The grant of a certificate of discharge under this section by the Accountant in Bankruptcy shall have the effect of discharging the [. . .] trustee from all liability (other than any liability arising from fraud) to the creditors or to the debtor in respect of any act or omission of the [. . .] trustee in exercising the functions conferred on him by this Act including, where he was also the interim trustee, the functions conferred on him as interim trustee.

(6) Where a certificate of discharge is granted under this section, the Accountant in Bankruptcy shall make an appropriate entry in the register of insolvencies and in the sederunt book.

(7) Where the [. . .] trustee has died, resigned office or been removed from office, the provisions of this section shall, subject to any necessary modifications, apply in relation to that [. . .] trustee or, if he has died, to his executor as they apply to a [. . .] trustee who has made a final division of the debtor's estate in accordance with the foregoing provisions of this Act.

[(8) This section does not apply in any case where the Accountant in Bankruptcy is the permanent trustee.]

## 58 Unclaimed dividends

(1) Any person, producing evidence of his right, may apply to the Accountant in Bankruptcy to receive a dividend deposited under section [57(1B)] [or 58A(3)] of this Act, if the application is made not later than 7 years after the date of such deposit.

(2) If the Accountant in Bankruptcy is satisfied of the applicant's right to the dividend, he shall authorise the appropriate bank or institution to pay to the applicant the amount of that dividend and of any interest which has accrued thereon.

(3) The Accountant in Bankruptcy shall, at the expiry of 7 years from the date of deposit of any unclaimed dividend or unapplied balance under section [57(1B)] [or 58A(3)] of this Act, hand over the deposit receipt or other voucher relating to such dividend or balance to the Secretary of State, who shall thereupon be entitled

to payment of the amount due, principal and interest, from the bank or institution
in which the deposit was made.

**[58A   Discharge of Accountant in Bankruptcy**
(1)   This section applies where the Accountant in Bankruptcy has acted as the
[. . .] trustee in any sequestration [including, where the Accountant in Bankruptcy
was the interim trustee, the functions of the interim trustee].
[. . .]
(3)   The Accountant in Bankruptcy shall deposit any unclaimed dividends and
any unapplied balances in an appropriate bank or institution.
(4)   The Accountant in Bankruptcy shall send to the debtor and to all creditors
known to him—
    (a)   a copy of [a determination of the Accountant in Bankruptcy's fees and
outlays calculated in accordance with regulations made under section 69A]; and
    (b)   a notice in writing stating—
      (i)   that the Accountant in Bankruptcy has commenced the procedure
under this Act leading to discharge in respect of his actings as [. . .] trustee;
      (ii)   that the sederunt book relating to the sequestration is available for
inspection [following a request made to the Accountant in Bankruptcy];
      [(iia)   that an application for a review may be made under subsection (4A)];
      (iii)   that an appeal may be made to the sheriff under subsection (5) below;
and
      (iv)   the effect of subsection (7) below.
[(4A)   The debtor or any creditor may apply to the Accountant in Bankruptcy
for a review of the discharge of the Accountant in Bankruptcy in respect of the
Accountant in Bankruptcy's actings as trustee.
(4B)   An application under subsection (4A) must be made before the expiry of
the period of 14 days beginning with the day on which notice is sent under subsection (4)(b).
(4C)   If an application under subsection (4A) is made, the Accountant in Bankruptcy must—
    (a)   take into account any representations made by an interested person
before the expiry of the period of 21 days beginning with the day on which the
application is made, and
    (b)   confirm or revoke the discharge before the expiry of the period of 28
days beginning with the day on which the application is made.]
[(5)   The debtor or any creditor may appeal to the sheriff against a decision by
the Accountant in Bankruptcy under subsection (4C)(b) before the expiry of the
period of 14 days beginning with the day on which the decision is made.]
[(6)   The decision of the sheriff on an appeal under subsection (5) is final.]
(7)   Where—
    (a)   the requirements of this section have been complied with; and
    (b)   no appeal to the sheriff is made under subsection (5) above or such an
appeal is made but is refused as regards the discharge of the Accountant in
Bankruptcy,
the Accountant in Bankruptcy shall be discharged from all liability (other than any
liability arising from fraud) to the creditors or to the debtor in respect of any act or
omission of the Accountant in Bankruptcy in exercising the functions of [. . .]
trustee in the sequestration.
[. . .]

**[58B   Assets discovered after trustee discharge: appointment of trustee**
(1)   This section applies where, after the trustee's discharge under section 57 or
58A but before the expiry of the period of 5 years from the date of sequestration,
the trustee or the Accountant in Bankruptcy becomes aware of any newly identified estate with a value of not less than £1000 (or such other sum as may be
prescribed).

(2)   In this section, 'newly identified estate' means any part of the debtor's estate which—

(a)   vested in the trustee in accordance with section 31 or 32, and

(b)   was not, before the trustee was discharged, known to the trustee.

(3)   The Accountant in Bankruptcy may—

(a)   in the case where the trustee was discharged under section 57—

(i)   on the application of the trustee who was discharged, reappoint that person as trustee on the debtor's estate, or

(ii)   appoint the Accountant in Bankruptcy as trustee on the debtor's estate,

(b)   in the case where the Accountant in Bankruptcy was discharged under section 58A, reappoint the Accountant in Bankruptcy as trustee on the debtor's estate.

(4)   The Accountant in Bankruptcy may make an appointment or reappointment under subsection (3) only if, in the opinion of the Accountant in Bankruptcy, the value of the newly identified estate is likely to exceed the costs of—

(a)   the appointment or reappointment, and

(b)   the recovery, management, realisation and distribution of the newly identified estate.

(5)   Where the trustee was discharged under section 57 and applies for re-appointment under subsection (3)(a)(i), the discharged trustee must provide to the Accountant in Bankruptcy the information mentioned in subsection (8)(a) to (c).

(6)   Where the trustee was discharged under section 57 and does not apply for reappointment under subsection (3)(a)(i), the discharged trustee must—

(a)   provide to the Accountant in Bankruptcy details of any newly identified estate that the discharged trustee becomes aware of, where that estate has a value which is not less than the value mentioned in subsection (1), and

(b)   if requested by the Accountant in Bankruptcy, provide to the Accountant in Bankruptcy the information mentioned in subsection (8)(b) and (c).

(7)   Where the Accountant in Bankruptcy was discharged under section 58A, the Accountant in Bankruptcy must record and consider the information mentioned in subsection (8).

(8)   The information is—

(a)   the estimated value of the newly identified estate,

(b)   the reason why the newly identified estate forms part of the debtor's estate,

(c)   the reason why the newly identified estate was not recovered,

(d)   the estimated outlays and remuneration of the trustee following an appointment or reappointment under subsection (3), and

(e)   the likely distribution under section 51 following an appointment or reappointment under subsection (3).

(9)   This section is without prejudice to any other right to take action following the discharge of the trustee.

## 58C   Assets discovered after trustee discharge: notice

(1)   The Accountant in Bankruptcy must notify the debtor and any other person the Accountant in Bankruptcy considers to have an interest—

(a)   where an application is made under section 58B(3)(a)(i), and

(b)   where the Accountant in Bankruptcy proposes to make an appointment or reappointment under section 58B(3)(a)(ii) or (b).

(2)   A notice under subsection (1) must inform the recipient that the person has a right to make representations to the Accountant in Bankruptcy in relation to the application or the proposed appointment or reappointment before the expiry of the period of 14 days beginning with the day on which the notice is given.

(3)   Before making an appointment or reappointment under section 58B, the Accountant in Bankruptcy must take into account any representations made by an interested person.

(4) If the Accountant in Bankruptcy makes an appointment or reappointment under section 58B, the Accountant in Bankruptcy must as soon as is practicable notify the debtor of the appointment or reappointment.

(5) A notice under subsection (4) must include information in relation to the debtor's duties to co-operate with the trustee under section 64.

**58D Assets discovered after trustee discharge: appeal**
Where the Accountant in Bankruptcy makes or refuses to make an order under section 58B, an interested person may, no later than 14 days after the date of the decision, appeal to the sheriff.]

*Voluntary trust deeds for creditors*

**59 Voluntary trust deeds for creditors**
Schedule 5 to this Act shall have effect in relation to trust deeds executed after the commencement of this section.

**[59A [Application for conversion to sequestration]**
(1) Where a member State liquidator proposes to [apply to the Accountant in Bankruptcy] for the conversion under Article 37 of the EC Regulation (conversion of earlier proceedings) of a protected trust deed into sequestration, an affidavit complying with section 59B of this Act must be prepared and sworn, and [submitted to the Accountant in Bankruptcy in support of the application].

(2) The [application] and the affidavit required under subsection (1) above shall be served upon—
    (a) the debtor;
    (b) the trustee;
    (c) such other person as may be prescribed.]

**[59B Contents of affidavit**
(1) The affidavit shall—
    (a) state that main proceedings have been opened in relation to the debtor in a member State other than the United Kingdom;
    (b) state that the member State liquidator believes that the conversion of the trust deed into a sequestration would prove to be in the interests of the creditors in the main proceedings;
    (c) contain such other information the member State liquidator considers will be of assistance to the [Accountant in Bankruptcy]—
        (i) in deciding whether to make an order under section 59C; and
        (ii) if the [Accountant in Bankruptcy] were to do so, in considering the need for any consequential provision that would be necessary or desirable; and
    (d) contain any other matters as may be prescribed.
(2) An affidavit under this section shall be sworn by, or on behalf of, the member State liquidator.]

**[59C [Power of Accountant in Bankruptcy]**
[(1) The Accountant in Bankruptcy may, after considering an application for conversion of a protected trust deed into a sequestration, make such order as the Accountant in Bankruptcy thinks fit.]

(2) If the [Accountant in Bankruptcy] makes an order for conversion into sequestration the order may contain all such consequential provisions as the [Accountant in Bankruptcy] deems necessary or desirable.

[(2A) The provisions of this Act shall apply to an order made by the [Accountant in Bankruptcy] under subsection (1) above as if it was a determination by the Accountant in Bankruptcy of a debtor application under section 12(1) of this Act and in relation to which the member State liquidator was a concurring creditor.]

(3) Where the [Accountant in Bankruptcy] makes an order for conversion into

sequestration under subsection (1) above, any expenses properly incurred as expenses of the administration of the trust deed in question shall be a first charge on the debtor's estate.]]

*Miscellaneous and supplementary*

## 60 Liabilities and rights of co-obligants

(1) Where a creditor has an obligant (in this section referred to as the 'co-obligant') bound to him along with the debtor for the whole or part of the debt, the co-obligant shall not be freed or discharged from his liability for the debt by reason of the discharge of the debtor or by virtue of the creditor's voting or drawing a dividend or assenting to, or not opposing—

(a)    the discharge of the debtor;

[. . .]

(2)   Where—

(a)    a creditor has had a claim accepted in whole or in part; and

(b)    a co-obligant holds a security over any part of the debtor's estate,

the co-obligant shall account to the [. . .] trustee so as to put the estate in the same position as if the co-obligant had paid the debt to the creditor and thereafter had had his claim accepted in whole or in part in the sequestration after deduction of the value of the security.

(3)   Without prejudice to any right under any rule of law of a co-obligant who has paid the debt, the co-obligant may require and obtain at his own expense from the creditor an assignation of the debt on payment of the amount thereof, and thereafter may in respect of that debt submit a claim, and vote and draw a dividend, if otherwise legally entitled to do so.

(4)   In this section a 'co-obligant' includes a cautioner.

## [60A Member State liquidator deemed creditor

For the purposes of this Act, and without prejudice to the generality of the right to participate referred to in paragraph 3 of Article 32 of the EC Regulation (exercise of creditors' rights) a member State liquidator appointed in relation to the debtor is deemed to be a creditor in the sum due to creditors in proceedings in relation to which he holds office.]

## [60B Trustee's duties concerning notices and copies of documents

(1)   This section applies where a member State liquidator has been appointed in relation to the debtor.

(2)   Where an interim [trustee or a] trustee is obliged to give notice to, or provide a copy of a document (including an order of court) to, the [sheriff] or the Accountant in Bankruptcy, the trustee shall [also] give notice or provide copies, as appropriate, to the member State liquidator.

(3)   Subsection (2) above is without prejudice to the generality of the obligations imposed by Article 31 of the EC Regulation (duty to co-operate and communicate information).]

## 61 Extortionate credit transactions

(1)   This section applies where the debtor is or has been a party to a transaction for, or involving, the provision to him of credit and his estate is sequestrated.

(2)   The [sheriff] may, on the application of the [. . .] trustee, make an order with respect to the transaction if the transaction is or was extortionate and was not entered into more than three years before the date of sequestration.

(3)   For the purposes of this section a transaction is extortionate if, having regard to the risk accepted by the person providing the credit—

(a)    the terms of it are or were such as to require grossly exorbitant payments to be made (whether unconditionally or in certain contingencies) in respect of the provision of the credit; or

(b)    it otherwise grossly contravened ordinary principles of fair dealing; and

it shall be presumed, unless the contrary is proved, that a transaction with
respect to which an application is made under this section is, or as the case may
be was, extortionate.

(4)   An order under this section with respect to any transaction may contain
such one or more of the following as the [sheriff] thinks fit—

(a)   provision setting aside the whole or part of any obligation created by the
transaction;

(b)   provision otherwise varying the terms of the transaction or varying the
terms on which any security for the purposes of the transaction is held;

(c)   provision requiring any person who is a party to the transaction to pay
to the [. . .] trustee any sums paid to that person, by virtue of the transaction, by
the debtor;

(d)   provision requiring any person to surrender to the [. . .] trustee any
property held by him as security for the purposes of the transaction;

(e)   provision directing accounts to be taken between any persons.

(5)   Any sums or property required to be paid or surrendered to the [. . .]
trustee in accordance with an order under this section shall vest in the [. . .]
trustee.

(6)   [. . .] But the powers conferred by this section shall be exercisable in relation to any transaction concurrently with any powers exercisable under this Act
in relation to that transaction as a gratuitous alienation or unfair preference.

(7)   In this section 'credit' has the same meaning as in the said Act of 1974.

## 62   Sederunt book and other documents

(1)   Subject to subsection (2) below, whoever by virtue of this Act for the time
being holds the sederunt book shall make it available for inspection at all
reasonable hours by any interested person.

(2)   As regards any case in which the person on whom a duty is imposed by
subsection (1) above is the Accountant in Bankruptcy, the [the Scottish Ministers
may by regulations]—

(a)   limit the period for which the duty is so imposed; and

(b)   prescribe conditions in accordance with which the duty shall be carried
out.

[(2A)   The trustee must insert in the sederunt book the information listed in
Schedule 3A to this Act.

(2B)   The Scottish Ministers may by regulations modify Schedule 3A.]

(3)   Any entry in the sederunt book shall be sufficient evidence of the facts
stated therein, except where it is founded on by the [. . .] trustee in his own
interest.

(4)   Notwithstanding any provision of this Act, the [. . .] trustee shall not be
bound to insert in the sederunt book any document of a confidential nature.

(5)   The [. . .] trustee shall not be bound to exhibit to any person other than a
commissioner or the Accountant in Bankruptcy any document in his possession of
a confidential nature.

(6)   An extract from the register of insolvencies bearing to be signed by the
Accountant in Bankruptcy shall be sufficient evidence of the facts stated therein.

## 63   [Power of court to cure defects in procedure]

(1)   The sheriff may, on the application of any person having an interest—

(a)   if there has been a failure to comply with any requirement of this Act or
any regulations made under it, make an order waiving any such failure and, so
far as practicable, restoring any person prejudiced by the failure to the position
he would have been in but for the failure;

(b)   if for any reason anything required or authorised to be done in, or in
connection with, the sequestration process cannot be done, make such order as
may be necessary to enable that thing to be done.

[(1A)  An order under subsection (1) may waive a failure to comply with a requirement mentioned in section 63A(1)(a) or (b) only if the failure relates to—

(a)  a document to be lodged with the sheriff,

(b)  a document issued by the sheriff, or

(c)  a time limit specified in relation to proceedings before the sheriff or a document relating to those proceedings.]

(2)  The sheriff, in an order under subsection (1) above, may impose such conditions, including conditions as to expenses, as he thinks fit and may—

(a)  authorise or dispense with the performance of any act in the sequestration process;

(b)  appoint as [. . .] trustee on the debtor's estate a person who would be eligible to be elected under section 24 of this Act, whether or not in place of an existing trustee;

(c)  extend or waive any time limit specified in or under this Act.

(3)  An application under subsection (1) above—

(a)  may at any time be remitted by the sheriff to the Court of Session, of his own accord or on an application by any person having an interest;

(b)  shall be so remitted, if the Court of Session so directs on an application by any such person,

if the sheriff or the Court of Session, as the case may be, considers that the remit is desirable because of the importance or complexity of the matters raised by the application.

[. . .]

### [63A  Power of Accountant in Bankruptcy to cure defects in procedure

(1)  The Accountant in Bankruptcy may make an order—

(a)  correcting a clerical or incidental error in a document required by or under this Act, or

(b)  waiving a failure to comply with a time limit—

(i)  which is specified by or under this Act, and

(ii)  for which no provision is made by or under this Act.

(2)  An order under subsection (1) may be made—

(a)  on the application of any person having an interest, or

(b)  without an application if the Accountant in Bankruptcy proposes to correct or waive a matter mentioned in subsection (1).

(3)  The applicant must notify all interested persons where an application is made under subsection (2)(a).

(4)  The Accountant in Bankruptcy must notify all interested persons where the Accountant in Bankruptcy proposes to make an order by virtue of subsection (2)(b).

(5)  A notice under subsection (3) or (4) must inform the recipient that the person has a right to make representations to the Accountant in Bankruptcy in relation to the application or the proposed order before the expiry of the period of 14 days beginning with the day on which the notice is given.

(6)  Before making an order under subsection (1), the Accountant in Bankruptcy must take into account any representations made by an interested person.

(7)  An order under subsection (1) may—

(a)  so far as practicable, restore any person prejudiced by the error or failure to the position that person would have been in but for the error or failure,

(b)  impose such conditions, including conditions as to expenses, as the Accountant in Bankruptcy thinks fit.

(8)  After making an order which affects a matter which is recorded in the Register of Inhibitions, the Accountant in Bankruptcy must without delay send a certified copy of the order to the Keeper of that register for recording in that register.

### 63B Decision under section 63A: review

(1)  An interested person may apply to the Accountant in Bankruptcy for a review of a decision of the Accountant in Bankruptcy to make, or refuse to make, an order under section 63A(1).

(2)  An application under subsection (1) must be made before the expiry of the period of 14 days beginning with the day of the decision.

(3)  If an application under subsection (1) is made, the Accountant in Bankruptcy must—

(a)  take into account any representations made by an interested person before the expiry of the period of 21 days beginning with the day on which the application is made, and

(b)  confirm, amend or revoke the decision before the expiry of the period of 28 days beginning with the day on which the application is made.

(4)  An interested person may appeal to the sheriff against a decision by the Accountant in Bankruptcy under subsection (3)(b) before the expiry of the period of 14 days beginning with the day of the decision.

(5)  The decision of the sheriff on an appeal under subsection (4) is final.]

### [63C Review of decisions by Accountant in Bankruptcy: grounds of appeal

(1)  For the avoidance of doubt, an appeal under a provision mentioned in subsection (2) may be made on—

(a)  a matter of fact,

(b)  a point of law, or

(c)  the merits.

(2)  The provisions are—

(a)  section 3A(7),

(b)  section 13A(11),

(c)  section 13B(7),

(d)  section 15(3D),

(e)  section 17G(5),

(f)  section 25A(8),

(g)  section 26A(5),

(h)  section 27(4),

(i)  section 28B(4),

(j)  section 29(4),

(k)  section 29(6H),

(l)  section 32C(5),

(m)  section 32H(5),

(n)  section 42(2D),

(o)  section 49(6D),

(p)  section 54B(6),

(q)  section 54G(6),

(r)  section 56J(8),

(s)  section 57(4),

(t)  section 58A(5),

(u)  section 63B(4),

(v)  paragraph 3(6) of Schedule 1.]

### 64 Debtor to co-operate with [. . .] trustee

(1)  The debtor shall take every practicable step, and in particular shall execute any document, which may be necessary to enable the [. . .] trustee to perform the functions conferred on him by this Act.

(2)  If the sheriff, on the application of the [. . .] trustee, is satisfied that the debtor has failed—

(a)  to execute any document in compliance with subsection (1) above, he may authorise the sheriff clerk to do so; and the execution of a document by the sheriff clerk under this paragraph shall have the like force and effect in all respects as if the document had been executed by the debtor;

(b)   to comply in any other respect with subsection (1) above, he may order the debtor to do so.

(3)   If the debtor fails to comply with an order of the sheriff under subsection (2) above, he shall be guilty of an offence.

(4)   In this section 'debtor' includes a debtor discharged under this Act.

(5)   A person convicted of an offence under subsection (3) above shall be liable—

(a)   on summary conviction, to a fine not exceeding the statutory maximum or—

(i)   to imprisonment for a term not exceeding 3 months; or

(ii)   if he has previously been convicted of an offence inferring dishonest appropriation of property or an attempt at such appropriation, to imprisonment for a term not exceeding 6 months,

or (in the case of either sub-paragraph) to both such fine and such imprisonment; or

(b)   on conviction on indictment to a fine or to imprisonment for a term not exceeding 2 years or to both.

### 65   Arbitration and compromise

(1)   The [. . .] trustee may (but if there are commissioners only with the consent of the commissioners, the creditors or the [sheriff])—

(a)   refer to arbitration any claim or question of whatever nature which may arise in the course of the sequestration; or

(b)   make a compromise with regard to any claim of whatever nature made against or on behalf of the sequestrated estate;

and the decree arbitral or compromise shall be binding on the creditors and the debtor.

(2)   Where any claim or question is referred to arbitration under this section, the Accountant in Bankruptcy may vary any time limit in respect of which any procedure under this Act has to be carried out.

[. . .]

### 66   Meetings of creditors and commissioners

Part I of Schedule 6 to this Act shall have effect in relation to meetings of creditors other than the statutory meeting; Part II of that Schedule shall have effect in relation to all meetings of creditors under this Act; and Part III of that Schedule shall have effect in relation to meetings of commissioners.

### 67   General offences by debtor etc

(1)   A debtor who during the relevant period makes a false statement in relation to his assets or his business or financial affairs to any creditor or to any person concerned in the administration of his estate shall be guilty of an offence, unless he shows that he neither knew nor had reason to believe that his statement was false.

(2)   A debtor, or other person acting in his interest whether with or without his authority, who during the relevant period destroys, damages, conceals [, disposes of] or removes from Scotland any part of the debtor's estate or any document relating to his assets or his business or financial affairs shall be guilty of an offence, unless the debtor or other person shows that he did not do so with intent to prejudice the creditors.

(3)   A debtor who is absent from Scotland and who after the date of sequestration of his estate fails, when required by the court, to come to Scotland for any purpose connected with the administration of his estate, shall be guilty of an offence.

(4)   A debtor, or other person acting in his interest whether with or without his authority, who during the relevant period falsifies any document relating to the

debtor's assets or his business or financial affairs, shall be guilty of an offence, unless the debtor or other person shows that he had no intention to mislead the [. . .] trustee, a commissioner or any creditor.

(5) If a debtor whose estate is sequestrated—

(a)    knows that a person has falsified any document relating to the debtor's assets or his business or financial affairs; and

(b)    fails, within one month of the date of acquiring such knowledge, to report his knowledge to the [. . .] trustee,

he shall be guilty of an offence.

(6)    A person who is absolutely insolvent and who during the relevant period transfers anything to another person for an inadequate consideration or grants any unfair preference to any of his creditors shall be guilty of an offence, unless the transferor or grantor shows that he did not do so with intent to prejudice the creditors.

(7)    A debtor who is engaged in trade or business shall be guilty of an offence if at any time in the period of one year ending with the date of sequestration of his estate, he pledges or disposes of, otherwise than in the ordinary course of his trade or business, any property which he has obtained on credit and has not paid for unless he shows that he did not intend to prejudice his creditors.

[. . .]

(9)    If a debtor, either alone or jointly with another person, obtains credit [—

(a)    to the extent of [£2000] (or such other sum as may be prescribed) or more; or

(b)    of any amount, where, at the time of obtaining credit, the debtor has debts amounting to £1,000 (or such other sum as may be prescribed) or more,]

without giving the person from whom he obtained it the relevant information about his status he shall be guilty of an offence.

[(9A)    For the purposes of calculating an amount of—

(a)    credit mentioned in subsection (9) above; or

(b)    debts mentioned in paragraph (b) of that subsection,

no account shall be taken of any credit obtained or, as the case may be, any liability for charges in respect of—

(i)    any of the supplies mentioned in section 70(4) of this Act; and

(ii)    any council tax within the meaning of section 99(1) of the Local Government Finance Act 1992 (c 14).]

(10)    For the purposes of subsection (9) above—

(a)    'debtor' means—

(i)    a debtor whose estate has been sequestrated,

(ii)    a person who has been adjudged bankrupt in England and Wales or Northern Ireland, [or

(iii)    a person subject to a bankruptcy restrictions order, or a bankruptcy restrictions undertaking, made in England or Wales,]

and who, in [the case mentioned in subparagraphs (i) or (ii) above], has not been discharged;

(b)    the reference to the debtor obtaining credit includes a reference to a case where goods are hired to him under a hire-purchase agreement or agreed to be sold to him under a conditional sale agreement; and

(c)    [the relevant information about the status of the debtor is the information that [—

(i)    his estate has been sequestrated and that he has not been discharged;

(ii)    he is an undischarged bankrupt in England and Wales or Northern Ireland; or

(iii)    he is subject to a bankruptcy restrictions order, or a bankruptcy restrictions undertaking, made in England or Wales, as the case may be.]

(11)    In this section—

(a)    'the relevant period' means the period commencing one year immediately before the date of sequestration of the debtor's estate and ending with his discharge;

(b)   references to intent to prejudice creditors shall include references to intent to prejudice an individual creditor.

[(11A)   A person shall be guilty of an offence under subsection (1), (2), (4), (5), (6) or (7) above if that person does or, as the case may be, fails to do, in any place in England and Wales or Northern Ireland, anything which would, if done or, as the case may be, not done in Scotland, be an offence under the subsection in question.]

(12)   A person convicted of any offence under this section shall be liable—

(a)   on summary conviction, to a fine not exceeding the statutory maximum or—

(i)   to imprisonment for a term not exceeding 3 months; or

(ii)   if he has previously been convicted of an offence inferring dishonest appropriation of property or an attempt at such appropriation, to imprisonment for a term not exceeding 6 months,

or (in the case of either sub-paragraph) to both such fine and such imprisonment; or

(b)   on conviction on indictment to a fine or—

(i)   in the case of an offence under subsection (1), (2), (4) or (7) above to imprisonment for a term not exceeding 5 years,

(ii)   in any other case to imprisonment for a term not exceeding 2 years,

or (in the case of either sub-paragraph) to both such fine and such imprisonment.

## 68   Summary proceedings

(1)   [Subject to subsection (1A) below] summary proceedings for an offence under this Act may be commenced at any time within the period of [12] months after the date on which evidence sufficient in the opinion of the Lord Advocate to justify the proceedings comes to his knowledge.

[(1A)   No such proceedings shall be commenced by virtue of this section more than three years after the commission of the offence.]

(2)   Subsection (3) of [section 136 of the Criminal Procedure (Scotland) Act 1995] (date of commencement of summary proceedings) shall have effect for the purposes of [this section] as it has effect for the purposes of that section.

(3)   For the purposes of subsection (1) above, a certificate of the Lord Advocate as to the date on which the evidence in question came to his knowledge is conclusive evidence of the date on which it did so.

## 69   [Outlays of insolvency practitioner in actings as interim trustee or trustee]

The Secretary of State may, by regulations, provide for the premium (or a proportionate part thereof) of any bond of caution or other security required, for the time being, to be given by an insolvency practitioner to be taken into account as part of the outlays of the insolvency practitioner in his actings as an interim trustee or [. . .] trustee.

## [69A   Fees for the Accountant in Bankruptcy

The Secretary of State may prescribe—

(a)   the fees and outlays to be payable to the Accountant in Bankruptcy in respect of the exercise of any of his functions under this Act [or the Insolvency Act 1986];

(b)   the time and manner in which such fees and outlays are to be paid; and

(c)   the circumstances, if any, in which the Accountant in Bankruptcy may allow exemption from payment or the remission or modification of payment of any fees or outlays payable or paid to him.]

## 70   Supplies by utilities

(1)   This section applies where on any day ('the relevant day')—

(a)   sequestration is awarded in a case where [a debtor application was made],

(b)    a warrant is granted under section 12(2) of this Act in a case where the petition was presented by a creditor or a trustee acting under a trust deed; or

(c)    the debtor grants a trust deed,

and in this section 'the office holder' means the interim trustee, the [. . .] trustee or the trustee acting under a trust deed, as the case may be.

(2)    If a request falling within subsection (3) below is made for the giving after the relevant day of any of the supplies mentioned in subsection (4) below, the supplier—

(a)    may make it a condition of the giving of the supply that the office holder personally guarantees the payment of any charges in respect of the supply; and

(b)    shall not make it a condition of the giving of the supply, or do anything which has the effect of making it a condition of the giving of the supply, that any outstanding charges in respect of a supply given to the debtor before the relevant day are paid.

(3)    A request falls within this subsection if it is made—

(a)    by or with the concurrence of the office holder; and

(b)    for the purposes of any business which is or has been carried on by or on behalf of the debtor.

(4)    The supplies referred to in subsection (2) above are—

(a)    a supply of gas by [a [gas supplier] within the meaning of Part I of the Gas Act 1986];

(b)    a supply of electricity by [an electricity supplier] within the meaning of Part I of the Electricity Act 1989;]

(c)    a supply of water by [Scottish Water];

[(d)    a supply of electronic communications services by a provider of a public communications service.

(5)    In subsection (4), 'communication services' do not include electronic communications services to the extent that they are used to broadcast or otherwise transmit programme services (within the meaning of the Communications Act 2003).]

[. . .]

#### [71A   Further duty of Accountant in Bankruptcy

The Accountant in Bankruptcy shall, on receiving any notice under section 109(1) of the Insolvency Act 1986 in relation to a community interest company, forward a copy of that notice to the Regulator of Community Interest Companies.]

#### [71B   Disqualification provisions: power to make orders

(1)    The Scottish Ministers may make an order under this section in relation to a disqualification provision.

(2)    A 'disqualification provision' is a provision made by or under any enactment which disqualifies (whether permanently or temporarily and whether absolutely or conditionally) a relevant debtor or a class of relevant debtors from—

(a)    being elected or appointed to an office or position;

(b)    holding an office or position; or

(c)    becoming or remaining a member of a body or group.

(3)    In subsection (2) above, the reference to a provision which disqualifies a person conditionally includes a reference to a provision which enables him to be dismissed.

(4)    An order under subsection (1) above may repeal or revoke the disqualification provision.

(5)    An order under subsection (1) above may amend, or modify the effect of, the disqualification provision—

(a)    so as to reduce the class of relevant debtors to whom the disqualification provision applies;

(b)   so as to extend the disqualification provision to some or all individuals who are subject to a bankruptcy restrictions order;

(c)   so that the disqualification provision applies only to some or all individuals who are subject to a bankruptcy restrictions order;

(d)   so as to make the application of the disqualification provision wholly or partly subject to the discretion of a specified person, body or group.

(6)   An order by virtue of subsection (5)(d) above may provide for a discretion to be subject to—

(a)   the approval of a specified person or body;

(b)   appeal to a specified person, body, court or tribunal.

(7)   The Scottish Ministers may be specified for the purposes of subsection (5)(d) or (6)(a) or (b) above.

(8)   In this section—

'bankruptcy restrictions order' includes—

[. . .]

(b)   a bankruptcy restrictions order made under paragraph 1 of Schedule 4A to the Insolvency Act 1986 (c 45); and

(c)   a bankruptcy restrictions undertaking entered into under paragraph 7 of that Schedule;

'relevant debtor' means a debtor—

(a)   whose estate has been sequestrated;

(b)   who has granted (or on whose behalf there has been granted) a trust deed;

(c)   who has been adjudged bankrupt by a court in England and Wales or in Northern Ireland; or

(d)   who, in England and Wales or in Northern Ireland, has made an agreement with his creditors for a composition in satisfaction of his debts or a scheme of arrangement of his affairs or for some other kind of settlement or arrangement.

(9)   An order under this section—

(a)   may make provision generally or for a specified purpose only;

(b)   may make different provision for different purposes; and

(c)   may make transitional, consequential or incidental provision.

(10)   An order under this section—

(a)   shall be made by statutory instrument; and

(b)   shall not be made unless a draft has been laid before and approved by a resolution of the Scottish Parliament.]

## [71C   Regulations: applications to Accountant in Bankruptcy etc

(1)   The Scottish Ministers may, by regulations, make provision in relation to the procedure to be followed in relation to—

(a)   an application to the Accountant in Bankruptcy under this Act,

(b)   an application to the Accountant in Bankruptcy for a review under this Act,

(c)   any other decision made by the Accountant in Bankruptcy under this Act.

(2)   In this section 'decision' includes any appointment, determination, direction, award, acceptance, rejection, adjudication, requirement, declaration, order or valuation made by the Accountant in Bankruptcy.

(3)   Regulations under subsection (1) may in particular make provision for or in connection with—

(a)   the procedure to be followed by the person making an application,

(b)   the form of any report or other document that may be required for the purposes of an application or a decision,

(c)   the form of a statement of undertakings that must be given by the debtor when making a debtor application,

(d)   time limits applying in relation to the procedure,

(e)   the procedure to be followed in connection with the production and recovery of documents relating to an application or a decision,

(f)   the procedure to be followed (including provision about those entitled to participate) in determining an application or making a decision, and

(g)   the procedure to be followed after an application is determined or a decision is made.

(4)   Regulations under subsection (1) may—

(a)   include such supplementary, incidental or consequential provision as the Scottish Ministers consider appropriate,

(b)   modify any enactment (including this Act).]

## 72   Regulations

[(1)   Subject to subsection (2) below] any power to make regulations under this Act shall be exercisable by statutory instrument subject to annulment in pursuance of a resolution of either House of Parliament [. . .].

[(1A)   Regulations under this Act may make different provision for different cases or classes of case.]

[(2)   No regulations such as are mentioned in subsection (3) below may be made unless a draft of the statutory instrument containing the regulations has been laid before, and approved by a resolution of, the Scottish Parliament.

(3)   The regulations are—

(a)   regulations made under—

(i)   subsection (2B)(a) and (4) of section 5;

[(ia)   section 5(2ZC),

(ib)   section 5(2ZD),]

[. . .]

[(iia)   section 5B(5);]

[(iib)   section 5C(2)(b),

(iic)   section 5D(1),

(iid)   section 32E(7),]

(iii)   section 39A(4)

[(iv)   section 71C(1) which contain provisions which add to, replace or omit any part of the text of an Act or an Act of the Scottish Parliament,

(v)   paragraph 2(7) of Schedule A1,]

of this Act; and

(b)   [. . .] regulations under paragraph 5 of Schedule 5 to this Act [. . .].]

## [72ZA   Modification of regulation making powers

Any power in any provision of this Act to make regulations may, insofar as that provision relates to a matter to which the EC Regulation applies, be exercised for the purpose of making provision in consequence of the EC Regulation.]

## [72A   Variation of references to time, money etc

For any reference in this Act to—

(a)   a period of time;

(b)   an amount of money; or

(c)   a fraction,

there shall be substituted a reference to such other period or, as the case may be, amount or fraction as may be prescribed.]

## 73   Interpretation

(1)   In this Act, unless the context otherwise requires—

'Accountant in Bankruptcy' shall be construed in accordance with section 1 of this Act;

'accounting period' shall be construed in accordance with section [52(2)] of this Act;

'act and warrant' means an act and warrant issued under section 25(2) of, or paragraph 2(2) of Schedule 2 to, this Act;

'apparent insolvency' and 'apparently insolvent' shall be construed in accordance with section 7 of this Act;

['appropriate bank or institution' means—

    (a)   the Bank of England,

    (b)   a person who has permission under Part 4 of the Financial Services and Markets Act 2000 to accept deposits,

    (c)   an EEA firm of the kind mentioned in paragraph 5(b) of Schedule 3 to that Act which has permission under paragraph 15 of that Schedule (as a result of qualifying for authorisation under paragraph 12 of that Schedule) to accept deposits, or

    (d)   a person who is exempt from the general prohibition in respect of accepting deposits as a result of an exemption order made under section 38(1) of that Act,

and the expressions in this definition must be read with section 22 of the Financial Services and Markets Act 2000, any relevant order under that section and Schedule 2 to that Act;]

'associate' shall be construed in accordance with section 74 of this Act;

['bankruptcy restrictions order' has the meaning given by section 56A(1) of this Act;

[. . .]

'business' means the carrying on of any activity, whether for profit or not;

['centre of main interests' has the same meaning as in the EC Regulation;]

'commissioner', except in the expression 'examining commissioner', shall be construed in accordance with section [4] of this Act;

['common financial tool' has the meaning given by section 5D(1),]

'court' means Court of Session or sheriff;

['creditor' includes a member State liquidator deemed to be a creditor under section 60A of this Act;]

['DAS register' has the meaning given by section 4A(4)(b),]

'date of sequestration' has the meaning assigned by section 12(4) of this Act;

'debtor' includes, without prejudice to the expression's generality, an entity whose estate may be sequestrated by virtue of section 6 of this Act, a deceased debtor or his executor or a person entitled to be appointed as executor to a deceased debtor;

['debtor application' means an application for sequestration made to the Accountant in Bankruptcy under sections 5(2)(a) [or (3)(a)] or 6(3)(a), (4)(a) or (6)(a) of this Act;]

['debtor contribution order' has the meaning given by section 32A(1),

'debtor's contribution' has the meaning given by section 5D(1),]

['the EC Regulation' means Council Regulation (EC) No 1346/2000 of 29th May 2000 on insolvency proceedings;

['enactment' includes an Act of the Scottish Parliament and any enactment comprised in subordinate legislation under such an Act;]

'establishment' has the meaning given by Article 2(h) of the EC Regulation;]

'examination' means a public examination under section 45 of this Act or a private examination under section 44 of this Act;

'examining commissioner' shall be construed in accordance with section 46(2) of this Act;

'interim trustee' shall be construed in accordance with section [2(5)] of this Act;

[. . .]

['main proceedings' means proceedings opened in accordance with Article 3(1) of the EC Regulation and falling within the definition of insolvency proceedings in Article 2(a) of the EC Regulation and—

(a)   in relation to England and Wales and Scotland, set out in Annex A to the EC Regulation under the heading 'United Kingdom'; and

(b)   in relation to another member State, set out in Annex A to the EC Regulation under the heading relating to that member State;

'member State liquidator' means a person falling within the definition of liquidator in Article 2(b) of the EC Regulation appointed in proceedings to which it applies in a member State other than the United Kingdom;]

['money adviser' has the meaning given by section 5C(2);]

'ordinary debt' shall be construed in accordance with section 51(1)(f) of this Act;

['original trustee' shall be construed in accordance with section 24(1)(a) of this Act;]

[. . .]

'postponed debt' has the meaning assigned by section 51(3) of this Act;

'preferred debt' has the meaning assigned by section 51(2) of this Act;

'prescribed' means prescribed by regulations made by the Secretary of State;

['protected trust deed' means a trust deed which has been granted protected status in accordance with regulations made under paragraph 5 of Schedule 5 to this Act;]

'qualified creditor' and 'qualified creditors' shall be construed in accordance with section 5(4) of this Act;

['qualified to act as an insolvency practitioner' is to be construed in accordance with section 390 of the Insolvency Act 1986;]

Provided that, until the coming into force of that section the expression shall instead mean satisfying such requirements (which, without prejudice to the generality of this definition, may include requirements as to the finding of caution) as may be prescribed for the purposes of this Act;

'register of insolvencies' has the meaning assigned by section [1A(1)(b)] of this Act;

'relevant person' has the meaning assigned by section 44(1)(b) of this Act;

['replacement trustee' shall be construed in accordance with section 24(1)(b) of this Act;]

['secondary proceedings' means proceedings opened in accordance with Articles 3(2) and 3(3) of the EC Regulation and falling within the definition of winding-up proceedings in Article 2(c) of the EC Regulation, and—

(a)   in relation to England and Wales and Scotland, set out in Annex B to the EC Regulation under the heading 'United Kingdom'; and

(b)   in relation to another member State, set out in Annex B to the EC Regulation under the heading relating to that member State;]

'secured creditor' means a creditor who holds a security for his debt over any part of the debtor's estate;

'security' means any security, heritable or moveable, or any right of lien, retention or preference;

'sederunt book' means the sederunt book maintained under section 3(1)(e) of this Act;

['sequestration proceedings' includes a debtor application and analogous expressions shall be construed accordingly;]

[. . .]

['statement of assets and liabilities' means a document (including a copy of a document) in such form as may be prescribed containing—

(i)   a list of the debtor's assets and liabilities;

(ii)   a list of his income and expenditure; and

(iii)   such other information as may be prescribed;]

['statement of undertakings' means the statement of debtor undertakings sent to the debtor under section 2(8) or, in the case of a debtor application, given by the debtor when making the application;]

'statutory meeting' has the meaning assigned by [section 20A] of this Act;

[. . .]

['temporary administrator' means a temporary administrator referred to by Article 38 of the EC Regulation; and

'territorial proceedings' means proceedings opened in accordance with Articles 3(2) and 3(4) of the EC Regulation and falling within the definition of insolvency proceedings in Article 2(a) of the EC Regulation, and—

    (a)   in relation to England and Wales and Scotland, set out in Annex A to the EC Regulation under the heading 'United Kingdom'; and

    (b)   in relation to another member State, set out in Annex A to the EC Regulation under the heading relating to that member State.]

'trust deed' has the meaning assigned by section 5(4A) of this Act;

['trustee' means trustee in the sequestration;

'trustee vote' shall be construed in accordance with section 24(1) of this Act;]

'unfair preference' means a preference created as is mentioned in subsection (1) of section 36 of this Act by a transaction to which subsection (4) of that section applies.

(2)   Any reference in this Act to a debtor being absolutely insolvent shall be construed as a reference to his liabilities being greater than his assets, and any reference to a debtor's estate being absolutely insolvent shall be construed accordingly.

(3)   Any reference in this Act to value of the creditors is, in relation to any matter, a reference to the value of their claims as accepted for the purposes of that matter.

(4)   Any reference in this Act to 'the creditors' in the context of their giving consent or doing any other thing shall, unless the context otherwise requires, be construed as a reference to the majority in value of such creditors as vote in that context at a meeting of creditors.

(5)   Any reference in this Act to any of the following acts by a creditor barring the effect of any enactment or rule of law relating to the limitation of actions in any part of the United Kingdom, namely—

    (a)   the presentation of a petition for sequestration;

    (b)   the concurrence in [a debtor application]; and

    (c)   the submission of a claim,

shall be construed as a reference to that act having the same effect, for the purposes of any such enactment or rule of law, as an effective acknowledgement of the creditor's claim; and any reference in this Act to any such enactment shall not include a reference to an enactment which implements or gives effect to any international agreement or obligation.

[(6)   Any reference in this Act, howsoever expressed, to the time when a petition for sequestration is presented shall be construed as a reference to the time when the petition is received by the [sheriff clerk].]

[(6A)   Any reference in this Act, howsoever expressed, to the time when a debtor application is made shall be construed as a reference to the time when the application is received by the Accountant in Bankruptcy.]

## 74  Meaning of 'associate'

(1)   Subject to subsection (7) below, for the purposes of this Act any question whether a person is an associate of another person shall be determined in accordance with the following provisions of this section (any reference, whether in those provisions or in regulations under the said subsection (7), to a person being an associate of another person being taken to be a reference to their being associates of each other).

(2)   A person is an associate of an individual if that person is the individual's [husband, wife or civil partner], or is a relative, or the [husband, wife or civil partner] of a relative, of the individual or of the individual's [husband, wife or civil partner].

(3)   A person is an associate of any person with whom he is in partnership, [and of any person who is an associate of any person with whom he is in partnership]; and a firm is an associate of any person who is a member of the firm.

(4)   For the purposes of this section a person is a relative of an individual if he is that individual's brother, sister, uncle, aunt, nephew, niece, lineal ancestor or lineal descendant treating—

(a)   any relationship of the half blood as a relationship of the whole blood and the stepchild or adopted child of any person as his child;

[. . .]

and references in this section to a [husband, wife or civil partner] include a former [husband, wife or civil partner] and a reputed [husband, wife or civil partner].

(5)   A person is an associate of any person whom he employs or by whom he is employed; and for the purposes of this subsection any director or other officer of a company shall be treated as employed by that company.

[(5A)   A company is an associate of another company—

(a)   if the same person has control of both, or a person has control of one and persons who are his associates, or he and persons who are his associates, have control of the other; or

(b)   if a group of two or more persons has control of each company, and the groups either consist of the same persons or could be regarded as consisting of the same persons by treating (in one or more cases) a member of either group as replaced by a person of whom he is an associate.

(5B)   A company is an associate of another person if that person has control of it or if that person and persons who are his associates together have control of it.

(5C)   For the purposes of this section a person shall be taken to have control of a company if—

(a)   the directors of the company or of another company which has control of it (or any of them) are accustomed to act in accordance with his directions or instructions; or

(b)   he is entitled to exercise, or control the exercise of, one third or more of the voting power at any general meeting of the company or of another company which has control of it,

and where two or more persons together satisfy either of the above conditions, they shall be taken to have control of the company.]

(6)   [In subsections (5), (5A), (5B) and (5C)] above, 'company' includes any body corporate (whether incorporated in Great Britain or elsewhere).

(7)   The Secretary of State may by regulations—

(a)   amend the foregoing provisions of this section so as to provide further categories of persons who, for the purposes of this Act, are to be associates of other persons; and

(b)   provide that any or all of subsections (2) to (6) above (or any subsection added by virtue of paragraph (a) above) shall cease to apply, whether in whole or in part, or shall apply subject to such modifications as he may specify in the regulations;

and he may in the regulations make such incidental or transitional provision as he considers appropriate.

**75**   [*Amendments, repeals and transitional provisions*]

## 76   Receipts and expenses

(1)   Any—

(a)   payments received by the Secretary of State under section 58(3) of this Act; or

(b)   amounts handed over to him in accordance with section 53 of this Act by virtue of the insertion provided for in paragraph 9 of Schedule 2 to this Act,

shall be paid by him into the Consolidated Fund.

(2)   There shall be paid out of moneys provided by Parliament—

(a) any amount of outlays and remuneration payable in accordance with section 53 of this Act by virtue of the insertion mentioned in subsection (1)(b) above;

(b) any administrative expenses incurred by the Secretary of State under this Act; and

(c) any increase attributable to this Act in the sums so payable under any other Act.

## 77 Crown application

The application of this Act to the Crown is to the Crown as creditor only.

## 78 Short title, commencement and extent

(1) This Act may be cited as the Bankruptcy (Scotland) Act 1985.

(2) This Act, except this section, shall come into force on such day as the Secretary of State may by order made by statutory instrument appoint; and different days may be so appointed for different purposes and for different provisions.

(3) An order under subsection (2) above may contain such transitional provisions and savings as appear to the Secretary of State necessary or expedient in connection with the provisions brought into force (whether wholly or partly) by the order.

(4) Without prejudice to section 75(3) to (5) of this Act, this Act applies to sequestrations as regards which the petition—

(a) is presented on or after the date of coming into force of section 5 of this Act; or

(b) was presented before, but in respect of which no award of sequestration has been made by, that date.

(5) This Act, except the provisions mentioned in subsection (6) below, extends to Scotland only.

(6) The provisions referred to in subsection (5) above are sections 8(5), 22(8) (including that subsection as applied by section 48(7)), 46, 55 and 73(5), paragraph 16(b) of Schedule 4 and paragraph 3 of Schedule 5.

## SCHEDULES

### [SCHEDULE A1
DEBTOR TO WHOM SECTION 5(2ZA) APPLIES: APPLICATION OF ACT
*(introduced by section 5(2ZE))*

*Modification of certain provisions of Act*

1—(1) Where section 5(2ZA) applies in relation to a debtor, this Act applies subject to the modifications mentioned in sub-paragraphs (2) to (6).

(2) Section 3(1) applies as if paragraphs (e) and (f) were omitted.

(3) Section 20 applies as if for subsection (1) there were substituted—

'(1) This section applies where the Accountant in Bankruptcy receives by virtue of section 5(6A) the statement of assets and liabilities in relation to a debtor to whom section 5(2ZA) applies.

(1A) As soon as practicable, the Accountant in Bankruptcy must prepare a statement of the debtor's affairs so far as within the knowledge of the Accountant in Bankruptcy stating that, because section 5(2ZA) applies to the debtor, no claims may be submitted by creditors under section 22 or 48.

(1B) The Accountant in Bankruptcy must send a copy of the statement prepared under subsection (1A) to every known creditor of the debtor.'.

(4) Section 43A applies as if for subsection (2) there were substituted—

'(2) The Accountant in Bankruptcy may at any time before the discharge of

the debtor require the debtor to give an account in writing, in such form as
may be prescribed, of the debtor's current state of affairs.'.
(5)  Section 58A applies as if—
  (a)  subsections (3) to (4C) and (7)(a) were omitted, and
  (b)  for subsection (5) there were substituted—
    '(5)  The debtor or any creditor may, before the expiry of the period of
    14 days beginning with the day on which the debtor is discharged under
    section 54C(1), appeal to the sheriff against the discharge of the Accoun-
    tant in Bankruptcy in respect of the Accountant in Bankruptcy's actings
    as trustee.'.
(6)  Sections 21A, 22, 23, 24, 25, 26 to 27, 48, 52 and 62(2A) do not apply.

*Accountant in Bankruptcy's duty to consider whether paragraph 1 should cease to apply*

2—(1)  This paragraph applies where paragraph 1 applies in relation to a
debtor.
(2)  If the Accountant in Bankruptcy considers that the circumstances mentioned in any of sub-paragraphs (3) to (6) apply in relation to the debtor, the
Accountant in Bankruptcy must consider whether paragraph 1 should cease to
apply in relation to the debtor.
(3)  The circumstances are—
  (a)  the Accountant in Bankruptcy becomes aware that the debtor application
submitted under section 5 contains an error, and
  (b)  the nature of the error is such that the debtor was not at that time a
debtor to whom section 5(2ZA) applies.
(4)  The circumstances are—
  (a)  the Accountant in Bankruptcy becomes aware that the debtor application
submitted under section 5 deliberately misrepresents or fails to state a fact that
was the case at the time of the application, and
  (b)  the nature of the misrepresentation or the omission of the fact is such
that the debtor was not at that time a debtor to whom section 5(2ZA) applies.
(5)  The circumstances are that, at any time after the date on which the debtor
application is made—
  (a)  the total value of the debtor's assets (leaving out of account any liabilities
and any assets that would not vest in a trustee under section 33(1)) exceeds
£5000 (or such other amount as may be prescribed), or
  (b)  the Accountant in Bankruptcy assesses the debtor under the common
financial tool as being able to make a contribution.
(6)  The circumstances are that, at any time after the date of sequestration—
  (a)  the Accountant in Bankruptcy is not satisfied that the debtor has co-
operated with the trustee, and
  (b)  the Accountant in Bankruptcy considers that it would be of financial
benefit to the estate of the debtor and in the interests of the creditors if
paragraph 1 were to cease to have effect.
(7)  The Scottish Ministers may by regulations modify this paragraph—
  (a)  by modifying the circumstances in which paragraph 1 ceases to have
effect,
  (b)  in consequence of any modification made under paragraph (a).

*Procedure where Accountant in Bankruptcy considers paragraph 1 should cease to apply*

3—(1)  If the Accountant in Bankruptcy considers under paragraph 2(2) that
paragraph 1 should cease to apply in relation to a debtor, the Accountant in
Bankruptcy must notify the debtor of that fact and the matters mentioned in
sub-paragraph (2).
(2)  The matters are—

(a) the circumstances mentioned in paragraph 2 which the Accountant in Bankruptcy considers apply in relation to the debtor, and

(b) that the debtor may make representations to the Accountant in Bankruptcy within the period of 14 days beginning with the giving of notification under sub-paragraph (1).

(3) On the expiry of the period mentioned in sub-paragraph (2)(b) and after having taken into account any representations made by the debtor under that sub-paragraph, the Accountant in Bankruptcy must decide whether paragraph 1 should cease to apply in relation to the debtor.

(4) If the Accountant in Bankruptcy decides that paragraph 1 should cease to apply in relation to the debtor, the Accountant in Bankruptcy must, as soon as practicable after reaching that decision, give notice in writing to the debtor of the decision and the effect of it.

### Debtor's right of appeal against decision under paragraph 3

4—(1) This paragraph applies where the Accountant in Bankruptcy gives notice to a debtor under paragraph 3(4).

(2) The debtor may appeal to the sheriff against the decision.

(3) An appeal must be lodged not later than 14 days after the day on which notice is given.

(4) If the sheriff grants the appeal, paragraph 1 continues to apply in relation to the debtor.

(5) If the sheriff refuses the appeal or if it is abandoned or withdrawn, paragraph 1 ceases to apply in relation to the debtor.

### Decision that paragraph 1 ceases to have effect: modification of certain provisions of Act

5—(1) Where paragraph 1 ceases to have effect in relation to a debtor, this Act applies subject to sub-paragraphs (2) to (4).

(2) The debtor must send to the trustee a statement of assets and liabilities—

(a) where no appeal is taken under paragraph 4, before the expiry of the period of 7 days beginning with the expiry of the period during which an appeal may be made under that paragraph,

(b) where an appeal is refused or, as the case may be, abandoned or withdrawn, before the expiry of the period of 7 days beginning with the day on which notice is given of the outcome of the appeal or, as the case may be, its abandonment or withdrawal.

(3) Section 21A applies as if in subsection (2), for 'sequestration is awarded' there were substituted ' paragraph 1 of Schedule A1 ceases to have effect in relation to the debtor '.

(4) Section 43A applies as if for subsection (2) there were substituted—

'(2) The trustee must require the debtor to give an account in writing, in such form as may be prescribed, of the debtor's current state of affairs—

(a) before the expiry of the period of 60 days beginning with the day on which paragraph 1 of Schedule A1 ceases to have effect in relation to the debtor,

(b) on the expiry of the period of 6 months beginning with the day on which the account is given under paragraph (a), and

(c) on the expiry of each subsequent period of 6 months.']

SCHEDULE 1

DETERMINATION OF AMOUNT OF CREDITOR'S CLAIM

Sections 5(5) and 22(9)

*Amount which may be claimed generally*

1—(1)  Subject to the provisions of this Schedule, the amount in respect of which a creditor shall be entitled to claim shall be the accumulated sum of principal and any interest which is due on the debt as at the date of sequestration.

(2)  If a debt does not depend on a contingency but would not be payable but for the sequestration until after the date of sequestration, the amount of the claim shall be calculated as if the debt were payable on the date of sequestration but subject to the deduction of interest at the rate specified in section 51(7) of this Act from the said date until the date for payment of the debt.

(3)  In calculating the amount of his claim, a creditor shall deduct any discount (other than any discount for payment in cash) which is allowable by contract or course of dealing between the creditor and the debtor or by the usage of trade.

*Claims for aliment and periodical allowance on divorce*

2—(1)  A person entitled to aliment, however arising, from a living debtor as at the date of sequestration, or from a deceased debtor immediately before his death, shall not be entitled to include in the amount of his claim—

(a)  any unpaid aliment for any period before the date of sequestration unless the amount of the aliment has been quantified by court decree or by any legally binding obligation which is supported by evidence in writing, and,

[(i)] in the case of spouses (or, where the aliment is payable to a divorced person in respect of a child, former spouses) [, or]

[(ii) in the case of civil partners (or, where the aliment is payable to a former civil partner in respect of a child after dissolution of a civil partnership, former civil partners),]

they were living apart during that period;

(b)  any aliment for any period after the date of sequestration.

(2)  Sub-paragraph (1) above shall apply to a periodical allowance payable on divorce [or on dissolution of a civil partnership]—

(a)  by virtue of a court order; or

(b)  under any legally binding obligation which is supported by evidence in writing,

as it applies to aliment and as if for the words from 'in the case' [, where they first occur] to 'they' there were substituted the words 'the payer and payee'.

*Debts depending on contingency*

3—(1)  Subject to sub-paragraph (2) below, the amount which a creditor shall be entitled to claim shall not include a debt in so far as its existence or amount depends upon a contingency.

(2)  On an application by the creditor—

(a)  to the [. . .] trustee; or

(b)  if there is no [. . .] trustee, to the [Accountant in Bankruptcy],

the [. . .] trustee or [Accountant in Bankruptcy] shall put a value on the debt in so far as it is contingent, and the amount in respect of which the creditor shall then be entitled to claim shall be that value but no more; and, where the contingent debt is an annuity, a cautioner may not then be sued for more than that value.

[(3) An interested person may apply to the Accountant in Bankruptcy for a review of a valuation under sub-paragraph (2) by the trustee.

(4) An application under sub-paragraph (3) must be made before the expiry of the period of 14 days beginning with the day of the valuation.

(5) If an application under subsection (3) is made, the Accountant in Bankruptcy must—

(a) take into account any representations made by an interested person before the expiry of the period of 21 days beginning with the day on which the application is made, and

(b) confirm or vary the valuation before the expiry of the period of 28 days beginning with the day on which the application is made.

(6) An interested person may appeal to the sheriff against a decision by the Accountant in Bankruptcy under subsection (5)(b) before the expiry of the period of 14 days beginning with the day of the decision.

(7) The Accountant in Bankruptcy may refer a case to the sheriff for a direction before making a decision under sub-paragraph (5)(b).

(8) An appeal to the sheriff under sub-paragraph (6) may not be made in relation to a matter on which the Accountant in Bankruptcy has applied to the sheriff for a direction under sub-paragraph (7).]

*[. . .]*

### Secured debts

5—(1) In calculating the amount of his claim, a secured creditor shall deduct the value of any security as estimated by him:

Provided that if he surrenders, or undertakes in writing to surrender, a security for the benefit of the debtor's estate, he shall not be required to make a deduction of the value of that security.

(2) The [. . .] trustee may, at any time after the expiry of 12 weeks from the date of sequestration, require a secured creditor at the expense of the debtor's estate to discharge the security or convey or assign it to the [. . .] trustee on payment to the creditor of the value specified by the creditor; and the amount in respect of which the creditor shall then be entitled to claim shall be any balance of his debt remaining after receipt of such payment.

(3) In calculating the amount of his claim, a creditor whose security has been realised shall deduct the amount (less the expenses of realisation) which he has received, or is entitled to receive, from the realisation.

### Valuation of claims against partners for debts of the partnership

6 Where a creditor claims in respect of a debt of a partnership, against the estate of one of its partners, the creditor shall estimate the value of—

(a) the debt to the creditor from the firm's estate where that estate has not been sequestrated; or

(b) the creditor's claim against that estate where it has been sequestrated, and deduct that value from his claim against the partner's estate; and the amount in respect of which he shall be entitled to claim on the partner's estate shall be the balance remaining after that deduction has been made.

[. . .]

SCHEDULE 3
PREFERRED DEBTS

Section 51

PART I
LIST OF PREFERRED DEBTS

[. . .]

*Contributions to occupational pension schemes, etc*

4   Any sum which is owed by the debtor and is a sum to which [Schedule 4 to the Pensions Schemes Act 1993] (contributions to occupational pension scheme and state scheme premiums) applies.

*Remuneration of employees, etc*

5—(1)   So much of any amount which—
    (a)   is owed by the debtor to a person who is or has been an employee of the debtor, and
    (b)   is payable by way of remuneration in respect of the whole or any part of the period of four months next before the relevant date,
as does not exceed the prescribed amount.
(2)   An amount owed by way of accrued holiday remuneration, in respect of any period of employment before the relevant date, to a person whose employment by the debtor has been terminated, whether before, on or after that date.
(3)   So much of any sum owed in respect of money advanced for the purpose as has been applied for the payment of a debt which, if it had not been paid, would have been a debt falling within sub-paragraph (1) or (2) above.

6   So much of any amount which—
    (a)   is ordered, whether before or after the relevant date, to be paid by the debtor under the Reserve Forces (Safeguard of Employment) Act 1985; and
    (b)   is so ordered in respect of a default made by the debtor before that date in the discharge of his obligations under that Act,
as does not exceed such amount as may be prescribed.

*Levies on coal and steel production*

[6A   Any sums due at the relevant date from the debtor in respect of—
    (a)   the levies on the production of coal and steel referred to in Articles 49 and 50 of the ECSC Treaty, or
    (b)   any surcharge for delay provided for in Article 50(3) of that Treaty and Article 6 of Decision 3/52 of the High Authority of the Coal and Steel Community.]

*[Debts owed to the Financial Services Compensation Scheme*

6AA Any debt owed by the debtor to the scheme manager of the Financial Services Compensation Scheme under section 215(2A) of the Financial Services and Markets Act 2000.]

*[Deposits covered by Financial Services Compensation Scheme*

6B   So much of any amount owed at the relevant date by the debtor in respect of an eligible deposit as does not exceed the compensation that would be payable in respect of the deposit under the Financial Services Compensation Scheme to the person or persons to whom the amount is owed.]

*[Other deposits*

6C   So much of any amount owed at the relevant date by the debtor to one or more eligible persons in respect of an eligible deposit as exceeds any compensation that would be payable in respect of the deposit under the Financial Services Compensation Scheme to that person or those persons.

6D   An amount owed at the relevant date by the debtor to one or more eligible persons in respect of a deposit that—

(a)   was made through a non-EEA branch of a credit institution authorised by the competent authority of an EEA state, and

(b)   would have been an eligible deposit if it had been made through an EEA branch of that credit institution.]

## PART II
## INTERPRETATION OF PART I

*Meaning of 'the relevant date'*

7   In Part I of this Schedule 'the relevant date' means—

(a)   in relation to a debtor (other than a deceased debtor), the date of sequestration; and

(b)   in relation to a deceased debtor, the date of his death.

[. . .]

[8D—(1)   For the purpose of paragraph 2(1D) of Part 1 of this Schedule—

(a)   where the whole of the accounting period to which any aggregates levy is attributable falls within the period of six months next before the relevant date ('the relevant period'), the whole amount of that levy shall be referable to the relevant period; and

(b)   in any other case the amount of any aggregates levy which shall be referable to the relevant period shall be the proportion of the levy which is equal to such proportion (if any) of the accounting period in question as falls within the relevant period.

(2)   In sub-paragraph (1) above 'accounting period' shall be construed in accordance with Part 2 of the Finance Act 2001.]

*Amounts payable by way of remuneration*

9—(1)   For the purposes of paragraph 5 of Part I of this Schedule a sum is payable by the debtor to a person by way of remuneration in respect of any period if—

(a)   it is paid as wages or salary (whether payable for time or for piece work or earned wholly or partly by way of commission) in respect of services rendered to the debtor in that period; or

(b)   it is an amount falling within sub-paragraph (2) below and is payable by the debtor in respect of that period.

(2)   An amount falls within this sub-paragraph if it is—

(a)   a guarantee payment under section 12(1) of the Employment Protection (Consolidation) Act 1978 (employee without work to do for a day or part of a day),

(b)   remuneration on suspension on medical grounds under section 19 of that Act,

(c)   any payment for the time off under section 27(3) (trade-union duties), 31(3) (looking for work, etc) or 31A(4) (ante-natal care) of that Act,

(d)   [. . .]

(e)   remuneration under a protective award made by an [employment tribunal] under section 101 of the Employment Protection Act 1975 (redundancy dismissal with compensation).

(3)   For the purposes of paragraph 5(2) of Part I of this Schedule, holiday remuneration shall be deemed, in the case of a person whose employment has been terminated by or in consequence of the award of sequestration of his employer's estate, to have accrued to that person in respect of any period of employment if, by virtue of that person's contract of employment or of any enactment (including an order made or direction given under any enactment), that remuneration would have accrued in respect of that period if that person's employment had continued until he became entitled to be allowed the holiday.

(4)   Without prejudice to the preceding provisions of this paragraph—

(a)   any remuneration payable by the debtor to a person in respect of a period of holiday or of absence from work through sickness or other good cause is deemed to be wages or, as the case may be, salary in respect of services rendered to the debtor in that period; and

(b)   references in this paragraph to remuneration in respect of a period of holiday include references to any sums which, if they had been paid, would have been treated for the purposes of the enactments relating to social services as earnings in respect of that period.


*[Meaning of scheme manager*

[9ZA   In paragraph 6AA 'the scheme manager' has the meaning given in section 212(1) of the Financial Services and Markets Act 2000.]]


*[Meaning of eligible deposit*

9A—(1)   In [paragraphs 6B to 6D] 'eligible deposit' means a deposit in respect of which the person, or any of the persons, to whom it is owed would be eligible for compensation under the Financial Services Compensation Scheme.

(2)   For [the purposes of those paragraphs and this paragraph] a 'deposit' means rights of the kind described in paragraph 22 of Schedule 2 to the Financial Services and Markets Act 2000 (deposits).]

[(3)   In paragraphs 6C and 6D, 'eligible person' means—

(a)   an individual, or

(b)   a micro-enterprise, a small enterprise or a medium-sized enterprise, each of those terms having the meaning given in Article 2.1(107) of the Directive 2014/59/EU of 15th May 2014 establishing a framework for the recovery and resolution of credit institutions and investment firms.

(4)   In paragraph 6D—

(a)   'credit institution' has the meaning given in Article 4.1(1) of the capital requirements regulation;

(b)   'EEA branch' means a branch, as defined in Article 4.1(17) of the capital requirements regulation, which is established in an EEA state;

(c)   'non-EEA branch' means a branch, as so defined, which is established in a country which is not an EEA state;

and for this purpose 'the capital requirements regulation' means Regulation (EU) No 575/2013 of the European Parliament and of the Council of 26th June 2013 on prudential requirements for credit institutions and investment firms and amending Regulation (EU) No 648/2012.]

*Transitional provisions*

10   Regulations under paragraph 5 or 6 of Part I of this Schedule may contain such transitional provisions as may appear to the Secretary of State necessary or expedient.


## SCHEDULE 3A

*[Contains information to be included in the Sederunt Book]*


[. . .]

## SCHEDULE 5
## VOLUNTARY TRUST DEEDS FOR CREDITORS

Section 59

*Remuneration of trustee*

1   Whether or not provision is made in the trust deed for auditing the trustee's accounts and for determining the method of fixing the trustee's remuneration or whether or not the trustee and the creditors have agreed on such auditing and the method of fixing the remuneration, the debtor, the trustee or any creditor may, at any time before the final distribution of the debtor's estate among the creditors, have the trustee's accounts audited by and his remuneration fixed by the Accountant in Bankruptcy.

*[Accountant in Bankruptcy's power to carry out audit]*

[1A   The Accountant in Bankruptcy may, at any time, audit the trustee's accounts and fix his remuneration.]

*Registration of notice of inhibition*

2—(1)   The trustee, from time to time after the trust deed has been delivered to him, may cause a notice in such form as shall be prescribed by the Court of Session by act of sederunt to be recorded in the register of inhibitions and adjudications; and such recording shall have the same effect as the recording in that register of letters of inhibition against the debtor.

(2)   The trustee, after the debtor's estate has been finally distributed among his creditors or the trust deed has otherwise ceased to be operative, shall cause to be so recorded a notice in such form as shall be prescribed as aforesaid recalling the notice recorded under sub-paragraph (1) above.

*Lodging of claim to bar effect of limitation of actions*

3   The submission of a claim by a creditor to the trustee acting under a trust deed shall bar the effect of any enactment or rule of law relating to limitation of actions in any part of the United Kingdom.

*Valuation of claims*

4   Unless the trust deed otherwise provides, Schedule 1 to this Act shall apply in relation to a trust deed as it applies in relation to a sequestration but subject to the following modifications—

(a)   in paragraphs 1, 2 and 5 for the word 'sequestration' wherever it occurs there shall be substituted the words 'granting of the trust deed';

(b)   in paragraph 3—
    (i)   in sub-paragraph (2), for the words from the beginning of paragraph
(a) to 'or sheriff' there shall be substituted the words 'the trustee'; and
        [. . .]

### Protected trust deeds

[5—(1)   The Scottish Ministers may by regulations make provision as to—
    (a)   the conditions which require to be fulfilled in order for a trust deed to be
granted the status of a protected trust deed;
    (b)   the consequences of a trust deed being granted that status;
    (c)   the rights of any creditor who does not accede to a trust deed which is
granted protected status;
    (d)   the extent to which a debtor may be discharged, by virtue of a protected
trust deed, from his liabilities or from such liabilities or class of liabilities as may
be prescribed in the regulations;
    (e)   the circumstances in which a debtor may bring to an end the operation
of a trust deed in respect of which the conditions provided for under sub-
paragraph (a) above are not fulfilled;
    (f)   the administration of the trust under a protected trust deed (including
provision about the remuneration payable to the trustee).
(2)   Regulations under this paragraph may—
    (a)   make provision enabling applications to be made to the court;
    [. . .]
    (b)   contain such amendments of this Act as appear to the Scottish Ministers
to be necessary in consequence of any other provision of the regulations.]

## SCHEDULE 7

## PART II
## RE-ENACTMENT OF CERTAIN PROVISIONS OF BANKRUPTCY (SCOTLAND)
## ACT 1913 (c 20)

### Arrestments and poindings

24—(1)   Subject to sub-paragraph (2) below, all arrestments and [attachments]
which have been executed within 60 days prior to the constitution of the apparent
insolvency of the debtor, or within four months thereafter, shall be ranked *pari
passu* as if they had all been executed on the same date.
    (2)   Any such arrestment which is executed on the dependence of an action
shall be followed up without undue delay.
    (3)   Any creditor judicially producing in a process relative to the subject of such
arrestment or [attachment] liquid grounds of debt or decree of payment within the
60 days or four months referred to in sub-paragraph (1) above shall be entitled to
rank as if he had executed an arrestment or [an attachment]; and if [in the meantime the first or any subsequent arrester obtains] a decree of furthcoming, and
recovers payment, or [an attaching] creditor carries through [an auction] [or
receives payment in respect of [an attached] article upon its redemption], he shall
be accountable for the sum recovered to those who, by virtue of this Act, may be
eventually found to have a right to a ranking *pari passu* thereon, and shall be liable
in an action at their instance for payment to them proportionately, after allowing
out of the fund the expense of such recovery.
    (4)   Arrestments executed for attaching the same effects of the debtor after the
period of four months subsequent to the constitution of his apparent insolvency
shall not compete with those within the said periods prior or subsequent thereto,

but may rank with each other on any reversion of the fund attached in accordance with any enactment or rule of law relating thereto.

(5) Any reference in the foregoing provisions of this paragraph to a debtor shall be construed as including a reference to any entity whose apparent insolvency may, by virtue of subsection [(4)] of section 7 of this Act, be constituted under subsection (1) of that section.

(6) This paragraph shall apply in respect of arrestments and poindings which have been executed either before or after the coming into force of this paragraph.

(7) The repeal of the Bankruptcy (Scotland) Act 1913 shall not affect the equalisation of arrestments and poindings (whether executed before or after the coming into force of this paragraph) in consequence of the constitution of notour bankruptcy under that Act.

[(8) Nothing in this paragraph shall apply to an earnings arrestment, a current maintenance arrestment or a conjoined arrestment order.]

*Exemptions from stamp duty or other duties for conveyances, deeds etc relating to sequestrated estates*

25 Any—

(a) conveyance, assignation, instrument, discharge, writing, or deed relating solely to the estate of a debtor which has been or may be sequestrated, either under this or any former Act, being estate which after the execution of such conveyance, assignation, instrument, discharge, writing, or deed, shall be and remain the property of such debtor, for the benefit of his creditors, or the [. . .] trustee appointed or chosen under or by virtue of such sequestration,

(b) discharge to such debtor,

(c) deed, assignation, instrument, or writing for reinvesting the debtor in the estate,

(d) article of roup or sale, or submission,

(e) other instrument or writing whatsoever relating solely to the estate of any such debtor; and

(f) other deed or writing forming part of the proceedings ordered under such sequestration,

shall be exempt from all stamp duties or other Government duty.

## DEBTORS (SCOTLAND) ACT 1987
### (1987, c 18)

## PART I
### EXTENSION OF TIME TO PAY DEBTS

*Time to pay directions on granting decree*

**1 Time to pay directions**

(1) Subject to subsections (3) to (5) below and to section 14 of this Act, [on an application by the debtor,] the court, on granting decree for payment of any principal sum of money [shall, if satisfied that it is reasonable in all the circumstances to do so, and having regard in particular to the matters mentioned in subsection (1A) below,] direct that any sum decerned for in the decree (including any interest claimed in pursuance of subsections (6) and (7) below) or any expenses in relation to which the decree contains a finding as to liability or both such sum and such expenses shall be paid—

(a) by such instalments, commencing at such time after the date of intimation by the creditor to the debtor of an extract of the decree containing the direction, payable at such intervals; or

(b)   as a lump sum at the end of such period following intimation as
mentioned in paragraph (a) above,
as the court may specify in the direction.

[(1A)   The matters referred to in subsection (1) above are—
(a)   the nature of and reasons for the debt in relation to which decree is
granted;
(b)   any action taken by the creditor to assist the debtor in paying that debt;
(c)   the debtor's financial position;
(d)   the reasonableness of any proposal by the debtor to pay that debt; and
(e)   the reasonableness of any refusal by the creditor of, or any objection by
the creditor to, and proposal by the debtor to pay that debt.]

(2)   A direction under subsection (1) above shall be known as a 'time to pay
direction'.

(3)   Where a court grants a decree which contains a finding as to liability for
expenses but does not at the same time make a time to pay direction, then
(whether or not the decree also decerns for payment of the expenses), it shall not
at any time thereafter be competent for the court to make a time to pay direction in
relation to those expenses.

(4)   Where a court grants a decree which contains a finding as to liability
for expenses and makes a time to pay direction in relation to those expenses
but—
(a)   does not decern for payment of the expenses; or
(b)   decerns for payment of the expenses as taxed by the auditor of court but
does not specify the amount of those expenses,
in relation to so much of the time to pay direction as relates to the expenses, the
reference in subsection (1) above to the date of intimation of an extract of the
decree containing the direction shall be treated as a reference to the date of intimation of an extract of a decree decerning for payment of the expenses, being an
extract specifying their amount.

(5)   It shall not be competent for the court to make a time to pay direction—
(a)   where the sum of money (exclusive of any interest and expenses) decerned
for exceeds [£25,000] or such amount as may be prescribed in regulations made
by the Lord Advocate;
(b)   where the decree contains an award of a capital sum on divorce or on
the granting of a declarator of nullity of marriage;
(c)   in connection with a maintenance order;
[(cc) in connection with a liability order within the meaning of the Child
Support Act 1991;]
(d)   in an action by or on behalf of [the Commissioners for Her Majesty's
Revenue and Customs] for payment of any sum recoverable [under or by virtue
of any enactment or under a contract settlement];
[. . .]
(f)   in an action for payment of—
[. . .]
(ii)   car tax due under the Car Tax Act 1983.
[. . .]

(6)   Without prejudice to section 2(5) of this Act, interest payable under a
decree containing a time to pay direction (other than interest awarded as a specific
sum in the decree) shall not be recoverable by the creditor except in accordance
with subsection (7) below.

(7)   A creditor who wishes to recover interest to which subsection (6) above
applies shall serve a notice on the debtor, not later than the date prescribed by Act
of Sederunt occurring—
(a)   in the case of a direction under subsection (1)(a) above, before the date
when the last instalment of the debt concerned (other than such interest) is
payable under the direction;

(b)   in the case of a direction under subsection (1)(b) above, before the end of the period specified in the direction,
stating that he is claiming such interest and specifying the amount of the interest claimed.

(8)   Any sum paid by a debtor under a time to pay direction shall not be ascribed to interest claimed in pursuance of subsections (6) and (7) above until the debt concerned (other than such interest) has been discharged.

[(8A)   In paragraph (d) of subsection (5) above, 'contract settlement' means an agreement made in connection with any person's liability to make a payment to the Commissioners for Her Majesty's Revenue and Customs under or by virtue of any enactment.]

[. . .]

## 2   Effect of time to pay direction on diligence

(1)   While a time to pay direction is in effect, it shall not be competent—
    (a)   to serve a charge for payment; or
    (b)   to commence or execute any of the following diligences—
        (i)   an arrestment and action of furthcoming or sale;
        (ii)   [an attachment;]
        (iii)   an earnings arrestment;
        (iv)   an adjudication for debt;
        [(v)   a money attachment;]
        *[(vi)   a land attachment;*
        *(vii)   a residual attachment]*
to enforce payment of the debt concerned.

(2)   While a time to pay direction is in effect an arrestment used on the dependence of the action or in security of the debt concerned shall remain in effect—
    (a)   if it has not been recalled; and
    (b)   to the extent that it has not been restricted under subsection (3) below,
but, while the direction is in effect, it shall not be competent to commence an action of furthcoming or sale following on such an arrestment.

[(2A)   Where the arrestment which remains in effect as mentioned in subsection (2) above is an arrestment such as is mentioned in subsection (1) of section 73J of this Act, while the time to pay direction is in effect—
    (a)   it shall not be competent to release funds under subsection (2) of that section; and
    (b)   the period during which the direction is in effect shall be disregarded for the purposes of determining whether the period mentioned in subsection (3) of that section has expired.]

[(2B)   While a time to pay direction is in effect an interim attachment shall remain in effect—
    (a)   if it has not been recalled; or
    (b)   to the extent that it has not been restricted under subsection (3) below.]

(3)   The court may, on making a time to pay direction, recall or restrict [an interim attachment or] an arrestment of the kind described in subsection (2) above.

(4)   If [an interim attachment or] an arrestment of the kind described in subsection (2) above is in effect, the court may order that the making of a time to pay direction and the recall or restriction of the [interim attachment or] arrestment shall be subject to the fulfilment by the debtor of such conditions within such period as the court thinks fit; and, where the court so orders, it shall postpone granting decree until such fulfilment or the end of that period, whichever is the earlier.

(5)   Where a time to pay direction is recalled or ceases to have effect, otherwise than—

(a)    under section 12(2)(a) of this Act; or

(b)    by reason of the debt concerned being paid or otherwise extinguished,

the debt in so far as it remains outstanding and interest thereon, whether or not awarded as a specific sum in the decree, shall, subject to any enactment or rule of law to the contrary, become enforceable by any diligence mentioned in subsection (1)(b) above.

[(5A)    Where—

(a)    a time to pay direction is recalled or ceases to have effect as mentioned in subsection (5) above; and

(b)    an arrestment such as is mentioned in section 73J(1) of this Act is in effect,

the clerk of court or sheriff clerk shall intimate the fact of that recall or cessation to the arrestee.]

### 3    Variation and recall of time to pay direction and arrestment

(1)    The court which granted a decree containing a time to pay direction may, on an application by the debtor or the creditor—

(a)    vary or recall the direction if it is satisfied that it is reasonable [in all the circumstances] to do so; or

(b)    if [an interim attachment or] an arrestment in respect of the debt concerned is in effect, recall or restrict the [interim attachment or] arrestment.

(2)    If [an interim attachment or] an arrestment in respect of the debt concerned is in effect, the court may order that any variation, recall or restriction under subsection (1) above shall be subject to the fulfilment by the debtor of such conditions as the court thinks fit.

(3)    The clerk of court or sheriff clerk shall as soon as is reasonably practicable intimate a variation under subsection (1) above to the debtor and to the creditor, and the variation shall come into effect on the date of such intimation.

### 4    Lapse of time to pay direction

(1)    If, on the day on which an instalment payable under a time to pay direction becomes due, there remains unpaid a sum, due under previous instalments, of not less than the aggregate of 2 instalments, the direction shall cease to have effect.

(2)    If at the end of the period of 3 weeks immediately following the day on which the last instalment payable under a time to pay direction becomes due, any part of the debt concerned remains outstanding, the direction shall cease to have effect.

(3)    If any sum payable under a time to pay direction under section 1(1)(b) of this Act remains unpaid 24 hours after the end of the period specified in the direction, the direction shall cease to have effect.

(4)    Where—

(a)    a decree for payment of a principal sum of money contains a finding as to liability for expenses and decree for payment of the expenses is subsequently granted; and

(b)    a time to pay direction is made in relation to both the principal sum and the expenses,

if under subsections (1) to (3) above the direction ceases to have effect in relation to the sum payable under either of the decrees, the direction shall also cease to have effect in relation to the sum payable under the other decree.

*Time to pay orders following charge or diligence*

### 5    Time to pay orders

(1)    Subject to section 14 of this Act, this section applies to a debt due under a decree or other document in respect of which—

(a)    a charge for payment has been served on the debtor;

(b)    an arrestment has been executed; or

(c)    an action of adjudication for debt has been commenced.

(2)   Subject to subsections (4) and (5) below, the sheriff [, on an application by the debtor, shall, if satisfied that it is reasonable in all the circumstances to do so, and having regard in particular to the matters mentioned in subsection (2A) below,] make an order that a debt to which this section applies (including any interest claimed in pursuance of subsections (6) and (7) below) so far as outstanding, shall be paid—

(a)    by such instalments, commencing at such time after the date of intimation in accordance with section 7(4) of this Act by the sheriff clerk to the debtor of the order under this subsection, payable at such intervals; or

(b)    as a lump sum at the end of such period following intimation as mentioned in paragraph (a) above,

as the sheriff may specify in the order.

[(2A)   The matters referred to in subsection (2) above are—

(a)    the nature of and reasons for the debt in relation to which the order is sought;

(b)    any action taken by the creditor to assist the debtor in paying that debt;

(c)    the debtor's financial position;

(d)    the reasonableness of any proposal by the debtor to pay that debt; and

(e)    the reasonableness of the objection by the creditor to the offer by the debtor to pay that debt.]

(3)   An order under subsection (2) above shall be known as a 'time to pay order'.

(4)   It shall not be competent for the sheriff to make a time to pay order—

(a)    where the amount of the debt outstanding at the date of the making of the application under subsection (2) above (exclusive of any interest) exceeds [£10,000] or such amount as may be prescribed in regulations made by the Lord Advocate;

(b)    where, in relation to the debt, a time to pay direction or a time to pay order has previously been made (whether such direction or order is in effect or not);

[. . .]

(d)    in relation to a debt including any sum recoverable by or on behalf of [the Commissioners of Her Majesty's Revenue and Customs [under or by virtue of any enactment or under a contract settlement]];

[. . .]

(f)    in relation to a debt including—

[. . .]

(ii)   car tax due under the Car Tax Act 1983.

[. . .]

(5)   Where in respect of a debt to which this section applies—

(a)    [articles belonging to the debtor have been attached and notice of an auction given under section 27(4) of the Debt Arrangement and Attachment (Scotland) Act 2002 (asp 17) but no auction has yet taken place;]

[(aa)   money owned by the debtor has been attached and removed;]

(b)    moveable property of the debtor has been arrested and in respect of the arrested property—

(i)   a decree in an action of furthcoming has been granted but has not been enforced; or

(ii)   a warrant of sale has been granted but the warrant has not been executed;

(c)    a decree in an action of adjudication for debt has been granted and the creditor has, with the debtor's consent or acquiescence, entered into possession of any property adjudged by the decree or has obtained a decree of mails and duties, or a decree of removing or ejection, in relation to any such property.

(d)    property owned by the debtor has been attached by residual attachment and a satisfaction order under section 136(2) of the 2007 Act has been made but not yet executed,]

it shall not be competent for the sheriff to make a time to pay order in respect of that debt until the diligence has been completed or has otherwise ceased to have effect.

[(5A)   Where, in respect of a debt to which this section applies, an arrestment such as is mentioned in subsection (1) of section 73J of this Act has been executed, the sheriff may make a time to pay order in respect of that debt only if less than 8 weeks of the period mentioned in subsection (3) of that section have expired.]

(6)    Without prejudice to section 9(12) of this Act, interest payable under a decree for payment of a debt in respect of which a time to pay order has been made (other than interest awarded as a specific sum in the decree) shall not be recoverable by the creditor except in accordance with subsection (7) below.

(7)    A creditor who wishes to recover interest to which subsection (6) above applies shall serve a notice on the debtor not later than the date prescribed by Act of Sederunt occurring—

(a)    in the case of an order under subsection (2)(a) above, before the date when the last instalment of the debt (other than such interest) is payable under the order;

(b)    in the case of an order under subsection (2)(b) above, before the end of the period specified in the order,

stating that he is claiming such interest and specifying the amount of the interest claimed.

(8)    Any sum paid by a debtor under a time to pay order shall not be ascribed to interest claimed in pursuance of subsections (6) and (7) above until the debt concerned (other than such interest) has been discharged.

[(8A)   In paragraph (d) of subsection (4) above, 'contract settlement' means an agreement made in connection with any person's liability to make a payment to the Commissioners for Her Majesty's Revenue and Customs under or by virtue of any enactment.]

[. . .]

## 6   Application for time to pay order

(1)    An application for a time to pay order shall specify, to the best of the debtor's knowledge, the amount of the debt outstanding as at the date of the making of the application and shall include an offer to pay it—

(a)    by specified instalments, payable at specified intervals; or

(b)    as a lump sum at the end of a specified period.

(2)    The sheriff clerk's duty under section 96(2)(b) of this Act to assist the debtor in the completion of certain forms shall, in relation to a form of application for a time to pay order, consist of a duty to assist him in the completion of the form in accordance with proposals for payment made by the debtor.

(3)    On receipt of an application for a time to pay order, the sheriff shall, if the application is properly made and unless it appears to him that the making of a time to pay order would not be competent, make an interim order sisting diligence as provided for in section 8(1) of this Act.

(4)    The sheriff may, where the debtor is unable to furnish the necessary information, make an order requiring the creditor, within such period as may be specified therein, to furnish to the sheriff such particulars of the decree or other document under which the debt is payable as may be prescribed by Act of Sederunt.

(5)    If a creditor fails to comply with an order under subsection (4) above the sheriff may, after giving the creditor an opportunity to make representations, make an order recalling or extinguishing any existing diligence, and interdicting the creditor from executing diligence, for the recovery of the debt.

(6)   Where the sheriff makes an interim order under subsection (3) above, the sheriff clerk shall as soon as is reasonably practicable—

(a)   serve a copy of the application for the time to pay order on the creditor informing him that he may object to the granting of the application within a period of 14 days after the date of service;

[(b)   serve on—

(i)   the creditor; and

(ii)   where an arrestment such as is mentioned in section 73J(1) of this Act is in effect, the arrestee,

a copy of the interim order; and

(c)   serve on the creditor a copy of any order under subsection (4) above.]

### 7   Disposal of application

(1)   If no objection is made in pursuance of section 6(6)(a) of this Act, the sheriff shall make a time to pay order in accordance with the application.

(2)   If such an objection is made, the sheriff shall not dispose of the application without first—

(a)   giving the debtor an opportunity to make representations; and

(b)   if agreement is not reached as to whether a time to pay order should be made or as to its terms, giving the parties an opportunity to be heard.

(3)   Where the sheriff refuses to make a time to pay order, he shall recall any interim order under section 6(3) of this Act.

(4)   The sheriff clerk shall as soon as is reasonably practicable—

(a)   intimate the decision of the sheriff on an application for a time to pay order (including any recall of an interim order under subsection (3) above) to the debtor [the creditor and, where an arrestment such as is mentioned in section 73J(1) of this Act is in effect, the arrestee]; and

(b)   if the sheriff has made a time to pay order, inform the creditor of the date when he intimated that fact to the debtor.

### 8   Effect of interim order on diligence

(1)   While an interim order under section 6(3) of this Act is in effect it shall not be competent in respect of the debt—

[(za)   to attach in execution of the decree any articles which have been attached by interim attachment;]

(a)   [to give, in relation to any articles which have been attached, notice of an auction under section 27(4) of the Debt Arrangement and Attachment (Scotland) Act 2002 (asp 17);]

[(aa)   to execute a money attachment;]

(b)   to execute an earnings arrestment;

(c)   [subject to subsection (1A) below,] where an arrestment of property belonging to the debtor (other than an arrestment of earnings in the hands of his employer) has been executed before or after the making of the interim order, to commence an action of furthcoming or sale, or to grant decree in any such action which has already been commenced, in pursuance of that arrestment;

(d)   to commence an action of adjudication for debt or, if such an action has already been commenced, to take any steps other than the registration of a notice of litigiosity in connection with the action, the obtaining and extracting of a decree in the action, the registration of an abbreviate of adjudication and the completion of title to property adjudged by the decree,

[(e)   subject to subsection (1C) below, to apply, under section 130(1) of the 2007 Act, for a residual attachment order].

[(1A)   Where the arrestment mentioned in subsection (1)(c) above is an arrestment such as is mentioned in subsection (1) of section 73J of this Act, while the interim order is in effect—

(a)   it shall not be competent to release funds under subsection (2) of that section; and

(b)   the period during which the order is in effect shall be disregarded for the purposes of determining whether the period mentioned in subsection (3) of that section has expired.

(1B)   Where, before the interim order is made—

(a)   a notice of land attachment is registered, it shall not be competent to take any steps other than—

(i)   serving, under subsection (5) of section 83 of the 2007 Act, a copy of that notice; and

(ii)   registering, under subsection (6) of that section, a certificate of service; or

(b)   a land attachment is created, it shall not be competent to make, under section 97(2) of the 2007 Act, an order granting a warrant for sale of the attached land.

(1C)   Where, before the interim order is made, a residual attachment order has been made, it shall not be competent—

(a)   to take any steps other than serving, under section 133(1) of the 2007 Act, a schedule of residual attachment; or

(b)   to make, under section 136(2) of the 2007 Act, a satisfaction order.]

(2)   An interim order under section 6(3) of this Act shall come into effect on intimation to the creditor under section 6(6)(b) of this Act and shall remain in effect until intimation of the sheriff's decision on the application for a time to pay order is made to the debtor and the creditor under section 7(4)(a) of this Act.

[. . .]

## 9   Effect of time to pay order on diligence

(1)   While a time to pay order is in effect, it shall not be competent—

(a)   to serve a charge for payment; or

(b)   to commence or execute any of the following diligences—

(i)   an arrestment and action of furthcoming or sale;

[(ii)   an attachment;]

(iii)   an earnings arrestment;

(iv)   an adjudication for debt;

[(v)   a money attachment;]

to enforce payment of the debt concerned.

(2)   On making a time to pay order, the sheriff in respect of the debt—

(a)   shall make an order recalling any existing earnings arrestment;

(b)   where the debt is being enforced by a conjoined arrestment order, shall—

(i)   if he, or another sheriff sitting in the same sheriff court, made the conjoined arrestment order, vary it so as to exclude the debt or, where no other debt or maintenance is being enforced by the order, recall the order;

(ii)   if a sheriff sitting in another sheriff court made the conjoined arrestment order, require intimation of the time to pay order to be made to a sheriff sitting there who shall so vary or, as the case may be, recall the conjoined arrestment order;

(c)   [where a notice of land attachment has been registered under section 83(1)(c) of the 2007 Act, shall make an order prohibiting the taking of any steps other than—

(i)   the serving, under subsection (5) of that section, of a copy of the notice; and

(ii)   the registration, under subsection (6) of that section, of a certificate of service;

[(ca)   where a residual attachment order has been made under section 132(2) of the 2007 Act, shall make an order prohibiting the taking of any steps other than the serving, under section 133(1) of the 2007 Act, of a schedule of residual attachment;

(cb)   may make an order recalling an interim attachment;]

(d)    may make an order recalling [an attachment];

(e)    may make an order recalling or restricting any arrestment other than an arrestment of the debtor's earnings in the hands of his employer.

(3)    If [an interim attachment, an attachment] or such an arrestment as is mentioned in subsection (2)(e) above is in effect, the sheriff may order that the making of a time to pay order [the recall of the interim attachment or the attachment] or the recall or restriction of the arrestment shall be subject to the fulfilment by the debtor of such conditions as the sheriff thinks fit.

(4)    [Subject to subsection (4A) below,] where the sheriff does not exercise the powers conferred on him by subsection [(2)(cb), (d) or (e)] above to recall a diligence, he shall order that no further steps shall be taken by the creditor in the diligence concerned other than, in the case of [an attachment, making a report of attachment under section 17 of the Debt Arrangement and Attachment (Scotland) Act 2002 (asp 17) or applying for an order under section 20(1) of that Act.]

[(4A)    Where, in relation to an arrestment such as is mentioned in subsection (1) of section 73J of this Act, the sheriff does not exercise the power conferred on him by subsection (2)(e) above to recall that arrestment, he shall make an order—

(a)    prohibiting, while the time to pay order is in effect, the release of funds under subsection (2) of section 73J of this Act; and

(b)    providing that the period during which the time to pay order is in effect shall be disregarded for the purposes of determining whether the period mentioned in subsection (3) of that section has expired.]

(5)    Any order made under subsection (2) or (4) above shall specify the diligence in relation to which it is made.

(6)    The sheriff shall not make an order under subsection [(2)(cb), (d) or (e)] above without first giving the creditor an opportunity to make representations.

(7)    The sheriff clerk shall, at the same time as he makes intimation under section 7(4)(a) of this Act—

(a)    intimate any order under subsection (2) or (4) above to the debtor and the creditor and the order shall come into effect on such intimation being made to the creditor;

(b)    intimate any order under subsection (2)(a) or (b) above to the employer [; and

(c)    where any order under subsection (4A) above is made in relation to an arrestment such as is mentioned in section 73J(1) of this Act is in effect, intimate that order to the arrestee.]

(8)    While an order under subsection (4) above is in effect it shall not be competent [. . .]—

(a)    [to sell articles which have been attached (other than by virtue of section 20(1) or 22(3) of the Debt Arrangement and Attachment (Scotland) Act (asp 17);]

(b)    [to grant] a decree of furthcoming or sale of arrested property.

(9)    For the purposes of section [24 of the Debt Arrangement and Attachment (Scotland) Act 2002 (asp 17)], the period during which an order under subsection (4) above is in effect shall be disregarded in calculating the period during which [an attachment] to which the order applies remains in effect.

(10)    Where, before the making of a time to pay order in respect of a debt, a charge to pay that debt has been served—

(a)    if the period for payment specified in the charge has not expired, the charge shall lapse on the making of the order;

(b)    if that period has expired, nothing in the time to pay order nor in any order under this section shall affect retrospectively the effect of the charge in the constitution of apparent insolvency within the meaning of section 7 of the Bankruptcy (Scotland) Act 1985.

(11)    If, when a time to pay order in relation to a debt is made, any diligence

enforcing it is in effect which is not specified in an order under subsection (2) or (4) above, the diligence shall remain in effect unless and until it is recalled under section 10(4) of this Act.

(12)   Where a time to pay order is recalled or ceases to have effect, otherwise than—

(a)   under section 12(2)(a) of this Act; or

(b)   by the debt payable under the order being paid or otherwise extinguished, the debt in so far as it remains outstanding (including interest thereon, whether or not awarded as a specific sum in the decree) shall, subject to any enactment or rule of law to the contrary, become enforceable by any diligence mentioned in subsection (1)(b) above; and, notwithstanding section [25 of the Debt Arrangement and Attachment (Scotland) Act 2002 (asp 17)], in this subsection 'diligence' includes, where the debt was, immediately before the time to pay order was made, being enforced by [an attachment] in any premises, [another attachment] in those premises.

## 10   Variation and recall of time to pay order and arrestment

(1)   The sheriff may, on an application by the debtor or the creditor—

(a)   vary or recall a time to pay order if he is satisfied that it is reasonable [in all the circumstances] to do so; or

(b)   if [an interim attachment, an attachment] or an arrestment in respect of the debt is in effect,

recall [the attachment] or recall or restrict the arrestment.

(2)   If [an interim attachment, an attachment] or an arrestment in respect of the debt is in effect, the sheriff may order that any variation, recall or restriction under subsection (1) above shall be subject to the fulfilment by the debtor of such conditions as the sheriff thinks fit.

(3)   The sheriff clerk shall as soon as is reasonably practicable intimate a variation under subsection (1) above to the debtor and to the creditor, and the variation shall come into effect on the date of such intimation.

(4)   Where, after a time to pay order has been made, it comes to the knowledge of the sheriff that the debt to which the order applies is being enforced by any of the diligences mentioned in section 9(1)(b) of this Act which was in effect when the time to pay order was made, the sheriff, after giving all interested parties an opportunity to be heard, may make—

(a)   an order recalling the time to pay order; or

(b)   any of the orders mentioned in subsection (2) or (4) of section 9 of this Act; and that section shall, subject to any necessary modifications, apply for the purposes of an order made under this paragraph as it applies for the purposes of an order made under either of those subsections.

## 11   Lapse of time to pay order

(1)   If, on the day on which an instalment payable under a time to pay order becomes due, there remains unpaid a sum, due under previous instalments, of not less than the aggregate of 2 instalments, the order shall cease to have effect.

(2)   If at the end of the period of 3 weeks immediately following the day on which the last instalment payable under a time to pay order becomes due, any part of the debt payable under the order remains outstanding, the order shall cease to have effect.

(3)   If any sum payable under a time to pay order under section 5(2)(b) of this Act remains unpaid 24 hours after the end of the period specified in the order, the order shall cease to have effect.

*Miscellaneous*

## 12   Sequestration and insolvency

(1)   While a time to pay direction or a time to pay order is in effect, the creditor

shall not be entitled to found on the debt concerned in presenting, or in concurring in the presentation of, a petition for the sequestration of the debtor's estate.

(2)   A time to pay direction or a time to pay order shall cease to have effect—

(a)   on the granting of an award of sequestration of the debtor's estate;

(b)   on the granting by the debtor of a voluntary trust deed whereby his estate is conveyed to a trustee for the benefit of his creditors generally; or

(c)   on the entering by the debtor into a composition contract with his creditors.

### 13   Saving of creditor's rights and remedies

(1)   No right or remedy of a creditor to enforce his debt shall be affected by—

(a)   a time to pay direction;

(b)   a time to pay order; or

(c)   an interim order under section 6(3) of this Act,

except as expressly provided in this Part of this Act.

(2)   The recall—

(a)   on the making of a time to pay direction or an order under section 3(1) of this Act, of an arrestment; or

(b)   on the making of a time to pay order or an order under section 10(1) of this Act, of an arrestment or [an attachment],

shall not prevent the creditor therein from being ranked by virtue of that arrestment or [attachment] pari passu under paragraph 24 of Schedule 7 to the Bankruptcy (Scotland) Act 1985 on the proceeds of any other arrestment or [attachment].

### 14   Circumstances where direction or order not competent or no longer effective

(1)   It shall be competent to make a time to pay direction or a time to pay order only in relation to a debtor who is an individual and only if, and to the extent that, the debtor is liable for payment of the debt concerned in either or both of the following capacities—

(a)   personally;

(b)   as a tutor of an individual or as a judicial factor loco tutoris, curator bonis or judicial factor loco absentis on an individual's estate.

(2)   A time to pay direction or a time to pay order shall cease to have effect on the death of the debtor or on the transmission of the obligation to pay the debt concerned during his lifetime to another person.

(3)   Where a time order for the payment by instalments of a sum owed under a regulated agreement or a security has been made under section 129(2)(a) of the Consumer Credit Act 1974 it shall not thereafter be competent to make a time to pay direction or a time to pay order in relation to that sum.

### 15   Interpretation of Part I

(1)   In this Part of this Act—

'adjudication for debt' does not include—

(a)   an adjudication on a *debitum fundi*;

[. . .]

(2)   In sections 1 to 4 of this Act—

'the court' means the Court of Session or the sheriff;

'the debt concerned' means the sum or expenses in respect of which a time to pay direction is made.

(3)   In sections 5 to 14 of this Act—

'debt' means the sum due by a debtor under a decree or other document (including any interest thereon and any expenses decerned for), and any expenses of diligence used to recover such sum which are chargeable against the debtor, but does not include—

(a)   any sum due under an order of court in criminal proceedings;

(b)   maintenance, whether due at the date of application for the time to pay order or not, or any capital sum awarded on divorce or on the granting of a declarator of nullity of marriage or any other sum due under a decree awarding maintenance or such a capital sum; or

(c)   any fine imposed—

(i)   for contempt of court;

(ii)   under any enactment, for professional misconduct; or

(iii)   for failure to implement an order under section 91 of the Court of Session Act 1868 (orders for specific performance of statutory duty);

'decree or other document' means—

(a)   a decree of the Court of Session or the sheriff;

[(aa)   a summary warrant;]

(b)   an extract of a document which is registered for execution in the Books of Council and Session or the sheriff court books;

(c)   an order or determination which by virtue of any enactment is enforceable as if it were an extract registered decree arbitral bearing a warrant for execution issued by the sheriff;

(d)   a civil judgment granted outside Scotland by a court, tribunal or arbiter which by virtue of any enactment or rule of law is enforceable in Scotland; and

(e)   a document or settlement which by virtue of an Order in Council made under section 13 of the Civil Jurisdiction and Judgments Act 1982 is enforceable in Scotland,

but does not include a maintenance order [, a liability order within the meaning of the Child Support Act 1991] [. . .];

'sheriff'—

(a)   in relation to a debt constituted by decree granted by a sheriff, means that sheriff or another sheriff sitting in the same sheriff court;

(b)   in any other case, means the sheriff having jurisdiction—

(i)   in the place where the debtor is domiciled;

(ii)   if the debtor is not domiciled in Scotland, in a place in Scotland where he carries on business; or

(iii)   if the debtor does not carry on business in Scotland, in a place where he has property which is not exempt from diligence;

and, for the purposes of sub-paragraphs (i) and (ii) above, the debtor's domicile shall be determined in accordance with section 41 of the Civil Jurisdiction and Judgments Act 1982.


[PART 1A
DILIGENCE ON THE DEPENDENCE

*Availability of diligence on the dependence*

**[15A   Diligence on the dependence of action**

(1)   Subject to subsection (2) below and to sections 15C to 15F of this Act, the Court of Session or the sheriff may grant warrant for diligence by—

(a)   arrestment; or

(b)   inhibition,

on the dependence of an action.

(2)   Warrant for—

(a)   arrestment on the dependence of an action is competent only where the action contains a conclusion for payment of a sum other than by way of expenses; and

(b)   inhibition on the dependence is competent only where the action contains—

(i)   such a conclusion; or

(ii) a conclusion for specific implement of an obligation to convey heritable property to the creditor or to grant in the creditor's favour a real right in security, or some other right, over such property.

(3) In this Part of this Act, 'action' includes, in the sheriff court—

(a) a summary cause;

(b) a small claim; and

(c) a summary application,

and references to 'summons', 'conclusion' and to cognate expressions shall be construed accordingly.]

## [15B Diligence on the dependence of petition

(1) Subject to subsection (2) below and to sections 15C to 15F of this Act, the Court of Session may grant warrant for diligence by—

(a) arrestment; or

(b) inhibition,

on the dependence of a petition.

(2) Warrant for—

(a) arrestment on the dependence of a petition is competent only where the petition contains a prayer for payment of a sum other than by way of expenses; and

(b) inhibition on the dependence is competent only where the petition contains—

(i) such a prayer; or

(ii) a prayer for specific implement of an obligation to convey heritable property to the creditor or to grant in the creditor's favour a real right in security, or some other right, over such property.

(3) The provisions of this Act (other than section 15A), of any other enactment and of any rule of law relating to diligence on the dependence of actions shall, in so far as is practicable and unless the contrary intention appears, apply to petitions in relation to which it is competent to grant warrant for such diligence and to the parties to them as they apply to actions and to parties to them.]

## [15C Diligence on the dependence to secure future or contingent debts

(1) It shall be competent for the court to grant warrant for diligence on the dependence where the sum concluded for is a future or contingent debt.

(2) In this section and in sections 15D to 15M of this Act, the 'court' means the court before which the action is depending.]

*Application for diligence on the dependence*

## [15D Application for diligence on the dependence

(1) A creditor may, at any time during which an action is in dependence, apply to the court for warrant for diligence by—

(a) arrestment; or

(b) inhibition,

on the dependence of the action.

(2) An application under subsection (1) above shall—

(a) be in (or as nearly as may be in) the form prescribed by Act of Sederunt;

(b) subject to subsection (3) below, be intimated to and provide details of—

(i) the debtor; and

(ii) any other person having an interest;

(c) state whether the creditor is seeking the grant, under section 15E(1) of this Act, of warrant for diligence on the dependence in advance of a hearing on the application under section 15F of this Act; and

(d) contain such other information as the Scottish Ministers may by regulations prescribe.

(3) An application under subsection (1) above need not be intimated where the

creditor is seeking the grant, under section 15E(1) of this Act, of warrant in advance of a hearing on the application under section 15F of this Act.

(4)   The court, on receiving an application under subsection (1) above, shall—

(a)   subject to section 15E of this Act, fix a date for a hearing on the application under section 15F of this Act; and

(b)   order the creditor to intimate that date to—

(i)   the debtor; and

(ii)   any other person appearing to the court to have an interest.]

**[15E   Grant of warrant without a hearing**

(1)   The court may, if satisfied as to the matters mentioned in subsection (2) below, make an order granting warrant for diligence on the dependence without a hearing on the application under section 15F of this Act.

(2)   The matters referred to in subsection (1) above are—

(a)   that the creditor has a prima facie case on the merits of the action;

(b)   that there is a real and substantial risk enforcement of any decree in the action in favour of the creditor would be defeated or prejudiced by reason of—

(i)   the debtor being insolvent or verging on insolvency; or

(ii)   the likelihood of the debtor removing, disposing of, burdening, concealing or otherwise dealing with all or some of the debtor's assets,

were warrant for diligence on the dependence not granted in advance of such a hearing; and

(c)   that it is reasonable in all the circumstances, including the effect granting warrant may have on any person having an interest, to do so.

(3)   The onus shall be on the creditor to satisfy the court that the order granting warrant should be made.

(4)   Where the court makes an order granting warrant for diligence on the dependence without a hearing on the application under section 15F of this Act, the court shall—

(a)   fix a date for a hearing under section 15K of this Act; and

(b)   order the creditor to intimate that date to—

(i)   the debtor; and

(ii)   any other person appearing to the court to have an interest.

(5)   Where a hearing is fixed under subsection (4)(a) above, section 15K of this Act shall apply as if an application had been made to the court for an order under that section.

(6)   Where the court refuses to make an order granting a warrant without a hearing under section 15F of this Act and the creditor insists in the application, the court shall—

(a)   fix a date for such a hearing on the application; and

(b)   order the creditor to intimate that date to—

(i)   the debtor; and

(ii)   any other person appearing to the court to have an interest.]

**[15F   Hearing on application**

(1)   At the hearing on an application for warrant for diligence on the dependence, the court shall not make any order without first giving—

(a)   any person to whom intimation of the date of the hearing was made; and

(b)   any other person the court is satisfied has an interest,

an opportunity to be heard.

(2)   The court may, if satisfied as to the matters mentioned in subsection (3) below, make an order granting warrant for diligence on the dependence.

(3)   The matters referred to in subsection (2) above are—

(a)   that the creditor has a prima facie case on the merits of the action;

(b)   that there is a real and substantial risk enforcement of any decree in the action in favour of the creditor would be defeated or prejudiced by reason of—

(i)   the debtor being insolvent or verging on insolvency; or

(ii) the likelihood of the debtor removing, disposing of, burdening, concealing or otherwise dealing with all or some of the debtor's assets,

were warrant for diligence on the dependence not granted; and

(c)    that it is reasonable in all the circumstances, including the effect granting warrant may have on any person having an interest, to do so.

(4)    The onus shall be on the creditor to satisfy the court that the order granting warrant should be made.

(5)    Where the court makes an order granting or, as the case may be, refusing warrant for diligence on the dependence, the court shall order the creditor to intimate that order to—

(a)    the debtor; and

(b)    any other person appearing to the court to have an interest.

(6)    Where the court makes an order refusing warrant for diligence on the dependence, the court may impose such conditions (if any) as it thinks fit.

(7)    Without prejudice to the generality of subsection (6) above, those conditions may require the debtor—

(a)    to consign into court such sum; or

(b)    to find caution or to give such other security,

as the court thinks fit.]

*Execution before service*

**[15G    Execution of diligence before service of summons**

(1)    This section applies where diligence by—

(a)    arrestment; or

(b)    inhibition,

on the dependence of an action is executed before service of the summons on the debtor.

(2)    Subject to subsection (3) below, if the summons is not served on the debtor before the end of the period of 21 days beginning with the day on which the diligence is executed, the diligence shall cease to have effect.

(3)    The court may, on the application of the creditor, make an order extending the period referred to in subsection (2) above.

(4)    In determining whether to make such an order the court shall have regard to—

(a)    the efforts of the creditor to serve the summons within the period of 21 days; and

(b)    any special circumstances preventing or obstructing service within that period.]

*Restriction on property attached*

**[15H    Sum attached by arrestment on dependence**

(1)    The court may, subject to subsection (2) below, when granting warrant for arrestment on the dependence, limit the sum which may be attached to funds not exceeding such amount as the court may specify.

(2)    The maximum amount which the court may specify under subsection (1) above shall be the aggregate of—

(a)    the principal sum concluded for;

(b)    a sum equal to 20 per cent of that sum or such other percentage as the Scottish Ministers may, by regulations, prescribe;

(c)    a sum equal to 1 year's interest on the principal sum at the judicial rate; and

(d)    any sum prescribed under subsection (3) below.

(3)    The Scottish Ministers may, by regulations, prescribe a sum which appears to them to be reasonable having regard to the expenses likely to be—

(a)    incurred by a creditor; and

(b)   chargeable against a debtor,
in executing an arrestment on the dependence.

(4)   For the avoidance of doubt, section 73F of this Act applies to any sum attached under this section.]

### [15J   Property affected by inhibition on dependence

Where the court grants warrant for diligence by inhibition on the dependence—

(a)   in a case where the action is brought for specific implement of an obligation—

(i)   to convey heritable property to the creditor;

(ii)   to grant in the creditor's favour a real right in security over such property; or

(iii)   to grant some other right over such property,

the court shall limit the property inhibited to that particular property; and

(b)   in any other case, the court may limit the property inhibited to such property as the court may specify.]

*Recall etc of diligence on the dependence*

### [15K   Recall or restriction of diligence on dependence

(1)   This section applies where warrant is granted for diligence on the dependence.

(2)   The debtor and any person having an interest may apply to the court for an order—

(a)   recalling the warrant;

(b)   restricting the warrant;

(c)   if an arrestment or inhibition has been executed in pursuance of the warrant—

(i)   recalling; or

(ii)   restricting,

that arrestment or inhibition;

(d)   determining any question relating to the validity, effect or operation of the warrant; or

(e)   ancillary to any order mentioned in paragraphs (a) to (d) above.

(3)   An application under subsection (2) above shall—

(a)   be in (or as nearly as may be in) the form prescribed by Act of Sederunt; and

(b)   be intimated to—

(i)   the creditor; and

(ii)   any other person having an interest.

(4)   At the hearing on the application under subsection (2) above, the court shall not make any order without first giving—

(a)   any person to whom intimation of the application was made; and

(b)   any other person the court is satisfied has an interest,

an opportunity to be heard.

(5)   Where the court is satisfied that the warrant is invalid it—

(a)   shall make an order—

(i)   recalling the warrant; and

(ii)   if an arrestment or inhibition has been executed in pursuance of the warrant, recalling that arrestment or inhibition; and

(b)   may make an order ancillary to any order mentioned in paragraph (a) above.

(6)   Where the court is satisfied that an arrestment or inhibition executed in pursuance of the warrant is incompetent, it—

(a)   shall make an order recalling that arrestment or inhibition; and

(b)   may make an order ancillary to any such order.

(7)   Subject to subsection (8) below, where the court is satisfied that the warrant is valid but that—

(a)   an arrestment or inhibition executed in pursuance of it is irregular or ineffective; or

(b)   it is reasonable in all the circumstances, including the effect granting warrant may have had on any person having an interest, to do so,

the court may make any order such as is mentioned in subsection (2) above.

(8)   If no longer satisfied as to the matters mentioned in subsection (9) below, the court—

(a)   shall make an order such as is mentioned in subsection (5)(a) above; and

(b)   may make an order such as is mentioned in subsection (5)(b) above.

(9)   The matters referred to in subsection (8) above are—

(a)   that the creditor has a prima facie case on the merits of the action;

(b)   that there is a real and substantial risk enforcement of any decree in the action in favour of the creditor would be defeated or prejudiced by reason of—

(i)   the debtor being insolvent or verging on insolvency; or

(ii)   the likelihood of the debtor removing, disposing of, burdening, concealing or otherwise dealing with all or some of the debtor's assets; and

(c)   that it is reasonable in all the circumstances, including the effect granting warrant may have had on any person having an interest, for the warrant or, as the case may be, any arrestment or inhibition executed in pursuance of it to continue to have effect.

(10)   The onus shall be on the creditor to satisfy the court that no order under subsection (5), (6), (7) or (8) above should be made.

(11)   In granting an application under subsection (2) above, the court may impose such conditions (if any) as it thinks fit.

(12)   Without prejudice to the generality of subsection (11) above, the court may impose conditions which require the debtor—

(a)   to consign into court such sum; or

(b)   to find such caution or to give such other security,

as the court thinks fit.

(13)   Where the court makes an order under this section, the court shall order the debtor to intimate that order to—

(a)   the creditor; and

(b)   any other person appearing to the court to have an interest.

(14)   This section applies irrespective of whether warrant for diligence on the dependence is obtained, or executed, before this section comes into force.]

## [15L   Variation of orders and variation or recall of conditions

(1)   Where—

(a)   an order restricting warrant for diligence on the dependence is made under section 15K(7); or

(b)   a condition is imposed by virtue of—

(i)   section 15F(6); or

(ii)   section 15K(11),

of this Act, the debtor may apply to the court for variation of the order or, as the case may be, variation or removal of the condition.

(2)   An application under subsection (1) above shall—

(a)   be in (or as nearly as may be in) the form prescribed by Act of Sederunt; and

(b)   be intimated to—

(i)   the creditor; and

(ii)   any other person having an interest.

(3)   At the hearing on the application under subsection (1) above, the court shall not make any order without first giving—

(a)   any person to whom intimation of the application was made; and

(b)   any other person the court is satisfied has an interest,

an opportunity to be heard.

(4)   On an application under subsection (1) above, the court may if it thinks fit—

(a)   vary the order; or

(b)   vary or remove the condition.

(5)   Where the court makes an order varying the order or, as the case may be, varying or removing the condition, the court shall order the debtor to intimate that order to—

(a)   the creditor; and

(b)   any other person appearing to the court to have an interest.]


*General and miscellaneous*


**[15M   Expenses of diligence on the dependence**

(1)   Subject to subsection (3)(a) below, a creditor shall be entitled to such expenses as the creditor incurs—

(a)   in obtaining warrant for diligence on the dependence; and

(b)   where an arrestment or inhibition is executed in pursuance of the warrant, in so executing the arrestment or inhibition.

(2)   Subject to subsection (3)(b) below, a debtor shall be entitled, where—

(a)   warrant for diligence on the dependence is granted; and

(b)   the court is satisfied that the creditor was acting unreasonably in applying for it,

to the expenses incurred in opposing that warrant.

(3)   The court may modify or refuse—

(a)   such expenses as are mentioned in subsection (1) above if it is satisfied that—

(i)   the creditor was acting unreasonably in applying for the warrant; or

(ii)   such modification or refusal is reasonable in all the circumstances and having regard to the outcome of the action; and

(b)   such expenses as are mentioned in subsection (2) above if it is satisfied as to the matter mentioned in paragraph (a)(ii) above.

(4)   Subject to subsections (1) to (3) above, the court may make such finding as it thinks fit in relation to such expenses as are mentioned in subsections (1) and (2) above.

(5)   Expenses incurred as mentioned in subsection (1) and (2) above in obtaining or, as the case may be, opposing an application for warrant shall be expenses of process.

(6)   Subsections (1) to (5) above are without prejudice to any enactment or rule of law as to the recovery of expenses chargeable against a debtor as are incurred in executing an arrestment or inhibition on the dependence of an action.]


**[15N   Application of this Part to admiralty actions**

This Part of this Act (other than sections 15H, 15J and 15M) shall apply, in so far as not inconsistent with the provisions of Part V of the Administration of Justice Act 1956 (c 46)(admiralty jurisdiction and arrestment of ships), to an arrestment on the dependence of an admiralty action as it applies to any other arrestment on the dependence.]]

[PART 3A
ARRESTMENT AND ACTION OF FURTHCOMING

**[73A   Arrestment and action of furthcoming to proceed only on decree or document of debt**

(1)   Arrestment and action of furthcoming or sale shall be competent only in execution of—

(a)   subject to subsection (2) below, a decree; or

(b)   a document of debt.

(2)   Arrestment and action of furthcoming or sale in execution of a summary warrant shall be competent only if—

(a)   the debtor has been charged to pay the debt due by virtue of the summary warrant; and

(b)   the period for payment specified in the charge has expired without payment being made.

(3)   Any rule of law, having effect immediately before the coming into force of this section, as to the decrees or documents on which arrestment and action of furthcoming or sale can proceed shall, in so far as inconsistent with this section, cease to have effect.

(4)   In this Part of this Act—

'decree' means—

(a)   a decree of the Court of Session, of the High Court of Justiciary or of the sheriff;

(b)   a decree of the Court of Teinds;

(c)   a summary warrant;

(d)   a civil judgment granted outside Scotland by a court, tribunal or arbiter which by virtue of any enactment or rule of law is enforceable in Scotland;

[(da)   a decision, court settlement or authentic instrument (within the meaning of Article 2 of the Maintenance Regulation) which is enforceable in Scotland by virtue of the Maintenance Regulation and the Civil Jurisdiction and Judgments (Maintenance) Regulations 2011;]

(e)   an order or determination which by virtue of any enactment is enforceable as if it were an extract registered decree arbitral bearing a warrant for execution issued by the sheriff;

(f)   a warrant granted, in criminal proceedings, for enforcement by civil diligence; or

(g)   a liability order within the meaning of section 33(2) of the Child Support Act 1991 (c 48),

being a decree, warrant, judgment, order or determination which, or an extract of which, authorises arrestment and action of furthcoming or sale; and

'document of debt' means—

(a)   a document registered for execution in the Books of Council and Session or the sheriff court books; or

(b)   a document or settlement which by virtue of an Order in Council under section 13 of the Civil Jurisdiction and Judgments Act 1982 (c 27) is enforceable in Scotland,

being a document or settlement which, or an extract of which, authorises arrestment and action of furthcoming or sale.

(5)   The Scottish Ministers may, by order, modify the definitions of 'decree' and 'document of debt' in subsection (4) above so as to—

(a)   add or remove types of decree or document to or, as the case may be, from those referred to in that provision; or

(b)   vary any of the descriptions of the types of decree or document there referred to.]

**[73B   Schedule of arrestment to be in prescribed form**

(1)   This section applies where a creditor arrests in execution of—

(a)   a decree and the creditor has not executed an arrestment on the dependence of the action; or

(b)   a document of debt.

(2)   The schedule of arrestment used in executing the arrestment shall be in (or as nearly as may be in) the form prescribed by the Scottish Ministers by regulations.]

### [73C   Arrestment on the dependence followed by decree

(1)   This section applies where a creditor obtains a decree (in this Part of this Act referred to as a 'final decree') in an action on the dependence of which the creditor has executed an arrestment.

(2)   The creditor shall, as soon as reasonably practicable, serve a copy of that final decree, in (or as nearly as may be in) the form prescribed by Act of Sederunt, on the arrestee.]

### [73E   Funds attached

(1)   Subsections (2) to (5) below apply—

(a)   where a creditor arrests in execution of—

(i)   a decree and the creditor has not executed an arrestment on the dependence of the action; or

(ii)   a document of debt; and

(b)   only to the extent that the arrestee holds funds due to the debtor the value of which, at the time the arrestment is executed, is or can be ascertained (whether or not that arrestee also holds other moveable property of the debtor).

(2)   Subject to subsection (4) below and to section 73F of this Act, the funds mentioned in subsection (1)(b) above attached by the arrestment shall be the lesser of—

(a)   the sum due by the arrestee to the debtor; or

(b)   the aggregate of—

(i)   the principal sum, in relation to which the decree or document is executed, owed by the debtor to the creditor;

(ii)   any judicial expenses chargeable against the debtor by virtue of the decree;

(iii)   the expenses of executing the arrestment;

(iv)   interest on the principal sum up to and including the date of service of the schedule of arrestment;

(v)   the interest on the principal sum which would be accrued in the period of 1 year beginning with the day after the date mentioned in sub-paragraph (iv) above;

(vi)   any interest on the expenses of executing the arrestment which is chargeable against the debtor; and

(vii)   any sum prescribed under subsection (3) below.

(3)   The Scottish Ministers may, by regulations, prescribe a sum which appears to them to be reasonable having regard to the average expenses likely to be incurred and chargeable against a debtor in a typical action of furthcoming.

(4)   Where—

(a)   the arrestee holds both funds due to and other moveable property of the debtor; and

(b)   the sum mentioned in paragraph (b) of subsection (2) above exceeds the sum mentioned in paragraph (a) of that subsection,

the arrestment shall, in addition to the funds equal to the sum mentioned in that paragraph (a), attach the whole moveable property so held.

(5)   Except as provided for in subsection (4) above, an arrestment to which this section applies shall not attach any moveable property of the debtor other than the sum attached under subsection (2) above.

(6)   Where, in a case to which subsections (2) to (5) above apply—

(a)   in addition to the funds mentioned in subsection (1)(b) above, the arrestee holds funds due to the debtor the value of which is not or cannot be ascertained; and

(b)   the sum mentioned in paragraph (a) of subsection (2) above exceeds the sum mentioned in paragraph (b) of that subsection,

the arrestment shall not attach any of the funds mentioned in paragraph (a) above.]

[73F   **Protection of minimum balance in certain bank accounts**

(1)   Subject to subsection (2) below, this section applies where—

(a)   a creditor arrests—

(i)   in pursuance of a warrant granted for diligence on the dependence of an action; or

(ii)   in execution of a decree or document of debt;

(b)   the arrestment attaches funds standing to the credit of a debtor in an account held by a bank or other financial institution; and

(c)   the debtor is an individual.

(2)   This section does not apply where the account is—

(a)   held in the name of a company, a limited liability partnership, a partnership or an unincorporated association; or

(b)   operated by the debtor as a trading account.

(3)   The arrestment shall—

(a)   in a case where the sum standing to the credit of the debtor exceeds the sum mentioned in subsection (4) below, attach only the balance above that sum; and

(b)   in any other case, attach no funds.

(4)   The sum referred to in subsection (3)(a) above is the sum first mentioned in column 1 of Table B in Schedule 2 to this Act (being the sum representing the net monthly earnings from which no deduction would be made under an earnings arrestment were such an arrestment in effect).

(5)   In subsection (1) above, 'bank or other financial institution' means—

(a)   the Bank of England;

(b)   a person who has permission under [Part 4A] of the Financial Services and Markets Act 2000 (c 8) to accept deposits;

(c)   an EEA firm of the kind mentioned in paragraph 5(b) of Schedule 3 to that Act which has permission under paragraph 15 of that schedule (as a result of qualifying for authorisation under paragraph 12 of that schedule) to accept deposits; or

(d)   a person who is exempt from the general prohibition in respect of accepting deposits as a result of an exemption order made under section 38(1) of that Act,

and the expressions in this definition shall be read with section 22 of that Act, any relevant order made under that section and Schedule 2 to that Act.

(6)   The Scottish Ministers may, by regulations—

(a)   modify subsection (2) above so as to—

(i)   add or remove types of account to or, as the case may be, from those referred to in that paragraph; or

(ii)   vary any of the descriptions of the types of account there referred to; and

(b)   modify the definition of 'bank or other financial institution' in subsection (5) above so as to—

(i)   add or remove types of financial institution to or, as the case may be, from those referred to in that provision; or

(ii)   vary any of the descriptions of the types of institution there referred to.]

**[73G Arrestee's duty of disclosure**

(1) This section applies where a creditor arrests—

(a) in pursuance of a warrant granted for diligence on the dependence of an action; or

(b) in execution of a decree or document of debt.

(2) The arrestee shall, before the expiry of the period mentioned in subsection (3) below, send to the creditor in (or as nearly as may be in) the form prescribed by the Scottish Ministers by regulations, the information mentioned in subsection (4) below.

(3) The period referred to in subsection (2) above is the period of 3 weeks beginning with the day on which the arrestment is executed.

(4) The information referred to in subsection (2) above is—

(a) where any property, other than funds due to the debtor, is attached—

(i) the nature of that property; and

(ii) the value of it in so far as known to the arrestee; and

(b) where any such funds are attached, the nature and value of those funds.

(5) The arrestee shall, at the same time as sending, under subsection (2) above, the information to the creditor, send a copy of it to—

(a) the debtor; and

(b) in so far as known to the arrestee, any person—

(i) who owns or claims to own attached property; or

(ii) to whom attached funds are or are claimed to be due,

solely or in common with the debtor.]

**[73H Failure to disclose information**

(1) Where an arrestee fails without reasonable excuse to send the prescribed form under section 73G(2) of this Act, the sheriff may, on the application of the creditor, make an order requiring the arrestee to pay to the creditor—

(a) the sum due to the creditor by the debtor; or

(b) the sum mentioned in section 73F(4) of this Act,

whichever is the lesser.

(2) Where the arrestee fails to send the prescribed form in relation to an arrestment on the dependence of an action, the sheriff—

(a) may not make an order under subsection (1) above until the creditor has served a copy of the final decree under section 73C(2) above; and

(b) may deal with the failure as a contempt of court.

(3) Where a sum is paid by virtue of an order under subsection (1) above—

(a) the debt owed by the debtor to the creditor shall be reduced by that sum; and

(b) the arrestee shall not be entitled to recover that sum from the debtor.

(4) An arrestee aggrieved by an order under subsection (1) above may, before the expiry of the period of 2 weeks beginning with the day on which the order is made, appeal, on point of law only, to the sheriff principal, whose decision shall be final.]

**[73J Automatic release of arrested funds**

(1) This section applies where—

(a) a creditor—

(i) obtains a final decree in an action on the dependence of which the creditor has executed an arrestment; or

(ii) arrests in execution of a decree or document of debt; and

(b) the arrestment attaches funds which are due to the debtor (whether or not it also attaches other moveable property of the debtor).

(2) Subject to section 73L of this Act, the arrestee—

(a) shall, on the expiry of the period mentioned in subsection (3) below, release to the creditor, from the attached funds, a sum calculated in accordance with section 73K of this Act; and

(b)   may, where a mandate authorises the arrestee to do so, release that sum before the expiry of that period.

(3)   The period referred to in subsection (2) above is the period of 14 weeks beginning with the date of service of a copy of the final decree under section 73C(2) of this Act or, as the case may be, the date of service of the schedule of arrestment.

(4)   In this section and in sections 73K to 73P of this Act, references to funds or sums due to or by any person do not include references to funds or sums due in respect of future or contingent debts.]

### [73K   Sum released under section 73J(2)

The sum released under section 73J(2) of this Act is the lowest of—

(a)   the sum attached by the arrestment;

(b)   the sum due by the arrestee to the debtor; or

(c)   the aggregate of—

(i)   the principal sum, in relation to which the decree or document is executed or, as the case may be, which is decerned for in the final decree, owed by the debtor to the creditor;

(ii)   any judicial expenses chargeable against the debtor by virtue of the decree or final decree;

(iii)   the expenses of executing the arrestment;

(iv)   interest on the principal sum up to and including the date of service of the schedule of arrestment or, as the case may be, the date of the final decree;

(v)   the interest on the principal sum which would be accrued in the period beginning with the day after the date mentioned in sub-paragraph (iv) above and ending on the day on which the funds are released under section 73J(2) of this Act; and

(vi)   any interest on the expenses of executing the arrestment which is chargeable against the debtor.]

### [73L   Circumstances preventing automatic release

(1)   No funds may be released under section 73J(2) of this Act where—

(a)   a person mentioned in subsection (2) below applies, by notice of objection, to the sheriff under section 73M(1) of this Act;

(b)   the debtor applies to the sheriff under section 73Q(2) of this Act;

(c)   an action of multiplepoinding is raised in relation to the funds attached by the arrestment; or

(d)   the arrestment is—

(i)   recalled;

(ii)   restricted; or

(iii)   otherwise ceases to have effect.

(2)   The persons referred to in subsection (1)(a) above are—

(a)   the debtor;

(b)   the arrestee; and

(c)   any other person to whom the funds are due solely or in common with the debtor (in this section and in sections 73M and 73N of this Act, the 'third party').]

### [73M   Notice of objection

(1)   Where section 73J of this Act applies—

(a)   the debtor;

(b)   the arrestee; or

(c)   a third party,

may, by notice of objection, apply to the sheriff for an order recalling or restricting the arrestment.

(2)   The notice of objection referred to in subsection (1) above shall—

(a)   be in (or as nearly as may be in) the form prescribed by Act of Sederunt;

(b)   be given to the persons mentioned in subsection (3) below before the
expiry of the period of 4 weeks beginning with the date of service of a copy of
the final decree under section 73C(2) of this Act or, as the case may be, the date
of service of the schedule of arrestment; and
    (c)   specify one or more of the grounds of objection mentioned in subsection
(4) below.
    (3)   The persons referred to in subsection (2)(b) above are—
        (a)   the creditor;
        (b)   the sheriff clerk;
        (c)   the debtor or, as the case may be, the arrestee; and
        (d)   in so far as known to the person objecting, any third party.
    (4)   The grounds of objection referred to in subsection (2)(c) above are—
        (a)   the warrant in execution of which the arrestment was executed is invalid;
        (b)   the arrestment has been executed incompetently or irregularly;
        (c)   the funds attached are due to the third party solely or in common with
the debtor.
    (5)   Where a person applies by notice of objection under subsection (1) above,
that person may not, subject to subsection (6) below, raise—
        (a)   an action of multiplepoinding; or
        (b)   subject to subsection (7) below, any other proceedings,
in relation to the funds attached.
    (6)   Subsection (5) above is without prejudice to the right of the person—
        (a)   to enter any such action or proceedings raised by any other person; and
        (b)   to raise such an action or proceedings where the sheriff makes, under
section 73N(5) of this Act, an order sisting the proceedings on the objection.
    (7)   A debtor who applies by notice of objection under subsection (1) above may
apply to the sheriff under section 73Q(2) of this Act and, in such a case, the sheriff
may deal with both applications at one hearing.]


**[73N   Hearings following notice of objection**
    (1)   Subject to subsection (5) below, before the expiry of the period of 8 weeks
beginning with the day on which an application by notice of objection is made
under section 73M(1) of this Act, the sheriff shall hold a hearing to determine the
objection.
    (2)   At the hearing under subsection (1) above, the sheriff shall not make any
order without first giving—
        (a)   the creditor;
        (b)   the arrestee;
        (c)   the debtor; and
        (d)   any third party,
an opportunity to be heard.
    (3)   Where the sheriff upholds the objection, the sheriff may make an order
recalling or restricting the arrestment.
    (4)   Where the sheriff rejects the objection, the sheriff may make an order
requiring a sum determined in the order to be released to the creditor—
        (a)   in a case where the period mentioned in section 73J(3) of this Act has not
expired, on the expiry of that period; or
        (b)   in any other case, as soon as reasonably practicable after the date on
which the order is made.
    (5)   Where—
        (a)   the sheriff is satisfied that it is more appropriate for the matters raised at
the hearing to be dealt with by—
            (i)   an action of multiplepoinding; or
            (ii)   other proceedings,
raised in relation to the funds attached; or

(b)   at any time before a decision is made under subsections (3) or (4) above, such an action is or other proceedings are raised,
the sheriff shall make an order sisting the proceedings on the objection.

(6)   The sheriff may make such other order as the sheriff thinks fit.

(7)   Where the sheriff makes an order under this section, the sheriff shall order the person who objected to intimate that order to such of the persons mentioned in subsection (2) above as the sheriff thinks fit.

(8)   A person aggrieved by a decision of the sheriff under this section may, before the expiry of the period of 14 days beginning with the day on which the decision is made, appeal, on point of law only, to the sheriff principal, whose decision shall be final.]

## [73P   Arrestee not liable for funds released in good faith

Where an arrestee releases funds under section 73J(2) of this Act in good faith but—

(a)   the warrant in execution of which the arrestment was executed is invalid; or

(b)   the arrestment was incompetently or irregularly executed,
the arrestee is not liable to the debtor or to any other person having an interest in the funds for damages for patrimonial loss caused by the release of funds.]

## [73Q   Application for release of property where arrestment unduly harsh

(1)   This section applies where—

(a)   a creditor—
(i)   obtains final decree in an action on the dependence of which the creditor executed an arrestment; or
(ii)   arrests in execution of a decree or document of debt; and

(b)   the arrestment attaches funds due to or other moveable property of the debtor.

(2)   The debtor may apply to the sheriff for an order—

(a)   providing that the arrestment ceases to have effect in relation to—
(i)   the funds or other property attached; or
(ii)   so much of those funds or that property as the sheriff specifies; and

(b)   requiring the arrestee to release the funds or property to the debtor.

(3)   An application under subsection (2) above shall be—

(a)   in (or as nearly as may be in) the form prescribed by Act of Sederunt;

(b)   made at any time during which the arrestment has effect; and

(c)   intimated to—
(i)   the creditor;
(ii)   the arrestee; and
(iii)   any other person appearing to have an interest.]

## [73R   Hearing on application under section 73Q for release of property

(1)   At the hearing on an application under section 73Q(2) of this Act, the sheriff shall not make any order without first giving—

(a)   the creditor;

(b)   the arrestee; and

(c)   any other person appearing to the court to have an interest,
an opportunity to be heard.

(2)   Subject to subsection (3) below, if the sheriff is satisfied that the arrestment is unduly harsh—

(a)   to the debtor; or

(b)   where the debtor is an individual, to any person such as is mentioned in subsection (4) below,
the sheriff shall make an order such as is mentioned in section 73Q(2) of this Act.

(3)   Before making an order under subsection (2) above the sheriff shall have regard to all the circumstances including, in a case where the debtor is an individual and funds are attached—

(a)   the source of those funds; and

(b)   where the source of those funds is or includes earnings, whether an earnings arrestment, current maintenance arrestment or conjoined arrestment order is in effect in relation to those earnings.

(4)   The persons referred to in subsection (2)(b) above are—

(a)   a spouse of the debtor;

(b)   a person living together with the debtor as husband and wife;

(c)   a civil partner of the debtor;

(d)   a person living with the debtor in a relationship which has the characteristics of the relationship between a husband and wife except that the person and the debtor are of the same sex;

(e)   a child of the debtor under the age of 16 years, including—

(i)   a stepchild; and

(ii)   any child brought up or treated by the debtor or any person mentioned in paragraph (b), (c) or (d) above as a child of the debtor or, as the case may be, that person.

(5)   Where the sheriff refuses to make an order under subsection (2) above, the sheriff may, in a case where funds are attached, make an order requiring a sum determined in the order to be released to the creditor—

(a)   in a case where the period mentioned in section 73J(3) of this Act has not expired, on the expiry of that period; or

(b)   in any other case, as soon as reasonably practicable after the date on which the order is made.

(6)   Where the sheriff makes an order under this section, the sheriff shall order the debtor to intimate that order to the persons mentioned in subsection (1) above.

(7)   A person aggrieved by a decision of the sheriff under this section may, before the expiry of the period of 14 days beginning with the day on which the decision is made, appeal, on point of law only, to the sheriff principal, whose decision shall be final.]

## [73S   Mandate to be in prescribed form

(1)   A mandate authorising an arrestee to pay over any funds or hand over other property attached by an arrestment shall be in (or as nearly as may be in) the form prescribed by the Scottish Ministers by regulations.

(2)   A mandate which is not in (or as nearly as may be in) the prescribed form is invalid.

(3)   Where—

(a)   a mandate is invalid by virtue of subsection (2) above; but

(b)   the arrestee pays over funds or hands over other property in accordance with that mandate,

the arrestee is not liable to the debtor or to any other person having an interest in the funds or property for damages for patrimonial loss caused by paying over the funds or handing over the property provided the arrestee acted in good faith.]

## [73T   Arrestment of ships etc

For the avoidance of doubt, this Part of this Act does not apply to the arrestment of a ship, cargo or other maritime property.]]

## PART VI
## WARRANTS FOR DILIGENCE AND CHARGES FOR PAYMENT

. . .

### 88 Warrants for diligence: special cases

(1) This section applies where a creditor has acquired by assignation intimated to the debtor, confirmation as executor, or otherwise a right to—

(a) a decree;

(b) an obligation contained in a document an extract of which, after the document has been registered in the Books of Council and Session or in sheriff court books, may be obtained containing warrant for execution;

(c) an order or determination which by virtue of any enactment is enforceable as if it were an extract registered decree arbitral bearing a warrant for execution issued by a sheriff,

either directly or through a third party from a person in whose favour the decree, order or determination was granted or who was the creditor in the obligation contained in the document.

(2) Where this section applies, the creditor who has acquired a right as mentioned in subsection (1) above may apply to the appropriate clerk for a warrant having the effect of authorising the execution at the instance of that creditor of any diligence authorised by an extract of the decree or document or by the order or determination, as the case may be.

(3) The applicant under subsection (2) above shall submit to the appropriate clerk—

(a) an extract of the decree or of the document registered as mentioned in subsection (1)(b) above or a certified copy of the order or determination; and

(b) the assignation (along with evidence of its intimation to the debtor), confirmation as executor or other document establishing the applicant's right.

(4) The appropriate clerk shall grant the warrant applied for under subsection (2) above if he is satisfied that the applicant's right is established.

(5) Where—

(a) a charge has already been served in pursuance of the decree, order, determination or registered document; and

(b) the applicant under subsection (2) above submits with his application the certificate of execution of the charge in addition to the documents mentioned in subsection (3) above,

a warrant granted under subsection (4) above shall authorise the execution at the instance of the applicant of diligence in pursuance of that charge.

(6) For the purposes of this section, 'the appropriate clerk' shall be—

(a) in the case of a decree granted by the Court of Session or a document registered (whether before or after such acquisition) in the Books of Council and Session, a clerk of court of the Court of Session;

(b) in the case of a decree granted by the High Court of Justiciary, a clerk of Justiciary;

(c) in the case of a decree granted by a sheriff or a document registered (whether before or after such acquisition) in the books of a sheriff court, the sheriff clerk of that sheriff court;

(d) in the case of such an order or determination as is mentioned in subsection (1)(c) above, any sheriff clerk.

### 89 Abolition of letters of horning, horning and poinding, poinding, and caption

The granting of letters of horning, letters of horning and poinding, letters of poinding and letters of caption shall cease to be competent.

**90   Provisions relating to charges for payment**

(1)   [. . .] the execution of [. . .] an earnings arrestment shall not be competent unless a charge for payment has been served on the debtor and the period for payment specified in the charge has expired without payment being made.

[(1A)   The following subsections of this section apply to any case where it is competent to execute diligence only if a charge for payment has been served on the debtor.]

[. . .]

(3)   The period for payment specified in any charge for payment served in pursuance of a warrant for execution shall be 14 days if the person on whom it is served is within the United Kingdom and 28 days if he is outside the United Kingdom or his whereabouts are unknown.

(4)   Any such charge shall be in the form prescribed by Act of Sederunt or Act of Adjournal.

(5)   Subject to subsection (6) below, where any such charge has been served, it shall not be competent to execute [diligence] by virtue of that charge more than 2 years after the date of such service.

(6)   A creditor may reconstitute his right to execute [diligence] by the service of a further charge for payment.

(7)   No expenses incurred in the service of a further charge for payment within the period of 2 years after service of the first charge shall be chargeable against the debtor.

(8)   Registration of certificates of execution of charges for payment in a register of hornings shall cease to be competent.

**91   Enforcement of certain warrants and precepts of sheriff anywhere in Scotland**

(1)   The following may be executed anywhere in Scotland—

(a)   a warrant for execution contained in an extract of a decree granted by a sheriff;

(b)   a warrant for execution inserted in an extract of a document registered in sheriff court books;

(c)   a summary warrant;

(d)   a warrant of a sheriff for arrestment on the dependence of an action or in security;

(e)   a precept (issued by a sheriff clerk) of arrestment in security of a liquid debt the term of payment of which has not arrived.

(2)   A warrant or precept mentioned in subsection (1) above may be executed by a sheriff officer of—

(a)   the court which granted it; or

(b)   the sheriff court district in which it is to be executed.


PART VII
MISCELLANEOUS AND GENERAL

. . .

**94   Ascription of sums recovered by diligence or while diligence is in effect**

(1)   This section applies to any sums recovered by any of the following diligences—

[. . .]

(b)   an earnings arrestment;

(c)   an arrestment and action of furthcoming or sale; or

(d)   a conjoined arrestment order in so far as it enforces an ordinary debt,

or paid to account of the sums recoverable by the diligence while the diligence is in effect.

(2)  A sum to which this section applies shall be ascribed to the following in the order in which they are mentioned—

(a)  the expenses already incurred in respect of—

(i)  the diligence;

(ii)  any previous diligence the expenses of which are chargeable against and recoverable from the debtor under section 93(5) of this Act;

(iii)  the execution of a current maintenance arrestment;

(b)  any interest, due under the decree or other document on which the diligence proceeds, which has accrued at the date of execution of the [. . .] earnings arrestment or arrestment, or in the case of an ordinary debt included in a conjoined arrestment order which has accrued at the date of application under section 60(2) or 62(5) of this Act;

(c)  any sum (including any expenses) due under the decree or other document, other than any expenses or interest mentioned in paragraphs (a) and (b) above.

### [95A  Prescription of arrestment

(1)  Subject to subsection (2) below, an arrestment which is not insisted in prescribes—

(a)  where it is on the dependence of an action, at the end of the period of 3 years beginning with the day on which a final interlocutor is obtained by the creditor for payment of all or part of a principal sum concluded for; or

(b)  where it is in execution of an extract decree or other extract registered document relating to a due debt, at the end of the period of 3 years beginning with the day on which the arrestment is executed.

(2)  Where the arrestment secures or enforces a future or contingent debt due to the creditor, it prescribes, if not insisted in, at the end of the period of 3 years beginning on the day on which the debt becomes due.

(3)  In a case where—

(a)  a time to pay direction;

(b)  an interim order under section 6(3) of this Act; or

(c)  a time to pay order,

has been made, there shall be disregarded, in computing the period at the end of which the arrestment prescribes, the period during which the time to pay direction, interim order or time to pay order is in effect.

(4)  Nothing in this section shall apply to an earnings arrestment, a current maintenance arrestment or a conjoined arrestment order.

(5)  Subsections (1) to (3) above apply irrespective of whether the arrestment is executed, or warrant for it obtained, before this section comes into force.

(6)  For the purposes of subsection (1)(a) above, a final interlocutor is obtained when an interlocutor cannot be recalled or altered and is not subject to review.]

### 102  Procedure in diligence proceeding on extract of registered document etc

(1)  The Court of Session may by Act of Sederunt—

(a)  regulate and prescribe the procedure and practice in; and

(b)  prescribe the form of any document to be used in, or for the purposes of, diligence of a kind specified in subsection (2) below.

(2)  The diligences referred to in subsection (1) above are diligences proceeding—

(a)  on an extract of a document which has been registered for execution in the Books of Council and Session or in sheriff court books; or

(b)  on an order or a determination which by virtue of any enactment is to be treated as if it were so registered.

SCHEDULE 2                                        Section 49

TABLE A: DEDUCTIONS FROM WEEKLY EARNINGS

| Net earnings | Deduction* |
|---|---|
| Not exceeding £106.17 | Nil |
| Exceeding £106.17 but not exceeding £383.74 | £4 or 19% of earnings exceeding £106.17, whichever is the greater |
| Exceeding £383.74 but not exceeding £576.92 | £52.74 plus 23% of earnings exceeding £383.74 |
| Exceeding £576.92 | £97.17 plus 50% of earnings exceeding £576.92 |

\*When applying a percentage the calculation should be done to two decimal places of a penny and the result rounded to the nearest whole penny, with an exact half penny being rounded down.

TABLE B: DEDUCTIONS FROM MONTHLY EARNINGS

| Net earnings | Deduction* |
|---|---|
| Not exceeding £460.06 | Nil |
| Exceeding £460.06 but not exceeding £1,662.88 | £15 or 19% of earnings exceeding £460.06, whichever is the greater |
| Exceeding £1,662.88 but not exceeding £2,500.00 | £228.54 plus 23% of earnings exceeding £1,662.88 |
| Exceeding £2,500.00 | £421.07 plus 50% of earnings exceeding £2,500.00 |

\*When applying a percentage the calculation should be done to two decimal places of a penny and the result rounded to the nearest whole penny, with an exact half penny being rounded down.

TABLE C: DEDUCTIONS FROM DAILY EARNINGS

| Net earnings | Deduction* |
|---|---|
| Not exceeding £15.12 | Nil |
| Exceeding £15.12 but not exceeding £54.68 | £0.50 or 19% of earnings exceeding £15.12, whichever is the greater |
| Exceeding £54.68 but not exceeding £82.19 | £7.52 plus 23% of earnings exceeding £54.68 |
| Exceeding £82.19 | £13.84 plus 50% of earnings exceeding £82.19 |

\*When applying a percentage the calculation should be done to two decimal places of a penny and the result rounded to the nearest whole penny, with an exact half penny being rounded down.

## CONSUMER PROTECTION ACT 1987
### (1987, c 43)

### PART I
### PRODUCT LIABILITY

**1 Purpose and construction of Part I**

(1) This Part shall have effect for the purpose of making such provision as is necessary in order to comply with the product liability Directive and shall be construed accordingly.

(2) In this Part, except in so far as the context otherwise requires—

[. . .]

'dependant' and 'relative' have the same meaning as they have in, respectively, the Fatal Accidents Act 1976 and the [Damages (Scotland) Act 2011];

'producer', in relation to a product, means—

(a) the person who manufactured it;

(b) in the case of a substance which has not been manufactured but has been won or abstracted, the person who won or abstracted it;

(c) in the case of a product which has not been manufactured, won or abstracted but essential characteristics of which are attributable to an industrial or other process having been carried out (for example, in relation to agricultural produce), the person who carried out that process;

'product' means any goods or electricity and (subject to subsection (3) below) includes a product which is comprised in another product, whether by virtue of being a component part or raw material or otherwise; and

'the product liability Directive' means the Directive of the Council of the European Communities, dated 25th July 1985, (No 85/374/EEC) on the approximation of the laws, regulations and administrative provisions of the member States concerning liability for defective products.

(3) For the purposes of this Part a person who supplies any product in which products are comprised, whether by virtue of being component parts or raw materials or otherwise, shall not be treated by reason only of his supply of that product as supplying any of the products so comprised.

**2 Liability for defective products**

(1) Subject to the following provisions of this Part, where any damage is caused wholly or partly by a defect in a product, every person to whom subsection (2) below applies shall be liable for the damage.

(2) This subsection applies to—

(a) the producer of the product;

(b) any person who, by putting his name on the product or using a trade mark or other distinguishing mark in relation to the product, has held himself out to be the producer of the product;

(c) any person who has imported the product into a member State from a place outside the member States in order, in the course of any business of his, to supply it to another.

(3) Subject as aforesaid, where any damage is caused wholly or partly by a defect in a product, any person who supplied the product (whether to the person who suffered the damage, to the producer of any product in which the product in question is comprised or to any other person) shall be liable for the damage if—

(a) the person who suffered the damage requests the supplier to identify one or more of the persons (whether still in existence or not) to whom subsection (2) above applies in relation to the product;

(b) that request is made within a reasonable period after the damage occurs and at a time when it is not reasonably practicable for the person making the request to identify all those persons; and

(c) the supplier fails, within a reasonable period after receiving the request, either to comply with the request or to identify the person who supplied the product to him.

[. . .]

(5)   Where two or more persons are liable by virtue of this Part for the same damage, their liability shall be joint and several.

(6)   This section shall be without prejudice to any liability arising otherwise than by virtue of this Part.

### 3   Meaning of 'defect'

(1)   Subject to the following provisions of the section, there is a defect in a product for the purposes of this Part if the safety of the product is not such as persons generally are entitled to expect; and for those purposes 'safety', in relation to a product, shall include safety with respect to products comprised in that product and safety in the context of risks of damage to property, as well as in the context of risks of death or personal injury.

(2)   In determining for the purposes of subsection (1) above what persons generally are entitled to expect in relation to a product all the circumstances shall be taken into account, including—

(a)   the manner in which, and purposes for which, the product has been marketed, its get-up, the use of any mark in relation to the product and any instructions for, or warnings with respect to, doing or refraining from doing anything with or in relation to the product;

(b)   what might reasonably be expected to be done with or in relation to the product; and

(c)   the time when the product was supplied by its producer to another;

and nothing in this section shall require a defect to be inferred from the fact alone that the safety of a product which is supplied after that time is greater than the safety of the product in question.

### 4   Defences

(1)   In any civil proceedings by virtue of this Part against any person ('the person proceeded against') in respect of a defect in a product it shall be a defence for him to show—

(a)   that the defect is attributable to compliance with any requirement imposed by or under any enactment or with any Community obligation; or

(b)   that the person proceeded against did not at any time supply the product to another; or

(c)   that the following conditions are satisfied, that is to say—

(i)   that the only supply of the product to another by the person proceeded against was otherwise than in the course of a business of that person's; and

(ii)   that section 2(2) above does not apply to that person or applies to him by virtue only of things done otherwise than with a view to profit; or

(d)   that the defect did not exist in the product at the relevant time; or

(e)   that the state of scientific and technical knowledge at the relevant time was not such that a producer of products of the same description as the product in question might be expected to have discovered the defect if it had existed in his products while they were under his control; or

(f)   that the defect—

(i)   constituted a defect in a product ('the subsequent product') in which the product in question had been comprised; and

(ii)   was wholly attributable to the design of the subsequent product or to compliance by the producer of the product in question with instructions given by the producer of the subsequent product.

(2)   In this section 'the relevant time', in relation to electricity, means the time at which it was generated, being a time before it was transmitted or distributed, and in relation to any other product, means—

(a) if the person proceeded against is a person to whom subsection (2) of section 2 above applies in relation to the product, the time when he supplied the product to another;

(b) if that subsection does not apply to that person in relation to the product, the time when the product was last supplied by a person to whom that subsection does apply in relation to the product.

## 5 Damage giving rise to liability

(1) Subject to the following provisions of this section, in this Part 'damages' means death or personal injury or any loss of or damage to any property (including land).

(2) A person shall not be liable under section 2 above in respect of any defect in a product for the loss of or any damage to the product itself or for the loss of or any damage to the whole or any part of any product which has been supplied with the product in question comprised in it.

(3) A person shall not be liable under section 2 above for any loss of or damage to any property which, at the time it is lost or damaged, is not—

(a) of a description of property ordinarily intended for private use, occupation or consumption; and

(b) intended by the person suffering the loss or damage mainly for his own private use, occupation or consumption.

(4) No damages shall be awarded to any person by virtue of this Part in respect of any loss of or damage to any property if the amount which would fall to be so awarded to that person, apart from this subsection and any liability for interest, does not exceed £275.

. . .

(8) Subsections (5) to (7) above shall not extend to Scotland.

## 6 Application of certain enactments etc

(1) Any damage for which a person is liable under section 2 above shall be deemed to have been caused—

(a) for the purposes of the Fatal Accidents Act 1976, by that person's wrongful act, neglect or default;

(b) for the purposes of section 3 of the Law Reform (Miscellaneous Provisions) (Scotland) Act 1940 (contribution among joint wrongdoers), by that person's wrongful act or negligent act or omission;

(c) for the purposes of [sections 3 to 6 of the Damages (Scotland) Act 2011] (rights of relatives of a deceased), by that person's act or omission, and

(d) for the purposes of Part II of the Administration of Justice Act 1982 (damages for personal injuries, etc—Scotland), by an act or omission giving rise to liability in that person to pay damages.

(2) Where—

(a) a person's death is caused wholly or partly by a defect in a product, or a person dies after suffering damage which has been so caused;

(b) a request such as mentioned in paragraph (a) of subsection (3) of section 2 above is made to a supplier of the product by that person's personal representatives or, in the case of a person whose death is caused wholly or partly by the defect, by any dependant or relative of that person; and

(c) the conditions specified in paragraphs (b) and (c) of that subsection are satisfied in relation to that request,

this Part shall have effect for the purposes of the Law Reform (Miscellaneous Provisions) Act 1934, the Fatal Accidents Acts 1976 and the [Damages (Scotland) Act 2011] as if liability of the supplier to that person under that subsection did not depend on that person having requested the supplier to identify certain persons or on the said conditions having been satisfied in relation to a request made by that person.

(3)   Section 1 of the Congenital Disabilities (Civil Liability) Act 1976 shall have effect for the purposes of this Part as if—

(a)   a person were answerable to a child in respect of an occurrence caused wholly or partly by a defect in a product if he is or has been liable under section 2 above in respect of any effect of the occurrence on a parent of the child, or would be so liable if the occurrence caused a parent of the child to suffer damage;

(b)   the provisions of this Part relating to liability under section 2 above applied in relation to liability by virtue of paragraph (a) above under the said section 1; and

(c)   subsection (6) of the said section 1 (exclusion of liability) were omitted.

(4)   Where any damage is caused partly by a defect in a product and partly by the fault of the person suffering the damage, the Law Reform (Contributory Negligence) Act 1945 and section 5 of the Fatal Accidents Act 1976 (contributory negligence) shall have effect as if the defect were the fault of every person liable by virtue of this Part for the damage caused by the defect.

(5)   In subsection (4) above 'fault' has the same meaning as in the said Act of 1945.

(6)   Schedule 1 to this Act shall have effect for the purpose of amending the Limitation Act 1980 and the Prescription and Limitation (Scotland) Act 1973 in their application in relation to the bringing of actions by virtue of this Part.

(7)   It is hereby declared that liability by virtue of this Part is to be treated as liability in tort for the purposes of any enactment conferring jurisdiction on any court with respect to any matter.

(8)   Nothing in this Part shall prejudice the operation of section 12 of the Nuclear Installations Act 1965 (rights to compensation for certain breaches of duties confined to rights under that Act).

## 7   Prohibition on exclusions from liability

The liability of a person by virtue of this Part to person who has suffered damage caused wholly or partly by a defect in a product, or to a dependant or relative of such a person, shall not be limited or excluded by any contract term, by any notice or by any other provision.

## 8   Power to modify Part I

(1)   Her Majesty may by Order in Council make such modifications of this Part and of any other enactment (including an enactment contained in the following Parts of this Act, or in an Act passed after this Act) as appear to Her Majesty in Council to be necessary or expedient in consequence of any modification of the product liability Directive which is made at any time after the passing of this Act.

(2)   An Order in Council under subsection (1) above shall not be submitted to Her Majesty in Council unless a draft of the Order has been laid before, and approved by a resolution of, each House of Parliament.

## 9   Application of Part I to Crown

(1)   Subject to subsection (2) below, this Part shall bind the Crown.

(2)   The Crown shall not, as regards the Crown's liability by virtue of this Part, be bound by this Part further than the Crown is made liable in tort or in reparation under the Crown Proceedings Act 1947, as that Act has effect from time to time.

## PART II
## CONSUMER SAFETY

[. . .]

**11  Safety regulations**

(1)  The Secretary of State may by regulations under this section ('safety regulations') make such provision as he considers appropriate [. . .] for the purpose of securing—

(a)  that goods to which this section applies are safe;

(b)  that goods to which this section applies which are unsafe, or would be unsafe in the hands of persons of a particular description, are not made available to persons generally or, as the case may be, to persons of that description, and

(c)  that appropriate information is, and inappropriate information is not, provided in relation to goods to which this section applies.

(2)  Without prejudice to the generality of subsection (1) above, safety regulations may contain provision—

(a)  with respect to the composition or contents, design, construction, finish or packing of goods to which this section applies, with respect to standards for such goods and with respect to other matters relating to such goods;

(b)  with respect to the giving, refusal, alteration or cancellation of approvals of such goods, of descriptions of such goods or of standards for such goods;

(c)  with respect to the conditions that may be attached to any approval given under the regulations;

(d)  for requiring such fees as may be determined by or under the regulations to be paid on the giving or alteration of any approval under the regulations and on the making of an application for such an approval or alteration;

(e)  with respect to appeals against refusals, alterations and cancellations of approvals given under the regulations and against the conditions contained in such approvals;

(f)  for requiring goods to which this section applies to be approved under the regulations or to conform to the requirements of the regulations or to descriptions or standards specified in or approved by or under the regulations;

(g)  with respect to the testing or inspection of goods to which this section applies (including provision for determining the standards to be applied in carrying out any test or inspection);

(h)  with respect to the way of dealing with goods of which some or all do not satisfy a test required by or under the regulations or a standard connected with a procedure so required;

(i)  for requiring a mark, warning or instruction or any other information relating to goods to be put on or to accompany the goods or to be used or provided in some other manner in relation to the goods, and for securing that inappropriate information is not given in relation to goods either by means of misleading marks or otherwise;

(j)  for prohibiting persons from supplying, or from offering to supply, agreeing to supply, exposing for supply or possessing for supply, goods to which this section applies and component parts and raw materials for such goods;

(k)  for requiring information to be given to any such person as may be determined by or under the regulations for the purpose of enabling that person to exercise any function conferred on him by the regulations.

(3)  Without prejudice as aforesaid, safety regulations may contain provision—

(a)  for requiring persons on whom functions are conferred by or under section 27 below to have regard, in exercising their functions so far as relating to any provision of safety regulations, to matters specified in a direction issued by the Secretary of State with respect to that provision;

(b)  for securing that a person shall not be guilty of an offence under section

12 below unless it is shown that the goods in question do not conform to a particular standard;

(c)   for securing that proceedings for such an offence are not brought in England and Wales except by or with the consent of the Secretary of State or the Director of Public Prosecutions;

(d)   for securing that proceedings for such an offence are not brought in Northern Ireland except by or with consent of the Secretary of State or the Director of Public Prosecutions for Northern Ireland;

(e)   for enabling a magistrate's court in England and Wales or Northern Ireland to try an information or, in Northern Ireland, a complaint in respect of such an offence if the information was laid or the complaint made within twelve months from the time when the offence was committed;

(f)   for enabling summary proceedings for such an offence to be brought in Scotland at any time within twelve months from the time when the offence was committed; and

(g)   for determining the persons by whom, and the manner in which, anything required to be done by or under the regulations is to be done.

(4)   Safety regulations shall not provide for any contravention of the regulations to be an offence.

(5)   Where the Secretary of State proposes to make safety regulations it shall be his duty before he makes them—

(a)   to consult such organisations as appear to him to be representative of interests substantially affected by the proposal;

(b)   to consult such other persons as he considers appropriate; and

(c)   in the case of proposed regulations relating to goods suitable for use at work to consult [the Health and Safety Executive] in relation to the application of the proposed regulations to Great Britain;

but the preceding provisions of this subsection shall not apply in the case of regulations which provide for the regulations to cease to have effect at the end of a period of not more than twelve months beginning with the day on which they come into force and which contain a statement that it appears to the Secretary of State that the need to protect the public requires that the regulations should be made without delay.

(6)   The power to make safety regulations shall be exercisable by statutory instrument subject to annulment in pursuance of a resolution of either House of Parliament and shall include power—

(a)   to make different provision for different cases; and

(b)   to make such supplemental, consequential and transitional provision as the Secretary of State considers appropriate.

(7)   This section applies to any goods other than—

(a)   growing crops and things comprised in land by virtue of being attached to it;

(b)   water, food, feeding stuff and fertiliser;

(c)   gas which is, is to be or has been supplied by a person authorised to supply it by or under [section 7A of the Gas Act 1986 (licensing of gas suppliers and gas shippers) or paragraph 5 of Schedule 2A to that Act (supply to very large customers an exception to prohibition on unlicensed activities)];

(d)   controlled drugs and licensed medicinal products.

## 12   Offences against the safety regulations

(1)   Where safety regulations prohibit a person from supplying or offering or agreeing to supply any goods or from exposing or possessing any goods for supply that person shall be guilty of an offence if he contravenes the prohibition.

(2)   Where safety regulations require a person who makes or processes any goods in the course of carrying on a business—

(a) to carry out a particular test or use a particular procedure in connection with the making or processing of the goods with a view to ascertaining whether the goods satisfy any requirements of such regulations; or

(b) to deal or not to deal in a particular way with a quantity of the goods of which the whole or part does not satisfy such a test or does not satisfy standards connected with such a procedure,

that person shall be guilty of an offence if he does not comply with the requirement.

(3) If a person contravenes a provision of safety regulations which prohibits or requires the provision, by means of a mark or otherwise, of information of a particular kind in relation to goods, he shall be guilty of an offence.

(4) Where safety regulations require any person to give information to another for the purpose of enabling that other to exercise any function, that person shall be guilty of an offence if—

(a) he fails without reasonable cause to comply with the requirement; or

(b) in giving the information which is required of him—

(i) he makes any statement which he knows is false in a material particular; or

(ii) he recklessly makes any statement which is false in a material particular.

(5) A person guilty of an offence under this section shall be liable on summary conviction to imprisonment for a term not exceeding six months or to a fine not exceeding level 5 on the standard scale or to both.

## 13 Prohibition notices and notices to warn

(1) The Secretary of State may—

(a) serve on any person a notice ('a prohibition notice') prohibiting that person, except with the consent of the Secretary of State, from supplying, or from offering to supply, agreeing to supply, exposing for supply or possessing for supply, any relevant goods which the Secretary of State considers are unsafe and which are described in the notice;

(b) serve on any person a notice ('a notice to warn') requiring that person at his own expense to publish, in a form and manner and on occasions specified in the notice, a warning about any relevant goods which the Secretary of State considers are unsafe, which that person supplies or has supplied and which are described in the notice.

(2) Schedule 2 to this Act shall have effect with respect to prohibition notices and notices to warn, and the Secretary of State may by regulations make provision specifying the manner in which information is to be given to any person under that Schedule.

(3) A consent given by the Secretary of State for the purposes of a prohibition notice may impose such conditions on the doing of anything for which the consent is required as the Secretary of State considers appropriate.

(4) A person who contravenes a prohibition notice or a notice to warn shall be guilty of an offence and liable on summary conviction to imprisonment for a term not exceeding six months or to a fine not exceeding level 5 on the standard scale or to both.

(5) The power to make regulations under subsection (2) above shall be exercisable by statutory instrument subject to annulment in pursuance of a resolution of either House of Parliament and shall include power—

(a) to make different provision for different cases; and

(b) to make such supplemental, consequential and transitional provision as the Secretary of State considers appropriate.

(6) In this section 'relevant goods' means—

(a) in relation to a prohibition notice, any goods to which section 11 above applies; and

(b)   in relation to a notice to warn, any goods to which that section applies or any growing crops or things comprised in land by virtue of being attached to it.

[(7)   A notice may not be given under this section in respect of any aspect of the safety of goods, or any risk or category of risk associated with goods, concerning which provision is contained in the General Product Safety Regulations 2005.]

### 14   Suspension notices

(1)   Where an enforcement authority has reasonable grounds for suspecting that any safety provision has been contravened in relation to any goods, the authority may serve a notice ('suspension notice') prohibiting the person on whom it is served, for such period ending not more than six months after the date of the notice as is specified therein, from doing any of the following things without the consent of the authority, that is to say, supplying the goods, offering to supply them, agreeing to supply them or exposing them for supply.

(2)   A suspension notice served by an enforcement authority in respect of any goods shall—

(a)   describe the goods in a manner sufficient to identify them;

(b)   set out the grounds on which the authority suspects that a safety provision has been contravened in relation to the goods, and

(c)   state that, and the manner in which, the person on whom the notice is served may appeal against the notice under section 15 below.

(3)   A suspension notice served by an enforcement authority for the purpose of prohibiting a person for any period from doing the things mentioned in subsection (1) above in relation to any goods may also require that person to keep the authority informed of the whereabouts throughout that period of any of those goods in which he has an interest.

(4)   Where a suspension notice has been served on any person in respect of any goods, no further such notice shall be served on that person in respect of the same goods unless—

(a)   proceedings against that person for an offence in respect of a contravention in relation to the goods of a safety provision (not being an offence under this section); or

(b)   proceedings for the forfeiture of the goods under section 16 or 17 below, are pending at the end of the period specified in the first-mentioned notice.

(5)   A consent given by an enforcement authority for the purposes of subsection (1) above may impose such conditions on the doing of anything for which the consent is required as the authority considers appropriate.

(6)   Any person who contravenes a suspension notice shall be guilty of an offence and liable on summary conviction to imprisonment for a term not exceeding six months or to a fine not exceeding level 5 on the standard scale or to both.

(7)   Where an enforcement authority serves a suspension notice in respect of any goods, the authority shall be liable to pay compensation to any person having an interest in the goods in respect of any loss or damage caused by reason of the service of the notice if—

(a)   there has been no contravention in relation to the goods of any safety provision; and

(b)   the exercise of the power is not attributable to any neglect or default by that person.

(8)   Any disputed question as to the right to or the amount of any compensation payable under this section shall be determined by arbitration or, in Scotland, by a single arbiter appointed, failing agreement between the parties, by the sheriff.

### 15   Appeals against suspension notices

(1)   Any person having an interest in any goods in respect of which a suspen-

sion notice is for the time being in force may apply for an order setting aside the notice.

(2)  An application under this section may be made—

(a)  to any magistrates' court in which proceedings have been brought in England and Wales or Northern Ireland—

(i)  for an offence in respect of a contravention in relation to the goods of any safety provision; or

(ii)  for the forfeiture of the goods under section 16 below;

(b)  where no such proceedings have been so brought, by way of complaint to a magistrates' court; or

(c)  in Scotland, by summary application to the sheriff.

(3)  On an application under this section to a magistrates' court in England and Wales or Northern Ireland the court shall make an order setting aside the suspension notice only if the court is satisfied that there has been no contravention in relation to the goods of any safety provision.

(4)  On an application under this section to the sheriff he shall make an order setting aside the suspension notice only if he is satisfied that at the date of making the order—

(a)  proceedings for an offence in respect of a contravention in relation to the goods of any safety provision; or

(b)  proceedings for the forfeiture of the goods under section 17 below, have not been brought or, having been brought, have been concluded.

(5)  Any person aggrieved by an order made under this section by a magistrates' court in England and Wales or Northern Ireland, or by a decision of such a court not to make such an order, may appeal against that order or decision—

(a)  in England and Wales, to the Crown Court;

(b)  in Northern Ireland, to the county court;

and an order so made may contain such provision as appears to the court to be appropriate for delaying the coming into force of the order pending the making and determination of any appeal (including any application under section 111 of the Magistrates' Courts Act 1980 or Article 146 of the Magistrates' Courts (Northern Ireland) Order 1981 (statement of case)).

**16**  [*Does not apply to Scotland.*]

### 17  Forfeiture: Scotland

(1)  In Scotland a sheriff may make an order for forfeiture of any goods in relation to which there has been a contravention of a safety provision—

(a)  on an application by the procurator-fiscal made in the manner specified in [section 134 of the Criminal Procedure (Scotland) Act 1995]; or

(b)  where a person is convicted of any offence in respect of any such contravention, in addition to any other penalty which the sheriff may impose.

(2)  The procurator-fiscal making an application under subsection (1)(a) above shall serve on any person appearing to him to be the owner of, or otherwise to have an interest in, the goods to which the application relates a copy of the application, together with a notice giving him the opportunity to appear at the hearing of the application to show cause why the goods should not be forfeited.

(3)  Service under subsection (2) above shall be carried out, and such service may be proved, in the manner specified for citation of accused in summary proceedings under the [Criminal Procedure (Scotland) Act 1995].

(4)  Any person upon whom notice is served under subsection (2) above and any other person claiming to be the owner of, or otherwise to have an interest in, goods to which an application under this section relates shall be entitled to appear at the hearing of the application to show cause why the goods should not be forfeited.

(5)  The sheriff shall not make an order following an application under subsection (1)(a) above—

(a)   if any person on whom notice is served under subsection (2) above does not appear, unless service of the notice on that person is proved; or

(b)   if no notice under subsection (2) above has been served, unless the court is satisfied that in the circumstances it was reasonable not to serve notice on any person.

(6)   The sheriff shall make an order under this section only if he is satisfied that there has been a contravention in relation to those goods of a safety provision.

(7)   For the avoidance of doubt it is declared that the sheriff may infer for the purposes of this section that there has been a contravention in relation to any goods of a safety provision if he is satisfied that any such provision has been contravened in relation to any goods which are representative of those goods (whether by reason of being of the same design or part of the same consignment or batch or otherwise).

(8)   Where an order for the forfeiture of any goods is made following an application by the procurator-fiscal under subsection (1)(a) above, any person who appeared, or was entitled to appear, to show cause why goods should not be forfeited may, within twenty-one days of the making of the order, appeal to the High Court by Bill of Suspension on the ground of an alleged miscarriage of justice; [and section 182(5)(a) to (e) of the Criminal Procedure (Scotland) Act 1995 shall apply to an appeal under this subsection as it applies to a stated case under Part X of that Act].

(9)   An order following an application under subsection (1)(a) above shall not take effect—

(a)   until the end of the period of twenty-one days beginning with the day after the day on which the order is made; or

(b)   if an appeal is made under subsection (8) above within that period, until the appeal is determined or abandoned.

(10)   An order under subsection (1)(b) above shall not take effect—

(a)   until the end of the period within which an appeal against the order could be brought under the Criminal Procedure (Scotland) Act 1995; or

(b)   if an appeal is made within that period, until the appeal is determined or abandoned.

(11)   Subject to subsection (12) below, goods forfeited under this section shall be destroyed in accordance with such directions as the sheriff may give.

(12)   If he thinks fit the sheriff may direct that the goods be released, to such person as he may specify, on condition that that person does not supply those goods to any other person otherwise than as mentioned in section 46(7)(a) or (b) below.

## 18   Power to obtain information

(1)   If the Secretary of State considers that, for the purpose of deciding whether—

(a)   to make, vary or revoke any safety regulations; or

(b)   to serve, vary or revoke a prohibition notice; or

(c)   to serve or revoke a notice to warn,

he requires information which another person is likely to be able to furnish, the Secretary of State may serve on the other person a notice under this section.

(2)   A notice served on any person under this section may require that person—

(a)   to furnish to the Secretary of State, within a period specified in the notice, such information as is so specified;

(b)   to produce such records as are specified in the notice at a time and place so specified and to permit a person appointed by the Secretary of State for the purpose to take copies of the records at that time and place.

(3)   A person shall be guilty of an offence if he—

(a)   fails, without reasonable cause, to comply with a notice served on him under this section; or

(b) in purporting to comply with a requirement which by virtue of paragraph (a) of subsection (2) above is contained in such a notice—

(i) furnishes information which he knows is false in a material particular; or

(ii) recklessly furnishes information which is false in a material particular.

(4) A person guilty of an offence under subsection (3) above shall—

(a) in the case of an offence under paragraph (a) of that subsection, be liable on summary conviction to a fine not exceeding level 5 on the standard scale; and

(b) in the case of an offence under paragraph (b) of that subsection be liable—

(i) on conviction on indictment, to a fine,

(ii) on summary conviction, to a fine not exceeding the statutory maximum.

## 19  Interpretation of Part II

(1) in this Part—

'controlled drug' means a controlled drug within the meaning of the Misuse of Drugs Act 1971;

'feeding stuff' and 'fertiliser' have the same meaning as in Part IV of the Agriculture Act 1970;

'food' does not include anything containing tobacco but, subject to that, has the same meaning as in the [Food Safety Act 1990] or, in relation to Northern Ireland, the same meaning as in the [Food (Northern Ireland) Order 1989];

'licensed medicinal product' means—

(a) any medicinal product within the meaning of the Medicines Act 1968 in respect of which a product licence within the meaning of that Act is for the time being in force;

(b) any other article or substance in respect of which any such licence is for the time being in force in pursuance of an order under section 104 or 105 of that Act (application of Act to other articles and substances); [or

(c) a veterinary medicinal product that has a marketing authorisation under the Veterinary Medicines Regulations 2006.]

'safe', in relation to any goods, means such that there is no risk, or no risk apart from one reduced to a minimum, that any of the following will (whether immediately or after a definite or indefinite period) cause the death of, or any personal injury to, any person whatsoever, that is to say—

(a) the goods;

(b) the keeping, use or consumption of the goods;

(c) the assembly of any of the goods which are, or are to be supplied unassembled;

(d) any emission or leakage from the goods or, as a result of the keeping, use or consumption of the goods, from anything else; or

(e) reliance on the accuracy of any measurement, calculation or other reading made by or by means of the goods,

and [. . .] 'unsafe' shall be construed accordingly;

'tobacco' includes any tobacco product within the meaning of the Tobacco Products Duty Act 1979 and any article or substance containing tobacco and intended for oral or nasal use.

(2) In the definition of 'safe' in subsection (1) above, references to the keeping, use or consumption of any goods are references to—

(a) the keeping, use or consumption of the goods by the persons by whom, and in all or any of the ways or circumstances in which, they might reasonably be expected to be kept, used or consumed; and

(b) the keeping, use or consumption of the goods either alone or in conjunction with other goods in conjunction with which they might reasonably be expected to be kept, used or consumed.

[. . .]

## PART IV
## ENFORCEMENT OF PARTS II AND III

### 27  Enforcement

(1)  Subject to the following provisions of this section—

(a)  it shall be the duty of every weights and measures authority in Great Britain to enforce within their area the safety provisions [. . .]; and

(b)  it shall be the duty of every district council in Northern Ireland to enforce within their area the safety provisions.

(2)  The Secretary of State may by regulations—

(a)  wholly or partly transfer any duty imposed by subsection (1) above on a weights and measures authority or a district council in Northern Ireland to such other person who has agreed to the transfer as is specified in the regulations;

(b)  relieve such an authority or council of any such duty so far as it is exercisable in relation to such goods as may be described in the regulations.

(3)  The power to make regulations under subsection (2) above shall be exercisable by statutory instrument subject to annulment in pursuance of a resolution of either House of Parliament and shall include power—

(a)  to make different provision for different cases; and

(b)  to make such supplemental, consequential and transitional provision as the Secretary of State considers appropriate.

[(3A)  For the investigatory powers available to a person for the purposes of the duty imposed by subsection (1), see Schedule 5 to the Consumer Rights Act 2015 (as well as section 29).]

(4)  Nothing in this section shall authorise any weights and measures authority, or any person on whom functions are conferred by regulations under subsection (2) above, to bring proceedings in Scotland for an offence.

[. . .]

### 29  Powers of search etc

(1)  Subject to the following provisions of this Part, a duly authorised officer of an enforcement authority may at any reasonable hour and on production, if required, of his credentials exercise [the power conferred by subsection (4)].

[. . .]

(4)  If the officer has reasonable grounds for suspecting that any goods are manufactured or imported goods which have not been supplied in the United Kingdom since they were manufactured or imported he may—

(a)  for the purpose of ascertaining whether there has been any contravention of any safety provision in relation to the goods, require any person carrying on a business, or employed in connection with a business, to produce any records relating to the business;

(b)  for the purpose of ascertaining (by testing or otherwise) whether there has been any such contravention, seize and detain the goods;

(c)  take copies of, or of any entry in, any records produced by virtue of paragraph (a) above.

[. . .]

(7)  If and to the extent that it is reasonably necessary to do so to prevent a contravention of any safety provision [. . .], the officer may, for the purpose of exercising his power under subsection (4) [. . .] above to seize any goods [. . .]—

(a)  require any person having authority to do so to open any container or to open any vending machine; and

(b)  himself open or break open any such container or machine where a requirement made under paragraph (a) above in relation to the container or machine has not been complied with.

## 30  Provisions supplemental to s 29

(1)  An officer seizing any goods [. . .] under section [29(4)] above shall inform the following persons that the goods [. . .] have been so seized, that is to say—

(a)   the person from whom they are seized; and

(b)   in the case of imported goods seized on any premises under the control of the Commissioners of Customs and Excise, the importer of those goods (within the meaning of the Customs and Excise Management Act 1979).

(2)   If a justice of the peace—

(a)   is satisfied by any written information on oath that there are reasonable grounds for believing either—

(i)   that any [. . .] records which any officer has power to inspect under section [29(4)] above are on any premises and that their inspection is likely to disclose evidence that there has been a contravention of any safety provision [. . .]; or

(ii)   that such a contravention has taken place, is taking place or is about to take place on any premises; and

(b)   is also satisfied by any such information either—

(i)   that admission to the premises has been or is likely to be refused and that notice of intention to apply for a warrant under this section has been given to the occupier; or

(ii)   that an application for admission, or the giving of such a notice, would defeat the object of entry or that the premises are unoccupied or that the occupier is temporarily absent and it might defeat the object of the entry to await his return, the justice may by warrant under his hand, which shall continue in force for a period of one month, authorise any officer of an enforcement authority to enter the premises, if need be by force.

(3)   An officer entering any premises by virtue of [. . .] a warrant under subsection (2) above may take with him such other persons and such equipment as may appear to him necessary.

(4)   On leaving any premises which a person is authorised to enter by a warrant under subsection (2) above, that person shall, if the premises are unoccupied or the occupier is temporarily absent, leave the premises as effectively secured against trespassers as he found them.

(5)   If any person who is not an officer of an enforcement authority purports to act as such under section [29(4)] above of this section he shall be guilty of an offence and liable on summary conviction to a fine not exceeding level 5 on the standard scale.

(6)   Where any goods seized by an officer under section [29(4)] above are submitted to a test, the officer shall inform the persons mentioned in subsection (1) above of the result of the test and, if—

(a)   proceedings are brought for an offence in respect of a contravention in relation to the goods of any safety provision [. . .] or for the forfeiture of the goods under section 16 or 17 above, or a suspension notice is served in respect of any goods; and

(b)   the officer is requested to do so and it is practicable to comply with the request, the officer shall allow any person who is a party to the proceedings or, as the case may be, has an interest in the goods to which the notice relates to have the goods tested.

(7)   The Secretary of State may by regulations provide that any test of goods seized under section [29(4)] above by an officer of an enforcement authority shall—

(a)   be carried out at the expense of the authority in a manner and by a person prescribed by or determined under the regulations; or

(b)   be carried out either as mentioned in paragraph (a) above or by the authority in a manner prescribed by the regulations.

(8)   The power to make regulations under subsection (7) above shall be exer-

cisable by statutory instrument subject to annulment in pursuance of a resolution of either House of Parliament and shall include power—

(a)   to make different provision for different cases; and

(b)   to make such supplemental, consequential and transitional provisions as the Secretary of State considers appropriate.

(9)   In the application of this section to Scotland, the reference in subsection (2) above to a justice of the peace shall include a reference to a sheriff and the references to written information on oath shall be construed as references to evidence on oath.

(10)   In the application of this section to Northern Ireland, the references in subsection (2) above to any information on oath shall be construed as references to any complaint on oath.

### 31   Power of customs officer to detain goods

(1)   A customs officer may, for the purpose of facilitating the exercise by an enforcement authority or officer of such an authority of any functions conferred on the authority or officer by or under Part II of this Act, or by [section 29(4) of this Act or Schedule 5 to the Consumer Rights Act 2015] in its application for the purposes of the safety provisions, seize any imported goods and detain them for not more than two working days.

(2)   Anything seized and detained under this section shall be dealt with during the period of its detention in such manner as the Commissioners of Customs and Excise may direct.

(3)   In subsection (1) above the reference to two working days is a reference to a period of forty-eight hours calculated from the time when the goods in question are seized but disregarding so much of any period as falls on a Saturday or Sunday or on Christmas Day, Good Friday or a day which is a bank holiday under the Banking and Financial Dealings Act 1971 in the part of the United Kingdom where the goods are seized.

(4)   In this section and section 32 below 'customs officer' means any officer within the meaning of the Customs and Excise Management Act 1979.

### 32   Obstruction of authorised officer

(1)   Any person who—

(a)   intentionally obstructs any officer of an enforcement authority who is acting in pursuance of [section 29(4)] or any customs officer who is [acting in pursuance of section 31]; or

(b)   intentionally fails to comply with any requirements made of him by any officer of an enforcement authority under [section 29(4)], or

(c)   without reasonable cause fails to give any officer of an enforcement authority who is so acting any other assistance or information which the officer may reasonably require of him for the purposes of the exercise of the officer's functions under [section 29(4)],

shall be guilty of an offence and liable on summary conviction to a fine not exceeding level 5 on the standard scale.

(2)   A person shall be guilty of an offence if, in giving any information which is required of him by virtue of subsection (1)(c) above—

(a)   he makes any statement which he knows is false in a material particular, or

(b)   he recklessly makes a statement which is false in a material particular.

(3)   A person guilty of an offence under subsection (2) above shall be liable—

(a)   on conviction on indictment to a fine;

(b)   on summary conviction, to a fine not exceeding the statutory maximum.

### 33   Appeals against detention of goods

(1)   Any person having an interest in any goods which are for the time being detained [section 29(4)] by an enforcement authority or by an officer of such an

authority may apply for an order requiring the goods to be released to him or to another person.

(2)   An application under this section may be made—

(a)   to any magistrates' court in which proceedings have been brought in England and Wales or Northern Ireland—

(i)   for an offence in respect of a contravention in relation to the goods of any safety provision [. . .]; or

(ii)   for the forfeiture of the goods under section 16 above;

(b)   where no such proceedings have been so brought, by way of complaint to a magistrates' court; or

(c)   in Scotland, by summary application to the sheriff [. . .].

(3)   On an application under this section to a magistrates' court or to the sheriff, an order requiring goods to be released shall be made only if the court or sheriff is satisfied—

(a)   that proceedings—

(i)   for an offence in respect of a contravention in relation to the goods of any safety provision [. . .]; or

(ii)   for the forfeiture of the goods under section 16 or 17 above,

have not been brought or, having been brought, have been concluded without the goods being forfeited; and

(b)   where no such proceedings have been brought, that more than six months have elapsed since the goods were seized.

(4)   [Does not apply to Scotland.]

### 34   Compensation for seizure and detention

(1)   Where an officer of an enforcement authority exercises any power under section [29(4)] above to seize and detain goods, the enforcement authority shall be liable to pay compensation to any person having an interest in the goods in respect of any loss or damage caused by reason of the exercise of the power if—

(a)   there has been no contravention in relation to the goods of any safety provision [. . .]; and

(b)   the exercise of the power is not attributable to any neglect or default by that person [. . .].

(2)   Any disputed question as to the right to or the amount of any compensation payable under this section shall be determined by arbitration or, in Scotland, by a single arbiter appointed, failing agreement between the parties, by the sheriff.

### 35   Recovery of expenses of enforcement

(1)   This section shall apply where a court—

(a)   convicts a person of an offence in respect of a contravention in relation to any goods of any safety provision [. . .]; or

(b)   makes an order under section 16 or 17 above for the forfeiture of any goods [. . .].

(2)   The court may (in addition to any other order it may make as to costs or expenses) order the person convicted or, as the case may be, any person having an interest in the goods to reimburse an enforcement authority for any expenditure which has been or may be incurred by that authority—

(a)   in connection with any seizure or detention of the goods by or on behalf of the authority; or

(b)   in connection with any compliance by the authority with directions given by the court for the purposes of any order for the forfeiture of the goods.

PART V
## MISCELLANEOUS AND SUPPLEMENTAL

**36** [*Amends Health and Safety at Work etc Act 1974*]

### 37 [Power of Commissioners for Revenue and Customs to disclose information]

(1) If they think it appropriate to do so for the purpose of facilitating the exercise by any person to whom subsection (2) below applies of any function conferred on that person by or under Part II of this Act, or by or under Part IV of this Act in its application for the purposes of the safety provisions, [the Commissioners for Her Majesty's Revenue and Customs] may authorise the disclosure to that person of any information obtained [or held] for the purposes of the exercise by [Her Majesty's Revenue and Customs] of their functions in relation to imported goods.

(2) This subsection applies to an enforcement authority and to any officer of an enforcement authority.

(3) A disclosure of information made to any person under subsection (1) above shall be made in such manner as may be directed by [the Commissioners for Her Majesty's Revenue and Customs] and may be made through such persons acting on behalf of that person as may be so directed.

(4) Information may be disclosed to a person under subsection (1) above whether or not the disclosure of the information has been requested by or on behalf of that person.

[. . .]

### 39 Defence of due diligence

(1) Subject to the following provisions of this section, in proceedings against any person for an offence to which this section applies it shall be a defence for that person to show that he took all reasonable steps and exercised all due diligence to avoid committing the offence.

(2) Where in any proceedings against any person for such an offence the defence provided by subsection (1) above involves an allegation that the commission of the offence was due—

(a)    to the act or default of another; or

(b)    to reliance on information given by another,

that person shall not, without the leave of the court, be entitled to rely on the defence unless, not less than seven clear days before the hearing of the proceedings, he has served a notice under subsection (3) below on the person bringing the proceedings.

(3) A notice under this subsection shall give such information identifying or assisting in the identification of the person who committed the act or default or gave the information as is in the possession of the person serving the notice at the time he serves it.

(4) It is hereby declared that a person shall not be entitled to rely on the defence provided by subsection (1) above by reason of his reliance on information supplied by another, unless he shows that it was reasonable in all the circumstances for him to have relied on the information, having regard in particular—

(a)    to the steps which he took, and those which might reasonably have been taken, for the purpose of verifying the information, and

(b)    to whether he had any reason to disbelieve the information.

(5) This section shall apply to an offence under section [. . .] 12(1), (2) or (3), 13(4) [, or 14(6)] above.

### 40 Liability of persons other than principal offender

(1) Where the commission by any person of an offence to which section 39 above applies is due to an act or default committed by some other person in the course of any business of his, the other person shall be guilty of the offence and

may be proceeded against and punished by virtue of this subsection whether or not proceedings are taken against the first-mentioned person.

(2)   Where a body corporate is guilty of an offence under this Act (including where it is so guilty by virtue of subsection (1) above) in respect of any act or default which is shown to have been committed with the consent or connivance of, or to be attributable to any neglect on the part of, any director, manager, secretary or other similar officer of the body corporate or any person who was purporting to act in any such capacity he, as well as the body corporate, shall be guilty of that offence and shall be liable to be proceeded against and punished accordingly.

(3)   Where the affairs of a body corporate are managed by its members, subsection (2) above shall apply in relation to the acts and defaults of a member in connection with his functions of management as if he were a director of the body corporate.

## 41   Civil proceedings

(1)   An obligation imposed by safety regulations shall be a duty owed to any person who may be affected by a contravention of the obligation and, subject to any provisions to the contrary in the regulations and to the defences and other incidents applying to actions for breach of statutory duty, a contravention of any such obligation shall be actionable accordingly.

(2)   This Act shall not be construed as conferring any other right of action in civil proceedings, apart from the right conferred by virtue of Part I of this Act, in respect of any loss or damage suffered in consequence of a contravention of a safety provision [. . .].

(3)   Subject to any provision to the contrary in the agreement itself, an agreement shall not be void or unenforceable by reason only of a contravention of a safety provision [. . .].

(4)   Liability by virtue of subsection (1) above shall not be limited or excluded by any contract term, by any notice or (subject to the power contained in subsection (1) above to limit or exclude it in safety regulations) by any other provision.

(5)   Nothing in subsection (1) above shall prejudice the operation of section 12 of the Nuclear Installations Act 1965 (rights to compensation for certain breaches of duties confined to rights under that Act).

(6)   In this section 'damage' includes personal injury and death.

## 42   Reports etc

(1)   It shall be the duty of the Secretary of State at least once in every five years to lay before each House of Parliament a report on the exercise during the period to which the report relates of the functions which under Part II of this Act, or under Part IV of this Act in its application for the purposes of the safety provisions, are exercisable by the Secretary of State, weights and measures authorities, district councils in Northern Ireland and persons on whom functions are conferred by regulations made under section 27(2) above.

(2)   The Secretary of State may from time to time prepare and lay before each House of Parliament such other reports on the exercise of those functions as he considers appropriate.

(3)   Every weights and measures authority, every district council in Northern Ireland and every person on whom functions are conferred by regulations under subsection (2) of section 27 above shall, whenever the Secretary of State so directs, make a report to the Secretary of State on the exercise of the functions exercisable by that authority or council under that section or by that person by virtue of any such regulations.

(4)   A report under subsection (3) above shall be in such form and shall contain such particulars as are specified in the direction of the Secretary of State.

(5)   The first report under subsection (1) above shall be laid before each House

of Parliament not more than five years after the laying of the last report under section 8(2) of the Consumer Safety Act 1978.

### 43 Financial provisions

(1) There shall be paid out of money provided by Parliament—

(a) any expenses incurred or compensation payable by a Minister of the Crown or Government department in consequence of any provision of this Act; and

(b) any increase attributable to this Act in the sums payable out of money so provided under any other Act.

(2) Any sums received by a Minister of the Crown or Government department by virtue of this Act shall be paid into the Consolidated Fund.

### 44 Service of documents etc

(1) Any documents required or authorised by virtue of this Act to be served on a person may be so served—

(a) by delivering it to him or by leaving it at his proper address or by sending it by post to him at that address; or

(b) if the person is a body corporate, by serving it in accordance with paragraph (a) above on the secretary or clerk of that body; or

(c) if the person is a partnership, by serving it in accordance with that paragraph on a partner or on a person having control or management of the partnership business.

(2) For the purposes of subsection (1) above, and for the purposes of section 7 of the Interpretation Act 1978 (which relates to the service of documents by post) in its application to that subsection, the proper address of any person on whom a document is to be served by virtue of this Act shall be his last known address except that—

(a) in the case of service on a body corporate or its secretary or clerk, it shall be the address of the registered or principal office of the body corporate;

(b) in the case of service on a partnership or a partner or a person having the control or management of a partnership business, it shall be the principal office of the partnership; and for the purposes of this subsection the principal office of a company registered outside the United Kingdom or of a partnership carrying on business outside the United Kingdom is its principal office within the United Kingdom.

(3) The Secretary of State may by regulations make provision for the manner in which any information is to be given to any person under any provision of Part IV of this Act.

(4) Without prejudice to the generality of subsection (3) above regulations made by the Secretary of State may prescribe the person, or manner of determining the person, who is to be treated for the purposes of section [. . .] 30 above as the person from whom goods were [. . .] seized where the goods were [. . .] seized from a vending machine.

(5) The power to make regulations under subsection (3) or (4) above shall be exercisable by statutory instrument subject to annulment in pursuance of a resolution of either House of Parliament and shall include power—

(a) to make different provision for different cases; and

(b) to make such supplemental, consequential and transitional provision as the Secretary of State considers appropriate.

### 45 Interpretation

(1) In this Act, except in so far as the context otherwise requires—

'aircraft' includes gliders, balloons and hovercraft;

'business' includes a trade or profession and the activities of a professional or trade association or of a local authority or other public authority;

'conditional sale agreement', 'credit-sale agreement' and 'hire-purchase agreement' have the same meanings as in the Consumer Credit Act 1974 but as if in the definitions in that Act 'goods' had the same meaning as in this Act;

'contravention' includes a failure to comply and cognate expressions shall be construed accordingly;

'enforcement authority' means the Secretary of State, any other Minister of the Crown in charge of a Government department, any such department and any authority, council or other person on whom functions under this Act are conferred by or under section 27 above;

'gas' has the same meaning as in Part I of the Gas Act 1986;

'goods' includes substances, growing crops and things comprised in land by virtue of being attached to it and any ship, aircraft or vehicle;

'information' includes accounts, estimates and returns;

'magistrates' court', in relation to Northern Ireland, means a court of summary jurisdiction;

'modifications' includes additions, alterations and omissions, and cognate expressions shall be construed accordingly;

'motor vehicle' has the same meaning as in [the Road Traffic Act 1988];

'notice' means a notice in writing;

'notice to warn' means a notice under section 13(1)(b) above;

'officer', in relation to an enforcement authority, means a person authorised in writing to assist the authority in carrying out its functions under or for the purposes of the enforcement of any of the safety provisions or of any of the provisions made by or under Part III of this Act;

'personal injury' includes any disease and any other impairment of a person's physical or mental condition;

'premises' includes any place and any ship, aircraft or vehicle;

'prohibition notice' means a notice under section 13(1)(a) above;

'records' includes any books or documents and any records in non-documentary form;

'safety provision' means [. . .] any provision of safety regulations, a prohibition notice or a suspension notice;

'safety regulations' means regulations under section 11 above;

'ship' includes any boat and any other description of vessel used in navigation;

'subordinate legislation' has the same meaning as in the Interpretation Act 1978;

'substance' means any natural or artificial substance, whether in solid, liquid or gaseous form or in the form of a vapour, and includes substances that are comprised in or mixed with other goods;

'supply' and cognate expressions shall be construed in accordance with section 46 below;

'suspension notice' means a notice under section 14 above.

(2)   Except in so far as the context otherwise requires, references in this Act to a contravention of a safety provision shall, in relation to any goods, include references to anything which would constitute such a contravention if the goods were supplied to any person.

(3)   References in this Act to any goods in relation to which any safety provision has been or may have been contravened shall include references to any goods which it is not reasonably practicable to separate from any such goods.

[. . .]

(5)   In Scotland, any reference in this Act to things comprised in land by virtue of being attached to it is a reference to moveables which have become heritable by accession to heritable property.

## 46   Meaning of 'supply'

(1)   Subject to the following provisions of this section, references in this Act to supplying goods shall be construed as references to doing any of the following, whether as principal or agent, that is to say—

(a)    selling, hiring out or lending the goods;

(b)    entering into a hire-purchase agreement to furnish the goods;

(c)    the performance of any contract for work and materials to furnish the goods;

(d)    providing the goods in exchange for any consideration [. . .] other than money;

(e)    providing the goods in or in connection with the performance of any statutory function; or

(f)    giving the goods as a prize or otherwise making a gift of the goods;

and, in relation to gas or water, those references shall be construed as including references to providing the service by which the gas or water is made available for use.

(2)    For the purposes of any reference in this Act to supplying goods, where a person ('the ostensible supplier') supplies goods to another person ('the customer') under a hire-purchase agreement, conditional sale agreement or credit-sale agreement or under an agreement for the hiring of goods (other than a hire-purchase agreement) and the ostensible supplier—

(a)    carries on the business of financing the provision of goods for others by means of such agreements; and

(b)    in the course of that business acquired his interest in the goods supplied to the customer as a means of financing the provision of them for the customer by a further person ('the effective supplier'),

the effective supplier and not the ostensible supplier shall be treated as supplying the goods to the customer.

(3)    Subject to subsection (4) below, the performance of any contract by the erection of any building or structure on any land or by the carrying out of any other building works shall be treated for the purposes of this Act as a supply of goods in so far as, but only in so far as, it involves the provision of any goods to any person by means of their incorporation into the building, structure or works.

(4)    Except for the purposes of, and in relation to, notices to warn [. . .], references in this Act to supplying goods shall not include references to supplying goods comprised in land where the supply is effected by the creation or disposal of an interest in the land.

(5)    Except in Part I of this Act references in this Act to a person's supplying goods shall be confined to references to that person's supplying goods in the course of a business of his, but for the purposes of this subsection it shall be immaterial whether the business is a business of dealing in the goods.

(6)    For the purposes of subsection (5) above goods shall not be treated as supplied in the course of a business if they are supplied, in pursuance of an obligation arising under or in connection with the insurance of the goods, to the person with whom they were insured.

(7)    Except for the purposes of, and in relation to, prohibition notices or suspension notices, references in [Part 2 or Part 4] of this Act to supplying goods shall not include—

(a)    references to supplying goods where the person supplied carries on a business of buying goods of the same description as those goods and repairing or reconditioning them,

(b)    references to supplying goods by a sale of articles as scrap (that is to say, for the value of materials included in the articles rather than for the value of the articles themselves).

(8)    Where any goods have at any time been supplied by being hired out or lent to any person, neither a continuation or renewal of the hire or loan (whether on the same or different terms) nor any transaction for the transfer after that time of any interest in the goods to the person to whom they were hired or lent shall be treated for the purposes of this Act as a further supply of the goods to that person.

(9)    A ship, aircraft or motor vehicle shall not be treated for the purposes of this

Act as supplied to any person by reason only that services consisting in the carriage of goods or passengers in that ship, aircraft or vehicle, or in its use for any other purpose, are provided to that person in pursuance of an agreement relating to the use of the ship, aircraft or vehicle for a particular period or for particular voyages, flights or journeys.

### 47  Savings for certain privileges

(1)  Nothing in this Act shall be taken as requiring any person to produce any records if he would be entitled to refuse to produce those records in any proceedings in any court on the ground that they are the subject of legal professional privilege or, in Scotland, that they contain a confidential communication made by or to an advocate or solicitor in that capacity, or as authorising any person to take possession of any records which are in the possession of a person who would be so entitled.

(2)  Nothing in this Act shall be construed as requiring a person to answer any question or give any information if to do so would incriminate that person or that person's spouse [or civil partner].

### 48  [*Minor and consequential amendments and repeals*]

### 49  [*Northern Ireland*]

### 50  Short title, commencement and transitional provision

(1)  This Act may be cited as the Consumer Protection Act 1987.

(2)  This Act shall come into force on such day as the Secretary of State may by order made by statutory instrument appoint, and different days may be so appointed for different provisions or for different purposes.

. . .


## SCHEDULE 2
## PROHIBITION NOTICES AND NOTICES TO WARN
Section 13


## PART I
## PROHIBITION NOTICES

1  A prohibition notice in respect of any goods shall—

(a)  state that the Secretary of State considers that the goods are unsafe;

(b)  set out the reasons why the Secretary of State considers that the goods are unsafe;

(c)  specify the day on which the notice is to come into force; and

(d)  state that the trader may at any time make representations in writing to the Secretary of State for the purpose of establishing that the goods are safe.

2—(1)  If representations in writing about a prohibition notice are made by the trader to the Secretary of State, it shall be the duty of the Secretary of State to consider whether to revoke the notice and—

(a)  if he decides to revoke it, to do so;

(b)  in any other case, to appoint a person to consider those representations, any further representations made (whether in writing or orally) by the trader about the notice and the statements of any witnesses examined under this Part of this Schedule.

(2)  Where the Secretary of State has appointed a person to consider representations about a prohibition notice, he shall serve a notification on the trader which—

(a)  states that the trader may make oral representations to the appointed person for the purpose of establishing that the goods to which the notice relates are safe; and

(b)   specifies the place and time at which the oral representations may be made.

(3)   The time specified in a notification served under sub-paragraph (2) above shall not be before the end of the period of twenty-one days beginning with the day on which the notification is served, unless the trader otherwise agrees.

(4)   A person on whom a notification has been served under sub-paragraph (2) above or his representative may, at the place and time specified in the notification—

(a)   make oral representations to the appointed person for the purpose of establishing that the goods in question are safe; and

(b)   call and examine witnesses in connection with representations.

3—(1)   Where representations in writing about a prohibition notice are made by the trader to the Secretary of State at any time after a person has been appointed to consider representations about that notice, then, whether or not the appointed person has made a report to the Secretary of State, the following provisions of this paragraph shall apply instead of paragraph 2 above.

(2)   The Secretary of State shall, before the end of the period of one month beginning with the day on which he receives the representations, serve a notification on the trader which states—

(a)   that the Secretary of State has decided to revoke the notice, has decided to vary it or, as the case may be, has decided neither to revoke nor to vary it; or

(b)   that, a person having been appointed to consider representations about the notice, the trader may, at a place and time specified in the notification, make oral representations to the appointed person for the purpose of establishing that the goods to which the notice relates are safe.

(3)   The time specified in a notification served for the purposes of sub-paragraph (2)(b) above shall not be before the end of the period of twenty-one days beginning with the day on which the notification is served, unless the trader otherwise agrees or the time is the time already specified for the purposes of paragraph 2(2)(b) above.

(4)   A person on whom a notification has been served for the purposes of sub-paragraph (2)(b) above or his representative may, at the place and time specified in the notification—

(a)   make oral representations to the appointed person for the purpose of establishing that the goods in question are safe; and

(b)   call and examine witnesses in connection with the representations.

4—(1)   Where a person is appointed to consider representations about a prohibition notice, it shall be his duty to consider—

(a)   any written representations made by the trader about the notice, other than those in respect of which a notification is served under paragraph 3(2)(a) above;

(b)   any oral representations made under paragraph 2(4) or 3(4) above; and

(c)   any statements made by witnesses in connection with the oral representations, and after considering any matters under this paragraph, to make a report (including recommendations) to the Secretary of State about the matters considered by him and the notice.

(2)   It shall be the duty of the Secretary of State to consider any report made to him under sub-paragraph (1) above and, after considering the report, to inform the trader of his decision with respect to the prohibition notice to which the report relates.

5—(1)   The Secretary of State may revoke or vary a prohibition notice by serving on the trader a notification stating that the notice is revoked or, as the case may be, is varied as specified in the notification.

(2)   The Secretary of State shall not vary a prohibition notice so as to make the effect of the notice more restrictive for the trader.

(3)   Without prejudice to the power conferred by section 13(2) of this Act, the service of a notification under sub-paragraph (1) above shall be sufficient to satisfy

the requirement of paragraph 4(2) above that the trader shall be informed of the Secretary of State's decision.

## PART II
## NOTICES TO WARN

6—(1) If the Secretary of State proposes to serve a notice to warn on any person in respect of any goods, the Secretary of State, before he serves the notice shall serve on that person a notification which—

(a) contains a draft of the proposed notice;

(b) states that the Secretary of State proposes to serve a notice in the form of the draft on that person;

(c) states that the Secretary of State considers that the goods described in the draft are unsafe;

(d) sets out the reasons why the Secretary of State considers that those goods are unsafe; and

(e) states that that person may make representations to the Secretary of State for the purpose of establishing that the goods are safe if, before the end of the period of fourteen days beginning with the day on which the notification is served, he informs the Secretary of State—

(i) of his intention to make representations; and

(ii) whether the representations will be made only in writing or both in writing and orally.

(2) Where the Secretary of State has served a notification containing a draft of a proposed notice to warn on any person, he shall not serve a notice to warn on that person in respect of the goods to which the proposed notice relates unless—

(a) the period of fourteen days beginning with the day on which the notification was served expires without the Secretary of State being informed as mentioned in sub-paragraph (1)(e) above;

(b) the period of twenty-eight days beginning with that day expires without any written representations being made by that person to the Secretary of State about the proposed notice; or

(c) the Secretary of State has considered a report about the proposed notice by a person appointed under paragraph 7(1) below.

7—(1) Where a person on whom a notification containing a draft of a proposed notice to warn has been served—

(a) informs the Secretary of State as mentioned in paragraph 6(1)(e) above before the end of the period of fourteen days beginning with the day on which the notification was served; and

(b) makes written representations to the Secretary of State about the proposed notice before the end of the period of twenty-eight days beginning with that day, the Secretary of State shall appoint a person to consider those representations, any further representations made by that person about the draft notice and the statements of any witnesses examined under this Part of this Schedule.

(2) Where—

(a) the Secretary of State has appointed a person to consider representations about a proposed notice to warn; and

(b) the person whose representations are to be considered has informed the Secretary of State for the purposes of paragraph 6(1)(e) above that the representations he intends to make will include oral representations, the Secretary of State shall inform the person intending to make the representations of the place and time at which oral representations may be made to the appointed person.

(3) Where a person on whom a notification containing a draft of a proposed notice to warn has been served is informed of a time for the purposes of sub-paragraph (2) above, that time shall not be—

(a)   before the end of the period of twenty-eight days beginning with the day on which the notification was served; or

(b)   before the end of the period of seven days beginning with the day on which that person is informed of the time.

(4)   A person who has been informed of a place and time for the purposes of sub-paragraph (2) above or his representative may, at that place and time—

(a)   make oral representations to the appointed person for the purpose of establishing that the goods to which the proposed notice relates are safe; and

(b)   call and examine witnesses in connection with the representations.

8—(1)   Where a person is appointed to consider representations about a proposed notice to warn, it shall be his duty to consider—

(a)   any written representations made by the person on whom it is proposed to serve the notice; and

(b)   in a case where a place and time has been appointed under paragraph 7(2) above for oral representations to be made by that person or his representative, any representations so made and any statements made by witnesses in connection with those representations,

and, after considering those matters to make a report (including recommendations) to the Secretary of State about the matters considered by him and the proposal to serve the notice.

(2)   It shall be the duty of the Secretary of State to consider any report made to him under sub-paragraph (1) above, and after considering the report, to inform the person on whom it was proposed that a notice to warn should be served of his decision with respect to the proposal.

(3)   If at any time after serving a notification on a person under paragraph 6 above the Secretary of State decides not to serve on that person either the proposed notice to warn or that notice with modifications, the Secretary of State shall inform that person of the decision, and nothing done for the purposes of any of the preceding provisions of this Part of this Schedule before that person was so informed shall—

(a)   entitle the Secretary of State subsequently to serve the proposed notice or the notice with modifications; or

(b)   require the Secretary of State, or any person appointed to consider representations about the proposed notice, subsequently to do anything in respect of, or in consequence of, any such representations.

(4)   Where a notification containing a draft of a proposed notice to warn is served on a person in respect of any goods, a notice to warn served on him in consequence of a decision made under sub-paragraph (2) above shall either be in the form of the draft or shall be less onerous than the draft.

9   The Secretary of State may revoke a notice to warn by serving on the person on whom the notice was served a notification stating that the notice is revoked.


PART III
GENERAL

10—(1)   Where in a notification served on any person under this Schedule the Secretary of State has appointed a time for the making of oral representations or the examination of witnesses, he may, by giving that person such notification as the Secretary of State considers appropriate, change that time to a later time or appoint further times at which further representations may be made or the examination of witnesses may be continued; and paragraphs 2(4), 3(4) and 7(4) above shall have effect accordingly.

(2)   For the purposes of this Schedule the Secretary of State may appoint a person (instead of the appointed person) to consider any representations or statements, if the person originally appointed, or last appointed under this sub-

paragraph, to consider those representations or statements has died or appears to the Secretary of State to be otherwise unable to act.

11   In this Schedule—

'the appointed person' in relation to a prohibition notice or a proposal to serve a notice to warn, means the person for the time being appointed under this Schedule to consider representations about the notice or, as the case may be, about the proposed notice;

'notification' means a notification in writing;

'trader', in relation to a prohibition notice, means the person on whom the notice is or was served.


## CARRIAGE OF GOODS BY SEA ACT 1992
### (1992, c 50)

### 1   Shipping documents etc to which Act applies

(1)   This Act applies to the following documents, that is to say—

(a)   any bill of lading;

(b)   any sea waybill; and

(c)   any ship's delivery order.

(2)   References in this Act to a bill of lading—

(a)   do not include references to a document which is incapable of transfer either by indorsement or, as a bearer bill, by delivery without indorsement; but

(b)   subject to that, do include references to a received for shipment bill of lading.

(3)   References in this Act to a sea waybill are references to any document which is not a bill of lading but—

(a)   is such a receipt for goods as contains or evidences a contract for the carriage of goods by sea; and

(b)   identifies the person to whom delivery of the goods is to be made by the carrier in accordance with that contract.

(4)   References in this Act to a ship's delivery order are references to any document which is neither a bill of lading nor a sea waybill but contains an undertaking which—

(a)   is given under or for the purposes of a contract for the carriage by sea of the goods to which the document relates, or of goods which include those goods; and

(b)   is an undertaking by the carrier to a person identified in the document to deliver the goods to which the document relates to that person.

(5)   The Secretary of State may by regulations make provision for the application of this Act to cases where [an electronic communications network] or any other information technology is used for effecting transactions corresponding to—

(a)   the issue of a document to which this Act applies;

(b)   the indorsement, delivery or other transfer of such a document; or

(c)   the doing of anything else in relation to such a document.

(6)   Regulations under subsection (5) above may—

(a)   make such modifications of the following provisions of this Act as the Secretary of State considers appropriate in connection with the application of this Act to any case mentioned in that subsection; and

(b)   contain supplemental, incidental, consequential and transitional provision;

and the power to make regulations under that subsection shall be exercisable by statutory instrument subject to annulment in pursuance of a resolution of either House of Parliament.

## 2  Rights under shipping documents

(1)  Subject to the following provisions of this section, a person who becomes—

(a)  the lawful holder of a bill of lading;

(b)  the person who (without being an original party to the contract of carriage) is the person to whom delivery of the goods to which a sea waybill relates is to be made by the carrier in accordance with that contract; or

(c)  the person to whom delivery of the goods to which a ship's delivery order relates is to be made in accordance with the undertaking contained in the order,

shall (by virtue of becoming the holder of the bill or, as the case may be, the person to whom delivery is to be made) have transferred to and vested in him all rights of suit under the contract of carriage as if he had been a party to that contract.

(2)  Where, when a person becomes the lawful holder of a bill of lading, possession of the bill no longer gives a right (as against the carrier) to possession of the goods to which the bill relates, that person shall not have any rights transferred to him by virtue of subsection (1) above unless he becomes the holder of the bill—

(a)  by virtue of a transaction effected in pursuance of any contractual or other arrangements made before the time when such a right to possession ceased to attach to possession of the bill; or

(b)  as a result of the rejection to that person by another person of goods or documents delivered to the other person in pursuance of any such arrangements.

(3)  The rights vested in any person by virtue of the operation of subsection (1) above in relation to a ship's delivery order—

(a)  shall be so vested subject to the terms of the order; and

(b)  where the goods to which the order relates form a part only of the goods to which the contract of carriage relates, shall be confined to rights in respect of the goods to which the order relates.

(4)  Where, in the case of any document to which this Act applies—

(a)  a person with any interest or right in or in relation to goods to which the document relates sustains loss or damage in consequence of a breach of the contract of carriage; but

(b)  subsection (1) above operates in relation to that document so that rights of suit in respect of that breach are vested in another person,

the other person shall be entitled to exercise those rights for the benefit of the person who sustained the loss or damage to the same extent as they could have been exercised if they had been vested in the person for whose benefit they are exercised.

(5)  Where rights are transferred by virtue of the operation of subsection (1) above in relation to any document, the transfer for which that subsection provides shall extinguish any entitlement to those rights which derives—

(a)  where that document is a bill of lading, from a person's having been an original party to the contract of carriage; or

(b)  in the case of any document to which this Act applies, from the previous operation of that subsection in relation to that document;

but the operation of that subsection shall be without prejudice to any rights which derive from a person's having been an original party to the contract contained in, or evidenced by, a sea waybill and, in relation to a ship's delivery order, shall be without prejudice to any rights deriving otherwise than from the previous operation of that subsection in relation to that order.

## 3  Liabilities under shipping documents

(1)  Where subsection (1) of section 2 of this Act operates in relation to any document to which this Act applies and the person in whom rights are vested by virtue of that subsection—

(a)   takes or demands delivery from the carrier of any of the goods to which the document relates;

(b)   makes a claim under the contract of carriage against the carrier in respect of any of those goods; or

(c)   is a person who, at a time before those rights were vested in him, took or demanded delivery from the carrier of any of those goods,

that person shall (by virtue of taking or demanding delivery or making the claim or, in a case falling within paragraph (c) above, of having the rights vested in him) become subject to the same liabilities under that contract as if he had been a party to that contract.

(2)   Where the goods to which a ship's delivery order relates form a part only of the goods to which the contract of carriage relates, the liabilities to which any person is subject by virtue of the operation of this section in relation to that order shall exclude liabilities in respect of any goods to which the order does not relate.

(3)   This section, so far as it imposes liabilities under any contract on any person, shall be without prejudice to the liabilities under the contract of any person as an original party to the contract.

## 4   Representations in bills of lading

A bill of lading which—

(a)   represents goods to have been shipped on board a vessel or to have been received for shipment on board a vessel; and

(b)   has been signed by the master of the vessel or by a person who was not the master but had the express, implied or apparent authority of the carrier to sign bills of lading,

shall, in favour of a person who has become the lawful holder of the bill, be conclusive evidence against the carrier of the shipment of the goods or, as the case may be, of their receipt for shipment.

## 5   Interpretation etc

(1)   In this Act—

'bill of lading', 'sea waybill' and 'ship's delivery order' shall be construed in accordance with section 1 above;

'the contract of carriage'—

(a)   in relation to a bill of lading or sea waybill, means the contract contained in or evidenced by that bill or waybill; and

(b)   in relation to a ship's delivery order, means the contract under or for the purposes of which the undertaking contained in the order is given;

'holder', in relation to a bill of lading, shall be construed in accordance with subsection (2) below;

'information technology' includes any computer or other technology by means of which information or other matter may be recorded or communicated without being reduced to documentary form.

[. . .]

(2)   References in this Act to the holder of a bill of lading are references to any of the following persons, that is to say—

(a)   a person with possession of the bill who, by virtue of being the person identified in the bill, is the consignee of the goods to which the bill relates;

(b)   a person with possession of the bill as a result of the completion, by delivery of the bill, of any indorsement of the bill or, in the case of a bearer bill, of any other transfer of the bill;

(c)   a person with possession of the bill as a result of any transaction by virtue of which he would have become a holder falling within paragraph (a) or (b) above had not the transaction been effected at a time when possession of the bill no longer gave a right (as against the carrier) to possession of the goods to which the bill relates;

and a person shall be regarded for the purposes of this Act as having become the lawful holder of a bill of lading wherever he has become the holder of the bill in good faith.

(3)   References in this Act to a person's being identified in a document include references to his being identified by a description which allows for the identity of the person in question to be varied, in accordance with the terms of the document, after its issue; and the reference in section 1(3)(b) of this Act to a document's identifying a person shall be construed accordingly.

(4)   Without prejudice to sections 2(2) and 4 above, nothing in this Act shall preclude its operation in relation to a case where the goods to which a document relates—

   (a)   cease to exist after the issue of the document; or
   (b)   cannot be identified (whether because they are mixed with other goods or for any other reason);

and references in this Act to the goods to which a document relates shall be construed accordingly.

(5)   The preceding provisions of this Act shall have effect without prejudice to the application, in relation to any case, of the rules (the Hague-Visby Rules) which for the time being have the force of law by virtue of section 1 of the Carriage of Goods by Sea Act 1971.

## 6   Short title, repeal, commencement and extent

(1)   This Act may be cited as the Carriage of Goods by Sea Act 1992.

(2)   The Bills of Lading Act 1855 is hereby repealed.

(3)   This Act shall come into force at the end of the period of two months beginning with the day on which it is passed; but nothing in this Act shall have effect in relation to any document issued before the coming into force of this Act.

(4)   This Act extends to Northern Ireland.

## CONTRACT (SCOTLAND) ACT 1997
### (1997, c 34)

## 1   Extrinsic evidence of additional contract term etc

(1)   Where a document appears (or two or more documents appear) to comprise all the express terms of a contract or unilateral voluntary obligation, it shall be presumed, unless the contrary is proved, that the document does (or the documents do) comprise all the express terms of the contract or unilateral voluntary obligation.

(2)   Extrinsic oral or documentary evidence shall be admissible to prove, for the purposes of subsection (1) above, that the contract or unilateral voluntary obligation includes additional express terms (whether or not written terms).

(3)   Notwithstanding the foregoing provisions of this section, where one of the terms in the document (or in the documents) is to the effect that the document does (or the documents do) comprise all the express terms of the contract or unilateral voluntary obligation, that term shall be conclusive in the matter.

(4)   This section is without prejudice to any enactment which makes provision as respects the constitution, or formalities of execution, of a contract or unilateral voluntary obligation.

## 2   Supersession

(1)   Where a deed is executed in implement, or purportedly in implement, of a contract, an unimplemented, or otherwise unfulfilled, term of the contract shall not be taken to be superseded by virtue only of that execution or of the delivery and acceptance of the deed.

(2)   Subsection (1) above is without prejudice to any agreement which the parties to a contract may reach (whether or not an agreement incorporated into the contract) as to supersession of the contract.

## 3  Damages for breach of contract of sale

Any rule of law which precludes the buyer in a contract of sale of property from obtaining damages for breach of that contract by the seller unless the buyer rejects the property and rescinds the contract shall cease to have effect.

## 4  Short title, extent etc

. . .

(3)  Section 1 of this Act applies only for the purposes of proceedings commenced on or after, and sections 2 and 3 only as respects contracts entered into on or after, the date on which this Act comes into force.

. . .

## DATA PROTECTION ACT 1998
### (1998, c 29)

## 7  Right of access to personal data*

(1)  Subject to the following provisions of this section and to [sections 8, 9 and 9A], an individual is entitled—

(a)  to be informed by any data controller whether personal data of which that individual is the data subject are being processed by or on behalf of that data controller,

(b)  if that is the case, to be given by the data controller a description of—

(i)  the personal data of which that individual is the data subject,

(ii)  the purposes for which they are being or are to be processed, and

(iii)  the recipients or classes of recipients to whom they are or may be disclosed,

(c)  to have communicated to him in an intelligible form—

(i)  the information constituting any personal data of which that individual is the data subject, and

(ii)  any information available to the data controller as to the source of those data, and

(d)  where the processing by automatic means of personal data of which that individual is the data subject for the purpose of evaluating matters relating to him such as, for example, his performance at work, his creditworthiness, his reliability or his conduct, has constituted or is likely to constitute the sole basis for any decision significantly affecting him, to be informed by the data controller of the logic involved in that decision-taking.

(2)  A data controller is not obliged to supply any information under subsection (1) unless he has received—

(a)  a request in writing, and

(b)  except in prescribed cases, such fee (not exceeding the prescribed maximum) as he may require.

[(3)  Where a data controller—

(a)  reasonably requires further information in order to satisfy himself as to the identity of the person making a request under this section and to locate the information which that person seeks, and

(b)  has informed him of that requirement,

the data controller is not obliged to comply with the request unless he is supplied with that further information.]

(4)  Where a data controller cannot comply with the request without disclosing information relating to another individual who can be identified from that information, he is not obliged to comply with the request unless—

*Section 7 is modified in relation to particular professions, namely health (SI 2000/413); education (SI 2000/414); social work (SI 2000/415; SI 2005/467; SI 2011/1034); and UK competent authority (SI 2014/3141).

(a)    the other individual has consented to the disclosure of the information to the person making the request, or

(b)    it is reasonable in all the circumstances to comply with the request without the consent of the other individual.

(5)    In subsection (4) the reference to information relating to another individual includes a reference to information identifying that individual as the source of the information sought by the request; and that subsection is not to be construed as excusing a data controller from communicating so much of the information sought by the request as can be communicated without disclosing the identity of the other individual concerned, whether by the omission of names or other identifying particulars or otherwise.

(6)    In determining for the purposes of subsection (4)(b) whether it is reasonable in all the circumstances to comply with the request without the consent of the other individual concerned, regard shall be had, in particular, to—

(a)    any duty of confidentiality owed to the other individual,

(b)    any steps taken by the data controller with a view to seeking the consent of the other individual,

(c)    whether the other individual is capable of giving consent, and

(d)    any express refusal of consent by the other individual.

(7)    An individual making a request under this section may, in such cases as may be prescribed, specify that his request is limited to personal data of any prescribed description.

(8)    Subject to subsection (4), a data controller shall comply with a request under this section promptly and in any event before the end of the prescribed period beginning with the relevant day.

(9)    If a court is satisfied on the application of any person who has made a request under the foregoing provisions of this section that the data controller in question has failed to comply with the request in contravention of those provisions, the court may order him to comply with the request.

(10)    In this section—

'prescribed' means prescribed by the [Secretary of State] by regulations;

'the prescribed maximum' means such amount as may be prescribed;

'the prescribed period' means forty days or such other period as may be prescribed;

'the relevant day', in relation to a request under this section, means the day on which the data controller receives the request or, if later, the first day on which the data controller has both the required fee and the information referred to in subsection (3).

(11)    Different amounts or periods may be prescribed under this section in relation to different cases.


## ELECTRONIC COMMUNICATIONS ACT 2000
### (2000, c 7)


### PART II
### FACILITATION OF ELECTRONIC COMMERCE, DATA STORAGE, ETC

### 7    Electronic signatures and related certificates

(1)    In any legal proceedings—

(a)    an electronic signature incorporated into or logically associated with a particular electronic communication or particular electronic data, and

(b)    the certification by any person of such a signature,

shall each be admissible in evidence in relation to any question as to the authenticity of the communication or data or as to the integrity of the communication or data.

(2) For the purposes of this section an electronic signature is so much of anything in electronic form as—

(a) is incorporated into or otherwise logically associated with any electronic communication or electronic data; and

(b) purports to be so incorporated or associated for the purpose of being used in establishing the authenticity of the communication or data, the integrity of the communication or data, or both.

(3) For the purposes of this section an electronic signature incorporated into or associated with a particular electronic communication or particular electronic data is certified by any person if that person (whether before or after the making of the communication) has made a statement confirming that—

(a) the signature,

(b) a means of producing, communicating or verifying the signature, or

(c) a procedure applied to the signature,

is (either alone or in combination with other factors) a valid means of establishing the authenticity of the communication or data, the integrity of the communication or data, or both.

## LIMITED LIABILITY PARTNERSHIPS ACT 2000
### (2000, c 12)

*Introductory*

### 1 Limited liability partnerships

(1) There shall be a new form of legal entity to be known as a limited liability partnership.

(2) A limited liability partnership is a body corporate (with legal personality separate from that of its members) which is formed by being incorporated under this Act; and—

(a) in the following provisions of this Act (except in the phrase 'oversea limited liability partnership'), and

(b) in any other enactment (except where provision is made to the contrary or the context otherwise requires),

references to a limited liability partnership are to such a body corporate.

(3) A limited liability partnership has unlimited capacity.

(4) The members of a limited liability partnership have such liability to contribute to its assets in the event of its being wound up as is provided for by virtue of this Act.

(5) Accordingly, except as far as otherwise provided by this Act or any other enactment, the law relating to partnerships does not apply to a limited liability partnership.

(6) The Schedule (which makes provision about the names and registered offices of limited liability partnerships) has effect.

*Incorporation*

### 2 Incorporation document etc

(1) For a limited liability partnership to be incorporated—

(a) two or more persons associated for carrying on a lawful business with a view to profit must have subscribed their names to an incorporation document,

[(b) the incorporation document or a copy of it must have been delivered to the registrar, and]

(c) there must have been so delivered a statement [. . .], made by either a solicitor engaged in the formation of the limited liability partnership or anyone who subscribed his name to the incorporation document, that the requirement imposed by paragraph (a) has been complied with.

(2)   The incorporation document must—

[. . .]

(b)   state the name of the limited liability partnership,

(c)   state whether the registered office of the limited liability partnership is to be situated in England and Wales, in Wales [, in Scotland or in Northern Ireland],

(d)   state the address of that registered office,

[(e)   give the required particulars of each of the persons who are to be members of the limited liability partnership on incorporation, and]

(f)   either specify which of those persons are to be designated members or state that every person who from time to time is a member of the limited liability partnership is a designated member.

[(2ZA)   The required particulars mentioned in subsection (2)(e) are the particulars required to be stated in the LLP's register of members and register of members' residential addresses.]

[. . .]

(3)   If a person makes a false statement under subsection (1)(c) which he—

(a)   knows to be false, or

(b)   does not believe to be true, he commits an offence.

(4)   A person guilty of an offence under subsection (3) is liable—

(a)   on summary conviction, to imprisonment for a period not exceeding six months or a fine not exceeding the statutory maximum, or to both, or

(b)   on conviction on indictment, to imprisonment for a period not exceeding two years or a fine, or to both.

### 3   Incorporation by registration

[(1)   The registrar, if satisfied that the requirements of section 2 are complied with, shall—

(a)   register the documents delivered under that section, and

(b)   give a certificate that the limited liability partnership is incorporated.]

[(1A)   The certificate must state—

(a)   the name and registered number of the limited liability partnership,

(b)   the date of its incorporation, and

(c)   whether the limited liability partnership's registered office is situated in England and Wales (or in Wales), in Scotland or in Northern Ireland.]

(2)   The registrar may accept the statement delivered under paragraph (c) of subsection (1) of section 2 as sufficient evidence that the requirement imposed by paragraph (a) of that subsection has been complied with.

(3)   The certificate shall either be signed by the registrar or be authenticated by his official seal.

(4)   The certificate is conclusive evidence that the requirements of section 2 are complied with and that the limited liability partnership is incorporated by the name specified in the incorporation document.

*Membership*

### 4   Members

(1)   On the incorporation of a limited liability partnership its members are the persons who subscribed their names to the incorporation document (other than any who have died or been dissolved).

(2)   Any other person may become a member of a limited liability partnership by and in accordance with an agreement with the existing members.

(3)   A person may cease to be a member of a limited liability partnership (as well as by death or dissolution) in accordance with an agreement with the other members or, in the absence of agreement with the other members as to cessation of membership, by giving reasonable notice to the other members.

(4)   A member of a limited liability partnership shall not be regarded for any

purpose as employed by the limited liability partnership unless, if he and the other members were partners in a partnership, he would be regarded for that purpose as employed by the partnership.

**[4A   Minimum membership for carrying on business**

(1)   This section applies where a limited liability partnership carries on business without having at least two members, and does so for more than 6 months.

(2)   A person who, for the whole or any part of the period that it so carries on business after those 6 months—

(a)   is a member of the limited liability partnership, and

(b)   knows that it is carrying on business with only one member,

is liable (jointly and severally with the limited liability partnership) for the payment of the limited liability partnership's debts contracted during the period or, as the case may be, that part of it.]

**5   Relationship of members etc**

(1)   Except as far as otherwise provided by this Act or any other enactment, the mutual rights and duties of the members of a limited liability partnership, and the mutual rights and duties of a limited liability partnership and its members, shall be governed—

(a)   by agreement between the members, or between the limited liability partnership and its members, or

(b)   in the absence of agreement as to any matter, by any provision made in relation to that matter by regulations under section 15(c).

(2)   An agreement made before the incorporation of a limited liability partnership between the persons who subscribe their names to the incorporation document may impose obligations on the limited liability partnership (to take effect at any time after its incorporation).

**6   Members as agents**

(1)   Every member of a limited liability partnership is the agent of the limited liability partnership.

(2)   But a limited liability partnership is not bound by anything done by a member in dealing with a person if—

(a)   the member in fact has no authority to act for the limited liability partnership by doing that thing, and

(b)   the person knows that he has no authority or does not know or believe him to be a member of the limited liability partnership.

(3)   Where a person has ceased to be a member of a limited liability partnership, the former member is to be regarded (in relation to any person dealing with the limited liability partnership) as still being a member of the limited liability partnership unless—

(a)   the person has notice that the former member has ceased to be a member of the limited liability partnership, or

(b)   notice that the former member has ceased to be a member of the limited liability partnership has been delivered to the registrar.

(4)   Where a member of a limited liability partnership is liable to any person (other than another member of the limited liability partnership) as a result of a wrongful act or omission of his in the course of the business of the limited liability partnership or with its authority, the limited liability partnership is liable to the same extent as the member.

**7   Ex-members**

(1)   This section applies where a member of a limited liability partnership has either ceased to be a member or—

(a)   has died,

(b)   has become bankrupt or had his estate sequestrated or has been wound up,

    (c)   has granted a trust deed for the benefit of his creditors, or

    (d)   has assigned the whole or any part of his share in the limited liability partnership (absolutely or by way of charge or security).

(2)   In such an event the former member or—

    (a)   his personal representative,

    (b)   his trustee in bankruptcy or permanent or interim trustee (within the meaning of the Bankruptcy (Scotland) Act 1985) or liquidator,

    (c)   his trustee under the trust deed for the benefit of his creditors, or

    (d)   his assignee,

may not interfere in the management or administration of any business or affairs of the limited liability partnership.

(3)   But subsection (2) does not affect any right to receive an amount from the limited liability partnership in that event.

## 8  Designated members

(1)   If the incorporation document specifies who are to be designated members—

    (a)   they are designated members on incorporation, and

    (b)   any member may become a designated member by and in accordance with an agreement with the other members,

and a member may cease to be a designated member in accordance with an agreement with the other members.

(2)   But if there would otherwise be no designated members, or only one, every member is a designated member.

(3)   If the incorporation document states that every person who from time to time is a member of the limited liability partnership is a designated member, every member is a designated member.

(4)   A limited liability partnership may at any time deliver to the registrar—

    (a)   notice that specified members are to be designated members, or

    (b)   notice that every person who from time to time is a member of the limited liability partnership is a designated member,

and, once it is delivered, subsection (1) (apart from paragraph (a)) and subsection (2), or subsection (3), shall have effect as if that were stated in the incorporation document.

    [. . .]

(6)   A person ceases to be a designated member if he ceases to be a member.

## 9  Registration of membership changes

(1)   A limited liability partnership must ensure that—

    (a)   where a person becomes or ceases to be a member or designated member, notice is delivered to the registrar within fourteen days, and

    (b)   where there is any change in the [particulars contained in its register of members or its register of members' residential addresses], notice is delivered to the registrar within [14 days].

(2)   Where all the members from time to time of a limited liability partnership are designated members, subsection (1)(a) does not require notice that a person has become or ceased to be a designated member as well as a member.

[(3)   A notice delivered under subsection (1) that relates to a person becoming a member or designated member must contain—

    (a)   a statement that the member or designated member consents to acting in that capacity, and

    (b)   in the case of a person becoming a member, a statement of the particulars of the new member that are required to be included in the limited liability partnership's register of members and its register of residential addresses.]

[(3ZA)  Where—

    (a)   a limited liability partnership gives notice of a change of a member's service address as stated in its register of members, and

(b)   the notice is not accompanied by notice of any resulting change in the particulars contained in its register of members' residential addresses,
the notice must be accompanied by a statement that no such change is required.]
  [. . .]
  (4)   If a limited liability partnership fails to comply with [this section], the partnership and every designated member commits an offence.
  (5)   But it is a defence for a designated member charged with an offence under subsection (4) to prove that he took all reasonable steps for securing that [this section] was complied with.
  (6)   A person guilty of an offence under subsection (4) is liable on summary conviction to a fine not exceeding level 5 on the standard scale.

*Regulations*

**14   Insolvency and winding up**
  (1)   Regulations shall make provision about the insolvency and winding up of limited liability partnerships by applying or incorporating, with such modifications as appear appropriate, [—
  (a)   in relation to a limited liability partnership registered in Great Britain, Parts 1 to 4, 6 and 7 of the Insolvency Act 1986;
  (b)   in relation to a limited liability partnership registered in Northern Ireland, Parts 2 to 5 and 7 of the Insolvency (Northern Ireland) Order 1989, and so much of Part 1 of that Order as applies for the purposes of those Parts.]
  (2)   Regulations may make other provision about the insolvency and winding up of limited liability partnerships, and provision about the insolvency and winding up of oversea limited liability partnerships, by—
  (a)   applying or incorporating, with such modifications as appear appropriate, any law relating to the insolvency or winding up of companies or other corporations which would not otherwise have effect in relation to them, or
  (b)   providing for any law relating to the insolvency or winding up of companies or other corporations which would otherwise have effect in relation to them not to apply to them or to apply to them with such modifications as appear appropriate.
  (3)   In this Act 'oversea limited liability partnership' means a body incorporated or otherwise established outside [the United Kingdom] and having such connection with [the United Kingdom], and such other features, as regulations may prescribe.

**15   Application of company law etc**
Regulations may make provision about limited liability partnerships and oversea limited liability partnerships (not being provision about insolvency or winding up) by—
  (a)   applying or incorporating, with such modifications as appear appropriate, any law relating to companies or other corporations which would not otherwise have effect in relation to them,
  (b)   providing for any law relating to companies or other corporations which would otherwise have effect in relation to them not to apply to them or to apply to them with such modifications as appear appropriate, or
  (c)   applying or incorporating, with such modifications as appear appropriate, any law relating to partnerships.

## DEBT ARRANGEMENT AND ATTACHMENT (SCOTLAND) ACT 2002
### (2002, asp 17)

PART 1

THE DEBT ARRANGEMENT SCHEME

### 1  Debt arrangement scheme

This Part of this Act constitutes a scheme (to be known as the 'debt arrangement scheme') under which [persons] may arrange for their debts to be paid under debt payment programmes.

### 2  Debt payment programmes

(1)  A debt payment programme is a programme which provides for the payment of money owed by a debtor.

[(1A)  Subsection (1) above is subject to any provision in regulations made under section 7A(1) below.]

(2)  The Scottish Ministers may, on an application by a debtor, approve any debt payment programme set out in the application.

(3)  Such an application [. . .] shall—

(a)  specify, to the best of the debtor's knowledge and belief, in relation to each debt which the debtor is proposing to be paid under the debt payment programme—

(i)  the amount outstanding;

(ii)  the creditor to whom the debt is due; and

(iii)  the period for which the debt has been due;

(b)  set out the arrangements under which those debts are, in accordance with the provisions of the programme, to be paid, in particular specifying—

(i)  the amounts which the debtor proposes to pay under the programme;

(ii)  the proposed regularity of those payments;

(iii)  the manner in which those payments are to be made; and

(iv)  the manner in which, and period over which, each of the debts included in the programme is to be paid;

(c)  specify the name and address of the person (the 'payments distributor') who is to—

(i)  receive payments from the debtor; and

(ii)  pay, on behalf of the debtor, the debts included in the programme, in accordance with the provisions of the programme; and

(d)  contain such other information (including information relating to the debtor's financial circumstances), and be in such form, as may be prescribed.

(4)  Such an application shall, subject to any contrary provision in regulations made under section 7(1) [or 7A(1)] below, incorporate the consent, indicated in the prescribed form, of all the debtor's creditors.

(5)  A person's name and address shall not be specified in an application for approval of a debt payment programme as a payments distributor unless that person has been approved by the Scottish Ministers as a person suitable to carry out the functions of a payments distributor.

### 3  Money advice

(1)  A debtor is not entitled to make an application for the approval, or the variation, of a debt payment programme unless the debtor has obtained the advice of a money adviser in relation to—

(a)  the debtor's financial circumstances;

(b)  the effect of the proposed programme or, as the case may be, the proposed variation of the programme; and

(c)  the preparation of the application.

(2)  Such an application shall—

(a)  contain a [. . .] declaration by the money adviser who provided the advice referred to in subsection (1) above that such advice has been given; and

(b)  specify the name and address of the money adviser.

[(3)  Subsections (1) and (2) above are subject to any contrary provision in regulations made under section 7(1) below.]

### 4  Effect of debt payment programmes

(1)  Where a debt payment programme has been approved or varied, the debts specified in the application for the approval or, as the case may be, the variation shall be paid in accordance with the programme.

(2)  It is not competent—

(a)  to serve a charge for payment in respect of; or

(b)  [subject to] subsection (2A),] to commence or execute any diligence to enforce payment of; or

[(c)  to commit a debtor to prison under section 4 of the Civil Imprisonment (Scotland) Act 1882, except for the purposes of section 40A of the Child Support Act 1991, in respect of,]

any debt owed by a debtor who has debts which are being paid under an approved debt payment programme.

[(2A)  Despite subsection (2)(b), it is competent to—

(a)  auction an attached article where—

(i)  notice has been given to the debtor under section 27(4) below; or

(ii)  an article has been removed, or notice of removal has been given, under section 53 below;

(b)  implement a decree of furthcoming;

(c)  implement a decree or order for sale of a ship (or a share of it) or cargo.

[. . .]

(3)  A creditor is not entitled to found on any debt owed by such a debtor in presenting, or concurring in the presentation of, a petition for the sequestration of the debtor's estate.

(4)  There is to be disregarded, for the purposes of the exercise by a creditor of any rights to enforce a debt or remedies to like effect, any period during which the debtor's debts were subject to an approved debt payment programme.

(5)  The debts referred to in subsections (2) to (4) above are restricted to—

(a)  those to which the debtor's debt payment programme relates; and

(b)  any other debts owed to creditors who have been given notice, in the prescribed form, of the approval of the debt payment programme.

### 5  Variation of debt payment programmes

(1)  The Scottish Ministers may, on an application by the debtor or by any creditor, approve the variation of a debt payment programme.

(2)  The Scottish Ministers may not consider an application for approval of a variation under subsection (1) above unless—

(a)  where the application is made by the debtor, a copy of the application has been given to each creditor who is owed a debt which is being paid under the debt payment programme; or

(b)  where the application is made by a creditor, a copy of the application has been given to the debtor and to each other creditor who is owed such a debt.

(3)  Such an application may seek the variation of any condition which is attached to the approval of the programme or, as the case may be, a previous variation of the programme.

(4)  An application for the variation of a debt payment programme shall—

(a)  contain such information, and be in such form, as may be prescribed;

[. . .]

## 6   Deduction from earnings

(1)   Where an approved debt payment programme requires sums to be paid to the payments distributor by way of deduction of the debtor's earnings from employment, the debtor shall provide an instruction, in the prescribed form, to the person by whom the debtor is employed to make—

(a)   deductions from the debtor's earnings; and

(b)   payments of the amounts deducted to the payments distributor, in accordance with the provisions of the debt payment programme.

(2)   It is the duty of the employer to comply with any instruction so provided.

## 7   Debt payment programmes: power to make further provision

(1)   The Scottish Ministers may, by regulations, make such further provision as they think fit in connection with—

(a)   applications for the approval, or for the variation, of debt payment programmes;

(b)   the manner in which such programmes are to operate, including conditions with which debtors, creditors, payments distributors or money advisers must comply;

(c)   the effect of such programmes; and

(d)   the effect of the failure of an employer to comply with the duty under section 6(2) above.

(2)   The regulations may, in particular, make provision about—

(a)   the class of person who may or may not make an application for the approval, or the variation, of a debt payment programme;

(b)   the class of debt in respect of which such an application may or may not be made;

[(ba)   circumstances in which some or all of the functions of a money adviser under section 3 above may instead be carried out by an approved intermediary;

(bb)   circumstances in which a debtor is entitled to make an application for the approval, or the variation, of a debt payment programme where the debtor has not obtained advice under section 3(1) above;

(bc)   the manner in which—

(i)   the seeking of the consent of creditors to applications for approval of debt payment programmes; or

(ii)   the making of such applications,

affects the rights and remedies of creditors or other third parties.]

[(bd)   the method of assessing the amount of a debtor's assets, income, liabilities and expenditure in considering applications for the approval, or the variation, of a debt payment programme;]

(c)   the matters to which the Scottish Ministers are to have regard in determining whether to approve such an application;

(d)   the conditions which may or may not be attached to an approval of such an application;

(e)   circumstances in which such an application will not be approved;

(f)   appeals against determinations by the Scottish Ministers on such applications;

(g)   circumstances in which the consent for the purposes of section 2(4) above of a creditor or creditors generally may be dispensed with;

(h)   circumstances in which a creditor may object to—

(i)   the dispensation of the creditor's consent; or

(ii)   the approval of such an application, and the manner in which such objection may be made;

(i)   the remitting of any such application in respect of which a creditor has made an objection to the sheriff for determination;

(j)   the manner in which a debt payment programme may be varied;

(k)   the priority in which debts are to be paid under a debt payment programme;

(l)   the ingathering and sale or other disposal of assets and the distribution to creditors of amounts so realised;

(m)   the period for which a debt payment programme is to remain in operation;

(n)   circumstances in which, and the procedure under which, any such period can, in relation to a particular debt payment programme, be shortened or extended;

(o)   circumstances in which a debt payment programme is to cease to have effect;

(p)   subject to section 4 above, the manner in which a debt payment programme affects the rights or remedies of a creditor or other third party;

(q)   circumstances in which creditors are to notify debtors of the right to make such an application and the effect of the failure of a creditor to provide that notice;

(r)   the class of person who may act as a payments distributor;

(s)   the class of person who may act as a money adviser;

[(sa)   the class of person who may act as an approved intermediary;]

(t)   the functions of a payments distributor;

(u)   the functions of a money adviser;

[(ua)   the functions of an approved intermediary;]

[(ub)   the remuneration of the payments distributors and money advisers;]

(v)   the establishment and maintenance by the Scottish Ministers of a register of debt payment programmes and applications for the approval, and variation, of such programmes;

(w)   the information which is to be kept in such a register;

(x)   the manner in which that information is to be kept and in which it, or any part of it, is to be made available to the public; and

(y)   the determination, and charging, by the Scottish Ministers of fees in respect of—

(i)   the consideration of applications for the approval, or the variation, of a debt payment programme; and

(ii)   the provision of information recorded in the register of debt payment programmes.

(3)   The regulations may also—

(a)   make different provision in relation to such different types of debtors, debts or other matters as may be described by the Scottish Ministers;

(b)   provide that such different provision is to have effect only for such period as is specified by the Scottish Ministers; and

(c)   provide that, on the expiry of that period, the Scottish Ministers may determine that the different provision to which they relate is to—

(i)   continue to have effect without limit of time;

(ii)   continue to have effect for such further period as may be determined by the Scottish Ministers; or

(iii)   cease to have effect.

(4)   The regulations may also modify any enactment (including this Act), instrument or document for the purposes of making such further provision as is mentioned in subsection (1) above.

**[7A   Debt payment programmes: power to make provision about debt relief**

(1)   The Scottish Ministers may, by regulations, make such further provision as they think fit in connection with debt payment programmes for the purposes of—

(a)   enabling such programmes to provide for the payment of part only of money owed by debtors; and

(b)   on the completion of such programmes or otherwise, enabling any liability of debtors to pay any part of such money owed as is outstanding to be discharged.

(2) The regulations may, in particular, make provision about—

(a) the minimum proportion or percentage of debts which shall be paid under such debt payment programmes;

(b) without prejudice to section 7(2)(h) to (j) above, the consent of creditors for the purposes of section 2(4) above (including the circumstances in which consent by a majority by number or in value shall be sufficient);

(c) the effect of such programmes on debtors' liabilities for interest, fees, penalties and other charges in relation to debts being paid under such programmes;

(d) the effect of such programmes on the rights of creditors to charge interest, fees, penalties or other charges in relation to debts being paid under such programmes;

(e) circumstances in which, on completion of such programmes or otherwise, any liability of debtors to pay—

(i) part of any debts as are outstanding; or

(ii) any interest, fees, penalties or other charges in relation to such debts,

is to be discharged.

(3) Subsections (3) and (4) of section 7 above apply for the purposes of regulations under this section as they apply for the purposes of regulations under subsection (1) of that section.]

## 8 Functions of the Scottish Ministers

(1) The Scottish Ministers may by order provide that their functions under this Part of this Act may be performed on their behalf by such other person as may be specified in the order.

(2) Such an order does not allow regulations under this Part of this Act or any further order under this section to be made by any person other than the Scottish Ministers.

(3) Such an order may make different provision for different functions.

## 9 Interpretation of Part

(1) In this Part of this Act—

['approved intermediary' means any person, not being a money adviser, who has been approved by the Scottish Ministers as a person who may give advice to a debtor for the purposes of section 3(1) above.]

'money adviser' means any person who has been approved by the Scottish Ministers as a person who may give advice to a debtor for the purposes of section 3(1) above; and

'prescribed' means prescribed by regulations made by the Scottish Ministers.

[. . .]

[PART 1A
INTERIM ATTACHMENT

*Interim attachment*

## [9A Interim attachment

(1) Subject to sections 9B to 9E below, the court may grant warrant for diligence by attachment of corporeal moveable property owned (whether alone or in common) by the debtor on the dependence of an action (such attachment is to be known as interim attachment).

(2) Warrant for interim attachment is competent only where an action contains a conclusion for payment of a sum other than by way of expenses.

(3)   This Part of this Act shall apply to petitions in the Court of Session and to parties to them as it applies to actions and to parties to them.

(4)   In this Part of this Act—

'action' includes, in the sheriff court—

(a)   a summary cause;

(b)   a small claim; and

(c)   a summary application,

and references to 'summons', 'conclusion' and to cognate expressions shall be construed accordingly;

'court' means—

(a)   the court before which the action is in dependence; or

(b)   where, by virtue of section 9L(1)(a) below, the interim attachment has effect after the creditor obtains a final interlocutor for payment, the court which granted that interlocutor;

'creditor' means the party who concludes for payment and who seeks, obtains or executes warrant for interim attachment;

'debtor' means the party against whom the conclusion for payment is addressed; and expressions used in this Part of this Act have, unless the context otherwise requires, the same meanings as those expressions have in Part 2 of this Act.]

### [9B   Articles exempt from interim attachment

It is not competent to attach by interim attachment—

(a)   any article within a dwellinghouse;

(b)   any article which, by virtue of section 11 below, it is not competent to attach;

(c)   a mobile home which is the only or principal residence of a person other than the debtor;

(d)   any article of a perishable nature or which is likely to deteriorate substantially and rapidly in condition or value; or

(e)   where the debtor is engaged in trade, any article acquired by the debtor—

(i)   to be sold by the debtor (whether or not after adaptation); or

(ii)   as a material for a process of manufacturing for sale by the debtor, in the ordinary course of that trade.]

*Application for interim attachment*

### [9C   Application for warrant for interim attachment

(1)   A creditor may, at any time during which an action is in dependence, apply to the court for warrant for interim attachment.

(2)   An application under subsection (1) above shall—

(a)   be in (or as nearly as may be in) the form prescribed by Act of Sederunt;

(b)   subject to subsection (3) below, be intimated to and provide details of—

(i)   the debtor; and

(ii)   any other person having an interest;

(c)   state whether the creditor is seeking the grant, under section 9D(1) below, of warrant for interim attachment in advance of a hearing on the application under section 9E below; and

(d)   contain such other information as the Scottish Ministers may by regulations prescribe.

(3)   An application under subsection (1) above need not be intimated where the creditor is seeking the grant, under section 9D(1) below, of warrant in advance of a hearing on the application under section 9E below.

(4)   The court, on receiving an application under subsection (1) above, shall—

(a)   subject to section 9D below, fix a date for a hearing on the application under section 9E below; and

(b)   order the creditor to intimate that date to—

  (i) the debtor; and

  (ii) any other person appearing to the court to have an interest.]

### [9D Grant of warrant without a hearing

(1) The court may, if satisfied as to the matters mentioned in subsection (2) below, make an order granting warrant for interim attachment without a hearing on the application under section 9E below.

(2) The matters referred to in subsection (1) above are—

  (a) that the creditor has a prima facie case on the merits of the action;

  (b) that there is a real and substantial risk enforcement of any decree in the action in favour of the creditor would be defeated or prejudiced by reason of—

   (i) the debtor being insolvent or verging on insolvency; or

   (ii) the likelihood of the debtor removing, disposing of, burdening, concealing or otherwise dealing with all or some of the debtor's assets,

were warrant for interim attachment not granted in advance of such a hearing; and

  (c) that it is reasonable in all the circumstances, including the effect granting warrant may have on any person having an interest, to do so.

(3) The onus shall be on the creditor to satisfy the court that the order granting warrant should be made.

(4) Where the court makes an order granting warrant for interim attachment without a hearing on the application under section 9E below, the court shall—

  (a) fix a date for a hearing under section 9M below; and

  (b) order the creditor to intimate that date to—

   (i) the debtor; and

   (ii) any other person appearing to the court to have an interest.

(5) Where a hearing is fixed under subsection (4)(a) above, section 9M (except subsection (11)) below shall apply as if an application had been made to the court for an order under that section.

(6) Where the court refuses to make an order granting warrant without a hearing under section 9E below and the creditor insists in the application, the court shall—

  (a) fix a date for such a hearing on the application; and

  (b) order the creditor to intimate that date to—

   (i) the debtor; and

   (ii) any other person appearing to the court to have an interest.]

### [9E Hearing on application

(1) At the hearing on an application for warrant for interim attachment, the court shall not make any order without first giving—

  (a) any person to whom intimation of the date of the hearing was made; and

  (b) any other person appearing to the court to have an interest,

an opportunity to be heard.

(2) The court may, if satisfied as to the matters mentioned in subsection (3) below, make an order granting warrant for interim attachment.

(3) The matters referred to in subsection (2) above are—

  (a) that the creditor has a prima facie case on the merits of the action;

  (b) that there is a real and substantial risk enforcement of any decree in the action in favour of the creditor would be defeated or prejudiced by reason of—

   (i) the debtor being insolvent or verging on insolvency; or

   (ii) the likelihood of the debtor removing, disposing of, burdening, concealing or otherwise dealing with all or some of the debtor's assets,

were warrant for interim attachment not granted; and

  (c) that it is reasonable in all the circumstances, including the effect granting warrant may have on any person having an interest, to do so.

(4) The onus shall be on the creditor to satisfy the court that the order granting warrant should be made.

(5) Where the court makes an order granting or, as the case may be, refusing warrant for interim attachment, the court shall order the creditor to intimate that order to—

(a) the debtor; and

(b) any other person appearing to the court to have an interest.

(6) Where the court makes an order refusing warrant for interim attachment, the court may impose such conditions (if any) as it thinks fit.

(7) Without prejudice to the generality of subsection (6) above, those conditions may require the debtor—

(a) to consign into court such sum; or

(b) to find caution or to give such other security,

as the court thinks fit.]

*Execution of interim attachment*

**[9F Execution of interim attachment**

(1) Sections 12, 13, 15 and (subject to subsection (6) below) 17 below apply to execution of an interim attachment as they apply to execution of an attachment.

(2) The officer shall, immediately after executing an interim attachment, complete a schedule such as is mentioned in subsection (3) below (in this Part of this Act, a 'schedule of interim attachment').

(3) The schedule of interim attachment—

(a) shall be—

(i) in (or as nearly as may be in) the form prescribed by Act of Sederunt; and

(ii) signed by the officer; and

(b) shall specify—

(i) the articles attached; and

(ii) their value, so far as ascertainable.

(4) The officer shall—

(a) give a copy of the schedule of interim attachment to the debtor; or

(b) where it is not practicable to do so—

(i) give a copy of the schedule to a person present at the place where the interim attachment was executed; or

(ii) where there is no such person, leave a copy of the schedule at that place.

(5) References in this Part of this Act to the day on which an interim attachment is executed are references to the day on which the officer complies with subsection (4) above.

(6) The application of section 17 below shall be subject to the following modifications—

(a) subsections (3)(b) and (4) shall not apply;

(b) in subsections (1), (5) and (6), the references to the sheriff shall be construed as references to the court; and

(c) in subsection (6)(b), the reference to the sheriff clerk shall, in the case of an action in the Court of Session, be construed as a reference to the clerk of the court.]

**[9G Execution of interim attachment before service**

(1) This section applies where an interim attachment is executed before the service of the summons on the debtor.

(2) Subject to subsection (3) below, if the summons is not served on the debtor before the end of the period of 21 days beginning with the day on which the interim attachment is executed, the attachment shall cease to have effect.

(3) The court may, on the application of the creditor, make an order extending the period referred to in subsection (2) above.

(4)   In determining whether to make such an order the court shall have regard to—

(a)   the efforts of the creditor to serve the summons within the period of 21 days; and

(b)   any special circumstances preventing or obstructing service within that period.]

*Interim attachment: further procedure*

**[9H   Order for security of attached articles**

(1)   The court may, on an application, at any time after articles have been attached—

(a)   by the creditor;

(b)   the officer; or

(c)   the debtor,

make an order for the security of any of the attached articles.

(2)   An application for an order under subsection (1) above shall—

(a)   be in (or as nearly as may be in) the form prescribed by Act of Sederunt; and

(b)   be intimated—

(i)   where it is made by the creditor or the officer, to the debtor;

(ii)   where it is made by the debtor, to the creditor and the officer.

(3)   At the hearing on the application under subsection (1) above, the court shall not make any order without first giving—

(a)   any person to whom intimation of the application was made; and

(b)   any other person the court is satisfied has an interest,

an opportunity to be heard.]

*Interim attachment: effects*

**[9J   Unlawful acts after interim attachment**

Section 21 (except subsections (3) and (15)) below applies to an interim attachment as it applies to an attachment with the following modifications—

(a)   in subsections (10) and (11), the references to the sheriff shall be construed as references to the court; and

(b)   in subsection (12), the references to sections 51 and 54(1) below shall be of no effect.]

**[9K   Articles belonging to or owned in common by a third party**

(1)   Where—

(a)   a third party claims to own an article attached by interim attachment; and

(b)   the court, on the application of the third party, makes an order stating that it is satisfied that the claim is valid,

the interim attachment of that article shall cease to have effect.

(2)   Where—

(a)   a third party claims to own an article attached by interim attachment in common with the debtor;

(b)   the court, on the application of the third party, makes an order stating that it is satisfied—

(i)   that the claim is valid; and

(ii)   that the continued attachment of the article would be unduly harsh to the third party,

the interim attachment of that article shall cease to have effect.

(3)   Subsection (2) of section 34 below applies where a third party makes an

application for the purposes of subsection (1)(b) above as it applies where a third party makes an application for the purposes of subsection (1)(b)(ii) of that section.

(4)   Where the attachment of an article ceases, by virtue of an order under subsection (1) or (2) above, to have effect, the officer may attach other articles which are owned by the debtor and kept at the place at which the original interim attachment was executed.]

**[9L   Duration of interim attachment**

(1)   An interim attachment shall, unless recalled, have effect only until—

(a)   subject to subsections (2), (4) and (7) below, where—

(i)   the creditor obtains a final interlocutor for payment of all or part of a principal sum concluded for in the action on the dependence of which warrant for interim attachment was granted;

(ii)   the creditor obtains a final interlocutor in the creditor's favour in respect of another remedy concluded for in that action; or

(iii)   the final interlocutor is of absolvitor or dismissal and the court grants decree under and for the purposes of section 9Q(1)(b) below,

the expiry of the period of 6 months after the action is disposed of;

(b)   where—

(i)   the final interlocutor is of absolvitor or dismissal; and

(ii)   no decree under and for the purposes of section 9Q(1)(b) below is granted,

the granting of that interlocutor; or

(c)   the creditor consents, by virtue of subsection (3) below, to the interim attachment ceasing to have effect in relation to every article attached.

(2)   An interim attachment shall have effect in relation to a specific article only until the article is attached by the creditor in execution of any such final interlocutor or decree as is mentioned in subsection (1)(a) above.

(3)   The creditor may at any time consent in writing to the interim attachment ceasing to have effect in relation to a specific article attached; and the attachment shall cease to have effect when that consent is notified to the court.

(4)   The court may, on an application by the creditor, extend the period mentioned in subsection (1)(a) above but only if—

(a)   the application is made before the expiry of the period mentioned in that subsection; and

(b)   the court is satisfied that exceptional circumstances make it reasonable to grant the application.

(5)   An application under subsection (4) above shall—

(a)   be in (or as nearly as may be in) the form prescribed by Act of Sederunt; and

(b)   be intimated by the creditor to—

(i)   the debtor; and

(ii)   any other person having an interest.

(6)   The court shall order the creditor to intimate any decision under subsection (4) above disposing of the application under that subsection to—

(a)   the debtor; and

(b)   any other person appearing to the court to have an interest.

(7)   Where such an application is made but not disposed of before the date on which the interim attachment would, but for this subsection, cease to have effect, the interim attachment shall continue to have effect until the application is disposed of.

(8)   In calculating the period mentioned in subsection (1)(a) above, any period during which—

(a)   a time to pay direction under section 1(1) of the Debtors (Scotland) Act 1987 (c 18); or

(b)   an order under—

(i)   section 6(3) of that Act (interim order sisting diligence); or

(ii)  section 9(4) of that Act (diligence sisted if not recalled on making of time to pay order),

is in effect shall be disregarded.

(9)   For the purposes of subsection (1) above—

(a)   a final interlocutor is obtained when an interlocutor—

(i)   cannot be recalled or altered; and

(ii)  is not subject to review; and

(b)   an action is disposed of on the date on which the final interlocutor mentioned in paragraph (a) of that subsection is obtained unless, on a later date, the creditor obtains a final interlocutor for expenses in the action, in which case it is disposed of on that later date.]


*Recall etc of interim attachment*

**[9M   Recall or restriction of interim attachment**

(1)   This section applies where warrant is granted for interim attachment.

(2)   The debtor and any person having an interest may apply to the court for an order—

(a)   recalling the warrant;

(b)   restricting the warrant;

(c)   if an interim attachment has been executed in pursuance of the warrant—

(i)   recalling; or

(ii)  restricting,

that attachment;

(d)   determining any question relating to the validity, effect or operation of the warrant; or

(e)   ancillary to any order mentioned in paragraphs (a) to (d) above.

(3)   An application under subsection (2) above shall—

(a)   be in (or as nearly as may be in) the form prescribed by Act of Sederunt; and

(b)   be intimated to—

(i)   the creditor; and

(ii)  any other person having an interest.

(4)   At the hearing on the application under subsection (2) above, the court shall not make any order without first giving—

(a)   any person to whom intimation of the application was made; and

(b)   any other person the court is satisfied has an interest,

an opportunity to be heard.

(5)   Where the court is satisfied that the warrant is invalid it—

(a)   shall make an order—

(i)   recalling the warrant; and

(ii)  if interim attachment has been executed in pursuance of the warrant, recalling that interim attachment; and

(b)   may make an order ancillary to any order mentioned in paragraph (a) above.

(6)   Where the court is satisfied that an interim attachment executed in pursuance of the warrant is incompetent, it—

(a)   shall make an order recalling the interim attachment; and

(b)   may make an order ancillary to any such order.

(7)   Subject to subsection (8) below, where the court is satisfied that the warrant is valid but that—

(a)   an interim attachment executed in pursuance of it is irregular or ineffective; or

(b) it is reasonable in all the circumstances, including the effect granting warrant may have had on any person having an interest, to do so,
the court may, subject to subsection (11) below, make any order such as is mentioned in subsection (2) above.

(8) If no longer satisfied as to the matters mentioned in subsection (9) below, the court—

(a) shall make an order such as is mentioned in subsection (5)(a) above; and

(b) may make an order such as is mentioned in subsection (5)(b) above.

(9) The matters referred to in subsection (8) above are—

(a) that the creditor has a prima facie case on the merits of the action;

(b) that there is a real and substantial risk enforcement of any decree in the action in favour of the creditor would be defeated or prejudiced by reason of—

(i) the debtor being insolvent or verging on insolvency; or

(ii) the likelihood of the debtor removing, disposing of, burdening, concealing or otherwise dealing with all or some of the debtor's assets; and

(c) that it is reasonable in all the circumstances, including the effect granting warrant may have had on any person having an interest, for the warrant or, as the case may be, any interim attachment executed in pursuance of it to continue to have effect.

(10) The onus shall be on the creditor to satisfy the court that no order under subsection (5), (6), (7) or (8) above should be made.

(11) Where—

(a) by virtue of section 9L(1)(a) above, the interim attachment continues to have effect after the creditor obtains a final interlocutor for payment; and

(b) the period of six months mentioned in that paragraph has not expired,
the court shall not make an order under subsection (7) above.

(12) In granting an application under subsection (2) above, the court may impose such conditions (if any) as it thinks fit.

(13) Without prejudice to the generality of subsection (12) above, those conditions may require the debtor—

(a) to consign into court such sum; or

(b) to find such caution or to give such other security,
as the court thinks fit.

(14) Where the court makes an order under this section, the court shall order the debtor to intimate that order to—

(a) the creditor; and

(b) any other person appearing to the court to have an interest.]

## [9N Variation of orders and variation or recall of conditions

(1) Where—

(a) an order restricting warrant for interim attachment is made under section 9M(7) above; or

(b) a condition is imposed under—

(i) section 9E(6) above; or

(ii) section 9M(12) above,
the debtor may apply to the court for variation of the order or, as the case may be, variation or removal of the condition.

(2) An application under subsection (1) above shall—

(a) be in (or as nearly as may be in) the form prescribed by Act of Sederunt; and

(b) be intimated to—

(i) the creditor; and

(ii) any other person having an interest.

(3) At the hearing on the application under subsection (1) above, the court shall not make any order without first giving—

(a)    any person to whom intimation of the application was made; and

(b)    any other person the court is satisfied has an interest,

an opportunity to be heard.

(4)    On an application under subsection (1) above, the court may if it thinks fit—

(a)    vary the order; or

(b)    vary or remove the condition.

(5)    Where the court makes an order varying the order or, as the case may be, varying or removing the condition, the court shall order the debtor to intimate that order to—

(a)    the creditor; and

(b)    any other person appearing to the court to have an interest.]

*General and miscellaneous provisions*

**[9P    Expenses of interim attachment**

(1)    Subject to subsection (3)(a) below, a creditor shall be entitled to the expenses incurred—

(a)    in obtaining warrant for interim attachment; and

(b)    where an interim attachment is executed in pursuance of the warrant, in so executing that attachment.

(2)    Subject to subsection (3)(b) below, a debtor shall be entitled, where—

(a)    warrant for interim attachment is granted; and

(b)    the court is satisfied that the creditor was acting unreasonably in applying for it,

to the expenses incurred in opposing that warrant.

(3)    The court may modify or refuse—

(a)    such expenses as are mentioned in subsection (1) above if it is satisfied that—

(i)    the creditor was acting unreasonably in applying for the warrant; or

(ii)    such modification or refusal is reasonable in all the circumstances and having regard to the outcome of the action; and

(b)    such expenses as are mentioned in subsection (2) above if it is satisfied as to the matter mentioned in paragraph (a)(ii) above.

(4)    Subject to subsections (1) to (3) above, the court may make such findings as it thinks fit in relation to such expenses as are mentioned in subsections (1) and (2) above.

(5)    Expenses incurred as mentioned in subsections (1) and (2) above in obtaining or, as the case may be, opposing an application for warrant shall be expenses of process.]

**[9Q    Recovery of expenses of interim attachment**

(1)    Subject to subsection (4) below, any expenses chargeable against the debtor which are incurred in executing an interim attachment shall be recoverable only by attachment—

(a)    in execution of a decree granted by virtue of—

(i)    the conclusion for payment in the action on the dependence of which the warrant for interim attachment was granted; or

(ii)    another conclusion in the creditor's favour in that action; or

(b)    where the final interlocutor in the action is of absolvitor or dismissal, in execution of a decree granted under and for the purposes of this subsection.

(2)    Where any such expenses cease to be recoverable in pursuance of subsection (1) above, they cease to be chargeable against the debtor.

(3)    Subsection (4) below applies where interim attachment is—

(a)    recalled under section 2(3), 3(1)(b), 9(2)(cb) or 10(1)(b) of the 1987 Act in relation to a time to pay direction or order;

(b)  in effect immediately before the date of sequestration (within the meaning of the Bankruptcy (Scotland) Act 1985 (c 66)) of the debtor's estate;

(c)  in effect immediately before the appointment of an administrator under Part II of the Insolvency Act 1986 (c 45);

(d)  in effect against property of the debtor immediately before a floating charge attaches all or part of that property under section 53(7)(attachment on appointment of receiver by holder of charge) or 54(6)(attachment on appointment of receiver by court) of the 1986 Act;

(e)  in effect immediately before the commencement of the winding up, under Part IV or V of the 1986 Act, of the debtor; or

(f)  rendered unenforceable by virtue of the creditor entering into a composition contract or acceding to a trust deed for creditors or by virtue of the subsistence of a protected trust deed within the meaning of Schedule 5 to the 1985 Act.

(4)  Where this subsection applies—

(a)  the expenses of the interim attachment which were chargeable against the debtor remain so chargeable; and

(b)  if the debtor's obligation to pay the expenses is not discharged under or by virtue of the time to pay direction or order, sequestration, appointment, receivership, winding up, composition contract or trust deed for creditors,

those expenses are recoverable in pursuance of subsection (1) above.]

## [9R  Ascription of sums recovered while interim attachment is in effect

(1)  This section applies where—

(a)  any amounts are—

(i)  secured by an interim attachment; and

(ii)  while the attachment is in effect, paid to account of the amounts recoverable from the debtor; and

(b)  that interim attachment ceases to have effect.

(2)  Such amounts shall be ascribed to the following in the order in which they are mentioned—

(a)  the expenses incurred in—

(i)  obtaining warrant for; and

(ii)  executing,

the interim attachment;

(b)  any interest which has accrued, in relation to a sum due under a decree granted by virtue of the conclusion in relation to which warrant for interim attachment was granted, as at the date of execution;

(c)  any sum due under that decree together with such interest as has accrued after that date.

(3)  Where an interim attachment is followed by an attachment in execution of a decree granted by virtue of the conclusion in relation to which the warrant for the interim attachment was granted, section 41 below shall apply to amounts to which this section applies as it applies to amounts to which that section applies.]

## [9S  Ranking of interim attachment

For the purposes of any enactment or rule of law as to ranking or preference—

(a)  where—

(i)  an interim attachment has been executed; and

(ii)  the creditor has, without undue delay, obtained an interlocutor for payment of all or part of the sum concluded for,

that interim attachment shall be treated as if it were an attachment by virtue of section 10 below of the property attached, executed when the interim attachment was executed; and

(b)   where an interim attachment has ceased to have effect in relation to any article by virtue of section 9L(2) above, the attachment of the article in question shall be taken to have been executed when the interim attachment was executed.]]

## PART 2
## ATTACHMENT

### *Attachment*

**10   Attachment**
(1)   There shall be a form of diligence over corporeal moveable property for recovery of money owed; it is to be known as attachment.
(2)   Attachment is exigible only in execution of a decree or document of debt and only upon property owned (whether alone or in common) by the debtor.
(3)   Attachment is competent only where—
    [(a)   the debtor has been charged to pay the debt;
    (b)   the period for payment specified in the charge has expired without payment being made; and
    (c)   where the debtor is an individual, the creditor has, no earlier than 12 weeks before taking any steps to execute the attachment, provided the debtor with a debt advice and information package.]
    [. . .]
(5)   In this section—
'debt advice and information package' means a document or bundle of documents containing such information (including information regarding the availability of money advice within the debtor's locality), and in such form, as the Scottish Ministers may determine;
'decree' means—
    (a)   a decree of the Court of Session, of the High Court of Justiciary or of the sheriff;
    (b)   a decree of the Court of Teinds;
    (c)   a summary warrant;
    (d)   a civil judgment granted outside Scotland by a court, tribunal or arbiter which by virtue of any enactment or rule of law is enforceable in Scotland;
    (e)   an order or determination which by virtue of any enactment is enforceable as if it were an extract registered decree arbitral bearing a warrant for execution issued by the sheriff;
    (f)   a warrant granted, in criminal proceedings, for enforcement by civil diligence;
    (g)   an order under section 114 of the Companies Clauses Consolidation (Scotland) Act 1845 (c 17);
    (h)   a determination under section 46 of the Harbours, Docks and Piers Clauses Act 1847 (c 27); or
    (i)   a liability order within the meaning of section 33(2) of the Child Support Act 1991 (c 48), being a decree, warrant, judgment, order or determination which, or an extract of which, authorises attachment; and
'document of debt' means—
        (a)   a document registered for execution in the Books of Council and Session or the sheriff court books; or
        (b)   a document or settlement which by virtue of an Order in Council made under section 13 of the Civil Jurisdiction and Judgments Act 1982 (c 27) is enforceable in Scotland,
being a document, bill or settlement which, or an extract of which, authorises attachment.

(6)   The Scottish Ministers may by order modify the definitions of 'decree' and 'document of debt' in subsection (5) above so as to—

(a)   add or remove types of decree or document to or, as the case may be, from those referred to in that provision; or

(b)   vary any of the descriptions of the types of decree or document there referred to.

(7)   In this Act, references to attaching are references to the execution of attachment.

### 11   Articles exempt from attachment

(1)   It is not competent to attach—

(a)   any implements, tools of trade, books or other equipment reasonably required for the use of the debtor in the practice of the debtor's profession, trade or business and not exceeding in aggregate value £1,000 or such amount as may be prescribed in regulations made by the Scottish Ministers;

(b)   any vehicle, the use of which is so reasonably required by the debtor, not exceeding in value £1,000 or such amount as may be prescribed in regulations made by the Scottish Ministers;

(c)   a mobile home which is the debtor's only or principal residence;

(d)   any tools or other equipment reasonably required for the purpose of keeping in good order and condition any garden or yard adjacent to, or associated with, a dwellinghouse in which the debtor resides;

[(e)   any money.]

(2)   The Scottish Ministers may by regulations modify subsection (1) above so as to—

(a)   add or remove types of articles to or, as the case may be, from those referred to in that provision; or

(b)   vary any of the descriptions of the types of articles there referred to.

[(3)   It is not competent to attach cargo which it is competent to arrest by virtue of section 47C of the Administration of Justice Act 1965 (c 46) (competence of arresting cargo.)]*

[(3)   In subsection (1)(e) above, 'money' has the same meaning as in section 175 of the Bankruptcy and Diligence etc (Scotland) Act 2007 (asp 3).]*

*Subsection (3) inserted twice, by Bankruptcy and Diligence etc (Scotland) Act 2007 Sch 4 para 11 and by Sch 5 para 11 respectively.

### 12   Times when attachment is not competent

(1)   It is not competent to execute an attachment on—

(a)   a Sunday;

(b)   a day which is a public holiday in the area in which the attachment is to be executed; or

(c)   such other day as may be prescribed by Act of Sederunt.

(2)   The execution of an attachment shall not—

(a)   begin before 8 am or after 8 pm; or

(b)   be continued after 8 pm,

unless the officer has obtained prior authority from the sheriff for such commencement or continuation.

### 13   Presumption of ownership

(1)   An officer may, when executing an attachment, proceed on the assumption that the debtor owns, solely or in common with a third party, any article which is in the possession of the debtor.

(2)   The officer shall, before attaching any article, make enquiries of any person who is present at the place at which the article is situated as to the ownership of

the article (and in particular shall enquire as to whether there is any person who owns the article in common with the debtor).

(3)   The officer may not proceed on the assumption mentioned in subsection (1) above where the officer knows or ought to know that the contrary is the case.

(4)   The officer is not precluded from relying on that assumption by reason only of one or both of the following circumstances—

(a)   that the article belongs to a class which is commonly held under a hire, hire-purchase or conditional sale agreement or on some other limited title of possession;

(b)   that an assertion has been made that the article is not owned by the debtor.

### [13A   Schedule of attachment

(1)   The officer must, immediately after executing an attachment, complete a schedule such as is mentioned in subsection (2) below (in this section, the 'attachment schedule').

(2)   An attachment schedule—

(a)   must be in (or as nearly as may be in) the form prescribed by Act of Sederunt; and

(b)   must specify—

(i)   the articles attached; and

(ii)   their value, so far as ascertainable.

(3)   The officer must—

(a)   give a copy of the attachment schedule to the debtor; or

(b)   where it is not practicable to do so—

(i)   give a copy of the schedule to a person present at the place where the attachment was executed; or

(ii)   where there is no such person, leave a copy of it at that place.

(4)   An attachment is executed on the day on which the officer complies with subsection (3) above.]

*Attachment of articles kept outwith dwellinghouses etc*

### 14   Procedure for attachment of articles kept outwith dwellinghouses etc

Sections 15 to [19A] below apply only in relation to the attachment of articles which are—

(a)   kept outwith a dwellinghouse; or

(b)   mobile homes which are not the only or principal residence of the debtor.

### 15   [Valuation]

(1)   An officer may be open shut and lockfast places for the purposes of executing an attachment.

(2)   When executing an attachment the officer shall, subject to subsection (3) below, value the articles being attached at the price which they are likely to fetch if sold on the open market.

(3)   Where the officer considers that an article is such that a valuation by a professional valuer or other suitably skilled person is appropriate, the officer shall arrange for such a valuation and a valuation so arranged shall proceed on the basis set out in subsection (2) above.

### 16   Attachment of mobile homes

(1)   Where a mobile home which is the only or principal residence of a person other than the debtor has been attached—

(a)   the officer shall give notice to that other person of that fact; and

(b)   the sheriff may, on an application by the debtor or that other person, order that the attachment of the mobile home is to cease to have effect.

(2)   The sheriff—

(a)   shall consider any application for an order under subsection (1) above which is made before the date which is 14 days after the date on which the mobile home is attached; and

(b)    may, on cause shown, consider any such application which is made at any time after that date but before the date on which the attached mobile home is auctioned.

## 17    Report of attachment

(1)    The officer shall, within 14 days of the execution of an attachment (or such longer period as the sheriff on cause shown may allow on application by the officer), make to the sheriff a report of the attachment.

(2)    A report made under subsection (1) above shall—

(a)    be in the form prescribed by Act of Sederunt; and

(b)    be signed by the officer.

(3)    Such a report shall specify—

(a)    whether any person, in response to enquiries made under section 13(2) above, asserted that any attached article is not owned by the debtor (or is owned in common by the debtor and a third party);

(b)    whether any attached article has been redeemed under section 18(1) below.

(4)    Such a report need not be made in respect of any article or vehicle which has been sold in pursuance of an order made under section 20(1)(b) or, as the case may be, 22(3) below.

(5)    The sheriff may refuse to receive such a report on the ground that it has not been made and signed in accordance with subsections (1) and (2) above.

(6)    If the sheriff so refuses—

(a)    the attachment to which the report relates is to cease to have effect; and

(b)    the sheriff clerk shall intimate the refusal to—

(i)    the debtor; and

(ii)    if another person is in possession of the attached articles, that person.

## 18    Redemption

(1)    Subject to any order made under section 20(1)(b) below, the debtor is entitled, within 14 days of the date on which an article is attached, to redeem that article.

(2)    The amount for which such an article may be redeemed is the value fixed under subsection (2) or (3) of section 15 above.

(3)    The officer shall, on receiving payment from the debtor for the redemption of an attached article, grant a receipt in the form prescribed by Act of Sederunt to the debtor.

(4)    The attachment of the article is, on the grant of such a receipt, to cease to have effect.

(5)    Where an article is redeemed after the officer has made a report under section 17(1) above in respect of the attachment, the officer shall report the redemption as soon as is reasonably practicable to the sheriff.

## 19    Removal and auction of attached articles

(1)    [An officer] may, after the report of attachment has been received by the sheriff—

(a)    make arrangements for the auction of the attached articles; and

(b)    on the date specified in the notice given under section 27(4) below, remove the attached articles from the place at which they are kept.

(2)    The officer may open shut and lockfast places for the purpose of so removing the attached articles.

(3)    The officer may not remove any vehicle in respect of which an application for an order under subsection (1) or (3) of section 22 below has been made but not disposed of.

(4)    The officer may remove to the place at which the auction is to be held such

attached articles as, if sold at their values fixed under subsection (2) or, as the case may be, (3) of section 15 above, would realise in aggregate the sum recoverable at the time of the auction.

(5)   The remaining attached articles will cease to be subject to attachment.

(6)   An attached article shall not, subject to any order made under section 20(1)(b) or 22(3) below, be auctioned before the date which is 7 days after the date on which the article is removed by the officer from the place at which it was attached.

### [19A   Urgent removal of attached articles

(1)   The officer may at any time remove an attached article without notice if—
    (a)   the officer considers it necessary for—
        (i)   the security; or
        (ii)   the preservation of the value,
  of the article; and
    (b)   there is insufficient time to obtain an order under section 20(1)(a) below.

(2)   The officer shall remove an article under subsection (1) above—
    (a)   to the nearest convenient premises of the debtor or the person in possession of the articles; or
    (b)   if—
        (i)   no such premises are available; or
        (ii)   the officer considers such premises to be unsuitable,
  to the nearest suitable secure premises.

(3)   Subsections (2) and (6) of section 19 above shall apply to this section as they apply to that section.]

### Attachment: further procedure

### 20   Order for security of articles or sale of articles which are perishable etc

(1)   The sheriff may, on an application by the creditor, the officer or the debtor, at any time after articles have been attached make an order—
    (a)   for the security of any of the attached articles;
    (b)   in relation to any of the articles which are of a perishable nature or which are likely to deteriorate substantially and rapidly in condition or value, for the creditor or the officer to make arrangements for their immediate sale and for any proceeds of the sale to be consigned in court.

(2)   An application for an order under subsection (1) above—
    (a)   by the creditor or the officer, shall be intimated by the creditor or, as the case may be, the officer to the debtor;
    (b)   by the debtor, shall be intimated to the creditor and the officer, [—
        (i)   who attached articles; or
        (ii)   who is authorised to arrange the auction,]
  at the time when it is made.

(3)   A decision of the sheriff to make an order under subsection (1)(b) above shall not be subject to appeal.

(4)   Any sum consigned in court in pursuance of an order made under subsection (1)(b) above shall, where an attachment ceases to have effect before the auction of attached articles is held, be paid to the creditor to the extent necessary to meet the sum recoverable, any surplus thereof being paid to the debtor.

### 21   Unlawful acts after attachment

(1)   The debtor or person in possession of an attached article shall not move it from the place at which it was attached.

(2)   If an article is so moved—
    (a)   the debtor or, as the case may be, the person in possession of the attached articles is acting in breach of the attachment; and
    (b)   the sheriff may, on an application by the creditor or by the officer, by

order authorise the attachment of other articles which are owned by the debtor and kept at the place at which the original attachment was executed.

(3) Subsection (1) above does not apply in relation to any vehicle in respect of which an application for an order under subsection (1) or (3) of section 22 below has been made but not disposed of.

(4) The debtor shall not sell, make a gift of or otherwise relinquish ownership of any attached article.

(5) If an attached article is so sold, gifted or otherwise disposed of the debtor is acting in breach of the attachment.

(6) Any person who wilfully damages or destroys any article which that person knows has been attached is acting in breach of the attachment.

(7) Where an attached article is stolen, the debtor shall give notice to the creditor and the officer [—

    (i) who attached articles; or

    (ii) who is authorised to arrange the auction,]

of that fact and of any related claim which the debtor makes, or intends to make, under a contract of insurance.

(8) Any debtor who fails to give notice as required by subsection (7) above is acting in breach of the attachment.

(9) Any act which is, under subsection (2), (5), (6) or (8) above, a breach of the attachment may be dealt with as a contempt of court.

(10) Where attached articles are damaged, destroyed or stolen the sheriff, on an application by the creditor or by the officer, may by order authorise—

    (a) the attachment of other articles which are owned by the debtor and kept at the place at which the original attachment was executed;

    (b) the revaluation of any damaged article in accordance with subsection (2) or (3) of section 15 above.

(11) Where the debtor or any third party who knows that an article is attached—

    (a) moves it from the place at which the attachment was executed, and it is—

        (i) damaged, destroyed, lost or stolen; or

        (ii) acquired from or through the debtor or, as the case may be, the third party by another person without knowledge of the attachment and for value; or

    (b) wilfully damages or destroys it,

the sheriff may order the debtor or, as the case may be, the third party to consign the sum set out in subsection (12) below in court.

(12) That sum is—

    (a) where the article has been damaged but not so damaged as to make it worthless, a sum equal to the difference between the value of the article fixed under subsection (2) or (3) of section 15 above or, as the case may be, under section 51 or 54(1) below and the value of the article so damaged; or

    (b) in any other case, a sum equal to the value of the article as fixed under subsection (2) or (3) of section 15 above or, as the case may be, under section 51 or 54(1) below.

(13) For the purposes of subsection (12)(a) above, the officer shall, subject to subsection (14) below, value a damaged article at the price which it is likely to fetch if sold in that condition on the open market.

(14) Where the officer considers that a damaged article is such that a valuation by a professional valuer or other suitably skilled person is appropriate, the officer shall arrange for such a valuation and a valuation so arranged shall proceed on the basis set out in subsection (13) above.

(15) Any sum consigned in court in pursuance of an order made under subsection (11) above shall, where the attachment of a damaged article ceases to have effect before it is auctioned, be paid to the creditor to the extent necessary to meet the sum recoverable, any surplus thereof being paid to the debtor.

## 22   Release of vehicle from attachment

(1)   The sheriff may, on an application by the debtor and on being satisfied that the auction of any vehicle which has been attached would be unduly harsh in the circumstances, make an order—

(a)   providing that the attachment of the vehicle is to cease to have effect; and

(b)   where the vehicle has been removed by the officer from the place at which it was attached, requiring the officer to return the vehicle to that place.

(2)   The sheriff may not make an order under subsection (1) above unless the value of the vehicle (as fixed under subsection (2) or (3) of section 15 above) does not exceed £1,000 or such other amount as may be prescribed in regulations made by the Scottish Ministers.

(3)   Where the value (as fixed under subsection (2) or (3) of section 15 above) of an attached vehicle does exceed £1,000 or, as the case may be, such other pre-scribed amount the sheriff may, on an application by the debtor and on being satisfied that the auction of any vehicle which has been attached would be unduly harsh in the circumstances, make an order requiring the officer to—

(a)   make arrangements for the immediate sale of the vehicle;

(b)   pay to the debtor from any proceeds of such sale the sum of £1,000 (or such lesser amount as the sheriff may specify); and

(c)   consign any surplus remaining in court.

(4)   Where the amount realised on the sale of a vehicle in pursuance of an order has been made under subsection (3) above is less than the amount which the officer is required by that order to pay to the debtor, the order shall be deemed to have required the officer to pay the amount realised only.

(5)   Where the officer is unable to sell the vehicle in pursuance of an order made under subsection (3) above within 14 days of the date on which the order was made, the attachment of that vehicle is to cease to have effect.

(6)   The sheriff may consider an application for an order under subsection (1) or (3) above only where it is made within 14 days of the date on which the vehicle is attached.

## 23   Appeals against valuation

(1)   Where the sheriff is satisfied that the aggregate of the values of attached articles fixed under section 15(2) or (3) above or, as the case may be, section 51 or 54(1) below is substantially below the aggregate of the prices which they are likely to fetch if sold on the open market, the sheriff may, on or before the day which immediately precedes the day on which the articles are to be auctioned, order that the attachment is to cease to have effect.

(2)   The sheriff may make an order under subsection (1) above on the appli-cation of the debtor or on the sheriff's own accord.

(3)   The sheriff shall not make such an order without first giving the debtor and the creditor—

(a)   an opportunity to make representations; and

(b)   if either party wishes to be heard, an opportunity to be heard.

## 24   Duration of attachment

(1)   An attachment shall, subject to subsections (6), (7) and (8) below, have effect only until—

(a)   the earlier of—

(i)   the date which is six months after the date on which the article is attached; and

(ii)   the date which is 28 days after the date on which the attached article is removed by the officer from the place at which it was attached; or

(b)   such other date as may be specified in an order made under subsection (2) or section 29(4)(b) below or in an exceptional attachment order.

(2)  Where the sheriff is satisfied—

(a)   that, if the date on which an attachment is to cease to have effect were to be substituted with a later date, the debtor is likely to comply with an agreement between the creditor and the debtor for the payment of the sum recoverable by instalments or otherwise; or

(b)   that the auction of the attached articles cannot take place before the date on which the attachment is to cease to have effect due to circumstances for which the creditor cannot be held responsible and that the attachment ceasing to have effect on that date would prejudice the creditor,

the sheriff may, on an application by the creditor or by the officer, by order provide that the attachment is to remain in effect until such later date as the sheriff considers reasonable in the circumstances.

(3)  Where the period for which an attachment is to have effect is extended by an order made under subsection (2) above, an application may be made for another order under that subsection so as to further extend that period.

(4)  The sheriff may consider an application for an order under subsection (2) above only where it is made during the period in respect of which an extension is being sought.

(5)  A decision of the sheriff on such an application shall be intimated to the debtor by the sheriff clerk.

(6)  Where such an application is made but not disposed of before the date on which the attachment in respect of which it is made would, but for this subsection, cease to have effect, the attachment shall continue to have effect until the application is disposed of.

(7)  Where such an application is—

(a)   made on the ground referred to in paragraph (a) of subsection (2) above; and

(b)   refused by the sheriff within 14 days of the date on which the attachment in respect of which it is made would, but for this subsection, cease to have effect,

the attachment shall continue to have effect until the date which is 14 days after the date of the refusal.

(8)  Where—

(a)   arrangements for an auction of attached articles are, under section 29(1) below, cancelled; and

(b)   the agreement in respect of which the cancellation is made is breached by the debtor,

the period which begins with the date on which the report of agreement was made under section 29(3) below and which ends with the date on which the debtor breaches the agreement is to be disregarded in determining the date on which the attachment is, under subsection (1) above, to cease to have effect.

## 25  Second attachment at same place

(1)  Subject to—

(a)   section 9(12) (which provides that a debt which remains outstanding on the recall or cessation of a time to pay order may be enforced by certain diligences) of the Debtors (Scotland) Act 1987 (c 18);

(b)   any order made under subsection (2)(b) or (10)(a) of section 21 above; and

(c)   sections 34(3) and 35(4) below,

where articles are attached (or are purported to be attached) at any place, it is not competent to attach other articles kept at that place to enforce the same debt unless those other articles are brought to that place after the execution of the first attachment.

(2)  It is not competent to attach any article in respect of which an attachment has—

(a)    previously been executed in enforcement of the same debt; and

(b)    ceased, by virtue of section 16, 18(4), 22(1), 34(1), 35(3), 55(2) or 56(4) of this Act, to have effect.

### 26  Invalidity and cessation of attachment

(1)   Where, at any time before the auction of an article which has been or purports to have been attached, the sheriff is satisfied that—

(a)    the attachment has ceased to have effect; or, as the case may be

(b)    the purported attachment is invalid (by reason of the attachment being incompetent or otherwise),

the sheriff shall make an order declaring that to be the case and may make such consequential order as appears to the sheriff to be necessary in the circumstances.

(2)   An order under subsection (1) above may be made on an application by the debtor or on the sheriff's own initiative.

(3)   Where such an order is made on the sheriff's own initiative, the sheriff clerk shall intimate the order to the debtor.

(4)   The sheriff shall not make an order under subsection (1) above without first giving the debtor and the creditor—

(a)    an opportunity to make representations; and

(b)    if either party wishes to be heard, an opportunity to be heard.

(5)   Where—

(a)    an order is made under subsection (1) above; and

(b)    [an officer] has removed the article from the place at which it was, or purported to be, attached,

the officer shall return the article to the place from which it was removed.

(6)   The sheriff shall give reasons for a refusal to grant an order under subsection (1) above.

*Auction of attached articles*

### 27  Notice of public auction

(1)   The auction of attached articles shall, subject to subsections (2) and (3) below, be by public auction held in an auction room.

(2)   If it is impractical to hold the auction of an attached article in an auction room the auction may be held at such other place (other than the debtor's dwellinghouse) as the officer considers appropriate.

(3)   The auction of other articles which have been attached together with an article which is to be auctioned at a place other than an auction room may, if the officer considers it appropriate (having had regard, in particular, to the expenses which are likely to be incurred in connection with the auction), also be held at that other place.

(4)   The officer [. . .] shall give notice to the debtor and to any other person in possession of the attached articles of—

(a)    the date on which the auction is to be held;

(b)    the location of the auction room or, as the case may be, the other place at which the auction is to be held; and

(c)    where sections 15 to 19 above apply in relation to the attached articles, the date arranged for the removal of those attached articles from the place at which they are kept.

(5)   The officer shall advertise the auction by public notice.

### 28  Alteration of arrangements for removal or auction

(1)   Subject to subsection (2) below and without prejudice to section 29(4) below, the creditor or the officer is not, after notice has been given under section 27(4) above to the debtor, entitled to arrange—

(a)    a new date for the auction; or

(b)   where [sections 15 to 19A] above apply in relation to the attached articles, a new date for the removal of those articles from the place where they are kept.

(2)   Where, for any reason for which neither the creditor nor the officer is responsible, it is not possible—

(a)   for the auction to be held on the date specified in the notice given under section 27(4) above; or

(b)   for the attached articles to be removed from the place where they are kept on the date so specified,

the creditor may instruct the officer to arrange a new date for the auction or, as the case may be, a new date for the removal and the officer shall intimate the new date to the debtor and to any other person in possession of the attached articles.

(3)   A new date arranged under subsection (2) above shall not in any case be fewer than 7 days after the date of intimation under that subsection.

## 29   Cancellation of auctions

(1)   The officer may, for the purposes of enabling the sum recoverable to be paid in accordance with an agreement between the creditor and the debtor, cancel arrangements for an auction of attached articles.

(2)   The officer may not cancel the arrangements for such an auction on more than two occasions.

(3)   Where an auction has been cancelled the officer shall—

(a)   make to the sheriff a report of the agreement reached; and

(b)   arrange for the return of any attached articles which have been removed for auction to the place from which they were removed.

(4)   The sheriff, if satisfied on an application by the creditor that the debtor is in breach of any agreement which has been reported under subsection (3) above, may by order provide—

(a)   if the arrangements for the auction of the attached articles can still be implemented in accordance with the provisions of this Part and Part 3 of this Act, that the officer may resume making arrangements for the auction in accordance with those provisions;

(b)   if for any reason for which neither the creditor nor the officer is responsible arrangements for the auction cannot be implemented in accordance with those provisions, that the provisions of this Part and Part 3 of this Act which prevent such implementation are not to apply for the purposes of the attachment and auction of those articles.

(5)   The sheriff shall not make an order under subsection (4) above without first giving the debtor—

(a)   an opportunity to make representations; and

(b)   if the debtor so wishes, an opportunity to be heard.

## 30   Auction

(1)   The officer shall attend the auction and maintain a record of the attached articles which are sold.

(2)   Such a record shall specify the amount for which each attached article is sold.

(3)   The officer shall be accompanied at the auction by another person who shall witness the proceedings.

(4)   Any attached article exposed for sale in the auction may be purchased by—

(a)   any creditor, including the creditor on whose behalf the article was attached;

(b)   a third party who owns the attached article in common with the debtor.

## 31   Disposal of proceeds of auction

(1)   The officer shall, subject to section 37 (effect of sequestration on diligence) of the Bankruptcy (Scotland) Act 1985 (c 66), dispose of the proceeds of the auction by—

(a)  retaining such amount as necessary to meet the fees and outlays of the officer;

(b)  paying to the creditor the remainder of the proceeds of auction so far as necessary to meet the sum recoverable; and

(c)  paying to the debtor any surplus remaining.

[(1A)  Where an article is sold at the auction at a price below the value of the article, the difference between that price and that value shall, prior to the proceeds of the auction being disposed of under subsection (1) above, be credited against the sum recoverable.

(1B)  Where—

(a)  an article to which subsection (1A) above applies has been damaged and revalued under section 21(10)(b) above;

(b)  the damage was not caused by the fault of the debtor; and

(c)  no sum has been consigned into court by a third party under section 21(11) above,

the revaluation shall be disregarded for the purposes of subsection (1A) above.]

(2)  Where the sum recoverable is not realised by the proceeds of auction and any article remains unsold after being exposed for auction—

(a)  ownership of the article shall, without prejudice to the rights of any third party, pass to the creditor; and

(b)  the value of that article shall be credited against the sum recoverable.

(3)  Where the value of unsold articles exceeds the amount of the sum recoverable which remains outstanding, subsection (2) above shall operate only in relation to such of those articles which have, in aggregate, the value which is nearest to the amount which remains outstanding.

(4)  The references in subsections [(1A),] (2)(b) and (3) above to the value of an article are references to the value of the article as fixed under subsection (2) or (3) of section 15 above or, as the case may be, section 51 or 54(1) below.

(5)  Where the creditor does not uplift an article within 3 working days after the day on which the auction is held the ownership of the article shall revert to the person who owned the article before the operation of subsection (2)(a) above.

(6)  For the purposes of this section—

'proceeds of auction' include any amount—

(a)  consigned in court in pursuance of an order made under section 21(11), 20(1)(b), 22(3) or 50(5) of this Act;

(b)  received by the officer in respect of a transfer, under section 35(2) below, of the debtor's interest in any article owned in common by the debtor and a third party,

but do not include any amount which the officer is required to pay to the debtor in pursuance of an order under section 22(3) above; and

'working day' means a day which is not—

(a)  a Saturday;

(b)  a Sunday;

(c)  New Year's Day;

(d)  2nd January;

(e)  Good Friday;

(f)  Easter Monday;

(g)  Christmas Day;

(h)  Boxing Day; or

(i)  any other day which is a public holiday in the area in which the auction is held.

## 32  Report of auction

(1)  The officer who arranged the auction shall, within the period of 14 days

after the date on which the auction is held, make to the sheriff a report in the form prescribed by Act of Sederunt (a 'report of auction').

(2) A report of auction shall—

(a) specify—

(i) any attached articles which have been sold;

(ii) the amount for which they have been sold;

(iii) any attached articles which remain unsold;

[(iiia) any sums paid by the debtor to account of the sum recoverable;]

(iv) any chargeable expenses;

(v) any surplus paid to the debtor; and

(vi) any balance due by or to the debtor;

(b) refer to any article in respect of which—

(i) an attachment has, under section 34(1) below or in pursuance of an order made under section 35(3) below, ceased to have effect;

(ii) the debtor's interest has, under section 35(2) below, transferred to a third party;

(c) contain a declaration by the officer that all the information contained within it is, to the best of the officer's knowledge, true; and

(d) be signed by the officer and the witness who attended the auction.

(3) If the officer—

(a) without reasonable excuse makes a report of auction after the expiry of the period mentioned in subsection (1) above; or

(b) wilfully refuses to make, or delays making, a report of auction after the expiry of that period,

the sheriff may make an order providing that the officer is liable for the chargeable expenses, either in whole or in part.

(4) An order made under subsection (3) above does not prejudice the right of the sheriff to report the matter to the Court of Session or the sheriff principal under section 79(1)(b) (investigation of alleged misconduct by a messenger-at-arms or sheriff officer) of the Debtors (Scotland) Act 1987 (c 18).

## 33 Audit of report of auction

(1) The sheriff shall remit the report of auction to the auditor of court who shall—

(a) tax the chargeable expenses;

(b) certify the balance due by or to the debtor following the auction; and

(c) make a report to the sheriff.

(2) The auditor of court shall not alter the report of auction without first providing all interested persons an opportunity to make representations.

(3) The auditor of court shall not charge a fee in respect of the report made under subsection (1)(c) above.

(4) On receipt of a report made under subsection (1)(c) above the sheriff shall make an order—

(a) declaring the balance due by or to the debtor, as certified by the auditor of court;

(b) declaring such a balance after making modifications to the balance so certified; or

(c) where the sheriff is satisfied that there has been a substantial irregularity in the execution of the attachment (other than the timing of the report of auction), declaring the attachment and auction to be void.

(5) An order made under subsection (4)(c) above may make such consequential provision as the sheriff thinks fit.

(6) An order made under subsection (4)(c) above shall not affect the title of a person to any article acquired by that person at the auction, or subsequently, in good faith.

(7)   The sheriff may not make an order under subsection (4)(b) or (c) above without first

[(a)   giving—

(i)   the debtor;

(ii)   the creditor; and

(iii)   any third party who claims ownership (whether alone or in common with the debtor) of any attached article,

an opportunity to make representations; or

(b)   holding a hearing.]

(8)   The sheriff clerk shall intimate the sheriff's order under subsection (4) above to the [persons mentioned in subsection (7)(a) above].

*General and miscellaneous provisions*

### 34   Articles belonging to a third party

(1)   Where at any time before an attached article is auctioned—

(a)   a third party claims to own the article; and

(b)   either—

(i)   the officer is satisfied that the claim is valid and neither the debtor nor any other person in possession of the article disputes the claim; or

(ii)   the sheriff, on an application by the third party, makes an order stating that the sheriff is [satisfied that the claim is valid],

the attachment of that article is to cease to have effect.

(2)   The making of an application to the sheriff for the purposes of subsection (1)(b)(ii) above does not preclude the third party making the application from taking any other proceedings for the recovery of an article which is owned by the third party.

(3)   Where the attachment of an article ceases, under subsection (1) above, to have effect, the officer may attach other articles which are owned by the debtor and kept at the place at which the original attachment was executed.

### 35   Articles in common ownership

(1)   Articles which are owned in common by a debtor and a third party may be attached and disposed of in satisfaction of the debts of the debtor.

(2)   Where at any time before an attached article is auctioned—

(a)   a third party claims to own the article in common with the debtor;

(b)   either—

(i)   the officer is satisfied that the claim is valid; or

(ii)   the sheriff, on an application by the third party, makes an order stating that the sheriff is so satisfied; and

(c)   the third party pays to the officer a sum equal to the value of the debtor's interest in the article,

the debtor's interest in the article shall transfer to the third party.

(3)   Where the sheriff is satisfied—

(a)   that an article which has been removed from the place at which it was attached is owned in common by the debtor and a third party; and

(b)   that the auction of the article would be unduly harsh to the third party in the circumstances,

the sheriff may, on an application by the third party before the attached article is auctioned, order that the attachment of that article is to cease to have effect.

(4)   Where—

(a)   the debtor's interest in an article owned in common by the debtor and a third party is, under subsection (2) above, transferred to the third party; or

(b)   the attachment of an article which is so owned ceases, in pursuance of an order made under subsection (3) above, to have effect,

the officer may attach other articles which are owned by the debtor and kept at the place at which the original attachment was executed.

**36 Procedure where articles in common ownership are sold at auction**

(1) This subsection applies where—

(a) a third party claimed, before an attached article was auctioned, to own the article in common with the debtor;

(b) the debtor's interest in the article has not transferred to the third party under section 35(2) above;

(c) the attachment of the article has not, by virtue of an order made under section 35(3) above, ceased to have effect;

(d) the third party's interest in the article has, following the auction of the article, been transferred to another person; and

(e) either—

(i) the third party's claim is, after that transfer of interest, admitted by the creditor and the debtor; or

(ii) where the third party's claim is not so admitted, the sheriff, on an application by the third party after that transfer of interest, is satisfied that the claim is valid.

(2) Where subsection (1) above applies, the creditor shall—

(a) where the article has been sold at the auction, pay to the third party the fraction of the proceeds of the sale of the article which corresponded to the third party's interest in the article; or

(b) where the ownership of the article has passed to the creditor under section 31(2)(a) above, pay to the third party the fraction of the value of the article which corresponded to the third party's interest in the article.

(3) The reference in subsection (2)(b) above to the value of an article is a reference to the value of the article as fixed under subsection (2) or (3) of section 15 above or, as the case may be, section 51 or 54(1) below.

**37 Attachment terminated by payment or tender of full amount owing**

An attachment is to cease to have effect if the sum recoverable is—

(a) paid to the creditor, the officer or any other person who has authority to receive payment on behalf of the creditor; or

(b) tendered to any of those persons and the tender is not accepted within a reasonable time.

**38 Assistance to debtor**

The sheriff clerk shall, if requested by the debtor—

(a) provide the debtor with information as to the procedures available to him under any provision of this Part or Part 3 of this Act; and

(b) assist the debtor in the completion of any form required in connection with any proceedings under any provision of this Part or Part 3 of this Act,

but the sheriff clerk shall not be liable for any error or omission by him in performing the duties imposed on him by this section.

**39 Expenses chargeable in relation to attachment etc**

(1) Schedule 1 to this Act has effect for the purposes of determining the liability, as between the creditor and the debtor, for expenses incurred in serving a charge and in the process of attachment and auction.

(2) The Scottish Ministers may by order modify that schedule so as to—

(a) add or remove types of expenses to or, as the case may be, from those referred to in that schedule; or

(b) vary any of the descriptions of the types of expenses there referred to.

**40 Recovery from debtor of expenses of attachment**

(1) Subject to subsections (2) and (4) below, any expenses chargeable against the debtor which are incurred in an attachment (including the service of the charge preceding it and the auction following it) are recoverable from the debtor by the attachment concerned but not by any other legal process, and any such expenses

which have not been recovered by the time the attachment and auction is completed will cease to be chargeable against the debtor.

(2)   The sheriff shall grant decree for payment of—

(a)   any expenses awarded by the sheriff against the debtor in favour of the creditor under paragraph 4 or 7 of schedule 1 to this Act; or

(b)   any additional sum of expenses awarded by the sheriff against the debtor in favour of the creditor under paragraph 5 of that schedule.

(3)   Subsection (4) below applies where an attachment is—

(a)   recalled under [section 9(2)(d) or (10)(b)] (effect of time to pay order on diligence) of the Debtors (Scotland) Act 1987 (c 18) in relation to a time to pay order;

(b)   in effect immediately before the date of sequestration (within the meaning of the Bankruptcy (Scotland) Act 1985 (c 66)) of the debtor's estate;

(c)   in effect immediately before the [appointment of an administrator] under Part II of the Insolvency Act 1986 (c 45);

(d)   in effect against property of the debtor immediately before a floating charge attaches to all or part of that property under section 53(7) (attachment on appointment of receiver by holder of charge) or 54(6) (attachment on appointment of receiver by court) of that Act of 1986;

(e)   in effect immediately before the commencement of the winding up, under Part IV or V of that Act of 1986, of the debtor; or

(f)   rendered unenforceable by virtue of the creditor entering into a composition contract or acceding to a trust deed for creditors or by virtue of the subsistence of a protected trust deed within the meaning of Schedule 5 to the Bankruptcy (Scotland) Act 1985 (c 66).

(4)   Where this subsection applies—

(a)   the expenses of the attachment which were chargeable against the debtor remain so chargeable; and

(b)   if the debtor's obligation to pay the expenses is not discharged under or by virtue of the time to pay order, sequestration, [appointment], receivership, winding up, composition contract or trust deed for creditors, those expenses are recoverable by further attachment.

### 41   Ascription of sums recovered by attachment or while attachment is in effect

(1)   This section applies to any amounts recovered by an attachment or paid to account of the amounts recoverable by the attachment while the attachment is in effect.

(2)   An amount to which this section applies shall be ascribed to the following in the order in which they are mentioned—

(a)   the expenses already incurred in respect of—

(i)   the attachment;

[(ia)   any previous interim attachment the expenses of which are chargeable against and recoverable from the debtor under section 9Q(1)(a) of this Act;]

(ii)   any previous diligence the expenses of which are chargeable against and recoverable from the debtor under section 40(4) above or section 93(5) of the Debtors (Scotland) Act 1987 (c 18);

(b)   any interest, due under the decree or other document of debt on which the attachment proceeds, which has accrued at the date of execution of the attachment;

(c)   any sum (including any expenses) due under the decree or other document of debt, other than any expenses or interest mentioned in paragraphs (a) and (b) above.

### 42   Restriction on fees payable by debtor

No fees shall be payable by a debtor in connection with—

(a)   any application by the debtor;

(b)   objections by the debtor to an application by any other person; or
(c)   a hearing held,

under any provision of this Part or Part 3 of this Act, to any officer of any office or department connected with the Court of Session or the sheriff court the expenses of which are paid wholly or partly out of the Scottish Consolidated Fund.

**43, 44**   [*Amending provisions*]

### 45   Interpretation of this Part and Parts 3 and 4

In this Part and in Parts 3 and 4 of this Act—

'chargeable expenses' means expenses chargeable against the debtor in accordance with this Part of this Act;

'dwellinghouse' does not include—

(a)   a garage, even although it forms part of the structure or building which consists of or includes the dwellinghouse; or

(b)   other structures or buildings used in connection with the dwellinghouse, but does include a mobile home or other place used as a dwelling;

'exceptional attachment order' has the meaning given by section 47(1) below;

'mobile home' means a caravan, houseboat or other moveable structure used as a dwelling;

'non-essential assets' has the meaning given by schedule 2 to this Act;

'officer' means the officer of court appointed by a creditor;

'sum recoverable' means the debt in respect of which the attachment is executed together with any interest thereon and any chargeable expenses; and

'summary warrant' means a summary warrant granted under, or by virtue of, any enactment.

PART 3
ATTACHMENT OF ARTICLES KEPT IN DWELLINGHOUSES:
SPECIAL PROCEDURE

### 46   Restriction on attachment of articles kept in dwellinghouses

Articles kept in a dwellinghouse may be attached but only—

(a)   in pursuance of an exceptional attachment order; and
(b)   otherwise in accordance with this Part of this Act.

### 47   Exceptional attachment order

(1)   The sheriff may, on an application by the creditor and on being satisfied that there are exceptional circumstances, order that an attachment of non-essential assets of the debtor's kept in any dwellinghouse specified in the application may take place; such an order shall be called an 'exceptional attachment order'.

(2)   An exceptional attachment order shall—

(a)   authorise the attachment, removal and auction of non-essential assets of the debtor's which are, at the time when an attachment is executed in pursuance of the order, kept in any dwellinghouse specified in the application for the order;

(b)   specify a period during which the order is to be executed; and

(c)   empower the officer to open shut and lockfast places for the purpose of executing the order.

(3)   In considering whether to make such an order the sheriff shall have regard to the matters set out in subsection (4) below.

(4)   Those matters are—

(a)   the nature of the debt (and, in particular, whether the debt incurred relates to any tax or duty or to any trade or business carried on by the debtor);

(b)   whether the debtor resides in the dwellinghouse specified in the application;

(c)   whether the debtor carries on a trade or business in that dwellinghouse;

(d)   whether money advice has been given to the debtor;

(e)   whether any direction made under section 1 (time to pay directions) of the Debtors (Scotland) Act 1987 (c 18), or order made under section 5 (time to pay orders) of that Act, in respect of the debt, or any other debt, has lapsed under section 4 (lapse of time to pay directions) or, as the case may be, section 11 (lapse of time to pay orders), of that Act of 1987;

(f)   any agreement between the debtor and creditor for the settlement of the debt;

(g)   any declaration or representation made, or document lodged, by or on behalf of the debtor which relates to—

    (i)   the existence of any non-essential assets owned by the debtor;

    (ii)   where they exist, their value; or

    (iii)   the debtor's financial circumstances [; and

(h)   whether an application by the debtor for approval of a debt payment programme under Part 1 of this Act has been refused or approved, and if approved, whether that programme has been varied, or is revoked or completed.]

(5)   Before deciding whether to make an exceptional attachment order, the sheriff may make—

(a)   an order for a visit to the debtor by a person specified in the order for the purposes of giving money advice to the debtor; or

(b)   such other order as the sheriff thinks fit.

(6)   The Scottish Ministers may by order modify subsection (4) above so as to—

(a)   add or remove matters to or, as the case may be, from those referred to in that subsection; or

(b)   vary any of the descriptions of the matters there referred to.

## 48   Exceptional circumstances

(1)   The reference in section 47(1) above to the sheriff being satisfied that there are exceptional circumstances is to be regarded as a reference to the sheriff being satisfied—

(a)   that the creditor has taken reasonable steps to negotiate (or seek to negotiate) a settlement of the debt;

(b)   that the creditor has executed, or so far as it is reasonable to do so has attempted to execute—

    (i)   an arrestment and action of forthcoming or sale; and

    (ii)   an earnings arrestment, in order to secure payment of the debt;

(c)   that there is a reasonable prospect that the sum recovered from an auction of the debtor's non-essential assets would be at least equal to the aggregate of the following—

    (i)   a reasonable estimate of any chargeable expenses; and

    (ii)   £100 or such other amount as may be specified by order made by the Scottish Ministers; and

(d)   that, having had regard to the matters set out in section 47(4) above and any other matters which the sheriff considers appropriate, it would be reasonable in the circumstances to grant the exceptional attachment order.

(2)   For the purposes of subsection (1)(b) above, a creditor who has not proceeded with the diligences referred to in that subsection on the ground that so proceeding would be unlikely to recover the aggregate of—

(a)   a reasonable estimate of the expenses likely to be incurred by the creditor in exercising the diligences; and

(b)   £100 or such other amount as may be specified by order made by the Scottish Ministers, is to be treated as having attempted to execute those diligences in so far as it is reasonable to do so.

## 49   Power of entry

(1)   Notwithstanding the authorisation in an exceptional attachment order to

open shut and lockfast places, the officer shall not enter a dwellinghouse to execute the order unless the officer—

(a)   at the intended time of entry, is satisfied as to the condition set out in subsection (2) below; or

(b)   has, at least 4 days before the intended date of entry, served notice on the debtor setting out that intention and specifying that date.

(2)   That condition is that there appears to the officer to be a person present who—

(a)   is aged 16 years or over; and

(b)   is not, because of the person's age, knowledge of English, mental illness, mental or physical disability or otherwise, unable to understand the consequences of the procedure being carried out.

(3)   Where the sheriff is satisfied that the requirement of service under subsection (1)(b) above is likely to prejudice the execution of the order the sheriff may, on an application by the officer, dispense with that requirement.

(4)   An application for a dispensation under subsection (3) above need not be intimated to the debtor.

### 50   Unlawful acts before attachment

(1)   It shall be regarded as a breach of an exceptional attachment order—

(a)   for the debtor or any other person who knows that the order has been made to, without the consent of the sheriff, move any article which forms part of the debtor's non-essential assets from the dwellinghouse in which it is kept; or

(b)   for the debtor, without the consent of the sheriff, to sell, make a gift of or otherwise relinquish ownership of any such article,

before an attachment is executed in pursuance of the order.

(2)   Any person who—

(a)   knows that an exceptional attachment order has been made; and

(b)   before an attachment is executed in pursuance of the order, wilfully damages or destroys any article which forms part of the debtor's non-essential assets,

shall be regarded as acting in breach of the order.

(3)   Where, at any time after an exceptional attachment order has been made, an article which forms part of the debtor's non-essential assets is stolen, the debtor shall give notice to the creditor, the officer and the sheriff who granted the order of that fact and of any related claim which the debtor makes, or intends to make, under a contract of insurance.

(4)   Any failure by the debtor to give notice as required by subsection (3) above is to be regarded as acting in breach of the order.

(5)   Where a debtor or any third party who knows that an exceptional attachment order has been made and that an article forms part of the debtor's non-essential assets—

(a)   moves it from the dwellinghouse in which it is kept before an attachment is executed in pursuance of the order, and it is—

(i)   damaged, destroyed, lost or stolen; or

(ii)   acquired from or through the debtor or, as the case may be, the third party by another person without knowledge of order and for value; or

(b)   wilfully damages or destroys it,

the sheriff may order the debtor or, as the case may be, the third party to consign the sum set out in subsection (6) below in court.

(6)   That sum shall be—

(a)   where the article has been damaged but not so damaged as to make it worthless, a sum equal to the difference between the value of the article before it was damaged and the value of the article so damaged; or

(b)   where the damaged article is worthless, a sum equal to the value of the article before it was so damaged.

(7)   Any reference in subsection (6) above to the value of an article is a reference to the officer's best estimate of the amount which the article is or, as the case may be, was likely to realise on sale by auction.

(8)   Any sum consigned in court in pursuance of an order made under subsection (5) above shall, where that order ceases to have effect before an auction is held in execution of the order, be paid to the creditor to the extent necessary to meet the sum recoverable, any surplus thereof being paid to the debtor.

### 51   Valuation

When executing an attachment in pursuance of an exceptional attachment order the officer shall value the articles being attached at the price which they are likely to fetch if sold on the open market.

### 52   Articles with sentimental value

(1)   An officer may not, in executing an exceptional attachment order, attach any articles which the officer considers likely to be of sentimental value to the debtor.

(2)   Subsection (1) above applies only where the aggregate of the values of articles considered likely to be of that type (as fixed by the officer under section 51 above) does not exceed £150 or such other amount as may be prescribed in regulations made by the Scottish Ministers.

### 53   Removal of articles attached in dwellinghouse

(1)   The officer shall, unless the officer considers it impractical to do so, immediately remove any article which is attached in execution of an exceptional attachment order from the dwellinghouse in which it is attached.

(2)   If an article is not immediately removed from the dwellinghouse in which it is attached, the officer shall give notice to the debtor and to any other person in possession of the article of the date arranged for the removal of the article from that dwellinghouse.

(3)   The officer may remove from the dwellinghouse only such attached articles as, if sold at their values fixed under section 51 above, would realise in aggregate the sum recoverable.

### 54   Professional valuation

(1)   The officer may, if the officer considers it appropriate, arrange for an attached article to be valued by a professional valuer or other suitably skilled person.

(2)   Any such valuer or other person shall value an attached article at the price which it is likely to fetch if sold on the open market.

(3)   If such a valuer or other person values an attached article at an amount other than the amount at which that article was valued by the officer when executing the attachment, the officer shall notify the debtor of the value arrived at by the valuer or other person.

### 55   Release of articles from attachment

(1)   An article attached in execution of an exceptional attachment order shall not, subject to any order made under section 20(1)(b) above, be auctioned before the date which is 7 days after the date on which the article was removed by the officer from the dwellinghouse in which it was attached.

(2)   The sheriff may, on an application by the debtor, make an order—

(a)   providing that the attachment of an article attached in execution of an exceptional attachment order is to cease to have effect; and

(b)   requiring the officer to return the article to the dwellinghouse at which it was attached.

(3)   Where the sheriff is satisfied that—

(a)   the attachment of an article is not competent; or

(b)    the auction of an attached article would be unduly harsh in the circumstances,
the sheriff shall grant an order under subsection (2) above in respect of the article.

(4)    Where the sheriff is satisfied that—

(a)    articles likely to be of sentimental value to the debtor were kept in a dwellinghouse when an exceptional attachment order was executed in the dwellinghouse;

(b)    those articles are likely to realise, on sale by auction, an aggregate amount not exceeding £150 or such other amount as may be prescribed in regulations made under section 52(2) above; and

(c)    an article of that type has been attached in execution of the exceptional attachment order, the sheriff shall grant an order under subsection (2) above in respect of the attached article.

(5)    The sheriff may consider an application for an order under subsection (2) above only where it is made during the period in which the article which is subject of the application may not, by virtue of subsection (1) above, be auctioned.

## 56   Redemption

(1)    Subject to any order made under section 20(1)(b) above, the debtor is entitled, within 7 days of the date on which an article is attached, to redeem that article.

(2)    The amount for which such an article may be redeemed is the value fixed under section 51 or 54(1) above.

(3)    The officer shall, on receiving payment from the debtor for the redemption of an attached article, grant a receipt in the form prescribed by Act of Sederunt to the debtor.

(4)    The attachment of the article is, on the grant of such a receipt, to cease to have effect.

## 57   Appeals

(1)    An appeal made against any decision of a sheriff made under or for the purposes of this Part or, where the appeal relates to the attachment of articles kept in a dwellinghouse, under or for the purposes of Part 2 of this Act may be made only—

(a)    to the sheriff principal;

(b)    with the leave of the sheriff; and

(c)    on a point of law.

(2)    The decision of the sheriff principal on such an appeal is final.

PART 4
ABOLITION OF POINDINGS AND WARRANT SALES

## 58   Abolition of poindings and warrant sales

(1)    It is not, subject to section 59 below, competent to enforce payment of a debt by poinding or warrant sale; and any enactment or rule of law allowing such enforcement shall cease to have effect.

(2)    The following provisions of the Debtors (Scotland) Act 1987 (c 18) are repealed—

(a)    Part II;

(b)    section 74(2);

(c)    Schedule 1; and

(d)    Schedule 5.

## 59   Savings

(1)    The provisions set out in subsection (5) below continue to have effect in relation to a poinding in respect of which a warrant sale has been completed before 30 December 2002 as if sections 58(2) above and 61 below had not come into force.

(2)    Subject to subsection (3) below, those provisions also continue to have that

effect in relation to a poinding executed before that date in respect of which a warrant sale has not been completed before that date.

(3) The saving provided for in subsection (2) above—

(a) has effect only if the poinding was executed at a place other than a dwellinghouse; and

(b) continues to have effect after 31 March 2003 only if a warrant sale is completed in respect of the poinding on or before that date.

(4) A summary warrant which, before 30 December 2002, authorised a poinding and sale in accordance with Schedule 5 to the Debtors (Scotland) Act 1987 (c 18) is to be treated on and after that date as authorising an attachment.

(5) The provisions referred to in subsections (1) and (2) above are—

(a) paragraph 24 of Schedule 7 to the Bankruptcy (Scotland) Act 1985 (c 66);

(b) the provisions of the Act of 1987 mentioned in section 58(2) above; and

(c) the provisions of the Act of 2002 mentioned in paragraph 29 of schedule 3 to this Act.

## PART 5
### MISCELLANEOUS AND GENERAL

**60 Application of this Act to sequestration for rent and arrestment**

[. . .]

(2) It is not competent for [the landlord's] hypothec to arise in any article—

(a) of the type described in section 11(1);

[. . .]

(3) An arrestment (other than an arrestment of a debtor's earnings in the hands of the debtor's employer) of any article of the type mentioned in paragraph (a) or (b) of subsection (2) above is incompetent.

[. . .]

**[60A Electronic signatures**

(1) This section applies where—

(a) a report or declaration under this Act requires to be signed; and

(b) provision is made by virtue of this Act or any other enactment permitting the report or declaration to be an electronic communication.

(2) Where the report or declaration is an electronic communication, the requirement is satisfied by a certified electronic signature.

(3) Subsection (2) above is to be read in accordance with section 7(2) and (3) of the Electronic Communications Act 2000 (c7) (electronic signatures and certification).]

**61** [Minor and consequential amendments and repeals]

**62** [Regulations and orders]

**63 Crown application**

This Act binds the Crown acting in its capacity as a creditor or employer.

**64 Short title and commencement**

(1) This Act may be cited as the Debt Arrangement and Attachment (Scotland) Act 2002.

(2) Subject to subsections (3) and (4) below, this Act (except this section and sections 43 and 62 above) comes into force on 30 December 2002.

. . .

## SCHEDULE 2
## NON-ESSENTIAL ASSETS

1   For the purposes of Part 3 of this Act, 'non-essential assets' are, subject to paragraph 2 below, corporeal moveable property of the debtor's which is kept in a dwellinghouse.

2   None of the following is a non-essential asset for the purposes of Part 3 of this Act—

(a)   an article specified in paragraph 3 below;

(b)   an article described in paragraph 4 below; and

(c)   an article the attachment of which is (by virtue of section 11(1) above or otherwise) incompetent.

3   The articles referred to in paragraph 2(a) above are—

(a)   clothing reasonably required for the use of the debtor or any member of the debtor's household;

(b)   implements, tools of trade, books or other equipment reasonably required for the use of any member of the debtor's household in the practice of such member's profession, trade or business, not exceeding in aggregate value £1,000 or such other amount as may be prescribed in regulations made by the Scottish Ministers;

(c)   medical aids or medical equipment reasonably required for the use of the debtor or any member of the debtor's household;

(d)   books or other articles reasonably required for the education or training of the debtor or any member of the debtor's household not exceeding in aggregate value £1,000 or such other amount as may be prescribed in regulations made by the Scottish Ministers;

(e)   articles reasonably required for the care or upbringing of a child who is a member of the debtor's household;

(f)   toys for the use of any child who is a member of the debtor's household.

4   The articles referred to in paragraph 2(b) above are the following so far as they are reasonably required, at the time of the attachment, for the use of the debtor or a member of the debtor's household—

(a)   beds or bedding;

(b)   household linen;

(c)   chairs or settees;

(d)   tables;

(e)   food;

(f)   lights or light fittings;

(g)   heating appliances;

(h)   curtains;

(i)   floor coverings;

(j)   furniture, equipment or utensils used for storing, cooking or eating food;

(k)   refrigerators;

(l)   articles used for cleaning, drying, mending, or pressing clothes;

(m)   articles used for cleaning the dwellinghouse;

(n)   furniture used for storing—

(i)   clothing, bedding or household linen;

(ii)   articles used for cleaning the dwellinghouse; or

(iii)   utensils used for cooking or eating food;

(o)   articles used for safety in the dwellinghouse;

(p)   tools used for maintenance or repair of the dwellinghouse or of household articles;

(q)   computers and accessory equipment;

(r)   microwave ovens;

(s)   radios;

(t)   telephones;

    (u)    televisions.

5    The Scottish Ministers may by regulations modify paragraph 4 above so as to—

    (a)    add or remove types of articles to or, as the case may be, from those referred to in that paragraph; or

    (b)    vary any of the descriptions of the types of articles there referred to.

. . .

## BANKRUPTCY AND DILIGENCE ETC (SCOTLAND) ACT 2007
### (2007 asp 3)

### PART 5
### INHIBITION

*Creation*

### 146   Certain decrees and documents of debt to authorise inhibition without need for letters of inhibition

(1)    Inhibition in execution is competent to enforce—

    (a)    payment of a debt constituted by a decree or document of debt;

    (b)    subject to subsection (2) below, an obligation to perform a particular act (other than payment) contained in a decree.

(2)    Inhibition under subsection (1)(b) above is competent only if the decree is a decree—

    (a)    in an action containing an alternative conclusion or crave for payment of a sum other than by way of expenses; or

    (b)    for specific implement of an obligation to convey heritable property to the creditor or to grant in the creditor's favour a real right in security, or some other right, over such property.

(3)–(5)   *[amending provisions]*

(6)    It is not competent for the Court of Session to grant letters of inhibition.

(7)    In a case where inhibition is executed under subsection (1)(b) above—

    (a)    sections 165 and 166 of this Act do not apply; and

    (b)    sections 158, 159, 160 and 163 of this Act have effect as if references to a 'debtor' or 'creditor' were references to the debtor or creditor in the obligation.

(8)    In this Part—

'decree' has the meaning given by section 221 of this Act, except that paragraphs (c), (g) and (h) of the definition of 'decree' in that section do not apply; and

'document of debt' has the meaning given by section 221 of this Act.

(9)    The Scottish Ministers may by order modify the definitions of 'decree' and 'document of debt' in subsection (8) above by—

    (a)    adding types of decree or document to;

    (b)    removing types of decree or document from; or

    (c)    varying the description of,

the types of decree or document to which those definitions apply.

### 147   Provision of debt advice and information package when executing inhibition

Where the debtor is an individual, a schedule of inhibition served in execution of an inhibition under section 146(1) of this Act (other than an inhibition such as is mentioned in section 146(2)(b)) must be accompanied with a debt advice and information package.

### 148   Registration of inhibition

(1)    An inhibition is registered only by registering—

    (a)    the schedule of inhibition; and

    (b)    the certificate of execution of the inhibition,

in the Register of Inhibitions.

(2)   References in any enactment to registering or, as the case may be, recording an inhibition must, unless the context otherwise requires, be construed as references to registration in accordance with subsection (1) above.

(3)   The—

(a)   schedule of inhibition; and

(b)   certificate of execution of the inhibition,

must be in (or as nearly as may be in) the form prescribed by the Scottish Ministers by regulations.

**149**   *[Amends Titles to Land Consolidation (Scotland) Act 1868.]*

*Effect*

**150   Property affected by inhibition**

(1)   Subject to section 153 of this Act, inhibition may affect any heritable property.

(2)   Any enactment or rule of law by virtue of which inhibition may affect other property ceases to have effect.

(3)   For the purposes of subsection (1) above and section 157 of the 1868 Act, a person acquires property at the beginning of the day on which the deed conveying or otherwise granting a real right in the property is delivered to that person.

**151   Effect on inhibition to enforce obligation when alternative decree granted**

Where—

(a)   an inhibition is executed to enforce a decree such as is mentioned in section 146(2)(a) of this Act; and

(b)   decree is subsequently granted in terms of the alternative conclusion or crave mentioned in that section,

the inhibition continues to have effect for the purposes of enforcing payment of the debt constituted by that subsequent decree.

**152   Effect of conversion of limited inhibition on the dependence to inhibition in execution**

[(1)]   [Subject to subsection (2) below,] where—

(a)   a creditor obtains a decree for payment of all or part of a principal sum concluded or craved for in proceedings on the dependence of which warrant for inhibition was granted; and

(b)   the warrant was limited to specified property by virtue of section 15J(b) of the 1987 Act (property affected by inhibition on dependence),

[any inhibition on the dependence which, on decree, becomes an inhibition in execution of that decree, is no longer limited to that property].

[(2)   Subsection (1) above has effect from the beginning of the day on which—

(a)   an extract of the decree (or a copy of the interlocutor certified by the clerk of court); and

(b)   a notice in (or as nearly as may be in) the form set out in the Schedule to the Bankruptcy and Diligence etc (Scotland) Act 2007 (Inhibition) Order 2009, are registered in the Register of Inhibitions.]

**153   Property affected by inhibition to enforce obligation to convey heritable property**

Where a decree such as is mentioned in section 146(2)(b) of this Act is granted, any inhibition executed to enforce that decree is limited to the property to which the decree relates.

**154   Inhibition not to confer a preference in ranking**

(1)   An inhibition does not confer any preference in any—

(a)   sequestration;

    (b)    insolvency proceedings; or
    (c)    other process in which there is ranking.
    (2)    Subsection (1) above does not affect any preference claimed in—
    (a)    a sequestration;
    (b)    insolvency proceedings; or
    (c)    any other process,
where the inhibition has effect before this section comes into force.
    (3)    For the avoidance of doubt, in this section, 'other process' includes the process, under section 27(1) of the Conveyancing and Feudal Reform (Scotland) Act 1970 (c 35), of applying the proceeds of sale where a creditor in a standard security has effected a sale of the security subjects.
    (4)    In this section, 'insolvency proceedings' means—
    (a)    winding up;
    (b)    receivership;
    (c)    administration; and
    (d)    proceedings in relation to a company voluntary arrangement,
within the meaning of the Insolvency Act 1986 (c 45).

*Termination*

. . .

### 157   Inhibition terminated by payment of full amount owing
    (1)    This section applies where—
    (a)    an inhibition executed to enforce payment of a debt has effect; and
    (b)    a sum is paid, in respect of the debt constituted by the decree or document of debt authorising the inhibition, to the creditor, [an officer of court] or any other person who has authority to receive payment on behalf of the creditor.
    (2)    Where the sum paid amounts to the sum of—
    (a)    the debt (including any interest due under the decree or document of debt);
    (b)    the expenses incurred by the creditor in executing an inhibition (referred to in this section and in sections 165 and 166 as the 'inhibition expenses'); and
    (c)    the expenses of discharging the inhibition,
the inhibition ceases to have effect.
    (3)    Any rule of law to the effect that an inhibition ceases to have effect on payment or tender of the debt constituted by the decree or document of debt is abolished.
    (4)    This section and sections 165 and 166 of this Act do not apply to an inhibition on the dependence of an action.

### 158   Inhibition terminated by compliance with obligation to perform
Where—
    (a)    an inhibition executed to enforce an obligation to perform a particular act (other than payment) contained in a decree has effect; and
    (b)    the debtor has complied with the decree,
the inhibition ceases to have effect.

### 159   Termination of inhibition when property acquired by third party
    (1)    Notwithstanding section 160 of this Act, an inhibition ceases to have effect (and is treated as never having had effect) in relation to property if a person acquires the property (or a right in the property) in good faith and for adequate consideration.
    (2)    For the purposes of subsection (1) above, a person acquires property (or a right in the property) when the deed conveying (or granting the right in) the property is delivered to the person.
    (3)    An acquisition under subsection (1) above may be from the inhibited debtor

or any other person who has acquired the property or right (regardless of whether that person acquired in good faith or for value).

(4) For the purposes of subsection (1) above, a person is presumed to have acted in good faith if the person—

(a) is unaware of the inhibition; and

(b) has taken all reasonable steps to discover the existence of an inhibition affecting the property.

*Breach*

### 160 Breach of inhibition

An inhibited debtor breaches the inhibition when the debtor delivers a deed—

(a) conveying; or

(b) otherwise granting a right in,

property over which the inhibition has effect to a person other than the inhibiting creditor.

### 161 Prescription of right to reduce transactions in breach of inhibition

For the avoidance of doubt, section 8(1) of the Prescription and Limitation (Scotland) Act 1973 (c 52) (extinction of certain rights relating to property by pre-scriptive period of 20 years) applies to the right of an inhibitor to have a deed granted in breach of an inhibition reduced.

### 163 Reduction of lease granted in breach of inhibition

(1) This section applies where an inhibited debtor grants a lease of property affected by the inhibition.

(2) A lease which, on the date an action of reduction of the lease is raised, has an unexpired duration of not less than 5 years is reducible.

(3) A lease which, on the date an action of reduction of the lease is raised, has an unexpired duration of less than 5 years may be reduced only if the Court of Session is satisfied that it would be fair and reasonable in all the circumstances to do so.

(4) In calculating the unexpired duration of a lease for the purposes of sub-sections (2) and (3) above—

(a) any provision in the lease (however expressed) enabling the lease to be terminated earlier than the date on which the lease would otherwise terminate must be disregarded; and

(b) where the lease includes provision (however expressed) requiring the landlord to renew it, the duration of any such renewed lease must be added to the duration of the original lease.

*General and miscellaneous*

### 165 Expenses of inhibition

(1) Subject to subsection (3) below, the inhibition expenses are chargeable against the debtor.

(2) Inhibition expenses are recoverable from the debtor by land attachment or residual attachment executed for the purpose of enforcing payment of the debt to which the inhibition relates but not by any other legal process.

(3) Where a creditor has executed an inhibition, the expenses of only one fur-ther inhibition in relation to the debt to which the first inhibition relates are chargeable against the debtor as inhibition expenses.

(4) For the purposes of a sequestration or other process in which there is rank-ing, the inhibition expenses must be treated as part of the debt constituted by the decree or document of debt authorising the inhibition.

### 166 Ascription

(1) This section applies where—

(a)    an inhibition has effect; and

(b)    any sums are paid to account of the sums recoverable from the debtor by virtue of the decree or document of debt authorising the inhibition.

(2)    Such sums must be ascribed to the following in the order in which they are mentioned—

(a)    the expenses which are chargeable against the debtor incurred in respect of any diligence (other than the inhibition) authorised by the decree or document of debt;

(b)    the inhibition expenses;

(c)    any interest which has accrued, at the date on which the inhibition takes effect, on the debt constituted by the decree or document of debt;

(d)    the debt constituted by the decree or document of debt together with such interest as has accrued after the date on which the inhibition takes effect.

**168    Inhibition effective against judicial factor**

(1)    Notwithstanding the appointment of a judicial factor on a debtor's estate, an inhibition has effect.

(2)    But subsection (1) above does not apply in a case where—

(a)    a judicial factor is appointed under section 11A of the Judicial Factors (Scotland) Act 1889 (c 39) (application for judicial factor on deceased person's estate); and

(b)    the inhibition was effective against the debtor prior to the debtor's death.


PART 11
MAILLS AND DUTIES, SEQUESTRATION FOR RENT AND LANDLORD'S
HYPOTHEC

. . .

*Landlord's hypothec and sequestration for rent*

**208    Abolition of sequestration for rent and restriction of landlord's hypothec**

(1)    The diligence of sequestration for rent is abolished and any enactment or rule of law enabling an action of sequestration for rent to be raised ceases to have effect.

(2)    Notwithstanding that abolition, the landlord's hypothec—

(a)    continues, subject to subsections (3) to (9) below, as a right in security over corporeal moveable property kept in or on the subjects let; and—

(b)    ranks accordingly in any—

(i)    sequestration;

(ii)    insolvency proceedings; or

(iii)    other process in which there is ranking,

in respect of that property.

(3)    The landlord's hypothec no longer arises in relation to property which is kept—

(a)    in a dwellinghouse;

(b)    on agricultural land; or

(c)    on a croft.

(4)    It no longer arises in relation to property which is owned by a person other than the tenant.

(5)    Property which is acquired by a person from the tenant—

(a)    in good faith; or

(b)    where the property is acquired after an interdict prohibiting the tenant from disposing of or removing items secured by the hypothec has been granted in favour the landlord, in good faith and for value,

ceases to be subject to the hypothec upon acquisition by the person.

(6)   Subsection (5)(b) above does not affect the tenant's liability for breach of the interdict.

(7)   Where property is owned in common by the tenant and a third party, any right of hypothec arises only to the extent of the tenant's interest in that property.

(8)   The landlord's hypothec—

    (a)   is security for rent due and unpaid only; and

    (b)   subsists for so long as that rent remains unpaid.

(9)   Any enactment or rule of law relating to the landlord's hypothec ceases to have effect in so far as it is inconsistent with subsections (2) to (8) above.

(10)   Subsections (1) to (3), (8) and (9) above do not affect an action of sequestration for rent brought before this section comes into force.

(11)   Subsection (3) above does not affect a landlord's right of hypothec which arose before and subsists on the coming into force of this section.

(12)   In subsection (2) above, 'insolvency proceedings' means—

    (a)   winding up;

    (b)   receivership;

    (c)   administration; and

    (d)   proceedings in relation to a company voluntary arrangement,

within the meaning of the Insolvency Act 1986 (c 45).

(13)   In subsection (3) above—

'agricultural land' has the same meaning as in section 1(2) of the Agricultural Holdings (Scotland) Act 1991 (c 55);

'croft' has the same meaning as in section 3(1) of the Crofters (Scotland) Act 1993 (c 44); and

'dwellinghouse' includes—

    (a)   a mobile home or other place used as a dwelling; and

    (b)   any other structure or building used in connection with the dwellinghouse.

# CONSUMER INSURANCE (DISCLOSURE AND REPRESENTATIONS) ACT 2012
## (2012, c 6)

*Main definitions*

## 1  Main definitions

In this Act—

'consumer insurance contract' means a contract of insurance between—

    (a)   an individual who enters into the contract wholly or mainly for purposes unrelated to the individual's trade, business or profession, and

    (b)   a person who carries on the business of insurance and who becomes a party to the contract by way of that business (whether or not in accordance with permission for the purposes of the Financial Services and Markets Act 2000);

'consumer' means the individual who enters into a consumer insurance contract, or proposes to do so;

'insurer' means the person who is, or would become, the other party to a consumer insurance contract.

*Pre-contract and pre-variation information*

## 2  Disclosure and representations before contract or variation

(1)   This section makes provision about disclosure and representations by a consumer to an insurer before a consumer insurance contract is entered into or varied.

(2)  It is the duty of the consumer to take reasonable care not to make a misrepresentation to the insurer.

(3)  A failure by the consumer to comply with the insurer's request to confirm or amend particulars previously given is capable of being a misrepresentation for the purposes of this Act (whether or not it could be apart from this subsection).

(4)  The duty set out in subsection (2) replaces any duty relating to disclosure or representations by a consumer to an insurer which existed in the same circumstances before this Act applied.

(5)  Accordingly—

(a)  any rule of law to the effect that a consumer insurance contract is one of the utmost good faith is modified to the extent required by the provisions of this Act, and

(b)  the application of section 17 of the Marine Insurance Act 1906 (contracts of marine insurance are of utmost good faith), in relation to a contract of marine insurance which is a consumer insurance contract, is subject to the provisions of this Act.

### 3  Reasonable care

(1)  Whether or not a consumer has taken reasonable care not to make a misrepresentation is to be determined in the light of all the relevant circumstances.

(2)  The following are examples of things which may need to be taken into account in making a determination under subsection (1)—

(a)  the type of consumer insurance contract in question, and its target market,

(b)  any relevant explanatory material or publicity produced or authorised by the insurer,

(c)  how clear, and how specific, the insurer's questions were,

(d)  in the case of a failure to respond to the insurer's questions in connection with the renewal or variation of a consumer insurance contract, how clearly the insurer communicated the importance of answering those questions (or the possible consequences of failing to do so),

(e)  whether or not an agent was acting for the consumer.

(3)  The standard of care required is that of a reasonable consumer: but this is subject to subsections (4) and (5).

(4)  If the insurer was, or ought to have been, aware of any particular characteristics or circumstances of the actual consumer, those are to be taken into account.

(5)  A misrepresentation made dishonestly is always to be taken as showing lack of reasonable care.

*Qualifying misrepresentations*

### 4  Qualifying misrepresentations: definition and remedies

(1)  An insurer has a remedy against a consumer for a misrepresentation made by the consumer before a consumer insurance contract was entered into or varied only if—

(a)  the consumer made the misrepresentation in breach of the duty set out in section 2(2), and

(b)  the insurer shows that without the misrepresentation, that insurer would not have entered into the contract (or agreed to the variation) at all, or would have done so only on different terms.

(2)  A misrepresentation for which the insurer has a remedy against the consumer is referred to in this Act as a 'qualifying misrepresentation'.

(3)  The only such remedies available are set out in Schedule 1.

### 5  Qualifying misrepresentations: classification and presumptions

(1)  For the purposes of this Act, a qualifying misrepresentation (see section 4(2)) is either—

    (a)    deliberate or reckless, or

    (b)    careless.

(2)   A qualifying misrepresentation is deliberate or reckless if the consumer—

    (a)    knew that it was untrue or misleading, or did not care whether or not it was untrue or misleading, and

    (b)    knew that the matter to which the misrepresentation related was relevant to the insurer, or did not care whether or not it was relevant to the insurer.

(3)   A qualifying misrepresentation is careless if it is not deliberate or reckless.

(4)   It is for the insurer to show that a qualifying misrepresentation was deliberate or reckless.

(5)   But it is to be presumed, unless the contrary is shown—

    (a)    that the consumer had the knowledge of a reasonable consumer, and

    (b)    that the consumer knew that a matter about which the insurer asked a clear and specific question was relevant to the insurer.

*Specific issues*

## 6  Warranties and representations

(1)   This section applies to representations made by a consumer—

    (a)    in connection with a proposed consumer insurance contract, or

    (b)    in connection with a proposed variation to a consumer insurance contract.

(2)   Such a representation is not capable of being converted into a warranty by means of any provision of the consumer insurance contract (or of the terms of the variation), or of any other contract (and whether by declaring the representation to form the basis of the contract or otherwise).

## 7  Group insurance

(1)   This section applies where—

    (a)    a contract of insurance is entered into by a person ('A') in order to provide cover for another person ('C'), or is varied or extended so as to do so,

    (b)    C is not a party to the contract,

    (c)    so far as the cover for C is concerned, the contract would have been a consumer insurance contract if entered into by C rather than by A, and

    (d)    C provided information directly or indirectly to the insurer before the contract was entered into, or before it was varied or extended to provide cover for C.

(2)   So far as the cover for C is concerned—

    (a)    sections 2 and 3 apply in relation to disclosure and representations by C to the insurer as if C were proposing to enter into a consumer insurance contract for the relevant cover with the insurer, and

    (b)    subject to subsections (3) to (5) and the modifications in relation to the insurer's remedies set out in Part 3 of Schedule 1, the remainder of this Act applies in relation to the cover for C as if C had entered into a consumer insurance contract for that cover with the insurer.

(3)   Section 4(1)(b) applies as if it read as follows—

    '(b)    the insurer shows that without the misrepresentation, that insurer would not have agreed to provide cover for C at all, or would have done so only on different terms.'

(4)   If there is more than one C, a breach on the part of one of them of the duty imposed (by virtue of subsection (2)(a)) by section 2(2) does not affect the contract so far as it relates to the others.

(5)   Nothing in this section affects any duty owed by A to the insurer, or any remedy which the insurer may have against A for breach of such a duty.

**8 Insurance on life of another**

(1) This section applies in relation to a consumer insurance contract for life insurance on the life of an individual ('L') who is not a party to the contract.

(2) If this section applies—

(a) information provided to the insurer by L is to be treated for the purposes of this Act as if it were provided by the person who is the party to the contract, but

(b) in relation to such information, if anything turns on the state of mind, knowledge, circumstances or characteristics of the individual providing the information, it is to be determined by reference to L and not the party to the contract.

**9 Agents**

Schedule 2 applies for determining, for the purposes of this Act only, whether an agent through whom a consumer insurance contract is effected is the agent of the consumer or of the insurer.

**10 Contracting out**

(1) A term of a consumer insurance contract, or of any other contract, which would put the consumer in a worse position as respects the matters mentioned in subsection (2) than the consumer would be in by virtue of the provisions of this Act is to that extent of no effect.

(2) The matters are—

(a) disclosure and representations by the consumer to the insurer before the contract is entered into or varied, and

(b) any remedies for qualifying misrepresentations (see section 4(2)).

(3) This section does not apply in relation to a contract for the settlement of a claim arising under a consumer insurance contract.

*Final provision*

**11 Consequential provision**

(1) Any rule of law to the same effect as the following is abolished in relation to consumer insurance contracts—

(a) section 18 of the Marine Insurance Act 1906 (disclosure by assured),

(b) section 19 of that Act (disclosure by agent effecting insurance),

(c) section 20 of that Act (representations pending negotiation of contract).

(2) [Amends the Marine Insurance Act 1906.]

(3) [Amends the Road Traffic Act 1988.]

(4) [Applies to Northern Ireland.]

**12 Short title, commencement, application and extent**

(1) This Act may be cited as the Consumer Insurance (Disclosure and Representations) Act 2012.

(2) *Section 1 and this section come into force on the day on which this Act is passed, but otherwise this Act comes into force on such day as the Treasury may by order made by statutory instrument appoint.*

(3) *An order under subsection (2) may not appoint a day sooner than the end of the period of 1 year beginning with the day on which this Act is passed.*

(4) *This Act applies only in relation to consumer insurance contracts entered into, and variations to consumer insurance contracts agreed, after the Act comes into force.*

*In the case of group insurance (see section 7), that includes the provision of cover for C by means of an insurance contract entered into by A after the Act comes into force, or varied or extended so as to do so after the Act comes into force.*

(5) Nothing in this Act affects the circumstances in which a person is bound by the acts or omissions of that person's agent.

(6) Apart from the provisions listed in subsection (7), this Act extends to England and Wales, Scotland and Northern Ireland.

(7)   In section 11—
    (a)   subsection (3) extends to England and Wales and Scotland only;
    (b)   subsection (4) extends to Northern Ireland only.

## SCHEDULE 1
## INSURERS' REMEDIES FOR QUALIFYING MISREPRESENTATIONS
Section 4(3)

## PART 1
## CONTRACTS

### General

1   This Part of this Schedule applies in relation to qualifying misrepresentations made in connection with consumer insurance contracts (for variations to them, see Part 2).

### Deliberate or reckless misrepresentations

2   If a qualifying misrepresentation was deliberate or reckless, the insurer—
    (a)   may avoid the contract and refuse all claims, and
    (b)   need not return any of the premiums paid, except to the extent (if any) that it would be unfair to the consumer to retain them.

### Careless misrepresentations—claims

3   If the qualifying misrepresentation was careless, paragraphs 4 to 8 apply in relation to any claim.

4   The insurer's remedies are based on what it would have done if the consumer had complied with the duty set out in section 2(2), and paragraphs 5 to 8 are to be read accordingly.

5   If the insurer would not have entered into the consumer insurance contract on any terms, the insurer may avoid the contract and refuse all claims, but must return the premiums paid.

6   If the insurer would have entered into the consumer insurance contract, but on different terms (excluding terms relating to the premium), the contract is to be treated as if it had been entered into on those different terms if the insurer so requires.

7   In addition, if the insurer would have entered into the consumer insurance contract (whether the terms relating to matters other than the premium would have been the same or different), but would have charged a higher premium, the insurer may reduce proportionately the amount to be paid on a claim.

8   'Reduce proportionately' means that the insurer need pay on the claim only X% of what it would otherwise have been under an obligation to pay under the terms of the contract (or, if applicable, under the different terms provided for by virtue of paragraph 6), where—

$$X = \frac{\text{Premium actually charged}}{\text{Higher premium}} \times 100$$

*Careless misrepresentations—treatment of contract for the future*

9—(1) This paragraph—
  (a) applies if the qualifying misrepresentation was careless, but
  (b) does not relate to any outstanding claim.
(2) Paragraphs 5 and 6 (as read with paragraph 4) apply as they apply where a claim has been made.
(3) Paragraph 7 (as read with paragraph 4) applies in relation to a claim yet to be made as it applies in relation to a claim which has been made.
(4) If by virtue of sub-paragraph (2) or (3), the insurer would have either (or both) of the rights conferred by paragraph 6 or 7, the insurer may—
  (a) give notice to that effect to the consumer, or
  (b) terminate the contract by giving reasonable notice to the consumer.
(5) But the insurer may not terminate a contract under sub-paragraph (4)(b) if it is wholly or mainly one of life insurance.
(6) If the insurer gives notice to the consumer under sub-paragraph (4)(a), the consumer may terminate the contract by giving reasonable notice to the insurer.
(7) If either party terminates the contract under this paragraph, the insurer must refund any premiums paid for the terminated cover in respect of the balance of the contract term.
(8) Termination of the contract under this paragraph does not affect the treatment of any claim arising under the contract in the period before termination.
(9) Nothing in this paragraph affects any contractual right to terminate the contract.

## PART 2
## VARIATIONS

10 This Part of this Schedule applies in relation to qualifying misrepresentations made in connection with variations to consumer insurance contracts.

11 If the subject-matter of a variation can reasonably be treated separately from the subject-matter of the rest of the contract, Part 1 of this Schedule applies (with any necessary modifications) in relation to the variation as it applies in relation to a contract.

12 Otherwise, Part 1 applies (with any necessary modifications) as if the qualifying misrepresentation had been made in relation to the whole contract (for this purpose treated as including the variation) rather than merely in relation to the variation.

## PART 3
## MODIFICATIONS FOR GROUP INSURANCE

13 Part 1 is to be read subject to the following modifications in relation to cover provided for C under a group insurance contract as mentioned in section 7 (and in this Part 'A' and 'C' mean the same as in that section).

14 References to the consumer insurance contract (however described) are to that part of the contract which provides for cover for C.

15 References to claims and premiums are to claims and premiums in relation to that cover.

16 The reference to the consumer is to be read—
  (a) in paragraph 2(b), as a reference to whoever paid the premiums, or the part of them that related to the cover for C,
  (b) in paragraph 9(4) and (6), as a reference to A.

PART 4
SUPPLEMENTARY

17   Section 84 of the Marine Insurance Act 1906 (return of premium for failure of consideration) is to be read subject to the provisions of this Schedule in relation to contracts of marine insurance which are consumer insurance contracts.

SCHEDULE 2
RULES FOR DETERMINING STATUS OF AGENTS

Section 9

1   This Schedule sets out rules for determining, for the purposes of this Act only, whether an agent through whom a consumer insurance contract is effected is acting as the agent of the consumer or of the insurer.

2   The agent is to be taken as the insurer's agent in each of the following cases—

(a)   when the agent does something in the agent's capacity as the appointed representative of the insurer for the purposes of the Financial Services and Markets Act 2000 (see section 39 of that Act),

(b)   when the agent collects information from the consumer, if the insurer had given the agent express authority to do so as the insurer's agent,

(c)   when the agent enters into the contract as the insurer's agent, if the insurer had given the agent express authority to do so.

3—(1)   In any other case, it is to be presumed that the agent is acting as the consumer's agent unless, in the light of all the relevant circumstances, it appears that the agent is acting as the insurer's agent.

(2)   Some factors which may be relevant are set out below.

(3)   Examples of factors which may tend to confirm that the agent is acting for the consumer are—

(a)   the agent undertakes to give impartial advice to the consumer,

(b)   the agent undertakes to conduct a fair analysis of the market,

(c)   the consumer pays the agent a fee.

(4)   Examples of factors which may tend to show that the agent is acting for the insurer are—

(a)   the agent places insurance of the type in question with only one of the insurers who provide insurance of that type,

(b)   the agent is under a contractual obligation which has the effect of restricting the number of insurers with whom the agent places insurance of the type in question,

(c)   the insurer provides insurance of the type in question through only a small proportion of the agents who deal in that type of insurance,

(d)   the insurer permits the agent to use the insurer's name in providing the agent's services,

(e)   the insurance in question is marketed under the name of the agent,

(f)   the insurer asks the agent to solicit the consumer's custom.

4—(1)   If it appears to the Treasury that the list of factors in sub-paragraph (3) or (4) of paragraph 3 has become outdated, the Treasury may by order made by statutory instrument bring the list up to date by amending the sub-paragraph so as to add, omit or alter any factor.

(2)   A statutory instrument containing an order under sub-paragraph (1) may not be made unless a draft of the instrument has been laid before and approved by a resolution of each House of Parliament.

## INSURANCE ACT 2015*
## (2015, c 4)

## PART 1
## INSURANCE CONTRACTS: MAIN DEFINITIONS

### 1  Insurance contracts: main definitions

In this Act (apart from Part 6)—

'consumer insurance contract' has the same meaning as in the Consumer Insurance (Disclosure and Representations) Act 2012;

'non-consumer insurance contract' means a contract of insurance that is not a consumer insurance contract;

'insured' means the party to a contract of insurance who is the insured under the contract, or would be if the contract were entered into;

'insurer' means the party to a contract of insurance who is the insurer under the contract, or would be if the contract were entered into;

'the duty of fair presentation' means the duty imposed by section 3(1).

## PART 2
## THE DUTY OF FAIR PRESENTATION

### 2  Application and interpretation

(1)   This Part applies to non-consumer insurance contracts only.

(2)   This Part applies in relation to variations of non-consumer insurance contracts as it applies to contracts, but—

(a)   references to the risk are to be read as references to changes in the risk relevant to the proposed variation, and

(b)   references to the contract of insurance are to the variation.

### 3  The duty of fair presentation

(1)   Before a contract of insurance is entered into, the insured must make to the insurer a fair presentation of the risk.

(2)   The duty imposed by subsection (1) is referred to in this Act as 'the duty of fair presentation'.

(3)   A fair presentation of the risk is one—

(a)   which makes the disclosure required by subsection (4),

(b)   which makes that disclosure in a manner which would be reasonably clear and accessible to a prudent insurer, and

(c)   in which every material representation as to a matter of fact is substantially correct, and every material representation as to a matter of expectation or belief is made in good faith.

(4)   The disclosure required is as follows, except as provided in subsection (5)—

(a)   disclosure of every material circumstance which the insured knows or ought to know, or

(b)   failing that, disclosure which gives the insurer sufficient information to put a prudent insurer on notice that it needs to make further enquiries for the purpose of revealing those material circumstances.

(5)   In the absence of enquiry, subsection (4) does not require the insured to disclose a circumstance if—

(a)   it diminishes the risk,

(b)   the insurer knows it,

(c)   the insurer ought to know it,

(d)   the insurer is presumed to know it, or

(e)   it is something as to which the insurer waives information.

---

*The Insurance Act 2015 comes into force on 12 August 2016.

(6)   Sections 4 to 6 make further provision about the knowledge of the insured and of the insurer, and section 7 contains supplementary provision.

## 4   Knowledge of insured

(1)   This section provides for what an insured knows or ought to know for the purposes of section 3(4)(a).

(2)   An insured who is an individual knows only—

(a)   what is known to the individual, and

(b)   what is known to one or more of the individuals who are responsible for the insured's insurance.

(3)   An insured who is not an individual knows only what is known to one or more of the individuals who are—

(a)   part of the insured's senior management, or

(b)   responsible for the insured's insurance.

(4)   An insured is not by virtue of subsection (2)(b) or (3)(b) taken to know confidential information known to an individual if—

(a)   the individual is, or is an employee of, the insured's agent; and

(b)   the information was acquired by the insured's agent (or by an employee of that agent) through a business relationship with a person who is not connected with the contract of insurance.

(5)   For the purposes of subsection (4) the persons connected with a contract of insurance are—

(a)   the insured and any other persons for whom cover is provided by the contract, and

(b)   if the contract re-insures risks covered by another contract, the persons who are (by virtue of this subsection) connected with that other contract.

(6)   Whether an individual or not, an insured ought to know what should reasonably have been revealed by a reasonable search of information available to the insured (whether the search is conducted by making enquiries or by any other means).

(7)   In subsection (6) 'information' includes information held within the insured's organisation or by any other person (such as the insured's agent or a person for whom cover is provided by the contract of insurance).

(8)   For the purposes of this section—

(a)   'employee', in relation to the insured's agent, includes any individual working for the agent, whatever the capacity in which the individual acts,

(b)   an individual is responsible for the insured's insurance if the individual participates on behalf of the insured in the process of procuring the insured's insurance (whether the individual does so as the insured's employee or agent, as an employee of the insured's agent or in any other capacity), and

(c)   'senior management' means those individuals who play significant roles in the making of decisions about how the insured's activities are to be managed or organised.

## 5   Knowledge of insurer

(1)   For the purposes of section 3(5)(b), an insurer knows something only if it is known to one or more of the individuals who participate on behalf of the insurer in the decision whether to take the risk, and if so on what terms (whether the individual does so as the insurer's employee or agent, as an employee of the insurer's agent or in any other capacity).

(2)   For the purposes of section 3(5)(c), an insurer ought to know something only if—

(a)   an employee or agent of the insurer knows it, and ought reasonably to have passed on the relevant information to an individual mentioned in subsection (1), or

(b)   the relevant information is held by the insurer and is readily available to an individual mentioned in subsection (1).

(3)   For the purposes of section 3(5)(d), an insurer is presumed to know—

(a)    things which are common knowledge, and

(b)    things which an insurer offering insurance of the class in question to insureds in the field of activity in question would reasonably be expected to know in the ordinary course of business.

### 6   Knowledge: general

(1)   For the purposes of sections 3 to 5, references to an individual's knowledge include not only actual knowledge, but also matters which the individual suspected, and of which the individual would have had knowledge but for deliberately refraining from confirming them or enquiring about them.

(2)   Nothing in this Part affects the operation of any rule of law according to which knowledge of a fraud perpetrated by an individual ('F') either on the insured or on the insurer is not to be attributed to the insured or to the insurer (respectively), where—

(a)    if the fraud is on the insured, F is any of the individuals mentioned in section 4(2)(b) or (3), or

(b)    if the fraud is on the insurer, F is any of the individuals mentioned in section 5(1).

### 7   Supplementary

(1)   A fair presentation need not be contained in only one document or oral presentation.

(2)   The term 'circumstance' includes any communication made to, or information received by, the insured.

(3)   A circumstance or representation is material if it would influence the judgement of a prudent insurer in determining whether to take the risk and, if so, on what terms.

(4)   Examples of things which may be material circumstances are—

(a)    special or unusual facts relating to the risk,

(b)    any particular concerns which led the insured to seek insurance cover for the risk,

(c)    anything which those concerned with the class of insurance and field of activity in question would generally understand as being something that should be dealt with in a fair presentation of risks of the type in question.

(5)   A material representation is substantially correct if a prudent insurer would not consider the difference between what is represented and what is actually correct to be material.

(6)   A representation may be withdrawn or corrected before the contract of insurance is entered into.

### 8   Remedies for breach

(1)   The insurer has a remedy against the insured for a breach of the duty of fair presentation only if the insurer shows that, but for the breach, the insurer—

(a)    would not have entered into the contract of insurance at all, or

(b)    would have done so only on different terms.

(2)   The remedies are set out in Schedule 1.

(3)   A breach for which the insurer has a remedy against the insured is referred to in this Act as a 'qualifying breach'.

(4)   A qualifying breach is either—

(a)    deliberate or reckless, or

(b)    neither deliberate nor reckless.

(5)   A qualifying breach is deliberate or reckless if the insured —

(a)    knew that it was in breach of the duty of fair presentation, or

(b)    did not care whether or not it was in breach of that duty.

(6)   It is for the insurer to show that a qualifying breach was deliberate or reckless.

PART 3
## WARRANTIES AND OTHER TERMS

### 9   Warranties and representations

(1)   This section applies to representations made by the insured in connection with—

    (a)   a proposed non-consumer insurance contract, or

    (b)   a proposed variation to a non-consumer insurance contract.

(2)   Such a representation is not capable of being converted into a warranty by means of any provision of the non-consumer insurance contract (or of the terms of the variation), or of any other contract (and whether by declaring the representation to form the basis of the contract or otherwise).

### 10   Breach of warranty

(1)   Any rule of law that breach of a warranty (express or implied) in a contract of insurance results in the discharge of the insurer's liability under the contract is abolished.

(2)   An insurer has no liability under a contract of insurance in respect of any loss occurring, or attributable to something happening, after a warranty (express or implied) in the contract has been breached but before the breach has been remedied.

(3)   But subsection (2) does not apply if—

    (a)   because of a change of circumstances, the warranty ceases to be applicable to the circumstances of the contract,

    (b)   compliance with the warranty is rendered unlawful by any subsequent law, or

    (c)   the insurer waives the breach of warranty.

(4)   Subsection (2) does not affect the liability of the insurer in respect of losses occurring, or attributable to something happening—

    (a)   before the breach of warranty, or

    (b)   if the breach can be remedied, after it has been remedied.

(5)   For the purposes of this section, a breach of warranty is to be taken as remedied—

    (a)   in a case falling within subsection (6), if the risk to which the warranty relates later becomes essentially the same as that originally contemplated by the parties,

    (b)   in any other case, if the insured ceases to be in breach of the warranty.

(6)   A case falls within this subsection if—

    (a)   the warranty in question requires that by an ascertainable time something is to be done (or not done), or a condition is to be fulfilled, or something is (or is not) to be the case, and

    (b)   that requirement is not complied with.

(7)   In the Marine Insurance Act 1906—

    (a)   in section 33 (nature of warranty), in subsection (3), the second sentence is omitted,

    (b)   section 34 (when breach of warranty excused) is omitted.

### 11   Terms not relevant to the actual loss

(1)   This section applies to a term (express or implied) of a contract of insurance, other than a term defining the risk as a whole, if compliance with it would tend to reduce the risk of one or more of the following—

    (a)   loss of a particular kind,

    (b)   loss at a particular location,

    (c)   loss at a particular time.

(2)   If a loss occurs, and the term has not been complied with, the insurer may not rely on the non-compliance to exclude, limit or discharge its liability under the contract for the loss if the insured satisfies subsection (3).

(3)   The insured satisfies this subsection if it shows that the non-compliance with the term could not have increased the risk of the loss which actually occurred in the circumstances in which it occurred.

(4)   This section may apply in addition to section 10.

PART 4
FRAUDULENT CLAIMS

**12   Remedies for fraudulent claims**

(1)   If the insured makes a fraudulent claim under a contract of insurance—

(a)   the insurer is not liable to pay the claim,

(b)   the insurer may recover from the insured any sums paid by the insurer to the insured in respect of the claim, and

(c)   in addition, the insurer may by notice to the insured treat the contract as having been terminated with effect from the time of the fraudulent act.

(2)   If the insurer does treat the contract as having been terminated—

(a)   it may refuse all liability to the insured under the contract in respect of a relevant event occurring after the time of the fraudulent act, and

(b)   it need not return any of the premiums paid under the contract.

(3)   Treating a contract as having been terminated under this section does not affect the rights and obligations of the parties to the contract with respect to a relevant event occurring before the time of the fraudulent act.

(4)   In subsections (2)(a) and (3), 'relevant event' refers to whatever gives rise to the insurer's liability under the contract (and includes, for example, the occurrence of a loss, the making of a claim, or the notification of a potential claim, depending on how the contract is written).

**13   Remedies for fraudulent claims: group insurance**

(1)   This section applies where—

(a)   a contract of insurance is entered into with an insurer by a person ('A'),

(b)   the contract provides cover for one or more other persons who are not parties to the contract ('the Cs'), whether or not it also provides cover of any kind for A or another insured party, and

(c)   a fraudulent claim is made under the contract by or on behalf of one of the Cs ('CF').

(2)   Section 12 applies in relation to the claim as if the cover provided for CF were provided under an individual insurance contract between the insurer and CF as the insured; and, accordingly—

(a)   the insurer's rights under section 12 are exercisable only in relation to the cover provided for CF, and

(b)   the exercise of any of those rights does not affect the cover provided under the contract for anyone else.

(3)   In its application by virtue of subsection (2), section 12 is subject to the following particular modifications—

(a)   the first reference to 'the insured' in subsection (1)(b) of that section, in respect of any particular sum paid by the insurer, is to whichever of A and CF the insurer paid the sum to; but if a sum was paid to A and passed on by A to CF, the reference is to CF,

(b)   the second reference to 'the insured' in subsection (1)(b) is to A or CF,

(c)   the reference to 'the insured' in subsection (1)(c) is to both CF and A,

(d)   the reference in subsection (2)(b) to the premiums paid under the contract is to premiums paid in respect of the cover for CF.

## PART 5
## GOOD FAITH AND CONTRACTING OUT

*Good faith*

### 14  Good faith

(1)   Any rule of law permitting a party to a contract of insurance to avoid the contract on the ground that the utmost good faith has not been observed by the other party is abolished.

(2)   Any rule of law to the effect that a contract of insurance is a contract based on the utmost good faith is modified to the extent required by the provisions of this Act and the Consumer Insurance (Disclosure and Representations) Act 2012.

(3)   Accordingly—

(a)   in section 17 of the Marine Insurance Act 1906 (marine insurance contracts are contracts of the utmost good faith), the words from ', and' to the end are omitted, and

(b)   the application of that section (as so amended) is subject to the provisions of this Act and the Consumer Insurance (Disclosure and Representations) Act 2012.

(4)   In section 2 of the Consumer Insurance (Disclosure and Representations) Act 2012 (disclosure and representations before contract or variation), subsection (5) is omitted.

*Contracting out*

### 15  Contracting out: consumer insurance contracts

(1)   A term of a consumer insurance contract, or of any other contract, which would put the consumer in a worse position as respects any of the matters provided for in Part 3 or 4 of this Act than the consumer would be in by virtue of the provisions of those Parts (so far as relating to consumer insurance contracts) is to that extent of no effect.

(2)   In subsection (1) references to a contract include a variation.

(3)   This section does not apply in relation to a contract for the settlement of a claim arising under a consumer insurance contract.

### 16  Contracting out: non-consumer insurance contracts

(1)   A term of a non-consumer insurance contract, or of any other contract, which would put the insured in a worse position as respects representations to which section 9 applies than the insured would be in by virtue of that section is to that extent of no effect.

(2)   A term of a non-consumer insurance contract, or of any other contract, which would put the insured in a worse position as respects any of the other matters provided for in Part 2, 3 or 4 of this Act than the insured would be in by virtue of the provisions of those Parts (so far as relating to non-consumer insurance contracts) is to that extent of no effect, unless the requirements of section 17 have been satisfied in relation to the term.

(3)   In this section references to a contract include a variation.

(4)   This section does not apply in relation to a contract for the settlement of a claim arising under a non-consumer insurance contract.

### 17  The transparency requirements

(1)   In this section, 'the disadvantageous term' means such a term as is mentioned in section 16(2).

(2)   The insurer must take sufficient steps to draw the disadvantageous term to the insured's attention before the contract is entered into or the variation agreed.

(3)   The disadvantageous term must be clear and unambiguous as to its effect.

(4)   In determining whether the requirements of subsections (2) and (3) have

been met, the characteristics of insured persons of the kind in question, and the circumstances of the transaction, are to be taken into account.

(5)   The insured may not rely on any failure on the part of the insurer to meet the requirements of subsection (2) if the insured (or its agent) had actual knowledge of the disadvantageous term when the contract was entered into or the variation agreed.

## 18   Contracting out: group insurance contracts

(1)   This section applies to a contract of insurance referred to in section 13(1)(a); and in this section—

'A' and 'the Cs' have the same meaning as in section 13,

'consumer C' means an individual who is one of the Cs, where the cover provided by the contract for that individual would have been a consumer insurance contract if entered into by that person rather than by A, and

'non-consumer C' means any of the Cs who is not a consumer C.

(2)   A term of the contract of insurance, or any other contract, which puts a consumer C in a worse position as respects any matter dealt with in section 13 than that individual would be in by virtue of that section is to that extent of no effect.

(3)   A term of the contract of insurance, or any other contract, which puts a non-consumer C in a worse position as respects any matter dealt with in section 13 than that person would be in by virtue of that section is to that extent of no effect, unless the requirements of section 17 have been met in relation to the term.

(4)   Section 17 applies in relation to such a term as it applies to a term mentioned in section 16(2), with references to the insured being read as references to A rather than the non-consumer C.

(5)   In this section references to a contract include a variation.

(6)   This section does not apply in relation to a contract for the settlement of a claim arising under a contract of insurance to which this section applies.


*[PART 6 amends the Third Parties (Rights Against Insurers Act 2010.]*


PART 7
GENERAL

## 21   Provision consequential on Part 2

(1)   The provision made by this section is consequential on Part 2 of this Act.

(2)   In the Marine Insurance Act 1906, sections 18 (disclosure by assured), 19 (disclosure by agent effecting insurance) and 20 (representations pending negotiation of contract) are omitted.

(3)   Any rule of law to the same effect as any of those provisions is abolished.

(4)   *[Amends the Road Traffic Act 1988]*

(5)   *[Applies to Northern Ireland]*

(6)   In section 11 of the Consumer Insurance (Disclosure and Representations) Act 2012 (consequential provision), subsections (1) and (2) are omitted.

## 22   Application etc of Parts 2 to 5

(1)   Part 2 (and section 21) and section 14 apply only in relation to—

   (a)   contracts of insurance entered into after the end of the relevant period, and

   (b)   variations, agreed after the end of the relevant period, to contracts of insurance entered into at any time.

(2)   Parts 3 and 4 of this Act apply only in relation to contracts of insurance entered into after the end of the relevant period, and variations to such contracts.

(3)   In subsections (1) and (2) 'the relevant period' means the period of 18 months beginning with the day on which this Act is passed.

(4) Unless the contrary intention appears, references in Parts 2 to 5 to something being done by or in relation to the insurer or the insured include its being done by or in relation to that person's agent.

### 23  Extent, commencement and short title

(1) This Act extends to England and Wales, Scotland and Northern Ireland, except for—

(a)  section 21(4), which does not extend to Northern Ireland; and

(b)  section 21(5), which extends to Northern Ireland only.

(2) This Act (apart from Part 6 and this section) comes into force at the end of the period of 18 months beginning with the day on which it is passed.

(3) In Part 6—

(a)  section 19 comes into force at the end of the period of two months beginning with the day on which this Act is passed; and

(b)  section 20 and Schedule 2 come into force on the day appointed under section 21(2) of the Third Parties (Rights against Insurers) Act 2010 for the coming into force of that Act.

(4) This section comes into force on the day on which this Act is passed.

(5) This Act may be cited as the Insurance Act 2015.

SCHEDULE 1

INSURERS' REMEDIES FOR QUALIFYING BREACHES

Section 8(2).

PART 1

CONTRACTS

*General*

1  This Part of this Schedule applies to qualifying breaches of the duty of fair presentation in relation to non-consumer insurance contracts (for variations to them, see Part 2).

*Deliberate or reckless breaches*

2  If a qualifying breach was deliberate or reckless, the insurer—

(a)  may avoid the contract and refuse all claims, and

(b)  need not return any of the premiums paid.

*Other breaches*

3  Paragraphs 4 to 6 apply if a qualifying breach was neither deliberate nor reckless.

4  If, in the absence of the qualifying breach, the insurer would not have entered into the contract on any terms, the insurer may avoid the contract and refuse all claims, but must in that event return the premiums paid.

5  If the insurer would have entered into the contract, but on different terms (other than terms relating to the premium), the contract is to be treated as if it had been entered into on those different terms if the insurer so requires.

6—(1) In addition, if the insurer would have entered into the contract (whether the terms relating to matters other than the premium would have been the same or different), but would have charged a higher premium, the insurer may reduce proportionately the amount to be paid on a claim.

(2) In sub-paragraph (1), 'reduce proportionately' means that the insurer need pay on the claim only X% of what it would otherwise have been under an obliga-

tion to pay under the terms of the contract (or, if applicable, under the different terms provided for by virtue of paragraph 5), where—

$$X = \frac{\text{Premium actually charged}}{\text{Higher premium}} \times 100$$

## PART 2
## VARIATIONS

### *General*

7   This Part of this Schedule applies to qualifying breaches of the duty of fair presentation in relation to variations to non-consumer insurance contracts.

### *Deliberate or reckless breaches*

8   If a qualifying breach was deliberate or reckless, the insurer—
   (a)   may by notice to the insured treat the contract as having been terminated with effect from the time when the variation was made, and
   (b)   need not return any of the premiums paid.

### *Other breaches*

9—(1)   This paragraph applies if—
   (a)   a qualifying breach was neither deliberate nor reckless, and
   (b)   the total premium was increased or not changed as a result of the variation.
(2)   If, in the absence of the qualifying breach, the insurer would not have agreed to the variation on any terms, the insurer may treat the contract as if the variation was never made, but must in that event return any extra premium paid.
(3)   If sub-paragraph (2) does not apply—
   (a)   if the insurer would have agreed to the variation on different terms (other than terms relating to the premium), the variation is to be treated as if it had been entered into on those different terms if the insurer so requires, and
   (b)   paragraph 11 also applies if (in the case of an increased premium) the insurer would have increased the premium by more than it did, or (in the case of an unchanged premium) the insurer would have increased the premium.

10—(1)   This paragraph applies if—
   (a)   a qualifying breach was neither deliberate nor reckless, and
   (b)   the total premium was reduced as a result of the variation.
(2)   If, in the absence of the qualifying breach, the insurer would not have agreed to the variation on any terms, the insurer may treat the contract as if the variation was never made, and paragraph 11 also applies.
(3)   If sub-paragraph (2) does not apply—
   (a)   if the insurer would have agreed to the variation on different terms (other than terms relating to the premium), the variation is to be treated as if it had been entered into on those different terms if the insurer so requires, and
   (b)   paragraph 11 also applies if the insurer would have increased the premium, would not have reduced the premium, or would have reduced it by less than it did.

*Proportionate reduction*

11—(1)  If this paragraph applies, the insurer may reduce proportionately the amount to be paid on a claim arising out of events after the variation.

(2)  In sub-paragraph (1), 'reduce proportionately' means that the insurer need pay on the claim only Y% of what it would otherwise have been under an obligation to pay under the terms of the contract (whether on the original terms, or as varied, or under the different terms provided for by virtue of paragraph 9(3)(a) or 10(3)(a), as the case may be), where—

$$Y = \frac{\text{Total premium actually charged}}{P} \times 100$$

(3)  In the formula in sub-paragraph (2), 'P'—

(a)   in a paragraph 9(3)(b) case, is the total premium the insurer would have charged,

(b)   in a paragraph 10(2) case, is the original premium,

(c)   in a paragraph 10(3)(b) case, is the original premium if the insurer would not have changed it, and otherwise the increased or (as the case may be) reduced total premium the insurer would have charged.

## PART 3
### Supplementary

*Relationship with section 84 of the Marine Insurance Act 1906*

12  Section 84 of the Marine Insurance Act 1906 (return of premium for failure of consideration) is to be read subject to the provisions of this Schedule in relation to contracts of marine insurance which are non-consumer insurance contracts.

. . .

## CONSUMER RIGHTS ACT 2015
### (2015, c 15)

### PART 1
### CONSUMER CONTRACTS FOR GOODS, DIGITAL CONTENT AND SERVICES

### CHAPTER 1
### Introduction

**1  Where Part 1 applies**

(1)  This Part applies where there is an agreement between a trader and a consumer for the trader to supply goods, digital content or services, if the agreement is a contract.

(2)  It applies whether the contract is written or oral or implied from the parties' conduct, or more than one of these combined.

(3)  Any of Chapters 2, 3 and 4 may apply to a contract—

  (a)   if it is a contract for the trader to supply goods, see Chapter 2;

  (b)   if it is a contract for the trader to supply digital content, see Chapter 3 (also, subsection (6));

  (c)   if it is a contract for the trader to supply a service, see Chapter 4 (also, subsection (6)).

(4)  In each case the Chapter applies even if the contract also covers something covered by another Chapter (a mixed contract).

(5)  Two or all three of those Chapters may apply to a mixed contract.

(6)  For provisions about particular mixed contracts, see—

  (a)   section 15 (goods and installation);

  (b)   section 16 (goods and digital content).

(7)  For other provision applying to contracts to which this Part applies, see Part 2 (unfair terms).

**2  Key definitions**

(1)  These definitions apply in this Part (as well as the definitions in section 59).

(2)  'Trader' means a person acting for purposes relating to that person's trade, business, craft or profession, whether acting personally or through another person acting in the trader's name or on the trader's behalf.

(3)  'Consumer' means an individual acting for purposes that are wholly or mainly outside that individual's trade, business, craft or profession.

(4)  A trader claiming that an individual was not acting for purposes wholly or mainly outside the individual's trade, business, craft or profession must prove it.

(5)  For the purposes of Chapter 2, except to the extent mentioned in subsection (6), a person is not a consumer in relation to a sales contract if—

  (a)   the goods are second hand goods sold at public auction, and

  (b)   individuals have the opportunity of attending the sale in person.

(6)  A person is a consumer in relation to such a contract for the purposes of—

  (a)   sections 11(4) and (5), 12, 28 and 29, and

  (b)   the other provisions of Chapter 2 as they apply in relation to those sections.

(7)  'Business' includes the activities of any government department or local or public authority.

(8)  'Goods' means any tangible moveable items, but that includes water, gas and electricity if and only if they are put up for supply in a limited volume or set quantity.

(9)  'Digital content' means data which are produced and supplied in digital form.

## CHAPTER 2
## Goods

*What goods contracts are covered?*

**3 Contracts covered by this Chapter**

(1) This Chapter applies to a contract for a trader to supply goods to a consumer.

(2) It applies only if the contract is one of these (defined for the purposes of this Part in sections 5 to 8)—

(a) a sales contract;

(b) a contract for the hire of goods;

(c) a hire-purchase agreement;

(d) a contract for transfer of goods.

(3) It does not apply—

(a) to a contract for a trader to supply coins or notes to a consumer for use as currency;

(b) to a contract for goods to be sold by way of execution or otherwise by authority of law;

(c) to a contract intended to operate as a mortgage, pledge, charge or other security;

(d) in relation to England and Wales or Northern Ireland, to a contract made by deed and for which the only consideration is the presumed consideration imported by the deed;

(e) in relation to Scotland, to a gratuitous contract.

(4) A contract to which this Chapter applies is referred to in this Part as a 'contract to supply goods'.

(5) Contracts to supply goods include—

(a) contracts entered into between one part owner and another;

(b) contracts for the transfer of an undivided share in goods;

(c) contracts that are absolute and contracts that are conditional.

(6) Subsection (1) is subject to any provision of this Chapter that applies a section or part of a section to only some of the kinds of contracts listed in subsection (2).

(7) A mixed contract (see section 1(4)) may be a contract of any of those kinds.

**4 Ownership of goods**

(1) In this Chapter ownership of goods means the general property in goods, not merely a special property.

(2) For the time when ownership of goods is transferred, see in particular the following provisions of the Sale of Goods Act 1979 (which relate to contracts of sale)—

section 16: goods must be ascertained

section 17: property passes when intended to pass

section 18: rules for ascertaining intention

section 19: reservation of right of disposal

section 20A: undivided shares in goods forming part of a bulk

section 20B: deemed consent by co-owner to dealings in bulk goods

**5 Sales contracts**

(1) A contract is a sales contract if under it—

(a) the trader transfers or agrees to transfer ownership of goods to the consumer, and

(b) the consumer pays or agrees to pay the price.

(2) A contract is a sales contract (whether or not it would be one under subsection (1)) if under the contract—

(a) goods are to be manufactured or produced and the trader agrees to supply them to the consumer,

(b) on being supplied, the goods will be owned by the consumer, and

(c) the consumer pays or agrees to pay the price.

(3) A sales contract may be conditional (see section 3(5)), but in this Part 'conditional sales contract' means a sales contract under which—

(a) the price for the goods or part of it is payable by instalments, and

(b) the trader retains ownership of the goods until the conditions specified in the contract (for the payment of instalments or otherwise) are met;

and it makes no difference whether or not the consumer possesses the goods.

### 6 Contracts for the hire of goods

(1) A contract is for the hire of goods if under it the trader gives or agrees to give the consumer possession of the goods with the right to use them, subject to the terms of the contract, for a period determined in accordance with the contract.

(2) But a contract is not for the hire of goods if it is a hire-purchase agreement.

### 7 Hire-purchase agreements

(1) A contract is a hire-purchase agreement if it meets the two conditions set out below.

(2) The first condition is that under the contract goods are hired by the trader in return for periodical payments by the consumer (and 'hired' is to be read in accordance with section 6(1)).

(3) The second condition is that under the contract ownership of the goods will transfer to the consumer if the terms of the contract are complied with and—

(a) the consumer exercises an option to buy the goods,

(b) any party to the contract does an act specified in it, or

(c) an event specified in the contract occurs.

(4) But a contract is not a hire-purchase agreement if it is a conditional sales contract.

### 8 Contracts for transfer of goods

A contract to supply goods is a contract for transfer of goods if under it the trader transfers or agrees to transfer ownership of the goods to the consumer and—

(a) the consumer provides or agrees to provide consideration otherwise than by paying a price, or

(b) the contract is, for any other reason, not a sales contract or a hire-purchase agreement.

*What statutory rights are there under a goods contract?*

### 9 Goods to be of satisfactory quality

(1) Every contract to supply goods is to be treated as including a term that the quality of the goods is satisfactory.

(2) The quality of goods is satisfactory if they meet the standard that a reasonable person would consider satisfactory, taking account of—

(a) any description of the goods,

(b) the price or other consideration for the goods (if relevant), and

(c) all the other relevant circumstances (see subsection (5)).

(3) The quality of goods includes their state and condition; and the following aspects (among others) are in appropriate cases aspects of the quality of goods—

(a) fitness for all the purposes for which goods of that kind are usually supplied;

(b) appearance and finish;

(c) freedom from minor defects;

(d) safety;

(e) durability.

(4)   The term mentioned in subsection (1) does not cover anything which makes the quality of the goods unsatisfactory—

(a)   which is specifically drawn to the consumer's attention before the contract is made,

(b)   where the consumer examines the goods before the contract is made, which that examination ought to reveal, or

(c)   in the case of a contract to supply goods by sample, which would have been apparent on a reasonable examination of the sample.

(5)   The relevant circumstances mentioned in subsection (2)(c) include any public statement about the specific characteristics of the goods made by the trader, the producer or any representative of the trader or the producer.

(6)   That includes, in particular, any public statement made in advertising or labelling.

(7)   But a public statement is not a relevant circumstance for the purposes of subsection (2)(c) if the trader shows that—

(a)   when the contract was made, the trader was not, and could not reasonably have been, aware of the statement,

(b)   before the contract was made, the statement had been publicly withdrawn or, to the extent that it contained anything which was incorrect or misleading, it had been publicly corrected, or

(c)   the consumer's decision to contract for the goods could not have been influenced by the statement.

(8)   In a contract to supply goods a term about the quality of the goods may be treated as included as a matter of custom.

(9)   See section 19 for a consumer's rights if the trader is in breach of a term that this section requires to be treated as included in a contract.

## 10   Goods to be fit for particular purpose

(1)   Subsection (3) applies to a contract to supply goods if before the contract is made the consumer makes known to the trader (expressly or by implication) any particular purpose for which the consumer is contracting for the goods.

(2)   Subsection (3) also applies to a contract to supply goods if—

(a)   the goods were previously sold by a credit-broker to the trader,

(b)   in the case of a sales contract or contract for transfer of goods, the consideration or part of it is a sum payable by instalments, and

(c)   before the contract is made, the consumer makes known to the credit-broker (expressly or by implication) any particular purpose for which the consumer is contracting for the goods.

(3)   The contract is to be treated as including a term that the goods are reasonably fit for that purpose, whether or not that is a purpose for which goods of that kind are usually supplied.

(4)   Subsection (3) does not apply if the circumstances show that the consumer does not rely, or it is unreasonable for the consumer to rely, on the skill or judgment of the trader or credit-broker.

(5)   In a contract to supply goods a term about the fitness of the goods for a particular purpose may be treated as included as a matter of custom.

(6)   See section 19 for a consumer's rights if the trader is in breach of a term that this section requires to be treated as included in a contract.

## 11   Goods to be as described

(1)   Every contract to supply goods by description is to be treated as including a term that the goods will match the description.

(2)   If the supply is by sample as well as by description, it is not sufficient that the bulk of the goods matches the sample if the goods do not also match the description.

(3)   A supply of goods is not prevented from being a supply by description just because—

    (a)   the goods are exposed for supply, and

    (b)   they are selected by the consumer.

(4)   Any information that is provided by the trader about the goods and is information mentioned in paragraph (a) of Schedule 1 or 2 to the Consumer Contracts (Information, Cancellation and Additional Charges) Regulations 2013 (SI 2013/3134) (main characteristics of goods) is to be treated as included as a term of the contract.

(5)   A change to any of that information, made before entering into the contract or later, is not effective unless expressly agreed between the consumer and the trader.

(6)   See section 2(5) and (6) for the application of subsections (4) and (5) where goods are sold at public auction.

(7)   See section 19 for a consumer's rights if the trader is in breach of a term that this section requires to be treated as included in a contract.

## 12   Other pre-contract information included in contract

(1)   This section applies to any contract to supply goods.

(2)   Where regulation 9, 10 or 13 of the Consumer Contracts (Information, Cancellation and Additional Charges) Regulations 2013 (SI 2013/3134) required the trader to provide information to the consumer before the contract became binding, any of that information that was provided by the trader other than information about the goods and mentioned in paragraph (a) of Schedule 1 or 2 to the Regulations (main characteristics of goods) is to be treated as included as a term of the contract.

(3)   A change to any of that information, made before entering into the contract or later, is not effective unless expressly agreed between the consumer and the trader.

(4)   See section 2(5) and (6) for the application of this section where goods are sold at public auction.

(5)   See section 19 for a consumer's rights if the trader is in breach of a term that this section requires to be treated as included in the contract.

## 13   Goods to match a sample

(1)   This section applies to a contract to supply goods by reference to a sample of the goods that is seen or examined by the consumer before the contract is made.

(2)   Every contract to which this section applies is to be treated as including a term that—

    (a)   the goods will match the sample except to the extent that any differences between the sample and the goods are brought to the consumer's attention before the contract is made, and

    (b)   the goods will be free from any defect that makes their quality unsatisfactory and that would not be apparent on a reasonable examination of the sample.

(3)   See section 19 for a consumer's rights if the trader is in breach of a term that this section requires to be treated as included in a contract.

## 14   Goods to match a model seen or examined

(1)   This section applies to a contract to supply goods by reference to a model of the goods that is seen or examined by the consumer before entering into the contract.

(2)   Every contract to which this section applies is to be treated as including a term that the goods will match the model except to the extent that any differences between the model and the goods are brought to the consumer's attention before the consumer enters into the contract.

(3)   See section 19 for a consumer's rights if the trader is in breach of a term that this section requires to be treated as included in a contract.

### 15   Installation as part of conformity of the goods with the contract
(1)   Goods do not conform to a contract to supply goods if—
    (a)   installation of the goods forms part of the contract,
    (b)   the goods are installed by the trader or under the trader's responsibility, and
    (c)   the goods are installed incorrectly.
(2)   See section 19 for the effect of goods not conforming to the contract.

### 16   Goods not conforming to contract if digital content does not conform
(1)   Goods (whether or not they conform otherwise to a contract to supply goods) do not conform to it if—
    (a)   the goods are an item that includes digital content, and
    (b)   the digital content does not conform to the contract to supply that content (for which see section 42(1)).
(2)   See section 19 for the effect of goods not conforming to the contract.

### 17   Trader to have right to supply the goods etc
(1)   Every contract to supply goods, except one within subsection (4), is to be treated as including a term—
    (a)   in the case of a contract for the hire of goods, that at the beginning of the period of hire the trader must have the right to transfer possession of the goods by way of hire for that period,
    (b)   in any other case, that the trader must have the right to sell or transfer the goods at the time when ownership of the goods is to be transferred.
(2)   Every contract to supply goods, except a contract for the hire of goods or a contract within subsection (4), is to be treated as including a term that—
    (a)   the goods are free from any charge or encumbrance not disclosed or known to the consumer before entering into the contract,
    (b)   the goods will remain free from any such charge or encumbrance until ownership of them is to be transferred, and
    (c)   the consumer will enjoy quiet possession of the goods except so far as it may be disturbed by the owner or other person entitled to the benefit of any charge or encumbrance so disclosed or known.
(3)   Every contract for the hire of goods is to be treated as including a term that the consumer will enjoy quiet possession of the goods for the period of the hire except so far as the possession may be disturbed by the owner or other person entitled to the benefit of any charge or encumbrance disclosed or known to the consumer before entering into the contract.
(4)   This subsection applies to a contract if the contract shows, or the circumstances when they enter into the contract imply, that the trader and the consumer intend the trader to transfer only—
    (a)   whatever title the trader has, even if it is limited, or
    (b)   whatever title a third person has, even if it is limited.
(5)   Every contract within subsection (4) is to be treated as including a term that all charges or encumbrances known to the trader and not known to the consumer were disclosed to the consumer before entering into the contract.
(6)   Every contract within subsection (4) is to be treated as including a term that the consumer's quiet possession of the goods—
    (a)   will not be disturbed by the trader, and
    (b)   will not be disturbed by a person claiming through or under the trader, unless that person is claiming under a charge or encumbrance that was disclosed or known to the consumer before entering into the contract.
(7)   If subsection (4)(b) applies (transfer of title that a third person has), the contract is also to be treated as including a term that the consumer's quiet possession of the goods—
    (a)   will not be disturbed by the third person, and
    (b)   will not be disturbed by a person claiming through or under the third

person, unless the claim is under a charge or encumbrance that was disclosed or known to the consumer before entering into the contract.

(8)   In the case of a contract for the hire of goods, this section does not affect the right of the trader to repossess the goods where the contract provides or is to be treated as providing for this.

(9)   See section 19 for a consumer's rights if the trader is in breach of a term that this section requires to be treated as included in a contract.

**18   No other requirement to treat term about quality or fitness as included**

(1)   Except as provided by sections 9, 10, 13 and 16, a contract to supply goods is not to be treated as including any term about the quality of the goods or their fitness for any particular purpose, unless the term is expressly included in the contract.

(2)   Subsection (1) is subject to provision made by any other enactment (whenever passed or made).

*What remedies are there if statutory rights under a goods contract are not met?*

**19   Consumer's rights to enforce terms about goods**

(1)   In this section and sections 22 to 24 references to goods conforming to a contract are references to—

(a)   the goods conforming to the terms described in sections 9, 10, 11, 13 and 14,

(b)   the goods not failing to conform to the contract under section 15 or 16, and

(c)   the goods conforming to requirements that are stated in the contract.

(2)   But, for the purposes of this section and sections 22 to 24, a failure to conform as mentioned in subsection (1)(a) to (c) is not a failure to conform to the contract if it has its origin in materials supplied by the consumer.

(3)   If the goods do not conform to the contract because of a breach of any of the terms described in sections 9, 10, 11, 13 and 14, or if they do not conform to the contract under section 16, the consumer's rights (and the provisions about them and when they are available) are—

(a)   the short-term right to reject (sections 20 and 22);

(b)   the right to repair or replacement (section 23); and

(c)   the right to a price reduction or the final right to reject (sections 20 and 24).

(4)   If the goods do not conform to the contract under section 15 or because of a breach of requirements that are stated in the contract, the consumer's rights (and the provisions about them and when they are available) are—

(a)   the right to repair or replacement (section 23); and

(b)   the right to a price reduction or the final right to reject (sections 20 and 24).

(5)   If the trader is in breach of a term that section 12 requires to be treated as included in the contract, the consumer has the right to recover from the trader the amount of any costs incurred by the consumer as a result of the breach, up to the amount of the price paid or the value of other consideration given for the goods.

(6)   If the trader is in breach of the term that section 17(1) (right to supply etc) requires to be treated as included in the contract, the consumer has a right to reject (see section 20 for provisions about that right and when it is available).

(7)   Subsections (3) to (6) are subject to section 25 and subsections (3)(a) and (6) are subject to section 26.

(8)   Section 28 makes provision about remedies for breach of a term about the time for delivery of goods.

(9)   This Chapter does not prevent the consumer seeking other remedies—

(a)   for a breach of a term that this Chapter requires to be treated as included in the contract,

(b)    on the grounds that, under section 15 or 16, goods do not conform to the contract, or

(c)    for a breach of a requirement stated in the contract.

(10)   Those other remedies may be ones—

(a)    in addition to a remedy referred to in subsections (3) to (6) (but not so as to recover twice for the same loss), or

(b)    instead of such a remedy, or

(c)    where no such remedy is provided for.

(11)   Those other remedies include any of the following that is open to the consumer in the circumstances—

(a)    claiming damages;

(b)    seeking specific performance;

(c)    seeking an order for specific implement;

(d)    relying on the breach against a claim by the trader for the price;

(e)    for breach of an express term, exercising a right to treat the contract as at an end.

(12)   It is not open to the consumer to treat the contract as at an end for breach of a term that this Chapter requires to be treated as included in the contract, or on the grounds that, under section 15 or 16, goods do not conform to the contract, except as provided by subsections (3), (4) and (6).

(13)   In this Part, treating a contract as at an end means treating it as repudiated.

(14)   For the purposes of subsections (3)(b) and (c) and (4), goods which do not conform to the contract at any time within the period of six months beginning with the day on which the goods were delivered to the consumer must be taken not to have conformed to it on that day.

(15)   Subsection (14) does not apply if—

(a)    it is established that the goods did conform to the contract on that day, or

(b)    its application is incompatible with the nature of the goods or with how they fail to conform to the contract.

## 20   Right to reject

(1)    The short-term right to reject is subject to section 22.

(2)    The final right to reject is subject to section 24.

(3)    The right to reject under section 19(6) is not limited by those sections.

(4)    Each of these rights entitles the consumer to reject the goods and treat the contract as at an end, subject to subsections (20) and (21).

(5)    The right is exercised if the consumer indicates to the trader that the consumer is rejecting the goods and treating the contract as at an end.

(6)    The indication may be something the consumer says or does, but it must be clear enough to be understood by the trader.

(7)    From the time when the right is exercised—

(a)    the trader has a duty to give the consumer a refund, subject to subsection (18), and

(b)    the consumer has a duty to make the goods available for collection by the trader or (if there is an agreement for the consumer to return rejected goods) to return them as agreed.

(8)    Whether or not the consumer has a duty to return the rejected goods, the trader must bear any reasonable costs of returning them, other than any costs incurred by the consumer in returning the goods in person to the place where the consumer took physical possession of them.

(9)    The consumer's entitlement to receive a refund works as follows.

(10)   To the extent that the consumer paid money under the contract, the consumer is entitled to receive back the same amount of money.

(11)   To the extent that the consumer transferred anything else under the

contract, the consumer is entitled to receive back the same amount of what the consumer transferred, unless subsection (12) applies.

(12)   To the extent that the consumer transferred under the contract something for which the same amount of the same thing cannot be substituted, the consumer is entitled to receive back in its original state whatever the consumer transferred.

(13)   If the contract is for the hire of goods, the entitlement to a refund extends only to anything paid or otherwise transferred for a period of hire that the consumer does not get because the contract is treated as at an end.

(14)   If the contract is a hire-purchase agreement or a conditional sales contract and the contract is treated as at an end before the whole of the price has been paid, the entitlement to a refund extends only to the part of the price paid.

(15)   A refund under this section must be given without undue delay, and in any event within 14 days beginning with the day on which the trader agrees that the consumer is entitled to a refund.

(16)   If the consumer paid money under the contract, the trader must give the refund using the same means of payment as the consumer used, unless the consumer expressly agrees otherwise.

(17)   The trader must not impose any fee on the consumer in respect of the refund.

(18)   There is no entitlement to receive a refund—
    (a)   if none of subsections (10) to (12) applies,
    (b)   to the extent that anything to which subsection (12) applies cannot be given back in its original state, or
    (c)   where subsection (13) applies, to the extent that anything the consumer transferred under the contract cannot be divided so as to give back only the amount, or part of the amount, to which the consumer is entitled.

(19)   It may be open to a consumer to claim damages where there is no entitlement to receive a refund, or because of the limits of the entitlement, or instead of a refund.

(20)   Subsection (21) qualifies the application in relation to England and Wales and Northern Ireland of the rights mentioned in subsections (1) to (3) where—
    (a)   the contract is a severable contract,
    (b)   in relation to the final right to reject, the contract is a contract for the hire of goods, a hire-purchase agreement or a contract for transfer of goods, and
    (c)   section 26(3) does not apply.

(21)   The consumer is entitled, depending on the terms of the contract and the circumstances of the case—
    (a)   to reject the goods to which a severable obligation relates and treat that obligation as at an end (so that the entitlement to a refund relates only to what the consumer paid or transferred in relation to that obligation), or
    (b)   to exercise any of the rights mentioned in subsections (1) to (3) in respect of the whole contract.

## 21   Partial rejection of goods

(1)   If the consumer has any of the rights mentioned in section 20(1) to (3), but does not reject all of the goods and treat the contract as at an end, the consumer—
    (a)   may reject some or all of the goods that do not conform to the contract, but
    (b)   may not reject any goods that do conform to the contract.

(2)   If the consumer is entitled to reject the goods in an instalment, but does not reject all of those goods, the consumer—
    (a)   may reject some or all of the goods in the instalment that do not conform to the contract, but
    (b)   may not reject any goods in the instalment that do conform to the contract.

(3)   If any of the goods form a commercial unit, the consumer cannot reject some of those goods without also rejecting the rest of them.

(4)   A unit is a 'commercial unit' if division of the unit would materially impair the value of the goods or the character of the unit.

(5)   The consumer rejects goods under this section by indicating to the trader that the consumer is rejecting the goods.

(6)   The indication may be something the consumer says or does, but it must be clear enough to be understood by the trader.

(7)   From the time when a consumer rejects goods under this section—

(a)   the trader has a duty to give the consumer a refund in respect of those goods (subject to subsection (10)), and

(b)   the consumer has a duty to make those goods available for collection by the trader or (if there is an agreement for the consumer to return rejected goods) to return them as agreed.

(8)   Whether or not the consumer has a duty to return the rejected goods, the trader must bear any reasonable costs of returning them, other than any costs incurred by the consumer in returning those goods in person to the place where the consumer took physical possession of them.

(9)   Section 20(10) to (17) apply to a consumer's right to receive a refund under this section (and in section 20(13) and (14) references to the contract being treated as at an end are to be read as references to goods being rejected).

(10)   That right does not apply—

(a)   if none of section 20(10) to (12) applies,

(b)   to the extent that anything to which section 20(12) applies cannot be given back in its original state, or

(c)   to the extent that anything the consumer transferred under the contract cannot be divided so as to give back only the amount, or part of the amount, to which the consumer is entitled.

(11)   It may be open to a consumer to claim damages where there is no right to receive a refund, or because of the limits of the right, or instead of a refund.

(12)   References in this section to goods conforming to a contract are to be read in accordance with section 19(1) and (2), but they also include the goods conforming to the terms described in section 17.

(13)   Where section 20(21)(a) applies the reference in subsection (1) to the consumer treating the contract as at an end is to be read as a reference to the consumer treating the severable obligation as at an end.

## 22   Time limit for short-term right to reject

(1)   A consumer who has the short-term right to reject loses it if the time limit for exercising it passes without the consumer exercising it, unless the trader and the consumer agree that it may be exercised later.

(2)   An agreement under which the short-term right to reject would be lost before the time limit passes is not binding on the consumer.

(3)   The time limit for exercising the short-term right to reject (unless subsection (4) applies) is the end of 30 days beginning with the first day after these have all happened—

(a)   ownership or (in the case of a contract for the hire of goods, a hire-purchase agreement or a conditional sales contract) possession of the goods has been transferred to the consumer,

(b)   the goods have been delivered, and

(c)   where the contract requires the trader to install the goods or take other action to enable the consumer to use them, the trader has notified the consumer that the action has been taken.

(4)   If any of the goods are of a kind that can reasonably be expected to perish after a shorter period, the time limit for exercising the short-term right to reject in

relation to those goods is the end of that shorter period (but without affecting the time limit in relation to goods that are not of that kind).

(5)  Subsections (3) and (4) do not prevent the consumer exercising the short-term right to reject before something mentioned in subsection (3)(a), (b) or (c) has happened.

(6)  If the consumer requests or agrees to the repair or replacement of goods, the period mentioned in subsection (3) or (4) stops running for the length of the waiting period.

(7)  If goods supplied by the trader in response to that request or agreement do not conform to the contract, the time limit for exercising the short-term right to reject is then either—

(a)    7 days after the waiting period ends, or

(b)    if later, the original time limit for exercising that right, extended by the waiting period.

(8)  The waiting period—

(a)    begins with the day the consumer requests or agrees to the repair or replacement of the goods, and

(b)    ends with the day on which the consumer receives goods supplied by the trader in response to the request or agreement.

## 23  Right to repair or replacement

(1)  This section applies if the consumer has the right to repair or replacement (see section 19(3) and (4)).

(2)  If the consumer requires the trader to repair or replace the goods, the trader must—

(a)    do so within a reasonable time and without significant inconvenience to the consumer, and

(b)    bear any necessary costs incurred in doing so (including in particular the cost of any labour, materials or postage).

(3)  The consumer cannot require the trader to repair or replace the goods if that remedy (the repair or the replacement)—

(a)    is impossible, or

(b)    is disproportionate compared to the other of those remedies.

(4)  Either of those remedies is disproportionate compared to the other if it imposes costs on the trader which, compared to those imposed by the other, are unreasonable, taking into account—

(a)    the value which the goods would have if they conformed to the contract,

(b)    the significance of the lack of conformity, and

(c)    whether the other remedy could be effected without significant inconvenience to the consumer.

(5)  Any question as to what is a reasonable time or significant inconvenience is to be determined taking account of—

(a)    the nature of the goods, and

(b)    the purpose for which the goods were acquired.

(6)  A consumer who requires or agrees to the repair of goods cannot require the trader to replace them, or exercise the short-term right to reject, without giving the trader a reasonable time to repair them (unless giving the trader that time would cause significant inconvenience to the consumer).

(7)  A consumer who requires or agrees to the replacement of goods cannot require the trader to repair them, or exercise the short-term right to reject, without giving the trader a reasonable time to replace them (unless giving the trader that time would cause significant inconvenience to the consumer).

(8)  In this Chapter, 'repair' in relation to goods that do not conform to a contract, means making them conform.

## 24  Right to price reduction or final right to reject

(1)  The right to a price reduction is the right—

(a)   to require the trader to reduce by an appropriate amount the price the consumer is required to pay under the contract, or anything else the consumer is required to transfer under the contract, and

(b)   to receive a refund from the trader for anything already paid or otherwise transferred by the consumer above the reduced amount.

(2)   The amount of the reduction may, where appropriate, be the full amount of the price or whatever the consumer is required to transfer.

(3)   Section 20(10) to (17) applies to a consumer's right to receive a refund under subsection (1)(b).

(4)   The right to a price reduction does not apply—

(a)   if what the consumer is (before the reduction) required to transfer under the contract, whether or not already transferred, cannot be divided up so as to enable the trader to receive or retain only the reduced amount, or

(b)   if anything to which section 20(12) applies cannot be given back in its original state.

(5)   A consumer who has the right to a price reduction and the final right to reject may only exercise one (not both), and may only do so in one of these situations—

(a)   after one repair or one replacement, the goods do not conform to the contract;

(b)   because of section 23(3) the consumer can require neither repair nor replacement of the goods; or

(c)   the consumer has required the trader to repair or replace the goods, but the trader is in breach of the requirement of section 23(2)(a) to do so within a reasonable time and without significant inconvenience to the consumer.

(6)   There has been a repair or replacement for the purposes of subsection (5)(a) if—

(a)   the consumer has requested or agreed to repair or replacement of the goods (whether in relation to one fault or more than one), and

(b)   the trader has delivered goods to the consumer, or made goods available to the consumer, in response to the request or agreement.

(7)   For the purposes of subsection (6) goods that the trader arranges to repair at the consumer's premises are made available when the trader indicates that the repairs are finished.

(8)   If the consumer exercises the final right to reject, any refund to the consumer may be reduced by a deduction for use, to take account of the use the consumer has had of the goods in the period since they were delivered, but this is subject to subsections (9) and (10).

(9)   No deduction may be made to take account of use in any period when the consumer had the goods only because the trader failed to collect them at an agreed time.

(10)   No deduction may be made if the final right to reject is exercised in the first 6 months (see subsection (11)), unless—

(a)   the goods consist of a motor vehicle, or

(b)   the goods are of a description specified by order made by the Secretary of State by statutory instrument.

(11)   In subsection (10) the first 6 months means 6 months beginning with the first day after these have all happened—

(a)   ownership or (in the case of a contract for the hire of goods, a hire-purchase agreement or a conditional sales contract) possession of the goods has been transferred to the consumer,

(b)   the goods have been delivered, and

(c)   where the contract requires the trader to install the goods or take other action to enable the consumer to use them, the trader has notified the consumer that the action has been taken.

(12)   In subsection (10)(a) 'motor vehicle'—

(a)    in relation to Great Britain, has the same meaning as in the Road Traffic Act 1988 (see sections 185 to 194 of that Act);

(b)    in relation to Northern Ireland, has the same meaning as in the Road Traffic (Northern Ireland) Order 1995 (SI 1995/2994 (NI 18)) (see Parts I and V of that Order).

(13)   But a vehicle is not a motor vehicle for the purposes of subsection (10)(a) if it is constructed or adapted—

(a)    for the use of a person suffering from some physical defect or disability, and

(b)    so that it may only be used by one such person at any one time.

(14)   An order under subsection (10)(b)—

(a)    may be made only if the Secretary of State is satisfied that it is appropriate to do so because of significant detriment caused to traders as a result of the application of subsection (10) in relation to goods of the description specified by the order;

(b)    may contain transitional or transitory provision or savings.

(15)   No order may be made under subsection (10)(b) unless a draft of the statutory instrument containing it has been laid before, and approved by a resolution of, each House of Parliament.

*Other rules about remedies under goods contracts*

### 25   Delivery of wrong quantity

(1)   Where the trader delivers to the consumer a quantity of goods less than the trader contracted to supply, the consumer may reject them, but if the consumer accepts them the consumer must pay for them at the contract rate.

(2)   Where the trader delivers to the consumer a quantity of goods larger than the trader contracted to supply, the consumer may accept the goods included in the contract and reject the rest, or may reject all of the goods.

(3)   Where the trader delivers to the consumer a quantity of goods larger than the trader contracted to supply and the consumer accepts all of the goods delivered, the consumer must pay for them at the contract rate.

(4)   Where the consumer is entitled to reject goods under this section, any entitlement for the consumer to treat the contract as at an end depends on the terms of the contract and the circumstances of the case.

(5)   The consumer rejects goods under this section by indicating to the trader that the consumer is rejecting the goods.

(6)   The indication may be something the consumer says or does, but it must be clear enough to be understood by the trader.

(7)   Subsections (1) to (3) do not prevent the consumer claiming damages, where it is open to the consumer to do so.

(8)   This section is subject to any usage of trade, special agreement, or course of dealing between the parties.

### 26   Instalment deliveries

(1)   Under a contract to supply goods, the consumer is not bound to accept delivery of the goods by instalments, unless that has been agreed between the consumer and the trader.

(2)   The following provisions apply if the contract provides for the goods to be delivered by stated instalments, which are to be separately paid for.

(3)   If the trader makes defective deliveries in respect of one or more instalments, the consumer, apart from any entitlement to claim damages, may be (but is not necessarily) entitled—

(a)    to exercise the short-term right to reject or the right to reject under section 19(6) (as applicable) in respect of the whole contract, or

(b)    to reject the goods in an instalment.

(4)  Whether paragraph (a) or (b) of subsection (3) (or neither) applies to a consumer depends on the terms of the contract and the circumstances of the case.

(5)  In subsection (3), making defective deliveries does not include failing to make a delivery in accordance with section 28.

(6)  If the consumer neglects or refuses to take delivery of or pay for one or more instalments, the trader may—

(a)  be entitled to treat the whole contract as at an end, or

(b)  if it is a severable breach, have a claim for damages but not a right to treat the whole contract as at an end.

(7)  Whether paragraph (a) or (b) of subsection (6) (or neither) applies to a trader depends on the terms of the contract and the circumstances of the case.

## 27  Consignation, or payment into court, in Scotland

(1)  Subsection (2) applies where—

(a)  a consumer has not rejected goods which the consumer could have rejected for breach of a term mentioned in section 19(3) or (6),

(b)  the consumer has chosen to treat the breach as giving rise only to a claim for damages or to a right to rely on the breach against a claim by the trader for the price of the goods, and

(c)  the trader has begun proceedings in court to recover the price or has brought a counter-claim for the price.

(2)  The court may require the consumer—

(a)  to consign, or pay into court, the price of the goods, or part of the price, or

(b)  to provide some other reasonable security for payment of the price.

Other rules about goods contracts.

## 28  Delivery of goods

(1)  This section applies to any sales contract.

(2)  Unless the trader and the consumer have agreed otherwise, the contract is to be treated as including a term that the trader must deliver the goods to the consumer.

(3)  Unless there is an agreed time or period, the contract is to be treated as including a term that the trader must deliver the goods—

(a)  without undue delay, and

(b)  in any event, not more than 30 days after the day on which the contract is entered into.

(4)  In this section—

(a)  an 'agreed' time or period means a time or period agreed by the trader and the consumer for delivery of the goods;

(b)  if there is an obligation to deliver the goods at the time the contract is entered into, that time counts as the 'agreed' time.

(5)  Subsections (6) and (7) apply if the trader does not deliver the goods in accordance with subsection (3) or at the agreed time or within the agreed period.

(6)  If the circumstances are that—

(a)  the trader has refused to deliver the goods,

(b)  delivery of the goods at the agreed time or within the agreed period is essential taking into account all the relevant circumstances at the time the contract was entered into, or

(c)  the consumer told the trader before the contract was entered into that delivery in accordance with subsection (3), or at the agreed time or within the agreed period, was essential,

then the consumer may treat the contract as at an end.

(7)  In any other circumstances, the consumer may specify a period that is appropriate in the circumstances and require the trader to deliver the goods before the end of that period.

(8)  If the consumer specifies a period under subsection (7) but the goods are

not delivered within that period, then the consumer may treat the contract as at an end.

(9)   If the consumer treats the contract as at an end under subsection (6) or (8), the trader must without undue delay reimburse all payments made under the contract.

(10)   If subsection (6) or (8) applies but the consumer does not treat the contract as at an end—

(a)   that does not prevent the consumer from cancelling the order for any of the goods or rejecting goods that have been delivered, and

(b)   the trader must without undue delay reimburse all payments made under the contract in respect of any goods for which the consumer cancels the order or which the consumer rejects.

(11)   If any of the goods form a commercial unit, the consumer cannot reject or cancel the order for some of those goods without also rejecting or cancelling the order for the rest of them.

(12)   A unit is a 'commercial unit' if division of the unit would materially impair the value of the goods or the character of the unit.

(13)   This section does not prevent the consumer seeking other remedies where it is open to the consumer to do so.

(14)   See section 2(5) and (6) for the application of this section where goods are sold at public auction.

## 29   Passing of risk

(1)   A sales contract is to be treated as including the following provisions as terms.

(2)   The goods remain at the trader's risk until they come into the physical possession of—

(a)   the consumer, or

(b)   a person identified by the consumer to take possession of the goods.

(3)   Subsection (2) does not apply if the goods are delivered to a carrier who—

(a)   is commissioned by the consumer to deliver the goods, and

(b)   is not a carrier the trader named as an option for the consumer.

(4)   In that case the goods are at the consumer's risk on and after delivery to the carrier.

(5)   Subsection (4) does not affect any liability of the carrier to the consumer in respect of the goods.

(6)   See section 2(5) and (6) for the application of this section where goods are sold at public auction.

## 30   Goods under guarantee

(1)   This section applies where—

(a)   there is a contract to supply goods, and

(b)   there is a guarantee in relation to the goods.

(2)   'Guarantee' here means an undertaking to the consumer given without extra charge by a person acting in the course of the person's business (the 'guarantor') that, if the goods do not meet the specifications set out in the guarantee statement or in any associated advertising—

(a)   the consumer will be reimbursed for the price paid for the goods, or

(b)   the goods will be repaired, replaced or handled in any way.

(3)   The guarantee takes effect, at the time the goods are delivered, as a contractual obligation owed by the guarantor under the conditions set out in the guarantee statement and in any associated advertising.

(4)   The guarantor must ensure that—

(a)   the guarantee sets out in plain and intelligible language the contents of the guarantee and the essential particulars for making claims under the guarantee,

(b)   the guarantee states that the consumer has statutory rights in relation to the goods and that those rights are not affected by the guarantee, and

(c)   where the goods are offered within the territory of the United Kingdom, the guarantee is written in English.

(5)   The contents of the guarantee to be set out in it include, in particular—

(a)   the name and address of the guarantor, and

(b)   the duration and territorial scope of the guarantee.

(6)   The guarantor and any other person who offers to supply to consumers the goods which are the subject of the guarantee must, on request by the consumer, make the guarantee available to the consumer within a reasonable time, in writing and in a form accessible to the consumer.

(7)   What is a reasonable time is a question of fact.

(8)   If a person fails to comply with a requirement of this section, the enforcement authority may apply to the court for an injunction or (in Scotland) an order of specific implement against that person requiring that person to comply.

(9)   On an application the court may grant an injunction or (in Scotland) an order of specific implement on such terms as it thinks appropriate.

(10)   In this section—

'court' means—

(a)   in relation to England and Wales, the High Court or the county court,

(b)   in relation to Northern Ireland, the High Court or a county court, and

(c)   in relation to Scotland, the Court of Session or the sheriff;

'enforcement authority' means—

(a)   the Competition and Markets Authority,

(b)   a local weights and measures authority in Great Britain, and

(c)   the Department of Enterprise, Trade and Investment in Northern Ireland.


*Can a trader contract out of statutory rights and remedies under a goods contract?*

### 31   Liability that cannot be excluded or restricted

(1)   A term of a contract to supply goods is not binding on the consumer to the extent that it would exclude or restrict the trader's liability arising under any of these provisions—

(a)   section 9 (goods to be of satisfactory quality);

(b)   section 10 (goods to be fit for particular purpose);

(c)   section 11 (goods to be as described);

(d)   section 12 (other pre-contract information included in contract);

(e)   section 13 (goods to match a sample);

(f)   section 14 (goods to match a model seen or examined);

(g)   section 15 (installation as part of conformity of the goods with the contract);

(h)   section 16 (goods not conforming to contract if digital content does not conform);

(i)   section 17 (trader to have right to supply the goods etc);

(j)   section 28 (delivery of goods);

(k)   section 29 (passing of risk).

(2)   That also means that a term of a contract to supply goods is not binding on the consumer to the extent that it would—

(a)   exclude or restrict a right or remedy in respect of a liability under a provision listed in subsection (1),

(b)   make such a right or remedy or its enforcement subject to a restrictive or onerous condition,

(c)   allow a trader to put a person at a disadvantage as a result of pursuing such a right or remedy, or

(d)   exclude or restrict rules of evidence or procedure.

(3)   The reference in subsection (1) to excluding or restricting a liability also includes preventing an obligation or duty arising or limiting its extent.

(4)   An agreement in writing to submit present or future differences to arbitration is not to be regarded as excluding or restricting any liability for the purposes of this section.

(5)   Subsection (1)(i), and subsection (2) so far as it relates to liability under section 17, do not apply to a term of a contract for the hire of goods.

(6)   But an express term of a contract for the hire of goods is not binding on the consumer to the extent that it would exclude or restrict a term that section 17 requires to be treated as included in the contract, unless it is inconsistent with that term (and see also section 62 (requirement for terms to be fair)).

(7)   See Schedule 3 for provision about the enforcement of this section.

## 32   Contracts applying law of non-EEA State

(1)   If—

(a)   the law of a country or territory other than an EEA State is chosen by the parties to be applicable to a sales contract, but

(b)   the sales contract has a close connection with the United Kingdom,

this Chapter, except the provisions in subsection (2), applies despite that choice.

(2)   The exceptions are—

(a)   sections 11(4) and (5) and 12;

(b)   sections 28 and 29;

(c)   section 31(1)(d), (j) and (k).

(3)   For cases where those provisions apply, or where the law applicable has not been chosen or the law of an EEA State is chosen, see Regulation (EC) No 593/2008 of the European Parliament and of the Council of 17 June 2008 on the law applicable to contractual obligations.

CHAPTER 3

Digital content

What digital content contracts are covered?

## 33   Contracts covered by this Chapter

(1)   This Chapter applies to a contract for a trader to supply digital content to a consumer, if it is supplied or to be supplied for a price paid by the consumer.

(2)   This Chapter also applies to a contract for a trader to supply digital content to a consumer, if—

(a)   it is supplied free with goods or services or other digital content for which the consumer pays a price, and

(b)   it is not generally available to consumers unless they have paid a price for it or for goods or services or other digital content.

(3)   The references in subsections (1) and (2) to the consumer paying a price include references to the consumer using, by way of payment, any facility for which money has been paid.

(4)   A trader does not supply digital content to a consumer for the purposes of this Part merely because the trader supplies a service by which digital content reaches the consumer.

(5)   The Secretary of State may by order provide for this Chapter to apply to other contracts for a trader to supply digital content to a consumer, if the Secretary of State is satisfied that it is appropriate to do so because of significant detriment caused to consumers under contracts of the kind to which the order relates.

(6)   An order under subsection (5)—

(a)   may, in particular, amend this Act;

(b)   may contain transitional or transitory provision or savings.

(7)   A contract to which this Chapter applies is referred to in this Part as a 'contract to supply digital content'.

(8)   This section, other than subsection (4), does not limit the application of section 46.

(9)   The power to make an order under subsection (5) is exercisable by statutory instrument.

(10)   No order may be made under subsection (5) unless a draft of the statutory instrument containing it has been laid before, and approved by a resolution of, each House of Parliament.

*What statutory rights are there under a digital content contract?*

## 34   Digital content to be of satisfactory quality

(1)   Every contract to supply digital content is to be treated as including a term that the quality of the digital content is satisfactory.

(2)   The quality of digital content is satisfactory if it meets the standard that a reasonable person would consider satisfactory, taking account of—

(a)   any description of the digital content,

(b)   the price mentioned in section 33(1) or (2)(b) (if relevant), and

(c)   all the other relevant circumstances (see subsection (5)).

(3)   The quality of digital content includes its state and condition; and the following aspects (among others) are in appropriate cases aspects of the quality of digital content—

(a)   fitness for all the purposes for which digital content of that kind is usually supplied;

(b)   freedom from minor defects;

(c)   safety;

(d)   durability.

(4)   The term mentioned in subsection (1) does not cover anything which makes the quality of the digital content unsatisfactory—

(a)   which is specifically drawn to the consumer's attention before the contract is made,

(b)   where the consumer examines the digital content before the contract is made, which that examination ought to reveal, or

(c)   where the consumer examines a trial version before the contract is made, which would have been apparent on a reasonable examination of the trial version.

(5)   The relevant circumstances mentioned in subsection (2)(c) include any public statement about the specific characteristics of the digital content made by the trader, the producer or any representative of the trader or the producer.

(6)   That includes, in particular, any public statement made in advertising or labelling.

(7)   But a public statement is not a relevant circumstance for the purposes of subsection (2)(c) if the trader shows that—

(a)   when the contract was made, the trader was not, and could not reasonably have been, aware of the statement,

(b)   before the contract was made, the statement had been publicly withdrawn or, to the extent that it contained anything which was incorrect or misleading, it had been publicly corrected, or

(c)   the consumer's decision to contract for the digital content could not have been influenced by the statement.

(8)   In a contract to supply digital content a term about the quality of the digital content may be treated as included as a matter of custom.

(9)   See section 42 for a consumer's rights if the trader is in breach of a term that this section requires to be treated as included in a contract.

### 35  Digital content to be fit for particular purpose

(1)   Subsection (3) applies to a contract to supply digital content if before the contract is made the consumer makes known to the trader (expressly or by implication) any particular purpose for which the consumer is contracting for the digital content.

(2)   Subsection (3) also applies to a contract to supply digital content if—

    (a)   the digital content was previously sold by a credit-broker to the trader,

    (b)   the consideration or part of it is a sum payable by instalments, and

    (c)   before the contract is made, the consumer makes known to the credit-broker (expressly or by implication) any particular purpose for which the consumer is contracting for the digital content.

(3)   The contract is to be treated as including a term that the digital content is reasonably fit for that purpose, whether or not that is a purpose for which digital content of that kind is usually supplied.

(4)   Subsection (3) does not apply if the circumstances show that the consumer does not rely, or it is unreasonable for the consumer to rely, on the skill or judgment of the trader or credit-broker.

(5)   A contract to supply digital content may be treated as making provision about the fitness of the digital content for a particular purpose as a matter of custom.

(6)   See section 42 for a consumer's rights if the trader is in breach of a term that this section requires to be treated as included in a contract.

### 36  Digital content to be as described

(1)   Every contract to supply digital content is to be treated as including a term that the digital content will match any description of it given by the trader to the consumer.

(2)   Where the consumer examines a trial version before the contract is made, it is not sufficient that the digital content matches (or is better than) the trial version if the digital content does not also match any description of it given by the trader to the consumer.

(3)   Any information that is provided by the trader about the digital content that is information mentioned in paragraph (a), (j) or (k) of Schedule 1 or paragraph (a), (v) or (w) of Schedule 2 (main characteristics, functionality and compatibility) to the Consumer Contracts (Information, Cancellation and Additional Charges) Regulations 2013 (SI 2013/3134) is to be treated as included as a term of the contract.

(4)   A change to any of that information, made before entering into the contract or later, is not effective unless expressly agreed between the consumer and the trader.

(5)   See section 42 for a consumer's rights if the trader is in breach of a term that this section requires to be treated as included in a contract.

### 37  Other pre-contract information included in contract

(1)   This section applies to any contract to supply digital content.

(2)   Where regulation 9, 10 or 13 of the Consumer Contracts (Information, Cancellation and Additional Charges) Regulations 2013 (SI 2013/3134) required the trader to provide information to the consumer before the contract became binding, any of that information that was provided by the trader other than information about the digital content and mentioned in paragraph (a), (j) or (k) of Schedule 1 or paragraph (a), (v) or (w) of Schedule 2 to the Regulations (main characteristics, functionality and compatibility) is to be treated as included as a term of the contract.

(3)   A change to any of that information, made before entering into the contract or later, is not effective unless expressly agreed between the consumer and the trader.

(4) See section 42 for a consumer's rights if the trader is in breach of a term that this section requires to be treated as included in a contract.

### 38 No other requirement to treat term about quality or fitness as included

(1) Except as provided by sections 34 and 35, a contract to supply digital content is not to be treated as including any term about the quality of the digital content or its fitness for any particular purpose, unless the term is expressly included in the contract.

(2) Subsection (1) is subject to provision made by any other enactment, whenever passed or made.

### 39 Supply by transmission and facilities for continued transmission

(1) Subsection (2) applies where there is a contract to supply digital content and the consumer's access to the content on a device requires its transmission to the device under arrangements initiated by the trader.

(2) For the purposes of this Chapter, the digital content is supplied—

(a) when the content reaches the device, or

(b) if earlier, when the content reaches another trader chosen by the consumer to supply, under a contract with the consumer, a service by which digital content reaches the device.

(3) Subsections (5) to (7) apply where—

(a) there is a contract to supply digital content, and

(b) after the trader (T) has supplied the digital content, the consumer is to have access under the contract to a processing facility under arrangements made by T.

(4) A processing facility is a facility by which T or another trader will receive digital content from the consumer and transmit digital content to the consumer (whether or not other features are to be included under the contract).

(5) The contract is to be treated as including a term that the processing facility (with any feature that the facility is to include under the contract) must be available to the consumer for a reasonable time, unless a time is specified in the contract.

(6) The following provisions apply to all digital content transmitted to the consumer on each occasion under the facility, while it is provided under the contract, as they apply to the digital content first supplied—

(a) section 34 (quality);

(b) section 35 (fitness for a particular purpose);

(c) section 36 (description).

(7) Breach of a term treated as included under subsection (5) has the same effect as breach of a term treated as included under those sections (see section 42).

### 40 Quality, fitness and description of content supplied subject to modifications

(1) Where under a contract a trader supplies digital content to a consumer subject to the right of the trader or a third party to modify the digital content, the following provisions apply in relation to the digital content as modified as they apply in relation to the digital content as supplied under the contract—

(a) section 34 (quality);

(b) section 35 (fitness for a particular purpose);

(c) section 36 (description).

(2) Subsection (1)(c) does not prevent the trader from improving the features of, or adding new features to, the digital content, as long as—

(a) the digital content continues to match the description of it given by the trader to the consumer, and

(b) the digital content continues to conform to the information provided by the trader as mentioned in subsection (3) of section 36, subject to any change to that information that has been agreed in accordance with subsection (4) of that section.

(3)   A claim on the grounds that digital content does not conform to a term described in any of the sections listed in subsection (1) as applied by that subsection is to be treated as arising at the time when the digital content was supplied under the contract and not the time when it is modified.

### 41   Trader's right to supply digital content

(1)   Every contract to supply digital content is to be treated as including a term—

    (a)   in relation to any digital content which is supplied under the contract and which the consumer has paid for, that the trader has the right to supply that content to the consumer;

    (b)   in relation to any digital content which the trader agrees to supply under the contract and which the consumer has paid for, that the trader will have the right to supply it to the consumer at the time when it is to be supplied.

(2)   See section 42 for a consumer's rights if the trader is in breach of a term that this section requires to be treated as included in a contract.

*What remedies are there if statutory rights under a digital content contract are not met?*

### 42   Consumer's rights to enforce terms about digital content

(1)   In this section and section 43 references to digital content conforming to a contract are references to the digital content conforming to the terms described in sections 34, 35 and 36.

(2)   If the digital content does not conform to the contract, the consumer's rights (and the provisions about them and when they are available) are—

    (a)   the right to repair or replacement (see section 43);

    (b)   the right to a price reduction (see section 44).

(3)   Section 16 also applies if an item including the digital content is supplied.

(4)   If the trader is in breach of a term that section 37 requires to be treated as included in the contract, the consumer has the right to recover from the trader the amount of any costs incurred by the consumer as a result of the breach, up to the amount of the price paid for the digital content or for any facility within section 33(3) used by the consumer.

(5)   If the trader is in breach of the term that section 41(1) (right to supply the content) requires to be treated as included in the contract, the consumer has the right to a refund (see section 45 for provisions about that right and when it is available).

(6)   This Chapter does not prevent the consumer seeking other remedies for a breach of a term to which any of subsections (2), (4) or (5) applies, instead of or in addition to a remedy referred to there (but not so as to recover twice for the same loss).

(7)   Those other remedies include any of the following that is open to the consumer in the circumstances—

    (a)   claiming damages;

    (b)   seeking to recover money paid where the consideration for payment of the money has failed;

    (c)   seeking specific performance;

    (d)   seeking an order for specific implement;

    (e)   relying on the breach against a claim by the trader for the price.

(8)   It is not open to the consumer to treat the contract as at an end for breach of a term to which any of subsections (2), (4) or (5) applies.

(9)   For the purposes of subsection (2), digital content which does not conform to the contract at any time within the period of six months beginning with the day

on which it was supplied must be taken not to have conformed to the contract when it was supplied.

(10)   Subsection (9) does not apply if—

(a)   it is established that the digital content did conform to the contract when it was supplied, or

(b)   its application is incompatible with the nature of the digital content or with how it fails to conform to the contract.

### 43   Right to repair or replacement

(1)   This section applies if the consumer has the right to repair or replacement.

(2)   If the consumer requires the trader to repair or replace the digital content, the trader must—

(a)   do so within a reasonable time and without significant inconvenience to the consumer; and

(b)   bear any necessary costs incurred in doing so (including in particular the cost of any labour, materials or postage).

(3)   The consumer cannot require the trader to repair or replace the digital content if that remedy (the repair or the replacement)—

(a)   is impossible, or

(b)   is disproportionate compared to the other of those remedies.

(4)   Either of those remedies is disproportionate compared to the other if it imposes costs on the trader which, compared to those imposed by the other, are unreasonable, taking into account—

(a)   the value which the digital content would have if it conformed to the contract,

(b)   the significance of the lack of conformity, and

(c)   whether the other remedy could be effected without significant inconvenience to the consumer.

(5)   Any question as to what is a reasonable time or significant inconvenience is to be determined taking account of—

(a)   the nature of the digital content, and

(b)   the purpose for which the digital content was obtained or accessed.

(6)   A consumer who requires or agrees to the repair of digital content cannot require the trader to replace it without giving the trader a reasonable time to repair it (unless giving the trader that time would cause significant inconvenience to the consumer).

(7)   A consumer who requires or agrees to the replacement of digital content cannot require the trader to repair it without giving the trader a reasonable time to replace it (unless giving the trader that time would cause significant inconvenience to the consumer).

(8)   In this Chapter, 'repair' in relation to digital content that does not conform to a contract, means making it conform.

### 44   Right to price reduction

(1)   The right to a price reduction is the right to require the trader to reduce the price to the consumer by an appropriate amount (including the right to receive a refund for anything already paid above the reduced amount).

(2)   The amount of the reduction may, where appropriate, be the full amount of the price.

(3)   A consumer who has that right may only exercise it in one of these situations—

(a)   because of section 43(3)(a) the consumer can require neither repair nor replacement of the digital content, or

(b)   the consumer has required the trader to repair or replace the digital content, but the trader is in breach of the requirement of section 43(2)(a) to do so within a reasonable time and without significant inconvenience to the consumer.

(4)   A refund under this section must be given without undue delay, and in any

event within 14 days beginning with the day on which the trader agrees that the consumer is entitled to a refund.

(5)  The trader must give the refund using the same means of payment as the consumer used to pay for the digital content, unless the consumer expressly agrees otherwise.

(6)  The trader must not impose any fee on the consumer in respect of the refund.

### 45  Right to a refund

(1)  The right to a refund gives the consumer the right to receive a refund from the trader of all money paid by the consumer for the digital content (subject to subsection (2)).

(2)  If the breach giving the consumer the right to a refund affects only some of the digital content supplied under the contract, the right to a refund does not extend to any part of the price attributable to digital content that is not affected by the breach.

(3)  A refund must be given without undue delay, and in any event within 14 days beginning with the day on which the trader agrees that the consumer is entitled to a refund.

(4)  The trader must give the refund using the same means of payment as the consumer used to pay for the digital content, unless the consumer expressly agrees otherwise.

(5)  The trader must not impose any fee on the consumer in respect of the refund.

Compensation for damage to device or to other digital content

### 46  Remedy for damage to device or to other digital content

(1)  This section applies if—

  (a)  a trader supplies digital content to a consumer under a contract,

  (b)  the digital content causes damage to a device or to other digital content,

  (c)  the device or digital content that is damaged belongs to the consumer, and

  (d)  the damage is of a kind that would not have occurred if the trader had exercised reasonable care and skill.

(2)  If the consumer requires the trader to provide a remedy under this section, the trader must either—

  (a)  repair the damage in accordance with subsection (3), or

  (b)  compensate the consumer for the damage with an appropriate payment.

(3)  To repair the damage in accordance with this subsection, the trader must—

  (a)  repair the damage within a reasonable time and without significant inconvenience to the consumer, and

  (b)  bear any necessary costs incurred in repairing the damage (including in particular the cost of any labour, materials or postage).

(4)  Any question as to what is a reasonable time or significant inconvenience is to be determined taking account of—

  (a)  the nature of the device or digital content that is damaged, and

  (b)  the purpose for which it is used by the consumer.

(5)  A compensation payment under this section must be made without undue delay, and in any event within 14 days beginning with the day on which the trader agrees that the consumer is entitled to the payment.

(6)  The trader must not impose any fee on the consumer in respect of the payment.

(7)  A consumer with a right to a remedy under this section may bring a claim in civil proceedings to enforce that right.

(8)  The Limitation Act 1980 and the Limitation (Northern Ireland) Order 1989 (SI 1989/1339 (NI 11)) apply to a claim under this section as if it were an action founded on simple contract.

(9)  The Prescription and Limitation (Scotland) Act 1973 applies to a right to a remedy under this section as if it were an obligation to which section 6 of that Act applies.

*Can a trader contract out of statutory rights and remedies under a digital content contract?*

## 47  Liability that cannot be excluded or restricted

(1)  A term of a contract to supply digital content is not binding on the consumer to the extent that it would exclude or restrict the trader's liability arising under any of these provisions—

(a)  section 34 (digital content to be of satisfactory quality),

(b)  section 35 (digital content to be fit for particular purpose),

(c)  section 36 (digital content to be as described),

(d)  section 37 (other pre-contract information included in contract), or

(e)  section 41 (trader's right to supply digital content).

(2)  That also means that a term of a contract to supply digital content is not binding on the consumer to the extent that it would—

(a)  exclude or restrict a right or remedy in respect of a liability under a provision listed in subsection (1),

(b)  make such a right or remedy or its enforcement subject to a restrictive or onerous condition,

(c)  allow a trader to put a person at a disadvantage as a result of pursuing such a right or remedy, or

(d)  exclude or restrict rules of evidence or procedure.

(3)  The reference in subsection (1) to excluding or restricting a liability also includes preventing an obligation or duty arising or limiting its extent.

(4)  An agreement in writing to submit present or future differences to arbitration is not to be regarded as excluding or restricting any liability for the purposes of this section.

(5)  See Schedule 3 for provision about the enforcement of this section.

(6)  For provision limiting the ability of a trader under a contract within section 46 to exclude or restrict the trader's liability under that section, see section 62.

## CHAPTER 4
### Services

*What services contracts are covered?*

## 48  Contracts covered by this Chapter

(1)  This Chapter applies to a contract for a trader to supply a service to a consumer.

(2)  That does not include a contract of employment or apprenticeship.

(3)  In relation to Scotland, this Chapter does not apply to a gratuitous contract.

(4)  A contract to which this Chapter applies is referred to in this Part as a 'contract to supply a service'.

(5)  The Secretary of State may by order made by statutory instrument provide that a provision of this Chapter does not apply in relation to a service of a description specified in the order.

(6)  The power in subsection (5) includes power to provide that a provision of this Chapter does not apply in relation to a service of a description specified in the order in the circumstances so specified.

(7)  An order under subsection (5) may contain transitional or transitory provision or savings.

(8)  No order may be made under subsection (5) unless a draft of the statutory

instrument containing it has been laid before, and approved by a resolution of, each House of Parliament.

*What statutory rights are there under a services contract?*

### 49  Service to be performed with reasonable care and skill

(1)  Every contract to supply a service is to be treated as including a term that the trader must perform the service with reasonable care and skill.

(2)  See section 54 for a consumer's rights if the trader is in breach of a term that this section requires to be treated as included in a contract.

### 50  Information about the trader or service to be binding

(1)  Every contract to supply a service is to be treated as including as a term of the contract anything that is said or written to the consumer, by or on behalf of the trader, about the trader or the service, if—

    (a)  it is taken into account by the consumer when deciding to enter into the contract, or

    (b)  it is taken into account by the consumer when making any decision about the service after entering into the contract.

(2)  Anything taken into account by the consumer as mentioned in subsection (1)(a) or (b) is subject to—

    (a)  anything that qualified it and was said or written to the consumer by the trader on the same occasion, and

    (b)  any change to it that has been expressly agreed between the consumer and the trader (before entering into the contract or later).

(3)  Without prejudice to subsection (1), any information provided by the trader in accordance with regulation 9, 10 or 13 of the Consumer Contracts (Information, Cancellation and Additional Charges) Regulations 2013 (SI 2013/3134) is to be treated as included as a term of the contract.

(4)  A change to any of the information mentioned in subsection (3), made before entering into the contract or later, is not effective unless expressly agreed between the consumer and the trader.

(5)  See section 54 for a consumer's rights if the trader is in breach of a term that this section requires to be treated as included in a contract.

### 51  Reasonable price to be paid for a service

(1)  This section applies to a contract to supply a service if—

    (a)  the consumer has not paid a price or other consideration for the service,

    (b)  the contract does not expressly fix a price or other consideration, and does not say how it is to be fixed, and

    (c)  anything that is to be treated under section 50 as included in the contract does not fix a price or other consideration either.

(2)  In that case the contract is to be treated as including a term that the consumer must pay a reasonable price for the service, and no more.

(3)  What is a reasonable price is a question of fact.

### 52  Service to be performed within a reasonable time

(1)  This section applies to a contract to supply a service, if—

    (a)  the contract does not expressly fix the time for the service to be performed, and does not say how it is to be fixed, and

    (b)  information that is to be treated under section 50 as included in the contract does not fix the time either.

(2)  In that case the contract is to be treated as including a term that the trader must perform the service within a reasonable time.

(3)  What is a reasonable time is a question of fact.

(4)  See section 54 for a consumer's rights if the trader is in breach of a term that this section requires to be treated as included in a contract.

### 53 Relation to other law on contract terms

(1) Nothing in this Chapter affects any enactment or rule of law that imposes a stricter duty on the trader.

(2) This Chapter is subject to any other enactment which defines or restricts the rights, duties or liabilities arising in connection with a service of any description.

*What remedies are there if statutory rights under a services contract are not met?*

### 54 Consumer's rights to enforce terms about services

(1) The consumer's rights under this section and sections 55 and 56 do not affect any rights that the contract provides for, if those are not inconsistent.

(2) In this section and section 55 a reference to a service conforming to a contract is a reference to—

    (a) the service being performed in accordance with section 49, or

    (b) the service conforming to a term that section 50 requires to be treated as included in the contract and that relates to the performance of the service.

(3) If the service does not conform to the contract, the consumer's rights (and the provisions about them and when they are available) are—

    (a) the right to require repeat performance (see section 55);

    (b) the right to a price reduction (see section 56).

(4) If the trader is in breach of a term that section 50 requires to be treated as included in the contract but that does not relate to the service, the consumer has the right to a price reduction (see section 56 for provisions about that right and when it is available).

(5) If the trader is in breach of what the contract requires under section 52 (performance within a reasonable time), the consumer has the right to a price reduction (see section 56 for provisions about that right and when it is available).

(6) This section and sections 55 and 56 do not prevent the consumer seeking other remedies for a breach of a term to which any of subsections (3) to (5) applies, instead of or in addition to a remedy referred to there (but not so as to recover twice for the same loss).

(7) Those other remedies include any of the following that is open to the consumer in the circumstances—

    (a) claiming damages;

    (b) seeking to recover money paid where the consideration for payment of the money has failed;

    (c) seeking specific performance;

    (d) seeking an order for specific implement;

    (e) relying on the breach against a claim by the trader under the contract;

    (f) exercising a right to treat the contract as at an end.

### 55 Right to repeat performance

(1) The right to require repeat performance is a right to require the trader to perform the service again, to the extent necessary to complete its performance in conformity with the contract.

(2) If the consumer requires such repeat performance, the trader—

    (a) must provide it within a reasonable time and without significant inconvenience to the consumer; and

    (b) must bear any necessary costs incurred in doing so (including in particular the cost of any labour or materials).

(3) The consumer cannot require repeat performance if completing performance of the service in conformity with the contract is impossible.

(4) Any question as to what is a reasonable time or significant inconvenience is to be determined taking account of—

    (a) the nature of the service, and

    (b) the purpose for which the service was to be performed.

**56  Right to price reduction**

(1)   The right to a price reduction is the right to require the trader to reduce the price to the consumer by an appropriate amount (including the right to receive a refund for anything already paid above the reduced amount).

(2)   The amount of the reduction may, where appropriate, be the full amount of the price.

(3)   A consumer who has that right and the right to require repeat performance is only entitled to a price reduction in one of these situations—

(a)   because of section 55(3) the consumer cannot require repeat performance; or

(b)   the consumer has required repeat performance, but the trader is in breach of the requirement of section 55(2)(a) to do it within a reasonable time and without significant inconvenience to the consumer.

(4)   A refund under this section must be given without undue delay, and in any event within 14 days beginning with the day on which the trader agrees that the consumer is entitled to a refund.

(5)   The trader must give the refund using the same means of payment as the consumer used to pay for the service, unless the consumer expressly agrees otherwise.

(6)   The trader must not impose any fee on the consumer in respect of the refund.

*Can a trader contract out of statutory rights and remedies under a services contract?*

**57  Liability that cannot be excluded or restricted**

(1)   A term of a contract to supply services is not binding on the consumer to the extent that it would exclude the trader's liability arising under section 49 (service to be performed with reasonable care and skill).

(2)   Subject to section 50(2), a term of a contract to supply services is not binding on the consumer to the extent that it would exclude the trader's liability arising under section 50 (information about trader or service to be binding).

(3)   A term of a contract to supply services is not binding on the consumer to the extent that it would restrict the trader's liability arising under any of sections 49 and 50 and, where they apply, sections 51 and 52 (reasonable price and reasonable time), if it would prevent the consumer in an appropriate case from recovering the price paid or the value of any other consideration. (If it would not prevent the consumer from doing so, Part 2 (unfair terms) may apply.)

(4)   That also means that a term of a contract to supply services is not binding on the consumer to the extent that it would —

(a)   exclude or restrict a right or remedy in respect of a liability under any of sections 49 to 52,

(b)   make such a right or remedy or its enforcement subject to a restrictive or onerous condition,

(c)   allow a trader to put a person at a disadvantage as a result of pursuing such a right or remedy, or

(d)   exclude or restrict rules of evidence or procedure.

(5)   The references in subsections (1) to (3) to excluding or restricting a liability also include preventing an obligation or duty arising or limiting its extent.

(6)   An agreement in writing to submit present or future differences to arbitration is not to be regarded as excluding or restricting any liability for the purposes of this section.

(7)   See Schedule 3 for provision about the enforcement of this section.

## CHAPTER 5
### General and supplementary provisions

**58   Powers of the court**

(1)   In any proceedings in which a remedy is sought by virtue of section 19(3) or (4), 42(2) or 54(3), the court, in addition to any other power it has, may act under this section.

(2)   On the application of the consumer the court may make an order requiring specific performance or, in Scotland, specific implement by the trader of any obligation imposed on the trader by virtue of section 23, 43 or 55.

(3)   Subsection (4) applies if—

(a)   the consumer claims to exercise a right under the relevant remedies provisions, but

(b)   the court decides that those provisions have the effect that exercise of another right is appropriate.

(4)   The court may proceed as if the consumer had exercised that other right.

(5)   If the consumer has claimed to exercise the final right to reject, the court may order that any reimbursement to the consumer is reduced by a deduction for use, to take account of the use the consumer has had of the goods in the period since they were delivered.

(6)   Any deduction for use is limited as set out in section 24(9) and (10).

(7)   The court may make an order under this section unconditionally or on such terms and conditions as to damages, payment of the price and otherwise as it thinks just.

(8)   The 'relevant remedies provisions' are—

(a)   where Chapter 2 applies, sections 23 and 24;

(b)   where Chapter 3 applies, sections 43 and 44;

(c)   where Chapter 4 applies, sections 55 and 56.

**59   Interpretation**

(1)   These definitions apply in this Part (as well as the key definitions in section 2)—

'conditional sales contract' has the meaning given in section 5(3);

'Consumer Rights Directive' means Directive 2011/83/EU of the European Parliament and of the Council of 25 October 2011 on consumer rights, amending Council Directive 93/13/EEC and Directive 1999/44/EC of the European Parliament and of the Council and repealing Council Directive 85/577/EEC and Directive 97/7/EC of the European Parliament and of the Council;

'credit-broker' means a person acting in the course of a business of credit brokerage carried on by that person;

'credit brokerage' means—

(a)   introducing individuals who want to obtain credit to persons carrying on any business so far as it relates to the provision of credit,

(b)   introducing individuals who want to obtain goods on hire to persons carrying on a business which comprises or relates to supplying goods under a contract for the hire of goods, or

(c)   introducing individuals who want to obtain credit, or to obtain goods on hire, to other persons engaged in credit brokerage;

'delivery' means voluntary transfer of possession from one person to another;

'enactment' includes—

(a)   an enactment contained in subordinate legislation within the meaning of the Interpretation Act 1978,

(b)   an enactment contained in, or in an instrument made under, a Measure or Act of the National Assembly for Wales,

(c)   an enactment contained in, or in an instrument made under, an Act of the Scottish Parliament, and

(d)   an enactment contained in, or in an instrument made under, Northern Ireland legislation;

'producer', in relation to goods or digital content, means—

(a)   the manufacturer,

(b)   the importer into the European Economic Area, or

(c)   any person who purports to be a producer by placing the person's name, trade mark or other distinctive sign on the goods or using it in connection with the digital content.

(2)   References in this Part to treating a contract as at an end are to be read in accordance with section 19(13).

## 60   Changes to other legislation

Schedule 1 (amendments consequential on this Part) has effect.

## PART 2
## UNFAIR TERMS

*What contracts and notices are covered by this Part?*

## 61   Contracts and notices covered by this Part

(1)   This Part applies to a contract between a trader and a consumer.

(2)   This does not include a contract of employment or apprenticeship.

(3)   A contract to which this Part applies is referred to in this Part as a 'consumer contract'.

(4)   This Part applies to a notice to the extent that it—

(a)   relates to rights or obligations as between a trader and a consumer, or

(b)   purports to exclude or restrict a trader's liability to a consumer.

(5)   This does not include a notice relating to rights, obligations or liabilities as between an employer and an employee.

(6)   It does not matter for the purposes of subsection (4) whether the notice is expressed to apply to a consumer, as long as it is reasonable to assume it is intended to be seen or heard by a consumer.

(7)   A notice to which this Part applies is referred to in this Part as a 'consumer notice'.

(8)   In this section 'notice' includes an announcement, whether or not in writing, and any other communication or purported communication.

*What are the general rules about fairness of contract terms and notices?*

## 62   Requirement for contract terms and notices to be fair

(1)   An unfair term of a consumer contract is not binding on the consumer.

(2)   An unfair consumer notice is not binding on the consumer.

(3)   This does not prevent the consumer from relying on the term or notice if the consumer chooses to do so.

(4)   A term is unfair if, contrary to the requirement of good faith, it causes a significant imbalance in the parties' rights and obligations under the contract to the detriment of the consumer.

(5)   Whether a term is fair is to be determined—

(a)   taking into account the nature of the subject matter of the contract, and

(b)   by reference to all the circumstances existing when the term was agreed and to all of the other terms of the contract or of any other contract on which it depends.

(6)   A notice is unfair if, contrary to the requirement of good faith, it causes a significant imbalance in the parties' rights and obligations to the detriment of the consumer.

(7)   Whether a notice is fair is to be determined—

(a)    taking into account the nature of the subject matter of the notice, and

(b)    by reference to all the circumstances existing when the rights or obligations to which it relates arose and to the terms of any contract on which it depends.

(8)    This section does not affect the operation of—

(a)    section 31 (exclusion of liability: goods contracts),

(b)    section 47 (exclusion of liability: digital content contracts),

(c)    section 57 (exclusion of liability: services contracts), or

(d)    section 65 (exclusion of negligence liability).

## 63  Contract terms which may or must be regarded as unfair

(1)    Part 1 of Schedule 2 contains an indicative and non-exhaustive list of terms of consumer contracts that may be regarded as unfair for the purposes of this Part.

(2)    Part 1 of Schedule 2 is subject to Part 2 of that Schedule; but a term listed in Part 2 of that Schedule may nevertheless be assessed for fairness under section 62 unless section 64 or 73 applies to it.

(3)    The Secretary of State may by order made by statutory instrument amend Schedule 2 so as to add, modify or remove an entry in Part 1 or Part 2 of that Schedule.

(4)    An order under subsection (3) may contain transitional or transitory provision or savings.

(5)    No order may be made under subsection (3) unless a draft of the statutory instrument containing it has been laid before, and approved by a resolution of, each House of Parliament.

(6)    A term of a consumer contract must be regarded as unfair if it has the effect that the consumer bears the burden of proof with respect to compliance by a distance supplier or an intermediary with an obligation under any enactment or rule implementing the Distance Marketing Directive.

(7)    In subsection (6)—

'the Distance Marketing Directive' means Directive 2002/65/EC of the European Parliament and of the Council of 23 September 2002 concerning the distance marketing of consumer financial services and amending Council Directive 90/619/EEC and Directives 97/7/EC and 98/27/EC;

'distance supplier' means—

(a)    a supplier under a distance contract within the meaning of the Financial Services (Distance Marketing) Regulations 2004 (SI 2004/2095), or

(b)    a supplier of unsolicited financial services within the meaning of regulation 15 of those regulations;

'enactment' includes an enactment contained in subordinate legislation within the meaning of the Interpretation Act 1978;

'intermediary' has the same meaning as in the Financial Services (Distance Marketing) Regulations 2004;

'rule' means a rule made by the Financial Conduct Authority or the Prudential Regulation Authority under the Financial Services and Markets Act 2000 or by a designated professional body within the meaning of section 326(2) of that Act.

## 64  Exclusion from assessment of fairness

(1)    A term of a consumer contract may not be assessed for fairness under section 62 to the extent that—

(a)    it specifies the main subject matter of the contract, or

(b)    the assessment is of the appropriateness of the price payable under the contract by comparison with the goods, digital content or services supplied under it.

(2)    Subsection (1) excludes a term from an assessment under section 62 only if it is transparent and prominent.

(3)    A term is transparent for the purposes of this Part if it is expressed in plain and intelligible language and (in the case of a written term) is legible.

(4)  A term is prominent for the purposes of this section if it is brought to the consumer's attention in such a way that an average consumer would be aware of the term.

(5)  In subsection (4) 'average consumer' means a consumer who is reasonably well-informed, observant and circumspect.

(6)  This section does not apply to a term of a contract listed in Part 1 of Schedule 2.

### 65  Bar on exclusion or restriction of negligence liability

(1)  A trader cannot by a term of a consumer contract or by a consumer notice exclude or restrict liability for death or personal injury resulting from negligence.

(2)  Where a term of a consumer contract, or a consumer notice, purports to exclude or restrict a trader's liability for negligence, a person is not to be taken to have voluntarily accepted any risk merely because the person agreed to or knew about the term or notice.

(3)  In this section 'personal injury' includes any disease and any impairment of physical or mental condition.

(4)  In this section 'negligence' means the breach of—

(a)  any obligation to take reasonable care or exercise reasonable skill in the performance of a contract where the obligation arises from an express or implied term of the contract,

(b)  a common law duty to take reasonable care or exercise reasonable skill,

(c)  the common duty of care imposed by the Occupiers' Liability Act 1957 or the Occupiers' Liability Act (Northern Ireland) 1957, or

(d)  the duty of reasonable care imposed by section 2(1) of the Occupiers' Liability (Scotland) Act 1960.

(5)  It is immaterial for the purposes of subsection (4)—

(a)  whether a breach of duty or obligation was inadvertent or intentional, or

(b)  whether liability for it arises directly or vicariously.

(6)  This section is subject to section 66 (which makes provision about the scope of this section).

### 66  Scope of section 65

(1)  Section 65 does not apply to—

(a)  any contract so far as it is a contract of insurance, including a contract to pay an annuity on human life, or

(b)  any contract so far as it relates to the creation or transfer of an interest in land.

(2)  Section 65 does not affect the validity of any discharge or indemnity given by a person in consideration of the receipt by that person of compensation in settlement of any claim the person has.

(3)  Section 65 does not—

(a)  apply to liability which is excluded or discharged as mentioned in section 4(2)(a) (exception to liability to pay damages to relatives) of the Damages (Scotland) Act 2011, or

(b)  affect the operation of section 5 (discharge of liability to pay damages: exception for mesothelioma) of that Act.

(4)  Section 65 does not apply to the liability of an occupier of premises to a person who obtains access to the premises for recreational purposes if—

(a)  the person suffers loss or damage because of the dangerous state of the premises, and

(b)  allowing the person access for those purposes is not within the purposes of the occupier's trade, business, craft or profession.

### 67  Effect of an unfair term on the rest of a contract

Where a term of a consumer contract is not binding on the consumer as a result of this Part, the contract continues, so far as practicable, to have effect in every other respect.

### 68 Requirement for transparency

(1)   A trader must ensure that a written term of a consumer contract, or a consumer notice in writing, is transparent.

(2)   A consumer notice is transparent for the purposes of subsection (1) if it is expressed in plain and intelligible language and it is legible.

### 69 Contract terms that may have different meanings

(1)   If a term in a consumer contract, or a consumer notice, could have different meanings, the meaning that is most favourable to the consumer is to prevail.

(2)   Subsection (1) does not apply to the construction of a term or a notice in proceedings on an application for an injunction or interdict under paragraph 3 of Schedule 3.

*How are the general rules enforced?*

### 70 Enforcement of the law on unfair contract terms

(1)   Schedule 3 confers functions on the Competition and Markets Authority and other regulators in relation to the enforcement of this Part.

(2)   For provision about the investigatory powers that are available to those regulators for the purposes of that Schedule, see Schedule 5.

*Supplementary provisions*

### 71 Duty of court to consider fairness of term

(1)   Subsection (2) applies to proceedings before a court which relate to a term of a consumer contract.

(2)   The court must consider whether the term is fair even if none of the parties to the proceedings has raised that issue or indicated that it intends to raise it.

(3)   But subsection (2) does not apply unless the court considers that it has before it sufficient legal and factual material to enable it to consider the fairness of the term.

### 72 Application of rules to secondary contracts

(1)   This section applies if a term of a contract ('the secondary contract') reduces the rights or remedies or increases the obligations of a person under another contract ('the main contract').

(2)   The term is subject to the provisions of this Part that would apply to the term if it were in the main contract.

(3)   It does not matter for the purposes of this section—

    (a)   whether the parties to the secondary contract are the same as the parties to the main contract, or

    (b)   whether the secondary contract is a consumer contract.

(4)   This section does not apply if the secondary contract is a settlement of a claim arising under the main contract.

### 73 Disapplication of rules to mandatory terms and notices

(1)   This Part does not apply to a term of a contract, or to a notice, to the extent that it reflects—

    (a)   mandatory statutory or regulatory provisions, or

    (b)   the provisions or principles of an international convention to which the United Kingdom or the EU is a party.

(2)   In subsection (1) 'mandatory statutory or regulatory provisions' includes rules which, according to law, apply between the parties on the basis that no other arrangements have been established.

**74  Contracts applying law of non-EEA State**

(1)  If—

  (a)   the law of a country or territory other than an EEA State is chosen by the parties to be applicable to a consumer contract, but

  (b)   the consumer contract has a close connection with the United Kingdom, this Part applies despite that choice.

(2)  For cases where the law applicable has not been chosen or the law of an EEA State is chosen, see Regulation (EC) No. 593/2008 of the European Parliament and of the Council of 17 June 2008 on the law applicable to contractual obligations.

**75  Changes to other legislation**

Schedule 4 (amendments consequential on this Part) has effect.

**76  Interpretation of Part 2**

(1)   In this Part—

'consumer contract' has the meaning given by section 61(3);

'consumer notice' has the meaning given by section 61(7);

'transparent' is to be construed in accordance with sections 64(3) and 68(2).

(2)   The following have the same meanings in this Part as they have in Part 1—

'trader' (see section 2(2));

'consumer' (see section 2(3));

'goods' (see section 2(8));

'digital content' (see section 2(9)).

(3)   Section 2(4) (trader who claims an individual is not a consumer must prove it) applies in relation to this Part as it applies in relation to Part 1.

## PART 3
## MISCELLANEOUS AND GENERAL

### CHAPTER 1
### Enforcement etc

**77  Investigatory powers etc**

(1)   Schedule 5 (investigatory powers etc) has effect.

(2)   Schedule 6 (investigatory powers: consequential amendments) has effect.

[**78**   *Amends weights and measures legislation regarding unwrapped bread*]

[**79**   *Amends Enterprise Act 2002*]

[**80**   *Amends Communications Act 2003*]

### CHAPTER 2
### Competition

**81  Private actions in competition law**

Schedule 8 (private actions in competition law) has effect.

[**82**   *Amends Enterprise Act 2002*]

. . .

### CHAPTER 5
### Secondary ticketing

**90  Duty to provide information about tickets**

(1)  This section applies where a person ('the seller') re-sells a ticket for a recreational, sporting or cultural event in the United Kingdom through a secondary ticketing facility.

(2) The seller and each operator of the facility must ensure that the person who buys the ticket ('the buyer') is given the information specified in subsection (3), where this is applicable to the ticket.

(3) That information is—

(a) where the ticket is for a particular seat or standing area at the venue for the event, the information necessary to enable the buyer to identify that seat or standing area,

(b) information about any restriction which limits use of the ticket to persons of a particular description, and

(c) the face value of the ticket.

(4) The reference in subsection (3)(a) to information necessary to enable the buyer to identify a seat or standing area at a venue includes, so far as applicable—

(a) the name of the area in the venue in which the seat or standing area is located (for example the name of the stand in which it is located),

(b) information necessary to enable the buyer to identify the part of the area in the venue in which the seat or standing area is located (for example the block of seats in which the seat is located),

(c) the number, letter or other distinguishing mark of the row in which the seat is located, and

(d) the number, letter or other distinguishing mark of the seat.

(5) The reference in subsection (3)(c) to the face value of the ticket is to the amount stated on the ticket as its price.

(6) The seller and each operator of the facility must ensure that the buyer is given the information specified in subsection (7), where the seller is—

(a) an operator of the secondary ticketing facility,

(b) a person who is a parent undertaking or a subsidiary undertaking in relation to an operator of the secondary ticketing facility,

(c) a person who is employed or engaged by an operator of the secondary ticketing facility,

(d) a person who is acting on behalf of a person within paragraph (c), or

(e) an organiser of the event or a person acting on behalf of an organiser of the event.

(7) That information is a statement that the seller of the ticket is a person within subsection (6) which specifies the ground on which the seller falls within that subsection.

(8) Information required by this section to be given to the buyer must be given—

(a) in a clear and comprehensible manner, and

(b) before the buyer is bound by the contract for the sale of the ticket

(9) This section applies in relation to the re-sale of a ticket through a secondary ticketing facility only if the ticket is first offered for re-sale through the facility after the coming into force of this section.

## 91 Prohibition on cancellation or blacklisting

(1) This section applies where a person ('the seller') re-sells, or offers for re-sale, a ticket for a recreational, sporting or cultural event in the United Kingdom through a secondary ticketing facility.

(2) An organiser of the event must not cancel the ticket merely because the seller has re-sold the ticket or offered it for re-sale unless—

(a) a term of the original contract for the sale of the ticket—

(i) provided for its cancellation if it was re-sold by the buyer under that contract,

(ii) provided for its cancellation if it was offered for re-sale by that buyer, or

(iii) provided as mentioned in sub-paragraph (i) and (ii), and

(b) that term was not unfair for the purposes of Part 2 (unfair terms).

(3)   An organiser of the event must not blacklist the seller merely because the seller has re-sold the ticket or offered it for re-sale unless—

(a)   a term of the original contract for the sale of the ticket—

(i)   provided for the blacklisting of the buyer under that contract if it was re-sold by that buyer,

(ii)   provided for the blacklisting of that buyer if it was offered for re-sale by that buyer, or

(iii)   provided as mentioned in sub-paragraph (i) and (ii), and

(b)   that term was not unfair for the purposes of Part 2 (unfair terms).

(4)   In subsections (2) and (3) 'the original contract' means the contract for the sale of the ticket by an organiser of the event to a person other than an organiser of the event.

(5)   For the purposes of this section an organiser of an event cancels a ticket if the organiser takes steps which result in the holder for the time being of the ticket no longer being entitled to attend that event.

(6)   For the purposes of this section an organiser of an event blacklists a person if the organiser takes steps—

(a)   to prevent the person from acquiring a ticket for a recreational, sporting or cultural event in the United Kingdom, or

(b)   to restrict the person's opportunity to acquire such a ticket.

(7)   Part 2 (unfair terms) may apply to a term of a contract which, apart from that Part, would permit the cancellation of a ticket for a recreational, sporting or cultural event in the United Kingdom, or the blacklisting of the seller of such a ticket, in circumstances other than those mentioned in subsection (2) or (3).

(8)   Before the coming into force of Part 2, references to that Part in this section are to be read as references to the Unfair Terms in Consumer Contracts Regulations 1999 (SI 1999/2083).

(9)   This section applies in relation to a ticket that is re-sold or offered for re-sale before or after the coming into force of this section; but the prohibition in this section applies only to things done after its coming into force.

**92   Duty to report criminal activity**

(1)   This section applies where—

(a)   an operator of a secondary ticketing facility knows that a person has used or is using the facility in such a way that an offence has been or is being committed, and

(b)   the offence relates to the re-sale of a ticket for a recreational, sporting or cultural event in the United Kingdom.

(2)   The operator must, as soon as the operator becomes aware that a person has used or is using the facility as mentioned in subsection (1), disclose the matters specified in subsection (3) to—

(a)   an appropriate person, and

(b)   an organiser of the event (subject to subsection (5)).

(3)   Those matters are—

(a)   the identity of the person mentioned in subsection (1), if this is known to the operator, and

(b)   the fact that the operator knows that an offence has been or is being committed as mentioned in that subsection.

(4)   The following are appropriate persons for the purposes of this section—

(a)   a constable of a police force in England and Wales,

(b)   a constable of the police service of Scotland, and

(c)   a police officer within the meaning of the Police (Northern Ireland) Act 2000.

(5)   This section does not require an operator to make a disclosure to an organiser of an event if the operator has reasonable grounds for believing that to do so will prejudice the investigation of any offence.

(6)   References in this section to an offence are to an offence under the law of any part of the United Kingdom.

(7)   This section applies only in relation to an offence of which an operator becomes aware after the coming into force of this section.

### 93   Enforcement of this Chapter

(1)   A local weights and measures authority in Great Britain may enforce the provisions of this Chapter in its area.

(2)   The Department of Enterprise, Trade and Investment may enforce the provisions of this Chapter in Northern Ireland.

(3)   Each of the bodies referred to in subsections (1) and (2) is an 'enforcement authority' for the purposes of this Chapter.

(4)   Where an enforcement authority is satisfied on the balance of probabilities that a person has breached a duty or prohibition imposed by this Chapter, the authority may impose a financial penalty on the person in respect of that breach.

(5)   But in the case of a breach of a duty in section 90 or a prohibition in section 91 an enforcement authority may not impose a financial penalty on a person ('P') if the authority is satisfied on the balance of probabilities that—

    (a)   the breach was due to—

       (i)   a mistake,

       (ii)   reliance on information supplied to P by another person,

       (iii)   the act or default of another person,

       (iv)   an accident, or

       (v)   another cause beyond P's control, and

    (b)   P took all reasonable precautions and exercised all due diligence to avoid the breach.

(6)   A local weights and measures authority in England and Wales may impose a penalty under this section in respect of a breach which occurs in England and Wales but outside that authority's area (as well as in respect of a breach which occurs within that area).

(7)   A local weights and measures authority in Scotland may impose a penalty under this section in respect of a breach which occurs in Scotland but outside that authority's area (as well as in respect of a breach which occurs within that area).

(8)   Only one penalty under this section may be imposed on the same person in respect of the same breach.

(9)   The amount of a financial penalty imposed under this section—

    (a)   may be such as the enforcement authority imposing it determines, but

    (b)   must not exceed £5,000.

(10)   Schedule 10 (procedure for and appeals against financial penalties) has effect.

(11)   References in this section to this Chapter do not include section 94.

### 94   Duty to review measures relating to secondary ticketing

(1)   The Secretary of State must—

    (a)   review, or arrange for a review of, consumer protection measures applying to the re-sale of tickets for recreational, sporting or cultural events in the United Kingdom through secondary ticketing facilities,

    (b)   prepare a report on the outcome of the review or arrange for such a report to be prepared, and

    (c)   publish that report.

(2)   The report must be published before the end of the period of 12 months beginning with the day on which this section comes into force.

(3)   The Secretary of State must lay the report before Parliament.

(4)   In this section 'consumer protection measures' includes such legislation, rules of law, codes of practice and guidance as the Secretary of State considers relate to the rights of consumers or the protection of their interests.

**95   Interpretation of this Chapter**

(1)   In this Chapter—

'enforcement authority' has the meaning given by section 93(3);

'operator', in relation to a secondary ticketing facility, means a person who—

(a)   exercises control over the operation of the facility, and

(b)   receives revenue from the facility,

but this is subject to regulations under subsection (2);

'organiser', in relation to an event, means a person who—

(a)   is responsible for organising or managing the event, or

(b)   receives some or all of the revenue from the event;

'parent undertaking' has the meaning given by section 1162 of the Companies Act 2006;

'secondary ticketing facility' means an internet-based facility for the re-sale of tickets for recreational, sporting or cultural events;

'subsidiary undertaking' has the meaning given by section 1162 of the Companies Act 2006;

'undertaking' has the meaning given by section 1161(1) of the Companies Act 2006.

(2)   The Secretary of State may by regulations provide that a person of a description specified in the regulations is or is not to be treated for the purposes of this Chapter as an operator in relation to a secondary ticketing facility.

(3)   Regulations under subsection (2)—

(a)   are to be made by statutory instrument;

(b)   may make different provision for different purposes;

(c)   may include incidental, supplementary, consequential, transitional, transitory or saving provision.

(4)   A statutory instrument containing regulations under subsection (2) is not to be made unless a draft of the instrument has been laid before, and approved by a resolution of, each House of Parliament.

## CHAPTER 6
### General

**96   Power to make consequential provision**

(1)   The Secretary of State may by order made by statutory instrument make provision in consequence of this Act.

(2)   The power conferred by subsection (1) includes power—

(a)   to amend, repeal, revoke or otherwise modify any provision made by an enactment or an instrument made under an enactment (including an enactment passed or instrument made in the same Session as this Act);

(b)   to make transitional, transitory or saving provision.

(3)   A statutory instrument containing (whether alone or with other provision) an order under this section which amends, repeals, revokes or otherwise modifies any provision of primary legislation is not to be made unless a draft of the instrument has been laid before, and approved by a resolution of, each House of Parliament.

(4)   A statutory instrument containing an order under this section which does not amend, repeal, revoke or otherwise modify any provision of primary legislation is subject to annulment in pursuance of a resolution of either House of Parliament.

(5)   In this section—

'enactment' includes an Act of the Scottish Parliament, a Measure or Act of the National Assembly for Wales and Northern Ireland legislation;

'primary legislation' means—

(a)   an Act of Parliament,

(b) an Act of the Scottish Parliament,

(c) a Measure or Act of the National Assembly for Wales, and

(d) Northern Ireland legislation.

## 97 Power to make transitional, transitory and saving provision

(1) The Secretary of State may by order made by statutory instrument make transitional, transitory or saving provision in connection with the coming into force of any provision of this Act other than the coming into force of Chapter 3 or 4 of this Part in relation to Wales.

(2) The Welsh Ministers may by order made by statutory instrument make transitional, transitory or saving provision in connection with the coming into force of Chapter 3 or 4 of this Part in relation to Wales.

## 98 Financial provision

There is to be paid out of money provided by Parliament—

(a) any expenses incurred by a Minister of the Crown or a government department under this Act, and

(b) any increase attributable to this Act in the sums payable under any other Act out of money so provided.

## 99 Extent

(1) The amendment, repeal or revocation of any provision by this Act has the same extent as the provision concerned.

(2) Section 27 extends only to Scotland.

(3) Chapter 3 of this Part extends only to England and Wales.

(4) Subject to that, this Act extends to England and Wales, Scotland and Northern Ireland.

## 100 Commencement

(1) The provisions of this Act listed in subsection (2) come into force on the day on which this Act is passed.

(2) Those provisions are—

(a) section 48(5) to (8),

(b) Chapter 3 of this Part in so far as it confer powers to make regulations,

(c) section 88(5) to (11),

(d) this Chapter, and

(e) paragraph 12 of Schedule 5.

(3) Chapters 3 and 4 of this Part come into force—

(a) in relation to England, on such day as the Secretary of State may appoint by order made by statutory instrument;

(b) in relation to Wales, on such day as the Welsh Ministers may appoint by order made by statutory instrument.

(4) Chapter 5 of this Part comes into force at the end of the period of two months beginning with the day on which this Act is passed.

(5) The other provisions of this Act come into force on such day as the Secretary of State may appoint by order made by statutory instrument.

(6) An order under this section may appoint different days for different purposes.

## 101 Short title

This Act may be cited as the Consumer Rights Act 2015.

. . .

## SCHEDULE 2
## CONSUMER CONTRACT TERMS WHICH MAY BE REGARDED AS UNFAIR

### PART 1
### LIST OF TERMS

1   A term which has the object or effect of excluding or limiting the trader's liability in the event of the death of or personal injury to the consumer resulting from an act or omission of the trader.

2   A term which has the object or effect of inappropriately excluding or limiting the legal rights of the consumer in relation to the trader or another party in the event of total or partial non-performance or inadequate performance by the trader of any of the contractual obligations, including the option of offsetting a debt owed to the trader against any claim which the consumer may have against the trader.

3   A term which has the object or effect of making an agreement binding on the consumer in a case where the provision of services by the trader is subject to a condition whose realisation depends on the trader's will alone.

4   A term which has the object or effect of permitting the trader to retain sums paid by the consumer where the consumer decides not to conclude or perform the contract, without providing for the consumer to receive compensation of an equivalent amount from the trader where the trader is the party cancelling the contract.

5   A term which has the object or effect of requiring that, where the consumer decides not to conclude or perform the contract, the consumer must pay the trader a disproportionately high sum in compensation or for services which have not been supplied.

6   A term which has the object or effect of requiring a consumer who fails to fulfil his obligations under the contract to pay a disproportionately high sum in compensation.

7   A term which has the object or effect of authorising the trader to dissolve the contract on a discretionary basis where the same facility is not granted to the consumer, or permitting the trader to retain the sums paid for services not yet supplied by the trader where it is the trader who dissolves the contract.

8   A term which has the object or effect of enabling the trader to terminate a contract of indeterminate duration without reasonable notice except where there are serious grounds for doing so.

9   A term which has the object or effect of automatically extending a contract of fixed duration where the consumer does not indicate otherwise, when the deadline fixed for the consumer to express a desire not to extend the contract is unreasonably early.

10   A term which has the object or effect of irrevocably binding the consumer to terms with which the consumer has had no real opportunity of becoming acquainted before the conclusion of the contract.

11   A term which has the object or effect of enabling the trader to alter the terms of the contract unilaterally without a valid reason which is specified in the contract.

12   A term which has the object or effect of permitting the trader to determine the characteristics of the subject matter of the contract after the consumer has become bound by it.

13   A term which has the object or effect of enabling the trader to alter unilaterally without a valid reason any characteristics of the goods, digital content or services to be provided.

14   A term which has the object or effect of giving the trader the discretion to decide the price payable under the contract after the consumer has become bound

by it, where no price or method of determining the price is agreed when the consumer becomes bound.

15   A term which has the object or effect of permitting a trader to increase the price of goods, digital content or services without giving the consumer the right to cancel the contract if the final price is too high in relation to the price agreed when the contract was concluded.

16   A term which has the object or effect of giving the trader the right to determine whether the goods, digital content or services supplied are in conformity with the contract, or giving the trader the exclusive right to interpret any term of the contract.

17   A term which has the object or effect of limiting the trader's obligation to respect commitments undertaken by the trader's agents or making the trader's commitments subject to compliance with a particular formality.

18   A term which has the object or effect of obliging the consumer to fulfil all of the consumer's obligations where the trader does not perform the trader's obligations.

19   A term which has the object or effect of allowing the trader to transfer the trader's rights and obligations under the contract, where this may reduce the guarantees for the consumer, without the consumer's agreement.

20   A term which has the object or effect of excluding or hindering the consumer's right to take legal action or exercise any other legal remedy, in particular by—

(a)   requiring the consumer to take disputes exclusively to arbitration not covered by legal provisions,

(b)   unduly restricting the evidence available to the consumer, or

(c)   imposing on the consumer a burden of proof which, according to the applicable law, should lie with another party to the contract.

## PART 2
## SCOPE OF PART 1

### *Financial services*

21   Paragraph 8 (cancellation without reasonable notice) does not include a term by which a supplier of financial services reserves the right to terminate unilaterally a contract of indeterminate duration without notice where there is a valid reason, if the supplier is required to inform the consumer of the cancellation immediately.

22   Paragraph 11 (variation of contract without valid reason) does not include a term by which a supplier of financial services reserves the right to alter the rate of interest payable by or due to the consumer, or the amount of other charges for financial services without notice where there is a valid reason, if—

(a)   the supplier is required to inform the consumer of the alteration at the earliest opportunity, and

(b)   the consumer is free to dissolve the contract immediately.

Contracts which last indefinitely

23   Paragraphs 11 (variation of contract without valid reason), 12 (determination of characteristics of goods etc after consumer bound) and 14 (determination of price after consumer bound) do not include a term under which a trader reserves the right to alter unilaterally the conditions of a contract of indeterminate duration if—

(a)   the trader is required to inform the consumer with reasonable notice, and

(b)   the consumer is free to dissolve the contract.

*Sale of securities, foreign currency etc*

24   Paragraphs 8 (cancellation without reasonable notice), 11 (variation of contract without valid reason), 14 (determination of price after consumer bound) and 15 (increase in price) do not apply to—
    (a)   transactions in transferable securities, financial instruments and other products or services where the price is linked to fluctuations in a stock exchange quotation or index or a financial market rate that the trader does not control, and
    (b)   contracts for the purchase or sale of foreign currency, traveller's cheques or international money orders denominated in foreign currency.

*Price index clauses*

25   Paragraphs 14 (determination of price after consumer bound) and 15 (increase in price) do not include a term which is a price-indexation clause (where otherwise lawful), if the method by which prices vary is explicitly described.

SCHEDULE 3
ENFORCEMENT OF THE LAW ON UNFAIR CONTRACT TERMS AND
NOTICES

*Application of Schedule*

1   This Schedule applies to—
    (a)   a term of a consumer contract,
    (b)   a term proposed for use in a consumer contract,
    (c)   a term which a third party recommends for use in a consumer contract,
or
    (d)   a consumer notice.

*Consideration of complaints*

2—(1)   A regulator may consider a complaint about a term or notice to which this Schedule applies (a 'relevant complaint').
(2)   If a regulator other than the CMA intends to consider a relevant complaint, it must notify the CMA that it intends to do so, and must then consider the complaint.
(3)   If a regulator considers a relevant complaint, but decides not to make an application under paragraph 3 in relation to the complaint, it must give reasons for its decision to the person who made the complaint.

*Application for injunction or interdict*

3—(1)   A regulator may apply for an injunction or (in Scotland) an interdict against a person if the regulator thinks that—
    (a)   the person is using, or proposing or recommending the use of, a term or notice to which this Schedule applies, and
    (b)   the term or notice falls within any one or more of sub-paragraphs (2), (3) or (5).
(2)   A term or notice falls within this sub-paragraph if it purports to exclude or restrict liability of the kind mentioned in—
    (a)   section 31 (exclusion of liability: goods contracts),
    (b)   section 47 (exclusion of liability: digital content contracts),
    (c)   section 57 (exclusion of liability: services contracts), or

(d)   section 65(1) (business liability for death or personal injury resulting from negligence).

(3)   A term or notice falls within this sub-paragraph if it is unfair to any extent.

(4)   A term within paragraph 1(1)(b) or (c) (but not within paragraph 1(1)(a)) is to be treated for the purposes of section 62(4) and (5) (assessment of fairness) as if it were a term of a contract.

(5)   A term or notice falls within this sub-paragraph if it breaches section 68 (requirement for transparency).

(6)   A regulator may apply for an injunction or interdict under this paragraph in relation to a term or notice whether or not it has received a relevant complaint about the term or notice.

### Notification of application

4—(1)   Before making an application under paragraph 3, a regulator other than the CMA must notify the CMA that it intends to do so.

(2)   The regulator may make the application only if—

(a)   the period of 14 days beginning with the day on which the regulator notified the CMA has ended, or

(b)   before the end of that period, the CMA agrees to the regulator making the application.

### Determination of application

5—(1)   On an application for an injunction under paragraph 3, the court may grant an injunction on such conditions, and against such of the respondents, as it thinks appropriate.

(2)   On an application for an interdict under paragraph 3, the court may grant an interdict on such conditions, and against such of the defenders, as it thinks appropriate.

(3)   The injunction or interdict may include provision about—

(a)   a term or notice to which the application relates, or

(b)   any term of a consumer contract, or any consumer notice, of a similar kind or with a similar effect.

(4)   It is not a defence to an application under paragraph 3 to show that, because of a rule of law, a term to which the application relates is not, or could not be, an enforceable contract term.

(5)   If a regulator other than the CMA makes the application, it must notify the CMA of—

(a)   the outcome of the application, and

(b)   if an injunction or interdict is granted, the conditions on which, and the persons against whom, it is granted.

### Undertakings

6—(1)   A regulator may accept an undertaking from a person against whom it has applied, or thinks it is entitled to apply, for an injunction or interdict under paragraph 3.

(2)   The undertaking may provide that the person will comply with the conditions that are agreed between the person and the regulator about the use of terms or notices, or terms or notices of a kind, specified in the undertaking.

(3)   If a regulator other than the CMA accepts an undertaking, it must notify the CMA of—

(a)   the conditions on which the undertaking is accepted, and

(b)   the person who gave it.

*Publication, information and advice*

7—(1)   The CMA must arrange the publication of details of—
    (a)   any application it makes for an injunction or interdict under paragraph 3,
    (b)   any injunction or interdict under this Schedule, and
    (c)   any undertaking under this Schedule.
(2)   The CMA must respond to a request whether a term or notice, or one of a similar kind or with a similar effect, is or has been the subject of an injunction, interdict or undertaking under this Schedule.
(3)   Where the term or notice, or one of a similar kind or with a similar effect, is or has been the subject of an injunction or interdict under this Schedule, the CMA must give the person making the request a copy of the injunction or interdict.
(4)   Where the term or notice, or one of a similar kind or with a similar effect, is or has been the subject of an undertaking under this Schedule, the CMA must give the person making the request—
    (a)   details of the undertaking, and
    (b)   if the person giving the undertaking has agreed to amend the term or notice, a copy of the amendments.
(5)   The CMA may arrange the publication of advice and information about the provisions of this Part.
(6)   In this paragraph—
    (a)   references to an injunction or interdict under this Schedule are to an injunction or interdict granted on an application by the CMA under paragraph 3 or notified to it under paragraph 5, and
    (b)   references to an undertaking are to an undertaking given to the CMA under paragraph 6 or notified to it under that paragraph.

*Meaning of 'regulator'*

8—(1)   In this Schedule 'regulator' means—
    (a)   the CMA,
    (b)   the Department of Enterprise, Trade and Investment in Northern Ireland,
    (c)   a local weights and measures authority in Great Britain,
    (d)   the Financial Conduct Authority,
    (e)   the Office of Communications,
    (f)   the Information Commissioner,
    (g)   the Gas and Electricity Markets Authority,
    (h)   the Water Services Regulation Authority,
    (i)   the Office of Rail Regulation,
    (j)   the Northern Ireland Authority for Utility Regulation, or
    (k)   the Consumers' Association.
(2)   The Secretary of State may by order made by statutory instrument amend sub-paragraph (1) so as to add, modify or remove an entry.
(3)   An order under sub-paragraph (2) may amend sub-paragraph (1) so as to add a body that is not a public authority only if the Secretary of State thinks that the body represents the interests of consumers (or consumers of a particular description).
(4)   The Secretary of State must publish (and may from time to time vary) other criteria to be applied by the Secretary of State in deciding whether to add an entry to, or remove an entry from, sub-paragraph (1).
(5)   An order under sub-paragraph (2) may make consequential amendments to this Schedule (including with the effect that any of its provisions apply differently, or do not apply, to a body added to sub-paragraph (1)).
(6)   An order under sub-paragraph (2) may contain transitional or transitory provision or savings.
(7)   No order may be made under sub-paragraph (2) unless a draft of the statu-

tory instrument containing it has been laid before, and approved by a resolution of, each House of Parliament.

(8)   In this paragraph 'public authority' has the same meaning as in section 6 of the Human Rights Act 1998.

### Other definitions

9   In this Schedule—
'the CMA' means the Competition and Markets Authority;
'injunction' includes an interim injunction;
'interdict' includes an interim interdict.

### The Financial Conduct Authority

10   The functions of the Financial Conduct Authority under this Schedule are to be treated as functions of the Authority under the Financial Services and Markets Act 2000.

. . .

# PART II
# STATUTORY INSTRUMENTS

**COMMERCIAL AGENTS (COUNCIL DIRECTIVE) REGULATIONS 1993**
**(SI 1993/3053)**

PART I
GENERAL

### 2  Interpretation, application and extent

(1)   In these Regulations—

'commercial agent' means a self-employed intermediary who has continuing authority to negotiate the sale or purchase of goods on behalf of another person (the 'principal'), or to negotiate and conclude the sale or purchase of goods on behalf of and in the name of that principal; but shall be understood as not including in particular:

(i)   a person who, in his capacity as an officer of a company or association, is empowered to enter into commitments binding on that company or association;

(ii)  a partner who is lawfully authorised to enter into commitments binding on his partners;

(iii) a person who acts as an insolvency practitioner (as that expression is defined in section 388 of the Insolvency Act 1986) or the equivalent in any other jurisdiction;

'commission' means any part of the remuneration of a commercial agent which varies with the number or value of business transactions;

['EEA Agreement' means the Agreement on the European Economic Area signed at Oporto on 2nd May 1992 as adjusted by the Protocol signed at Brussels on 17th March 1993;

'member State' includes a State which is a contracting party to the EEA Agreement;]

'restraint of trade clause' means an agreement restricting the business activities of a commercial agent following termination of the agency contract.

(2)   These Regulations do not apply to—

(a)   commercial agents whose activities are unpaid;

(b)   commercial agents when they operate on commodity exchanges or in the commodity market;

(c)   the Crown Agents for Overseas Governments and Administrations, as set up under the Crown Agents Act 1979, or its subsidiaries.

(3)   The provisions of the Schedule to these Regulations have effect for the purpose of determining the persons whose activities as commercial agents are to be considered secondary.

(4)   These Regulations shall not apply to the persons referred to in paragraph (3) above.

(5)   These Regulations do not extend to Northern Ireland.

## PART II
## RIGHTS AND OBLIGATIONS

### 3  Duties of a commercial agent to his principal

(1)  In performing his activities a commercial agent must look after the interests of his principal and act dutifully and in good faith.

(2)  In particular, a commercial agent must—

(a)  make proper efforts to negotiate and, where appropriate, conclude the transactions he is instructed to take care of;

(b)  communicate to his principal all the necessary information available to him;

(c)  comply with reasonable instructions given by his principal.

### 4  Duties of a principal to his commercial agent

(1)  In his relations with his commercial agent a principal must act dutifully and in good faith.

(2)  In particular, a principal must—

(a)  provide his commercial agent with the necessary documentation relating to the goods concerned;

(b)  obtain for his commercial agent the information necessary for the performance of the agency contract, and in particular notify his commercial agent within a reasonable period once he anticipates that the volume of commercial transactions will be significantly lower than that which the commercial agent could normally have expected.

(3)  A principal shall, in addition, inform his commercial agent within a reasonable period of his acceptance or refusal of, and of any non-execution by him of, a commercial transaction which the commercial agent has procured for him.

### 5  Prohibition on derogation from regulations 3 and 4 and consequence of breach

(1)  The parties may not derogate from regulations 3 and 4 above.

(2)  The law applicable to the contract shall govern the consequence of breach of the rights and obligations under regulations 3 and 4 above.

## PART III
## REMUNERATION

### 6  Form and amount of remuneration in absence of agreement

(1)  In the absence of any agreement as to remuneration between the parties, a commercial agent shall be entitled to the remuneration that commercial agents appointed for the goods forming the subject of his agency contract are customarily allowed in the place where he carries on his activities and, if there is no such customary practice, a commercial agent shall be entitled to reasonable remuneration taking into account all the aspects of the transaction.

(2)  This regulation is without prejudice to the application of any enactment or rule of law concerning the level of remuneration.

(3)  Where a commercial agent is not remunerated (wholly or in part) by commission, regulations 7 to 12 below shall not apply.

### 7  Entitlement to commission on transactions concluded during agency contract

(1)  A commercial agent shall be entitled to commission on commercial transactions concluded during the period covered by the agency contract—

(a)  where the transaction has been concluded as a result of his action; or

(b)  where the transaction is concluded with a third party whom he has previously acquired as a customer for transactions of the same kind.

(2)  A commercial agent shall also be entitled to commission on transactions concluded during the period covered by the agency contract where he has an

exclusive right to a specific geographical area or to a specific group of customers and where the transaction has been entered into with a customer belonging to that area or group.

## 8 Entitlement to commission on transactions concluded after agency contract has terminated

Subject to regulation 9 below, a commercial agent shall be entitled to commission on commercial transactions concluded after the agency contract has terminated if—

(a) the transaction is mainly attributable to his efforts during the period covered by the agency contract and if the transaction was entered into within a reasonable period after that contract terminated; or

(b) in accordance with the conditions mentioned in regulation 7 above, the order of the third party reached the principal or the commercial agent before the agency contract terminated.

## 9 Apportionment of commission between new and previous commercial agents

(1) A commercial agent shall not be entitled to the commission referred to in regulation 7 above if that commission is payable, by virtue of regulation 8 above, to the previous commercial agent, unless it is equitable because of the circumstances for the commission to be shared between the commercial agents.

(2) The principal shall be liable for any sum due under paragraph (1) above to the person entitled to it in accordance with that paragraph, and any sum which the other commercial agent receives to which he is not entitled shall be refunded to the principal.

## 10 When commission due and date for payment

(1) Commission shall become due as soon as, and to the extent that, one of the following circumstances occurs:

(a) the principal has executed the transaction; or

(b) the principal should, according to his agreement with the third party, have executed the transaction; or

(c) the third party has executed the transaction.

(2) Commission shall become due at the latest when the third party has executed his part of the transaction or should have done so if the principal had executed his part of the transaction, as he should have.

(3) The commission shall be paid not later than on the last day of the month following the quarter in which it became due, and, for the purposes of these Regulations, unless otherwise agreed between the parties, the first quarter period shall run from the date the agency contract takes effect, and subsequent periods shall run from that date in the third month thereafter or the beginning of the fourth month, whichever is the sooner.

(4) Any agreement to derogate from paragraphs (2) and (3) above to the detriment of the commercial agent shall be void.

## 11 Extinction of right to commission

(1) The right to commission can be extinguished only if and to the extent that—

(a) it is established that the contract between the third party and the principal will not be executed; and

(b) that fact is due to a reason for which the principal is not to blame.

(2) Any commission which the commercial agent has already received shall be refunded if the right to it is extinguished.

(3) any agreement to derogate from paragraph (1) above to the detriment of the commercial agent shall be void.

## 12 Periodic supply of information as to commission due and right of inspection of principal's books

(1) The principal shall supply his commercial agent with a statement of the commission due, not later than the last day of the month following the quarter in which the commission has become due, and such statement shall set out the main components used in calculating the amount of the commission.

(2) A commercial agent shall be entitled to demand that he be provided with all the information (and in particular an extract from the books) which is available to his principal and which he needs in order to check the amount of the commission due to him.

(3) Any agreement to derogate from paragraphs (1) and (2) above shall be void.

(4) Nothing in this regulation shall remove or restrict the effect of, or prevent reliance upon, any enactment or rule of law which recognises the right of an agent to inspect the books of a principal.

### PART IV
### CONCLUSION AND TERMINATION OF THE AGENCY CONTRACT

## 13 Right to signed written statement of terms of agency contract

(1) The commercial agent and principal shall each be entitled to receive from the other, on request, a signed written document setting out the terms of the agency contract including any terms subsequently agreed.

(2) Any purported waiver of the right referred to in paragraph (1) above shall be void.

## 14 Conversion of agency contract after expiry of fixed period

An agency contract for a fixed period which continues to be performed by both parties after that period has expired shall be deemed to be converted into an agency contract for an indefinite period.

## 15 Minimum periods of notice for termination of agency contract

(1) Where an agency contract is concluded for an indefinite period either party may terminate it by notice.

(2) The period of notice shall be—
    (a) 1 month for the first year of the contract;
    (b) 2 months for the second year commenced;
    (c) 3 months for the third year commenced and for the subsequent years;
and the parties may not agree on any shorter periods of notice.

(3) If the parties agree on longer periods than those laid down in paragraph (2) above, the period of notice to be observed by the principal must not be shorter than that to be observed by the commercial agent.

(4) Unless otherwise agreed by the parties, the end of the period of notice must coincide with the end of a calendar month.

(5) The provisions of this regulation shall also apply to an agency contract for a fixed period where it is converted under regulation 14 above into an agency contract for an indefinite period subject to the proviso that the earlier fixed period must be taken into account in the calculation of the period of notice.

## 16 Savings with regard to immediate termination

These Regulations shall not affect the application of any enactment or rule of law which provides for the immediate termination of the agency contract—
    (a) because of the failure of one party to carry out all or part of his obligations under that contract; or
    (b) where exceptional circumstances arise.

## 17   Entitlement of commercial agent to indemnity or compensation on termination of agency contract

(1)   This regulation has effect for the purpose of ensuring that the commercial agent is, after termination of the agency contract, indemnified in accordance with paragraphs (3) to (5) below or compensated for damage in accordance with paragraphs (6) and (7) below.

(2)   Except where the agency [contract] otherwise provides, the commercial agent shall be entitled to be compensated rather than indemnified.

(3)   Subject to paragraph (9) and to regulation 18 below, the commercial agent shall be entitled to an indemnity if and to the extent that—

    (a)   he has brought the principal new customers or has significantly increased the volume of business with existing customers and the principal continues to derive substantial benefits from the business with such customers; and

    (b)   the payment of this indemnity is equitable having regard to all the circumstances and, in particular, the commission lost by the commercial agent on the business transacted with such customers.

(4)   The amount of the indemnity shall not exceed a figure equivalent to an indemnity for one year calculated from the commercial agent's average annual remuneration over the preceding five years and if the contract goes back less than five years the indemnity shall be calculated on the average for the period in question.

(5)   The grant of an indemnity as mentioned above shall not prevent the commercial agent from seeking damages.

(6)   Subject to paragraph (9) and to regulation 18 below, the commercial agent shall be entitled to compensation for the damage he suffers as a result of the termination of his relations with his principal.

(7)   For the purpose of these Regulations such damage shall be deemed to occur particularly when the termination takes place in either or both of the following circumstances, namely circumstances which—

    (a)   deprive the commercial agent of the commission which proper performance of the agency contract would have procured for him whilst providing his principal with substantial benefits linked to the activities of the commercial agent; or

    (b)   have not enabled the commercial agent to amortize the costs and expenses that he had incurred in the performance of the agency contract on the advice of his principal.

(8)   Entitlement to the indemnity or compensation for damage as provided for under paragraphs (2) to (7) above shall also arise where the agency contract is terminated as a result of the death of the commercial agent.

(9)   The commercial agent shall lose his entitlement to the indemnity or compensation for damage in the instances provided for in paragraphs (2) to (8) above if within one year following termination of his agency contract he has not notified his principal that he intends pursuing his entitlement.

## 18   Grounds for excluding payment of indemnity or compensation under regulation 17

The [indemnity or] compensation referred to in regulation 17 above shall not be payable to the commercial agent where—

    (a)   the principal has terminated the agency contract because of default attributable to the commercial agent which would justify immediate termination of the agency contract pursuant to regulation 16 above; or

    (b)   the commercial agent has himself terminated the agency contract, unless such termination is justified—

        (i)   by circumstances attributable to the principal, or

        (ii)   on grounds of the age, infirmity or illness of the commercial agent in consequence of which he cannot reasonably be required to continue his activities; or

(c)   the commercial agent, with the agreement of his principal, assigns his rights and duties under the agency contract to another person.

### 19   Prohibition on derogation from regulations 17 and 18

The parties may not derogate from regulations 17 and 18 to the detriment of the commercial agent before the agency contract expires.

### 20   Restraint of trade clauses

(1)   A restraint of trade clause shall be valid only if and to the extent that—

(a)   it is concluded in writing; and

(b)   it relates to the geographical area or the group of customers and the geographical area entrusted to the commercial agent and to the kind of goods covered by his agency under the contract.

(2)   A restraint of trade clause shall be valid for not more than two years after termination of the agency contract.

(3)   Nothing in this regulation shall affect any enactment or rule of law which imposes other restrictions on the validity or enforceability of restraint of trade clauses or which enables a court to reduce the obligations on the parties resulting from such clauses.

### PART V
### MISCELLANEOUS AND SUPPLEMENTAL

### 21   Disclosure of information

Nothing in these Regulations shall require information to be given where such disclosure would be contrary to public policy.

### 22   Service of notice etc

(1)   Any notice, statement or other document to be given or supplied to a commercial agent or to be given or supplied to the principal under these Regulations may be so given or supplied:

(a)   by delivering it to him;

(b)   by leaving it at his proper address addressed to him by name;

(c)   by sending it by post to him addressed either to his registered address or to the address of his registered or principal office;

or by any other means provided for in the agency contract.

(2)   Any such notice, statement or document may—

(a)   in the case of a body corporate, be given or served on the secretary or clerk of that body;

(b)   in the case of a partnership, be given to or served on any partner or on any person having the control or management of the partnership business.

### 23   Transitional provisions

(1)   Notwithstanding any provision in an agency contract made before 1st January 1994, these Regulations shall apply to that contract after that date and, accordingly any provision which is inconsistent with these Regulations shall have effect subject to them.

(2)   Nothing in these Regulations shall affect the rights and liabilities of a commercial agent or a principal which have accrued before 1st January 1994.

THE SCHEDULE Regulation 2(3)

1   The activities of a person as a commercial agent are to be considered secondary where it may reasonably be taken that the primary purpose of the arrangement with his principal is other than as set out in paragraph 2 below.

2   An arrangement falls within this paragraph if—

(a)   the business of the principal is the sale, or as the case may be purchase, of goods of a particular kind; and

(b)   the goods concerned are such that—

(i)   transactions are normally individually negotiated and concluded on a commercial basis, and

(ii)   procuring a transaction on one occasion is likely to lead to further transactions in those goods with that customer on future occasions, or to transactions in those goods with other customers in the same geographical area or among the same group of customers, and

that accordingly it is in the commercial interests of the principal in developing the market in those goods to appoint a representative to such customers with a view to the representative devoting effort, skill and expenditure from his own resources to that end.

3   The following are indications that an arrangement falls within paragraph 2 above, and the absence of any of them is an indication to the contrary—

(a)   the principal is the manufacturer, importer or distributor of the goods;

(b)   the goods are specifically identified with the principal in the market in question rather than, or to a greater extent than, with any other person;

(c)   the agent devotes substantially the whole of his time to representative activities (whether for one principal or for a number of principals whose interests are not conflicting);

(d)   the goods are not normally available in the market in question other than by means of the agent;

(e)   the arrangement is described as one of commercial agency.

4   The following are indications that an arrangement does not fall within paragraph 2 above—

(a)   promotional material is supplied direct to potential customers;

(b)   persons are granted agencies without reference to existing agents in a particular area or in relation to a particular group;

(c)   customers normally select the goods for themselves and merely place their orders through the agent.

5   The activities of the following categories of persons are presumed, unless the contrary is established, not to fall within paragraph 2 above—

Mail order catalogue agents for consumer goods.

Consumer credit agents.

**FINANCIAL SERVICES AND MARKETS ACT 2000 (REGULATED ACTIVITIES) ORDER 2001
(SI 2001/544)**

[CHAPTER 14A
REGULATED CREDIT AGREEMENTS

*The activities*

## 60B    Regulated credit agreements

(1)    Entering into a regulated credit agreement as lender is a specified kind of activity.

(2)    It is a specified kind of activity for the lender or another person to exercise, or to have the right to exercise, the lender's rights and duties under a regulated credit agreement.

(3)    In this article—

['credit agreement'—

(a)    in relation to an agreement other than a green deal plan, means an agreement between an individual or relevant recipient of credit ('A') and any other person ('B') under which B provides A with credit of any amount;

(b)    in relation to a green deal plan, has the meaning given by article 60LB;]

['exempt agreement' means a credit agreement which is an exempt agreement under articles 60C to 60H, but where only part of a credit agreement falls within a provision of articles 60C to 60H, only that part is an exempt agreement under those articles];

'regulated credit agreement' means any credit agreement which is not an exempt agreement.

## 60C    Exempt agreements: exemptions relating to the nature of the agreement

(1)    A credit agreement is an exempt agreement for the purposes of this Chapter in the following cases.

(2)    A credit agreement is an exempt agreement if it is a regulated mortgage contract or [if it is of a type described in article 61A(1) or (2) (mortgage contracts which are not regulated mortgage contracts)].

(3)    A credit agreement is an exempt agreement if—

(a)    the lender provides the borrower with credit exceeding £25,000, and

(b)    the agreement is entered into by the borrower wholly or predominantly for the purposes of a business carried on, or intended to be carried on, by the borrower.

(4)    A credit agreement is an exempt agreement if—

(a)    the lender provides the borrower with credit of £25,000 or less,

(b)    the agreement is entered into by the borrower wholly for the purposes of a business carried on, or intended to be carried on, by the borrower, and

[(c)    the agreement is a green deal plan made in relation to a property that is not a domestic property (as defined by article 60LB).]

(5)    For the purposes of paragraph (3), if an agreement includes a declaration which—

(a)    is made by the borrower,

(b)    provides that the agreement is entered into by the borrower wholly or predominantly for the purposes of a business carried on, or intended to be carried on, by the borrower, and

(c)    complies with rules made by the FCA for the purpose of this article,

the agreement is to be presumed to have been entered into by the borrower wholly or predominantly for the purposes specified in sub-paragraph (b) unless paragraph (6) applies.

(6)    This paragraph applies if, when the agreement is entered into—

(a)    the lender (or, if there is more than one lender, any of the lenders), or

(b)    any person who has acted on behalf of the lender (or, if there is more than one lender, any of the lenders) in connection with the entering into of the agreement,

knows or has reasonable cause to suspect that the agreement is not entered into by the borrower wholly or predominantly for the purposes of a business carried on, or intended to be carried on, by the borrower.

(7)    Paragraphs (5) and (6) also apply for the purposes of paragraph (4) but with the omission of the words 'or predominantly'.

(8)    A credit agreement is an exempt agreement if it is made in connection with trade in goods or services—

(a)    between the United Kingdom and a country outside the United Kingdom,

(b)    within a country [outside the United Kingdom], or

(c)    between countries outside the United Kingdom, and

the credit is provided to the borrower in the course of a business carried on by the borrower.

### 60D    Exempt agreements: exemption relating to the purchase of land for non-residential purposes

(1)    A credit agreement is an exempt agreement for the purposes of this Chapter if, at the time it is entered into, any sums due under it are secured by a legal [or equitable] mortgage on land and the condition in paragraph (2) is satisfied.

(2)    The condition is that less than 40% of the land is used, or is intended to be used, as or in connection with a dwelling—

(a)    by the borrower or a related person of the borrower, or

(b)    in the case of credit provided to trustees, by an individual who is a beneficiary of the trust or a related person of a beneficiary.

(3)    For the purposes of paragraph (2)—

(a)    the area of any land which comprises a building or other structure containing two or more storeys is to be taken to be the aggregate of the floor areas of each of those stories;

(b)    'related person' in relation to a person ('B') who is the borrower or (in the case of credit provided to trustees) a beneficiary of the trust, means—

(i)    B's spouse or civil partner,

(ii)    a person (whether or not of the opposite sex) whose relationship with B has the characteristics of the relationship between husband and wife, or

(iii)    B's parent, brother, sister, child, grandparent or grandchild.

[(4)    This article does not apply to an agreement of the type described in Article 3(1)(b) of the mortgages directive.]

### 60E    Exempt agreements: exemptions relating to the nature of the lender

(1)    A credit agreement is an exempt agreement for the purposes of this Chapter in the following cases.

(2)    [Subject to article 60HA, a relevant credit agreement] relating to the purchase of land is an exempt agreement if the lender is—

(a)    specified, or of a description specified, in rules made by the FCA under paragraph (3), or

(b)    a local authority.

(3)    The FCA may make rules specifying any of the following for the purpose of paragraph (2)—

(a)    an authorised person with permission to effect or carry out contracts of insurance;

(b)    a friendly society;

(c)    an organisation of employers or organisation of workers;

(d)    a charity;

(e)    an improvement company (within the meaning given by section 7 of the Improvement of Land Act 1899);

(f)    a body corporate named or specifically referred to in any public general Act;

(g)    a body corporate named or specifically referred to in, or in an order made under, a relevant housing provision;

(h)    a building society (within the meaning of the Building Societies Act 1986);

(i)    an authorised person with permission to accept deposits.

(4)    Rules under paragraph (3) may—

(a)    specify a particular person or class of persons;

(b)    be limited so as to apply only to agreements or classes of agreement specified in the rules.

(5)    [Subject to article 60HA, a relevant credit agreement] is an exempt agreement if it is—

(a)    secured by a legal [or equitable] mortgage on land,

(b)    that land is used or is intended to be used as or in connection with a dwelling, and

(c)    the lender is a housing authority.

(6)    A credit agreement is an exempt agreement if—

(a)    the lender is an investment firm or a credit institution, and

(b)    the agreement is entered into for the purpose of allowing the borrower to carry out a transaction relating to one or more financial instruments.

(7)    In this article—

'housing authority' means—

(a)    in England and Wales, the Homes and Communities Agency, the Welsh Ministers [, a company which is a wholly-owned subsidiary of the Welsh Ministers,] or a private registered provider (within the meaning of Part 2 of the Housing and Regeneration Act 2008);

(b)    in Scotland, the Scottish Ministers or a registered social landlord (within the meaning of the Housing (Scotland) Act 2010;

(c)    in Northern Ireland, the Northern Ireland Housing Executive;

'relevant credit agreement relating to the purchase of land' means—

(a)    a borrower-lender-supplier agreement financing—

(i)    the purchase of land, or

(ii)    provision of dwellings on land,

and secured by a legal [or equitable] mortgage on that land,

(b)    a borrower-lender agreement secured by a legal mortgage on land, or

(c)    a borrower-lender-supplier agreement financing a transaction which is a linked transaction in relation to—

(i)    an agreement falling within sub-paragraph (a), or

(ii)    an agreement falling within sub-paragraph (b) financing—

(aa)    the purchase of land,

(bb)    the provision of dwellings on land,

and secured by a legal [or equitable] mortgage on the land referred to in sub-paragraph (a) or the land referred to in paragraph (ii);

'relevant housing provision' means any of the following—

(a)    section 156(4) or 447(2)(a) of the Housing Act 1985,

(b)    section 156(4) of that Act as it has effect by virtue of section 17 of the Housing Act 1996 (the right to acquire), or

(c)    article 154(1)(a) of the Housing (Northern Ireland) Order 1981

[(7A)    In paragraph (7), in the definition of 'housing authority', in paragraph (a), 'wholly-owned subsidiary' has the same meaning as in section 1159 (meaning of 'subsidiary' etc) of the Companies Act 2006.

(7B)    For the purpose of paragraph (7A), the Welsh Ministers are to be treated as a body corporate.]

(8)    For the purposes of the definition of 'relevant credit agreement relating to the purchase of land', a transaction is, unless paragraph (9) applies, a 'linked transaction' in relation to a credit agreement ('the principal agreement') if—

(a)    it is (or will be) entered into by the borrower under the principal agreement or by a relative of the borrower,

(b)    it does not relate to the provision of security,

(c)    it does not form part of the principal agreement, and

(d)    one of the following conditions is satisfied—

(i)    the transaction is entered into in compliance with a term of the principal agreement;

(ii)    the principal agreement is a borrower-lender-supplier agreement and the transaction is financed, or to be financed, by the principal agreement;

(iii)    the following conditions are met—

(aa)    the other party is a person to whom paragraph (10) applies,

(bb)    the other party initiated the transaction by suggesting it to the borrower or the relative of the borrower, and

(cc)    the borrower or the relative of the borrower enters into the transaction to induce the lender to enter into the principal agreement or for another purpose related to the principal agreement or to a transaction financed or to be financed by the principal agreement.

(9)    This paragraph applies if the transaction is—

(a)    a contract of insurance,

(b)    a contract which contains a guarantee of goods, or

(c)    a transaction which comprises, or is effected under—

(i)    an agreement for the operation of an account (including any savings account) for the deposit of money, or

(ii)    an agreement for the operation of a current account, under which the customer ('C') may, by means of cheques or similar orders payable to C or to any other person, obtain or have the use of money held or made available by the person with whom the account is kept.

(10)    The persons to whom this paragraph applies are—

(a)    the lender;

(b)    the lender's associate;

(c)    a person who, in the negotiation of the transaction, is represented by a person who carries on an activity of the kind specified by article 36A (credit broking) by way of business who is or was also a negotiator in negotiations for the principal agreement;

(d)    a person who, at the time the transaction is initiated, knows that the principal agreement has been made or contemplates that it might be made.

**60F    Exempt agreements: exemptions relating to number of repayments to be made**

(1)    A credit agreement is an exempt agreement for the purposes of this Chapter in the following cases.

(2)    A credit agreement is an exempt agreement if—

(a)    the agreement is a borrower-lender-supplier agreement for fixed-sum credit[, other than a green deal plan],

(b)    the number of payments to be made by the borrower is not more than [twelve],

(c)    those payments are required to be made within a period of 12 months or less (beginning on the date of the agreement),

(d)    the credit is—

(i)    secured on land, or

(ii)    provided without interest or other [. . .] charges, and

(e)    paragraph (7) does not apply to the agreement.

(3)    A credit agreement is an exempt agreement if—

(a)    the agreement is a borrower-lender-supplier agreement for running-account credit,

(b)    the borrower is to make payments in relation to specified periods which must be, unless the agreement is secured on land, of 3 months or less,

(c)    the number of payments to be made by the borrower in repayment of the whole amount of credit provided in each such period is not more than one,

(d)    the credit is—

    (i)    secured on land, or

    (ii)    provided without interest or other significant charges, and

(e)    paragraph (7) does not apply to the agreement.

(4)    [Subject to article 60HA, a credit agreement] is an exempt agreement if—

(a)    the agreement is a borrower-lender-supplier agreement financing the purchase of land,

(b)    the number of payments to be made by the borrower is not more than four, and

(c)    the credit is—

    (i)    secured on land, or

    (ii)    provided without interest or other charges.

(5)    A credit agreement is an exempt agreement if—

(a)    the agreement is a borrower-lender-supplier agreement for fixed-sum credit,

(b)    the credit is to finance a premium under a contract of insurance relating to land or anything on land,

(c)    the lender is the lender under a credit agreement secured by a legal [or equitable] mortgage on that land,

(d)    the credit is to be repaid within the period (which must be 12 months or less) to which the premium relates,

(e)    in the case of an agreement secured on land, there is no charge forming part of the total charge for credit under the agreement other than interest at a rate not exceeding the rate of interest from time to time payable under the agreement mentioned at sub-paragraph (c),

(f)    in the case of an agreement which is not secured on land, the credit is provided without interest or other charges, and

(g)    the number of payments to be made by the borrower is not more than twelve.

(6)    A credit agreement is an exempt agreement if—

(a)    the agreement is a borrower-lender-supplier agreement for fixed-sum credit,

(b)    the lender is the lender under a credit agreement secured by a legal [or equitable] mortgage on land,

(c)    the agreement is to finance a premium under a contract of whole life insurance which provides, in the event of the death of the person on whose life the contract is effected before the credit referred to in sub-paragraph (b) has been repaid, for payment of a sum not exceeding the amount sufficient to meet the amount which, immediately after that credit has been advanced, would be payable to the lender in respect of that credit (including interest from time to time payable under that agreement),

(d)    in the case of an agreement secured on land, there is no charge forming part of the total charge for credit under the agreement other than interest at a rate not exceeding the rate of interest from time to time payable under the agreement mentioned at sub-paragraph (b),

(e)    in the case of an agreement which is not secured on land, the credit is provided without interest or other charges, and

(f)    the number of payments to be made by the borrower is not more than twelve.

(7)    This paragraph applies to—

(a)    agreements financing the purchase of land;

(b)    agreements which are conditional sale agreements or hire-purchase agreements;

(c)    agreements secured by a pledge (other than a pledge of documents of title or of bearer bonds).

[(8)  In this article, 'payment' means any payment which comprises or includes—

(a)    the repayment of capital, or

(b)    the payment of interest or any other charge which forms part of the total charge for credit.]

## 60G   Exempt agreements: exemptions relating to the total charge for credit

(1)    A credit agreement is an exempt agreement for the purposes of this Chapter in the following cases.

(2)    A credit agreement is an exempt agreement if—

(a)    it is a borrower-lender agreement, [. . .]

(b)    the lender is a credit union and the rate of the total charge for credit does not exceed 42.6 per cent[, and

(c)    paragraph (2A) applies to the agreement.]

[(2A)   This paragraph applies to the agreement if—

(a)    the agreement is not of a type described in Article 3(1) of the mortgages directive; or

(b)    the agreement is of such a type and—

(i)    the agreement is of a kind to which the mortgages directive does not apply by virtue of Article 3(2) of that directive,

(ii)    the agreement is a bridging loan within the meaning of Article 4(23) of the mortgages directive, or

(iii)    in relation to the agreement—

(aa)    the borrower receives timely information on the main features, risks and costs of the agreement at the pre-contractual stage, and

(bb)    any advertising of the agreement is fair, clear and not misleading.]

(3)    [Subject to paragraph (8), a credit agreement] is an exempt agreement if—

(a)    it is a borrower-lender agreement,

(b)    it is an agreement of a kind offered to a particular class of individual or relevant recipient of credit and not offered to the public generally,

(c)    it provides that the only charge included in the total charge for credit is interest,

(d)    interest under the agreement may not at any time be more than the sum of one per cent and the highest of the base rates published by the banks specified in paragraph (7)on the date 28 days before the date on which the interest is charged, and

(e)    paragraph (5) does not apply to the agreement.

(4)    [Subject to paragraph (8), a credit agreement] is an exempt agreement if—

(a)    it is a borrower-lender agreement,

(b)    it is an agreement of a kind offered to a particular class of individual or relevant recipient of credit and not offered to the public generally,

(c)    it does not provide for or permit an increase in the rate or amount of any item which is included in the total charge for credit,

(d)    the total charge for credit under the agreement is not more than the sum of one per cent and the highest of the base rates published by the banks specified in paragraph (7) on the date 28 days before the date on which the charge is imposed, and

(e)    paragraph (5) does not apply to the agreement.

(5)    This paragraph applies to an agreement if—

(a)    the total amount to be repaid by the borrower to discharge the borrower's indebtedness may vary according to a formula which is specified in the agreement and which has effect by reference to movements in the level of any index or other factor, or

[(b)  the agreement—

(i)  is not—

(aa)  secured on land, or

[(bb)  offered by a lender to a borrower as an incident of the borrower's employment with the lender or with an undertaking in the same group as the lender;] and

(ii)  does not meet the general interest test.]

(6)  For the purposes of [paragraphs (5) and (8)], an agreement meets the general interest test if—

(a)  the agreement is offered under an enactment with a general interest purpose, and

(b)  the terms on which the credit is provided are more favourable to the borrower than those prevailing on the market, either because the rate of interest is lower than that prevailing on the market, or because the rate of interest is no higher than that prevailing on the market but the other terms on which credit is provided are more favourable to the borrower.

(7)  The banks specified in this paragraph are—

(a)  the Bank of England;

(b)  Bank of Scotland;

(c)  Barclays Bank plc;

(d)  Clydesdale Bank plc;

(e)  Co-operative Bank Public Limited Company;

(f)  Coutts & Co;

(g)  National Westminster Bank Public Limited Company;

(h)  the Royal Bank of Scotland plc.

(8)  A credit agreement of a type described in Article 3(1) of the mortgages directive is an exempt agreement pursuant to paragraph (3) or (4) only if—

(a)  the agreement meets the general interest test;

(b)  the borrower receives timely information on the main features, risks and costs of the agreement at the pre-contractual stage; and

(c)  any advertising of the agreement is fair, clear and not misleading.]

**60H  Exempt agreements: exemptions relating to the nature of the borrower**

[(1)]  Subject to article 60HA, a credit agreement is an exempt agreement for the purposes of this Chapter if—

(a)  the borrower is an individual,

(b)  the agreement is either—

(i)  secured on land, or

[(ii)  for credit which exceeds £60,260 and is for a purpose other than—

(aa)  the renovation of residential property, or

(bb)  to acquire or retain property rights in land or in an existing or projected building,]

(c)  the agreement includes a declaration made by the borrower which provides that the borrower agrees to forgo the protection and remedies that would be available to the borrower if the agreement were a regulated credit agreement and which complies with rules made by the FCA for the purposes of this paragraph,

(d)  a statement has been made in relation to the income or assets of the borrower which complies with rules made by the FCA for the purposes of this paragraph,

(e)  the connection between the statement and the agreement complies with any rules made by the FCA for the purposes of this paragraph (including as to the period of time between the making of the statement and the agreement being entered into), and

(f)    a copy of the statement was provided to the lender before the agreement was entered into.

[(2)    Where a credit agreement would be an exempt agreement pursuant to this article but for paragraph (1)(b)(ii)(bb) or article 60HA, the FCA may treat the agreement as an exempt agreement except for the purpose of the application of the requirements of the mortgages directive.]

**[60HA    Exempt agreements: exemptions not permitted under the mortgages directive**

(1)    A credit agreement is not an exempt agreement pursuant to article 60E(2) or (5), 60F(4) or 60H(1) if—

(a)    the agreement is of a type described in Article 3(1) of the mortgages directive, and

(b)    paragraph (2) does not apply.

(2)    This paragraph applies if—

(a)    the agreement is of a kind to which the mortgages directive does not apply by virtue of Article 3(2) of that directive;

(b)    the agreement is a bridging loan within the meaning of Article 4(23) of that directive; or

(c)    the agreement is a restricted public loan in respect of which—

(i)    the borrower receives timely information on the main features, risks and costs at the pre-contractual stage; and

(ii)    any advertising is fair, clear and not misleading.

(3)    In paragraph (2)(c) 'restricted public loan' means a credit agreement that is—

(a)    offered to a particular class of borrower and not offered to the public generally;

(b)    offered under an enactment with a general interest purpose; and

(c)    provided on terms which are more favourable to the borrower than those prevailing on the market, because it meets one of the following conditions—

(i)    it is interest free;

(ii)    the rate of interest is lower than that prevailing on the market; or

(iii)    the rate of interest is no higher than that prevailing on the market but the other terms on which credit is provided are more favourable to the borrower.]

*Exclusions*

**60I    Arranging administration by authorised person**
A person ('A') who is not an authorised person does not carry on an activity of the kind specified by article 60B(2) in relation to a regulated credit agreement where A—

(a)    arranges for another person, who is an authorised person with permission to carry on an activity of that kind, to exercise or to have the right to exercise the lender's rights and duties under the agreement, or

(b)    exercises or has the right to exercise the lender's rights and duties under the agreement during a period of not more than one month beginning with the day on which any such arrangement comes to an end.

**60J    Administration pursuant to agreement with authorised person**
A person who is not an authorised person does not carry on an activity of the kind specified by article 60B(2) in relation to regulated credit agreement if that person exercises or has the right to exercise the lender's rights and duties under the agreement pursuant to an agreement with an authorised person who has permission to carry on an activity of the kind specified by article 60B(2).

**[60JA    Payment institutions**
(1)    There are excluded from article 60B activities carried on by a person who is

an EEA authorised payment institution exercising passport rights in the United Kingdom in accordance with Article 16(3) of the payment services directive.

(2)   Terms used in this article have the meanings given in Payment Services Regulations 2009.*

### 60JB   Electronic money institutions

(1)   There are excluded from article 60B activities carried on by a person who is an EEA authorised electronic money institution exercising passport rights in the United Kingdom in accordance with Article 16(3) of the payment services directive as applied by Article 6 of the electronic money directive.

(2)   Terms used in this article have the meanings given in the Electronic Money Regulations 2011.†]

### 60K   [Other exclusions]

Article 60B is also subject to [the exclusions in articles 72A (information society services), 72G (local authorities) and 72I (registered consumer buy-to-let mortgage firms)].

*Supplemental*

### 60L   Interpretation of Chapter 14A etc

(1)   In this Chapter—

'assignment', in relation to Scotland, means assignation;

'associate' means, in relation to a person ('P')—

    (a)   where P is an individual, any person who is or who has been—

        (i)   P's spouse or P's civil partner;

        (ii)   a relative of P, of P's spouse or of P's civil partner;

        (iii)   the spouse or civil partner of a relative of P or P's spouse or civil partner;

        (iv)   if P is a member of a partnership, any of P's partners and the spouse or civil partner of any such person;

    (b)   where P is a body corporate—

        (i)   any person who is a controller ('C') of P, and

        (ii)   any other person for whom C is a controller;

'borrower' means [(except in relation to green deal plans: see instead article 60LB)] a person who receives credit under a credit agreement or a person to whom the rights and duties of a borrower under a credit agreement have passed by assignment or operation of law;

'borrower-lender agreement' means—

    (a)   a credit agreement—

        (i)   to finance a transaction between the borrower and a person ('the supplier') other than the lender, and

        (ii)   which is not made by the lender under pre-existing arrangements, or in contemplation of future arrangements, between the lender and the supplier,

    (b)   a credit agreement to refinance any existing indebtedness of the borrower, whether to the lender or another person, or

    (c)   a credit agreement which is—

        (i)   an unrestricted-use credit agreement, and (ii) not made by the lender—

        (aa)   under pre-existing arrangements between the lender and a person other than the borrower ('the supplier'), and

        (bb)   in the knowledge that the credit is to be used to finance a transaction between the borrower and the supplier;

'borrower-lender-supplier agreement' means—

(a)    a credit agreement to finance a transaction between the borrower and the lender, whether forming part of that agreement or not;

(b)    a credit agreement—

(i)  to finance a transaction between the borrower and a person ('the supplier') other than the lender, and

(ii)  which is made by the lender under pre-existing arrangements, or in contemplation of future arrangements, between the lender and the supplier, or

(c)    a credit agreement which is—

(i)  an unrestricted-use credit agreement, and

(ii)  made by the lender under pre-existing arrangements between the lender and a person ('the supplier') other than the borrower in the knowledge that the credit is to be used to finance a transaction between the borrower and the supplier;

'conditional sale agreement' means an agreement for the sale of goods or land under which the purchase price or part of it is payable by instalments, and the property in the goods or land is to remain with the seller (notwithstanding that the buyer is to be in possession of the goods or land) until such conditions as to the payment of instalments or otherwise as may be specified in the agreement are fulfilled;

'credit' includes a cash loan and any other form of financial accommodation;

['credit agreement'—

(a)    in relation to an agreement other than a green deal plan, has the meaning given by article 60B;

(b)    in relation to a green deal plan, has the meaning given by article 60LB;]

'credit union' means a credit union within the meaning of—

(a)    the Credit Unions Act 1979;

(b)    the Credit Unions (Northern Ireland) Order 1985;

'deposit' (except where specified otherwise) means any sum payable by a borrower by way of deposit or down-payment, or credited or to be credited to the borrower on account of any deposit or down-payment, whether the sum is to be or has been paid to the lender or any other person, or is to be or has been discharged by a payment of money or a transfer or delivery of goods or other means;

'exempt agreement' has the meaning given by article 60B;

'finance' includes financing in whole or in part, and 'refinance' is to be read accordingly;

'fixed-sum credit' means a facility under a credit agreement whereby the borrower is enabled to receive credit (whether in one amount or by instalments) but which is not running-account credit;

'hire-purchase agreement' means an agreement—

(a)    which is not a conditional sale agreement,

(b)    under which goods are bailed or (in Scotland) hired to a person ('P') in return for periodical payments by P, and

(c)    the property in the goods will pass to P if the terms of the agreement are complied with and one or more of the following occurs—

(i)  the exercise by P of an option to purchase the goods;

(ii)  the doing by any party to the agreement of any other act specified in the agreement;

(iii)  the happening of any event specified in the agreement;

'legal [or equitable] mortgage' includes [a legal or equitable] charge and, in Scotland, a heritable security;

'lender' means [(except in relation to green deal plans: see instead article 60LB)]—

(a)    the person providing credit under a credit agreement, or

(b)    a person who exercises or has the right to exercise the rights and duties of a person who provided credit under such an agreement;

'payment' (except in article 60F) means a payment comprising or including an amount in respect of credit;

'regulated credit agreement' has the meaning given by article 60B;

'relative' means brother, sister, uncle, aunt, nephew, niece, lineal ancestor or lineal descendent;

'relevant recipient of credit' means—

(a)    a partnership consisting of two or three persons not all of whom are bodies corporate, or

(b)    an unincorporated body of persons which does not consist entirely of bodies corporate and is not a partnership;

'restricted-use credit agreement' means a credit agreement—

(a)    to finance a transaction between the borrower and the lender, whether forming part of that agreement or not,

(b)    to finance a transaction between the borrower and a person ('the supplier') other than the lender, or

(c)    to refinance any existing indebtedness of the borrower's, whether to the lender or another person;

'running-account credit' means a facility under a credit agreement under which the borrower or another person is enabled to receive from time to time from the lender or a third party cash, goods or services to an amount or value such that, taking into account payments made by or to the credit of the borrower, the credit limit (if any) is not at any time exceeded;

'security' in relation to a credit agreement, means a mortgage, charge, pledge, bond, debenture, indemnity, guarantee, bill, note or other right provided by the borrower or at the implied or express request of the borrower to secure the carrying out of the obligations of the borrower under the agreement;

'total charge for credit' has the meaning given in rules made by the FCA under article 60M;

'total price' means the total sum payable by the debtor under a hire-purchase agreement, including any sum payable on the exercise of an option to purchase but excluding any sum payable as a penalty or as compensation or damages for a breach of the agreement;

'unrestricted-use credit agreement' means a credit agreement which is not a restricted use credit agreement.

[(1A)    For the purposes of this Chapter, a credit agreement that is a green deal plan is to be treated as—

(a)    a borrower-lender-supplier agreement falling within paragraph (a) of the definition of 'borrower-lender-supplier agreement';

(b)    a restricted-use credit agreement falling within paragraph (a) of the definition of 'restricted-use credit agreement'].

(2)    For the purposes of the definition of 'restricted-use credit agreement'—

(a)    a credit agreement does not fall within the definition if the credit is in fact provided in such a way as to leave the borrower free to use it as the borrower chooses, even though certain uses would contravene that or any other agreement; and

(b)    an agreement may fall within paragraph (b) of the definition even though the identity of the supplier is unknown at the time the agreement is made.

(3)    For the purposes of the definition of 'borrower-lender agreement' [and the definition of 'borrower-lender-supplier agreement'], a credit agreement is, subject to paragraph (6), entered into under pre-existing arrangements between a lender and a supplier if it is entered into in accordance with, or in connection with, arrangements previously made between the lender (or the lender's associate) and the supplier (or the supplier's associate) unless the arrangements fall within paragraph (5).

(4)    For the purposes of the definition of 'borrower-lender agreement' [and the definition of 'borrower-lender-supplier agreement'], a credit agreement is entered

into in contemplation of future arrangements between a lender and a supplier if it is entered into in the expectation that arrangements will subsequently be made between the lender (or the lender's associate) and the supplier (or the supplier's associate) for the supply of cash, goods or services to be financed by the credit agreement unless the arrangements fall within paragraph (5).

(5)   Arrangements fall within this paragraph if they are—

(a)   for the making, in circumstances specified in the credit agreement, of payments to the supplier by the lender ('L') and L indicates that L is willing to make, in such circumstances, payments of the kind to suppliers generally, or

(b)   for the electronic transfer of funds from a current account held with an authorised person with permission to accept deposits (within the meaning given by article 3).

(6)   If a lender is an associate of the supplier's, the credit agreement is to be treated as entered into under pre-existing arrangements between the lender and the supplier unless the lender can show that this is not the case.

(7)   For the purposes of the definition of 'running-account credit', 'credit limit' means, as respects any period, the maximum debit balance which, under a credit agreement, is allowed to stand on the account during that period, disregarding any term of the agreement allowing that maximum to be exceeded on a temporary basis.

(8)   For the purposes of this Chapter, a person by whom goods are bailed or (in Scotland) hired to an individual or relevant recipient of credit under a hire-purchase agreement is to be taken to be providing that individual or person with fixed-sum credit to finance the transaction of an amount equal to the total price of the goods less the aggregate of the deposit (if any) and the total charge for credit.

(9)   For the purposes of this Chapter, where credit is provided otherwise than in sterling, it is to be treated as provided in sterling of an equivalent amount.

[(10)   For the purposes of this Chapter, where a provision specifies an amount of credit, running-account credit shall be taken not to exceed the amount specified in that provision ('the specified amount''') if—

(a)   the credit limit does not exceed the specified amount; or

(b)   the credit limit exceeds the specified amount, or there is no credit limit, and—

(i)   the borrower is not enabled to draw at any one time an amount which, so far as it represents credit, exceeds the specified amount; or

(ii)   the agreement provides that, if the debit balance rises above a given amount (not exceeding the specified amount), the rate of the total charge for credit increases or any other condition favouring the lender or the lender's associate comes into operation; or

(iii)   at the time the agreement is made it is probable, having regard to the terms of the agreement and any other relevant considerations, that the debit balance will not at any time rise above the specified amount.

(11)   For the purposes of this Chapter, an item entering into the total charge for credit is not to be treated as credit even though time is allowed for its payment.]

## [60LA   Meaning of consumer etc

(1)   For the purposes of sections 1G, 404E and 425A(18) of the Act (meaning of 'consumer'), in so far as those provisions relate to a person ('A') carrying on a regulated activity of the kind specified by—

(a)   article 60B (regulated credit agreements), or

(b)   article 64 (agreeing to carry on specified kinds of activity) in so far as that article relates to article 60B,

a person who is treated by A as a person who is or has been the borrower under a regulated credit agreement is to be treated as a 'consumer'.

(2)   For the purposes of section 328(8) of the Act (meaning of 'clients') in so far

as that provision relates to a person ('A') carrying on a regulated activity of the kind specified by—

(a)    article 60B (regulated credit agreements), or

(b)    article 64 (agreeing to carry on specified kinds of activity) in so far as that article relates to article 60B,

a person who is treated by A as a person who is or has been the borrower under a regulated credit agreement is to be treated as a 'client'.

(3)   In this article, 'borrower' includes (in addition to those persons included in the definition in article 60L [or, where the credit agreement is a green deal plan, article 60LB])—

(a)    any person providing a guarantee or indemnity under a regulated credit agreement, and

(b)    a person to whom the rights and duties of a person falling within sub-paragraph (a) have passed by assignment or operation of law.]

## [60LB    Green deal plans

(1)    A green deal plan is to be treated as a credit agreement for the purposes of this Order if (and only if)—

(a)    the property in relation to the plan is a domestic property at the time when the plan is commenced, or

(b)    if sub-paragraph (a) does not apply, the occupier or owner of the property who makes the arrangement for the plan is an individual or relevant recipient of credit.

(2)    In the application of this Order to a green deal credit agreement—

(a)    the lender is to be treated as being—

(i)    the green deal provider (within the meaning of Chapter 1 of Part 1 of the Energy Act 2011) for the plan, or

(ii)   a person who exercises or has the right to exercise the rights and duties of the green deal provider under the plan,

(b)    credit is to be treated as advanced under the agreement of an amount equal to the amount of the improvement costs, and

(c)    the advance of credit is to be treated as made on the completion of the installation of the energy efficiency improvements to the property (but this sub-paragraph is subject to any term of the green deal plan providing that part of the advance is to be treated as made on completion of any part of the installation).

(3)    A reference in a provision of this Order listed in the first column of the table in Schedule 4A to the borrower is, in the application of the provision in relation to a green deal credit agreement, to be read as a reference to—

(a)    a person who at the relevant time falls (or fell) within the description or descriptions specified in the corresponding entry in the second column of the table, or

(b)    if more than one description is specified and at the relevant time different persons fall (or fell) within the descriptions, each of those persons,

and except as provided by this paragraph, a person is not and is not to be treated as the borrower in relation to the agreement.

(4)    References in Schedule 4A to the 'improver', 'first bill payer', 'current bill payer' and 'previous bill payer' are to be read as follows—

(a)    a person is the 'improver' if the person—

(i)    is the owner or occupier of the property, and

(ii)   is the person who makes (or has made or proposes to make) the arrangement for the green deal plan;

(b)    a person is the 'first bill payer' if the person is liable to pay the energy bills for the property at the time when the green deal plan is commenced;

(c)    a person is the 'current bill payer' if the person is liable by virtue of section 1(6)(a) of the Energy Act 2011 to pay instalments under the plan as a result of being for the time being liable to pay the energy bills for the property;

(d)    a person is a 'previous bill payer' if, as a result of previously falling within sub-paragraph (c) for an earlier period, the person has an outstanding payment liability under the plan in respect of that period.

(5)    In this article—

'domestic property' means a building or part of a building that is occupied as a dwelling or (if not occupied) is intended to be occupied as a dwelling;

'energy bill' has the same meaning as in section 1 of the Energy Act 2011;

'energy efficiency improvements' has the meaning given by section 2(4) of the Energy Act 2011;

'green deal credit agreement' means a green deal plan that is to be treated as a credit agreement for the purposes of this Order by virtue of paragraph (1);

'improvement costs', in relation to a green deal plan, are the costs of the energy efficiency improvements to the property which are to be paid by instalments under the plan after the time when credit is to be treated as being advanced by virtue of paragraph (2) (but ignoring any interest or other charges for credit in determining those costs);

'occupier' and 'owner' have the same meanings as in Chapter 1 of Part 1 of the Energy Act 2011;

'property', in relation to a green deal plan, means the property to which the energy efficiency improvements under the plan are or are intended to be made.

(6)    For the purposes of this article—

(a)    a green deal plan is commenced when—

(i)    the occupier or owner of the property signs in the prescribed manner a document in relation to the plan in accordance with section 61(1) of the Consumer Credit Act 1974 (requirements as to form and content of regulated agreements)(1), or

(ii)    if the occupier or owner of the property does not sign such a document, the green deal plan is made;

(b)    a person is liable to pay the energy bills for a property at any time if the person would be treated as the bill payer for the property at that time for the purposes of Chapter 1 of Part 1 of the Energy Act 2011 (see section 2(3) and (10)).]

### 60M    Total charge for credit

(1)    The FCA may make rules specifying how the total charge for credit to the borrower under a credit agreement is to be determined for the purposes of this Chapter.

(2)    Rules made under paragraph (1) may in particular—

(a)    specify how the total charge for credit to a person who is, or is to become, the borrower under a credit agreement is to be determined;

(b)    specify what items are to be included in determining the total charge for credit and how the value of those items is to be determined;

(c)    specify the method of calculating the rate of the total charge for credit;

(d)    provide for the whole or part of the amount payable by the borrower or a relative of the borrower under a linked transaction (within the meaning given by article 60E(8)) to be included in the total charge for credit, whether or not the lender is a party to the transaction or derives a benefit from it.

## CHAPTER 14B
## REGULATED CONSUMER HIRE AGREEMENTS

*The activities*

### 60N   Regulated consumer hire agreements

(1)   Entering into a regulated consumer hire agreement as owner is a specified kind of activity.

(2)   It is a specified kind of activity for the owner or another person to exercise, or to have the right to exercise, the owner's rights and duties under a regulated consumer hire agreement.

(3)   In this Chapter—

'consumer hire agreement' means an agreement between a person ('the owner') and an individual or relevant recipient of credit ('the hirer') for the bailment or, in Scotland, the hiring, of goods to the hirer which—

    (a)   is not a hire-purchase agreement, and

    (b)   is capable of subsisting for more than three months;

'exempt agreement' means a consumer hire agreement which is an exempt agreement under articles 60O to 60Q;

'owner' means—

    (a)   the person who bails or, in Scotland, hires, goods under a [. . .] consumer hire agreement, or

    (b)   a person who exercises or has the right to exercise the rights and duties of a person who bailed or, in Scotland, hired, goods under such an agreement;

'regulated consumer hire agreement' means a consumer hire agreement which is not an exempt agreement.

### 60O   Exempt agreements: exemptions relating to nature of agreement

(1)   An agreement is an exempt agreement for the purposes of this Chapter if—

    (a)   the hirer is required by the agreement to make payments exceeding £25,000, and

    (b)   the agreement is entered into by the hirer wholly or predominantly for the purposes of a business carried on, or intended to be carried on, by the hirer.

(2)   For the purposes of paragraph (1), if an agreement includes a declaration which—

    (a)   is made by the hirer,

    (b)   provides that the agreement is entered into by the hirer wholly or predominantly for the purposes of a business carried on, or intended to be carried on, by the hirer, and

    (c)   complies with rules made by the FCA for the purposes of this article,

the agreement is to be presumed to have been entered into by the hirer wholly or predominantly for the purpose in sub-paragraph (b) unless paragraph (3) applies.

(3)   This paragraph applies if, when the agreement is entered into—

    (a)   the owner (or, if there is more than one owner, any of the owners), or

    (b)   any person who has acted on behalf of the owner (or, if there is more than one owner, any of the owners), in connection with the entering into of the agreement,

knows or has reasonable cause to suspect that the agreement is not entered into by the hirer wholly or predominantly for the purposes of a business carried on, or intended to be carried on, by the hirer.

(4)   For the purposes of this article, where credit is provided otherwise than in sterling, it is to be treated as provided in sterling of an equivalent amount.

### 60P   Exempt agreements: exemptions relating to supply of essential services

An agreement is an exempt agreement for the purposes of this Chapter if—

    (a)   the owner is a body corporate which is authorised by or under an enactment to supply gas, electricity or water, and

(b)    the subject of the agreement is a meter or metering equipment which is used (or is to be used) in connection with the supply of gas, electricity or water.

### 60Q    Exempt agreements: exemptions relating to the nature of the hirer

An agreement is an exempt agreement for the purposes of this Chapter if—

(a)    the hirer is an individual,

(b)    the agreement includes a declaration made by the hirer which provides that the hirer agrees to forgo the protection and remedies that would be available to the hirer if the agreement were a regulated consumer hire agreement and which complies with rules made by the FCA for the purposes of this paragraph,

(c)    a statement has been made in relation to the income or assets of the hirer which complies with rules made by the FCA for the purposes of this paragraph,

(d)    the connection between the statement and the agreement complies with any rules made by the FCA for the purposes of this paragraph (including as to the period of time between the making of the statement and the agreement being entered into), and

(e)    a copy of the statement was provided to the owner before the agreement was entered into.

*Exclusion*

### 60R    [Other exclusions]

Article 60N is subject to the exclusion in article 72A (information society services) [and the exclusion in article 72G (local authorities)].

*[Supplemental*

### 60S    Meaning of consumer etc

(1)    For the purposes of sections 1G, 404E and 425A of the Act (meaning of 'consumer'), in so far as those provisions relate to a person ('A') carrying on a regulated activity of the kind specified by—

(a)    article 60N (regulated consumer hire agreements), or

(b)    article 64 (agreeing to carry on specified kinds of activity) in so far as that article relates to article 60N,

a person who is treated by A as a person who is or has been the hirer under a regulated consumer hire agreement is to be treated as a 'consumer'.

(2)    For the purposes of section 328(8) of the Act (meaning of 'clients') in so far as that provision relates to a person ('A') carrying on a regulated activity of the kind specified by—

(a)    article 60N (regulated consumer hire agreements), or

(b)    article 64 (agreeing to carry on specified kinds of activity) in so far as that article relates to article 60N,

a person who is treated by A as a person who is or has been the hirer under a regulated consumer hire agreement is to be treated as a 'client'.

(3)    In this article, 'hirer' includes (in addition to those persons defined as 'the hirer' in the definition of 'consumer hire agreement' in article 60N(3))—

(a)    any person providing a guarantee or indemnity under a consumer hire agreement, and

(b)    a person to whom the rights and duties of a person falling within sub-paragraph (a) have passed by assignment or operation of law.]]

## LIMITED LIABILITY PARTNERSHIPS REGULATIONS 2001
### (SI 2001/1090)

### PART VI
### DEFAULT PROVISION

### 7 Default provision for limited liability partnerships

The mutual rights and duties of the members and the mutual rights and duties of the limited liability partnership and the members shall be determined, subject to the provisions of the general law and to the terms of any limited liability partnership agreement, by the following rules:

(1) All the members of a limited liability partnership are entitled to share equally in the capital and profits of the limited liability partnership.

(2) The limited liability partnership must indemnify each member in respect of payments made and personal liabilities incurred by him—

(a) in the ordinary and proper conduct of the business of the limited liability partnership; or

(b) in or about anything necessarily done for the preservation of the business or property of the limited liability partnership.

(3) Every member may take part in the management of the limited liability partnership.

(4) No member shall be entitled to remuneration for acting in the business or management of the limited liability partnership.

(5) No person may be introduced as a member or voluntarily assign an interest in a limited liability partnership without the consent of all existing members.

(6) Any difference arising as to ordinary matters connected with the business of the limited liability partnership may be decided by a majority of the members, but no change may be made in the nature of the business of the limited liability partnership without the consent of all the members.

(7) The books and records of the limited liability partnership are to be made available for inspection at the registered office of the limited liability partnership or at such other place as the members think fit and every member of the limited liability partnership may when he thinks fit have access to and inspect and copy any of them.

(8) Each member shall render true accounts and full information of all things affecting the limited liability partnership to any member or his legal representatives.

(9) If a member, without the consent of the limited liability partnership, carries on any business of the same nature as and competing with the limited liability partnership, he must account for and pay over to the limited liability partnership all profits made by him in that business.

(10) Every member must account to the limited liability partnership for any benefit derived by him without the consent of the limited liability partnership from any transaction concerning the limited liability partnership, or from any use by him of the property of the limited liability partnership, name or business connection.

### 8 Expulsion

No majority of the members can expel any member unless a power to do so has been conferred by express agreement between the members.

CONSUMER CREDIT (EU DIRECTIVE) REGULATIONS 2010
(SI 2010/1010)

PART 4
COMMENCEMENT, TRANSITIONAL AND SAVING PROVISION

. . .

**100 Application of regulations to agreements entered into before 1st February 2011**

(1) Subject to paragraphs (2) to (5) [regulations 101 and 101A] these Regulations apply only to a regulated consumer credit agreement entered into on or after 1st February 2011.

(2) The following regulations apply (from 1st February 2011) to a regulated consumer credit agreement which is an open-end agreement and is entered into before 11th June 2010—

[(za) regulation 22 (information to be provided on significant overdrawing without prior arrangement);]

(a) regulations 27 and 28 (information on change of interest rate etc);

(b) regulation 36 (assignment);

(c) regulations 37 to 39 (open-end agreements);

(d) regulation 46(b)(amendments to Enterprise Act 2002);

(e) regulation 63 (amendments to Consumer Credit (Running-Account Credit Information) Regulations 1983);

(f) regulation 69(b)(amendments to Enterprise Act 2002 (Part 8 Community Infringements Specified UK Laws) Order 2003);

(g) regulation 97 (amendments to Payment Services Regulations 2009).

(3) The following regulations apply (from 1st February 2011) to a regulated consumer credit agreement which is an open-end agreement and is entered into on or after 11th June 2010 and before 1st February 2011—

[(za) regulation 22 (information to be provided on significant overdrawing without prior arrangement);]

(a) regulation 25 (linked credit agreements);

(b) regulations 27 and 28 (information on change of interest rate etc);

(c) regulations 29 to 35 (early repayment);

(d) regulation 36 (assignment);

(e) regulations 37 to 39 (open-end agreements);

(f) regulation 46 (amendments to Enterprise Act 2002);

(g) regulations 59 to 62 (amendments to Consumer Credit (Settlement Information) Regulations 1983);

(h) regulation 63 (amendments to Consumer Credit (Running-Account Credit Information) Regulations 1983);

(i) regulation 69 (amendments to Enterprise Act 2002 (Part 8 Community Infringements Specified UK Laws) Order 2003);

(j) regulations 77 to 84 (amendments to Consumer Credit (Early Settlement) Regulations 2004);

(k) regulation 97 (amendments to Payment Services Regulations 2009).

(4) The following regulations apply (from 1st February 2011) to a regulated consumer credit agreement which not an open-end agreement and is entered into on or after 11th June 2010 and before 1st February 2011—

(a) regulation 25 (linked credit agreements);

(b) regulation 26 (statement of account);

(c) regulations 29 to 35 (early repayment);

(d) regulation 36 (assignment);

(e) regulation 46 (amendments to Enterprise Act 2002);

(f) regulations 59 to 62 (amendments to Consumer Credit (Settlement Information) Regulations 1983);

(g)   regulation 69 (amendments to Enterprise Act 2002 (Part 8 Community Infringements Specified UK Laws) Order 2003);

(h)   regulations 77 to 84 (amendments to Consumer Credit (Early Settlement) Regulations 2004).

(5)   Section 95A of the Consumer Credit Act 1974 (compensation for early repayment) applies in relation to an agreement by virtue of sub-paragraph (3)(c) or (4)(c) only where the debtor's entitlement to discharge his indebtedness arises by virtue of a notice made on or after 1st February 2011.

**101   Early application of regulations to certain agreements before 1st February 2011**

(1)   Where one of the conditions A to E is satisfied in relation to a prospective regulated consumer credit agreement on a date on or after 30th April 2010 and before 1st February 2011, Parts 1 to 3 of these Regulations apply to that agreement (and to any subsequent regulated consumer credit agreement entered into before 1st February 2011), from the date and time that the condition is satisfied.

(2)   Condition A is that information relating to the agreement is disclosed by a creditor or a credit intermediary before the agreement is made in compliance or in purported compliance with the Information Regulations 2010.

(3)   Condition B is that—

(a)   the agreement would, if made, be an agreement entered into at the debtor's request using a means of distance communication (other than voice telephony) which does not enable the provision before the agreement is made of the information referred to in regulation 3(4) of the Information Regulations 2010, and

(b)   the debtor is informed by the creditor before the agreement is made that the information referred to in regulation 3(4) of the Information Regulations 2010 will be disclosed immediately after the agreement is made in accordance with regulation 5 of those Regulations.

(4)   Condition C is that—

(a)   the agreement would, if made, be a distance agreement entered into by the debtor wholly or predominantly for the purposes of a business carried on, or intended to be carried on, by him, and

(b)   the debtor is informed by the creditor before the agreement is made that information referred to in regulation 3(4) of the Information Regulations 2010 will be disclosed immediately after the agreement is made in accordance with regulation 6 of those Regulations.

(5)   Condition D is that —

(a)   the agreement would, if made, be an authorised non-business overdraft agreement (other than a qualifying overdraft agreement referred to in paragraph (7)(b)),

(b)   the agreement would, if made, be one made at the debtor's request using a means of distance communication which does not enable the provision before the agreement is made of the information referred to in regulation 10(2) of the Information Regulations 2010, and

(c)   the creditor has informed the debtor before the agreement is made that a document containing the terms of the agreement will be provided immediately after the agreement is made as though the amendment made by regulation 9 of these Regulations (insertion of section 61B in the Consumer Credit Act 1974) applied.

(6)   Condition E is that the agreement would, if made, be a qualifying overdraft agreement and—

(a)   the creditor has provided a document containing the terms of the agreement before the agreement is made as though the amendment made by regulation 9 (insertion of section 61B in the Consumer Credit Act 1974) applied, or

(b) the creditor has informed the debtor before the agreement is made that a document containing the terms of the agreement will be provided at, or immediately after, the time the agreement is made as though the amendment made by regulation 9 applied.

(7) In paragraph (6) 'qualifying overdraft agreement' means—

(a) an authorised business overdraft agreement, or

(b) an authorised non-business overdraft agreement under which the creditor provides the debtor with credit exceeding £60,260 or which is secured on land.

[**101A**—(1) Where condition F is satisfied on a date on or after 26th August 2010 and before 1st February 2011 in relation to a prospective regulated consumer credit agreement falling within paragraph (2), Parts 1 to 3 of these Regulations apply to that agreement (and to any subsequent regulated consumer credit agreement entered into before 1st February 2011), from the date and time that the condition is satisfied.

(2) An agreement falls within this paragraph if it is an agreement which would, if made, be—

(a) an agreement under which the creditor provides the debtor with credit exceeding £60,260 and is not an authorised non-business overdraft agreement, or

(b) an agreement entered into by the debtor wholly or predominantly for the purposes of a business carried on, or intended to be carried on, by him.

(3) Condition F is that the Consumer Credit (Disclosure of Information) Regulations 2004 apply to the agreement, but the creditor—

(a) does what would be required by regulations 3(1)(a) and (c) of those Regulations (pre-contractual information requirement to disclose information and statements required by the Consumer Credit (Agreements) Regulations 1983) if the amendments to the Consumer Credit (Agreements) Regulations 1983 made by regulations 52 to 56 were in force; and

(b) also provides the debtor with a statement before the agreement is made that, if the creditor decides not to proceed with the agreement on the basis of information obtained from a credit reference agency, the creditor will, when informing the debtor of the decision—

(i) inform the debtor that this decision has been reached on the basis of information from a credit reference agency, and

(ii) provide the debtor with the particulars of the agency including its name, address and telephone number.]

## 102 Interpretation
In this Part—

(a) 'authorised business overdraft agreement', 'authorised non-business overdraft agreement', 'consumer credit agreement', 'creditor', 'debtor', 'open-end' and 'regulated' have the meanings given by section 189(1) of the Consumer Credit Act 1974;

(b) 'distance agreement' means any regulated consumer credit agreement made under an organised distance sales or service-provision scheme run by the creditor or on behalf of the creditor who, in any such case, for the purpose of that agreement makes exclusive use of one or more means of distance communication up to and including the time at which the agreement is made;

(c) 'Information Regulations 2010' means the Consumer Credit (Disclosure of Information) Regulations 2010;

(d) 'means of distance communication' means any means which, without the simultaneous physical presence of the creditor or a person acting on behalf of the creditor and of the debtor, may be used for the making of a regulated consumer credit agreement between the parties to that agreement.

## CONSUMER CREDIT (DISCLOSURE OF INFORMATION) REGULATIONS
### 2010
### (SI 2010/1013)

### 1  Citation, commencement and interpretation

(1)  These Regulations may be cited as the Consumer Credit (Disclosure of Information) Regulations 2010 and shall come into force on 30th April 2010.

(2)  In these Regulations—

'the Act' means the Consumer Credit Act 1974;

'advance payment' includes any deposit and in relation to a regulated consumer credit agreement includes also any part-exchange allowance in respect of any goods agreed in antecedent negotiations [. . .] to be taken by the creditor in part exchange but does not include a repayment of credit or any insurance premium or any amount entering into the total charge for credit;

'ancillary service' means a service that relates to the provision of credit under the agreement and includes in particular an insurance or payment protection policy;

'the APR' means the annual percentage rate of charge for credit determined in accordance with Schedule 2 to these Regulations and the [total charge for credit rules];

'cash price' in relation to any goods, services, land or other things means the price or charge at which the goods, services, land or other things may be purchased by, or supplied to, the debtor for cash account being taken of any discount generally available from the dealer or supplier in question;

'credit intermediary' has the same meaning as in [section 61A] of the Act;

'distance contract' means any regulated agreement made under an organised distance sales or service-provision scheme run by or on behalf of the creditor who, in any such case, for the purpose of that agreement makes exclusive use of one or more means of distance communication up to and including the time at which the agreement is made. For this purpose, 'means of distance communication' means any means which, without the simultaneous physical presence of the creditor or a person acting on behalf of the creditor and of the debtor, may be used for the making of a regulated agreement between the parties to that agreement;

'excluded pawn agreement' means a pawn agreement—

(a)  where the debtor is not a new customer of the creditor (see [paragraph (6)]), and

(b)  where, before the agreement is made, the creditor has not received a request from the debtor for the pre-contract credit information (see regulation 9);

'linked credit agreement' means a regulated consumer credit agreement which—

(a)  serves exclusively to finance an agreement for the supply of specific goods or the provision of a specific service or land, and

(b)  (i) where the supplier or service provider himself finances the credit for the debtor, or if it is financed by a third party, where the creditor uses the services of the supplier or service provider in connection with the preparation or making of the credit agreement, or

(ii)  where the specific goods or land or the provision of a specific service are explicitly specified in the credit agreement;

'pawn agreement' means a consumer credit agreement under which the creditor takes an article in pawn;

'pre-contract credit information' means the information specified in regulation 3(4);

'total amount of credit' means the credit limit or the total sums made available under a consumer credit agreement;

'total amount payable' means the sum of the total charge for credit and the total amount of credit payable under the agreement as well as any advance payment;

'total charge for credit' means the total charge for credit determined in accordance with the [total charge for credit rules] and the Schedule to these Regulations;

['the total charge for credit rules' means rules made by the Financial Conduct Authority under article 60M of the Financial Services and Markets Act 2000 (Regulated Activities) Order 2001 for the purposes of Chapter 14A of Part 2 of that Order;]

(3)   In these Regulations, a reference to a repayment is a reference to—

(a)   a repayment of the whole or any part of the credit,

(b)   a payment of the whole or any part of the total charge for credit, or

(c)   a combination of such repayments and payments.

(4)   In these Regulations, a reference to rate of interest is a reference to the interest rate expressed as a fixed or variable percentage applied on an annual basis to the amount of credit drawn down.

(5)   In these Regulations, a reference to an agreement includes a reference to a prospective agreement.

(6)   For the purposes of the definition of 'excluded pawn agreement' and regulation 8 the debtor is a new customer if the debtor has not entered into a pawn agreement with the creditor in the three years preceding the start of the negotiations antecedent to the agreement.

[. . .]

## 2   Agreements to which these Regulations apply

(1)   These Regulations apply in respect of a regulated consumer credit agreement, except as provided for in paragraphs (2) to (4).

(2)   These regulations do not apply to an agreement to which section 58 of the Act (opportunity for withdrawal from prospective land mortgage) applies.

(3)   These Regulations do not apply to an authorised non-business overdraft agreement which is—

(a)   for credit which exceeds £60,260 [unless it is a residential renovation agreement], or

(b)   secured on land.

(4)   Except as provided for in paragraph (5) these Regulations do not apply to an agreement—

(a)   under which the creditor provides the debtor with credit exceeding £60,260 [unless it is a residential renovation agreement],

(b)   secured on land,

(c)   entered into by the debtor wholly or predominantly for the purposes of a business also carried on, or intended to be carried on, by him, or

(d)   made before 1st February 2011.

(5)   These Regulations apply to an agreement mentioned in paragraph (4) (which is not also an agreement mentioned in paragraph (2) or (3)) where a creditor or, where applicable a credit intermediary, discloses or purports to disclose the pre-contract credit information in accordance with these Regulations rather than in accordance with the Consumer Credit (Disclosure of Information) Regulations 2004 or the Financial Services (Distance Marketing) Regulations 2004 (as the case may be).

[(6)   Article 60C(5) and (6) of the Financial Services and Markets Act 2000 (Regulated Activities) Order 2001 applies for the purposes of paragraph (4)(c).]

## 3   Information to be disclosed: agreements other than telephone contracts, non-telephone distance contracts, excluded pawn agreements and overdraft agreements

(1)   This regulation applies to an agreement other than—

[(a)   an agreement made by voice telephone communication where it is a distance contract and the debtor consents to the disclosure of the information referred to in regulation 4(2);

(aa)  an agreement made by voice telephone communication where it is not a distance contract (see regulation 4(3));]

(b)   an agreement made using a means of distance communication other than a voice telephone communication, which does not enable the provision of the pre-contract credit information before the agreement is made (see regulation 5);

(c)   an excluded pawn agreement;

(d)   an authorised non-business overdraft agreement (see regulations 10 and 11).

(2)  In good time before the agreement is made, the creditor must disclose to the debtor, in the manner set out in regulation 8, the pre-contract credit information.

(3)  Paragraph (2) does not require a creditor to disclose the pre-contract credit information where it has already been disclosed to the debtor by a credit intermediary in a manner which complies with paragraph (2).

(4)  For the purposes of these Regulations, the pre-contract credit information comprises—

(a)   the type of credit,

(b)   the identity and geographical address of the creditor and, where applicable, of the credit intermediary,

(c)   the total amount of credit to be provided under the agreement and the conditions governing the draw down of credit. In the case of an agreement for running-account credit, the total amount of credit may be expressed as a statement indicating the manner in which the credit limit will be determined where it is not practicable to express the limit as a sum of money,

(d)   the duration or minimum duration of the agreement or a statement that the agreement has no fixed or minimum duration,

(e)   in the case of—

(i)  credit in the form of deferred payment for specific goods, services or land, or

(ii)  a linked credit agreement,

a description of the goods, services or land and the cash price of each and the total cash price,

(f)   the rate of interest charged, any conditions applicable to that rate, where available, any reference rate on which that rate is based and any information on any changes to the rate of interest (including the periods that the rate applies, and any conditions or procedure applicable to changing the rate),

(g)   where different rates of interest are charged in different circumstances the creditor must provide the information in paragraph (f) in respect of each rate,

(h)   the APR and the total amount payable under the agreement illustrated (if not known) by way of a representative example mentioning all the assumptions used in order to calculate that rate and amount,

(i)   the amount (expressed as a sum of money), number (if applicable) and frequency of repayments to be made by the debtor and, where appropriate, the order in which repayments will be allocated to different outstanding balances charged at different rates of interest,

(j)   in the case of an agreement for running-account credit, the amount of each repayment is to be expressed as (a) a sum of money; (b) a specified proportion of a specified amount; (c) a combination of (a) or (b); or (d) in a case where the amount of any repayment cannot be expressed in accordance with (a), (b) or (c), a statement indicating the manner in which the amount will be determined,

(k)   if applicable, any charges for maintaining an account recording both payment transactions and draw downs, unless the opening of an account is optional, and any charge payable for using a method of payment in respect of payment transactions or draw downs,

(l)     any other charges payable deriving from the credit agreement and the conditions under which those charges may be changed,

(m)   if applicable, a statement that fees will be payable by the debtor to a notary on conclusion of the credit agreement,

(n)    the obligation, if any, to enter into a contract for ancillary services relating to the consumer credit agreement, in particular insurance services, where the conclusion of such a contract is compulsory in order to obtain the credit or to obtain it on the terms and conditions marketed,

(o)    the rate of interest applicable in the case of late payments and the arrangements for its adjustment, and, where applicable, any charges payable for default,

(p)    a warning regarding the consequences of missing payments (for example, the possibility of legal proceedings and the possibility that the debtor's home may be repossessed),

(q)    where applicable, any security to be provided by the debtor or on behalf of the debtor,

(r)     the existence or absence of a right of withdrawal,

(s)     the debtor's right of early repayment under section 94 of the Act, and where applicable, information concerning the creditor's right to compensation and the way in which that compensation will be determined,

(t)     the requirement for a creditor to inform a debtor in accordance with section 157(A1) of the Act that a decision not to proceed with a prospective regulated consumer credit agreement has been reached on the basis of information from a credit reference agency and of the particulars of that agency,

(u)    the debtor's right to be supplied under section 55C of the Act on request and free of charge, with a copy of the draft agreement except where—

(i)    the creditor is at the time of the request unwilling to proceed to the making of the agreement, or

(ii)   the agreement is an agreement referred to in regulation 2(4)(a) to (c) or a pawn agreement, and

(v)    if applicable, the period of time during which the creditor is bound by the pre-contract credit information.

(5)    For the purpose of the representative example referred to in paragraph (4)(h)—

(a) (i)    where the debtor has informed the creditor or credit intermediary of one or more components of his preferred credit, such as the duration of the consumer credit agreement or the total amount of credit, and

(ii)   where the creditor would in principle agree to offer credit on such terms,

the creditor or credit intermediary must take those components into account when calculating the representative APR and the total amount payable;

(b)    where the creditor uses the assumption set out in [the total charge for credit rules] the creditor must indicate that other draw down mechanisms for this type of consumer credit agreement may result in a higher APR;

(c)    subject to paragraph (a), in the case of an agreement for running-account credit, where the credit limit is not known at the date on which the pre-contract credit information is disclosed, the total amount of credit is to be assumed to be £1,200 or in a case where credit is to be provided subject to a maximum credit limit of less than £1,200, an amount equal to that maximum limit.

(6)    In the case of a consumer credit agreement under which repayments do not give rise to an immediate reduction in the total amount of credit advanced but are used to constitute capital as provided for under the agreement or under an ancillary agreement, the creditor or credit intermediary must provide a clear and

concise statement that such agreements do not provide for a guarantee of repayment of the total amount of credit drawn down under the credit agreement unless
such a guarantee is given.

### 4 Information to be disclosed: telephone contracts

(1) This regulation applies to an agreement (other than an authorised non-
business overdraft agreement) made by way of a voice telephone communication (whether or not it is a distance contract).

(2) Where the agreement is a distance contract and where the debtor explicitly
consents, the creditor must disclose the following information before the agreement is made—

(a) the identity of the person in contact with the debtor and that person's
link with the creditor,

(b) a description of the main characteristics of the credit agreement which
includes the information set out in regulation 3(4)(c), (d), (e), (f), (g), (h), (i) and
(j),

(c) the total price to be paid by the debtor to the creditor for the credit
including all taxes paid via the creditor or, if an exact price cannot be indicated,
the basis for the calculation of the price enabling the debtor to verify it,

(d) notice of the possibility that other taxes or costs may exist that are not
paid via the creditor or imposed by the creditor,

(e) whether or not there is—

(i) a right to withdraw under section 66A of the Act, or

(ii) a right to cancel under regulation 9 of the Financial Services (Distance
Marketing) Regulations 2004 and, where there is such a right, its duration and
the conditions for exercising it, including information on the amount which
the consumer may be required to pay in accordance with regulation 13 of
those Regulations, as well as the consequences of not exercising that right,

(f) that other information is available on request and the nature of that
information.

(3) Where the agreement is not a distance contract the creditor must disclose
the information in paragraph (2)(b) before the agreement is made.

(4) The creditor must disclose the pre-contract credit information in the
manner set out in regulation 8 immediately after the agreement is made.

### 5 Information to be disclosed: non-telephone distance contracts

(1) This regulation applies to an agreement (other than an authorised non-
business overdraft agreement) made—

(a) at the debtor's request, and

(b) using a means of distance communication other than a voice telephone
communication which does not enable the provision before the agreement is
made of the pre-contract credit information.

(2) The creditor must disclose the pre-contract credit information in the
manner set out in regulation 8 immediately after the agreement is made.

### 6 Information to be disclosed: distance contracts for the purpose of a business

(1) This regulation applies to an agreement that is a distance contract entered
into by the debtor wholly or predominantly for the purposes of a business carried
on, or intended to be carried on by him.

(2) Where the agreement is an agreement to which [regulations 3, 4 or 5]
would otherwise apply the creditor may comply with those regulations by disclosing the pre-contract credit information immediately after the agreement is
entered into.

[(3) Article 60C(5) and (6) of the Financial Services and Markets Act 2000
(Regulated Activities) Order 2001 applies for the purposes of paragraph (1).]

**7 Information about contractual terms and conditions: [regulations 3, 4 and 5]**

(1) This regulation applies to an agreement which is—

    (a) a distance contract to which [regulations 3, 4 or 5] applies, and

    (b) which is not entered into by the debtor wholly or predominantly for the purposes of a business carried on, or intended to be carried on, by him.

(2) The creditor must ensure that—

    (a) the information provided to the debtor pursuant to [regulations 3, 4 or 5] includes the contractual terms and conditions, and

    (b) the information provided to the debtor in relation to the contractual obligations which would arise if the distance contract were made accurately reflects the contractual obligations which would arise under the law presumed to be applicable to that contract.

[(3) Article 60C(5) and (6) of the Financial Services and Markets Act 2000 (Regulated Activities) Order 2001 applies for the purposes of paragraph (1).]

**8 Manner of disclosure**

(1) The pre-contract credit information must be disclosed by means of the form contained in Schedule 1.

(2) The form must be—

    (a) in writing, and

    (b) of a nature that enables the debtor to remove it from the place where it is disclosed to him.

(3) The form must be completed as specified in this paragraph—

    (a) the relevant pre-contract credit information is to be provided in the appropriate row,

    (b) the form is to be completed in accordance with the notes to that form,

    (c) the asterisks and notes may be deleted,

    (d) gridlines and boxes may be omitted, and

    (e) any information contained in the form must be clear and easily legible.

(4) Any additional information relating to the credit which is provided in writing by the creditor to the debtor must be provided in a separate document to the form.

(5) Where a consumer credit agreement is a multiple agreement containing more than one part for the purposes of section 18 of the Act, the pre-contract credit information in respect of each part may be provided in the same form provided that—

    (a) information that is not common to each part of the agreement is disclosed separately within the relevant section of the form, and

    (b) it is clear which information relates to which part.

**9 Information to be disclosed: pawn agreements**

(1) This Regulation applies to a pawn agreement.

(2) In good time before a pawn agreement is made (unless the debtor is a new customer), the creditor must inform the debtor of his right to receive the pre-contract credit information in the form contained in Schedule 1, free of charge, on request.

**10 Information to be disclosed: overdraft agreements**

(1) This regulation applies to an agreement which is an authorised non-business overdraft agreement.

(2) In good time before an authorised non-business overdraft agreement is made, the creditor must disclose to the debtor, the information in paragraph (3) in the manner set out in regulation 11.

(3) The information referred to in paragraph (2) is as follows—

    (a) the type of credit,

    (b) the identity and geographical address of the creditor and, where applicable, of the credit intermediary,

    (c)    the total amount of credit,

    (d)    the duration of the agreement,

    (e)    the rate of interest charged, any conditions applicable to that rate, any reference rate on which that rate is based and any information on any changes to the rate of interest (including the periods that the rate applies, and any conditions or procedure applicable to changing the rate),

    (f)    where different rates of interest are charged in different circumstances the creditor must provide the information in paragraph (e) in respect of each rate,

    (g)    the conditions and procedure for terminating the agreement,

    (h)    where applicable, an indication that the debtor may be requested to repay the amount of credit in full on demand at any time,

    (i)    the rate of interest applicable in the case of late payments and the arrangements for its adjustment, and, where applicable, any charges payable for default,

    (j)    the requirement for a creditor to inform a debtor in accordance with section 157(A1) of the Act that a decision not to proceed with a prospective regulated consumer credit agreement has been reached on the basis of information from a credit reference agency and of the particulars of that agency,

    (k)    the charges, other than the rates of interest, payable by the debtor under the agreement (and the conditions under which those charges may be varied),

    (l)    if applicable, the period of time during which the creditor is bound by the information set out in this paragraph.

(4)    Paragraph (2) does not apply to—

    (a)    an agreement made by a voice telephone communication (whether or not it is a distance contract),

    (b)    an agreement made at the debtor's request using a means of distance communication, other than a voice telephone communication, which does not enable the provision of the information required by paragraph (2) before the agreement is made, or

    (c)    an agreement that does not come within sub-paragraph (a) or (b) but where the debtor requests the overdraft be made available with immediate effect.

(5)    In the case of an agreement that falls within paragraph (4)(a) that is also a distance contract, where the debtor explicitly consents the creditor must disclose the following information before the agreement is made—

    (a)    the identity of the person in contact with the debtor and that person's link with the creditor,

    (b)    a description of the main characteristics of the financial service including at least the information in paragraph (3)(c), (e), (f), (h) and (k),

    (c)    the total price to be paid by the debtor to the creditor for the credit including all taxes paid via the creditor or, if an exact price cannot be indicated, the basis for the calculation of the price enabling the debtor to verify it,

    (d)    notice of the possibility that other taxes or costs may exist that are not paid via the creditor or imposed by the creditor,

    (e)    whether or not there is a right to cancel under regulation 9 of the Financial Services (Distance Marketing) Regulations 2004 and where there is such a right, its duration and the conditions for exercising it including information on the amount which the consumer may be required to pay in accordance with regulation 13 of those regulations, as well as the consequences of not exercising that right, and

    (f)    that other information is available on request and the nature of that information.

[(5A)    In the case of an agreement that falls within paragraph (4)(a) that is also a distance contract, where the debtor does not explicitly consent to the disclosure of the information in paragraph (5), the creditor must disclose the information in paragraph (3) to the debtor before the [agreement] is made.]

(6)   In the case of an agreement that falls within paragraph (4)(a) that is not a distance contract the creditor must disclose the information in paragraph (5)(b) before the agreement is made.

(7)   In the case of an agreement that is a distance contract to which this regulation applies the creditor must ensure that the information he provides to the debtor pursuant to this regulation regarding the contractual obligations which would arise if the distance contract were concluded, accurately reflects the contractual obligations which would arise under the law presumed to be applicable to that contract.

(8)   In the case of an agreement that falls within paragraph (4)(c), the creditor must disclose the information in paragraph (3)(c), (e), (f), (h), and (k) to the debtor before the agreement is made in the manner set out in regulation 11.

(9)   Where a current account is an agreement for two or more debtors jointly the creditor may comply with paragraphs (5), [(5A),] (6) or (8) by disclosing the information to one debtor provided that each of the debtors have given the creditor their consent that the creditor may not comply in each debtor's case with the relevant paragraph.

11—(1)   Where regulation 10(2) applies, the creditor must comply with that regulation by—
   (a)   disclosing the information by means of the European Consumer Credit Information form set out in Schedule 3 to these Regulations and as specified in paragraph (2), or
   (b)   disclosing the information in writing so that all information is equally prominent.
(2)   The specifications referred to in paragraph (1)(a) are that—
   (a)   the relevant information must be provided in the appropriate row,
   (b)   the form must be completed in accordance with the notes to that form,
   (c)   the asterisks and notes may be deleted,
   (d)   gridlines and boxes may be omitted, and
   (e)   any information contained in the form must be clear and easily legible.
(3)   Where regulation 10(8) applies, the creditor may provide the information orally.

## 12   Modifying agreements
(1)   Subject to paragraphs (2) to (4), these Regulations apply to a modifying agreement which varies or supplements an earlier agreement and which is, or is treated under section 82(3) of the Act as, a regulated agreement.

[(2)   Where a modifying agreement modifies an earlier consumer credit agreement, the requirements of regulations 3, 4 and 10 will be deemed to be satisfied if—
   (a)   in good time before the modifying agreement is made—
      (i)   the information specified by regulations 3(4) and 10(3) is disclosed to the debtor in respect of any provision of the earlier agreement which is varied or supplemented, and
      (ii)   the creditor informs the debtor in writing that the other information in the earlier agreement remains unchanged, and
   (b)   where the Financial Services (Distance Marketing) Regulations 2004 apply, the creditor complies with regulations 7 and 8 of those Regulations.]
(3)   Where a modifying agreement is made in a manner that does not allow the creditor to comply with the requirement in [paragraph (2)(a)(ii)], the creditor is deemed to have complied with that requirement if—
   (a)   before the agreement is made the creditor informs the debtor orally that the other information in the earlier agreement remains unchanged, and

(b) this is confirmed to the debtor in writing immediately after the agreement is made.

(4)  This regulation does not apply to an excluded pawn agreement.

Regulation 8(1)                    S C H E D U L E  1

PRE-CONTRACT CREDIT INFORMATION

(Standard European Consumer Credit Information)

## 1. Contact details

| | |
|---|---|
| Creditor.<br>Address.<br>Telephone number(s).*<br>E-mail, address.*<br>Fax number.*<br>Web address.* | [Identity.]<br>[Geographical address of the creditor to be used by the debtor.] |
| If applicable<br>Credit intermediary.<br>Address.<br>Telephone number(s).*<br>E-mail address.*<br>Fax number.*<br>Web address.* | [Identity.]<br>[Geographical address of the credit intermediary to be used by the debtor.] |

*This information is optional for the creditor. The row may be deleted if the information is not provided.

Wherever "if applicable" is indicated, the creditor must give the information relevant to the credit product or, if the information is not relevant for the type of credit considered, delete the respective information or the entire row, or indicate that the information is not applicable.

Indications between square brackets provide explanations for the creditor and must be replaced with the corresponding information.

## 2. Key features of the credit product

| | |
|---|---|
| The type of credit. | |
| The total amount of credit. This means the amount of credit to be provided under the proposed credit agreement or the credit limit. | [The amount is to be expressed as a sum of money. In the case of running-account credit, the total amount may be expressed as a statement indicating the manner in which the credit limit will be determined where it is not practicable to express the limit as a sum of money.] |
| How and when credit would be provided. | [Details of how and when any credit being advanced is to be drawn down.] |
| The duration of the credit agreement. | [The duration or minimum duration of the agreement or a statement that the agreement has no fixed or minimum duration.] |
| Repayments. If applicable: Your repayments will pay off what you owe in the following order. | [The amount (expressed as a sum of money), number (if applicable) and frequency of repayments to be made by the debtor. In the case of an agreement for running-account credit, the amount may be expressed as a sum of money or a specified proportion of a specified amount or both, or in a case where the amount of any repayment cannot be expressed as a sum of money or a specified proportion, a statement indicating the manner in which the amount will be determined. [The order in which repayments will be allocated to different outstanding balances charged at different rates of interest.] |
| The total amount you will have to pay. This means the amount you have borrowed plus interest and other costs. | [The amount payable by the debtor under the agreement (where necessary, illustrated by means of a representative example). The total amount payable will be the sum of the total amount of credit and the total charge for credit payable under the agreement as well as any advance payment where required. In the case of running account credit, where it is not practicable to express the limit as a sum of money, a credit limit of £1200 should be assumed. In a case where credit is to be provided subject to a maximum credit limit of less than £1200, an amount equal to that maximum limit. The total charge for credit is to be calculated using the relevant APR assumptions set out in Schedule 2 to the Consumer Credit (Disclosure of Information) Regulations 2010 and the Total Charge for Credit Regulations, and where appropriate the relevant components of the debtor's preferred credit.] |

| | |
|---|---|
| If applicable<br>[The proposed credit will be granted in the form of a deferred payment for goods or service.] or<br>[The proposed credit will be linked to the supply of specific goods or the provision of a service.]<br>Description of goods/services/land (as applicable).<br>Cash price. | [A list or other description]<br>[Cash price of goods or service.]<br>[Total cash price.] |
| If applicable<br>Security required.<br>This is a description of the security to be provided by you in relation to the credit agreement. | [Description of any security to be provided by or on behalf of the debtor.] |
| If applicable<br>Repayments will not immediately reduce the amount you owe. | [In the case of a credit agreement under which repayments do not give rise to an immediate reduction in the total amount of credit advanced but are used to constitute capital as provided by the agreement (or an ancillary agreement a clear and concise statement) where applicable, that the agreement does not provide for a guarantee of the repayment of the total amount of credit drawn down under the credit agreement.] |

## 3. Costs of the credit

| | |
|---|---|
| The rates of interest which apply to the credit agreement | [Details of the rate of interest charged, any conditions applicable to that rate, where available, any reference rate on which that rate is based and any information on changes to the rate of interest (including the periods that the rate applies, and any conditions or procedure applicable to changing the rate). Where different rates of interest are charged in different circumstances, the creditor must provide the above information in respect of each rate.] |
| Annual Percentage Rate of Charge (APR).<br>This is the total cost expressed as an annual percentage of the total amount of credit.<br>The APR is there to help you compare different offers. | [% if known. If the APR is not known a representative example (expressed as a %) mentioning all the necessary assumptions used for calculating the rate (as set out in Schedule 2 to the Consumer Credit (Disclosure of Information) Regulations 2010, the Total Charge for Credit Regulations and, where appropriate, the relevant components of the debtor's preferred credit).<br>Where the creditor uses the assumption set out in [. . .] the Total Charge for Credit Regulations, the creditor shall indicate that other draw down mechanisms for this type of agreement may result in a higher APR.] |

| | |
|---|---|
| If applicable<br>In order to obtain the credit or to obtain it on the terms and conditions marketed, you must take out:<br>—an insurance policy securing the credit, or<br>—another ancillary service contract.<br>If we do not know the costs of these services they are not included in the APR. | [Nature and description of any insurance or other ancillary service contract required.] |
| Related costs | |
| If applicable<br>You must have a separate account for recording both payment transactions and drawdowns. | [Details of any account or accounts that the creditor requires to be set up in order to obtain the credit together with the amount of any charge for this.] |
| If applicable<br>Charge for using a specific payment method. | [Specify means of payment and the amount of charge.] |
| If applicable<br>Any other costs deriving from the credit agreement.<br>If applicable<br>Conditions under which the above charges can be changed. | [Description and amount of any other charges not otherwise referred to in this form.]<br>[Details of the conditions under which any of the charges mentioned above can be changed.] |
| If applicable<br>You will be required to pay notarial fees. | [Description and amount of any fee.] |
| Costs in the case of late payments | Either<br>[A statement that there are no charges for late or missed payments.]<br>Or<br>[Applicable rate of interest in the case of late payments and arrangements for its adjustment and, where applicable any charges payable for default.] |
| Consequences of missing payments. | [A statement warning about the consequences of missing payments, including:<br>—a reference to possible legal proceedings and repossession of the debtor's home where this is a possibility, and<br>—the possibility of missing payments making it more difficult to obtain credit in the future.] |

## 4. Other important legal aspects

| | |
|---|---|
| Right of withdrawal. | Either:<br>[A statement that the debtor has the right to withdraw from the credit agreement before the end of 14 days beginning with the day after the day on which the agreement is made, or if information is provided after the agreement is made, the day on which the debtor receives a copy of the executed agreement under sections 61A or 63 of the Consumer Credit Act 1974, the day on which the debtor receives the information required in section 61A(3) of that Act or the day on which the creditor notifies the debtor of the credit limit, the first time it is provided, whichever is the latest.]<br>Or<br>[There is no right to withdraw from this agreement—if there is a right to cancel the agreement this should be stated.](a)<br>[If the right to cancel is under the Financial Services (Distance Marketing) Regulations 2004 refer to section 5 of the form.] |
| Early repayment.<br>If applicable<br>Compensation payable in the case of early repayment. | [A statement that the debtor has the right to repay the credit early at any time in full or partially.](b).<br>[Determination of the compensation (calculation method) in accordance with section 95A [(and, where applicable, section 95B)] of the Consumer Credit Act 1974.] |
| Consultation with a Credit Reference Agency(c). | [A statement that if the creditor decides not to proceed with a prospective regulated consumer credit agreement on the basis of information from a credit reference agency the creditor must, when informing the debtor of the decision, inform the debtor that it has been reached on the basis of information from a credit reference agency and of the particulars of that agency.] |
| Right to a draft credit agreement(d). | [A statement that the debtor has the right, upon request, to obtain a copy of the draft credit agreement free of charge, unless the creditor is unwilling at the time of the request to proceed to the conclusion of the credit agreement.] |
| If applicable<br>The period of time during which the creditor is bound by the pre-contractual information. | [This information is valid from [—] until [—].] or [Period of time during which the information on this form is valid.] |

(a) i.e. If there is a cancellation right in respect of an agreement involving credit in excess of £60,260.

(b) The words "or partially" may be excluded in the case of agreements secured on land.

(c) This requirement does not apply in the case of agreements secured on land.

(**d**) This requirement does not apply in the case of agreements secured on land, agreements for credit agreements exceeding £60,260, pawn agreements and business purpose agreements.

If applicable

## 5. Additional information in the case of distance marketing of financial services

| (a) concerning the creditor | |
|---|---|
| If applicable<br>The creditor's representative in your Member State of residence.<br>Address.<br>Telephone number(s).<br>E-mail address.*<br>Fax number.*<br>Web address.* | [i.e. where different from section 1.]<br>[Identity.]<br>[Geographical address to be used by the debtor.] |
| If applicable<br>Registration number. | [The Firm Reference Number (FRN) (if any) or Interim Permission Number (if any), and any other relevant registration number of the creditor.] |
| If applicable<br>The supervisory authority. | [The [Financial Conduct Authority] or any other relevant supervisory authority or both.] |
| (b) concerning the credit agreement | |
| If applicable(**a**)<br>Right to cancel the credit agreement. | [Practical instructions for exercising the right to cancel indicating, amongst other things, the period for exercising the right, the address to which notification of exercise of the right to cancel should be sent and the consequences of non- exercise of that right.] |
| If applicable<br>The law taken by the creditor as a basis for the establishment of relations with you before the conclusion of the credit agreement. | [English/other law] |
| If applicable<br>The law applicable to the credit agreement and/or the competent court. | [A statement concerning the law which governs the contract and the courts to which disputes may be referred.] |
| If applicable<br>Language to be used in connection with the credit agreement. | [Details of the language that the information and contractual terms will be supplied in and used, with your consent, for communication during the duration of the credit agreement.] |
| (c) concerning redress | |
| Access to out-of-court complaint and redress mechanism. | [Whether or not there is an out-of-court complaint and redress mechanism for the debtor and, if so, the methods of access to it.] |

*This information is optional for the creditor. The row may be deleted if the information is not provided.

(**a**) If the right to withdraw referred to in section 4 does not apply.

Regulation 1(2)                    SCHEDULE 2

PROVISIONS RELATING TO CALCULATION AND DISCLOSURE OF THE
TOTAL CHARGE FOR CREDIT AND APR

## 1. Assumptions about running-account credit
(a)    In the case of an agreement for running-account credit, the assumption in paragraph (b) shall have effect for the purpose of calculating the total charge for credit and any APR in place of any assumptions in [the total charge for credit rules] that might otherwise apply—
(b)    in a case where the credit limit applicable to the credit is not known at the time the pre-contract credit information is disclosed but it is known that it will be subject to a maximum limit of less than £1,200, the credit limit shall be assumed to be an amount equal to that maximum limit.

## 2. Permissible tolerances in disclosure of an APR
For the purposes of these Regulations, it shall be sufficient compliance with the requirement to show an APR if there is included in the pre-contract credit information—
(a)    a rate which exceeds the APR by not more than one,
(b)    a rate which falls short of the APR by not more than 0.1, or
(c)    in a case to which paragraph 3 or 4 of this Schedule applies, a rate determined in accordance with those paragraphs or whichever of them applies to that case.

## 3. Tolerance where repayments are nearly equal
In the case of an agreement under which all repayments but one are equal and that one repayment does not differ from any other repayment by more whole pence than there are repayments of credit, there may be included in the pre-contract credit information a rate found under [the total charge for credit rules] as if that one repayment were equal to the other repayments to be made under the agreement.

## 4. Tolerance where interval between relevant date and first repayment is greater than interval between repayments
In the case of an agreement under which-
(a)    three or more repayments are to be made at equal intervals, and
(b)    the interval between the relevant date and the first repayment is greater than the interval between the repayments,
there may be included in the pre-contract credit information a rate found under [the total charge for credit rules] as if the interval between the relevant date and the first repayment were shortened so as to be equal to the interval between repayments.

SCHEDULE 3             Regulation 11(1)

EUROPEAN CONSUMER CREDIT INFORMATION

## 1. Contact details

| | |
|---|---|
| Creditor.<br>Address.<br><br>Telephone number(s).*<br>E-mail address.*<br>Fax number.*<br>Web address.* | [Identity.]<br>[Geographical address of the creditor to be used by the debtor.] |
| If applicable<br>Credit intermediary.<br>Address.<br><br>Telephone number(s).*<br>E-mail address.*<br>Fax number.*<br>Web address.* | [Identity.]<br>[Geographical address of the credit intermediary to be used by the debtor.] |

\* This information is optional for the creditor. The row may be deleted if the information is not provided.

Wherever "if applicable" is indicated, the creditor must give the information relevant to the credit product or, if the information is not relevant for the type of credit considered, delete the respective information or the entire row or indicate that the information is not applicable.

Indications between square brackets provide explanations for the creditor and must be replaced with the corresponding information.

## 2. Description of the main features of the credit product

| | |
|---|---|
| The type of credit. | |
| The total amount of credit.<br>This means the amount of credit to be provided under the agreement or the credit limit. | [The amount is to be expressed as a sum of money. In the case of running account credit, the total amount may be expressed as a statement indicating the manner in which the credit limit will be determined where it is not practicable to express the limit as a sum of money.] |
| The duration of the credit agreement. | [The duration or minimum duration of the agreement or a statement that the agreement has no fixed or minimum duration.] |
| If applicable<br>Repayment of the credit. | [A statement informing the debtor that the debtor may be required to repay the amount of credit in full on demand at any time.] |

## 3. Costs of the credit

| | |
|---|---|
| The rates of interest which apply to the credit agreement. | [Details of the rates of interest charged, any conditions applicable to that rate, where available any reference rate on which that rate is based and any information on changes to the rate of interest (including the periods that the rate applies and any conditions or procedure applicable to changing the rate). Where different rates of interest are charged in different circumstances, the creditor must provide the above information in respect of each rate.] |
| If applicable<br>Costs.<br>If applicable<br>The conditions under which those costs may be changed. | [The costs applicable from the time the credit agreement is concluded.] |
| Costs in the case of late payments. | Either<br>[A statement that there are no charges for late or missed payments.]<br>Or<br>[Applicable rate of interest, in the case of late payments and arrangements for its adjustment and, where applicable, any charges payable for default.] |

## 4. Other important legal aspects

| | |
|---|---|
| Termination of the credit agreement. | [The conditions and procedure for termination of the credit agreement.] |
| Consultation with a credit reference agency. | [A statement that if the creditor decides not to proceed with a prospective regulated consumer credit agreement on the basis of information from a credit reference agency the creditor must, when informing the debtor of that decision, inform the debtor that it has been reached on the basis of information from a credit reference agency and of the particulars of that agency.] |
| If applicable<br>The period of time during which the creditor is bound by the pre-contractual information. | [This information is valid from [—] until [—] or<br>[Period of time during which the information on this form is valid.] |

If applicable

## 5. Additional information to be given in the case of distance marketing of financial services

| (a) concerning the creditor | |
|---|---|
| If applicable<br>The creditor's representative in [the UK] [your Member State of residence.]<br>Address.<br>Telephone number.*<br>E-mail address.*<br>Fax number.*<br>Web address.* | [i.e. where different from section 1.]<br>[Identity.]<br>[Geographical address to be used by the debtor.] |
| If applicable<br>Registration number. | [The Firm Reference Number (FRN) (if any) or Interim Permission Number (if any), and any other relevant registration number of the creditor.] |
| If applicable<br>The supervisory authority. | [The [Financial Conduct Authority] or any other relevant supervisory authority or both.] |
| (b) concerning the credit agreement | |
| If applicable<br>The law taken by the creditor as a basis for the establishment of relations with you before the conclusion of the credit contract. | [English/other law.] |
| If applicable<br>The law applicable to the credit agreement and/or the competent court. | [A statement concerning the law which governs the contract and the courts to which disputes may be referred.] |
| If applicable<br>Language to be used in connection your agreement. | [Details of the language that the information and contractual terms will be supplied in and used, with the debtor's consent, for communication during the duration of the credit agreement.] |
| (c) concerning redress | |
| Access to out- of-court complaint and redress mechanism. | [Whether or not there is an out-of-court complaint and redress mechanism for the debtor who is party to the distance contract and, if so, the methods of access to it.] |

* This information is optional for the creditor. The row may be deleted if the information is not provided.

# CONSUMER CONTRACTS (INFORMATION, CANCELLATION AND ADDITIONAL CHARGES) REGULATIONS 2013
## (SI 2013/3134)

## PART 1
## GENERAL

### 1 Citation and commencement

(1) These Regulations may be cited as the Consumer Contracts (Information, Cancellation and Additional Charges) Regulations 2013 and come into force on 13th June 2014.

(2) These Regulations apply in relation to contracts entered into on or after that date.

### 2 Regulations superseded

The following do not apply in relation to contracts entered into on or after 13th June 2014—

(a) the Consumer Protection (Distance Selling) Regulations 2000;

(b) the Cancellation of Contracts made in a Consumer's Home or Place of Work etc Regulations 2008.

### 3 Review

(1) The Secretary of State must before the end of each review period—

(a) carry out a review of these Regulations,

(b) set out the conclusions of the review in a report, and

(c) publish the report.

(2) In carrying out the review, the Secretary of State must, so far as is reasonable, have regard to what is done in other member States to implement Directive 2011/83/EU of the European Parliament and of the Council of 25 October 2011 on consumer rights, amending Council Directive 93/13/EEC and Directive 1999/44/EC of the European Parliament and of the Council and repealing Council Directive 85/577/EC and Directive 97/7/EC of the European Parliament and of the Council.

(3) The report must in particular—

(a) set out the objectives intended to be achieved by these Regulations,

(b) assess the extent to which those objectives have been achieved, and

(c) assess whether those objectives remain appropriate and, if so, the extent to which they could be achieved in a way that imposes less regulation.

(4) A review period is—

(a) the period of 5 years beginning with the day on which these Regulations come into force, and

(b) each successive period of 5 years.

### 4 'Consumer' and 'trader'

In these Regulations—

'consumer' means an individual acting for purposes which are wholly or mainly outside that individual's trade, business, craft or profession;

'trader' means a person acting for purposes relating to that person's trade, business, craft or profession, whether acting personally or through another person acting in the trader's name or on the trader's behalf.

### 5 Other definitions

In these Regulations—

'business' includes the activities of any government department or local or public authority;

'business premises' in relation to a trader means—

(a) any immovable retail premises where the activity of the trader is carried out on a permanent basis, or

(b)   any movable retail premises where the activity of the trader is carried out on a usual basis;

'CMA' means the Competition and Markets Authority;

'commercial guarantee', in relation to a contract, means any undertaking by the trader or producer to the consumer (in addition to the trader's duty to supply goods that are in conformity with the contract) to reimburse the price paid or to replace, repair or service goods in any way if they do not meet the specifications or any other requirements not related to conformity set out in the guarantee statement or in the relevant advertising available at the time of the contract or before it is entered into;

'court'—

(a)   in relation to England and Wales, means the county court or the High Court,

(b)   in relation to Northern Ireland, means a county court or the High Court, and

(c)   in relation to Scotland means the sheriff court or the Court of Session;

'delivery' means voluntary transfer of possession from one person to another;

'digital content' means data which are produced and supplied in digital form;

'distance contract' means a contract concluded between a trader and a consumer under an organised distance sales or service-provision scheme without the simultaneous physical presence of the trader and the consumer, with the exclusive use of one or more means of distance communication up to and including the time at which the contract is concluded;

'district heating' means the supply of heat (in the form of steam or hot water or otherwise) from a central source of production through a transmission and distribution system to heat more than one building;

'durable medium' means paper or email, or any other medium that—

(a)   allows information to be addressed personally to the recipient,

(b)   enables the recipient to store the information in a way accessible for future reference for a period that is long enough for the purposes of the information, and

(c)   allows the unchanged reproduction of the information stored;

'functionality' in relation to digital content includes region coding, restrictions incorporated for the purposes of digital rights management, and other technical restrictions;

'goods' means any tangible moveable items, but that includes water, gas and electricity if and only if they are put up for sale in a limited volume or a set quantity;

'off-premises contract' means a contract between a trader and a consumer which is any of these—

(a)   a contract concluded in the simultaneous physical presence of the trader and the consumer, in a place which is not the business premises of the trader;

(b)   a contract for which an offer was made by the consumer in the simultaneous physical presence of the trader and the consumer, in a place which is not the business premises of the trader;

(c)   a contract concluded on the business premises of the trader or through any means of distance communication immediately after the consumer was personally and individually addressed in a place which is not the business premises of the trader in the simultaneous physical presence of the trader and the consumer;

(d)   a contract concluded during an excursion organised by the trader with the aim or effect of promoting and selling goods or services to the consumer;

'on-premises contract' means a contract between a trader and a consumer which is neither a distance contract nor an off-premises contract;

'public auction' means a method of sale where—

(a)   goods or services are offered by a trader to consumers through a transparent, competitive bidding procedure run by an auctioneer,

(b)    the consumers attend or are given the possibility to attend in person, and

(c)    the successful bidder is bound to purchase the goods or services;

'sales contract' means a contract under which a trader transfers or agrees to transfer the ownership of goods to a consumer and the consumer pays or agrees to pay the price, including any contract that has both goods and services as its object;

'service' includes—

(a)    the supply of water, gas or electricity if they are not put up for sale in a limited volume or a set quantity, and

(b)    the supply of district heating;

'service contract' means a contract, other than a sales contract, under which a trader supplies or agrees to supply a service to a consumer and the consumer pays or agrees to pay the price.

## 6   Limits of application: general

(1)    These Regulations do not apply to a contract, to the extent that it is—

(a)    for—

(i)    gambling within the meaning of the Gambling Act 2005 (which includes gaming, betting and participating in a lottery); or

(ii)    in relation to Northern Ireland, for betting, gaming or participating lawfully in a lottery within the meaning of the Betting, Gaming, Lotteries and Amusements (Northern Ireland) Order 1985;

(b)    for services of a banking, credit, insurance, personal pension, investment or payment nature;

(c)    for the creation of immovable property or of rights in immovable property;

(d)    for rental of accommodation for residential purposes;

(e)    for the construction of new buildings, or the construction of substantially new buildings by the conversion of existing buildings;

(f)    for the supply of foodstuffs, beverages or other goods intended for current consumption in the household and which are supplied by a trader on frequent and regular rounds to the consumer's home, residence or workplace;

(g)    within the scope of Council Directive 90/314/EEC of 13 June 1990 on package travel, package holidays and package tours;

(h)    within the scope of Directive 2008/122/EC of the European Parliament and of the Council on the protection of consumers in respect of certain aspects of timeshare, long-term holiday product, resale and exchange contracts.

(2)    These Regulations do not apply to contracts—

(a)    concluded by means of automatic vending machines or automated commercial premises;

(b)    concluded with a telecommunications operator through a public telephone for the use of the telephone;

(c)    concluded for the use of one single connection, by telephone, internet or fax, established by a consumer;

(d)    under which goods are sold by way of execution or otherwise by authority of law.

(3)    Paragraph (1)(b) is subject to regulations 38(4) (ancillary contracts) and 40(3) (additional payments).

PART 2
INFORMATION REQUIREMENTS

Chapter 1
Provision of information

## 7 Application of Part 2

(1) This Part applies to on-premises, off-premises and distance contracts, subject to paragraphs (2), (3) and (4) and regulation 6.

(2) This Part does not apply to contracts to the extent that they are—

(a) for the supply of a medicinal product by administration by a prescriber, or under a prescription or directions given by a prescriber;

(b) for the supply of a product by a health care professional or a person included in a relevant list, under arrangements for the supply of services as part of the health service, where the product is one that, at least in some circumstances is available under such arrangements free or on prescription.

(3) This Part, except for regulation 14(1) to (5), does not apply to contracts to the extent that they are for passenger transport services.

(4) This Part does not apply to off-premises contracts under which the payment to be made by the consumer is not more than £42.

(5) In paragraph (2)—

'health care professional' and 'prescriber' have the meaning given by regulation 2(1) of the National Health Service (Pharmaceutical and Local Pharmaceutical Services) Regulations 2013;

'health service' means—

(a) the health service as defined by section 275(1) of the National Health Service Act 2006 or section 206(1) of the National Health Service (Wales) Act 2006,

(b) the health service as defined by section 108(1) of the National Health Service (Scotland) Act 1978, or

(c) any of the health services under section 2(1)(a) of the Health and Social Care (Reform) Act (Northern Ireland) 2009;

'medicinal product' has the meaning given by regulation 2(1) of the Human Medicines Regulations 2012;

'relevant list' means—

(d) a relevant list for the purposes of the National Health Service (Pharmaceutical and Local Pharmaceutical Services) Regulations 2013, or

(e) a list maintained under those Regulations.

## 8 Making information etc available to a consumer

For the purposes of this Part, something is made available to a consumer only if the consumer can reasonably be expected to know how to access it.

## 9 Information to be provided before making an on-premises contract

(1) Before the consumer is bound by an on-premises contract, the trader must give or make available to the consumer the information described in Schedule 1 in a clear and comprehensible manner, if that information is not already apparent from the context.

(2) Paragraph (1) does not apply to a contract which involves a day-to-day transaction and is performed immediately at the time when the contract is entered into.

(3) Any information that the trader gives the consumer as required by this regulation is to be treated as included as a term of the contract.

(4) A change to any of that information, made before entering into the contract or later, is not effective unless expressly agreed between the consumer and the trader.

## 10  Information to be provided before making an off-premises contract

(1)   Before the consumer is bound by an off-premises contract, the trader—

(a)   must give the consumer the information listed in Schedule 2 in a clear and comprehensible manner, and

(b)   if a right to cancel exists, must give the consumer a cancellation form as set out in part B of Schedule 3.

(2)   The information and any cancellation form must be given on paper or, if the consumer agrees, on another durable medium and must be legible.

(3)   The information referred to in paragraphs (l), (m) and (n) of Schedule 2 may be provided by means of the model instructions on cancellation set out in part A of Schedule 3; and a trader who has supplied those instructions to the consumer, correctly filled in, is to be treated as having complied with paragraph (1) in respect of those paragraphs.

(4)   If the trader has not complied with paragraph (1) in respect of paragraph (g), (h) or (m) of Schedule 2, the consumer is not to bear the charges or costs referred to in those paragraphs.

(5)   Any information that the trader gives the consumer as required by this regulation is to be treated as included as a term of the contract.

(6)   A change to any of that information, made before entering into the contract or later, is not effective unless expressly agreed between the consumer and the trader.

(7)   This regulation is subject to regulation 11.

## 11  Provision of information in connection with repair or maintenance contracts

(1)   If the conditions in paragraphs (2), (3) and (4) are met, regulation 10(1) does not apply to an off-premises contract where—

(a)   the contract is a service contract,

(b)   the consumer has explicitly requested the trader to supply the service for the purpose of carrying out repairs or maintenance,

(c)   the obligations of the trader and the consumer under the contract are to be performed immediately, and

(d)   the payment to be made by the consumer is not more than £170.

(2)   The first condition is that, before the consumer is bound by the contract, the trader gives or makes available to the consumer on paper or, if the consumer expressly agrees, on another durable medium—

(a)   the information referred to in paragraphs (b) to (d), (f) and (g) of Schedule 2,

(b)   an estimate of the total price, where it cannot reasonably be calculated in advance, and

(c)   where a right to cancel exists, a cancellation form as set out in part B of Schedule 3.

(3)   The second condition is that, before the consumer is bound by the contract, the trader gives or makes available to the consumer the information referred to in paragraphs (a), (l) and (o) of Schedule 2, either on paper or another durable medium or otherwise if the consumer expressly agrees.

(4)   The third condition is that the confirmation of the contract provided in accordance with regulation 12 contains the information required by regulation 10(1).

(5)   For the right to cancel where this regulation applies, see in particular—

(a)   regulation 28(1)(e) and (2) (cases where cancellation excluded: visit requested for urgent work);

(b)   regulation 36 (form of consumer's request, and consequences).

## 12  Provision of copy or confirmation of off-premises contracts

(1)   In the case of an off-premises contract, the trader must give the consumer—

(a)   a copy of the signed contract, or

(b)   confirmation of the contract.

(2)   The confirmation must include all the information referred to in Schedule 2 unless the trader has already provided that information to the consumer on a durable medium prior to the conclusion of the off-premises contract.

(3)   The copy or confirmation must be provided on paper or, if the consumer agrees, on another durable medium.

(4)   The copy or confirmation must be provided within a reasonable time after the conclusion of the contract, but in any event—

(a)   not later than the time of the delivery of any goods supplied under the contract, and

(b)   before performance begins of any service supplied under the contract.

(5)   If the contract is for the supply of digital content not on a tangible medium and the consumer has given the consent and acknowledgement referred to in regulation 37(1)(a) and (b), the copy or confirmation must include confirmation of the consent and acknowledgement.

### 13   Information to be provided before making a distance contract

(1)   Before the consumer is bound by a distance contract, the trader—

(a)   must give or make available to the consumer the information listed in Schedule 2 in a clear and comprehensible manner, and in a way appropriate to the means of distance communication used, and

(b)   if a right to cancel exists, must give or make available to the consumer a cancellation form as set out in part B of Schedule 3.

(2)   In so far as the information is provided on a durable medium, it must be legible.

(3)   The information referred to in paragraphs (l), (m) and (n) of Schedule 2 may be provided by means of the model instructions on cancellation set out in part A of Schedule 3; and a trader who has supplied those instructions to the consumer, correctly filled in, is to be treated as having complied with paragraph (1) in respect of those paragraphs.

(4)   Where a distance contract is concluded through a means of distance communication which allows limited space or time to display the information—

(a)   the information listed in paragraphs (a), (b), (f), (g), (h), (l) and (s) of Schedule 2 must be provided on that means of communication in accordance with paragraphs (1) and (2), but

(b)   the other information required by paragraph (1) may be provided in another appropriate way.

(5)   If the trader has not complied with paragraph (1) in respect of paragraph (g), (h) or (m) of Schedule 2, the consumer is not to bear the charges or costs referred to in those paragraphs.

(6)   Any information that the trader gives the consumer as required by this regulation is to be treated as included as a term of the contract.

(7)   A change to any of that information, made before entering into the contract or later, is not effective unless expressly agreed between the consumer and the trader.

### 14   Requirements for distance contracts concluded by electronic means

(1)   This regulation applies where a distance contract is concluded by electronic means.

(2)   If the contract places the consumer under an obligation to pay, the trader must make the consumer aware in a clear and prominent manner, and directly before the consumer places the order, of the information listed in paragraphs (a), (f), (g), (h), (s) and (t) of Schedule 2.

(3)   The trader must ensure that the consumer, when placing the order, explicitly acknowledges that the order implies an obligation to pay.

(4)   If placing an order entails activating a button or a similar function, the trader must ensure that the button or similar function is labelled in an easily

legible manner only with the words 'order with obligation to pay' or a correspond-ing unambiguous formulation indicating that placing the order entails an obli-gation to pay the trader.

(5) If the trader has not complied with paragraphs (3) and (4), the consumer is not bound by the contract or order.

(6) The trader must ensure that any trading website through which the con-tract is concluded indicates clearly and legibly, at the latest at the beginning of the ordering process, whether any delivery restrictions apply and which means of payment are accepted.

### 15 Telephone calls to conclude a distance contract

If the trader makes a telephone call to the consumer with a view to concluding a distance contract, the trader must, at the beginning of the conversation with the consumer, disclose—

(a) the trader's identity,
(b) where applicable, the identity of the person on whose behalf the trader makes the call, and
(c) the commercial purpose of the call.

### 16 Confirmation of distance contracts

(1) In the case of a distance contract the trader must give the consumer con-firmation of the contract on a durable medium.

(2) The confirmation must include all the information referred to in Schedule 2 unless the trader has already provided that information to the consumer on a durable medium prior to the conclusion of the distance contract.

(3) If the contract is for the supply of digital content not on a tangible medium and the consumer has given the consent and acknowledgment referred to in regulation 37(1)(a) and (b), the confirmation must include confirmation of the con-sent and acknowledgement.

(4) The confirmation must be provided within a reasonable time after the con-clusion of the contract, but in any event—

(a) not later than the time of delivery of any goods supplied under the contract, and
(b) before performance begins of any service supplied under the contract.

(5) For the purposes of paragraph (4), the confirmation is treated as provided as soon as the trader has sent it or done what is necessary to make it available to the consumer.

### 17 Burden of proof in relation to off-premises and distance contracts

(1) In case of dispute about the trader's compliance with any provision of regulations 10 to 16, it is for the trader to show that the provision was complied with.

(2) That does not apply to proceedings—

(a) for an offence under regulation 19, or
(b) relating to compliance with an injunction, interdict or order under regulation 45.

### 18 Effect on contract of failure to provide information

Every contract to which this Part applies is to be treated as including a term that the trader has complied with the provisions of—

(a) regulations 9 to 14, and
(b) regulation 16.

Chapter 2
Offences

**19   Offence relating to the failure to give notice of the right to cancel**
(1)   A trader is guilty of an offence if the trader enters into an off-premises contract to which regulation 10 applies but fails to give the consumer the information listed in paragraph (l), (m) or (n) of Schedule 2 in accordance with that regulation.
(2)   A person who is guilty of an offence under paragraph (1) is liable on summary conviction to a fine not exceeding level 5 on the standard scale.

**20   Defence of due diligence**
(1)   In any proceedings against a person (A) for an offence under regulation 19 it is a defence for A to prove—
    (a)   that the commission of the offence was due to—
        (i)   the act or default of another, or
        (ii)   reliance on information given by another, and
    (b)   that A took all reasonable precautions and exercised all due diligence to avoid the commission of such an offence by A or any person under A's control.
(2)   A person is not entitled to rely on the defence provided by paragraph (1) without leave of the court unless—
    (a)   that person has served on the prosecutor a notice in writing giving such information as was in that person's possession identifying or assisting in the identification of the other person; and
    (b)   the notice is served on the prosecutor not less than 7 days before the hearing of the proceedings or, in Scotland, 7 days before the intermediate diet or 14 days before the trial diet, whichever is earlier.

**21   Liability of persons other than the principal offender**
Where the commission by a person of an offence under regulation 19 is due to the act or default of another person, that other person is guilty of the offence and may be proceeded against and punished whether or not proceedings are taken against the first person.

**22   Offences committed by bodies of persons**
(1)   Where an offence under regulation 19 committed by a body corporate is proved—
    (a)   to have been committed with the consent or connivance of an officer of the body corporate or
    (b)   to be attributable to any neglect on the part of an officer of the body corporate,
the officer, as well as the body corporate, is guilty of the offence and liable to be proceeded against and punished accordingly.
(2)   In paragraph (1) a reference to an officer of a body corporate includes a reference to—
    (a)   a director, manager, secretary or other similar officer; and
    (b)   a person purporting to act as a director, manager, secretary or other similar officer.
(3)   Where an offence under regulation 19 committed in Scotland by a Scottish partnership is proved—
    (a)   to have been committed with the consent or connivance of a partner, or
    (b)   to be attributable to any neglect on the part of a partner,
that partner, as well as the partnership shall be guilty of the offence and liable to be proceeded against and punished accordingly.
(4)   In paragraph (3) a reference to a partner includes a person purporting to act as a partner.

**23   Duty to enforce**
(1)   Subject to paragraphs (2) and (3)—

(a)   it is the duty of every weights and measures authority in Great Britain to enforce regulation 19 within its area; and

(b)   it is the duty of the Department of Enterprise, Trade and Investment in Northern Ireland to enforce regulation 19 within Northern Ireland.

(2)   No proceedings for an offence under regulation 19 may be instituted in England and Wales except by or on behalf of an enforcement authority.

(3)   Nothing in paragraph (1) authorises any weights and measures authority to bring proceedings in Scotland for an offence.

### 24   Powers of investigation

(1)   If a duly authorised officer of an enforcement authority has reasonable grounds for suspecting that an offence has been committed under regulation 19, the officer may require a person carrying on or employed in a business to produce any document relating to the business, and take copies of it or any entry in it for the purposes of ascertaining whether such an offence has been committed.

(2)   If the officer has reasonable grounds for believing that any documents may be required as evidence in proceedings for such an offence, the officer may seize and detain them and shall, if the officer does so, inform the person from whom they are seized.

(3)   In this regulation 'document' includes information recorded in any form.

(4)   The reference in paragraph (1) to production of documents is, in the case of a document which contains information recorded otherwise than in a legible form, a reference to the production of a copy of the information in a legible form.

(5)   An officer seeking to exercise a power under this regulation must do so only at a reasonable hour and on production of the officer's identification and authority.

(6)   Nothing in this regulation requires a person to produce or provide, or authorises a person to inspect or take possession of, anything in respect of which a claim to legal professional privilege (in Scotland, to confidentiality of communications) could be maintained in legal proceedings.

### 25   Obstruction of authorised officers

(1)   A person commits an offence if that person—

(a)   intentionally obstructs an officer of an enforcement authority acting in pursuance of functions under regulation 24;

(b)   fails without reasonable cause to comply with any requirement properly made by such an officer under regulation 24; or

(c)   fails without reasonable cause to give such an officer any other assistance or information which the officer may reasonably require for the purpose of the performance of functions under regulation 24.

(2)   A person giving any information which is required from that person under paragraph (1)(c) is guilty of an offence if, in doing so, the person makes any statement knowing it to be false in a material particular.

(3)   A person guilty of an offence under paragraph (1) or (2) is liable on summary conviction to a fine not exceeding level 3 on the standard scale.

### 26   Freedom from self-incrimination

Nothing in regulation 24 or 25 is to be construed as requiring a person to answer any question or give any information if to do so might incriminate that person.

### PART 3
### RIGHT TO CANCEL

### 27   Application of Part 3

(1)   This Part applies to distance and off-premises contracts between a trader and a consumer, subject to paragraphs (2) and (3) and regulations 6 and 28.

(2)   This Part does not apply to contracts to the extent that they are—

(a)  for the supply of a medicinal product by administration by a prescriber, or under a prescription or directions given by a prescriber;

(b)  for the supply of a product by a health care professional or a person included in a relevant list, under arrangements for the supply of services as part of the health service, where the product is one that, at least in some circumstances is available under such arrangements free or on prescription;

(c)  for passenger transport services.

(3)  This Part does not apply to off-premises contracts under which the payment to be made by the consumer is not more than £42.

(4)  In paragraph (2)(a) and (b), expressions defined in regulation 7(5) have the meaning given there.

## 28  Limits of application: circumstances excluding cancellation

(1)  This Part does not apply as regards the following—

(a)  the supply of—

(i)  goods, or

(ii)  services, other than supply of water, gas, electricity or district heating, for which the price is dependent on fluctuations in the financial market which cannot be controlled by the trader and which may occur within the cancellation period;

(b)  the supply of goods that are made to the consumer's specifications or are clearly personalised;

(c)  the supply of goods which are liable to deteriorate or expire rapidly;

(d)  the supply of alcoholic beverages, where—

(i)  their price has been agreed at the time of the conclusion of the sales contract,

(ii)  delivery of them can only take place after 30 days, and

(iii)  their value is dependent on fluctuations in the market which cannot be controlled by the trader;

(e)  contracts where the consumer has specifically requested a visit from the trader for the purpose of carrying out urgent repairs or maintenance;

(f)  the supply of a newspaper, periodical or magazine with the exception of subscription contracts for the supply of such publications;

(g)  contracts concluded at a public auction;

(h)  the supply of accommodation, transport of goods, vehicle rental services, catering or services related to leisure activities, if the contract provides for a specific date or period of performance.

(2)  Sub-paragraph (e) of paragraph (1) does not prevent this Part applying to a contract for—

(a)  services in addition to the urgent repairs or maintenance requested, or

(b)  goods other than replacement parts necessarily used in making the repairs or carrying out the maintenance,

if the trader supplies them on the occasion of a visit such as is mentioned in that sub-paragraph.

(3)  The rights conferred by this Part cease to be available in the following circumstances—

(a)  in the case of a contract for the supply of sealed goods which are not suitable for return due to health protection or hygiene reasons, if they become unsealed after delivery;

(b)  in the case of a contract for the supply of sealed audio or sealed video recordings or sealed computer software, if the goods become unsealed after delivery;

(c)  in the case of any sales contract, if the goods become mixed inseparably (according to their nature) with other items after delivery.

## 29  Right to cancel

(1)  The consumer may cancel a distance or off-premises contract at any time in

the cancellation period without giving any reason, and without incurring any liability except under these provisions—

(a)  regulation 34(3) (where enhanced delivery chosen by consumer);

(b)  regulation 34(9) (where value of goods diminished by consumer handling);

(c)  regulation 35(5) (where goods returned by consumer);

(d)  regulation 36(4) (where consumer requests early supply of service).

(2)  The cancellation period begins when the contract is entered into and ends in accordance with regulation 30 or 31.

(3)  Paragraph (1) does not affect the consumer's right to withdraw an offer made by the consumer to enter into a distance or off-premises contract, at any time before the contract is entered into, without giving any reason and without incurring any liability.

**30  Normal cancellation period**

(1)  The cancellation period ends as follows, unless regulation 31 applies.

(2)  If the contract is—

(a)  a service contract, or

(b)  a contract for the supply of digital content which is not supplied on a tangible medium,

the cancellation period ends at the end of 14 days after the day on which the contract is entered into.

(3)  If the contract is a sales contract and none of paragraphs (4) to (6) applies, the cancellation period ends at the end of 14 days after the day on which the goods come into the physical possession of—

(a)  the consumer, or

(b)  a person, other than the carrier, identified by the consumer to take possession of them.

(4)  If the contract is a sales contract under which multiple goods are ordered by the consumer in one order but some are delivered on different days, the cancellation period ends at the end of 14 days after the day on which the last of the goods come into the physical possession of—

(a)  the consumer, or

(b)  a person, other than the carrier, identified by the consumer to take possession of them.

(5)  If the contract is a sales contract under which goods consisting of multiple lots or pieces of something are delivered on different days, the cancellation period ends at the end of 14 days after the day on which the last of the lots or pieces come into the physical possession of—

(a)  the consumer, or

(b)  a person, other than the carrier, identified by the consumer to take possession of them.

(6)  If the contract is a sales contract for regular delivery of goods during a defined period of more than one day, the cancellation period ends at the end of 14 days after the day on which the first of the goods come into the physical possession of—

(a)  the consumer, or

(b)  a person, other than the carrier, identified by the consumer to take possession of them.

**31  Cancellation period extended for breach of information requirement**

(1)  This regulation applies if the trader does not provide the consumer with the information on the right to cancel required by paragraph (l) of Schedule 2, in accordance with Part 2.

(2)  If the trader provides the consumer with that information in the period of 12 months beginning with the first day of the 14 days mentioned in regulation

30(2) to (6), but otherwise in accordance with Part 2, the cancellation period ends at the end of 14 days after the consumer receives the information.

(3)   Otherwise the cancellation period ends at the end of 12 months after the day on which it would have ended under regulation 30.

## 32   Exercise of the right to withdraw or cancel

(1)   To withdraw an offer to enter into a distance or off-premises contract, the consumer must inform the trader of the decision to withdraw it.

(2)   To cancel a contract under regulation 29(1), the consumer must inform the trader of the decision to cancel it.

(3)   To inform the trader under paragraph (2) the consumer may either—

(a)   use a form following the model cancellation form in part B of Schedule 3, or

(b)   make any other clear statement setting out the decision to cancel the contract.

(4)   If the trader gives the consumer the option of filling in and submitting such a form or other statement on the trader's website—

(a)   the consumer need not use it, but

(b)   if the consumer does, the trader must communicate to the consumer an acknowledgement of receipt of the cancellation on a durable medium without delay.

(5)   Where the consumer informs the trader under paragraph (2) by sending a communication, the consumer is to be treated as having cancelled the contract in the cancellation period if the communication is sent before the end of the period.

(6)   In case of dispute it is for the consumer to show that the contract was cancelled in the cancellation period in accordance with this regulation.

## 33   Effect of withdrawal or cancellation

(1)   If a contract is cancelled under regulation 29(1)—

(a)   the cancellation ends the obligations of the parties to perform the contract, and

(b)   regulations 34 to 38 apply.

(2)   Regulations 34 and 38 also apply if the consumer withdraws an offer to enter into a distance or off-premises contract.

## 34   Reimbursement by trader in the event of withdrawal or cancellation

(1)   The trader must reimburse all payments, other than payments for delivery, received from the consumer, subject to paragraph (10).

(2)   The trader must reimburse any payment for delivery received from the consumer, unless the consumer expressly chose a kind of delivery costing more than the least expensive common and generally acceptable kind of delivery offered by the trader.

(3)   In that case, the trader must reimburse any payment for delivery received from the consumer up to the amount the consumer would have paid if the consumer had chosen the least expensive common and generally acceptable kind of delivery offered by the trader.

(4)   Reimbursement must be without undue delay, and in any event not later than the time specified in paragraph (5) or (6).

(5)   If the contract is a sales contract and the trader has not offered to collect the goods, the time is the end of 14 days after—

(a)   the day on which the trader receives the goods back, or

(b)   if earlier, the day on which the consumer supplies evidence of having sent the goods back.

(6)   Otherwise, the time is the end of 14 days after the day on which the trader is informed of the consumer's decision to withdraw the offer or cancel the contract, in accordance with regulation 44.

(7)   The trader must make the reimbursement using the same means of payment

as the consumer used for the initial transaction, unless the consumer has expressly agreed otherwise.

(8)   The trader must not impose any fee on the consumer in respect of the reimbursement.

(9)   If (in the case of a sales contract) the value of the goods is diminished by any amount as a result of handling of the goods by the consumer beyond what is necessary to establish the nature, characteristics and functioning of the goods, the trader may recover that amount from the consumer, up to the contract price.

(10)   An amount that may be recovered under paragraph (9)—

(a)   may be deducted from the amount to be reimbursed under paragraph (1);

(b)   otherwise, must be paid by the consumer to the trader.

(11)   Paragraph (9) does not apply if the trader has failed to provide the consumer with the information on the right to cancel required by paragraph (l) of Schedule 2, in accordance with Part 2.

(12)   For the purposes of paragraph (9) handling is beyond what is necessary to establish the nature, characteristics and functioning of the goods if, in particular, it goes beyond the sort of handling that might reasonably be allowed in a shop.

(13)   Where the provisions of this regulation apply to cancellation of a contract, the contract is to be treated as including those provisions as terms.

### 35   Return of goods in the event of cancellation

(1)   Where a sales contract is cancelled under regulation 29(1), it is the trader's responsibility to collect the goods if—

(a)   the trader has offered to collect them, or

(b)   in the case of an off-premises contract, the goods were delivered to the consumer's home when the contract was entered into and could not, by their nature, normally be returned by post.

(2)   If it is not the trader's responsibility under paragraph (1) to collect the goods, the consumer must—

(a)   send them back, or

(b)   hand them over to the trader or to a person authorised by the trader to receive them.

(3)   The address to which goods must be sent under paragraph (2)(a) is—

(a)   any address specified by the trader for sending the goods back;

(b)   if no address is specified for that purpose, any address specified by the trader for the consumer to contact the trader;

(c)   if no address is specified for either of those purposes, any place of business of the trader.

(4)   The consumer must send off the goods under paragraph (2)(a), or hand them over under paragraph (2)(b), without undue delay and in any event not later than 14 days after the day on which the consumer informs the trader as required by regulation 32(2).

(5)   The consumer must bear the direct cost of returning goods under paragraph (2), unless—

(a)   the trader has agreed to bear those costs, or

(b)   the trader failed to provide the consumer with the information about the consumer bearing those costs, required by paragraph (m) of Schedule 2, in accordance with Part 2.

(6)   The contract is to be treated as including a term that the trader must bear the direct cost of the consumer returning goods under paragraph (2) where paragraph (5)(b) applies.

(7)   The consumer is not required to bear any other cost of returning goods under paragraph (2).

(8)   The consumer is not required to bear any cost of collecting goods under

paragraph (1) [unless the trader has offered to collect the goods and the consumer has agreed to bear the costs of the trader doing so.]

## 36  Supply of service in cancellation period

(1)   The trader must not begin the supply of a service before the end of the cancellation period provided for in regulation 30(1) unless the consumer—

(a)   has made an express request, and

(b)   in the case of an off-premises contract, has made the request on a durable medium.

(2)   In the case of a service other than supply of water, gas, electricity or district heating, the consumer ceases to have the right to cancel a service contract under regulation 29(1) if the service has been fully performed, and performance of the service began—

(a)   after a request by the consumer in accordance with paragraph (1), and

(b)   with the acknowledgement that the consumer would lose that right once the contract had been fully performed by the trader.

(3)   Paragraphs (4) to (6) apply where a contract is cancelled under regulation 29(1) and a service has been supplied in the cancellation period.

(4)   Where the service is supplied in response to a request in accordance with paragraph (1), the consumer must (subject to paragraph (6)) pay to the trader an amount—

(a)   for the supply of the service for the period for which it is supplied, ending with the time when the trader is informed of the consumer's decision to cancel the contract, in accordance with regulation 32(2), and

(b)   which is in proportion to what has been supplied, in comparison with the full coverage of the contract.

(5)   The amount is to be calculated—

(a)   on the basis of the total price agreed in the contract, or

(b)   if the total price is excessive, on the basis of the market value of the service that has been supplied, calculated by comparing prices for equivalent services supplied by other traders.

(6)   The consumer bears no cost for supply of the service, in full or in part, in the cancellation period, if—

(a)   the trader has failed to provide the consumer with the information on the right to cancel required by paragraph (l) of Schedule 2, or the information on payment of that cost required by paragraph (n) of that Schedule, in accordance with Part 2, or

(b)   the service is not supplied in response to a request in accordance with paragraph (1).

## 37  Supply of digital content in cancellation period

(1)   Under a contract for the supply of digital content not on a tangible medium, the trader must not begin supply of the digital content before the end of the cancellation period provided for in regulation 30(1), unless—

(a)   the consumer has given express consent, and

(b)   the consumer has acknowledged that the right to cancel the contract under regulation 29(1) will be lost.

(2)   The consumer ceases to have the right to cancel such a contract under regulation 29(1) if, before the end of the cancellation period, supply of the digital content has begun after the consumer has given the consent and acknowledgement required by paragraph (1).

(3)   Paragraph (4) applies where a contract is cancelled under regulation 29(1) and digital content has been supplied, not on a tangible medium, in the cancellation period.

(4)   The consumer bears no cost for supply of the digital content, in full or in part, in the cancellation period, if—

(a)   the consumer has not given prior express consent to the beginning of the performance of the digital content before the end of the 14-day period referred to in regulation 30,

(b)   the consumer gave that consent but did not acknowledge when giving it that the right to cancel would be lost, or

(c)   the trader failed to provide confirmation required by regulation 12(5) or 16(3).

## 38   Effects of withdrawal or cancellation on ancillary contracts

(1)   If a consumer withdraws an offer to enter into a distance or off-premises contract, or cancels such a contract under regulation 29(1), any ancillary contracts are automatically terminated, without any costs for the consumer, other than any costs under these provisions—

(a)   regulation 34(3) (where enhanced delivery chosen by consumer);

(b)   regulation 34(9) (where value of goods diminished by consumer handling);

(c)   regulation 35(5) (where goods returned by consumer);

(d)   regulation 36(4) (where consumer requests early supply of service).

(2)   When a trader is informed by a consumer under regulation 32(1) or (2) of a decision to withdraw an offer or cancel a contract, the trader must inform any other trader with whom the consumer has an ancillary contract that is terminated by paragraph (1).

(3)   An 'ancillary contract', in relation to a distance or off-premises contract (the 'main contract'), means a contract by which the consumer acquires goods or services related to the main contract, where those goods or services are provided—

(a)   by the trader, or

(b)   by a third party on the basis of an arrangement between the third party and the trader.

(4)   Regulation 6(1)(b) (exclusion of financial services contracts) does not limit the contracts that are ancillary contracts for the purposes of this regulation.

## PART 4
## PROTECTION FROM INERTIA SELLING AND ADDITIONAL CHARGES

## 39   Inertia selling

Before regulation 28 of the Consumer Protection from Unfair Trading Regulations 2008 (and in Part 5 of those Regulations) insert—

'27A Inertia selling

(1)   This regulation applies where a trader engages in the unfair commercial practice described in paragraph 29 of Schedule 1 (inertia selling).

(2)   The consumer is exempted from any obligation to provide consideration for the products supplied by the trader.

(3)   The absence of a response from the consumer following the supply does not constitute consent to the provision of consideration for, or the return or safekeeping of, the products.

(4)   In the case of an unsolicited supply of goods, the consumer may, as between the consumer and the trader, use, deal with or dispose of the goods as if they were an unconditional gift to the consumer.'.

## 40   Additional payments under a contract

(1)   Under a contract between a trader and a consumer, no payment is payable in addition to the remuneration agreed for the trader's main obligation unless, before the consumer became bound by the contract, the trader obtained the consumer's express consent.

(2)   There is no express consent (if there would otherwise be) for the purposes of this paragraph if consent is inferred from the consumer not changing a default option (such as a pre-ticked box on a website).

(3)   This regulation does not apply if the trader's main obligation is to supply

services within regulation 6(1)(b), but in any other case it applies even if an additional payment is for such services.

(4)  Where a trader receives an additional payment which, under this regulation, is not payable under a contract, the contract is to be treated as providing for the trader to reimburse the payment to the consumer.

### 41  Help-line charges over basic rate

(1)  Where a trader operates a telephone line for the purpose of consumers contacting the trader by telephone in relation to contracts entered into with the trader, a consumer contacting the trader must not be bound to pay more than the basic rate.

(2)  If in those circumstances a consumer who contacts a trader in relation to a contract is bound to pay more than the basic rate, the contract is to be treated as providing for the trader to pay to the consumer any amount by which the charge paid by the consumer for the call is more than the basic rate.

PART 5
### DELIVERY AND RISK

### 42  Time for delivery of goods

(1)  This regulation applies to any sales contract.

(2)  Unless the trader and the consumer have agreed otherwise, the contract is to be treated as including a term that the trader must deliver the goods to the consumer.

(3)  Unless there is an agreed time or period, the contract is to be treated as including a term that the trader must deliver the goods—

(a)  without undue delay, and

(b)  in any event, not more than 30 days after the day on which the contract is entered into.

(4)  In this regulation—

(a)  an 'agreed' time or period means a time or period agreed by the trader and the consumer for delivery of the goods, but

(b)  if there is an obligation to deliver the goods at the time the contract is entered into, that time counts as the 'agreed' time.

(5)  Paragraphs (6) and (7) apply if the trader does not deliver the goods in accordance with paragraph (3) or at the agreed time or within the agreed period.

(6)  If the circumstances are that—

(a)  the trader has refused to deliver the goods,

(b)  delivery of the goods at the agreed time or within the agreed period is essential taking into account all the relevant circumstances at the time the contract was entered into, or

(c)  the consumer told the trader before the contract was entered into that delivery in accordance with paragraph (3), or at the agreed time or within the agreed period, was essential,

then the consumer may treat the contract as at an end.

(7)  In any other circumstances, the consumer may specify a period that is appropriate in the circumstances and require the trader to deliver the goods before the end of that period.

(8)  If the consumer specifies a period under paragraph (7) but the goods are not delivered within that period, then the consumer may treat the contract as at an end.

(9)  If the consumer treats the contract as at an end under paragraph (6) or (8), the trader must without undue delay reimburse all payments made under the contract.

(10)  If paragraph (6) or (8) applies but the consumer does not treat the contract as at an end—

(a)   that does not prevent the consumer from cancelling the order for any of the goods or rejecting goods that have been delivered, and

(b)   the trader must without undue delay reimburse all payments made under the contract in respect of any goods for which the consumer cancels the order or which the consumer rejects.

(11)   If any of the goods form a commercial unit, then the consumer cannot reject or cancel the order for some of those goods without also rejecting or cancelling the order for the rest of them.

(12)   A unit is a 'commercial unit' if division of the unit would materially impair the value of the goods or the character of the unit.

(13)   This regulation does not prevent the consumer seeking other remedies where it is open to the consumer to do so.

### 43   Passing of risk

(1)   A sales contract is to be treated as including the following provisions as terms.

(2)   The goods remain at the trader's risk until they come into the physical possession of—

(a)   the consumer, or

(b)   a person identified by the consumer to take possession of the goods.

(3)   Paragraph (2) does not apply if the goods are delivered to a carrier who—

(a)   is commissioned by the consumer to deliver the goods, and

(b)   is not a carrier the trader named as an option for the consumer.

(4)   In that case the goods are at the consumer's risk on and after delivery to the carrier.

(5)   Paragraph (4) does not affect any liability of the carrier to the consumer in respect of the goods.

PART 6
ENFORCEMENT

### 44   Complaints

(1)   It is the duty of an enforcement authority to consider any complaint made to it about a contravention of these Regulations, unless—

(a)   the complaint appears to the authority to be frivolous or vexatious, or

(b)   another enforcement authority has notified the CMA that it agrees to consider the complaint.

(2)   If an enforcement authority has notified the CMA as mentioned in paragraph (1)(b), that authority is under a duty to consider the complaint.

(3)   The following are enforcement authorities for the purposes of these Regulations—

(a)   every local weights and measures authority in Great Britain;

(b)   the Department of Enterprise, Trade and Investment in Northern Ireland.

### 45   Orders to secure compliance

(1)   An enforcement authority may apply for an injunction, or in Scotland an interdict or order of specific implement, against any person who appears to the authority to be responsible for a contravention of these Regulations.

(2)   The court on an application under this regulation may grant an injunction, interdict or order on such terms as it thinks fit to secure compliance with these Regulations.

### 46   Notification of undertakings and orders to the CMA

An enforcement authority must notify the CMA—

(a)   of any undertaking given to it by or on behalf of any person who appears to it to be responsible for a contravention of these Regulations;

(b)   of the outcome of any application made by it under regulation 45, and of the terms of any undertaking given to the court or of any order made by the court;

(c)    of the outcome of any application made by it to enforce a previous order of the court.

PART 7
CONSEQUENTIAL AMENDMENTS

**47  Consequential amendments**
Schedule 4 makes amendments that are consequential on these Regulations.

Regulation 9(1)                         SCHEDULE 1
INFORMATION RELATING TO ON-PREMISES CONTRACTS

The information referred to in regulation 9(1) is—

(a)    the main characteristics of the [goods, services or digital content], to the extent appropriate to the medium of communication and to the [goods, services or digital content];

(b)    the identity of the trader (such as the trader's trading name), the geographical address at which the trader is established and the trader's telephone number;

(c)    the total price of the [goods, services or digital content] inclusive of taxes, or where the nature of the [goods, services or digital content] is such that the price cannot reasonably be calculated in advance, the manner in which the price is to be calculated;

(d)    where applicable, all additional delivery charges or, where those charges cannot reasonably be calculated in advance, the fact that such additional charges may be payable;

(e)    where applicable, the arrangements for payment, delivery, performance, and the time by which the trader undertakes to deliver the goods[, to perform the service or to supply the digital content];

(f)    where applicable, the trader's complaint handling policy;

(g)    in the case of a sales contract, a reminder that the trader is under a legal duty to supply goods that are in conformity with the contract;

(h)    where applicable, the existence and the conditions of after-sales services and commercial guarantees;

(i)    the duration of the contract, where applicable, or, if the contract is of indeterminate duration or is to be extended automatically, the conditions for terminating the contract;

(j)    where applicable, the functionality, including applicable technical protection measures, of digital content;

(k)    where applicable, any relevant compatibility of digital content with hardware and software that the trader is aware of or can reasonably be expected to have been aware of.

Regulations 10(1) and 13(1)        SCHEDULE 2
INFORMATION RELATING TO DISTANCE AND OFF-PREMISES
CONTRACTS

The information referred to in regulations 10(1) and 13(1) is (subject to the note at the end of this Schedule)—

(a)    the main characteristics of the [goods, services or digital content], to the extent appropriate to the medium of communication and to the [goods, services or digital content];

(b)    the identity of the trader (such as the trader's trading name);

(c)    the geographical address at which the trader is established and, where available, the trader's telephone number, fax number and e-mail address, to enable the consumer to contact the trader quickly and communicate efficiently;

(d)   where the trader is acting on behalf of another trader, the geographical address and identity of that other trader;

(e)   if different from the address provided in accordance with paragraph (c), the geographical address of the place of business of the trader, and, where the trader acts on behalf of another trader, the geographical address of the place of business of that other trader, where the consumer can address any complaints;

(f)   the total price of the [goods, services or digital content] inclusive of taxes, or where the nature of the [goods, services or digital content] is such that the price cannot reasonably be calculated in advance, the manner in which the price is to be calculated,

(g)   where applicable, all additional delivery charges and any other costs or, where those charges cannot reasonably be calculated in advance, the fact that such additional charges may be payable;

(h)   in the case of a contract of indeterminate duration or a contract containing a subscription, the total costs per billing period or (where such contracts are charged at a fixed rate) the total monthly costs;

(i)   the cost of using the means of distance communication for the conclusion of the contract where that cost is calculated other than at the basic rate;

(j)   the arrangements for payment, delivery, performance, and the time by which the trader undertakes to deliver the goods[, to perform the services or to supply the digital content];

(k)   where applicable, the trader's complaint handling policy;

(l)   where a right to cancel exists, the conditions, time limit and procedures for exercising that right in accordance with regulations 27 to 38;

(m)   where applicable, that the consumer will have to bear the cost of returning the goods in case of cancellation and, for distance contracts, if the goods, by their nature, cannot normally be returned by post, the cost of returning the goods;

(n)   that, if the consumer exercises the right to cancel after having made a request in accordance with regulation 36(1), the consumer is to be liable to pay the trader reasonable costs in accordance with regulation 36(4);

(o)   where under regulation 28, 36 or 37 there is no right to cancel or the right to cancel may be lost, the information that the consumer will not benefit from a right to cancel, or the circumstances under which the consumer loses the right to cancel;

(p)   in the case of a sales contract, a reminder that the trader is under a legal duty to supply goods that are in conformity with the contract;

(q)   where applicable, the existence and the conditions of after-sale customer assistance, after-sales services and commercial guarantees;

(r)   the existence of relevant codes of conduct, as defined in regulation 5(3)(b) of the Consumer Protection from Unfair Trading Regulations 2008, and how copies of them can be obtained, where applicable;

(s)   the duration of the contract, where applicable, or, if the contract is of indeterminate duration or is to be extended automatically, the conditions for terminating the contract;

(t)   where applicable, the minimum duration of the consumer's obligations under the contract;

(u)   where applicable, the existence and the conditions of deposits or other financial guarantees to be paid or provided by the consumer at the request of the trader;

(v)   where applicable, the functionality, including applicable technical protection measures, of digital content;

(w)   where applicable, any relevant compatibility of digital content with hardware and software that the trader is aware of or can reasonably be expected to have been aware of;

(x)   where applicable, the possibility of having recourse to an out-of-court complaint and redress mechanism, to which the trader is subject, and the methods for having access to it.

Note: In the case of a public auction, the information listed in paragraphs (b) to (e) may be replaced with the equivalent details for the auctioneer.

Regulations 10 and 13              SCHEDULE 3
INFORMATION ABOUT THE EXERCISE OF THE RIGHT TO CANCEL

A. Model instructions for cancellation

*Right to cancel*

You have the right to cancel this contract within 14 days without giving any reason.

The cancellation period will expire after 14 days from the day [See Note 1].

To exercise the right to cancel, you must inform us [See Note 2] of your decision to cancel this contract by a clear statement (eg a letter sent by post, fax or e-mail). You may use the attached model cancellation form, but it is not obligatory. [See Note 3]

To meet the cancellation deadline, it is sufficient for you to send your communication concerning your exercise of the right to cancel before the cancellation period has expired.

*Effects of cancellation*

If you cancel this contract, we will reimburse to you all payments received from you, including the costs of delivery (except for the supplementary costs arising if you chose a type of delivery other than the least expensive type of standard delivery offered by us).

We may make a deduction from the reimbursement for loss in value of any goods supplied, if the loss is the result of unnecessary handling by you.

We will make the reimbursement without undue delay, and not later than—
(a)   14 days after the day we receive back from you any goods supplied, or
(b)   (if earlier) 14 days after the day you provide evidence that you have returned the goods, or
(c)   if there were no goods supplied, 14 days after the day on which we are informed about your decision to cancel this contract.

We will make the reimbursement using the same means of payment as you used for the initial transaction, unless you have expressly agreed otherwise; in any event, you will not incur any fees as a result of the reimbursement. [See Note 4].

[See Note 5]

[See Note 6]

**Notes on instructions for completion:**

1.   Insert one of the following texts between inverted commas:
(a)   in the case of a service contract or a contract for the supply of digital content which is not supplied on a tangible medium: 'of the conclusion of the contract.';

(b)    in the case of a sales contract: 'on which you acquire, or a third party other than the carrier and indicated by you acquires, physical possession of the goods.';

(c)    in the case of a contract relating to multiple goods ordered by the consumer in one order and delivered separately: 'on which you acquire, or a third party other than the carrier and indicated by you acquires, physical possession of the last good.';

(d)    in the case of a contract relating to delivery of a good consisting of multiple lots or pieces: 'on which you acquire, or a third party other than the carrier and indicated by you acquires, physical possession of the last lot or piece.';

(e)    in the case of a contract for regular delivery of goods during a defined period of time: 'on which you acquire, or a third party other than the carrier and indicated by you acquires, physical possession of the first good.'.

2.    Insert your name, geographical address and, where available, your telephone number, fax number and e-mail address.

3.    If you give the option to the consumer to electronically fill in and submit information about the consumer's cancellation from the contract on your website, insert the following: 'You can also electronically fill in and submit the model cancellation form or any other clear statement on our website [insert Internet address]. If you use this option, we will communicate to you an acknowledgement of receipt of such a cancellation on a durable medium (eg by e-mail) without delay.'.

4.    In the case of sales contracts in which you have not offered to collect the goods in the event of cancellation insert the following: 'We may withhold reimbursement until we have received the goods back or you have supplied evidence of having sent back the goods, whichever is the earliest.'.

5.    If the consumer has received goods in connection with the contract

(a)    insert:

—'We will collect the goods.'; or,

—'You shall send back the goods or hand them over to us or ... [insert the name and geographical address, where applicable, of the person authorised by you to receive the goods], without undue delay and in any event not later than 14 days from the day on which you communicate your cancellation from this contract to us. The deadline is met if you send back the goods before the period of 14 days has expired.'

(b)    insert:

—'We will bear the cost of returning the goods.';

—'You will have to bear the direct cost of returning the goods.';

—If, in a distance contract, you do not offer to bear the cost of returning the goods and the goods, by their nature, cannot normally be returned by post: 'You will have to bear the direct cost of returning the goods, ... EUR [insert the amount].'; or if the cost of returning the goods cannot reasonably be calculated in advance: 'You will have to bear the direct cost of returning the goods. The cost is estimated at a maximum of approximately ... EUR [insert the amount].'; or

—If, in an off-premises contract, the goods, by their nature, cannot normally be returned by post and have been delivered to the consumer's home at the time of the conclusion of the contract: 'We will collect the goods at our own expense.'; and,

(c)   insert

—'You are only liable for any diminished value of the goods resulting from the handling other than what is necessary to establish the nature, characteristics and functioning of the goods.'

6. In the case of a service contract insert the following: 'If you requested to begin the performance of services during the cancellation period, you shall pay us an amount which is in proportion to what has been performed until you have communicated us your cancellation from this contract, in comparison with the full coverage of the contract.'.

## B. Model cancellation form

To [here the trader's name, geographical address and, where available, fax number and e-mail address are to be inserted by the trader]:

I/We [*] hereby give notice that I/We [*] cancel my/our [*] contract of sale of the following goods [*]/for the supply of the following service [*],

Ordered on [*]/received on [*],

Name of consumer(s),

Address of consumer(s),

Signature of consumer(s) (only if this form is notified on paper),

Date

[*] Delete as appropriate.

# PART III
# EU MATERIALS

REGULATION (EC) NO 593/2008 OF THE EUROPEAN PARLIAMENT AND
OF THE COUNCIL OF 17 JUNE 2008 ON THE LAW APPLICABLE TO
CONTRACTUAL OBLIGATIONS (ROME I)

Official Journal L 177, 04/07/2008 pp 6-16

THE EUROPEAN PARLIAMENT AND THE COUNCIL OF THE EUROPEAN UNION,

Having regard to the Treaty establishing the European Community, and in particular Article 61(c) and the second indent of Article 67(5) thereof,
    Having regard to the proposal from the Commission,
    Having regard to the opinion of the European Economic and Social Committee,
    Acting in accordance with the procedure laid down in Article 251 of the Treaty,

HAVE ADOPTED THIS REGULATION:

## CHAPTER I
## SCOPE

### Article 1. Material scope
    1.  This Regulation shall apply, in situations involving a conflict of laws, to contractual obligations in civil and commercial matters.
    It shall not apply, in particular, to revenue, customs or administrative matters.
    2.  The following shall be excluded from the scope of this Regulation:
    (a)  questions involving the status or legal capacity of natural persons, without prejudice to Article 13;
    (b)  obligations arising out of family relationships and relationships deemed by the law applicable to such relationships to have comparable effects, including maintenance obligations;
    (c)  obligations arising out of matrimonial property regimes, property regimes of relationships deemed by the law applicable to such relationships to have comparable effects to marriage, and wills and succession;
    (d)  obligations arising under bills of exchange, cheques and promissory notes and other negotiable instruments to the extent that the obligations under such other negotiable instruments arise out of their negotiable character;
    (e)  arbitration agreements and agreements on the choice of court;
    (f)  questions governed by the law of companies and other bodies, corporate or unincorporated, such as the creation, by registration or otherwise, legal capacity, internal organisation or winding-up of companies and other bodies, corporate or unincorporated, and the personal liability of officers and members as such for the obligations of the company or body;
    (g)  the question whether an agent is able to bind a principal, or an organ to

bind a company or other body corporate or unincorporated, in relation to a third party;

(h)    the constitution of trusts and the relationship between settlors, trustees and beneficiaries;

(i)    obligations arising out of dealings prior to the conclusion of a contract;]

(j)    insurance contracts arising out of operations carried out by organisations other than undertakings referred to in Article 2 of Directive 2002/83/EC of the European Parliament and of the Council of 5 November 2002 concerning life assurance the object of which is to provide benefits for employed or self-employed persons belonging to an undertaking or group of undertakings, or to a trade or group of trades, in the event of death or survival or of discontinuance or curtailment of activity, or of sickness related to work or accidents at work.

3.    This Regulation shall not apply to evidence and procedure, without prejudice to Article 18.

4.    In this Regulation, the term 'Member State' shall mean Member States to which this Regulation applies. However, in Article 3(4) and Article 7 the term shall mean all the Member States.

### Article 2. Universal application
Any law specified by this Regulation shall be applied whether or not it is the law of a Member State.

CHAPTER II
UNIFORM RULES

### Article 3. Freedom of choice
1.    A contract shall be governed by the law chosen by the parties. The choice shall be made expressly or clearly demonstrated by the terms of the contract or the circumstances of the case. By their choice the parties can select the law applicable to the whole or to part only of the contract.

2.    The parties may at any time agree to subject the contract to a law other than that which previously governed it, whether as a result of an earlier choice made under this Article or of other provisions of this Regulation. Any change in the law to be applied that is made after the conclusion of the contract shall not prejudice its formal validity under Article 11 or adversely affect the rights of third parties.

3.    Where all other elements relevant to the situation at the time of the choice are located in a country other than the country whose law has been chosen, the choice of the parties shall not prejudice the application of provisions of the law of that other country which cannot be derogated from by agreement.

4.    Where all other elements relevant to the situation at the time of the choice are located in one or more Member States, the parties' choice of applicable law other than that of a Member State shall not prejudice the application of provisions of Community law, where appropriate as implemented in the Member State of the forum, which cannot be derogated from by agreement.

5.    The existence and validity of the consent of the parties as to the choice of the applicable law shall be determined in accordance with the provisions of Articles 10, 11 and 13.

### Article 4. Applicable law in the absence of choice
1.    To the extent that the law applicable to the contract has not been chosen in accordance with Article 3 and without prejudice to Articles 5 to 8, the law governing the contract shall be determined as follows:

(a)    a contract for the sale of goods shall be governed by the law of the country where the seller has his habitual residence;

(b)    a contract for the provision of services shall be governed by the law of the country where the service provider has his habitual residence;

(c)    a contract relating to a right in rem in immovable property or to a tenancy of immovable property shall be governed by the law of the country where the property is situated;

(d)   notwithstanding point (c), a tenancy of immovable property concluded for temporary private use for a period of no more than six consecutive months shall be governed by the law of the country where the landlord has his habitual residence, provided that the tenant is a natural person and has his habitual residence in the same country;

(e)   a franchise contract shall be governed by the law of the country where the franchisee has his habitual residence;

(f)   a distribution contract shall be governed by the law of the country where the distributor has his habitual residence;

(g)   a contract for the sale of goods by auction shall be governed by the law of the country where the auction takes place, if such a place can be determined;

(h)   a contract concluded within a multilateral system which brings together or facilitates the bringing together of multiple third-party buying and selling interests in financial instruments, as defined by Article 4(1), point (17) of Directive 2004/39/EC, in accordance with non-discretionary rules and governed by a single law, shall be governed by that law.

2.   Where the contract is not covered by paragraph 1 or where the elements of the contract would be covered by more than one of points (a) to (h) of paragraph 1, the contract shall be governed by the law of the country where the party required to effect the characteristic performance of the contract has his habitual residence.

3.   Where it is clear from all the circumstances of the case that the contract is manifestly more closely connected with a country other than that indicated in paragraphs 1 or 2, the law of that other country shall apply.

4.   Where the law applicable cannot be determined pursuant to paragraphs 1 or 2, the contract shall be governed by the law of the country with which it is most closely connected.

### Article 5. Contracts of carriage

1.   To the extent that the law applicable to a contract for the carriage of goods has not been chosen in accordance with Article 3, the law applicable shall be the law of the country of habitual residence of the carrier, provided that the place of receipt or the place of delivery or the habitual residence of the consignor is also situated in that country. If those requirements are not met, the law of the country where the place of delivery as agreed by the parties is situated shall apply.

2.   To the extent that the law applicable to a contract for the carriage of passengers has not been chosen by the parties in accordance with the second subparagraph, the law applicable shall be the law of the country where the passenger has his habitual residence, provided that either the place of departure or the place of destination is situated in that country. If these requirements are not met, the law of the country where the carrier has his habitual residence shall apply.

The parties may choose as the law applicable to a contract for the carriage of passengers in accordance with Article 3 only the law of the country where:

(a)   the passenger has his habitual residence; or

(b)   the carrier has his habitual residence; or

(c)   the carrier has his place of central administration; or

(d)   the place of departure is situated; or

(e)   the place of destination is situated.

3.   Where it is clear from all the circumstances of the case that the contract, in the absence of a choice of law, is manifestly more closely connected with a country other than that indicated in paragraphs 1 or 2, the law of that other country shall apply.

### Article 6. Consumer contracts

1.   Without prejudice to Articles 5 and 7, a contract concluded by a natural

person for a purpose which can be regarded as being outside his trade or profession (the consumer) with another person acting in the exercise of his trade or profession (the professional) shall be governed by the law of the country where the consumer has his habitual residence, provided that the professional:

(a)   pursues his commercial or professional activities in the country where the consumer has his habitual residence, or

(b)   by any means, directs such activities to that country or to several countries including that country,

and the contract falls within the scope of such activities.

2.   Notwithstanding paragraph 1, the parties may choose the law applicable to a contract which fulfils the requirements of paragraph 1, in accordance with Article 3. Such a choice may not, however, have the result of depriving the consumer of the protection afforded to him by provisions that cannot be derogated from by agreement by virtue of the law which, in the absence of choice, would have been applicable on the basis of paragraph 1.

3.   If the requirements in points (a) or (b) of paragraph 1 are not fulfilled, the law applicable to a contract between a consumer and a professional shall be determined pursuant to Articles 3 and 4.

4.   Paragraphs 1 and 2 shall not apply to:

(a)   a contract for the supply of services where the services are to be supplied to the consumer exclusively in a country other than that in which he has his habitual residence;

(b)   a contract of carriage other than a contract relating to package travel within the meaning of Council Directive 90/314/EEC of 13 June 1990 on package travel, package holidays and package tours;

(c)   a contract relating to a right in rem in immovable property or a tenancy of immovable property other than a contract relating to the right to use immovable properties on a timeshare basis within the meaning of Directive 94/47/EC;

(d)   rights and obligations which constitute a financial instrument and rights and obligations constituting the terms and conditions governing the issuance or offer to the public and public take-over bids of transferable securities, and the subscription and redemption of units in collective investment undertakings in so far as these activities do not constitute provision of a financial service;

(e)   a contract concluded within the type of system falling within the scope of Article 4(1)(h)

### Article 7. Insurance contracts*

1.   This Article shall apply to contracts referred to in paragraph 2, whether or not the risk covered is situated in a Member State, and to all other insurance contracts covering risks situated inside the territory of the Member States. It shall not apply to reinsurance contracts.

2.   An insurance contract covering a large risk as defined in Article 5(d) of the First Council Directive 73/239/EEC of 24 July 1973 on the coordination of laws, regulations and administrative provisions relating to the taking-up and pursuit of the business of direct insurance other than life assurance shall be governed by the law chosen by the parties in accordance with Article 3 of this Regulation.

To the extent that the applicable law has not been chosen by the parties, the insurance contract shall be governed by the law of the country where the insurer has his habitual residence. Where it is clear from all the circumstances of the case that the contract is manifestly more closely connected with another country, the law of that other country shall apply.

3.   In the case of an insurance contract other than a contract falling within paragraph 2, only the following laws may be chosen by the parties in accordance with Article 3:

(a)  the law of any Member State where the risk is situated at the time of conclusion of the contract;

(b)  the law of the country where the policy holder has his habitual residence;

(c)  in the case of life assurance, the law of the Member State of which the policy holder is a national;

(d)  for insurance contracts covering risks limited to events occurring in one Member State other than the Member State where the risk is situated, the law of that Member State;

(e)  where the policy holder of a contract falling under this paragraph pursues a commercial or industrial activity or a liberal profession and the insurance contract covers two or more risks which relate to those activities and are situated in different Member States, the law of any of the Member States concerned or the law of the country of habitual residence of the policy holder.

Where, in the cases set out in points (a), (b) or (e), the Member States referred to grant greater freedom of choice of the law applicable to the insurance contract, the parties may take advantage of that freedom.

To the extent that the law applicable has not been chosen by the parties in accordance with this paragraph, such a contract shall be governed by the law of the Member State in which the risk is situated at the time of conclusion of the contract.

4.  The following additional rules shall apply to insurance contracts covering risks for which a Member State imposes an obligation to take out insurance:

(a)  the insurance contract shall not satisfy the obligation to take out insurance unless it complies with the specific provisions relating to that insurance laid down by the Member State that imposes the obligation. Where the law of the Member State in which the risk is situated and the law of the Member State imposing the obligation to take out insurance contradict each other, the latter shall prevail;

(b)  by way of derogation from paragraphs 2 and 3, a Member State may lay down that the insurance contract shall be governed by the law of the Member State that imposes the obligation to take out insurance.

5.  For the purposes of paragraph 3, third subparagraph, and paragraph 4, where the contract covers risks situated in more than one Member State, the contract shall be considered as constituting several contracts each relating to only one Member State.

6.  For the purposes of this Article, the country in which the risk is situated shall be determined in accordance with Article 2(d) of the Second Council Directive 88/357/EEC of 22 June 1988 on the coordination of laws, regulations and administrative provisions relating to direct insurance other than life assurance and laying down provisions to facilitate the effective exercise of freedom to provide services and, in the case of life assurance, the country in which the risk is situated shall be the country of the commitment within the meaning of Article 1(1)(g) of Directive 2002/83/EC.

## Article 8. Individual employment contracts

1.  An individual employment contract shall be governed by the law chosen by the parties in accordance with Article 3. Such a choice of law may not, however, have the result of depriving the employee of the protection afforded to him by provisions that cannot be derogated from by agreement under the law that, in the absence of choice, would have been applicable pursuant to paragraphs 2, 3 and 4 of this Article.

2.  To the extent that the law applicable to the individual employment contract has not been chosen by the parties, the contract shall be governed by the law of the country in which or, failing that, from which the employee habitually carries out his work in performance of the contract. The country where the work is habitually

carried out shall not be deemed to have changed if he is temporarily employed in another country.

3. Where the law applicable cannot be determined pursuant to paragraph 2, the contract shall be governed by the law of the country where the place of business through which the employee was engaged is situated.

4. Where it appears from the circumstances as a whole that the contract is more closely connected with a country other than that indicated in paragraphs 2 or 3, the law of that other country shall apply.

### Article 9. Overriding mandatory provisions

1. Overriding mandatory provisions are provisions the respect for which is regarded as crucial by a country for safeguarding its public interests, such as its political, social or economic organisation, to such an extent that they are applicable to any situation falling within their scope, irrespective of the law otherwise applicable to the contract under this Regulation.

2. Nothing in this Regulation shall restrict the application of the overriding mandatory provisions of the law of the forum.

3. Effect may be given to the overriding mandatory provisions of the law of the country where the obligations arising out of the contract have to be or have been performed, in so far as those overriding mandatory provisions render the performance of the contract unlawful. In considering whether to give effect to those provisions, regard shall be had to their nature and purpose and to the consequences of their application or non-application.

### Article 10. Consent and material validity

1. The existence and validity of a contract, or of any term of a contract, shall be determined by the law which would govern it under this Regulation if the contract or term were valid.

2. Nevertheless, a party, in order to establish that he did not consent, may rely upon the law of the country in which he has his habitual residence if it appears from the circumstances that it would not be reasonable to determine the effect of his conduct in accordance with the law specified in paragraph 1.

### Article 11. Formal validity

1. A contract concluded between persons who, or whose agents, are in the same country at the time of its conclusion is formally valid if it satisfies the formal requirements of the law which governs it in substance under this Regulation or of the law of the country where it is concluded.

2. A contract concluded between persons who, or whose agents, are in different countries at the time of its conclusion is formally valid if it satisfies the formal requirements of the law which governs it in substance under this Regulation, or of the law of either of the countries where either of the parties or their agent is present at the time of conclusion, or of the law of the country where either of the parties had his habitual residence at that time.

3. A unilateral act intended to have legal effect relating to an existing or contemplated contract is formally valid if it satisfies the formal requirements of the law which governs or would govern the contract in substance under this Regulation, or of the law of the country where the act was done, or of the law of the country where the person by whom it was done had his habitual residence at that time.

4. Paragraphs 1, 2 and 3 of this Article shall not apply to contracts that fall within the scope of Article 6. The form of such contracts shall be governed by the law of the country where the consumer has his habitual residence.

5. Notwithstanding paragraphs 1 to 4, a contract the subject matter of which is a right in rem in immovable property or a tenancy of immovable property shall be subject to the requirements of form of the law of the country where the property is situated if by that law:

(a)   those requirements are imposed irrespective of the country where the contract is concluded and irrespective of the law governing the contract; and

(b)   those requirements cannot be derogated from by agreement.

### Article 12. Scope of the law applicable

1.   The law applicable to a contract by virtue of this Regulation shall govern in particular:

(a)   interpretation;

(b)   performance;

(c)   within the limits of the powers conferred on the court by its procedural law, the consequences of a total or partial breach of obligations, including the assessment of damages in so far as it is governed by rules of law;

(d)   the various ways of extinguishing obligations, and prescription and limitation of actions;

(e)   the consequences of nullity of the contract.

2.   In relation to the manner of performance and the steps to be taken in the event of defective performance, regard shall be had to the law of the country in which performance takes place.

### Article 13. Incapacity

In a contract concluded between persons who are in the same country, a natural person who would have capacity under the law of that country may invoke his incapacity resulting from the law of another country, only if the other party to the contract was aware of that incapacity at the time of the conclusion of the contract or was not aware thereof as a result of negligence.

### Article 14. Voluntary assignment and contractual subrogation

1.   The relationship between assignor and assignee under a voluntary assignment or contractual subrogation of a claim against another person (the debtor) shall be governed by the law that applies to the contract between the assignor and assignee under this Regulation.

2.   The law governing the assigned or subrogated claim shall determine its assignability, the relationship between the assignee and the debtor, the conditions under which the assignment or subrogation can be invoked against the debtor and whether the debtor's obligations have been discharged.

3.   The concept of assignment in this Article includes outright transfers of claims, transfers of claims by way of security and pledges or other security rights over claims.

### Article 15. Legal subrogation

Where a person (the creditor) has a contractual claim against another (the debtor) and a third person has a duty to satisfy the creditor, or has in fact satisfied the creditor in discharge of that duty, the law which governs the third person's duty to satisfy the creditor shall determine whether and to what extent the third person is entitled to exercise against the debtor the rights which the creditor had against the debtor under the law governing their relationship.

### Article 16. Multiple liability

If a creditor has a claim against several debtors who are liable for the same claim, and one of the debtors has already satisfied the claim in whole or in part, the law governing the debtor's obligation towards the creditor also governs the debtor's right to claim recourse from the other debtors. The other debtors may rely on the defences they had against the creditor to the extent allowed by the law governing their obligations towards the creditor.

### Article 17. Set-off

Where the right to set-off is not agreed by the parties, set-off shall be governed by the law applicable to the claim against which the right to set-off is asserted.

### Article 18. Burden of proof

1.   The law governing a contractual obligation under this Regulation shall apply to the extent that, in matters of contractual obligations, it contains rules which raise presumptions of law or determine the burden of proof.

2.   A contract or an act intended to have legal effect may be proved by any mode of proof recognised by the law of the forum or by any of the laws referred to in Article 11 under which that contract or act is formally valid, provided that such mode of proof can be administered by the forum.

## CHAPTER III
## OTHER PROVISIONS

### Article 19. Habitual residence

1.   For the purposes of this Regulation, the habitual residence of companies and other bodies, corporate or unincorporated, shall be the place of central administration.

The habitual residence of a natural person acting in the course of his business activity shall be his principal place of business.

2.   Where the contract is concluded in the course of the operations of a branch, agency or any other establishment, or if, under the contract, performance is the responsibility of such a branch, agency or establishment, the place where the branch, agency or any other establishment is located shall be treated as the place of habitual residence.

3.   For the purposes of determining the habitual residence, the relevant point in time shall be the time of the conclusion of the contract.

### Article 20. Exclusion of renvoi

The application of the law of any country specified by this Regulation means the application of the rules of law in force in that country other than its rules of private international law, unless provided otherwise in this Regulation.

### Article 21. Public policy of the forum

The application of a provision of the law of any country specified by this Regulation may be refused only if such application is manifestly incompatible with the public policy (ordre public) of the forum.

### Article 22. States with more than one legal system*

1.   Where a State comprises several territorial units, each of which has its own rules of law in respect of contractual obligations, each territorial unit shall be considered as a country for the purposes of identifying the law applicable under this Regulation.

2.   A Member State where different territorial units have their own rules of law in respect of contractual obligations shall not be required to apply this Regulation to conflicts solely between the laws of such units.

### Article 23. Relationship with other provisions of Community law

With the exception of Article 7, this Regulation shall not prejudice the application of provisions of Community law which, in relation to particular matters, lay down conflict-of-law rules relating to contractual obligations.

### Article 24. Relationship with the Rome Convention

1.   This Regulation shall replace the Rome Convention in the Member States, except as regards the territories of the Member States which fall within the territorial scope of that Convention and to which this Regulation does not apply pursuant to Article 299 of the Treaty.

2.   In so far as this Regulation replaces the provisions of the Rome Convention, any reference to that Convention shall be understood as a reference to this Regulation.

**Article 25. Relationship with existing international conventions**

1. This Regulation shall not prejudice the application of international conventions to which one or more Member States are parties at the time when this Regulation is adopted and which lay down conflict-of-law rules relating to contractual obligations.

2. However, this Regulation shall, as between Member States, take precedence over conventions concluded exclusively between two or more of them in so far as such conventions concern matters governed by this Regulation.

**Article 26. List of Conventions**

1. By 17 June 2009, Member States shall notify the Commission of the conventions referred to in Article 25(1). After that date, Member States shall notify the Commission of all denunciations of such conventions.

2. Within six months of receipt of the notifications referred to in paragraph 1, the Commission shall publish in the Official Journal of the European Union:

(a) a list of the conventions referred to in paragraph 1;

(b) the denunciations referred to in paragraph 1.

**Article 27. Review clause**

1. By 17 June 2013, the Commission shall submit to the European Parliament, the Council and the European Economic and Social Committee a report on the application of this Regulation. If appropriate, the report shall be accompanied by proposals to amend this Regulation. The report shall include:

(a) a study on the law applicable to insurance contracts and an assessment of the impact of the provisions to be introduced, if any; and

(b) an evaluation on the application of Article 6, in particular as regards the coherence of Community law in the field of consumer protection.

2. By 17 June 2010, the Commission shall submit to the European Parliament, the Council and the European Economic and Social Committee a report on the question of the effectiveness of an assignment or subrogation of a claim against third parties and the priority of the assigned or subrogated claim over a right of another person. The report shall be accompanied, if appropriate, by a proposal to amend this Regulation and an assessment of the impact of the provisions to be introduced.

**Article 28. Application in time**

This Regulation shall apply to contracts concluded as from 17 December 2009.

## COUNCIL REGULATION (EU) NO 2015/848 OF 20 MAY ON INSOLVENCY PROCEEDINGS (RECAST)

Official Journal L 141, 05/06/2015 pp 19–72
THE EUROPEAN PARLIAMENT AND THE COUNCIL OF THE EUROPEAN UNION,
Having regard to the Treaty on the Functioning of the European Union, and in particular Article 81 thereof,
Having regard to the proposal from the European Commission,
After transmission of the draft legislative act to the national parliaments,
Having regard to the opinion of the European Economic and Social Committee,
Acting in accordance with the ordinary legislative procedure
HAVE ADOPTED THIS REGULATION:

CHAPTER I
GENERAL PROVISIONS

**Article 1. Scope**
1. This Regulation shall apply to public collective proceedings, including interim proceedings, which are based on laws relating to insolvency and in which, for the purpose of rescue, adjustment of debt, reorganisation or liquidation:

(a) a debtor is totally or partially divested of its assets and an insolvency practitioner is appointed;

(b) the assets and affairs of a debtor are subject to control or supervision by a court; or

(c) a temporary stay of individual enforcement proceedings is granted by a court or by operation of law, in order to allow for negotiations between the debtor and its creditors, provided that the proceedings in which the stay is granted provide for suitable measures to protect the general body of creditors, and, where no agreement is reached, are preliminary to one of the proceedings referred to in point (a) or (b).

Where the proceedings referred to in this paragraph may be commenced in situations where there is only a likelihood of insolvency, their purpose shall be to avoid the debtor's insolvency or the cessation of the debtor's business activities.

The proceedings referred to in this paragraph are listed in Annex A.

2. This Regulation shall not apply to proceedings referred to in paragraph 1 that concern:

(a) insurance undertakings;

(b) credit institutions;

(c) investment firms and other firms, institutions and undertakings to the extent that they are covered by Directive 2001/24/EC; or

(d) collective investment undertakings.

**Article 2. Definitions**
For the purposes of this Regulation:

(1) 'collective proceedings' means proceedings which include all or a significant part of a debtor's creditors, provided that, in the latter case, the proceedings do not affect the claims of creditors which are not involved in them;

(2) 'collective investment undertakings' means undertakings for collective investment in transferable securities (UCITS) as defined in Directive 2009/65/EC of the European Parliament and of the Council and alternative investment funds (AIFs) as defined in Directive 2011/61/EU of the European Parliament and of the Council;

(3) 'debtor in possession' means a debtor in respect of which insolvency proceedings have been opened which do not necessarily involve the appointment of an insolvency practitioner or the complete transfer of the rights and duties to

administer the debtor's assets to an insolvency practitioner and where, therefore, the debtor remains totally or at least partially in control of its assets and affairs;

(4) 'insolvency proceedings' means the proceedings listed in Annex A;

(5) 'insolvency practitioner' means any person or body whose function, including on an interim basis, is to:

(i) verify and admit claims submitted in insolvency proceedings;

(ii) represent the collective interest of the creditors;

(iii) administer, either in full or in part, assets of which the debtor has been divested;

(iv) liquidate the assets referred to in point (iii); or

(v) supervise the administration of the debtor's affairs.

The persons and bodies referred to in the first subparagraph are listed in Annex B;

(6) 'court' means:

(i) in points (b) and (c) of Article 1(1), Article 4(2), Articles 5 and 6, Article 21(3), point (j) of Article 24(2), Articles 36 and 39, and Articles 61 to 77, the judicial body of a Member State;

(ii) in all other articles, the judicial body or any other competent body of a Member State empowered to open insolvency proceedings, to confirm such opening or to take decisions in the course of such proceedings;

(7) 'judgment opening insolvency proceedings' includes:

(i) the decision of any court to open insolvency proceedings or to confirm the opening of such proceedings; and

(ii) the decision of a court to appoint an insolvency practitioner;

(8) 'the time of the opening of proceedings' means the time at which the judgment opening insolvency proceedings becomes effective, regardless of whether the judgment is final or not;

(9) 'the Member State in which assets are situated' means, in the case of:

(i) registered shares in companies other than those referred to in point (ii), the Member State within the territory of which the company having issued the shares has its registered office;

(ii) financial instruments, the title to which is evidenced by entries in a register or account maintained by or on behalf of an intermediary ('book entry securities'), the Member State in which the register or account in which the entries are made is maintained;

(iii) cash held in accounts with a credit institution, the Member State indicated in the account's IBAN, or, for cash held in accounts with a credit institution which does not have an IBAN, the Member State in which the credit institution holding the account has its central administration or, where the account is held with a branch, agency or other establishment, the Member State in which the branch, agency or other establishment is located;

(iv) property and rights, ownership of or entitlement to which is entered in a public register other than those referred to in point (i), the Member State under the authority of which the register is kept;

(v) European patents, the Member State for which the European patent is granted;

(vi) copyright and related rights, the Member State within the territory of which the owner of such rights has its habitual residence or registered office;

(vii) tangible property, other than that referred to in points (i) to (iv), the Member State within the territory of which the property is situated;

(viii) claims against third parties, other than those relating to assets referred to in point (iii), the Member State within the territory of which the third party required to meet the claims has the centre of its main interests, as determined in accordance with Article 3(1);

(10) 'establishment' means any place of operations where a debtor carries out or has carried out in the 3-month period prior to the request to open main in-

solvency proceedings a non-transitory economic activity with human means and assets;

(11)  'local creditor' means a creditor whose claims against a debtor arose from or in connection with the operation of an establishment situated in a Member State other than the Member State in which the centre of the debtor's main interests is located;

(12)  'foreign creditor' means a creditor which has its habitual residence, domicile or registered office in a Member State other than the State of the opening of proceedings, including the tax authorities and social security authorities of Member States;

(13)  'group of companies' means a parent undertaking and all its subsidiary undertakings;

(14)  'parent undertaking' means an undertaking which controls, either directly or indirectly, one or more subsidiary undertakings. An undertaking which prepares consolidated financial statements in accordance with Directive 2013/34/EU of the European Parliament and of the Council shall be deemed to be a parent undertaking.

### Article 3.   International jurisdiction

1.   The courts of the Member State within the territory of which the centre of the debtor's main interests is situated shall have jurisdiction to open insolvency proceedings ('main insolvency proceedings'). The centre of main interests shall be the place where the debtor conducts the administration of its interests on a regular basis and which is ascertainable by third parties.

In the case of a company or legal person, the place of the registered office shall be presumed to be the centre of its main interests in the absence of proof to the contrary. That presumption shall only apply if the registered office has not been moved to another Member State within the 3-month period prior to the request for the opening of insolvency proceedings.

In the case of an individual exercising an independent business or professional activity, the centre of main interests shall be presumed to be that individual's principal place of business in the absence of proof to the contrary. That presumption shall only apply if the individual's principal place of business has not been moved to another Member State within the 3-month period prior to the request for the opening of insolvency proceedings.

In the case of any other individual, the centre of main interests shall be presumed to be the place of the individual's habitual residence in the absence of proof to the contrary. This presumption shall only apply if the habitual residence has not been moved to another Member State within the 6-month period prior to the request for the opening of insolvency proceedings.

2.   Where the centre of the debtor's main interests is situated within the territory of a Member State, the courts of another Member State shall have jurisdiction to open insolvency proceedings against that debtor only if it possesses an establishment within the territory of that other Member State. The effects of those proceedings shall be restricted to the assets of the debtor situated in the territory of the latter Member State.

3.   Where insolvency proceedings have been opened in accordance with paragraph 1, any proceedings opened subsequently in accordance with paragraph 2 shall be secondary insolvency proceedings.

4.   The territorial insolvency proceedings referred to in paragraph 2 may only be opened prior to the opening of main insolvency proceedings in accordance with paragraph 1 where

(a)   insolvency proceedings under paragraph 1 cannot be opened because of the conditions laid down by the law of the Member State within the territory of which the centre of the debtor's main interests is situated; or

(b)   the opening of territorial insolvency proceedings is requested by:

(i) a creditor whose claim arises from or is in connection with the operation of an establishment situated within the territory of the Member State where the opening of territorial proceedings is requested; or

(ii) a public authority which, under the law of the Member State within the territory of which the establishment is situated, has the right to request the opening of insolvency proceedings.

When main insolvency proceedings are opened, the territorial insolvency proceedings shall become secondary insolvency proceedings.

### Article 4. Examination as to jurisdiction

1. A court seised of a request to open insolvency proceedings shall of its own motion examine whether it has jurisdiction pursuant to Article 3. The judgment opening insolvency proceedings shall specify the grounds on which the jurisdiction of the court is based, and, in particular, whether jurisdiction is based on Article 3(1) or (2).

2. Notwithstanding paragraph 1, where insolvency proceedings are opened in accordance with national law without a decision by a court, Member States may entrust the insolvency practitioner appointed in such proceedings to examine whether the Member State in which a request for the opening of proceedings is pending has jurisdiction pursuant to Article 3. Where this is the case, the insolvency practitioner shall specify in the decision opening the proceedings the grounds on which jurisdiction is based and, in particular, whether jurisdiction is based on Article 3(1) or (2).

### Article 5. Judicial review of the decision to open main insolvency proceedings

1. The debtor or any creditor may challenge before a court the decision opening main insolvency proceedings on grounds of international jurisdiction.

2. The decision opening main insolvency proceedings may be challenged by parties other than those referred to in paragraph 1 or on grounds other than a lack of international jurisdiction where national law so provides.

### Article 6. Jurisdiction for actions deriving directly from insolvency proceedings and closely linked with them

1. The courts of the Member State within the territory of which insolvency proceedings have been opened in accordance with Article 3 shall have jurisdiction for any action which derives directly from the insolvency proceedings and is closely linked with them, such as avoidance actions.

2. Where an action referred to in paragraph 1 is related to an action in civil and commercial matters against the same defendant, the insolvency practitioner may bring both actions before the courts of the Member State within the territory of which the defendant is domiciled, or, where the action is brought against several defendants, before the courts of the Member State within the territory of which any of them is domiciled, provided that those courts have jurisdiction pursuant to Regulation (EU) No 1215/2012.

The first subparagraph shall apply to the debtor in possession, provided that national law allows the debtor in possession to bring actions on behalf of the insolvency estate.

3. For the purpose of paragraph 2, actions are deemed to be related where they are so closely connected that it is expedient to hear and determine them together to avoid the risk of irreconcilable judgments resulting from separate proceedings.

### Article 7. Applicable law

1. Save as otherwise provided in this Regulation, the law applicable to insolvency proceedings and their effects shall be that of the Member State within the territory of which such proceedings are opened (the 'State of the opening of proceedings').

2. The law of the State of the opening of proceedings shall determine the

conditions for the opening of those proceedings, their conduct and their closure. In particular, it shall determine the following:

(a) the debtors against which insolvency proceedings may be brought on account of their capacity;

(b) the assets which form part of the insolvency estate and the treatment of assets acquired by or devolving on the debtor after the opening of the insolvency proceedings;

(c) the respective powers of the debtor and the insolvency practitioner;

(d) the conditions under which set-offs may be invoked;

(e) the effects of insolvency proceedings on current contracts to which the debtor is party;

(f) the effects of the insolvency proceedings on proceedings brought by individual creditors, with the exception of pending lawsuits;

(g) the claims which are to be lodged against the debtor's insolvency estate and the treatment of claims arising after the opening of insolvency proceedings;

(h) the rules governing the lodging, verification and admission of claims;

(i) the rules governing the distribution of proceeds from the realisation of assets, the ranking of claims and the rights of creditors who have obtained partial satisfaction after the opening of insolvency proceedings by virtue of a right in rem or through a set-off;

(j) the conditions for, and the effects of closure of, insolvency proceedings, in particular by composition;

(k) creditors' rights after the closure of insolvency proceedings;

(l) who is to bear the costs and expenses incurred in the insolvency proceedings;

(m) the rules relating to the voidness, voidability or unenforceability of legal acts detrimental to the general body of creditors.

### Article 8. Third parties' rights in rem

1. The opening of insolvency proceedings shall not affect the rights in rem of creditors or third parties in respect of tangible or intangible, moveable or immoveable assets, both specific assets and collections of indefinite assets as a whole which change from time to time, belonging to the debtor which are situated within the territory of another Member State at the time of the opening of proceedings.

2. The rights referred to in paragraph 1 shall, in particular, mean:

(a) the right to dispose of assets or have them disposed of and to obtain satisfaction from the proceeds of or income from those assets, in particular by virtue of a lien or a mortgage;

(b) the exclusive right to have a claim met, in particular a right guaranteed by a lien in respect of the claim or by assignment of the claim by way of a guarantee;

(c) the right to demand assets from, and/or to require restitution by, anyone having possession or use of them contrary to the wishes of the party so entitled;

(d) a right in rem to the beneficial use of assets.

3. The right, recorded in a public register and enforceable against third parties, based on which a right in rem within the meaning of paragraph 1 may be obtained shall be considered to be a right in rem.

4. Paragraph 1 shall not preclude actions for voidness, voidability or unenforceability as referred to in point (m) of Article 7(2).

### Article 9. Set-off

1. The opening of insolvency proceedings shall not affect the right of creditors to demand the set-off of their claims against the claims of a debtor, where such a set-off is permitted by the law applicable to the insolvent debtor's claim.

2. Paragraph 1 shall not preclude actions for voidness, voidability or unenforceability as referred to in point (m) of Article 7(2).

### Article 10.  Reservation of title
1.   The opening of insolvency proceedings against the purchaser of an asset shall not affect sellers' rights that are based on a reservation of title where at the time of the opening of proceedings the asset is situated within the territory of a Member State other than the State of the opening of proceedings.

2.   The opening of insolvency proceedings against the seller of an asset, after delivery of the asset, shall not constitute grounds for rescinding or terminating the sale and shall not prevent the purchaser from acquiring title where at the time of the opening of proceedings the asset sold is situated within the territory of a Member State other than the State of the opening of proceedings.

3.   Paragraphs 1 and 2 shall not preclude actions for voidness, voidability or unenforceability as referred to in point (m) of Article 7(2).

### Article 11.  Contracts relating to immoveable property
1.   The effects of insolvency proceedings on a contract conferring the right to acquire or make use of immoveable property shall be governed solely by the law of the Member State within the territory of which the immoveable property is situated.

2.   The court which opened main insolvency proceedings shall have jurisdiction to approve the termination or modification of the contracts referred to in this Article where:
   (a)   the law of the Member State applicable to those contracts requires that such a contract may only be terminated or modified with the approval of the court opening insolvency proceedings; and
   (b)   no insolvency proceedings have been opened in that Member State.

### Article 12.  Payment systems and financial markets
1.   Without prejudice to Article 8, the effects of insolvency proceedings on the rights and obligations of the parties to a payment or settlement system or to a financial market shall be governed solely by the law of the Member State applicable to that system or market.

2.   Paragraph 1 shall not preclude any action for voidness, voidability or unenforceability which may be taken to set aside payments or transactions under the law applicable to the relevant payment system or financial market.

### Article 13.  Contracts of employment
1.   The effects of insolvency proceedings on employment contracts and relationships shall be governed solely by the law of the Member State applicable to the contract of employment.

2.   The courts of the Member State in which secondary insolvency proceedings may be opened shall retain jurisdiction to approve the termination or modification of the contracts referred to in this Article even if no insolvency proceedings have been opened in that Member State.

The first subparagraph shall also apply to an authority competent under national law to approve the termination or modification of the contracts referred to in this Article.

### Article 14.  Effects on rights subject to registration
The effects of insolvency proceedings on the rights of a debtor in immoveable property, a ship or an aircraft subject to registration in a public register shall be determined by the law of the Member State under the authority of which the register is kept.

### Article 15.  European patents with unitary effect and Community trade marks
For the purposes of this Regulation, a European patent with unitary effect, a Community trade mark or any other similar right established by Union law may be included only in the proceedings referred to in Article 3(1).

### Article 16. Detrimental acts

Point (m) of Article 7(2) shall not apply where the person who benefited from an act detrimental to all the creditors provides proof that:

(a) the act is subject to the law of a Member State other than that of the State of the opening of proceedings; and

(b) the law of that Member State does not allow any means of challenging that act in the relevant case.

### Article 17. Protection of third-party purchasers

Where, by an act concluded after the opening of insolvency proceedings, a debtor disposes, for consideration, of:

(a) an immoveable asset;

(b) a ship or an aircraft subject to registration in a public register; or

(c) securities the existence of which requires registration in a register laid down by law;

the validity of that act shall be governed by the law of the State within the territory of which the immoveable asset is situated or under the authority of which the register is kept.

### Article 18. Effects of insolvency proceedings on pending lawsuits or arbitral proceedings

The effects of insolvency proceedings on a pending lawsuit or pending arbitral proceedings concerning an asset or a right which forms part of a debtor's insolvency estate shall be governed solely by the law of the Member State in which that lawsuit is pending or in which the arbitral tribunal has its seat.

### CHAPTER II
### RECOGNITION OF INSOLVENCY PROCEEDINGS

### Article 19. Principle

1. Any judgment opening insolvency proceedings handed down by a court of a Member State which has jurisdiction pursuant to Article 3 shall be recognised in all other Member States from the moment that it becomes effective in the State of the opening of proceedings.

The rule laid down in the first subparagraph shall also apply where, on account of a debtor's capacity, insolvency proceedings cannot be brought against that debtor in other Member States.

2. Recognition of the proceedings referred to in Article 3(1) shall not preclude the opening of the proceedings referred to in Article 3(2) by a court in another Member State. The latter proceedings shall be secondary insolvency proceedings within the meaning of Chapter III.

### Article 20. Effects of recognition

1. The judgment opening insolvency proceedings as referred to in Article 3(1) shall, with no further formalities, produce the same effects in any other Member State as under the law of the State of the opening of proceedings, unless this Regulation provides otherwise and as long as no proceedings referred to in Article 3(2) are opened in that other Member State.

2. The effects of the proceedings referred to in Article 3(2) may not be challenged in other Member States. Any restriction of creditors' rights, in particular a stay or discharge, shall produce effects vis-à-vis assets situated within the territory of another Member State only in the case of those creditors who have given their consent.

### Article 21. Powers of the insolvency practitioner

1. The insolvency practitioner appointed by a court which has jurisdiction pursuant to Article 3(1) may exercise all the powers conferred on it, by the law of the State of the opening of proceedings, in another Member State, as long as no other

insolvency proceedings have been opened there and no preservation measure to the contrary has been taken there further to a request for the opening of insolvency proceedings in that State. Subject to Articles 8 and 10, the insolvency practitioner may, in particular, remove the debtor's assets from the territory of the Member State in which they are situated.

2.   The insolvency practitioner appointed by a court which has jurisdiction pursuant to Article 3(2) may in any other Member State claim through the courts or out of court that moveable property was removed from the territory of the State of the opening of proceedings to the territory of that other Member State after the opening of the insolvency proceedings. The insolvency practitioner may also bring any action to set aside which is in the interests of the creditors.

3.   In exercising its powers, the insolvency practitioner shall comply with the law of the Member State within the territory of which it intends to take action, in particular with regard to procedures for the realisation of assets. Those powers may not include coercive measures, unless ordered by a court of that Member State, or the right to rule on legal proceedings or disputes.

### Article 22.   Proof of the insolvency practitioner's appointment
The insolvency practitioner's appointment shall be evidenced by a certified copy of the original decision appointing it or by any other certificate issued by the court which has jurisdiction.

A translation into the official language or one of the official languages of the Member State within the territory of which it intends to act may be required. No legalisation or other similar formality shall be required.

### Article 23.   Return and imputation
1.   A creditor which, after the opening of the proceedings referred to in Article 3(1), obtains by any means, in particular through enforcement, total or partial satisfaction of its claim on the assets belonging to a debtor situated within the territory of another Member State, shall return what it has obtained to the insolvency practitioner, subject to Articles 8 and 10.

2.   In order to ensure the equal treatment of creditors, a creditor which has, in the course of insolvency proceedings, obtained a dividend on its claim shall share in distributions made in other proceedings only where creditors of the same ranking or category have, in those other proceedings, obtained an equivalent dividend.

### Article 24.   Establishment of insolvency registers
1.   Member States shall establish and maintain in their territory one or several registers in which information concerning insolvency proceedings is published ('insolvency registers'). That information shall be published as soon as possible after the opening of such proceedings.

2.   The information referred to in paragraph 1 shall be made publicly available, subject to the conditions laid down in Article 27, and shall include the following ('mandatory information'):

(a)   the date of the opening of insolvency proceedings;

(b)   the court opening insolvency proceedings and the case reference number, if any;

(c)   the type of insolvency proceedings referred to in Annex A that were opened and, where applicable, any relevant subtype of such proceedings opened in accordance with national law;

(d)   whether jurisdiction for opening proceedings is based on Article 3(1), 3(2) or 3(4);

(e)   if the debtor is a company or a legal person, the debtor's name, registration number, registered office or, if different, postal address;

(f)   if the debtor is an individual whether or not exercising an independent business or professional activity, the debtor's name, registration number, if any, and postal address or, where the address is protected, the debtor's place and date of birth;

(g)   the name, postal address or e-mail address of the insolvency practitioner, if any, appointed in the proceedings;

(h)   the time limit for lodging claims, if any, or a reference to the criteria for calculating that time limit;

(i)   the date of closing main insolvency proceedings, if any;

(j)   the court before which and, where applicable, the time limit within which a challenge of the decision opening insolvency proceedings is to be lodged in accordance with Article 5, or a reference to the criteria for calculating that time limit.

3.   Paragraph 2 shall not preclude Member States from including documents or additional information in their national insolvency registers, such as directors' disqualifications related to insolvency.

4.   Member States shall not be obliged to include in the insolvency registers the information referred to in paragraph 1 of this Article in relation to individuals not exercising an independent business or professional activity, or to make such information publicly available through the system of interconnection of those registers, provided that known foreign creditors are informed, pursuant to Article 54, of the elements referred to under point (j) of paragraph 2 of this Article.

Where a Member State makes use of the possibility referred to in the first subparagraph, the insolvency proceedings shall not affect the claims of foreign creditors who have not received the information referred to in the first subparagraph.

5.   The publication of information in the registers under this Regulation shall not have any legal effects other than those set out in national law and in Article 55(6).

### Article 25.   Interconnection of insolvency registers

1.   The Commission shall establish a decentralised system for the interconnection of insolvency registers by means of implementing acts. That system shall be composed of the insolvency registers and the European e-Justice Portal, which shall serve as a central public electronic access point to information in the system. The system shall provide a search service in all the official languages of the institutions of the Union in order to make available the mandatory information and any other documents or information included in the insolvency registers which the Member States choose to make available through the European e-Justice Portal.

2.   By means of implementing acts in accordance with the procedure referred to in Article 87, the Commission shall adopt the following by 26 June 2019:

(a)   the technical specification defining the methods of communication and information exchange by electronic means on the basis of the established interface specification for the system of interconnection of insolvency registers;

(b)   the technical measures ensuring the minimum information technology security standards for communication and distribution of information within the system of interconnection of insolvency registers;

(c)   minimum criteria for the search service provided by the European e-Justice Portal based on the information set out in Article 24;

(d)   minimum criteria for the presentation of the results of such searches based on the information set out in Article 24;

(e)   the means and the technical conditions of availability of services provided by the system of interconnection; and

(f)   a glossary containing a basic explanation of the national insolvency proceedings listed in Annex A.

### Article 26.   Costs of establishing and interconnecting insolvency registers

1.   The establishment, maintenance and future development of the system of

interconnection of insolvency registers shall be financed from the general budget of the Union.

2. Each Member State shall bear the costs of establishing and adjusting its national insolvency registers to make them interoperable with the European e-Justice Portal, as well as the costs of administering, operating and maintaining those registers. This shall be without prejudice to the possibility to apply for grants to support such activities under the Union's financial programmes.

### Article 27. Conditions of access to information via the system of interconnection

1. Member States shall ensure that the mandatory information referred to in points (a) to (j) of Article 24(2) is available free of charge via the system of interconnection of insolvency registers.

2. This Regulation shall not preclude Member States from charging a reasonable fee for access to the documents or additional information referred to in Article 24(3) via the system of interconnection of insolvency registers.

3. Member States may make access to mandatory information concerning individuals who are not exercising an independent business or professional activity, and concerning individuals exercising an independent business or professional activity when the insolvency proceedings are not related to that activity, subject to supplementary search criteria relating to the debtor in addition to the minimum criteria referred to in point (c) of Article 25(2).

4. Member States may require that access to the information referred to in paragraph 3 be made conditional upon a request to the competent authority. Member States may make access conditional upon the verification of the existence of a legitimate interest for accessing such information. The requesting person shall be able to submit the request for information electronically by means of a standard form via the European e-Justice Portal. Where a legitimate interest is required, it shall be permissible for the requesting person to justify his request by electronic copies of relevant documents. The requesting person shall be provided with an answer by the competent authority within 3 working days.

The requesting person shall not be obliged to provide translations of the documents justifying his request, or to bear any costs of translation which the competent authority may incur.

### Article 28. Publication in another Member State

1. The insolvency practitioner or the debtor in possession shall request that notice of the judgment opening insolvency proceedings and, where appropriate, the decision appointing the insolvency practitioner be published in any other Member State where an establishment of the debtor is located in accordance with the publication procedures provided for in that Member State. Such publication shall specify, where appropriate, the insolvency practitioner appointed and whether the jurisdiction rule applied is that pursuant to Article 3(1) or (2).

2. The insolvency practitioner or the debtor in possession may request that the information referred to in paragraph 1 be published in any other Member State where the insolvency practitioner or the debtor in possession deems it necessary in accordance with the publication procedures provided for in that Member State.

### Article 29. Registration in public registers of another Member State

1. Where the law of a Member State in which an establishment of the debtor is located and this establishment has been entered into a public register of that Member State, or the law of a Member State in which immovable property belonging to the debtor is located, requires information on the opening of insolvency proceedings referred to in Article 28 to be published in the land register, company register or any other public register, the insolvency practitioner or the debtor in possession shall take all the necessary measures to ensure such a registration.

2. The insolvency practitioner or the debtor in possession may request such

registration in any other Member State, provided that the law of the Member State where the register is kept allows such registration.

### Article 30.   Costs
The costs of the publication and registration provided for in Articles 28 and 29 shall be regarded as costs and expenses incurred in the proceedings.

### Article 31.   Honouring of an obligation to a debtor
1.   Where an obligation has been honoured in a Member State for the benefit of a debtor who is subject to insolvency proceedings opened in another Member State, when it should have been honoured for the benefit of the insolvency practitioner in those proceedings, the person honouring the obligation shall be deemed to have discharged it if he was unaware of the opening of the proceedings.

2.   Where such an obligation is honoured before the publication provided for in Article 28 has been effected, the person honouring the obligation shall be presumed, in the absence of proof to the contrary, to have been unaware of the opening of insolvency proceedings. Where the obligation is honoured after such publication has been effected, the person honouring the obligation shall be presumed, in the absence of proof to the contrary, to have been aware of the opening of proceedings.

### Article 32.   Recognition and enforceability of other judgments
1.   Judgments handed down by a court whose judgment concerning the opening of proceedings is recognised in accordance with Article 19 and which concern the course and closure of insolvency proceedings, and compositions approved by that court, shall also be recognised with no further formalities. Such judgments shall be enforced in accordance with Articles 39 to 44 and 47 to 57 of Regulation (EU) No 1215/2012.

The first subparagraph shall also apply to judgments deriving directly from the insolvency proceedings and which are closely linked with them, even if they were handed down by another court.

The first subparagraph shall also apply to judgments relating to preservation measures taken after the request for the opening of insolvency proceedings or in connection with it.

2.   The recognition and enforcement of judgments other than those referred to in paragraph 1 of this Article shall be governed by Regulation (EU) No 1215/2012 provided that that Regulation is applicable.

### Article 33.   Public policy
Any Member State may refuse to recognise insolvency proceedings opened in another Member State or to enforce a judgment handed down in the context of such proceedings where the effects of such recognition or enforcement would be manifestly contrary to that State's public policy, in particular its fundamental principles or the constitutional rights and liberties of the individual.

### CHAPTER III
### SECONDARY INSOLVENCY PROCEEDINGS

### Article 34.   Opening of proceedings
Where main insolvency proceedings have been opened by a court of a Member State and recognised in another Member State, a court of that other Member State which has jurisdiction pursuant to Article 3(2) may open secondary insolvency proceedings in accordance with the provisions set out in this Chapter. Where the main insolvency proceedings required that the debtor be insolvent, the debtor's insolvency shall not be re-examined in the Member State in which secondary insolvency proceedings may be opened. The effects of secondary insolvency proceedings shall be restricted to the assets of the debtor situated within the territory of the Member State in which those proceedings have been opened.

### Article 35.  Applicable law

Save as otherwise provided for in this Regulation, the law applicable to secondary insolvency proceedings shall be that of the Member State within the territory of which the secondary insolvency proceedings are opened.

### Article 36.  Right to give an undertaking in order to avoid secondary insolvency proceedings

1.  In order to avoid the opening of secondary insolvency proceedings, the insolvency practitioner in the main insolvency proceedings may give a unilateral undertaking (the 'undertaking') in respect of the assets located in the Member State in which secondary insolvency proceedings could be opened, that when distributing those assets or the proceeds received as a result of their realisation, it will comply with the distribution and priority rights under national law that creditors would have if secondary insolvency proceedings were opened in that Member State. The undertaking shall specify the factual assumptions on which it is based, in particular in respect of the value of the assets located in the Member State concerned and the options available to realise such assets.

2.  Where an undertaking has been given in accordance with this Article, the law applicable to the distribution of proceeds from the realisation of assets referred to in paragraph 1, to the ranking of creditors' claims, and to the rights of creditors in relation to the assets referred to in paragraph 1 shall be the law of the Member State in which secondary insolvency proceedings could have been opened. The relevant point in time for determining the assets referred to in paragraph 1 shall be the moment at which the undertaking is given.

3.  The undertaking shall be made in the official language or one of the official languages of the Member State where secondary insolvency proceedings could have been opened, or, where there are several official languages in that Member State, the official language or one of the official languages of the place in which secondary insolvency proceedings could have been opened.

4.  The undertaking shall be made in writing. It shall be subject to any other requirements relating to form and approval requirements as to distributions, if any, of the State of the opening of the main insolvency proceedings.

5.  The undertaking shall be approved by the known local creditors. The rules on qualified majority and voting that apply to the adoption of restructuring plans under the law of the Member State where secondary insolvency proceedings could have been opened shall also apply to the approval of the undertaking. Creditors shall be able to participate in the vote by distance means of communication, where national law so permits. The insolvency practitioner shall inform the known local creditors of the undertaking, of the rules and procedures for its approval, and of the approval or rejection of the undertaking.

6.  An undertaking given and approved in accordance with this Article shall be binding on the estate. If secondary insolvency proceedings are opened in accordance with Articles 37 and 38, the insolvency practitioner in the main insolvency proceedings shall transfer any assets which it removed from the territory of that Member State after the undertaking was given or, where those assets have already been realised, their proceeds, to the insolvency practitioner in the secondary insolvency proceedings.

7.  Where the insolvency practitioner has given an undertaking, it shall inform local creditors about the intended distributions prior to distributing the assets and proceeds referred to in paragraph 1. If that information does not comply with the terms of the undertaking or the applicable law, any local creditor may challenge such distribution before the courts of the Member State in which main insolvency proceedings have been opened in order to obtain a distribution in accordance with the terms of the undertaking and the applicable law. In such cases, no distribution shall take place until the court has taken a decision on the challenge.

8.  Local creditors may apply to the courts of the Member State in which main

insolvency proceedings have been opened, in order to require the insolvency practitioner in the main insolvency proceedings to take any suitable measures necessary to ensure compliance with the terms of the undertaking available under the law of the State of the opening of main insolvency proceedings.

9. Local creditors may also apply to the courts of the Member State in which secondary insolvency proceedings could have been opened in order to require the court to take provisional or protective measures to ensure compliance by the insolvency practitioner with the terms of the undertaking.

10. The insolvency practitioner shall be liable for any damage caused to local creditors as a result of its non-compliance with the obligations and requirements set out in this Article.

11. For the purpose of this Article, an authority which is established in the Member State where secondary insolvency proceedings could have been opened and which is obliged under Directive 2008/94/EC of the European Parliament and of the Council to guarantee the payment of employees' outstanding claims resulting from contracts of employment or employment relationships shall be considered to be a local creditor, where the national law so provides.

**Article 37. Right to request the opening of secondary insolvency proceedings**
1. The opening of secondary insolvency proceedings may be requested by:
   (a) the insolvency practitioner in the main insolvency proceedings;
   (b) any other person or authority empowered to request the opening of insolvency proceedings under the law of the Member State within the territory of which the opening of secondary insolvency proceedings is requested.
2. Where an undertaking has become binding in accordance with Article 36, the request for opening secondary insolvency proceedings shall be lodged within 30 days of having received notice of the approval of the undertaking.

**Article 38. Decision to open secondary insolvency proceedings**
1. A court seised of a request to open secondary insolvency proceedings shall immediately give notice to the insolvency practitioner or the debtor in possession in the main insolvency proceedings and give it an opportunity to be heard on the request.
2. Where the insolvency practitioner in the main insolvency proceedings has given an undertaking in accordance with Article 36, the court referred to in paragraph 1 of this Article shall, at the request of the insolvency practitioner, not open secondary insolvency proceedings if it is satisfied that the undertaking adequately protects the general interests of local creditors.
3. Where a temporary stay of individual enforcement proceedings has been granted in order to allow for negotiations between the debtor and its creditors, the court, at the request of the insolvency practitioner or the debtor in possession, may stay the opening of secondary insolvency proceedings for a period not exceeding 3 months, provided that suitable measures are in place to protect the interests of local creditors.

The court referred to in paragraph 1 may order protective measures to protect the interests of local creditors by requiring the insolvency practitioner or the debtor in possession not to remove or dispose of any assets which are located in the Member State where its establishment is located unless this is done in the ordinary course of business. The court may also order other measures to protect the interest of local creditors during a stay, unless this is incompatible with the national rules on civil procedure.

The stay of the opening of secondary insolvency proceedings shall be lifted by the court of its own motion or at the request of any creditor if, during the stay, an agreement in the negotiations referred to in the first subparagraph has been concluded.

The stay may be lifted by the court of its own motion or at the request of any creditor if the continuation of the stay is detrimental to the creditor's rights, in particular if the negotiations have been disrupted or it has become evident that they are unlikely to be concluded, or if the insolvency practitioner or the debtor in possession has infringed the prohibition on disposal of its assets or on removal of them from the territory of the Member State where the establishment is located.

4. At the request of the insolvency practitioner in the main insolvency proceedings, the court referred to in paragraph 1 may open a type of insolvency proceedings as listed in Annex A other than the type initially requested, provided that the conditions for opening that type of proceedings under national law are fulfilled and that that type of proceedings is the most appropriate as regards the interests of the local creditors and coherence between the main and secondary insolvency proceedings. The second sentence of Article 34 shall apply.

### Article 39. Judicial review of the decision to open secondary insolvency proceedings

The insolvency practitioner in the main insolvency proceedings may challenge the decision to open secondary insolvency proceedings before the courts of the Member State in which secondary insolvency proceedings have been opened on the ground that the court did not comply with the conditions and requirements of Article 38.

### Article 40. Advance payment of costs and expenses

Where the law of the Member State in which the opening of secondary insolvency proceedings is requested requires that the debtor's assets be sufficient to cover in whole or in part the costs and expenses of the proceedings, the court may, when it receives such a request, require the applicant to make an advance payment of costs or to provide appropriate security.

### Article 41. Cooperation and communication between insolvency practitioners

1. The insolvency practitioner in the main insolvency proceedings and the insolvency practitioner or practitioners in secondary insolvency proceedings concerning the same debtor shall cooperate with each other to the extent such cooperation is not incompatible with the rules applicable to the respective proceedings. Such cooperation may take any form, including the conclusion of agreements or protocols.

2. In implementing the cooperation set out in paragraph 1, the insolvency practitioners shall:

(a) as soon as possible communicate to each other any information which may be relevant to the other proceedings, in particular any progress made in lodging and verifying claims and all measures aimed at rescuing or restructuring the debtor, or at terminating the proceedings, provided appropriate arrangements are made to protect confidential information;

(b) explore the possibility of restructuring the debtor and, where such a possibility exists, coordinate the elaboration and implementation of a restructuring plan;

(c) coordinate the administration of the realisation or use of the debtor's assets and affairs; the insolvency practitioner in the secondary insolvency proceedings shall give the insolvency practitioner in the main insolvency proceedings an early opportunity to submit proposals on the realisation or use of the assets in the secondary insolvency proceedings.

3. Paragraphs 1 and 2 shall apply mutatis mutandis to situations where, in the main or in the secondary insolvency proceedings or in any territorial insolvency proceedings concerning the same debtor and open at the same time, the debtor remains in possession of its assets.

### Article 42. Cooperation and communication between courts

1. In order to facilitate the coordination of main, territorial and secondary insolvency proceedings concerning the same debtor, a court before which a request to open insolvency proceedings is pending, or which has opened such proceed-

ings, shall cooperate with any other court before which a request to open insolvency proceedings is pending, or which has opened such proceedings, to the extent that such cooperation is not incompatible with the rules applicable to each of the proceedings. For that purpose, the courts may, where appropriate, appoint an independent person or body acting on its instructions, provided that it is not incompatible with the rules applicable to them.

2. In implementing the cooperation set out in paragraph 1, the courts, or any appointed person or body acting on their behalf, as referred to in paragraph 1, may communicate directly with, or request information or assistance directly from, each other provided that such communication respects the procedural rights of the parties to the proceedings and the confidentiality of information.

3. The cooperation referred to in paragraph 1 may be implemented by any means that the court considers appropriate. It may, in particular, concern:

(a) coordination in the appointment of the insolvency practitioners;

(b) communication of information by any means considered appropriate by the court;

(c) coordination of the administration and supervision of the debtor's assets and affairs;

(d) coordination of the conduct of hearings;

(e) coordination in the approval of protocols, where necessary.

### Article 43. Cooperation and communication between insolvency practitioners and courts

1. In order to facilitate the coordination of main, territorial and secondary insolvency proceedings opened in respect of the same debtor:

(a) an insolvency practitioner in main insolvency proceedings shall cooperate and communicate with any court before which a request to open secondary insolvency proceedings is pending or which has opened such proceedings;

(b) an insolvency practitioner in territorial or secondary insolvency proceedings shall cooperate and communicate with the court before which a request to open main insolvency proceedings is pending or which has opened such proceedings; and

(c) an insolvency practitioner in territorial or secondary insolvency proceedings shall cooperate and communicate with the court before which a request to open other territorial or secondary insolvency proceedings is pending or which has opened such proceedings;

to the extent that such cooperation and communication are not incompatible with the rules applicable to each of the proceedings and do not entail any conflict of interest.

2. The cooperation referred to in paragraph 1 may be implemented by any appropriate means, such as those set out in Article 42(3).

### Article 44. Costs of cooperation and communication

The requirements laid down in Articles 42 and 43 shall not result in courts charging costs to each other for cooperation and communication.

### Article 45. Exercise of creditors' rights

1. Any creditor may lodge its claim in the main insolvency proceedings and in any secondary insolvency proceedings.

2. The insolvency practitioners in the main and any secondary insolvency proceedings shall lodge in other proceedings claims which have already been lodged in the proceedings for which they were appointed, provided that the interests of creditors in the latter proceedings are served by doing so, subject to the right of creditors to oppose such lodgement or to withdraw the lodgement of their claims where the law applicable so provides.

3. The insolvency practitioner in the main or secondary insolvency proceedings

shall be entitled to participate in other proceedings on the same basis as a creditor, in particular by attending creditors' meetings.

### Article 46. Stay of the process of realisation of assets

1. The court which opened the secondary insolvency proceedings shall stay the process of realisation of assets in whole or in part on receipt of a request from the insolvency practitioner in the main insolvency proceedings. In such a case, it may require the insolvency practitioner in the main insolvency proceedings to take any suitable measure to guarantee the interests of the creditors in the secondary insolvency proceedings and of individual classes of creditors. Such a request from the insolvency practitioner may be rejected only if it is manifestly of no interest to the creditors in the main insolvency proceedings. Such a stay of the process of realisation of assets may be ordered for up to 3 months. It may be continued or renewed for similar periods.

2. The court referred to in paragraph 1 shall terminate the stay of the process of realisation of assets:

(a) at the request of the insolvency practitioner in the main insolvency proceedings;

(b) of its own motion, at the request of a creditor or at the request of the insolvency practitioner in the secondary insolvency proceedings if that measure no longer appears justified, in particular, by the interests of creditors in the main insolvency proceedings or in the secondary insolvency proceedings.

### Article 47. Power of the insolvency practitioner to propose restructuring plans

1. Where the law of the Member State where secondary insolvency proceedings have been opened allows for such proceedings to be closed without liquidation by a restructuring plan, a composition or a comparable measure, the insolvency practitioner in the main insolvency proceedings shall be empowered to propose such a measure in accordance with the procedure of that Member State.

2. Any restriction of creditors' rights arising from a measure referred to in paragraph 1 which is proposed in secondary insolvency proceedings, such as a stay of payment or discharge of debt, shall have no effect in respect of assets of a debtor that are not covered by those proceedings, without the consent of all the creditors having an interest.

### Article 48. Impact of closure of insolvency proceedings

1. Without prejudice to Article 49, the closure of insolvency proceedings shall not prevent the continuation of other insolvency proceedings concerning the same debtor which are still open at that point in time.

2. Where insolvency proceedings concerning a legal person or a company in the Member State of that person's or company's registered office would entail the dissolution of the legal person or of the company, that legal person or company shall not cease to exist until any other insolvency proceedings concerning the same debtor have been closed, or the insolvency practitioner or practitioners in such proceedings have given consent to the dissolution.

### Article 49. Assets remaining in the secondary insolvency proceedings

If, by the liquidation of assets in the secondary insolvency proceedings, it is possible to meet all claims allowed under those proceedings, the insolvency practitioner appointed in those proceedings shall immediately transfer any assets remaining to the insolvency practitioner in the main insolvency proceedings.

### Article 50. Subsequent opening of the main insolvency proceedings

Where the proceedings referred to in Article 3(1) are opened following the opening of the proceedings referred to in Article 3(2) in another Member State, Articles 41, 45, 46, 47 and 49 shall apply to those opened first, in so far as the progress of those proceedings so permits.

### Article 51. Conversion of secondary insolvency proceedings

1. At the request of the insolvency practitioner in the main insolvency proceedings, the court of the Member State in which secondary insolvency proceedings have been opened may order the conversion of the secondary insolvency proceedings into another type of insolvency proceedings listed in Annex A, provided that the conditions for opening that type of proceedings under national law are fulfilled and that that type of proceedings is the most appropriate as regards the interests of the local creditors and coherence between the main and secondary insolvency proceedings.

2. When considering the request referred to in paragraph 1, the court may seek information from the insolvency practitioners involved in both proceedings.

### Article 52. Preservation measures

Where the court of a Member State which has jurisdiction pursuant to Article 3(1) appoints a temporary administrator in order to ensure the preservation of a debtor's assets, that temporary administrator shall be empowered to request any measures to secure and preserve any of the debtor's assets situated in another Member State, provided for under the law of that Member State, for the period between the request for the opening of insolvency proceedings and the judgment opening the proceedings.

CHAPTER IV
### PROVISION OF INFORMATION FOR CREDITORS AND LODGEMENT OF THEIR CLAIMS

### Article 53. Right to lodge claims

Any foreign creditor may lodge claims in insolvency proceedings by any means of communication, which are accepted by the law of the State of the opening of proceedings. Representation by a lawyer or another legal professional shall not be mandatory for the sole purpose of lodging of claims.

### Article 54. Duty to inform creditors

1. As soon as insolvency proceedings are opened in a Member State, the court of that State having jurisdiction or the insolvency practitioner appointed by that court shall immediately inform the known foreign creditors.

2. The information referred to in paragraph 1, provided by an individual notice, shall in particular include time limits, the penalties laid down with regard to those time limits, the body or authority empowered to accept the lodgement of claims and any other measures laid down. Such notice shall also indicate whether creditors whose claims are preferential or secured in rem need to lodge their claims. The notice shall also include a copy of the standard form for lodging of claims referred to in Article 55 or information on where that form is available.

3. The information referred to in paragraphs 1 and 2 of this Article shall be provided using the standard notice form to be established in accordance with Article 88. The form shall be published in the European e-Justice Portal and shall bear the heading 'Notice of insolvency proceedings' in all the official languages of the institutions of the Union. It shall be transmitted in the official language of the State of the opening of proceedings or, if there are several official languages in that Member State, in the official language or one of the official languages of the place where insolvency proceedings have been opened, or in another language which that State has indicated it can accept, in accordance with Article 55(5), if it can be assumed that that language is easier to understand for the foreign creditors.

4. In insolvency proceedings relating to an individual not exercising a business or professional activity, the use of the standard form referred to in this Article shall not be obligatory if creditors are not required to lodge their claims in order to have their claims taken into account in the proceedings.

### Article 55. Procedure for lodging claims

1. Any foreign creditor may lodge its claim using the standard claims form to be established in accordance with Article 88. The form shall bear the heading 'Lodgement of claims' in all the official languages of the institutions of the Union.

2. The standard claims form referred to in paragraph 1 shall include the following information:

(a) the name, postal address, e-mail address, if any, personal identification number, if any, and bank details of the foreign creditor referred to in paragraph 1;

(b) the amount of the claim, specifying the principal and, where applicable, interest and the date on which it arose and the date on which it became due, if different;

(c) if interest is claimed, the interest rate, whether the interest is of a legal or contractual nature, the period of time for which the interest is claimed and the capitalised amount of interest;

(d) if costs incurred in asserting the claim prior to the opening of proceedings are claimed, the amount and the details of those costs;

(e) the nature of the claim;

(f) whether any preferential creditor status is claimed and the basis of such a claim;

(g) whether security in rem or a reservation of title is alleged in respect of the claim and if so, what assets are covered by the security interest being invoked, the date on which the security was granted and, where the security has been registered, the registration number; and

(h) whether any set-off is claimed and, if so, the amounts of the mutual claims existing on the date when insolvency proceedings were opened, the date on which they arose and the amount net of set-off claimed.

The standard claims form shall be accompanied by copies of any supporting documents.

3. The standard claims form shall indicate that the provision of information concerning the bank details and the personal identification number of the creditor referred to in point (a) of paragraph 2 is not compulsory.

4. When a creditor lodges its claim by means other than the standard form referred to in paragraph 1, the claim shall contain the information referred to in paragraph 2.

5. Claims may be lodged in any official language of the institutions of the Union. The court, the insolvency practitioner or the debtor in possession may require the creditor to provide a translation in the official language of the State of the opening of proceedings or, if there are several official languages in that Member State, in the official language or one of the official languages of the place where insolvency proceedings have been opened, or in another language which that Member State has indicated it can accept. Each Member State shall indicate whether it accepts any official language of the institutions of the Union other than its own for the purpose of the lodging of claims.

6. Claims shall be lodged within the period stipulated by the law of the State of the opening of proceedings. In the case of a foreign creditor, that period shall not be less than 30 days following the publication of the opening of insolvency proceedings in the insolvency register of the State of the opening of proceedings. Where a Member State relies on Article 24(4), that period shall not be less than 30 days following a creditor having been informed pursuant to Article 54.

7. Where the court, the insolvency practitioner or the debtor in possession has doubts in relation to a claim lodged in accordance with this Article, it shall give the creditor the opportunity to provide additional evidence on the existence and the amount of the claim.

## CHAPTER V
## INSOLVENCY PROCEEDINGS OF MEMBERS OF A GROUP OF COMPANIES

### Section 1: Cooperation and communication

**Article 56.  Cooperation and communication between insolvency practitioners**

1.  Where insolvency proceedings relate to two or more members of a group of companies, an insolvency practitioner appointed in proceedings concerning a member of the group shall cooperate with any insolvency practitioner appointed in proceedings concerning another member of the same group to the extent that such cooperation is appropriate to facilitate the effective administration of those proceedings, is not incompatible with the rules applicable to such proceedings and does not entail any conflict of interest. That cooperation may take any form, including the conclusion of agreements or protocols.

2.  In implementing the cooperation set out in paragraph 1, insolvency practitioners shall:

(a)  as soon as possible communicate to each other any information which may be relevant to the other proceedings, provided appropriate arrangements are made to protect confidential information;

(b)  consider whether possibilities exist for coordinating the administration and supervision of the affairs of the group members which are subject to insolvency proceedings, and if so, coordinate such administration and supervision;

(c)  consider whether possibilities exist for restructuring group members which are subject to insolvency proceedings and, if so, coordinate with regard to the proposal and negotiation of a coordinated restructuring plan.

For the purposes of points (b) and (c), all or some of the insolvency practitioners referred to in paragraph 1 may agree to grant additional powers to an insolvency practitioner appointed in one of the proceedings where such an agreement is permitted by the rules applicable to each of the proceedings. They may also agree on the allocation of certain tasks amongst them, where such allocation of tasks is permitted by the rules applicable to each of the proceedings.

**Article 57.  Cooperation and communication between courts**

1.  Where insolvency proceedings relate to two or more members of a group of companies, a court which has opened such proceedings shall cooperate with any other court before which a request to open proceedings concerning another member of the same group is pending or which has opened such proceedings to the extent that such cooperation is appropriate to facilitate the effective administration of the proceedings, is not incompatible with the rules applicable to them and does not entail any conflict of interest. For that purpose, the courts may, where appropriate, appoint an independent person or body to act on its instructions, provided that this is not incompatible with the rules applicable to them.

2.  In implementing the cooperation set out in paragraph 1, courts, or any appointed person or body acting on their behalf, as referred to in paragraph 1, may communicate directly with each other, or request information or assistance directly from each other, provided that such communication respects the procedural rights of the parties to the proceedings and the confidentiality of information.

3.  The cooperation referred to in paragraph 1 may be implemented by any means that the court considers appropriate. It may, in particular, concern:

(a)  coordination in the appointment of insolvency practitioners;

(b)  communication of information by any means considered appropriate by the court;

(c)  coordination of the administration and supervision of the assets and affairs of the members of the group;

(d)  coordination of the conduct of hearings;

(e)  coordination in the approval of protocols where necessary.

### Article 58.   Cooperation and communication between insolvency practitioners and courts

An insolvency practitioner appointed in insolvency proceedings concerning a member of a group of companies:

(a)   shall cooperate and communicate with any court before which a request for the opening of proceedings in respect of another member of the same group of companies is pending or which has opened such proceedings; and

(b)   may request information from that court concerning the proceedings regarding the other member of the group or request assistance concerning the proceedings in which he has been appointed;

to the extent that such cooperation and communication are appropriate to facilitate the effective administration of the proceedings, do not entail any conflict of interest and are not incompatible with the rules applicable to them.

### Article 59.   Costs of cooperation and communication in proceedings concerning members of a group of companies

The costs of the cooperation and communication provided for in Articles 56 to 60 incurred by an insolvency practitioner or a court shall be regarded as costs and expenses incurred in the respective proceedings.

### Article 60.   Powers of the insolvency practitioner in proceedings concerning members of a group of companies

1.   An insolvency practitioner appointed in insolvency proceedings opened in respect of a member of a group of companies may, to the extent appropriate to facilitate the effective administration of the proceedings:

(a)   be heard in any of the proceedings opened in respect of any other member of the same group;

(b)   request a stay of any measure related to the realisation of the assets in the proceedings opened with respect to any other member of the same group, provided that:

(i)   a restructuring plan for all or some members of the group for which insolvency proceedings have been opened has been proposed under point (c) of Article 56(2) and presents a reasonable chance of success;

(ii)   such a stay is necessary in order to ensure the proper implementation of the restructuring plan;

(iii)   the restructuring plan would be to the benefit of the creditors in the proceedings for which the stay is requested; and

(iv)   neither the insolvency proceedings in which the insolvency practitioner referred to in paragraph 1 of this Article has been appointed nor the proceedings in respect of which the stay is requested are subject to coordination under Section 2 of this Chapter;

(c)   apply for the opening of group coordination proceedings in accordance with Article 61.

2.   The court having opened proceedings referred to in point (b) of paragraph 1 shall stay any measure related to the realisation of the assets in the proceedings in whole or in part if it is satisfied that the conditions referred to in point (b) of paragraph 1 are fulfilled.

Before ordering the stay, the court shall hear the insolvency practitioner appointed in the proceedings for which the stay is requested. Such a stay may be ordered for any period, not exceeding 3 months, which the court considers appropriate and which is compatible with the rules applicable to the proceedings.

The court ordering the stay may require the insolvency practitioner referred to in paragraph 1 to take any suitable measure available under national law to guarantee the interests of the creditors in the proceedings.

The court may extend the duration of the stay by such further period or periods as it considers appropriate and which are compatible with the rules applicable to the proceedings, provided that the conditions referred to in points (b)(ii) to (iv) of paragraph 1 continue to be fulfilled and that the total duration of the stay (the initial period together with any such extensions) does not exceed 6 months.

## Section 2: Coordination

### *Subsection 1: Procedure*

### Article 61.  Request to open group coordination proceedings

1.  Group coordination proceedings may be requested before any court having jurisdiction over the insolvency proceedings of a member of the group, by an insolvency practitioner appointed in insolvency proceedings opened in relation to a member of the group.

2.  The request referred to in paragraph 1 shall be made in accordance with the conditions provided for by the law applicable to the proceedings in which the insolvency practitioner has been appointed.

3.  The request referred to in paragraph 1 shall be accompanied by:

(a)  a proposal as to the person to be nominated as the group coordinator ('the coordinator'), details of his or her eligibility pursuant to Article 71, details of his or her qualifications and his or her written agreement to act as coordinator;

(b)  an outline of the proposed group coordination, and in particular the reasons why the conditions set out in Article 63(1) are fulfilled;

(c)  a list of the insolvency practitioners appointed in relation to the members of the group and, where relevant, the courts and competent authorities involved in the insolvency proceedings of the members of the group;

(d)  an outline of the estimated costs of the proposed group coordination and the estimation of the share of those costs to be paid by each member of the group.

### Article 62.  Priority rule

Without prejudice to Article 66, where the opening of group coordination proceedings is requested before courts of different Member States, any court other than the court first seised shall decline jurisdiction in favour of that court.

### Article 63.  Notice by the court seised

1.  The court seised of a request to open group coordination proceedings shall give notice as soon as possible of the request for the opening of group coordination proceedings and of the proposed coordinator to the insolvency practitioners appointed in relation to the members of the group as indicated in the request referred to in point (c) of Article 61(3), if it is satisfied that:

(a)  the opening of such proceedings is appropriate to facilitate the effective administration of the insolvency proceedings relating to the different group members;

(b)  no creditor of any group member expected to participate in the proceedings is likely to be financially disadvantaged by the inclusion of that member in such proceedings; and

(c)  the proposed coordinator fulfils the requirements laid down in Article 71.

2.  The notice referred to in paragraph 1 of this Article shall list the elements referred to in points (a) to (d) of Article 61(3).

3.  The notice referred to in paragraph 1 shall be sent by registered letter, attested by an acknowledgment of receipt.

4.  The court seised shall give the insolvency practitioners involved the opportunity to be heard.

### Article 64.  Objections by insolvency practitioners

1.  An insolvency practitioner appointed in respect of any group member may object to:

(a) the inclusion within group coordination proceedings of the insolvency proceedings in respect of which it has been appointed; or

(b) the person proposed as a coordinator.

2. Objections pursuant to paragraph 1 of this Article shall be lodged with the court referred to in Article 63 within 30 days of receipt of notice of the request for the opening of group coordination proceedings by the insolvency practitioner referred to in paragraph 1 of this Article.

The objection may be made by means of the standard form established in accordance with Article 88.

3. Prior to taking the decision to participate or not to participate in the coordination in accordance with point (a) of paragraph 1, an insolvency practitioner shall obtain any approval which may be required under the law of the State of the opening of proceedings for which it has been appointed.

### Article 65. Consequences of objection to the inclusion in group coordination

1. Where an insolvency practitioner has objected to the inclusion of the proceedings in respect of which it has been appointed in group coordination proceedings, those proceedings shall not be included in the group coordination proceedings.

2. The powers of the court referred to in Article 68 or of the coordinator arising from those proceedings shall have no effect as regards that member, and shall entail no costs for that member.

### Article 66. Choice of court for group coordination proceedings

1. Where at least two-thirds of all insolvency practitioners appointed in insolvency proceedings of the members of the group have agreed that a court of another Member State having jurisdiction is the most appropriate court for the opening of group coordination proceedings, that court shall have exclusive jurisdiction.

2. The choice of court shall be made by joint agreement in writing or evidenced in writing. It may be made until such time as group coordination proceedings have been opened in accordance with Article 68.

3. Any court other than the court seised under paragraph 1 shall decline jurisdiction in favour of that court.

4. The request for the opening of group coordination proceedings shall be submitted to the court agreed in accordance with Article 61.

### Article 67. Consequences of objections to the proposed coordinator

Where objections to the person proposed as coordinator have been received from an insolvency practitioner which does not also object to the inclusion in the group coordination proceedings of the member in respect of which it has been appointed, the court may refrain from appointing that person and invite the objecting insolvency practitioner to submit a new request in accordance with Article 61(3).

### Article 68. Decision to open group coordination proceedings

1. After the period referred to in Article 64(2) has elapsed, the court may open group coordination proceedings where it is satisfied that the conditions of Article 63(1) are met. In such a case, the court shall:

(a) appoint a coordinator;

(b) decide on the outline of the coordination; and

(c) decide on the estimation of costs and the share to be paid by the group members.

2. The decision opening group coordination proceedings shall be brought to the notice of the participating insolvency practitioners and of the coordinator.

### Article 69. Subsequent opt-in by insolvency practitioners

1. In accordance with its national law, any insolvency practitioner may request,

after the court decision referred to in Article 68, the inclusion of the proceedings in respect of which it has been appointed, where:

(a) there has been an objection to the inclusion of the insolvency proceedings within the group coordination proceedings; or

(b) insolvency proceedings with respect to a member of the group have been opened after the court has opened group coordination proceedings.

2. Without prejudice to paragraph 4, the coordinator may accede to such a request, after consulting the insolvency practitioners involved, where

(a) he or she is satisfied that, taking into account the stage that the group coordination proceedings has reached at the time of the request, the criteria set out in points (a) and (b) of Article 63(1) are met; or

(b) all insolvency practitioners involved agree, subject to the conditions in their national law.

3. The coordinator shall inform the court and the participating insolvency practitioners of his or her decision pursuant to paragraph 2 and of the reasons on which it is based.

4. Any participating insolvency practitioner or any insolvency practitioner whose request for inclusion in the group coordination proceedings has been rejected may challenge the decision referred to in paragraph 2 in accordance with the procedure set out under the law of the Member State in which the group coordination proceedings have been opened.

### Article 70. Recommendations and group coordination plan

1. When conducting their insolvency proceedings, insolvency practitioners shall consider the recommendations of the coordinator and the content of the group coordination plan referred to in Article 72(1).

2. An insolvency practitioner shall not be obliged to follow in whole or in part the coordinator's recommendations or the group coordination plan.

If it does not follow the coordinator's recommendations or the group coordination plan, it shall give reasons for not doing so to the persons or bodies that it is to report to under its national law, and to the coordinator.

*Subsection 2: General provisions*

### Article 71. The coordinator

1. The coordinator shall be a person eligible under the law of a Member State to act as an insolvency practitioner.

2. The coordinator shall not be one of the insolvency practitioners appointed to act in respect of any of the group members, and shall have no conflict of interest in respect of the group members, their creditors and the insolvency practitioners appointed in respect of any of the group members.

### Article 72. Tasks and rights of the coordinator

1. The coordinator shall:

(a) identify and outline recommendations for the coordinated conduct of the insolvency proceedings;

(b) propose a group coordination plan that identifies, describes and recommends a comprehensive set of measures appropriate to an integrated approach to the resolution of the group members' insolvencies. In particular, the plan may contain proposals for:

(i) the measures to be taken in order to re-establish the economic performance and the financial soundness of the group or any part of it;

(ii) the settlement of intra-group disputes as regards intra-group transactions and avoidance actions;

(iii) agreements between the insolvency practitioners of the insolvent group members.

2. The coordinator may also:

(a) be heard and participate, in particular by attending creditors' meetings, in any of the proceedings opened in respect of any member of the group;

(b) mediate any dispute arising between two or more insolvency practitioners of group members;

(c) present and explain his or her group coordination plan to the persons or bodies that he or she is to report to under his or her national law;

(d) request information from any insolvency practitioner in respect of any member of the group where that information is or might be of use when identifying and outlining strategies and measures in order to coordinate the proceedings; and

(e) request a stay for a period of up to 6 months of the proceedings opened in respect of any member of the group, provided that such a stay is necessary in order to ensure the proper implementation of the plan and would be to the benefit of the creditors in the proceedings for which the stay is requested; or request the lifting of any existing stay. Such a request shall be made to the court that opened the proceedings for which a stay is requested.

3. The plan referred to in point (b) of paragraph 1 shall not include recommendations as to any consolidation of proceedings or insolvency estates.

4. The coordinator's tasks and rights as defined under this Article shall not extend to any member of the group not participating in group coordination proceedings.

5. The coordinator shall perform his or her duties impartially and with due care.

6. Where the coordinator considers that the fulfilment of his or her tasks requires a significant increase in the costs compared to the cost estimate referred to in point (d) of Article 61(3), and in any case, where the costs exceed 10% of the estimated costs, the coordinator shall:

(a) inform without delay the participating insolvency practitioners; and

(b) seek the prior approval of the court opening group coordination proceedings.

### Article 73. Languages

1. The coordinator shall communicate with the insolvency practitioner of a participating group member in the language agreed with the insolvency practitioner or, in the absence of an agreement, in the official language or one of the official languages of the institutions of the Union, and of the court which opened the proceedings in respect of that group member.

2. The coordinator shall communicate with a court in the official language applicable to that court.

### Article 74. Cooperation between insolvency practitioners and the coordinator

1. Insolvency practitioners appointed in relation to members of a group and the coordinator shall cooperate with each other to the extent that such cooperation is not incompatible with the rules applicable to the respective proceedings.

2. In particular, insolvency practitioners shall communicate any information that is relevant for the coordinator to perform his or her tasks.

### Article 75. Revocation of the appointment of the coordinator

The court shall revoke the appointment of the coordinator of its own motion or at the request of the insolvency practitioner of a participating group member where:

(a) the coordinator acts to the detriment of the creditors of a participating group member; or

(b) the coordinator fails to comply with his or her obligations under this Chapter.

**Article 76.   Debtor in possession**
The provisions applicable, under this Chapter, to the insolvency practitioner shall also apply, where appropriate, to the debtor in possession.

**Article 77.   Costs and distribution**
   1.   The remuneration for the coordinator shall be adequate, proportionate to the tasks fulfilled and reflect reasonable expenses.
   2.   On having completed his or her tasks, the coordinator shall establish the final statement of costs and the share to be paid by each member, and submit this statement to each participating insolvency practitioner and to the court opening coordination proceedings.
   3.   In the absence of objections by the insolvency practitioners within 30 days of receipt of the statement referred to in paragraph 2, the costs and the share to be paid by each member shall be deemed to be agreed. The statement shall be submitted to the court opening coordination proceedings for confirmation.
   4.   In the event of an objection, the court that opened the group coordination proceedings shall, upon the application of the coordinator or any participating insolvency practitioner, decide on the costs and the share to be paid by each member in accordance with the criteria set out in paragraph 1 of this Article, and taking into account the estimation of costs referred to in Article 68(1) and, where applicable, Article 72(6).
   5.   Any participating insolvency practitioner may challenge the decision referred to in paragraph 4 in accordance with the procedure set out under the law of the Member State where group coordination proceedings have been opened.

CHAPTER VI
DATA PROTECTION

**Article 78.   Data protection**
   1.   National rules implementing Directive 95/46/EC shall apply to the processing of personal data carried out in the Member States pursuant to this Regulation, provided that processing operations referred to in Article 3(2) of Directive 95/46/EC are not concerned.
   2.   Regulation (EC) No 45/2001 shall apply to the processing of personal data carried out by the Commission pursuant to this Regulation.

**Article 79.   Responsibilities of Member States regarding the processing of personal data in national insolvency registers**
   1.   Each Member State shall communicate to the Commission the name of the natural or legal person, public authority, agency or any other body designated by national law to exercise the functions of controller in accordance with point (d) of Article 2 of Directive 95/46/EC, with a view to its publication on the European e-Justice Portal.
   2.   Member States shall ensure that the technical measures for ensuring the security of personal data processed in their national insolvency registers referred to in Article 24 are implemented.
   3.   Member States shall be responsible for verifying that the controller, designated by national law in accordance with point (d) of Article 2 of Directive 95/46/EC, ensures compliance with the principles of data quality, in particular the accuracy and the updating of data stored in national insolvency registers.
   4.   Member States shall be responsible, in accordance with Directive 95/46/EC, for the collection and storage of data in national databases and for decisions taken to make such data available in the interconnected register that can be consulted via the European e-Justice Portal.
   5.   As part of the information that should be provided to data subjects to enable them to exercise their rights, and in particular the right to the erasure of data,

Member States shall inform data subjects of the accessibility period set for personal data stored in insolvency registers.

### Article 80. Responsibilities of the Commission in connection with the processing of personal data

1. The Commission shall exercise the responsibilities of controller pursuant to Article 2(d) of Regulation (EC) No 45/2001 in accordance with its respective responsibilities defined in this Article.

2. The Commission shall define the necessary policies and apply the necessary technical solutions to fulfil its responsibilities within the scope of the function of controller.

3. The Commission shall implement the technical measures required to ensure the security of personal data while in transit, in particular the confidentiality and integrity of any transmission to and from the European e-Justice Portal.

4. The obligations of the Commission shall not affect the responsibilities of the Member States and other bodies for the content and operation of the inter-connected national databases run by them.

### Article 81. Information obligations

Without prejudice to the information to be given to data subjects in accordance with Articles 11 and 12 of Regulation (EC) No 45/2001, the Commission shall inform data subjects, by means of publication through the European e-Justice Portal, about its role in the processing of data and the purposes for which those data will be processed.

### Article 82. Storage of personal data

As regards information from interconnected national databases, no personal data relating to data subjects shall be stored in the European e-Justice Portal. All such data shall be stored in the national databases operated by the Member States or other bodies.

### Article 83. Access to personal data via the European e-Justice Portal

Personal data stored in the national insolvency registers referred to in Article 24 shall be accessible via the European e-Justice Portal for as long as they remain accessible under national law.

CHAPTER VII

TRANSITIONAL AND FINAL PROVISIONS

### Article 84. Applicability in time

1. The provisions of this Regulation shall apply only to insolvency proceedings opened after 26 June 2017. Acts committed by a debtor before that date shall continue to be governed by the law which was applicable to them at the time they were committed.

2. Notwithstanding Article 91 of this Regulation, Regulation (EC) No 1346/2000 shall continue to apply to insolvency proceedings which fall within the scope of that Regulation and which have been opened before 26 June 2017.

### Article 85. Relationship to Conventions

. . .

2. The Conventions referred to in paragraph 1 shall continue to have effect with regard to proceedings opened before the entry into force of Regulation (EC) No 1346/2000. 3. This Regulation shall not apply:

(a) in any Member State, to the extent that it is irreconcilable with the obligations arising in relation to bankruptcy from a convention concluded by that Member State with one or more third countries before the entry into force of Regulation (EC) No 1346/2000;

(b) in the United Kingdom of Great Britain and Northern Ireland, to the extent that is irreconcilable with the obligations arising in relation to bankruptcy and the winding-up of insolvent companies from any arrangements with the Commonwealth existing at the time Regulation (EC) No 1346/2000 entered into force.

### Article 86. Information on national and Union insolvency law

1. The Member States shall provide, within the framework of the European Judicial Network in civil and commercial matters established by Council Decision 2001/470/EC, and with a view to making the information available to the public, a short description of their national legislation and procedures relating to insolvency, in particular relating to the matters listed in Article 7(2).

2. The Member States shall update the information referred to in paragraph 1 regularly.

3. The Commission shall make information concerning this Regulation available to the public.

### Article 87. Establishment of the interconnection of registers

The Commission shall adopt implementing acts establishing the interconnection of insolvency registers as referred to in Article 25. Those implementing acts shall be adopted in accordance with the examination procedure referred to in Article 89(3).

### Article 88. Establishment and subsequent amendment of standard forms

The Commission shall adopt implementing acts establishing and, where necessary, amending the forms referred to in Article 27(4), Articles 54 and 55 and Article 64(2). Those implementing acts shall be adopted in accordance with the advisory procedure referred to in Article 89(2).

### Article 89. Committee procedure

1. The Commission shall be assisted by a committee. That committee shall be a committee within the meaning of Regulation (EU) No 182/2011.

2. Where reference is made to this paragraph, Article 4 of Regulation (EU) No 182/2011 shall apply.

3. Where reference is made to this paragraph, Article 5 of Regulation (EU) No 182/2011 shall apply.

### Article 90. Review clause

1. No later than 27 June 2027, and every 5 years thereafter, the Commission shall present to the European Parliament, the Council and the European Economic and Social Committee a report on the application of this Regulation. The report shall be accompanied where necessary by a proposal for adaptation of this Regulation.

2. No later than 27 June 2022, the Commission shall present to the European Parliament, the Council and the European Economic and Social Committee a report on the application of the group coordination proceedings. The report shall be accompanied where necessary by a proposal for adaptation of this Regulation.

3. No later than 1 January 2016, the Commission shall submit to the European Parliament, the Council and the European Economic and Social Committee a study on the cross-border issues in the area of directors' liability and disqualifications.

4. No later than 27 June 2020, the Commission shall submit to the European Parliament, the Council and the European Economic and Social Committee a study on the issue of abusive forum shopping.

### Article 91. Repeal

Regulation (EC) No 1346/2000 is repealed.

References to the repealed Regulation shall be construed as references to this Regulation and shall be read in accordance with the correlation table set out in Annex D to this Regulation.

**Article 92.  Entry into force**
This Regulation shall enter into force on the twentieth day following that of its publication in the Official Journal of the European Union.
    It shall apply from 26 June 2017, with the exception of:
    (a)   Article 86, which shall apply from 26 June 2016;
    (b)   Article 24(1), which shall apply from 26 June 2018; and
    (c)   Article 25, which shall apply from 26 June 2019.
    This Regulation shall be binding in its entirety and directly applicable in the Member States in accordance with the Treaties.

Done at Strasbourg, 20 May 2015.


## ANNEX A
Insolvency proceedings referred to in point (4) of Article 2


. . .
UNITED KINGDOM
– Winding-up by or subject to the supervision of the court,
– Creditors' voluntary winding-up (with confirmation by the court),
– Administration, including appointments made by filing prescribed documents with the court,
–Voluntary arrangements under insolvency legislation,
– Bankruptcy or sequestration.


## ANNEX B
Insolvency practitioners referred to in point (5) of Article 2


. . .
UNITED KINGDOM
– Liquidator,
– Supervisor of a voluntary arrangement,
– Administrator,
– Official Receiver,
– Trustee,
– Provisional Liquidator,
– Interim Receiver,
– Judicial factor.

# INDEX OF STATUTES